Teaching
for Reconciliation

Ronald Thomas Habermas, M.Div. (North American Baptist Seminary); M.A. (Wheaton Graduate School); Ph.D. (Michigan State University). Associate professor of Christian education and coordinator of the Master of Arts in Christian Education degree program, Columbia Biblical Seminary and Graduate School of Missions.

Klaus Issler, Th.M. (Dallas Theological Seminary); M.A. (University of California, Riverside); Ph.D. (Michigan State University). Associate professor of Christian education, Talbot School of Theology, Biola University.

Teaching for Reconciliation

Foundations and Practice
of Christian Educational Ministry

Ronald Habermas
and Klaus Issler

Foreword by
Lawrence O. Richards

BAKER BOOK HOUSE
Grand Rapids, Michigan 49516

Printed in the United States of America

Library of Congress Cataloging-in-Publication Data

Habermas, Ronald T.
  Teaching for reconciliation : foundations and practice of Christian educational ministry / Ronald Habermas and Klaus Issler ; foreword by Lawrence O. Richards.
    p.   cm.
  Includes bibliographical references and indexes.
  ISBN 0-8010-4367-0
  1. Christian education. I. Issler, Klaus Dieter. II. Title.
BV1471.2.H23   1992
268—dc20   92-25728

*We lovingly dedicate this book
to our wives,
Mary and Beth.*

Contents

List of Tables and Figures

Tables

Figures

Foreword

It's not easy to eat an elephant, however you go about it. An elephant is big. And parts of it are thick and tough. Even so, it's nourishing. And if you're unhappy with the thin, greasy patties you get in fast-food eateries, you will appreciate the fact that you can chew on an elephant for a long, *long* time.

Ron Habermas and Klaus Issler have succeeded in helping us eat an elephant the only way it can be done—one bite at a time.

The elephant in this case, of course, is that massive beast, Christian educational ministry. For a long time too many evangelicals have trivialized educational ministry, whittling the discipline down until its vital issues can be ignored or easily dismissed. But it will be hard for anyone to whittle down the vision shared by Habermas and Issler in this fine book. They challenge us to think seriously. What they say isn't easy to grasp, but it's not supposed to be. It isn't a rehash of familiar evangelical jargon. And it isn't hype, promoting the next fad. It really *is* an elephant—chewy, tough in parts, but definitely nourishing. And definitely worth digesting.

I suspect that those who work in various disciplines watch with interest to see who will emerge as leading thinkers in the next generation. I know I have, and it is personally rewarding to see the quality and depth of thought exhibited in this work by two young professors of Christian education.

I won't be so bold as to tell you what you're about to read. But I do want to note two things. First, Christian education is essentially *theological:* Our understandings must be rooted in relevant, revealed truth. Second, Christian education is *a science:* Our understandings often grow out of questions raised by the social sciences, and our answers can frequently be expressed through paradigms and in terms drawn from the social sciences. I am particularly pleased to see the mastery of both biblical and behavioral science material exhibited by Habermas and Issler. They demonstrate a capacity that certainly establishes them as leaders in their field.

Lawrence O. Richards, Ph.D.
Hudson, Florida

Acknowledgments

During this project we have experienced both individual and corporate support. For Ron, initial ideas for this book were nurtured several years ago. They emerged from preliminary studies in the Tower Scholar Program at Union Theological Seminary in Richmond, Virginia. Sara Little, in particular, was instrumental in this process through her useful seminar for Tower Scholar participants and her personal words of encouragement. For Klaus, some of the key concepts of the book took form during a semester when he and colleague Bob Radcliffe worked together and team-taught a course at Western Conservative Baptist Seminary. Stimulating conversations of diverse topics were standard fare at those weekly lesson planning meetings. Bob reviewed earlier versions of chapters and provided encouragement and thoughtful criticism.

We also wish to thank the following school administrators for their support over the past six years: Elmer Towns, dean of the School of Religion, Liberty University, Lynchburg, Virginia; Ken Mulholland, dean of Columbia Biblical Seminary and Graduate School of Missions, South Carolina; Jim Sweeney, vice president of Academic Affairs, Western Conservative Baptist Seminary, Portland, Oregon; and Bing Hunter, dean of Talbot School of Theology, Biola University, La Mirada, California.

Furthermore we are indebted to several co-workers for their assistance. For Ron, to the following school staff for superb assistance in putting the manuscripts together: Wanda Brown, Clita Clark, Patsy Pattison, Cathy Rex, Georgia Roberts, and Denise Wright; for Klaus, for research help provided by graduate assistants and library staff and to faculty colleagues who read portions of the manuscript or provided feedback on concepts from the book: Audrey Arnst, Gerry Breshears, Rodger Bufford, Wayne Colwell, Beverly Wong Ginn, Chris Haymond, John Hu, Betty Lu Johnstone, Darryl Keeney, Bob Krupp, J. P. Moreland, Bill Roth, and Bob Saucy.

We likewise express gratitude to our students over these half-dozen years. They have been not only recipients but also participants in shaping this textbook. We thank them for their patience, prayers, and insight.

Next, we want to thank three extraordinary people at Baker Book House. Allan Fisher was the first to show interest in and affirmation for this work. Although some early concepts for this text changed many times, Allan remained constant. He expressed confidence in two writers who had several dreams but no published books. Jim Weaver followed Allan's leadership. Jim's faithful communication over the years buoyed us and kept us on course. His collaborative style produced an unusually strong editor-author relationship. Associate copyeditor Maria E. denBoer provided helpful comments and critiques, too. Her abilities, like that of an experienced seamstress, skillfully synthesized the many parts of this book.

Special appreciation goes to our families who saw this project through from a different angle: Mary, Elizabeth, Melissa, and Susan; Beth, Daniel, and Ruth. For the countless times we said, "Yes, I *must* work on it again this Saturday," or "No, I really can't take a break this minute"; and for the numerous moments we promised, "I'll be right there; I've got only one more paragraph to finish," or "just one more revision and I should be done," we express our thanks for their patience and support.

Finally, we offer praise to God for his providential direction throughout this project. Our prayers are that his truth will be heralded and his kingdom advanced.

Introduction

Remember the White Rabbit in Lewis Carroll's *Alice in Wonderland?* He stumbled upon an important—albeit mysterious—note, discovered in the presence of the royal court. In his confusion and nervousness, the rabbit asked the king where he should start reading the lost document. His Majesty advised, "Begin at the beginning and go on till you come to the end; then stop."

What took the king only one sentence to say has taken us nearly six years. During those years we've attempted to produce a foundations-to-practice textbook in Christian education. At first we thought our job would be fairly straightforward. Just "begin at the beginning," we reminded each other. Countless revisions later, we settled on what you hold in your hands.

Having "come to the end," we've decided to "stop." In reality, we view this stop to be more of a "pause," a time to catch our breath. To use an analogy, we feel like we've been on a never-ending roller-coaster. And, it's only natural to expect that when you experience an exhilarating six-year ride on those rails, and then get off, you continue "riding" long after the park closes. So, while we're still feeling the ride's effects, permit us to share with you what this book is all about.

First, *we value the fact that God speaks to us.* The centrality of his special revelation lays the text's foundation or infrastructure. Yet supplementary insights from his general revelation are also acknowledged. Complementary social science truth provides the book's framework or superstructure.

Second, *we are convinced that theory drives practice.* We have included only those theories that are substantive and sound, as well as relevant to ministry.

Third, *we recognize that life and faith are replete with paradoxes.* As often as possible, we state God's truth within sets of tensions or polarities. This mindset prevents us from giving simple answers to complex questions.

Fourth, *we anticipate our readership,* those who will come along on the ride with us. In particular, we anticipate the diverse challenges they will bring along: from undergraduates to graduate students, from Christian education majors to those who take only one CE course. Accordingly, we try to fashion each chapter with necessary and creative content, while offering detailed endnotes, figures, tables, and illustrations for students who desire more in-depth information. Furthermore, we purposefully arrange each chapter with various kinds of meaningful interaction activities. We hope these features will provide all participants with a memorable ride.

Fifth, *we believe in Christian education.* This fact might appear a bit strange, at first. But we are fully convinced that a comprehensive perspective on Christian education has been sold short. The church has settled for a truncated version of its divine instructional task. Unless we reclaim a truer, fuller picture of Christian education, we will continue in our bewildered state of hit-or-miss teaching and random learning.

Finally, and perhaps most important, *we claim God's power to reconcile.* Until we permit "God with us" to radically reconcile all things to himself as the Savior of the world—for all intents and purposes—we figuratively remain with the babe in Bethlehem. We hope that this textbook will be one resource to assist Christian educators in the uncompromising, lifelong task of reconciliation.

Your fellow ambassadors,

Ron Habermas
Klaus Issler
December 1991

Part 1

Educational Ministry Foundations

1 Boxes and Blind Men

Now You See It, Now . . .

Like a mirage, what *you* see is not always what *others* see. Analyze the word puzzle below. What images initially form in your mind? What is the author describing?

A [person] stands at home, dressed in very peculiar clothing, and facing odds of 9 to 1. The future holds a number of possibilities, all difficult. One is that the [person] will be found "out" or even worse, out of the game. Another is the need for sacrifice. Still another is that the player may be reduced to stealing. And even if there is a positive outcome, it will certainly involve running for one's life, facing down in the earth, covered with dirt, perhaps twisting an ankle, but always straining so that the back bends and the arms are always aching and the sweat runs down the face. And the sun burns, or the rains come, but even if the game is called, it will start again tomorrow.

And why? Why go through all this?

In order to return home.[1]

Most Americans would not describe our national pastime, baseball, in these terms. But that's only because we're too close to it. We're familiar with its jargon and strategies—too familiar. People who have never witnessed this sport may, indeed, explain their first encounter with baseball this way.

The same is true of Christian education. Many of us are so close, we take things for granted: our goals, our lesson plans, our students. But it's time for a change. The purpose of this book is to challenge the familiar, traditional ways we look at Christian education.[2] Figuratively, we must exchange our standard camera lens for a wide-angle one.

For instance, we need to go beyond discussions about which teaching method is best. We must first ask, "How does any method imply broader presumptions about teaching?" Instead of uncritically accepting any curriculum, we should investigate what is *not* being taught in our selected material. Likewise, what "hidden curriculum" is communicated?

As you read the previous analogy of baseball, no doubt your view of that sport expanded. Correspondingly, we anticipate that interaction with this book will stretch your current concept of education that is Christian.[3] Catch the challenge to see the bigger picture.

The cartoon below sneaks a peek at what's to follow. It portrays one critique of traditional teaching patterns.

Many Christian teachers adhere to the father's lesson in shooting free throws. Simply put: When teachers teach, students learn. Unfortunately, too much of what passes for Christian education follows this basketball lesson plan. It's clear that the son learned *something*. But what?

Think about It

1. Name at least two "lessons" the son learned that were not the father's aim.
   Lesson 1: _____

Lesson 2: _____

2. Give at least one example of how a student in a Christian education setting might learn the exact *opposite lesson* that the teacher planned. _____

_____

_____

Down Home Wisdom

Remember Mark Twain's adventurous tale of the street-wise teenager, Huckleberry Finn? One day, Huck was chatting with Mary Jane, Peter Wilks' red-headed daughter. During their conversation, the young man talked about the Sheffield church where Mary Jane's uncle preached. Huck's unedited comments would provoke most believers today, because this teenager charged that the Sheffield congregation had not one—but *seventeen*—preachers! Upon hearing this alarming report, Mary Jane screeched:

"Seventeen! My land! Why, I wouldn't set out such a string as that, not if I *never* got to glory. It must take 'em a week."
"Shucks, they don't *all* of 'em preach the same day—only *one* of 'em."
"Well, then, what does the rest of 'em do?"
"Oh, nothing much. Loll around, pass the plate—and one thing or another. But mainly they don't do nothing."

Figure 1.1

Biblical Pictures of the Church

In 2 Corinthians 2:15, Paul compares believers to sweet-smelling fragrance, to the aroma of incense. Consider each verse below and ask the following questions: What is the image being portrayed? What is its purpose or meaning? What are the implications for ministry? By synthesizing these biblical images, we can begin the foundational task of determining a Christian philosophy for teaching ministry.

Picture and Text	Meaning	Ministry Implication
Athletes in a Foot Race (1 Cor. 9:24–25)		
Aliens and Strangers in the World (1 Pet. 2:11)		
Bride of Christ (Eph. 5:23–27; Rev. 19:7)		
Body of Christ (1 Cor. 12:27)		
Children of God (John 1:12)		
Household of God (1 Tim. 3:15; 5:1–2)		
Holy Temple (Eph. 2:21–22)		
Holy Instrument (2 Tim. 2:20–21)		
Light of the World (Matt. 5:14)		
Mature Adult (Eph. 4:13)		
Newborn Babes (1 Pet. 2:1)		
Royal Priesthood (1 Pet. 2:9)		
Salt of the Earth (Matt. 5:13)		
Sheep (John 10:11–16)		
Soldiers in Battle (Eph. 6:10–17)		

"Well, then, what are they *for?*"
"Why, they're for *style*. Don't you know nothing?"[4]

More than a hundred years have passed since Mark Twain created this image of the church. Perhaps it's a picture of overindulgence. Or it is a portrait of questionable perspectives, if not values. For some people, this image has not changed, but is as vivid as the day Twain reinforced it with his pen.

Whether we know it or not, we all hold images of the church. We each possess mental snapshots of God's people. The church may look like a fortress. It may well be the picture of a hospital or a school or a soup line. Figure 1.1 identifies several biblical metaphors of the church. Which ones are familiar to you? Which pictures strike you as unusual?

Think about It

---

1. List six metaphors in Figure 1.1 that are familiar to you. Give two ministry implications.

   _____

   _____

2. Which word pictures strike you as somewhat unusual?

   _____

   _____

3. Which images seem to conflict with other images?[5]

   _____

   _____

Whatever picture of the church you have, your image includes *purpose* (What is it believers are to do?) and your view of *people* (How are Christians similar and dissimilar to unbelievers?). In addition, your mental snapshot of the church expresses thoughts about learning *processes* (In what areas should people mature? How do we motivate them? How do we work with them to see evidence of growth?).

Everybody holds at least one picture of the church. These pictures reveal more about our views of teaching ministry than we realize. Purposes, people, and processes for growth and learning are but a few extended categories. To put it another way, it is fair to say we all possess a philosophy of educational ministry. All of us have assumptions and convictions about why we are here, about why the church exists, and about what we are called to do. It may be a bit fuzzy, but we all operate by some game plan.

The real test is, first, to become aware of our position and, then, to evaluate it. Every time pastors step into a pulpit they say something about their educational philosophy of ministry. In particular, they communicate several deep-seated views about teaching and learning. What they actually say gives insight into their perceived "purposes." For example, if pastors typically close with an altar call, they're making a statement about the intentional place of evangelism in the church's worship.

To whom pastors preach (i.e., the congregation) indicates something of their view of "people." For example, some ministers reserve evangelistic messages for groups they know are not yet Christians. Conversely, they present nurturing messages to believers, those who are guided by the indwelling Holy Spirit. Their perceptions about people influence their sermons.

How pastors actually deliver their messages identifies their preferred "processes of growth"—what they believe about patterns of learning. For example, preachers who include their sermon outlines in the bulletin encourage listeners to take notes. Their views of instruction and learning retention emerge. Creative pastors who utilize mime and drama in their preaching make a different type of philosophical comment about how people learn.

Think about It

Contemplate the sermons you've heard recently. Assess these presentations, according to the trio of categories above:

1. What did they preach? (i.e., their topics) _____

   _____

2. To whom did they preach? (i.e., believers or nonbelievers)

   _____

   _____

3. How did they preach? (i.e., what audio-visual equipment was used?)

   _____

   _____

Make a few summary statements about these pastors' philosophy of educational ministry: _____

_____

It comes down to this: Philosophies of educational ministry are personal. From time to time, these views may become public. But only when we are consciously aware of our position, and then evaluate it, will we be more effective in God's work. In pulpits around the world, Sunday after Sunday, philosophies are on display. That's a given. The same could be said of youth work, prison ministries, or neighborhood outreach. The question is: How biblical are these approaches to ministry? Specifically, are these approaches thoroughly Christian expressions of teaching and learning?

Negatively stated, ministry philosophies left unattended may do irreparable damage to the kingdom. In this regard, philosophies of educational ministry are like long-distance phone service; if you don't choose one, one will be chosen for you.[6]

A Parable to Ponder

Jesus spoke in parables to help people think, discern, and choose. The story below has the same aims. It is a peculiar tale, written by a leading evangelical.[7] Your first

---

Figure 1.2

Parrot Fish

They say you get to see spiders and little red snakes. Or tiny green men six inches tall. I saw parrot fish. What's more, I heard them.

I gotta quit, that's all there is to it. I shake so bad in the morning that I can hardly get the bottle to my lips. And sometimes the bottle's already empty.

You know, I've quit twice already—seven months the first time, three the second. So I can do it if I really try. But it's my nerves. If only that fool doctor could sort out my nerves, I'd never touch another drop. I'm no alcoholic, though I admit I've got a problem.

Matter of fact, I can't stand the booze here in Jamaica. Rum. Foul stuff. I just hold my nose and swallow it.

See, I got this job teaching scuba diving to tourists. You don't really teach 'em anything—just watch so they don't get into trouble. Afterward they treat you in the bar . . .

I got a little something in my room too. It's against hotel regulations for the staff, but I got one bottle in the flush tank above the toilet, plus a large after-shave bottle and a largish cologne bottle. Sounds pretty sneaky, but it's the only way I can get to sleep.

But these fish. Parrot fish ten feet long! I know it sounds crazy, and that's what has me scared.

But I know a parrot fish when I see one, though these were the first that ever talked.

The thing about going below is the silence, know what I mean? Well, the silence is no more. This time the crazy things talked—booming, screeching parrot-fish talk through echoing waters. You can't scream under water, but I screamed inside my guts.

There was this woman parrot fish with glasses on. "Convention? I defy convention! I intend to be free," she screeched.

The silence came again. None of them seemed to notice me. As the moments passed my heart beat less fiercely. Dim green water and bubbles. Then I jumped like a thousand needles were being pushed through my skin as a professor fish squeaked, "And what do you mean by *free? No.*" The lady parrot fish was about to interrupt. "No. Let me make my question clear. In concrete terms, what do you want to be free to do?"

The other fish opened their great mouths and closed them again. The female's eyes narrowed, like she could tell he was still a momma's boy. She began to talk coldly. "Take the surface above us— this silly, wavy, inconsistent plane. Who in Neptune's name decreed that we must always stay below it? Who's to say what is moral and what is immoral? Don't interrupt me till I finish! The thing our ancestors were pleased to call the surface of the ocean is no moral absolute but an arbitrary line established by custom and prejudice. It's not real. In some cultures the line to which we attach such importance is completely ignored. How can I possibly harm anyone by crossing it if I want to? Humans go above and below it. Their morality permits it. And flying fish . . ."

A chorus of protest rose at the mention of flying fish. Words like *flippies, commufish,* the *bomb, fishist,* the *effluvient society* and *extreme right-fin politics* battered my ears and befuddled my brain. Some fish paled visibly.

I got scared. Not 'cause the arguments were any good, but because the fish were so mad. They fought with words like drunks fight with broken beer bottles. They were carving one another up. No one was listening. They were so mad they didn't care whether they hurt or got hurt. It was a brawl in a bar. You could almost see the smashed mirrors, the wrecked chairs, the filth.

It quieted down after a while, and one of the younger fish said, "I like this freedom bit. Like you say, the thing is not to hurt anybody. And if nobody else gets hurt, why not do what you like?"

The younger fish seemed to like this.

The professor and the female with glasses began to speak at the same time. The female won out, which was a pity since she just liked to grab the scene.

"I went on the beach last night."

There were gasps of admiration.

"And I ate with a knife and fork."

"With knife and fork . . . !" ". . . and fork!" ". . . and fork!" echoed among the coral.

"Why not?"

"Sure, why not?" echoed the younger fish who liked the freedom idea.

"Humans do," she continued.

"What are forks?" asked a very young fish, amid general snickers from the preadolescents and serious looks from their elders. "Don't laugh at her," said the female with glasses. "We were all green once. They're plastic things, dear, with four sharp spines you can stick your fins into. They're designed for pushing food into your mouth."

The female had everyone's ear.

"Oh, potato chips and paper . . ."

"Highly indigestible, I would have thought," the professor-type piped.

"Delicious," the female chirped. (Nobody was really in a position to disagree.) "And anyway, I was free. I didn't have to be bound by water. I refuse to spend the rest of my life restricted by the confines of the puny ocean. I refuse to be forced always to suck insipid seafood through my mouth. What's more, I had an experience on the beach that changed my whole life."

A pause ensued, which the female enjoyed for as long as she dared; then, "I laid eggs on the sand."

For a moment, everything stood still. I felt shocked myself, though I don't know why. Neither sound nor movement broke the tension until one fish said softly, "Neptune, I feel sick. You gotta draw the line somewhere. Oh, Neptune . . ." Slowly he turned and swam away into the shadows. The rest stayed on, nervous and jittery.

The young fish who liked freedom said, "I'm not shocked. The ocean's changed in the last ten years. We can't live in the past. We may not always be right, but at least we're not hypocrites, pretending to follow standards we see no sense in. We gotta find out what we really want. We're free."

A fancy pastor-type drifted into the center, cleared his throat, and said, "Some interesting issues have been raised (indeed, I might say, provocative and challenging issues). The whole discussion has been conducted on a mature and responsible level. Personally, I feel I've learned a great deal. Though I'm not certain what advantages there were to laying eggs on sand." He seemed to think he was being funny and the professor smiled and nodded. "It is perhaps inconsistent with our concept of Neptune to think of the matter in outmodedly rigid terms. There is nothing sinful about laying eggs. There is nothing bad about sand. And it might be, under certain circumstances, a very meaningful thing to do to lay eggs on sand. After all, freedom is Neptune's gift to us."

Maybe my head was clearing. At any rate, the fish were returning to their normal size. One old parrot fish, who seemed to shrink more slowly than the rest, was staring me right in the eye, never moving a fin. He was the first to notice me, and as I stared back he winked, ever so slowly.

I winked back. I wasn't sure what we were winking about, but I didn't want to offend him. Anyway, I was still scared.

"Freedom," he said contemptuously. "Freedom is doing what you were made to do and doing it with all you've got."

The rest of the fish had disappeared, and the old fish himself was growing smaller. I wanted to ask him more, but there was no time. Yet he still held my eye and his voice was powerful and strong. "Knives and forks! Potato chips!" His scorn made me cringe. "Watch!"

It was the last word I heard. He turned in a flash and was sliding through blue-green water, hovering, twisting, darting, gliding. Four other fish joined him in the frolic, their movements one, as though I had quintuple vision. Each twist was clean and perfectly timed. I was watching a ballet so taut and sharp that the toughest discipline on earth would never reproduce it. Yet suddenly I knew I was watching freedom. Freedom for fish.

But for me? The pressure in my tank was down, and I began to think of the bottle of rum in the flush tank of my bathroom. I turned for home.

So freedom is doing what you were made to do, and doing it with all you've got. What was I made to do? I felt freest when I had three or four ounces of hard liquor inside me. Free from the ugliness of reality. Were feeling free and being free the same? After all, what was I made for?

It was worth a second thought—maybe even a sober thought.

Source: White (1984, pp. 162–66).

question might be: "Does this story have *anything* to do with Christian education?" But, be patient. The "aha" moment will come, eventually.

For the most part, the parable presented in Figure 1.2 takes place under water, and the purposes of life are communicated by fish! There are at least two main points you want to look for:

1. The female parrot fish proposes an unorthodox view of freedom. As she

does, ask yourself, "What is used to support her claims?"

2. The old parrot fish upholds the same ideal: freedom. But his viewpoint is radically different than the female fish's. Ask: "What's his definition of freedom? What accompanying evidences of support exist?"

Purposes—including how they are defined—shape many different personal perspectives. Purposes radically distinguish our educational ministries. Even believers are not all after the same thing. If we take time to delineate our objectives—and, then, make comparisons—we will discover some surprising results. For instance, what distinguishes education that is Christian from other kinds of instruction? In large measure, differing purposes set it apart.[8] This is also the case in the parable.[9]

Think about It

Take a parallel example: schooling. What are some prominent goals of public schools? List three or four that come to mind. _____

_____

In what ways might private school (Christian or otherwise) aims be different from public school aims? List a couple of distinctions. _____

_____

Provide two aims of home schooling that might be unique, compared to the other two institutions.

_____

_____

Every educator has aims, whether stated or not. Furthermore, every teacher has assumptions behind each aim, whether known or not. Education that is Christian, by definition, is guided by God's Word. Our

educational objectives are necessarily drawn from this source of revelation.

Biblical Guidelines

Consider two Scripture passages relevant to Christian educational ministries. Each plots the non-negotiable routes that teachers must follow.

Twin Commands for All Saints

Every believer, at one time or another, has heard the Great Commission (Matt. 28:18–20). Many have memorized it: "Then Jesus came to them and said, 'All authority in heaven and on earth has been given to me. Therefore go and make disciples of all nations, baptizing them in the name of the Father and of the Son and of the Holy Spirit, and teaching them to obey everything I have commanded you. And surely I am with you always, to the very end of the age.'"

When this passage is taught, most Christians typically dissect Matthew's final commandment into two basic tasks, evangelism and discipleship. But a great irony is perpetuated by traditional instruction of the Great Commission: Nine times out of ten these memory-etched verses are misused. Believers isolate and reinforce the call for witness, not Christ-likeness. We settle on new birth, not nurture. Evangelism is elevated to the exclusion of discipleship.

Honestly ask yourself: When do you most often hear these closing words of the first Gospel? The answer is: at missions conferences, outreach seminars, and evangelism training sessions. And that's fine.

But when was the last time you heard the Great Commission employed for discipleship and Christian education concerns; to implement a Scripture memory program; to encourage meaningful community service; to assist the poor; to worship God with genuine and thankful hearts? These are overt indications of obeying Christ in everything he has commanded (Matt. 28:20a). A careful and obedient student of Scripture recognizes that the imperative to nurture is explicit; salvation is implicit.

The dichotomy between evangelism and discipleship (which minimizes the latter) is not without consequence. The absence of sound instruction for believers caused one seasoned dean and former missionary to conclude: "The world-wide Church has seen burgeoning growth in the past decades. But we have failed to train young converts. To use an analogy, church growth has been mile-wide, but Christian education only inch-deep."[10]

In sum, we need more—and better—Christian teaching. Education that is Christian is synonymous with discipleship. Both involve instruction. Both expect growth. Both last a lifetime. Both incorporate comprehensive nurture. Both represent complex learning approaches. Both are confronted by the Lord's challenge—"teaching them to obey everything I have commanded you."

An Educational Pattern for the Church

Sometimes the best way to define a subject is to comprehend what it does *not* mean. Recall the Book of Hebrews. The au-dience addressed in this inspired letter portray a deplorable spiritual state. They are thoroughly immature. Yet this negative condition is salvaged for a positive cause. Read Hebrews 5:11–6:3. The ultimate objective of the faith is featured as the need to "go on to maturity" (6:1a) in Christ. In Hebrews 5:11–13[11] an intentional contrast is set up: where the audience is (regarding this ultimate objective) and where they *should* be. Table 1.1 provides an overview.

How are these saints to grow up? There are at least three biblical guidelines. Generally, they represent sequential movement toward spiritual maturity. But caution should be taken, for this threesome is not a lock-step, guaranteed formula for Christ-likeness.

Believe Truth—Hebrews 6:1b–2 acknowledges that certain theological constructs anchor our faith. We must believe in something: God's truth.

Apply Truth—Genuine acceptance of truth surpasses (yet includes) "head knowledge." Behaviors change. Values are altered (Heb. 5:14a).

Evidence Truth—Hebrews 5:14b states that wisdom emerges from faithful life application of truth. (Other virtues are

Table 1.1

The Immaturity Gap of the Hebrew Audience

Where They Were	Where They Should Have Been
They could not understand "hard-to-explain" teachings (v. 11a).	They should have been able to grasp "much" (more) concerning the faith (v. 11a).
They were "slow to learn" (v. 11b).	They ought to have been teachers by this time (v. 12a).
They needed "elementary truths" (v. 12b).	They could not digest "solid food" (v. 12e).
They required "someone to teach . . . [them] God's word all over again" (v. 12c).	
They were in "need [of] milk" (v. 12d).	
They were still "infants" (v. 13a).	
They were "not acquainted with the teaching about righteousness" (v. 13b).	

Source: Based on Heb. 5:11–14.

also produced, comparable to "fruit" [see Gal. 5:22–23a]).

The three components, again, must not be viewed as some magic formula. They do represent dominant phases of spiritual maturity.[12] Suffice it to say that Christian teachers must be serious about Scripture. We need to adapt biblical principles to contemporary teaching opportunities.[13]

A Helpful Model

How are we to frame our educational ministry? What ideological concepts make sense? One useful approach, employed throughout this book, was created by philosophy professor William K. Frankena.[14] Our modified version of Frankena's theory is presented in Figure 1.3.[15]

In simple terms, Box A expresses the ideals of living.[16] These might be seen as God's directives. The source of these directives is eternal and divine. God's Word identifies what we should do.

Box B is grounded in the real world, since its sources include temporal means (e.g., scientific studies). In contrast to stating what we should do, Box B describes what *is*. The difference between Box A and Box B is the difference between *prescription* and *de-*

Figure 1.3

A Modification of Frankena's Theory

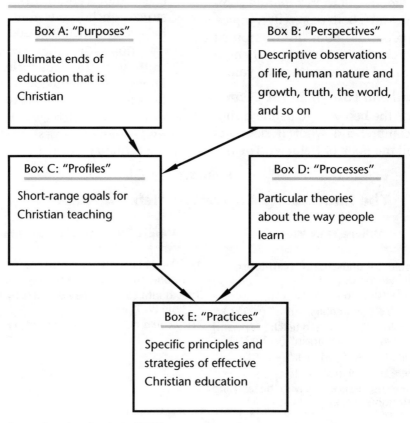

Source: Based on Frankena (1965).

Figure 1.4
Acts 17 and the Frankena Boxes

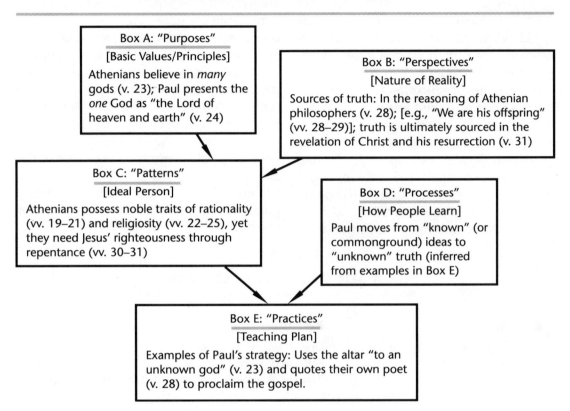

Box A: "Purposes"
[Basic Values/Principles]
Athenians believe in *many* gods (v. 23); Paul presents the *one* God as "the Lord of heaven and earth" (v. 24)

Box B: "Perspectives"
[Nature of Reality]
Sources of truth: In the reasoning of Athenian philosophers (v. 28); [e.g., "We are his offspring" (vv. 28–29)]; truth is ultimately sourced in the revelation of Christ and his resurrection (v. 31)

Box C: "Patterns"
[Ideal Person]
Athenians possess noble traits of rationality (vv. 19–21) and religiosity (vv. 22–25), yet they need Jesus' righteousness through repentance (vv. 30–31)

Box D: "Processes"
[How People Learn]
Paul moves from "known" (or commonground) ideas to "unknown" truth (inferred from examples in Box E)

Box E: "Practices"
[Teaching Plan]
Examples of Paul's strategy: Uses the altar "to an unknown god" (v. 23) and quotes their own poet (v. 28) to proclaim the gospel.

scription. Box A provides ultimate aims, while Box B points out the ways we see those aims (and related matters) through our particular "glasses," our "perspectives."

Boxes A and B complement each other; one cannot be sacrificed unless at the expense of the other. Combined, they express our worldview. Box A speaks of our values, originating from theological and philosophical bases.[17] Box B points out our assumptions about life, gained through researched data and personal experiences. Specifically, it centers on issues of human nature and human growth.[18]

Box C combines these two categories. Frankena (1965, p. 8) describes this synthesis as the "list of excellencies to be produced." We call them short-range goals.

Box C lists the intermediate steps toward our ultimate objective (i.e., Box A).[19]

Box D asks "How do people learn?" Typically, theories about learning and teaching pertain to this fourth category.[20]

Box E suggests the practical plan of Christian educational philosophy. It's where the "rubber meets the road." To use a comparison, Box A stands for ultimate aims; Box C depicts the intermediate aims; Box E produces the immediate aims—what we actually do, week in and week out. Figure 1.3 illustrates these five boxes.

Fish Flashback
The "Parrot Fish" parable should make more sense now. The Frankena model offers a new set of wide-angle lenses with which to view and to assess the parable.

How does the Frankena model assist you in evaluating this parable?

First, recall that each fish in the story valued the ultimate purpose of freedom (Box A). Yet, when assumptions behind that single word were verbalized, two totally divergent views emerged.

Philosophies of education that are Christian operate much the same way. Virtually all evangelicals, for example, identify the church's ultimate aims using words like "glorifying God," "obeying God," "loving God," "evangelism," and "discipleship." The problem, however, is that such generalities—when left alone—contribute to fuzzy thinking. Particulars must be spelled out.

In the fish parable, for instance, the eventual conflict occurred only after the female parrot fish began to voice her assumptions about life under and above the water. Specifically, it began with her unorthodox perception (Box B) that the ocean surface was really an "arbitrary line," that it was morally permissible to cross over it. Her reasoning? Humans had crossed over already. The perspectives of reality she expressed (including those of the gullible younger fish) were markedly dissimilar from those of the old parrot fish. His one constraint (i.e., "doing what you were made to do") clearly put him at odds with the anything-goes freedom of the others.[21]

Figure 1.5

Schematic Overview of the Book

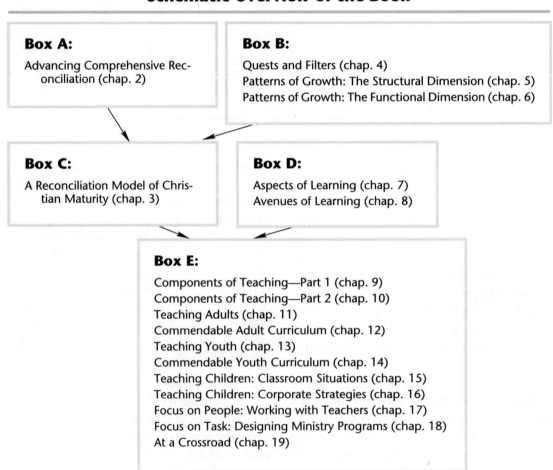

Box A:

Advancing Comprehensive Reconciliation (chap. 2)

Box B:

Quests and Filters (chap. 4)
Patterns of Growth: The Structural Dimension (chap. 5)
Patterns of Growth: The Functional Dimension (chap. 6)

Box C:

A Reconciliation Model of Christian Maturity (chap. 3)

Box D:

Aspects of Learning (chap. 7)
Avenues of Learning (chap. 8)

Box E:

Components of Teaching—Part 1 (chap. 9)
Components of Teaching—Part 2 (chap. 10)
Teaching Adults (chap. 11)
Commendable Adult Curriculum (chap. 12)
Teaching Youth (chap. 13)
Commendable Youth Curriculum (chap. 14)
Teaching Children: Classroom Situations (chap. 15)
Teaching Children: Corporate Strategies (chap. 16)
Focus on People: Working with Teachers (chap. 17)
Focus on Task: Designing Ministry Programs (chap. 18)
At a Crossroad (chap. 19)

Finally, short-range and immediate goals (Boxes C and E) express ultimate (Box A) and temporal (Box B) worlds in the parable. The nontraditional fish generally spoke of changing times. They saw the need to break away from the past. Particularly for the female fish, this meant eating potato chips, using a plastic knife and fork, and laying her eggs on the sand. These radical mid-range goals were logical extensions of her combined Box A and B positions.

Similarly, the old fish's intermediate aims were complementary to his Box A and B views. His definition of freedom, followed by his actions, verified this consistency: "Freedom [Box A] is doing what you were made to do and doing it with all you've got [Box B]." The brilliant underwater ballet that followed was the Box C and E composite of the ultimate and the temporal worlds valued by the elder fish. The author's description of this stirring ballet turned an otherwise static *A* into a dynamic expression of *C* and *E*. "Suddenly I knew I was watching freedom. Freedom for fish." This energetic display put feet (or fins!) to theory.

The Frankena theory can be summarized in various ways.[22] One way is to correlate this theory with the table of contents. Instead of sequential chapter order, Figure 1.5 reveals a *topical* ordering. This schematic design identifies the basic rationale for this book.

Conclusion

In his first letter, Peter commands the church: "Always be prepared to give an answer to everyone who asks you to give the reason for the hope that you have" (3:15b). The Greek word for answer (*apologia*) is the English equivalent for apologetics. In other words, Peter recognizes the value of an intentional faith defense. A lesser-known command immediately follows: "But do this with gentleness and respect, keeping a clear conscience, so that those who speak maliciously against your good behavior in Christ may be ashamed of their slander" (3:15c–16). These verses, like two sweeping brushstrokes, broadly depict the twin aims for this book.

On the one hand, the aims of awareness and communication are present. This brushstroke paints the significance of knowing our faith position. Also, we Christian teachers must explain the prominent theological and philosophical foundation that upholds our beliefs. Peter compares this foundation with the "answer [for] . . . the reason for the hope." On the other hand, this book portrays the aims of responsible choices and lifestyles. This brushstroke paints the importance of evaluation, freedom of selection, and life implementation. Peter cites the goal of "good behavior in Christ" at this point. "Clear conscience" is a second, related outcome.

In the end, these aims express the balance of good theory and good practice. It is knowing *why* we do *what* we do. Foundation is coupled with function. That's the making of commendable instruction. If we maintain a responsible blend of theory and practice, our educational debates will not be restricted to questions of superior methodology. We won't get bogged down by petty controversies pertaining to age-level trends. Miniscule curricular comparisons will not represent our primary concerns. Certainly these subjects will eventually find their way into our final analysis of Christian educational ministry. But they will not typify our point of departure. They will not consume our initial and vital energies.

As we assume a broader base, we sidestep the trivialities of our professional discipline. We overcome the blindness that restricts our effectiveness.[23]

Once upon a time, six blind men tried to describe an elephant. Each attempted to convince the other, as they touched the huge beast.

"It's a sturdy wall," the first one shouted, feeling the elephant's side.

"No, more like a spear," said the second. He caressed a smooth, sharp tusk.

"What do you mean? A snake! The elephant compares to a large snake," the third exclaimed. His hands failed to contain the elephant's sizable, squirming trunk.

"It is clear that this animal is like a tree," the fourth blind man testified. "Can't you see this enormous base?" he asked, wrapping his arms around one leg.

"All lies!" denounced the fifth. "It's a mighty fan. Don't you feel that breeze?" he quizzed, standing by one ear.

Ignoring the others, the sixth man declared: "A rope, I tell you! Feel here," holding up the tail.

Each person fought tenaciously for his viewpoint. None left his location near the beast. None contemplated an alternative perspective. None tolerated another opinion.

Each blind man was partly right, but all were totally wrong.

Think about It

Extend the analogy of this story to Christian educational ministry. Name at least four myths of Christian education you've encountered. What partly right, but totally wrong images of Christian teaching and learning have you heard? List them.

1. _____
2. _____
3. _____
4. _____

Convictions, experiences, denominational persuasions, theological backgrounds—all of these factors and more color our limited understanding of Christian nurture and instruction. Like the insights of a half-dozen blind men, our own myopic and competing views of Christian teaching are often inaccurate.

Consider six of our own comparable, "blind" reports that we advance in the church today. Each prohibits a comprehensive meaning of Christian education. The first report equates Christian teaching solely with Sunday school. A second traditional report links Christian instruction exclusively with childhood church programs. Some people correlate Christian instruction with the Christian school movement. Others prefer a restrictive association with higher education (i.e., colleges and seminaries). Not to be outdone, certain individuals focus on the evangelistic or pastoral dimensions of Christian teaching; they might stress home Bible studies or outreach groups. Finally, a popular report includes any training in the home; burgeoning home schooling efforts partially affirm this category.

Each blind man was partly right but all were totally wrong.

The contemporary church is obligated to correct such narrow misconceptions of Christian educational ministry. We need a wide-angle frame of reference. To settle for anything less keeps us groping like blind people.

We must come to know *why* we believe *what* we believe.

2 Advancing Comprehensive Reconciliation

A man read an ad claiming a certain chain saw could cut five cords of wood per hour. After several oak trees on his property were leveled by a storm, he decided to test the ad's guarantee.

After a week of exhaustion and frustration, he marched back to the store.

"What's wrong?" the clerk asked.

"I demand a refund!" the man shouted. "I used that saw for five days and didn't stack a single cord. You said I'd get five per hour. Pay me back!"

"Let me see that chain saw," the clerk answered defensively, snatching the saw. He jerked the rip cord. The engine turned over instantly, "W-w-w-h-h-h-r-r."

The startled customer jumped back, shouting, "What's *that* noise?"

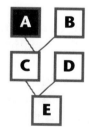

Following the directions helps us avoid undue stress and failure. Embarrassment can be avoided. Adhering to instructions is especially critical when it comes to ultimate directives from

God's Word. We do well to follow the Owner's Manual.[1]

Now, for a pop quiz! Without looking back, explain the specific contents of the five Frankena boxes.

Box A: _____

Box B: _____

Box C: _____

Box D: _____

Box E: _____

How well did you do?

A Common Triangle

Box A helps us identify the "big picture" of God's truth: Who we are? Why we are here? Where we are going? When these significant topics are analyzed through the grid of Scripture, a helpful structure for teaching emerges: Christian educational ministry should always be fashioned by the triadic relationship of God, people, and creation.

Anthony A. Hoekema offers a stimulating study of the *imago Dei* (God's image in people).[2] Hoekema captures the best of God's grace and purposes, along with the realistic restrictions of humanity. Balancing theology with day-to-day living, Hoekema describes the meaning of our being in God's image in terms of a "triangle":

- "To be a human being is to be directed toward God."
- "To be a human being is to be directed toward one's fellowmen."
- "To be a human being is to rule over nature" (1986, pp. 75–78).

All three parts are interconnected and indispensable. "When we love the neighbor and when we work responsibly with God's creation, we are at the same time serving God."[3] No other part of creation can fulfill our lifelong responsibilities like we can—not even angels.[4] In the final analysis, Jesus Christ—the True Image of God—fulfilled this threefold obligation. When it comes to our similar trio of responsibilities, we can look to the Incarnate One.

- Christ was "wholly directed toward God," as indicated by his unswerving desire to obey the Father. He pronounced: "My food is to do the will of him who sent me and to finish his work" (John 4:34).
- Christ was "wholly directed toward the neighbor," as shown by his life testimony: "For even the Son of Man did not come to be served, but to serve, and to give his life as a ransom for many" (Mark 10:45).
- Christ "rules over nature," as recorded by his miracles—from his first at Cana through his last at the tomb.[5]

Randolph Crump Miller also employs a parallel three-part construction to identify the church's teaching task. Miller (1956, p. 55) proposes that "the purpose of Christian education is to make men whole." He particularly focuses on the value of synthesizing elements of growth: "Integration occurs when relationships between *persons* are secure, when there is a personal encounter with *God* . . . when there is an organic relationship between a man and his *environment*."[6]

Nicholas Wolterstorff builds upon this triadic formation, adding a fourth dimension. Wolterstorff includes the negative effects of the fall (1980, pp. 9–10, emphasis added): "In freedom man revolted against God and refused to live in trustful obedience, preferring instead to act as if he were self-normed. Thereupon he became confused about his responsibilities and defected from them. He mutilated the *earth*. He victimized his *fellows*. He squandered *his abilities*. He set up surrogate *gods*."[7]

If you were to summarize your life up to this point, what would you say? What single word or phrase captures, in a nutshell, who you are or what you have accomplished?_____

_____

Now, try to do the same to the Scriptures. Summarize the Bible in a word or phrase. Would you say something like "God's love letter to people" or "the secret to life and the afterlife"? What would your phrase be?

_____

_____

Using your last response, what singular, overarching purpose statement can you make about God's will for us, as believers?

_____

_____

The Reconciliation Model

Following a thorough study of the New Testament, Ralph P. Martin introduces the unifying biblical motif of reconciliation.[8] He maintains that this concept advances three significant subpoints of Christian theology. First, reconciliation must encounter "all components of a chaotic sin-infested world." All reality became unglued when Adam and Eve disobeyed a holy God. Demonic forces were unleashed. Created order turned into confusion. Reconciliation affirms the cosmic catastrophe of sin.

Second, the "message of reconciliation includes a full range of restored relationships." God's saving work in Christ initiates the process of restoration between Creator and individual creatures. Likewise, it commences other chain-reaction events. The prospect of renewed social ties emerges. As God's power is appropriated, barriers are broken down. Antagonism gives way to peace.

Third, reconciliation has personal benefits. In Galatians 2:20 Paul testifies that "I have been crucified with Christ . . . but Christ lives in me." Accordingly, Martin states that whether in the first-person singular ("I") or plural ("we"), the apostolic witness values first-hand blessings in Christ. Reconciliation is real and personal.[9]

Linguistic Roots

Reconciliation involves both a resolving of differences and a restoring of harmony. Fundamentally, the term means "to reestablish friendship."[10] When further scrutinized, "reconciliation" (or, the return to a state of conciliation) provides a helpful word picture. The Latin word *concilium* gives us the English equivalent of "union, gathering, meeting"; in short, the word "council." It illustrates a renewed meeting of like-minded individuals. Furthermore, this Latin word means "to bring together," "unite," "win over."[11]

The prominent Greek verb used to express reconciliation (*katallassō*) means to exchange one thing for another. William Barclay (1964, p. 165) notes that this meaning has had wide-ranging applications, from simple monetary exchange to Aristotle's reference that mercenary soldiers willingly bartered their lives for worldly gain. In New Testament theology, of course, the word is used to convey God's gift of atonement and righteousness through his Son's sacrifice. Paul expresses God's unmerited favor through a contrast: "For if, when we were God's enemies, we were reconciled [from the verb *katallassō*] to him through the death of his Son, how much more, having been reconciled [*katallassō*], shall we be saved through his life!" (Rom. 5:10).

A Provocative Passage

Reconciliation is a comprehensive concept. It embraces evangelism and acknowledges discipleship. Reconciliation offers both theological soundness and practical direction for daily life. God's plan is for believers to serve as ministers of restoration.

Reconsider Wolterstorff's earlier commentary. Determining the fall's consequences, he specifies four categories pertinent to reconciliation:

- Between the individual and *God*
- Between the individual and *self*
- Between the individual and *others*
- Between the individual and *creation*[12]

When God acts, he does so completely. He is thorough and impartial. Consequently, when we look at his reconciling gift in Christ, we observe the universal dimensions of restoration at work. All of creation felt the transforming effects of the cross. Our mission—in Christ—is to not dismiss any aspect of reconciliation:

Therefore, if anyone is in Christ, he is a new creation; the old has gone, the new has come! All this is from God, who reconciled us to himself through Christ and gave us the ministry of reconciliation: that God was reconciling the world to himself in Christ, not counting men's sins against them. And he has committed to us the message of reconciliation. We are therefore Christ's ambassadors, as though God were making his appeal through us. We implore you on Christ's behalf: Be reconciled to God. God made him who had no sin to be sin for us, so that in him we might become the righteousness of God. As God's fellow workers

we urge you not to receive God's grace in vain. (2 Cor. 5:17–6:1)

In brief, these six verses summarize the Christian's view of and purpose in life. Regardless of our particular giftedness and callings, we are reminded what it is that unites us in Christ. This passage of Scripture advances every dimension of reconciliation. It is the Magna Charta for all believers, our authority, directive, and liberation.

First, the *message of reconciliation* is noted at least three times: "God . . . reconciled us to himself through Christ" (5:18a). This historic act was intended for "the world" in such a way that God would "not [be] counting men's sins against them" (v. 19a). Moreover, "God made him [Christ] who had no sin to be sin for us, so that in him we might become the righteousness of God" (v. 21).

Second, a *metamorphosis through reconciliation* has been experienced. Divine transformation begins. Unprecedented change occurs within every genuine believer. "Therefore, if anyone is in Christ, he is a new creation; the old has gone, the new has come!" (v. 17).

Third, *messengers for reconciliation* appear. The true church comprises all who have been (and who are being) transformed. Paul refers to believers as "God's fellow workers" (6:1). No fewer than eight times in six short verses are the words "we" and "us" utilized. Specifically, Paul acknowledges that God "gave *us* the ministry of reconciliation" (v. 18b), and God "committed to *us* the message of reconciliation" (v. 19b).

Fourth, the *ministry of reconciliation* emerges from Paul's letter. The second half of verse 18 raises this precise phrase. Without mincing words, Paul concludes: "We are therefore Christ's ambassadors" (v. 20a). Such a phrase may elicit several images in our minds. Paul promotes the value of a worthy, though difficult, vocation. Our daily life-task is to allow "God . . . [to make] his appeal through us" (v. 20b). Among other concerns, this task includes our "cultural mandate"—the complementary duties of being rulers over and stewards of the environment.

Figure 2.1 summarizes these four features from 2 Corinthians 5:17–6:1. Categories that require reconciliation are paired with God's plan for resolution.

How Did We Get Here?

A brief sketch of human history facilitates our comprehension of reconciliation. It is helpful to picture history as separate acts of a play—the unfolding drama of God's creation, so to speak. Three acts are prominent; the third act contains three sub-

Figure 2.1

Reconciliation: Requirements and Resolutions

Requirement		Resolution
• Between the individual and *God*	→	by the *MESSAGE*
• Between the individual and *self*	→	by the *METAMORPHOSIS*
• Between the individual and *others*	→	by the *MESSENGERS*
• Between the individual and *creation*	→	by the *MINISTRY*

Source: Based on 2 Cor. 5:17–6:1.

scenes. (See Figure 2.2 for an overview of God's work in history.)

Concentrate especially on the three "acts" of God.

Figure 2.2

God's Plan for Reconciliation

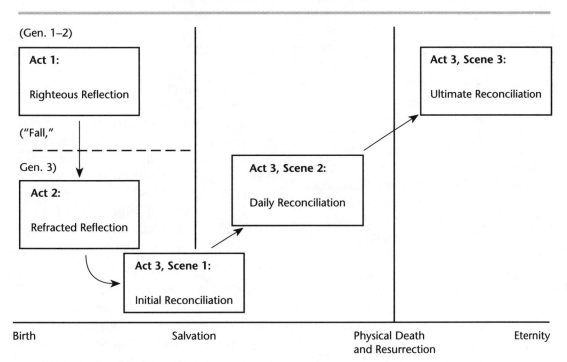

Note: Act 3 represents *Rejuvenated Reconciliation*. All three "scenes" derive from Act 3.

Act 1: Righteous Reflection—As the curtain opens on God's creative work in history, everything is perfect. In particular, people perfectly reflect their Creator.

Act 2: Refracted Reflection—Darkness permeates the stage, subsequent to Adam and Eve's rebellion. The backdrop of sin leads to gloom and despair.

Act 3: Rejuvenated Reflection—Through Christ's redeeming sacrifice, potential restoration is realized. Three subscenes comprise this third act, the last of which exalts the Creator.

Act 1: Righteous Reflection

When God created his world he called it "good" (Gen. 1:10, 12, 18, 21, 25). He formed the first man and woman. "Very good," the Creator decreed (Gen. 1:31). The world was flawless and perfect. It is impossible for us to fully grasp this perfection, this side of the fall.

At least three aspects of Righteous Reflection existed at that time. Mary VanderGoot (1987, p. 142) puts her finger on the first aspect: "In the world that God created, that was not marred by sin, humankind imaged God by willing rightly and by knowing truly, not merely by willing and reasoning per se. What is most essential to the image of God in us, and thus to our definition as persons, is the relationship of God the creator with us the creatures he made."

Being created in God's image sets the critical theological tone for biblical anthropology. It best indicates the character of our pre-fallen parents. Likewise, it describes the nature of *every* person subsequent to the fall,[13] Christian as well as atheist. What does it mean to be in God's image? Hoekema (1986, pp. 68–73) suggests two broad categories: the *structural* element and the *functional* element. The former refers to who people *are* (their essence). The latter centers on what people *do* (their performance). To illustrate,

among other God-given gifts, people reflect their Maker by having the capacity to speak (structure). What they actually say when they communicate represents function.[14]

The perfect state of our first parents involved far more than righteous companionship with the Creator. Vertical relationship always mirrors horizontal ties with all creation. As VanderGoot (1987, p. 142) points out, the second aspect of this initial sinless state "was not only a perfect harmony with the creator, but also perfect harmony among all the creatures God made. The image of paradise is one in which each creature had a place among all the others. And the place of the original man and woman was to be special caretakers of the other creatures that the Lord had made."

One indication of humankind's unique task to care for all of God's creation was Adam's privilege of naming every one of God's creatures (Gen. 2:15, 19–20). The apex of creation was in tune with every corner of the "triangle." No fearful mistrust existed, no breach of relationships. It was quite similar to what creation's future reality will look like. God will fully restore his creation; the wolf will live with the lamb, the leopard with the goat, the calf with the lion (Isa. 11:6).

But there was still more. The initial state of perfection assured harmony among all people as well. The third aspect points to a perfect partnership within the first family (Gen. 1:27–28; 2:21–24).

All three aspects of humankind's sinless condition are demonstrated in Figure 2.3. Righteous Reflection comprehensively embraced every relationship.

Act 2: Refracted Reflection

No sooner had perfection been established then things turned sour because of sin. Each "triangle corner" felt the devastating jolt of sin's effects. Nothing escaped its ruin.

Figure 2.3

Relationships of Righteous Reflection

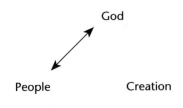

Aspect 1: Perfect harmony between the *Creator and people*

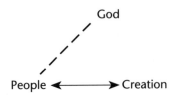

Aspect 2: Perfect harmony between *people and the rest of creation*

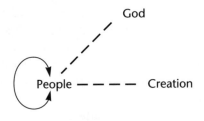

Aspect 3: Perfect harmony *among people themselves* [*Note*: This phase connotes harmony with self *and* harmony with others.]

VanderGoot (1987, p. 143) correctly assesses the universal destruction resulting from our willful rebellion: "Everything in us and about us was touched by the distorting consequences of sin: our wills became corrupt, our understanding blurred, our human relationships stressful, our guardianship of the other creatures unreliable, our feelings bent, and our actions inadequate."

Figure 2.4 graphically portrays this devastation. Broken relationships exist at every point.[15]

First, sin necessarily marred our first parents' perfect union with God. The twin emotions of guilt and fear pointed to this separation (see Gen. 3:8–10).[16] Second, Satan (embodied in the serpent) was set at odds with people (Gen. 3:14–15). Third, pain in childbirth would represent strife within all human relationships.[17] Finally, discord between the total cosmos and the entire human race was sown, portrayed by the cursed ground (Gen. 3:17–19).

"Refracted Reflection" best describes this second act of God's unfolding drama, since refraction means "to break off." The Latin word *refractarius* describes an obstinate and unmanageable relationship. To put it an-

Figure 2.4

Relationships of Refracted Reflection

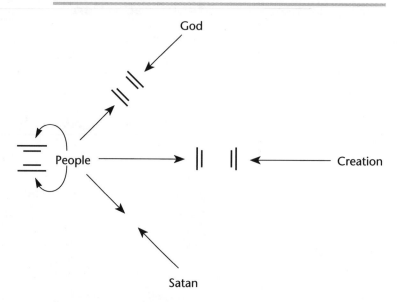

other way, all human relationships were "broken off" from earlier perfect harmony. Contentiousness remained. People still mirrored their Creator. But now, the image was the distorted reflection of an amusement park mirror.

In all, seven expressions of refraction are found in Genesis 3. Table 2.1 provides a summary, having many overlapping points.[18]

Think about It

Choose three of the seven expressions of refraction from Table 2.1 and write them here:

1. _____
2. _____
3. _____

Beside each selection, provide at least two examples of sin's consequences, other than those given in Table 2.1

Act 3: Rejuvenated Reflection

In the middle of God's judgments is the promise of the coming Messiah (Gen. 3:15). The grace of God intervenes. Justice and hope are offered to the human race.

In Genesis 6, a prototype of God's ultimate plan for reconciliation is played out

Table 2.1

Implications of Refracted Reflection

- *Theological* refraction (involving God, people, and Satan)
- *Cosmological* refraction ("thorns and thistles")
- *Vocational* refraction (the "painful toil" of hard work)
- *Physiological* refraction (eventual physical deterioration into "dust")
- *Psychological* refraction (personal guilt and shame)
- *Sociological* refraction (interpersonal conflict, symbolized by birth pangs)
- *Ecological* refraction (never-ending conflict between people and creation)

through the flood. The temporal salvation of Noah, his family, and the animals in the ark prefigure God's future work on Calvary's cross. Even the postflood restoration of the earth points toward future, comprehensive reconciliation. Genesis 8:21–22 and 9:12–16 articulate a covenant for all creation, not just for people.

Of course, Christ's reconciling atonement was far superior and more permanent than the Noahic and the Mosaic covenants. (This fact stands as the premise for the entire Book of Hebrews.)

God's sovereign plan for Rejuvenated Reflection is not without its own complex structure. Three subscenes appear. All Act 3 features are mentioned in Colossians 1:19–23:

> For God was pleased to have all his fullness dwell in him, and through him to reconcile to himself all things, whether things on earth or things in heaven, by making peace through his blood, shed on the cross. Once you were alienated from God and were enemies in your minds because of your evil behavior. But now he has reconciled you by Christ's physical body through death to present you holy in his sight, without blemish and free from accusation—if you continue in your faith, established and firm, not moved from the hope held out in the gospel. This is the gospel that you heard and that has been proclaimed to every creature under heaven, and of which I, Paul, have become a servant.

Scene 1: Initial Reconciliation (Col. 1:19–21)
Whoever trusts Jesus as personal Savior receives instantaneous inheritance in God's kingdom. This promise became a historical reality through the reconciling act of Christ's sacrifice. The Bible says God was "making peace through his blood, shed on the cross" (v. 20). This verse is to be literally rendered "having *made* peace" (a past action with continuing results). Paul con-

sciously contrasts historic time sequence, saying that those "who were *once* . . . alienated from God" (v. 21) are "*now* . . . reconciled" (v. 22).[19]

Lewis B. Smedes comments on reconciliation, using a parallel verse (2 Cor. 5:17). Paul is not pleading the cause, Smedes says, for people to *become* "new creations" in Christ. Nor is Paul discussing what *may become* of believers at some future date. Rather, change occurs instantaneously.

Smedes (1970, pp. 104–5) proceeds to reinforce the importance of the cross' historicity. "God reconciled us to Himself by means of a particular occurrence at a particular place during three particular hours that could have been measured on anyone's clock." Moreover, Smedes affirms the value of time apologetically.[20]

It must never be forgotten that reconciliation restores "*all* things" to God (Col. 1:20). In fact, Paul purposefully adds "whether things on earth or things in heaven." Oftentimes, evangelicals live as though God's restoration is exclusively for us. We dupe ourselves into thinking that reconciliation is restricted to private instances of salvation. But God's work at Calvary was comprehensive. *All* of creation is affected.[21]

Scene 2: Daily Reconciliation (Col. 1:23)
"This world is not my home. I'm just-a passin' through." Many of the spirituals correctly present the Christian life as a pilgrimage. Peter testifies of this pilgrim travel, calling his readers "aliens and strangers in the world" (1 Pet. 2:11a). The Hall of Faith chapter in the Bible (Heb. 11) characterizes several noble pilgrims. Faithful living should link Daily Reconciliation with Initial and Ultimate Reconciliation. Paul leaves no doubt about this fact, saying that temporal evidences (fruit) of holy living objectively affirm God's reconciliation. The phrase "If you continue in your faith" (v. 23a) is sharply juxtaposed with unfaithful charac-

ter—"not moved from the hope held out in the gospel" (v. 23b).

Recall that the anthropological portion of the Reconciliation Model consists of two subsections. *Intra*personal features of reconciliation involve duty to self. Paul specifies our private responsibilities of renewed mind and renewed behavior. Both require continual sanctification (Col. 1:21). *Inter*personal decrees for reconciliation are scattered throughout Scripture. This is especially seen in synonymous commands. Imperatives for peace, for instance, include verses like Hebrews 12:14: "Make every effort to live in peace with all men and to be holy; without holiness no one will see the Lord." Paul's letter to Rome keeps the same focus, but has an even more conditional tone: "If it is possible, as far as it depends on you, live at peace with everyone" (Rom. 12:18).[22]

Think about It

1. How is Hebrews 12:14 different from Romans 12:18? _____

   _____

2. Paraphrase Romans 12:18.

   _____

   _____

3. Pretend you're counseling a person who is finding it difficult to work with another employee. What advice do you give that person, based on your understanding of these two verses?

   _____

   _____

Interpersonal reconciliation simply expresses one facet of the *imago Dei*. Proverbs 14:31 promotes a more complex formula: "He who oppresses the poor shows contempt for their Maker, but whoever is kind to the needy honors God" (cf. Prov. 17:5a). James extends the same formula. It is inconsistent to praise God, then to "curse men, who have been made in God's likeness" (3:9). Of course, cursing is not limited to verbal abuse. As the previous proverb demonstrates, any form of oppression counts. John C. Maxwell (1989, p. 11) explains, "What's the key to relating to others? It's putting yourself in someone else's place instead of putting them in their place." This formula takes the shape of an equation: *As we treat people, so we treat God.*

Other passages of Scriptures affirm this equation. Consider Matthew 25:31–46. Here, the righteous are ultimately distinguished from the unrighteous, since the former express their sincere devotion to the Lord through:

- nourishing the hungry and thirsty
- welcoming the stranger
- clothing the naked
- caring for the sick
- visiting the imprisoned

The unrighteous, by contrast, stand at the opposite end of the judgment continuum. They fail to assist the same needy groups of people.

The righteous genuinely question their reward (vv. 37–39). "How was it," they ponder out loud, "that our interpersonal kindnesses were actually taken as kindness to the King (Christ)?" In other words, the righteous act kindly because it is inherently right; there is no need for extrinsic reward. The unrighteous ask the identical question of the King (v. 44). The way they frame their question, however, is dissimilar. A paraphrase of their inquiry could read: "Lord, had we *known* it was you we were helping through these needy people, we *would* have responded appropriately." In other words, the unrighteous fail to accomplish the inherently moral task. They are motivated solely by external reward. Before they act, they have to be promised some personal benefit.

The King pronounces equitable judgment in both cases: "Whatever you did [or "did not do"] for one of the least of these [brothers of mine] you did for me" (vv. 40, 45).

Bill Hybels (1987, p. 64) makes the following application: "Empathy [or compassion] does not come naturally to us hard-hearted people. We have to slow down and make a determined effort to put ourselves in other people's shoes. We need to ask ourselves how it would feel to be in their situations."[23]

In addition to these expressions of reconciling ministry, we should not neglect our responsibility to the environment, God's creation. The church must lead the way in ecological reform. We must set the pace when it comes to sound stewardship. Unfortunately, not much attention has been given to this concern in evangelical circles; there are very few educational resources.[24]

Scene 3: Ultimate Reconciliation (Col. 1:22)

Now we face the dilemma. If we have been immediately reconciled, why don't we feel and act like it? Why don't we always have victory over sin? Unfortunately we are stuck between *the now* and *the not yet.*[25]

Besides Initial and Daily Restoration, Paul deliberates on the coming day when Christians will be presented to God "holy . . . without blemish and free from accusation" (Col. 1:22). The futuristic tone is as certain as the victory is sealed—not now, but one day. Although the outcome is sure, believers must not live "so heavenly-minded, they are no earthly-good." Smedes (1970, p. 108) cautions against such a mindset, providing a realistic response to Ultimate Reconciliation:

But if we assume, as we must, that the Christian has here and now been liberat-

ed from the kingdom of darkness and given asylum in the land of light, that the "powers" have fallen, that the "god of this age" has been defeated, that "old things have passed away and the new has come," we are in agony. But it is the agony of one who knows that things have really changed and are going to change; only the man who knows in faith that something has happened and is going to happen is likely to cry, "How long?"

Francis Schaeffer draws similar conclusions. He concentrates on the continuous tension between Ultimate and Daily Reconciliation. Regarding the latter responsibility, his assessment of evangelicals is that we have failed miserably. Schaeffer's (1970, p. 68) solution is found in what he calls "substantial healing," a phrase connoting two prominent church tasks. First, we must continually attempt to restore creation, recognizing that our daily efforts and results will be limited. This reflects faithful—yet realistic—thinking.

Second, we must try to reconcile creation, by keeping *ultimate* restoration in mind as our motivation. This shows hopeful—and idealistic—thought. "On the basis of the fact that there is going to be total redemption in the future, not only of man but of all creation, the Christian who believes the Bible should be the man who—with God's help and in the power of the Holy Spirit—is treating nature *now* in the direction of the way nature will be *then.*"

Conclusion

Figure 2.5 portrays the composite picture of God's reconciling plan as outlined in this chapter. Although actual progression toward Ultimate Reconciliation is much more fluid and dynamic, this linear model stresses discrete categories and sequences of events. By adding Christ as the Mediator of

Figure 2.5
God's Plan to Reconcile All Creation

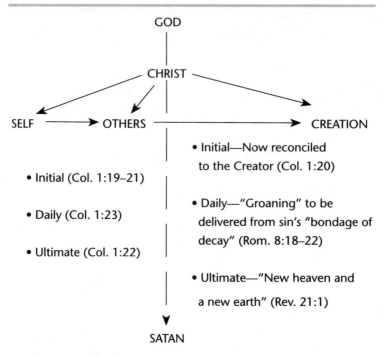

The dotted line from Christ to Satan indicates
that technically Satan will not be reconciled with
the rest of creation. Yet, it is useful to observe
the facts about him, according to the three-scene structure.

- Initial—Defeat by Christ secured in the Garden (Gen. 3:15)

- Daily—Given limited authority as "the ruler of the
  kingdom of the air" (Eph. 2:2)

- Ultimate—Eternal suffering and torment (Rev. 20:10)

all reconciliation and by subdividing the anthropological component into "self" and "others," the previous version of the Reconciliation Model is updated. Also, each of the three scenes from Act 3 (Rejuvenated Reconciliation) can be expanded.

'Til Faith Do Us Part

Commitment in reconciliation can be compared to marriage. In marriage, a person says "I do" at some historical place and point in time. So, too, the obedient believer commences the spiritual pilgrimage by saying "I do" at the altar of salvation. Ideally both commitments are for a lifetime. Each decision is daily reaffirmed and strengthened. Deeper levels of loyalty are sought. Fidelity, sincerity, and unrestricted love are prerequisites for both marriage and faith.

By way of contrast, when the commitment of faith is minimized, the result is the "cheap grace" that Dietrich Bonhoeffer despised—easy believism. Similarly, as wedding vows are cheapened, the onslaught of broken marriages in this generation is no surprise. The marriage and faith analogy is presented in Table 2.2. The three phases of commitment compare with the three scenes of our Reconciliation Model.

Think about It

Expand Table 2.2 using your own insights. What additional parallels can you make between the commitments made in faith and marriage? _____

_____

_____

_____

Furthering the analogy of faith and marriage, the wedding bands symbolize wholehearted commitment. Personal values complement the costly metal and jewels within the rings. A continuous circle represents faithfulness. Perhaps similar mementos should be given on the day a person accepts Christ as Savior. Such visual reminders encourage steadfastness. We intentionally celebrate wedding anniversaries. Why not annually celebrate our rebirth?

Age-Appropriate Applications

What are the daily indicators of reconciliation? What does a reconciling person look like? It isn't enough just to know *about* God. The Pharisees accomplished this goal quite well. Knowledge is important, but incomplete for maturing believers. We must drop the preposition "about." We should daily "know" our heavenly Father through a growing, intimate relationship.[26]

Contemplate this reconciling duty from an age-specific perspective. Consider just one reconciling task: our personal relationship with God in prayer. A young child's understanding of prayer is classified under "things that Christians do." Prayer is seen as a checklist item to complete, like brushing your teeth, just one more thing to do before turning off the lights. A young child should be guided to see prayer as some-

---

Table 2.2

The Marriage-Faith Analogy

The *Initial* Commitment	At a historical point in time we say, "I do" at the altars of marriage and faith.
The *Daily* Commitment: Affecting Thoughts and Choices	Daily choosing to be faithful—saying "Yes" to one person requires saying "No" to all others—influences our thoughts and choices. (Notice how idolatry is often linked with adultery. See 1 Cor. 5:9–11; 10:7–8.)
Affecting Feelings and Attitudes	Daily choosing to resolve destructive emotions encourages self-control and fidelity (see Eph. 4:26–27).
Affecting Behaviors and Lifestyles	Daily choosing a posture of mutual submission is necessary for growth (see 1 Cor. 7:3–4).
The *Ultimate* Commitment	"I do" lasts 'til death do us part."

thing Christians do *in relationship with their Father.* This expanded classification goes beyond facts *about* God to fellowship *with* him.

Teenagers should be encouraged to mature and expand their view of reconciliation. They should pursue their relationship with God as they would a strong friendship; they should develop a prayer life with the same fervor as meaningful communication with closest confidants.

Adults should not view prayer as something to do in a relationship or even as part of the relationship itself. Both are ultimately tied to a reward system: Motivation is attributed to what *I* get out of it (i.e., good gifts and good friends, respectively). From time to time, there may be a legitimate place for these two prayer perspectives, but it must not be the mature believer's predominant image. Prayer should be inherently valued as a privilege of an endearing relationship. Specifically, we must view prayer as a necessary component of our covenant with God. We must help adults talk to the Father as they would to a cherished friend, to share their highs and lows. In contrast to the teen perspective, adults must not expect something in return. Often, God is quite silent. That silence should not diminish the commitment to the relationship.

In the end, then, our duty as leaders in Christian educational ministry is to promote peace and restoration. Our lifelong task as ambassadors of peace must focus on God, self, others, and all of creation.

But our never-ending task must also be age-shaped. Young children see prayer as *rules* of Christian relationship—asking for personal favors. Teenagers view prayer as *rituals*—acting according to certain interpersonal customs. Adults visualize prayer as *rights* (or privileges) of spiritual stewardship—being committed to principled loyalty, regardless of reward. Each position values age-appropriate instructional applications.

As Christian teachers, two broad implications surface. First, we must model reconciliation, consistent with these truths. Second, we instructors must be sensitive to phases of growth in our students and seek maturity via relevant strategies.[27]

We must help all individuals respond to God. We must create environments that encourage a sincere passion for the Creator. No dimension of human experience should be abandoned. How we think, feel, choose, and live are important to God—and they should be important to us, as educators.

One evaluative question rises above all others: "Does it foster restoration?" Nothing short of reconciliation will do.

3 A Reconciliation Model of Christian Maturity

Dog Day Afternoon

I never thought it would happen. Two unthinkable events occurred within one month's time. First, Mary and I broke down and gave in to the pressure. After eighteen years of marriage and thirteen years of childrearing, we bought our first family pet: a hamster. Granted, it was a compromise. Both of us came from large families. We had experienced an array of pets during our own childhoods, from turtles and snakes to cats and German shepherds. In spite of this—or because of it—for years we clung to the same old arguments against any pet: "They're too difficult to take care of." "Who watches it while we're away?" "What if they die?"

The first unthinkable event of hamster ownership quickly brought all the "what ifs" to reality. Our family went on a va-

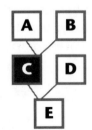

cation. After three days, our house-sitter called us to say that Alvin had passed on. It took us eight days to get the courage to tell the kids.

When we got home, we replaced Alvin with Betsy. That's when the second unthinkable event happened. Betsy escaped from her cage. After hours of hunting in vain, Mary suggested that we give in again: We brought Jackson into the house to find Betsy. Jackson was the neighborhood hound. "You mean that, after almost twenty years of marriage without pets, you want to bring an 'outdoor' dog into *our* neatly kept house?" I challenged. I was shocked! I knew Mary was desperate, but what she said made sense: "That's what those types of dogs are made to do—track animals," she reasoned. "That's their one outstanding characteristic." And she was right.

We share this story to highlight this chapter's purpose. Believers must continually ask: What is the outstanding task that we have? What were we "made to do"?

In the Rearview Mirror

In Chapter 2 we claimed that the Christian's ultimate task is reconciliation. The term represents a biblically sound objective. God initiated this focus through his Son. The church subsequently assumed the responsibility. Numerous imperatives from Scripture call for related aims of peace, unity, and fellowship. Specifically, believers are directed to restore harmony, mend broken ties, bring back erring believers, and regain the lost.

We also spoke about four particular categories of faith and life that require reconciliation. Restored relationships include those with God, self, others, and creation. If reconciliation is seen as comprehensive— and it must—Christian leaders should never neglect any feature of this foursome.[1]

Foundational Considerations of Maturity

With reconciliation as our ultimate objective, how can we Christian educators subdivide this lifelong task?[2] What intermediate aims or subpoints exist? How do we know if we are accomplishing God's overarching mandate? What is it we were "made to do"?

Ultimate Purpose and Subgoals[3]

As we investigate the integrated parts of reconciliation, it is important to analyze New Testament patterns. A well-known Scripture passage, Acts 2:42–47, details the intermediate aims of early Christians. This passage delineates the component parts of our ultimate educational purpose.

> They devoted themselves to the apostles' teaching and to the fellowship, to the breaking of bread and to prayer. Everyone was filled with awe, and many wonders and miraculous signs were done by the apostles. All the believers were together and had everything in common. Selling their possessions and goods, they gave to anyone as he had need. Every day they continued to meet together in the temple courts. They broke bread in their homes and ate together with glad and sincere hearts, praising God and enjoying the favor of all the people. And the Lord added to their number daily those who were being saved.

This passage does not exhaust the directives entrusted to God's people. But it does provide a superb list of subpoints pertinent to reconciliation. Specifically, the church's responsibilities can be broken down into four themes:

- Communion[4]
- Community

Figure 3.1

The Reconciled Church's Responsibilities

THEME	LOGO	SUPPORT IN SCRIPTURE	PRIMARY FOCUS
COMMUNION		"prayer" (v. 42) "praising God" (v. 47)	the Reconciler (God)
COMMUNITY		"devoted to . . . the fellowship" (v. 42) "together and had everything in common" (v. 44)	the reconcilable people
CHARACTER		"devoted to the apostles' teaching" (v. 42)	the reconciling process
COMMISSION		"selling their possessions . . . they gave to anyone as he had need" (v. 45)	the reconciliatory proclamation

- Character
- Commission

Figure 3.1 correlates these four themes with directives from Acts 2. Notice how the match-ups parallel doctrinal features of reconciliation.

The Four Themes

"Communion" is central to all four themes. The word highlights our essential relationship with God. Communion reflects our primary *vertical* tie. The three remaining themes are predominantly *horizontal*. J. I. Packer (1973, p. 29) observes:

What were we made for? To know God. . . . What is the "eternal life" that Jesus gives? Knowledge of God. "This is life eternal, that they might know thee, the only true God, and Jesus Christ, whom thou hast sent" (John 17:3). What is the best

thing in life, bringing more joy, delight, and contentment, than anything else? Knowledge of God. . . . Once you become aware that the main business that you are here for is to know God, most of life's problems fall into place of their own accord.

In Acts 2:42, 47, the early church fulfilled Communion obligations through prayer and praise. Their knowledge of God—in the most comprehensive, experiential sense—increased. Faith blossomed within these worshipers. As these believers maintained the centrality of Communion, a proper ordering of the four themes emerged. As this vertical dimension was heeded, the remaining responsibilities were better accomplished.

Perhaps the fact most often highlighted in Acts 2 is fellowship. We've coined it "Community." Voluntarily, believers devoted themselves to each other. Sophisticated social growth and accountability were evidenced. This second theme points to the reconcilable people in God's redemptive plan. Frederick Buechner (1969, pp. 45–47) suggests a practical metaphor. Affirming John Donne's "No man is an island," Buechner calls for believers to be "bridge-builders"— what he labels *pontifex*. In this way the kingdom of God is built.[5]

"Character" speaks of personal growth. Among other matters, dedication to God's Word elicits such worthy ends. Believers, transformed on the first day of Pentecost, commenced Character formation through the apostles' teaching (v. 42). The reputation of the church—along with its size—had both qualitative and quantitative growth. Christians were "enjoying the favor of all the people" (v. 47a). Their testimony affirmed the moral dimension of Character. Packer (1988, p. 33) connects the themes of Communion and Character. Forgiveness provides the link, since this is how Christian maturity begins: "However unloved and worthless we once felt, and however much self-hate and condemnation we once

nursed, we must now see that by loving us enough to redeem us God gave us value, and by forgiving us completely, he obligated us to forgive ourselves and made it sin for us not to."

The theme of Character originates in divine forgiveness. The reason why the early believers were "enjoying the favor" of the populace was because, for the first time, they were freed from sin's slavery. As Packer states, God's forgiveness also brings *value.* To accept the Father's forgiveness is to appropriate our self-worth.[6] Genuine Christian Character starts with a new view of personhood.

Finally, "Commission" provides the church with its marching orders. Evangelism is pivotal. Yet, a more comprehensive understanding of "good news" is required. Early believers, for instance, were known for their sacrificial love expressed in material gifts. Since they gave the proceeds of possessions they sold to *"anyone"* who was needy (v. 45), even nonbelievers benefited.[7] Our divine calling, giftedness, and vocation attend to the theme of Commission. Com-

Table 3.1

Reconciliation Themes

	Communion	**Community**	**Character**	**Commission**
Description	Praising God by acknowledging and obeying his revelation	Experiencing genuine fellowship through the common bond of Christ	Being individually nurtured to grow into the Son's image	Sharing the good news of Christ's love; ministering to needy people; applying God's truth to life and vocation
Duty	To bring joy to God; to strengthen the divine-human relationship; to grow in faith and love	To knit believers together in love, stressing social/moral maturity in the church	To facilitate personal holistic growth toward Christ-likeness	To help people know God and become like his Son through God's calling and gifts

menting on this term, Buechner (1969, p. 31) states: "It means for us simply that we must be careful with our lives, for Christ's sake, because it would seem that they are the only lives we are going to have in this puzzling and perilous world, and so they are very precious and what we do with them matters enormously."

How do we instructors know if we are accomplishing what God calls us to teach? What specific evidence can we use for the evaluation of personal maturity? How do we best help others mature? What signs of growth will we see? In this section, two major topics are discussed. First, the four themes of the Reconciliation Model of maturity are further scrutinized. Second, practical examples of education are examined. Table 3.1 offers descriptions and duties of the themes.

Communion

Gordon R. Lewis and Bruce A. Demarest (1987, p. 122) note that "The comprehensive purpose of special revelation is the reestablishment of the full communion of sinful people with God." James Houston (1989, p. 56) comments that "Many people have an internal division between what they think and what they do, between belief and action. In fact, many religious people see their faith as a set of beliefs they agree to, rather than as a living relationship with God." Communion with God begins with meaningful communication patterns like prayer and worship. Eugene Peterson (1987, p. 29) admonishes: "Prayer means that we deal with God and then with the world." In Psalm 139 David shows us that God knows us better than we know ourselves.

- "O LORD, you have searched me and you know me" (v. 1).
- "Before a word is on my tongue you know it completely, O LORD" (v. 4).

- "For you created my inmost being; you knit me together in my mother's womb" (v. 13).

Communion is being honest with God—sharing our doubts, hurts, anger, bitterness, and despair. Conversely, it includes expressions of joy, thanksgiving, and praise. In short, Communion portrays the essence of a healthy, intimate relationship. Whatever promotes these aims advances the practical side of Communion. A parallel, biblical phrase for this theme is "faith." Godly leaders in Scripture were known as men and women *of faith*, because they steadfastly communed with the Creator. On this point, Peterson (1987, p. 28) advances a stern warning: "Pastors who imitate the preaching and moral action of the prophets without also imitating the prophets' deep praying and worship so evident in the Psalms are an embarrassment to the faith and an encumbrance to the church."

Think about It

When was the last time you were honest about your relationship with God? How did you express your growth—through sincere doubts or genuine thanksgiving?

Read Psalm 55. State your first reactions to David's honesty. _____

_____

List two problems that troubled David. Note where these difficulties are found in the psalm.

1. (verse   )— _____
2. (verse   )— _____

List two assurances or promises that David identifies. Give the respective verses.

1. (verse   )— _____
2. (verse   )— _____

Follow David's lead. Contemplate one area of your Communion with God. Where do you need to be more honest and transparent in your prayers? What promise will you claim for your needs?

Community

Community is to fellowship what Communion is to worship. Both seek relational integrity. Several passages in Scripture depict this analogy: Our faith in God affirms our love for one another (John 13:34–35). This must be the litmus test of all mature congregations. Conversely, we are "liars" if we say we love God but hate our spiritual kin (1 John 4:20–21). A vivid application of this dual association surfaces in Matthew 5:20–26. If, while we are worshiping God (i.e., Communion), we recall an interpersonal offense (i.e., Community), we are to promptly cease our worship, become reconciled, and return to worship. It is impossible to divorce this vertical-horizontal obligation, according to the Bible.[8]

Think about It

What particular sins might be estranging you from your brother or sister in Christ? What sins inhibit your effectiveness as a Christian educator? A critical tongue? An unforgiving spirit? Gossip? Ungodly cliques? Or is it the *absence* of positive, social behavior: failure to encourage, to offer gratitude, to comfort?

Character

One practical dimension of this third theme resides in the need to guard our thought life. Paul frequently reminds us of this responsibility: "Finally, brothers, whatever is true, whatever is noble, whatever is right, whatever is pure, whatever is lovely, whatever is admirable—if anything is excellent or praiseworthy—think about such things" (Phil. 4:8).

But godly Character means much more. The prophet Micah provides substantive dimensions of Character: "And what does the LORD require of you? To act justly and to love mercy and to walk humbly with your God" (Mic. 6:8). Living by this meter stick demands that we incarnate comprehensive issues of justice, mercy, and humility in our classrooms.

Think about It

With your students, how do you promote fairness? Do you remedy situations where learners are oppressed by others or by their environment? How do you offer mercy instead of harshness?

Put negatively, is your ministry characterized by arrogance or even aloofness?

Perhaps the phrase "moral growth" best defines the theme of godly Character. Although the words "spirituality" and "morality" are not synonymous, a close association exists between them. Recall that when Jesus spoke of future judgment, he equated inherently moral deeds with spiritual vitality and reward (Matt. 25:31–40).

Commission

What facilitates godly stewardship? It starts with a confident calling, mission, and purpose. We've titled it "Commission." This challenge includes the call to good works (Eph. 2:10), the implementation of spiritual giftedness (Eph. 4:16), and genuine service to the needy (Acts 20:35). All three subduties can be consciously prompted by thoughtful teachers. Even those who instruct young children should intentionally address these objectives. Christ-honoring behaviors must be commended; potential gifts (such as mercy, hospitality, and wisdom) should be recognized; and opportunities for service ministries should be provided. Many of us fondly recall childhood experiences of serving in our churches and neighborhoods.

Dallas Willard (1988, p. 51) reminds us that Commission includes ecological concerns as well. He ties this fourth theme to the doctrine of anthropology:

> Perhaps our present tendency to have pets and zoos, to be fond of living creatures and domesticate them, and our amazing powers to train and control other creatures on the planet are but dim reflections of the divine intention for us.
>
> Our care about the extinction of species and our general feeling of responsibility and concern for the fate of animals, plants, and even the earth also speaks of this divine intention. Scientists talk easily and often of our responsibility to care for the oceans and forests and wild, living things. This urge toward such responsibility is, I think, only a manifestation of the *imago Dei* originally implanted in humankind and still not wholly destroyed.

William Diehl (1991) advances a provocative dimension of Commission. He suggests specific ways to help laypersons daily express their faith to the world: (1) the ministry of *competency*—for people to be the best at what they do, by utilizing their talents and gifts[9]; (2) the ministry of *presence*—for Christians to exhibit their faith in God via interpersonal relationships, offering a listening ear and prayers of intercession; (3) the ministry of *ethics*—for laypeople to translate Scripture into tough decision-making choices; (4) the ministry of *change*—for believers to alter socioeconomic structures with justice as their motivation; and (5) the ministry of *values*—for laypersons to reassess personal lifestyles and comprehensive stewardship issues.

John testifies of one household church, "I have no greater joy than to hear that my children are walking in the truth" (3 John 4). Commission undergirds this broad witness. It provides the opportunity to display faith in action. For all intents and purposes, Commission is contrasted with Community. Typically, the former is associated with the ministries *outside* the church; the latter *within* the fellowship. Exceptions to this contrast include those who are gifted to vocations *within* the body of Christ.[10]

Think about It

Given the "outside" nature of Commission, state three ways that teachers could encourage their students to obey this theme (avoid common statements like "witnessing" and "evangelizing"). Ask yourself, "What would 'walking in the truth' look like for students?"

1. _____
2. _____
3. _____

Table 3.2 details the practical instructional aims of the four themes. This table is intended to promote a better understanding of the maturity model.

How Perspectives Influence Themes[11]

It only makes sense that an ultimate objective affects pertinent subgoals. What might not be as apparent, however, is that the *perspectives* that people hold also affect these same goals, our themes. For example, consider two Sunday school teachers of schoolage children who expressly accept the ultimate purpose of reconciliation. One instructor sees children as miniature adults, while the other views each age group inde-

Table 3.2

Practical Instructional Aims

Communion	1. To encourage Bible study and worship. 2. To think critically about our prayers, raising pertinent questions about theology and spiritual maturity and challenging unexamined ideas (e.g., "Does God answer the prayers of the unrighteous?").
Community	1. To encourage emulation of peers and other persons who exhibit Christ-like character. 2. To scrutinize the model's total lifestyle, rejecting sinful behaviors or contradicting inconsistencies; to resolve conflict between believers; to learn when and how to disagree.
Character	1. To encourage virtuous qualities such as "strength, love, and self-discipline" (2 Tim. 1:7, NEB). 2. To foster teachable attitudes and correct harmful dispositions; to alter habits that are counterproductive to godliness; to promote self-assessment and personal goal setting.
Commission	1. To encourage fruitful evidences of tithing, evangelism, and giftedness. 2. To break down barriers to kingdom building; to support advocacy of the poor and needy; to promote comprehensive strategies that advance the cause of reconciliation.

pendently. More likely than not, the *means* by which both teachers instruct their students will vary because of their diverse perspectives. This topic takes into account broad views about people, truth, and lifestyle. Such perspectives are not merely subjective, but are based on findings from science and empirical information about these three subjects.

Extremes to Avoid

The key is balance and inclusion. If we teachers direct our learners toward only one or two of these themes, our effectiveness will be weakened. We must strive to avoid extreme interpretations of the Christian life and education.

The Tabernacle Temptation

By admitting his preference to stay on the Mount of Transfiguration and to build three tabernacles, Peter succumbed to this temptation (see Matt. 17:1–8). The Communion theme is totally misrepresented. The dualistic thinking of Greek culture appears in Peter's desires; a dichotomy emerges between the spiritual world (i.e., the

good) and the material world (i.e., the evil). Peter wanted to remain with the former and ignore the latter. Indicators of this neglect are self-righteous attitudes, little or no non-Christian contact, and a prevailing legalism. The tabernacle temptation is pervasive and subtle. Even the best intentions lead godly teachers down this path of isolationism and ineffectiveness.

The Country Club

Here, the theme of Community is exclusively (and unbiblically) highlighted. "The church exists," club members contend, "to meet its own needs." Socials are important. Conformity is expected. "We look out for one another. We're family."

Whereas fellowship *is* critical, country clubbers forget the mandate to witness to an unregenerate society (Acts 1:8). They forget that God providentially nudged the church out of its "Jerusalem" with an ensuing persecution (Acts 8:1). Some commentators believe that God's action was purposely directed toward the country club mind set. Think for a minute how we, even unconsciously, give into this temptation.

How can we educators specifically confront this temptation?

The Tightrope Walker

Henri Nouwen (1989, pp. 35–39) believes that many Christians distort the theme of Character. He confesses to personally falling into this temptation: "I came to see that I had lived most of my life as a tightrope artist trying to walk on a high, thin cable from one tower to the other, always waiting for the applause when I had not fallen off and broken my leg." Tightrope walkers view life and ministry from an extreme, individualistic stance. Not only do they remove themselves from the world, but they distance themselves from other believers. In so doing, they remove themselves from reality. Effective service as church leaders is diminished because no one can be discipled. Nobody can replicate their high-wire act. Character formation is erroneously viewed as private.

The Martha Syndrome

Some people believe that the difference between Mary and Martha is one of personality style (Luke 10:38–42). An alternate way of understanding this passage, however, is to acknowledge different emphases: Mary intentionally listened at Jesus' feet, whereas "Martha was distracted by all the preparations that had to be made" (v. 40). In other words, Martha placed a disproportionate emphasis on Commission. Ministry and vocation were translated into busyness. Christian workaholism resulted.

Think about It

Provide brief responses to the following questions:

1. Why are each of the four extremes above so tempting? What makes each attractive?

a. "Tabernacle Temptation"

_____

b. "Country Club" _____

_____

c. "Tightrope Walker"

_____

d. "Martha Syndrome"

_____

2. Pretend that your best friend has succumbed to one of these patterns. Circle one of the letters (a, b, c, or d) above, which you want to consider. In two or three sentences, what advice would you give to your friend?

_____

3. Provide your own example of each of these four extremes. How have you seen these misinterpretations of maturity demonstrated?

a. "Tabernacle Temptation"

_____

b. "Country Club"

_____

c. "Tightrope Walker"

_____

d. "Martha Syndrome"

_____

The tabernacle temptation, country club, tightrope walker, and Martha syndrome are properly checked by balance. We, as well as our students, must integrate all four Reconciliation themes. We must value comprehensive Christian educational ministry. One of the ways we maintain maturity is to guard against false assumptions. Review the four extremes above. Each features at least one major myth. What would you cite as the misconception of each?[12]

Practical Considerations of Maturity

Besides the theoretical foundations that frame the Reconciliation Model, practical considerations are also important.[13] Specific educational activities per theme are evident. In later chapters, age-appropriate methods are discussed.[14] Table 3.3, however, offers no such limits. Rather, it presents a potpourri of exercises geared at diverse environments: for public and private use; for in-class and out-of-class settings; for typical and atypical activities.

Think about It

Table 3.3 suggests practical ideas for teaching. What additional activities would you suggest for each theme in Christian education? Put your ideas in their respective categories.

Communion _____

_____

Community _____

_____

Table 3.3

Practical Instructional Activities

Communion	Community	Character	Commission
• Praying • Singing • Reading worshipful passages from the Bible or other books • Writing and reading reverent poetry • Analyzing useful guidelines about worship from the Bible, relevant books, and tapes • Leading a creative worship • Participation in worshipful drama or mime • Giving cheerfully • Using leisure time to glorify God • Honoring the Creator with a special gift or project	• Sharing with prayer partners • Bearing one another's burdens • Helping others develop their gifts • Eating together • Going on a church retreat • Interceding for others • Rejoicing with others • Participation in meaningful leisure activities • Developing accountability partners • Studying a controversial issue with those who hold alternative views; learning to agree to disagree • Counseling others • Providing services to the needy	• Memorizing Scripture • Praying • Meditating • Studying relevant Scripture passages on maturity • Analyzing ways to apply God's truth to one's life • Studying helpful tapes and books of godly men and women • Utilizing case studies with ethical dilemmas • Keeping a journal of answers to prayer • Discovering and developing spiritual giftedness • Promoting holistic health • Observing the Spirit's work through personal evidence of spiritual fruit	• Praying for non-Christian friends • Reading books on evangelism and discipleship • Sharing the gospel with a specific neighborhood group • Befriending an international student • Caring for needy individuals or families • Raising money for world hunger relief • Praying for unreached people • Consciously exhibiting lifestyle evangelism • Attending to ecological concerns • Becoming involved in social action and "cup of cold water" services • Supporting local parachurch ministries (e.g., childcare; outreach; rescue missions) • Demonstrating godly business ethics • Participating in community programs

Character _____

_____

Commission _____

_____

Conclusion

"Getting right with God" captures the best way to initiate personal reconciliation. Look at it from God's vantage point. The One who made us knows the precise prescription for our well-being. Accordingly, Communion means peace with God. We possess this assurance through our Savior. Paul says "we have peace with God through our Lord Jesus Christ" (Rom. 5:1).

Peace with God is not meant to stagnate through privatistic faith. Christian maturity should also produce peace-makers. It is not coincidental that those who actively pursue peace "will be called sons of God" (Matt. 5:9). Several times believers are intentionally directed to "live in peace with each other" (1 Thess. 5:13b; see also Col. 3:15; Titus 3:2). These commands point to practical aspects of Community.

Believers also need the peace of God. Peace *with* God commemorates our initial and immediate reconciliation. It is a historic event. The peace *of* God is more akin to daily personal reconciliation; it is an ongoing choice we make. Speaking about this task, Paul gives Christians at Philippi two directives for God's peace. First, don't worry about anything (Phil. 4:6a). Second, "present your requests to God" with thanksgiving and petition (Phil. 4:6b). The result? The peace *of* God (Phil. 4:7). We've termed it Character development.

Finally, whatever promotes "peaceful living" pertains to godly behavior. Our reconciling conduct must extend beyond the church to include peaceful coexistence with all creation. Paul reminds his spiritual son, Timothy, to join all believers and "live peaceful and quiet lives in all godliness and holiness" (1 Tim. 2:2). Commission means to "live at peace with *everyone*"—even non-believers.[15] This final theme includes all people as well as the rest of creation.

In other words, the educational themes of Christian maturity compare and contrast in this manner:

- *Communion* points to the "message of reconciliation"
- *Community* emphasizes the "messengers for reconciliation"
- *Character* attests to the "metamorphosis through reconciliation"
- *Commission* acknowledges the "ministry of reconciliation"

In the end, the model of maturity must not be read as a quick-fix formula. It should not be interpreted as some brash notion of accomplishment. It must not be misunderstood as a presumptuous statement of sinlessness. Rather, it speaks of breadth. It confronts the whole of education that is Christian. Through the four practical themes, our ultimate objective is better understood. Also, our instructional activities are more substantially grounded by these themes. We can assess whether or not educational strategies have any extrinsic merit. "Is there a bigger picture—a larger purpose—to our methods?" we must constantly ask.

This chapter's content is inextricably connected with the next two. All three chapters center on the four themes. The *theological* argument for this foursome has been advanced in this chapter. Chapter 4 proposes the *philosophical* (and anthropological) argument. Finally, Chapter 5 demonstrates the *psychological* argument for the four-part design of Christian maturity.

4 Universal Quests and Unique Filters

Playing Sherlock Holmes

Do you enjoy solving mysteries? Try your hand at these two brain-teasers.[1]

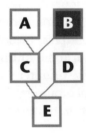

1. You enter a room. Romeo and Juliet lie dead on the floor. Broken glass and water surround them. The cat peeks out from behind a curtain. How did they die?
2. A woman enters a store to purchase something for her house. She asks the price. The clerk replies, "The cost of one is 39 cents. The cost of twenty-five is 78 cents. The cost of 144 is $1.17." What is the woman buying?

How did you solve the "Romeo and Juliet" mystery? Were they murdered? Was it suicide? Were they poisoned? Shot to death? Drowned? Did they bleed to death from the broken glass? These explanations are feasible, *if* you make a fundamental assumption: that Romeo and Juliet are people. But what if you change your assumption? What if the pair are *goldfish*—and the cat was left unattended?

Likewise, in the second case, many people falsely assume that 1, 25, and 144 stand for the quantity of purchased objects. But what if these figures *are* the actual objects? What if the woman was purchasing house numbers, representing her address? Following that assumption, "144" costs exactly three times what "1" costs.

In a sense, it comes down to perspective—the way we look at things.

Now, contemplate more serious matters: the gospel and culture. Whether we know it or not, we cling to numerous assumptions and perspectives pertinent to our faith. It's only human. But we can't be satisfied with simply accepting these biases, for some emerge from our sinful natures.

Think about It[2]

Listed below are issues that believers from various denominations deem important. Decide which statements you think are universal (and essential) to all Christians; check the blank to the *left* of each letter. Then, discern which statements you believe are cultural (and negotiable) for the church; check the blank to the *right* of each letter.

"Essential" or "Negotiable"

___ A.___ Greet believers with a holy kiss.
___ B.___ Don't sue other Christians.
___ C.___ Women should be veiled when they pray in church.
___ D.___ Wash the feet of participants at the Lord's Supper (Eucharist).
___ E.___ Lay hands on a pastoral candidate at ordination.
___ F.___ Worship without musical instruments.
___ G.___ Abstain from eating blood.
___ H.___ Abstain from fornication.
___ I.___ Always use unleavened bread and wine at the Lord's Supper (Eucharist).
___ J.___ Anoint with oil for healing.
___ K.___ Women should not teach men.
___ L.___ Women should not wear pearls or gold or braid their hair.
___ M.___ Don't ever drink wine.
___ N.___ Men should not have long hair.
___ O.___ Slavery is permissible, if slaves are treated well.
___ P.___ Stay single.
___ Q.___ Seek the gift of tongues.
___ R.___ Seek the gift of healing.
___ S.___ Seek the gift of signs and wonders.
___ T.___ Lift your hands when you pray.
___ U.___ Lift your hands when you pray in private.
___ V.___ Nonworking people don't eat.
___ W.___ Say "Amen" to conclude prayer.
___ X.___ Believers should be baptized by immersion.

If you're like most people, you discovered that this exercise was not as easy as it first appeared. "Essential" and "negotiable" are, at times, tough to differentiate.

1. Review your selection of "essential" items. Give two reasons or principles for how you determined their "essential" rating.

a._____

_____

b. _____

_____

2. Which statements had no explicit correlation with Scripture? List the first half-dozen you rated "negotiable" by *letter* only: _____

_____

_____

_____

3. State two overall assumptions you discovered you were making about Christian guidelines for behavior in this exercise:

a. _____

b. _____

An Overview

In this chapter, we will analyze perspectives. We all possess them. They represent how we look at life. In fact, "looking" provides a helpful analogy. On the one hand, everyone looks at life similarly. Perhaps you have heard the phrase "universal quests." In anthropology, it's called a "theory of man." Noted anthropologist Walter Goldschmidt (1966, p. 133) asks, "What is the nature of man? . . . What . . . are the recurrent problems of human interactions? What are the tenable solutions to these problems? What are the secondary consequences to such solutions?"

On the other hand, compared with others, we also observe life dissimilarly. We hold biases. We have diverse experiences. We maintain different values and convictions. All these contribute to what we've called "unique filters." Charles Kraft (1979, p. 26, emphasis added) extends the visual analogy:

Individuals and groups, for example, organize their perceptions of reality so as to ignore, distort, or exaggerate its features in ways that differ to a greater or lesser

extent from the organized perceptions of that reality described by other individuals and groups. We understand in terms of the *pictures of reality inside our heads,* via the lenses of our cultural and psychological cameras (or glasses). If those lenses are, for some reason or other (such as sickness, limitedness of experience, perversity, etc.) dirty or distorting (as with a camera out of focus), the way we perceive reality is greatly affected.

Technically speaking, our universal quests and our unique filters collectively form our worldview. Both frame the "reality inside our heads." Each has a valuable contribution to make when it comes to understanding how we live and interpret life, from the way we react to the evening news to the vocations we choose.

Comprehending the Meaning of Worldview

Missiologist Lloyd Kwast (1981, p. 363) defines our common tie with humanity as follows:

At the very heart of any culture is its world view, answering the most basic question: *"What is real?"* This area of culture concerns itself with the great "ultimate" questions of reality. . . . Who are they? Where did they come from? Is there anything or anyone else occupying reality that should be taken into consideration? Is what they see really all there is, or is there something else, or something more? Is right now the only time that is important? Or do events in the past and the future significantly impact their present experience?

Such life perceptions or worldviews may be conscious or unconscious. Regardless, they're potent. For they lie "at the very heart of culture, touching, interacting with, and strongly influencing every other aspect of the culture" (Kraft 1979, p. 53).

Various analogies have been employed to explain the meaning of worldview. Some prefer the idea of conceptual organizer. Others use the word to express patterns by which participants in a culture behave. The phrase "central control box" has been coined.[3] Clifford Geertz (1972) speaks in terms of mapping. First, there are maps of perceived reality. These grids are used to interpret and to understand life experiences. Second, there are maps for directing behavior. They plot our life responses. Jesus utilized this same two-part scheme of thinking and acting, when he contrasted worldly leadership with the godly alternative: "You *know* that the rulers of the Gentiles lord it over them," he began, stressing the "thinking" function of their cultural interpretation, how they conceptualized leadership. Then the Master Teacher ventured further: "and their high officials *exercise authority over them*" (Matt. 20:25). "Acting" is emphasized, the way that leaders lived. Accordingly, Jesus challenges his followers to a new lifestyle. Servanthood offers an alternative approach to thinking about and acting through leadership.

Alan Tippett suggests that a major historical cause for missionary ineffectiveness is unevaluated worldviews. Western individualism and competitiveness are two specific factors that are often unassessed. For example, traditionally it was difficult for some North American missionaries to understand how certain non-Western groups made decisions via consensus. They were dumbfounded when entire villages decided to follow Christ at the same time. Tippett (1987, p. 91) recalls one striking incident:

Not all missionaries know how to handle a group conversion movement of some hundreds of persons coming together to the Christian faith. *I know of one case of missionaries saying this could not be of the Spirit of God and so held the inquirers off at gun point, because they thought the only mode of conversion was the form they had known at home.* They did not recognize that this rejection of paganism had come after months of multi-individual discussion in their proper decision making institutions for matters of religious change.

Paul Hiebert goes to great lengths to show how Westerners assume too much about our worldview. It surprises us when we discover different—especially opposite—positions from ours. His comments are not restricted to issues of Christianity and missions per se.[4] It's not difficult to envision how Western biases lead to counterproductivity on foreign soil. Hiebert's (1985, pp. 112–37) shortened list of seven unchecked worldviews are provided in Table 4.1. For every one of his statements (major and minor points alike), the author suggests alternative ways to perceive reality. As you examine his condensed list, ask yourself if you've ever questioned these perspectives. Or, like many Westerners, have you taken them for granted?

Table 4.1

The Western Perspective

1. We assume that we live in a *real and rational world.*
   This perception includes related ideas like:
   - dualistic separation between natural and supernatural worlds
   - dichotomized notions of worth between people and the rest of creation
   - judging people by what they own—an extension of the right of private ownership belief
   - "progress" means "bigger and better"

2. We accept an *analytical approach* to life. This perception includes related ideas like:
   - superiority of "either-or" thinking (e.g., "work is serious business; play is fun")
   - planning is critical; personal choice and responsibilities should be emphasized
   - utilitarianism—or pragmatism—is normative; whatever "works" (i.e., accomplishes the job) is "right"

3. We believe in a *mechanistic* way of living. This perception includes related ideas like:
   - "doing" is more important than "being" or "becoming"
   - success is based on measurable results
   - "assembly-line" perspectives are valued over craftsmanship of an entire product

4. We uphold *individualism*. This perception includes related ideas like:
   - the search for private identity
   - an emphasis on self-reliance
   - casual, superficial relationships in groups
   - the strong need to be accepted and liked
   - promoting "the exclusive right to use and dispose of property"
   - a high regard for human life; humanitarianism

5. We (theoretically) stand for *equality*. This perception includes related ideas like:
   - the rejection of social hierarchies; the desire for informal structures
   - acceptance of competition and free enterprise
   - the tendency to be direct and confrontational in our relationships
   - cooperation with others, if personal goals are attained

6. We treasure *time over space*. This perception includes related ideas like:
   - time seen as "linear" not "cyclical"
   - orientation toward the future, not the past
   - youth esteemed over age

7. We perceive life via *sight* more than other senses. This perception includes related ideas like:
   - the inclination to communicate abstract (versus concrete) ideas
   - acceptance of literate over nonliterate forms of communication (e.g., story, dance, rituals)

- attributing status to people of knowledge (versus wisdom)
- valuing systematic thinking over effective or experiential realities

Source: Adapted from Hiebert (1985, pp. 112–37).

Think about It

Review Hiebert's seven categories in Table 4.1. Superimpose his categories over another culture's worldview, different than yours. Choose a culture with which you are familiar. In other words, imagine a cross-cultural Christian education setting. For each of Hiebert's seven points, state one example of how Christian instruction could be rendered ineffective, if the unexamined Western perspective is employed in another culture. (*Note:* If you are not familiar with a non-Western culture first-hand, recall what you have heard and read from others' experiences.) An example of Hiebert's "individualism" has been supplied. It comes from Tippett's earlier illustration.

Complete the blank, by finishing this sentence: "Christian education could be ineffective cross-culturally, if we . . ."

1. _____
2. _____
3. _____
4. Believe that all public confessions of faith must be expressed as individuals, not as groups.
5. _____
6. _____
7. _____

Distinguishing Quests from Filters

Worldviews are as natural to us as breathing. Our views of reality are developed (among other influences) by our experiences, convictions, and levels of maturity. Two major components make up every worldview:

- *Quests*—Four universal questions about life, raised throughout our lives.
- *Filters*—Three major perceptual screens, which directly affect our responses to the four quests.

Both components are equally important. In fact, they're inseparable. Stated simply, "quests" deal with *what* we question. "Filters" deal with *how* we question, that is, how we interpret our quests.

Charles Kraft alludes to the tension between quests and filters by referring to the concept of critical realism. This is the combination of external reality and our percep-

tion of it. Citing virtually all four quests along with the concept of filters, Kraft (1979, p. 28) defines critical realism as the assumption that "whether we are dealing with the reality of the physical environment, the reality of human nature and psychology, or the reality of divine revelation [quests], the process of coming to know always involves the process of theory and model building on the part of the observer [filters]." Kraft compares his definition to Paul's testimony: "Now we see but a poor reflection as in a mirror" (1 Cor. 13:12a). Kraft adds, "We cannot now see as God sees—objectively, as things really are."

Table 4.2

Functions and Forms

FUNCTIONS	FORMS
(Nonrelative human needs)	(Relative means to satisfy functions)
1. Obtaining food	a. Hunting b. Agriculture c. Exchange/purchase
2. Providing shelter	a. Lean-to b. House
3. Providing for children	a. Nuclear family b. Extended family
4. Protecting against external threats	a. Individual weapons b. Community protection groups c. Armies
5. Transmitting knowledge	a. Imitation b. Informal instruction c. Formal instruction
6. Maintaining the social system	a. Taboos b. Laws c. Police force d. Ethnocentrism e. Patriotism
7. Relating with the supracultural God	a. Belief systems b. Ritual c. Prayer d. Worship

Source: Modified from Kraft (1979, p. 91).

Table 4.3

Cultural Conceptions of Sin

Fact: The Bible says that all people are separated from God by sin (Rom. 3:23).
Question: How is the concept of "sin" expressed in different cultures?

HEBREW	GREEK	AMERICAN	AFRICAN
1. Idolatry	1. Going astray	1. Meaninglessness of	1. Fear of evil spirits
2. Breaking a covenant	2. Falling short of per-	life	2. Breaking relation-
3. Missing the mark	fection	2. Self-centeredness	ships with one's
4. Transgressing a law	3. Unrighteousness	3. Loneliness	kinship group
5. Rebelling	4. Lawlessness		

Source: Modified from Kraft (1979, p. 91).

One of the most beneficial ways to differentiate between quests and filters is to borrow a parallel comparison between *function* and *form* in anthropology. "Function" identifies universal human needs; they are static and nonrelative. "Form" pertains to societal structures and patterns by which the functions are addressed; they are dynamic and culture-specific. Kraft (1979, p. 91) provides a useful chart of these differences (see Table 4.2).

Examine item 7 in Table 4.2. How would these questions about spiritual realities change in different settings? How would a Christian teacher, for instance, communicate the universal principle of sin and still respect cultural-specific filters? Again, Kraft (1979, p. 95) offers a useful illustration (see Table 4.3).

Kraft's (1979, p. 99) insights provide one final comparison of the differences between quests (functions) and filters (forms):

The principle here seems to be that *Christianness lies primarily in the functions served and the meanings conveyed by the cultural forms employed,* rather than in the forms themselves. Indeed, at this very point we can most clearly see beyond mere relativism. If it is true, as we contend, that God seeks to work in terms of cultural forms

(which are relative), it is for the purpose of leading people into a relationship with himself. . . . That is, God seeks to use and to cooperate with human beings in the continued use of relative cultural forms to express absolute supracultural meanings. *The forms of culture are important not for their own sake but for the sake of that which they convey.* And an appropriate fit between form and content is all-important.

Quests

Eugene Nida (1964, p. 55) insists that "the similarities that unite mankind as a cultural 'species' are much greater than the differences that separate." In part, he is referring to common quests. Such similarities are significant enough to "provide a basis for mutual understanding." George R. Knight also reminds us of our common bond. He particularly accentuates our need for a belief-system, the glue that holds our worldview together. Some people choose to put their trust in that which makes sense to them. Others prefer something that feels right or offers personal satisfaction. Still others rely on tradition or authority for answers. Regardless, every individual looks to something or someone for solutions to life's disturbing problems. Knight (1980, p. 27, emphasis added) clarifies:

> Through the study of basic questions man is forced to realize his smallness and helplessness in the universe. He must realize that nothing can be known for certain in the sense of final and ultimate proof that is open and acceptable to all men. *Every person*—the skeptic and the agnostic, the scientist and the businessman, the Hindu and the Christian—*lives by a faith*. The acceptance of a particular position in metaphysics [i.e., reality] and epistemology [i.e., truth] is a "faith-choice" made by individuals and it entails a commitment to a way of life.

Such "faith-choices" affect the quests of our worldview. Again, this holds our views of reality together.

Think about It

Pretend you belong to an international task force formed by the United Nations. Your duty consists of advising the Security Council of prominent human concerns, by answering the challenge: "What do all people question in life? What are their foundational questions?"

But the challenge is complicated by this limitation: You cannot explicitly use any theological terms or church jargon. You must use concepts that are familiar to the officials to whom you report.

What would you say about twenty-first-century people? What does our society reveal about its members' rudimentary concerns? What specific illustrations, ideas, or analogies would you choose, in order to verify your responses? Write a couple of thoughts here:_____

_____
_____

When challenged by the overwhelming task of summarizing such concerns, we need not despair. Francis Schaeffer (1968, p. 87) plots our course when he posits that Christianity must be viewed as a "system" providing "answers to the basic needs of modern man." Neither time nor space permits an analysis of all Schaeffer's insights. But note where he begins: "The *first basic need* is caused by the lack of certainty regarding the reality of individual personality. Every man is in tension until he finds a satisfactory answer to the problem of *who he himself is*" (1968, p. 87).

In other words, the point of departure is *identity formation*. It touches every person. It so pervades both scriptural and scientific studies that it is worthy of our full attention. This comprehensive topic helps unlock the study of the quests. Several authorities, from a wide range of scientific disciplines,[5] address the eminent task of identity formation. Collectively, they make a strong case for its nomination as a premier need.

Specifically related to issues of self-worth, Erik Erikson (1968, p. 24) concludes that "identity is never 'established' as an 'achievement.'" The search for identity is unlike other human task accomplishments. It cannot be equated with such terminating exploits as high school diplomas and retirement. In fact, the question of identity lasts a lifetime. Erikson (1968, p. 211) defines identity as a "forever to-be-revised sense of reality." He combines individual drives with social expectations. Rollo May (1953, p. 32) adds that "*Every* human being gets much of his sense of his own reality out of what others say to him or think about him." Rolf E. Muus (1988, p. 55) unites the life-space component of identity with life crises: "Any time a major role change takes place, such as one's first job, marriage, parenthood, divorce, unemployment, serious illness, wid-

Table 4.4

Universal Human Quests

Box B Quests	Needs Addressed	Lifelong Questions	Box C Themes
Search for Immortality	Belief Needs	"What is ultimate reality?"	Communion
Search for Intimacy	Belonging Needs	"How should I relate?"	Community
Search for Integrity	Being Needs	"Who am I morally?"	Character
Search for Industry	Behavior Needs	"What must I accomplish?"	Commission

owhood, or retirement, *identity issues re-emerge."*

The bottom line is this: Identity formation generates a formidable expression of universal human need.[6] It reveals the core of the four quests.

One way to determine the compound nature of identity formation is to isolate three complementary facets of Erikson's psychosocial theory: (1) *Industry,* which enhances identity through personal accomplishment; (2) *Intimacy,* which correlates with identity via relationship building; and (3) *Integrity,* which specifies how identity extends from character formation.[7] In one sense, these three phases owe particular allegiance to specific life segments.[8] In a much broader sense, however, the essence and demands of this threesome (like the life-span concerns of identity formation itself) cannot be restricted to any single age.[9]

In addition to Erikson's phases of Industry, Intimacy, and Integrity, John Stott (1988) cites another dimension of human experience that affects identity formation. He labels it the "quest for transcendence." In brief, Stott (1988, p. 125) defines this term as "the search for ultimate reality beyond the material universe." Building on Erikson's three alliterated phrases, Stott's

contribution compares to the lifelong search for *immortality.* Fowler's (1981, p. 17) concept of "shared center(s) of value and power" parallels Stott's contribution. Levinson (1978) affirms this "wish for immortality" as well, describing it as "one of the strongest and least malleable of human motives" (p. 215). Much more than a human drive for survival, Levinson analyzes this need to be a "concern with meaning . . . [and] significant value for myself and the world" (p. 216).

In part, this fourth quest represents the search for a relevant belief system. It is our anticipation of and our hope for truth and purpose outside ourselves.

By way of review, Table 4.4 summarizes the universal human quests. Representative statements of lifelong questions are provided along with matching human needs. Finally, the four themes from Chapter 3 are correlated with their respective issues.

Filters

Recall that our worldviews combine quests *and* filters. Whereas the former are universal (public), the latter are particular (private). Kraft (1979, p. 29) states that we each "see reality *not as it is but always from inside our heads."* Therefore, models or theories about worldviews are necessarily "limited and inadequate ways of imagining what is not observable" (Barbour 1974, p. 38). Hiebert (1976/1983, p. 6) employs an analogy to characterize our subjectivity: "Human beings live, as it were, in a house with only a few windows of tinted and curved glass, through which we can see the outside world. The glass colors and distorts our observations, but its effects can be determined only with much difficulty."

A. F. C. Wallace (1956) calls this personalized feature of worldview our "mazeways." Commenting on this term, Hiebert (1976/1983, p. 391) holds that "no two individuals share the same mazeway, not even within the same society or segment of society." R. M. Keesing and F. M. Keesing (1971, p. 21) expand the implications of our subjectivity without forecasting doom. Certainly human restrictions apply, they concede. Yet, potential also exists for understanding ourselves better.

> To view other people's ways of life in terms of our own cultural glasses is called ethnocentrism. Becoming conscious of, and analytical about, our own cultural glasses is a painful business. We do it best by learning about other people's glasses. Although we can never take our glasses off to find out what the world is "really like," or try looking through anyone else's without ours on as well, we can at least learn a good deal about our own prescription.

One Sunday morning, young Melissa struck a perplexed pose as she climbed into the car. She shared matching dresses with her two sisters. But she didn't share their quiet spirits. Restlessly, the first-grader inquired, "Are we going to that church where people other than the pastor pray?"

For a minute, Melissa's parents reflected her puzzled look. They didn't have a clue about what she was asking. Then the light came on. Melissa had just described a local congregation where believers mutually expressed their needs. They publicly prayed for one another; no single individual performed this priestly function for all.

Melissa had visited this gathering only two or three times. But it didn't take long for her to notice a distinguishing quality within the worship service. In contrast to traditional churches she had experienced—where one person (the pastor) prayed—a new category emerged: "[a] church where people *other* than the pastor pray." Melissa had just created an alternative filter for the subject "churches."

Think about It

Contemplate the following questions and write a few words of response to each.

1. Consider two or three church services where you perceived differences in the ways things were accomplished. List what was different (e.g., order of worship; types of hymns sung; approach to the sermon; special music; etc.).

   _____

   _____

   _____

2. Suggest a couple "filters" you used as you compared these church services (e.g., the filter of whether or not altar calls were critical features of each service). _____

   _____

   _____

Not only do all people see their world through universal quests, but everyone does so through three private screens: the filters of people, truth, and lifestyle (or values).[10] Everyone holds diverse perspectives of reality or personal ethics. Each of us uniquely interprets our worlds, figuratively attaching our price tags.

Ancient Filters

Before the twelve spies enter the Promised Land, Moses gives them explicit instructions. Notice the polarized tensions he raises in his questions (Num. 13:17–20).

- Are the people "strong or weak"? (v. 18)
- Are the people "few or many"? (v. 18)
- Is their land "good or bad"? (v. 19)
- Are the towns "unwalled or fortified"? (v. 19)
- Is the soil "fertile or poor"? (v. 20)
- Are there trees on it or not? (v. 20)

The instructions are precise, specific, and objective. In fact, they could not be more so. No doubt Moses anticipates a unanimous reply from the spies. But we know how the story ends. We know there was a split vote. Why? *Filters.*

Initially, all twelve verify the land's splendor. They admit "it does flow with milk and honey!" (v. 27); there are no dissenting voices. But, before the crowd's excitement mounts, contrary reports surface. Ten of twelve declare, "We can't attack those people; they are stronger than we are" (v. 31). Remember their analogy? "We seemed like grasshoppers in our own eyes, and we looked the same to them" (v. 33). The ten go beyond the facts. They subjectively *interpret* the facts. Personal filters sway their reports.

Caleb and Joshua also have perspectives. And their conclusions lead them to the exact opposite view. Caleb pleads, "We should go up and take possession of the land, for we can certainly do it" (v. 30).

What makes the difference? Why do two people draw the opposite conclusion of the ten? Simply, they hold alternative filters.

First, look at their filter of *people.* Joshua and Caleb refuse to accept the majority report; a "grasshopper mentality" is unthinkable for this godly pair. Joshua and Caleb lose their patience with the fickle assembly (Num. 14:6–9). They tear their clothes in despair, crying, "Do not be afraid of the people of the land, because we will swallow them up" (v. 9a).

Second, their perspective of *truth* is different. The two men trust in the reality of God's existence. They place confidence in his promise. They believe he can win battles for them. Recall their unwavering faith in this truth: "The LORD . . . *will* lead us into that land, a land flowing with milk and honey" (v. 8). Consequently, the twosome believe in the reality of heavenly intervention. They denounce their defenseless enemy, proclaiming that "Their protection is gone" (v. 9b).

Third, note the pair's distinct philosophy of *lifestyle.* The value-laden motto of Joshua and Caleb is simple: "the LORD is with us" (v. 9c). Ethics and priorities are molded by this motto. People, truth, and lifestyle take on alternative shapes for this noble team of two. The filters of their dynamic faith transform their views.

Again, it is significant to review what Moses requested of the twelve. He expected a report on the objective facts about Canaan. Yet, during the forty-day research of the Promised Land, each man filtered the *objective* questions through *subjective* screens. It is impossible to keep from completely doing otherwise.

Filters are ever-present. Filters are powerful, and they are very persuasive.

It's not too difficult to deduce that different filters produce different values and behaviors. Diverse assumptions of reality yield alternative worldviews.

Evening Filters

When Nicodemus comes to Jesus at night, what intrigues him are the Lord's "miraculous signs" (John 3:2). Jesus' credibility is acknowledged, for the ruling counsel member tells the Messiah that "God [is] . . . with him." Yet in the course of dialogue, Jesus shifts discussion from his miraculous *ministry* to his *message:* "no one can see the kingdom of God unless he is born again" (v. 3b).

With that statement, flashing lights and clanging bells are set off inside Nicodemus' head!

Have you ever experienced a conversation where you say to yourself, "This discussion isn't going anywhere! We just keep talking past each other"? That's the way it was between the Lord and Nicodemus. Specifically, their filters were so diametrically opposed that effective communication was hampered. Read John 3:1–12. But this time, as you read these well-known verses, identify as many examples of counterproductive communication as you can.

Contrast the trifocal categories: What is being said about the nature of people? What conflicting statements concerning truth can you locate? How do values within lifestyle clash?[11]

Think about It

What instances did you find of counterproductive communication? Below, give specific examples (with corresponding verses) of trifocal discrepancies.

1. Where did you observe ineffective discussion concerning the nature of people because of diverse filters? _____

   _____

2. How did differing filters of truth limit their communication?

   _____

   _____

3. What conflicting views of lifestyle (or values) did you discover? _____

   _____

Table 4.5 summarizes the John 3 encounter. Notice the trifocal differences once again.

Conclusion[12]

Albert Einstein once commented that we live in an era of perfect means and confused goals. The following bizarre tale features confusion of both ends and means.

Several centuries ago, a curious but deadly plague appeared in a small village in Lithuania. What was curious about this disease was its grip on its victim; as soon as a person contracted it, he would go into a very deep, almost deathlike coma. Most individuals would die within twenty-four hours, but occasionally a hardy soul would make it back to the full bloom of health. The problem was that since early eighteenth century medical technology was not very advanced, the unafflicted had quite a difficult time telling whether a victim was dead or alive. This didn't matter too much, though, because most of the people were, in fact, dead.

Then one day it was discovered that someone had been buried alive. This alarmed the townspeople, so they called a town meeting to decide what should be done to prevent such a situation from happening again. After much discussion, most people agreed on the following solution. They decided to put food and water in every casket next to the body. They would even put an air hole up from the casket to the earth's surface. These procedures would be expensive, but they would

Table 4.5

John 3—Clashing Filters

	Nicodemus' Filters	Jesus' Filters
What is the nature and purpose of *people?* Are people only physical or are they spiritual as well?	"Born again" must mean literal rebirth. First, a man cannot be born when he is old (v. 4a). Second, a man cannot enter a second time into his mother's womb (v. 4b).	Jesus acknowledges a real, material world (those "born of water" [v. 5]) and a spiritual world (those "born of . . . the Spirit" [v. 5]). Jesus also distinguishes two realms of reality and personhood ("flesh" and "Spirit" [v. 6]).
What is *truth?* Which sources of truth help us determine what to believe?	Nicodemus' view of truth affects his earlier view of people. His respect for truth (via human senses and experience) tells him "born again" *must* be biological rebirth. Being "born again" breaks all known, natural laws. Even after Jesus' first explanation (vv. 5–8), Nicodemus' last response (v. 9) is "You've got to be joking!" Nicodemus' view of truth is limited to human experience and reasoning.	Again, Jesus claims that truth is both material and spiritual. His primary analogy is the wind (v. 8). Jesus employs a play on words; the Greek word *pneuma* is translated "wind" and "Spirit." Jesus helps Nicodemus connect both realities. Jesus criticizes claims that only humanly verifiable experiences are "real." Jesus affirms wind is "real" because we see its effects, even though we do not know its origin or destiny. Then he parallels spiritual rebirth: We cannot determine the details of the spiritual world, but it is quite real.
What is valuable in *life?* What is worth living for?	Nicodemus' view of life motivates him to see Christ, to see signs of God's presence (v. 2). These valued signs become ends in themselves.	Jesus focuses on the greater value behind the miracles: the *kingdom of God* (vv. 3, 5). To contrast the two positions: Nicodemus sets his eyes on temporal means; Jesus stresses eternal ends (see vv. 12, 15, 16).

be more than worthwhile if they would save some people's lives.

Another group came up with a second, less expensive, right answer. They proposed implanting a twelve inch long stake in every coffin lid directly over where the victim's heart would be. Then whatever doubts there were about whether the person was dead or alive would be eliminated as soon as the coffin lid was closed.[13]

Think about It

Ponder these questions and jot down brief responses.

1. What motivated the townspeople who came up with the more expensive solution? _____

_____

_____

2. Describe the thinking process of the second group, who proposed a less expensive plan. _____

_____

_____

3. Obviously, one of the major differences between the two groups centered on their view of people. Think about diverse congregations with which you are familiar. Provide at least two dif-

ferent understandings of people within those local churches.

_____

The Lithuanian legend is a story of conflicting ends and means. What distinguishes the two, opposite plans of the tale are the villagers' divergent thought patterns—specifically their analytical questions. Von Oech (1983, p. 26) correctly interprets the Lithuanian legend: "Whereas the first group asked, 'What should we do in the event we bury somebody *alive?*' the second group wondered, 'How can we make sure everyone we bury is *dead?*'"

To put it another way, the former individuals waved the banner "Life—at all

Figure 4.1

Quests and Filters

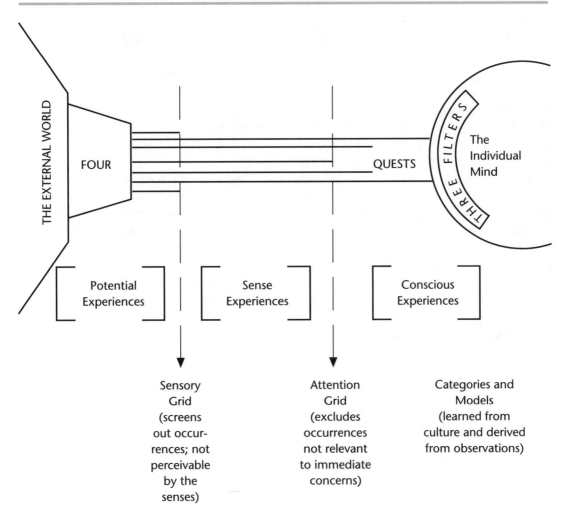

Source: Adapted from Hiebert (1976/1983, p. 6).

costs." The latter's slogan read: "Life—if it isn't too expensive." Two competing perspectives appear, two conflicting worldviews, namely, the perceived value of rescuing people who may be alive versus assuring survivors that all buried were dead. Also, a related set of perspectives exists: more expensive solutions are worthwhile if lives are spared versus a "cheaper is better" mentality. When combined, these two sets of perspectives yield polarized short-term plans: food, water, and air hole versus a foot-long stake!

A worldview comprises universal quests and unique filters. Eugene Nida (1960, pp. 90–91, emphasis added) concisely underscores the value of both elements. We educators can profit considerably from his advice. The comments pertain to a critical factor of teaching and learning: how to structure or organize curriculum.[14] "The fundamental processes of reasoning of all people are essentially the same, but the premises on which such reasoning rests and the basic categories that influence the judgment of different peoples are somewhat different. . . . *Men differ . . . not so much in their reasoning powers as in their starting points.*"

A modification of Hiebert's (1976/1983, p. 6) diagram helps us to visualize the tensions between our universal search and our unique perceptions of life[15] (see Figure 4.1).

Finally, teachers who are sensitive to quests and filters become more understanding of their students' worlds. They serve as more effective leaders. Assessing one's own position on these two issues tends to produce ownership. Valuing the positions of others produces empathy and respect for choice. In short, these qualities lead to more fruitful ministry and to more caring witness.[16]

This, in part, is what J. Herbert Kane (1981, pp. 62–69) envisions of believers who adopt a "world Christian" perspective. Kane's comments blend the compatible concerns of education and mission. He specifically focuses on the relevance of worldviews. His pertinent thoughts are especially insightful, given the "shrinking" nature of global conditions and their effects on the church. As you read Kane's seven descriptions, contemplate which statement challenges you to grow in the formation of your personal worldview. Which one helps to shape a better understanding of your quests and filters? World Christians

1. seek to increase their knowledge of world affairs.
2. broaden their view of the church.
3. want to increase their understanding of the Christian mission.
4. enlarge the scope of their prayer life.
5. go abroad if opportunity affords.
6. change their lifestyle.
7. recognize their personal responsibility for world missions.

5 Patterns of Growth: The Structural Dimension

Introduction

Think about It

Remember these familiar choruses?

Deep and wide, Deep and wide
There's a Fountain flowing deep and wide,
Deep and wide, Deep and wide,
There's a Fountain flowing deep and wide.—Herbert G. Tovey

Climb, climb up sunshine mountain, Heav'nly breezes blow;
Climb, climb up sunshine mountain, Faces all aglow.
Turn, turn from sin and doubting, Looking to the sky;
Climb, climb up sunshine mountain, You and I.—E. Pate

1. What do these songs mean?
2. For additional insight, interview others for their opinions. Be sure to include one or two children, teenagers, and adults. Then contrast their responses.

As a reference point, compare your views and findings with the comments in Tables 5.1 and 5.2.[1] Notice the variation of responses, particularly between the children's comments and those of teens and adults. In general, the children's interpretations represent rudimentary perceptions, simple word pictures of literal reality. Teen and adult insights reveal more sophisticated figurative connotations.

Characteristics of Human Nature

These interview comments illustrate how we tend to think at various age levels. They give us a peek at the complexity and wonder of human nature. Humankind reveals God's creative work at its best. Since humanity has been created in the image of God, it was possible for God to take on human form. The incarnation of our Lord, the second person of the Godhead, affirmed the inherent value and goodness of human nature, as originally ordained in the Garden of Eden (Gen. 1:31). Luke 2:52 records Jesus' maturation and growth.[2]

Growth and Change

The Bible verifies differences in cognitive ability. In his famous "love chapter" Paul states, "When I was a child, I talked like a child, I thought like a child, I reasoned like a child. When I became a man, I put childish ways behind me" (1 Cor. 13:11). Paul implies that, for children, it is quite appropriate to talk, to think, and to reason like children. Much more is expected of adults. The difference lies in the distinctive meanings of child*likeness* and child*ishness*.[3] God's

Table 5.1

Interpretations of "Deep and Wide"

Child

6 yrs. "It's a fun song about a big ocean."

9 yrs. "This is a fun song with motions. The 'deep' is about a waterfall falling off a rocky hill and everyone is looking; and the 'wide' is the ocean."

10 yrs. "Uh, it's talking about a spider—I don't know."

Teen

13 yrs. "This song doesn't mean much of anything, just a lot of motions."

15 yrs. "God is infinite. He is everywhere. God is so pure [the fountain]."

16 yrs. "That's probably the fountain of spiritual water, maybe the Holy Spirit."

Adult

42 yrs. "This is a good action song to get everybody loosened up. The word 'river' should be substituted for 'fountain,' because a river flows more so than a fountain."

45 yrs. "I take it as God's gracious nature and mercy, the fountain being the blood."

60 yrs. "It speaks of the love of God as being immeasurable. But even a good Buddhist could sing the same thing. It's not particularly a 'Christian' song."

Table 5.2

Interpretations of "Climb Up Sunshine Mountain"

Child

6 yrs. "I am climbing up a ladder to the sun. My face gets nice and warm from the sunshine."

7 yrs. "It means to climb up to Jesus, to heaven by doing the right thing."

9 yrs. "I see a person climbing a mountain. He is carrying a stick because it is a rocky mountain. But he is singing a song and thinking of the faces of all those people he knows."

Teen

13 yrs. "We are all climbing up this mountain where there is all this sun. And because [of this] . . . the heavenly breezes are there to cool us off. When we climb we are to leave our sins behind and stop worrying."

15 yrs. "You are in the presence of God and all the sins don't matter. It's just peace and love and all that."

16 yrs. "It means that maybe if you shed light on your problems, they tend to go away or you see how small they can be."

Adult

23 yrs. "It talks about where heaven is, you and I, where Christ is, I guess. Where God is. I don't know."

45 yrs. "It's figuratively speaking—it's like going to heaven, a transit from earth to heaven; faces aglow because of the glory of heaven. We'd have turned from sin here on earth."

53 yrs. "I grew up in the church and this was a cute song with fun motions. I think it is a positive song, if not strictly theological."

plan is that we should grow toward maturity. We evidence growth through the divinely designed developmental process. We experience tremendous changes.

In this chapter and the following chapter we identify what constitutes "normal" growth.[4] If a five-year-old is extremely thin, small, and cannot speak or walk, we suspect that something is not right. As with physical development, other areas of growth also follow fairly predictable patterns. Consequently, we can be alerted when growth is abnormally arrested.

Comprehending holistic developmental patterns challenges us to keep on growing. Complacency is not an option. Figuratively speaking, we have the potential of being eight-cylinder engines, but may be running on only three or four cylinders. With Paul as our model, we must press on to full maturity: "Not that I have already obtained all this, or have already been made perfect, but I press on to take hold of that for which Christ Jesus took hold of me" (Phil. 3:12).

The New Testament often speaks of growth: "But grow in the grace and knowledge of our Lord and Savior, Jesus Christ" (2 Pet. 3:18).[5] Besides maturity in our thinking, we should experience other kinds of growth. Luke describes Jesus' childhood, mentioning specific areas of growth: "And Jesus grew in wisdom (cognitive) and stature (physical) and in favor with God (faith) and man (social)" (Luke 2:52; cf. 1 Sam. 2:26). Some domains of growth are apparent (e.g., physical development); others are more difficult to assess (e.g., social development).

Structure and Function

Basic to any Christian understanding of personhood is the crucial concept that all people are created in God's image. Anthony Hoekema (1986, pp. 68–73) suggests that "image" encompasses both structural and functional dimensions. The *structural* dimension refers to our hereditary capacities, both material (e.g., muscular mobility of the body) and immaterial (e.g., mind, conscience). The *functional* dimension refers to the proper use of these capacities according to God's purpose and will (e.g., speaking the truth in love rather than cursing someone).

Employing an analogy from the construction industry, the structural dimension illustrates the human superstructure: the supportive components of persons, including the *physical* domain, the *cognitive* domain, and the *personality* domain. This instrumental superstructure frames the functional dimension of human development. The functional dimension represents the infrastructure of our being, the core of personhood. In a study of theological imperatives in Chapter 3, this infrastructure emerged as four themes of Christian maturity. Four related universal human quests derived from philosophical and anthropological insights surfaced in the previous chapter. In this chapter, a psychological perspective is addressed:

Functional Domains of Growth	Themes
Faith development	Communion
Social development	Community
Moral development	Character
Vocational development	Commission

For two main reasons we have placed each of the domains within their respective clusters. First, the common tie in the structural dimension is that the physical, cognitive, and personality domains each have innate at-birth factors that affect their development. This is more obvious in physical development, but even the temperament traits of personality are affected by heredity. Second, at the moment of regeneration (our second birth), God primarily makes major changes in the "functional" dimension: We are made alive and indwelt by the Spirit (faith—Rom. 8:8; Eph. 2:1–5); we become members of the body of Christ and are baptized into it (social—1 Cor. 12:12–14); our conscience is cleansed (moral—Heb. 9:14; 1 Pet. 3:21); we are gifted to serve the common good of the body (vocational—1 Cor. 12:7, 11). Changes in the structural dimension will primarily occur when we receive our glorified bodies (Rom. 8:23; 1 Cor. 15:50–54).

Figure 5.1 displays a graphic overview of these dimensions; Table 5.3 presents a verbal summary.[6]

Without the foundation of structure there can be no function. And without proper functioning, people cannot fulfill their life purpose: to glorify God (1 Cor. 10:31). By way of illustration, a watch is created by its designer primarily to measure and register time (and secondarily to function as an attractive piece of jewelry). To attempt to use a watch for any other purpose (e.g., to hammer a nail or to brush our teeth) would yield poor results and may permanently hinder the watch from fulfilling its legitimate purpose. So the structural endowments of humankind must be considered in accord with the functional purposes of the Great Designer.

Figure 5.1
An Integrated View of Personhood

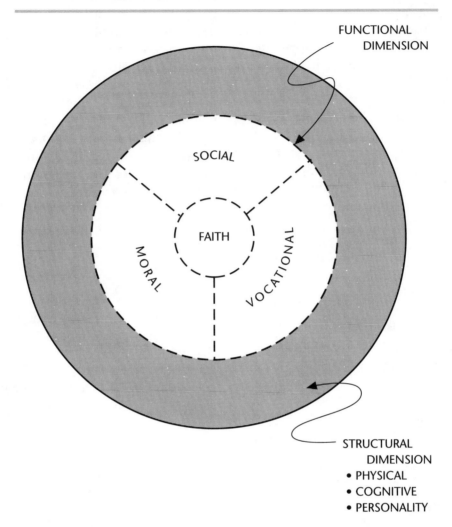

FUNCTIONAL
DIMENSION

SOCIAL

FAITH

MORAL

VOCATIONAL

STRUCTURAL
DIMENSION
• PHYSICAL
• COGNITIVE
• PERSONALITY

Note: The dotted lines indicate interaction within the four "functional" domains, as well as between the functional and structural dimensions.

Elijah and the Domains of Human Nature

Most believers are well acquainted with Elijah's triumphant victory over Baal on Mount Carmel in 1 Kings 18. However, some may not be aware of his subsequent personal battle. In 1 Kings 19:2–3, Elijah becomes fearful *(personality [emotional] domain)* of Queen Jezebel's death threat. He runs for his life, fleeing to a desert near Beersheba. Fears escalate to paranoia. He severs ties with his servant *(social domain)*. Elijah privately journeys a day farther into the desert (vv. 3–4). Exhausted, he confesses to low esteem *(personality [identity] domain)*, culminating in his request to die (v. 4).

Initially, God delays addressing Elijah's legitimate fears and meets the prophet's *physi-*

cal needs. God provides nourishment and rest over a two-day period (vv. 5–8). A special meeting between God and Elijah is forthcoming *(faith domain)*. Refreshed, Elijah travels forty days to Mount Horeb, the mountain of God (vv. 8–9). God first engages Elijah's *cognitive* capacities through conversation. He elicits Elijah's perceptions of the situation (vv. 10–14). For emphasis, God asks twice, "What are you doing here?" Elijah answers, "I have been very zealous for the LORD God Almighty. The Israelites have rejected your covenant, broken down your altars, and put your prophets to death with the sword. I am the only one left, and now they are trying to kill me, too" (vv. 10, 14).

Several warning flags go up. The prophet's reply reveals particular concerns.

1. Elijah is troubled about the issue of *faith.* He perceives his faithfulness to God. But is there a reciprocal response? God won the battle at Mount Carmel, but he seems to be losing the war to Baal.
2. The man of God senses his isolation *(social domain):* No other godly prophets of God remain.
3. Elijah is anxious over the issue of justice *(moral domain):* God's prophets have been murdered and Elijah is next in line.
4. Only Elijah is left to serve as God's messenger. Nobody will carry on the ministry after his death *(vocational domain).*

God has already met Elijah's *physical* needs. Now he communicates to Elijah (using the *cognitive domain)* in each remaining, troubled domain. God reveals himself in powerful ways to Elijah, using the natural vehicles of wind, earthquake, and fire. Through these means God addresses Elijah's *faith, intellect,* and *personality (emo-*

tions). In addition, God says he has reserved seven thousand who have not worshiped Baal *(faith, social, vocational domains).* God promises to deal with the acknowledged murderers through his instruments of judgment *(moral domain),* Hazael of Aram and Jehu of Israel. Furthermore, God supplies a companion *(social domain),* Elisha. Elisha will serve alongside Elijah. This young apprentice will continue the prophetic ministry after Elijah is gone *(vocational domain).* Elijah is fully nurtured and ready to return as God's prophet. The Creator met his needs in *each human domain.*

Think about It

Contemplate the past year or two of your life.

1. Single out significant growth spurts you have experienced in any of the domains listed below.

Domains of "Structural" Development
Physical: Cognitive: Personality:

Domains of "Functional" Development
Faith: Social: Moral: Vocational:

2. If you were forced to choose, in which domain have you experienced the most growth at this point in your life? Why do you think this is so?
3. In which domain have you experienced minimal growth? What explanations would you give for your reply?

In the remaining part of this chapter we will attend to the structural domains, the easily observable arenas of human growth: physical, cognitive, and personality development.[7] Because our "functional" growth to maturity is filtered through the givens of these three "structural" domains, each of us will vary in how we express our Christianity. We have been given differing physical shapes and faces, differing cognitive capabilities, and differing temperaments. Just like snowflakes, each of us presents a unique expression of the abundant life. No cookie-cutter cult here! These three structural arenas are instrumental to the cultivation of all four "functional" domains, which will be explained in the next chapter.

Physical Growth

An acorn will eventually become an oak tree, not an apple tree, seaweed, or bird. The basic design is inherent within the seed, which will mature with proper nurture (e.g., sun, mineral-rich earth, water, etc.). In the same way, God has placed a design within the human seed. With appropriate nurturing, we will grow to an adult form. The word "growth" is best associated with the botanical sphere, conveying the imagery of progress dependent on the genetic code within the seed.

Configuration and Timing

In each seed, both the *configuration* of the final adult form and the general *developmental pattern* (i.e., timing and sequence) toward that final form have already been determined. Within that configurational design there is great variability of form (e.g., height, weight, facial features, skin color, hair, and eyes) and levels of physical ability.

In addition to this configuration, the maturational pattern deserves consideration. Both *sequence* and *time* are a part of this pattern. Proper sequence dictates that

adults must first be children. We experience fairly predictable bodily changes from birth to the senior years. These changes affect our mobility and capacity for action. For example, the onset of puberty, around the age of twelve, a critical milestone of physical development, announces that adulthood with all its potential is just around the corner. This particular milestone involves both primary and secondary bodily changes. In addition, significant cognitive and personality factors emerge. It takes approximately fifteen to twenty years to reach the basic capabilities of adult functioning.[8]

As with the configurational design of the adult form, there is some variability in the timing of adult functioning. A positive, nurturing environment encourages human growth along "normal" chronology. But when growth has been slowed down, appropriate intervention will be necessary to facilitate progressive movement. A very negative and repressive environment may slow down growth to the extent that some adult capabilities may never reach optimum levels of functioning. This axiom is borne out by historical accounts of children who have grown up in wilderness settings or who have been deprived of human contact for long periods of time.[9] Understanding the scope of our physical abilities and the various changes that occur can help us comprehend the inherent possibilities and constraints of each of our students.

A Christian Perspective

A study of the physical domain also highlights the continuities and discontinuities of persons with the rest of God's creation. Some of our physical endowments are common to other creatures, such as a capacity to see and move. Yet, other capacities are unique to humankind. For example, we have received distinctive physical features like the twenty-eight subcutaneous facial muscles by which we are able to smile or frown (Cosgrove 1987, p. 30). Our vocal tract was designed specifically for the complexities of human speech (pp. 42–44).[10] Despite these wonderful endowments, Paul reminds believers that we currently "groan inwardly" as we await "the redemption of our bodies" (Rom. 8:23). For, ultimately, our physical bodies will be changed. We will be clothed with immortality in glorified bodies (1 Cor. 15:52) as we enter a new state of existence (2 Pet. 3:13).[11]

Cognitive Growth

Children and adults actually *think differently*. In the maturation process a person's knowledge base expands (a *quantitative* change); the logic of how that person thinks also changes. This growth represents an increase in complexity (a *qualitative* change). Based on the pioneering work of Swiss psychologist Jean Piaget,[12] four general levels of qualitative reasoning have been identified. We all grow through these levels from birth to the young adult years.

A simplified illustration of Piaget's findings is described below, using the game of "Monopoly." Picture in your mind several people playing this game. Representing various mental stages, contrast how each participant approaches the game.

Sensorimotor Period (approx. birth through 2 years):[13] Small children place houses, hotels, and dice in their mouth. They chew on the "Get out of jail free" card.

Preoperational Period (approx. 2 through 7 years): Preschoolers play "at" Monopoly, but intuitively make up their own rules. They can't understand the instructions because they have difficulty playing in turn and exchanging amounts of money (rents owed and

money possessed). Generally, they fail to comprehend the goals of the game.

Concrete Operational Period (approx. 7 through 11 years): School-aged children understand the basic instructions. They are able to follow the rules. But they can't deal with hypothetical transactions concerning mortgages, loans, and complex bargaining with other players.

Formal Operational Period (approx. 12 years and up): Teens and adults are no longer tied to concrete and tangible rules. They are able to engage in the complex hypothetical transactions unique to each game (Dworetzky 1981, p. 316).

One seminary student remembers how his mother wisely explained an abstract concept in concrete terms appropriate to his developmental level:

> In about fourth grade I began to struggle with the word "love." I knew what "like" meant—I like my dog, my teachers. But this girl meant more to me, it must be "love." One day I asked my mom about how I could know if I was in "love." She gave the perfect "concrete" example that clearly established in my ten-year-old mind what true love was. She said, "Love is when you look forward to talking to a person as much as you like to look at Christmas toy catalogs." Oh, I didn't know it was that serious. Immediately I knew I wasn't in love, or even close.[14]

The point is that children do not think the same way that adults think. Figure 5.2 portrays the difference between *quantitative* and *qualitative* change. Two series of shapes have been placed on a continuum beginning with birth (on the left) and moving toward adulthood (on the right). In the first row of symbols, the increasing circle size suggests our understanding of previous information is

Figure 5.2

Quantitative and Qualitative Mental Growth

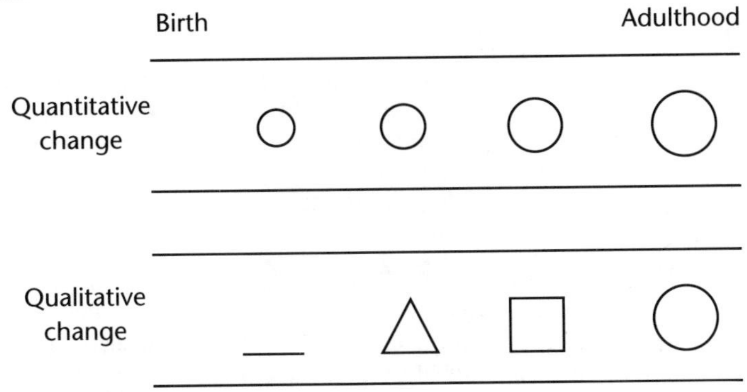

Birth			Adulthood

Quantitative change

Qualitative change

proportionally enlarged. In the second row, the changing geometric shapes (from line to triangle to square to circle[15]) imply that each new stage of thinking introduces significantly new dimensions for processing information. Each stage represents a fundamentally different way of thinking than previous stages. The technical definitions for this four-stage theory of qualitative cognitive development, advanced by Piaget, are provided in Figure 5.3.[16]

New ways of thinking appear at each level. The change may be compared to shifting gears in a car with a manual transmission. The ratio of each gear differs to provide increased potential for power and speed. To move the engine to a desired upper level the driver shifts to the subsequent gear. An appropriate order is followed: first, second, third, fourth, and overdrive.[17]

Practice and Performance

In Piaget's research, a significant distinction is made between capability and performance. Although children and adults have the capability of a certain thinking level (the focus of Piaget's research), they may not regularly perform at that level. For example, just because someone owns the car in the above illustration, does not mean that person can use it to its greatest poten-

tial. This inability may be due either to a lack of training and experience, or because the current circumstances do not demand or allow full use. If driving is restricted to the city, the driver may never use the overdrive gear. Full performance comes through regular practice in diverse settings.

The same is true with cognitive development. Although some adults have the potential to use complex levels of thinking (formal operations), they may actually employ a less sophisticated one (e.g., concrete operations). A similar point is suggested in Hebrews 5:11–14: "But solid food is for the mature, who by constant use have trained themselves to distinguish good from evil." The author held high expectations of his audience's *capability:* "by this time you *ought* to be teachers" (v. 12a). But their *performance* was substandard: "you need someone to teach you the elementary truths of God's word all over again. You need milk, not solid food!" (v. 12b). Their performance indicated poor stewardship of their capabilities.

As teachers, we sometimes hinder the full use of God-given mental abilities in our students. This occurs, for instance, when we give them "the right answers" at moments when they should think through the ques-

Table 5.3

Piaget's Stages of Cognitive Development

—— *Sensorimotor Period* (birth–18 months/2 years)

Infants explore their world primarily through their sensory perceptions and motor activities—what Piaget called "practical intelligence." During these early years they develop various concepts (e.g., cause and effect, space and time, object permanence, a sense of self) and abilities (e.g., intentional behavior, symbolic representation of physical actions, rudimentary communication skills).

 ### *Preoperational Period* (approx. 2–7 years)

Toddlers and preschoolers begin to explore the world on a symbolic level: mental images, drawings, dreams, make-believe play, gestures, and language. Children imitate the activities of adults and thus learn to adjust to the world. In the latter part of this period, children's concepts are still fuzzy and somewhat confused—what Piaget calls "semilogical." For example, young children believe everything has a reason and a purpose, and that the whole world shares the same feelings and thoughts as they do.

 ### *Concrete Operational Period* (approx. 7–11 years)

School-aged children are capable of true "operational" thinking using concrete objects to organize and classify them mentally. Children can now master four mathematical operations: addition, subtraction (i.e., reversal of addition), multiplication, and division (i.e., reversal of multiplication). But thought is mainly limited to their own concrete, physical experiences.

◯ *Formal Operational Period* (appearing at approx. 11 years)

A new world of mental operations is open to adolescents: thinking about thoughts and ideas, not just concrete, physical objects. The beginnings of full adult reasoning powers become available so that adolescents can now consider abstract and hypothetical concepts, inductive and deductive logic, and the generation and testing of hypotheses.

Sources: Piaget and Inhelder (1969); Pulaski (1980).

Key term: Mental operations—logical actions of the mind beyond simply imitating or representing what is being or has been observed (i.e., memory).

---

tions themselves. We circumvent their growth process. Just because someone correctly recites a doctrinal statement does not guarantee full comprehension of its meaning. Implications for Bible memorization programs should be apparent.

As Paul illustrates in 1 Corinthians 13:11, we must move beyond our childlike reasoning, especially in understanding God's Word. Listen to the reflections of one high school student, following a re-reading of Herman Melville's novel, *Moby Dick:*

"When I read this as a kid I thought it was just a neat whaling story: how to harpoon, the dangers of the sea. Now it seems different. Why is the Captain so obsessed with this whale? Does it have some special meaning?" (Sprinthall and Sprinthall 1990, p. 119). Similarly, adults may assume they understand the main intentions and messages of Scripture when, actually, they have only a cursory awareness. They may have regularly attended Sunday school as children. They may be acquainted with many

Table 5.4

Structural and Functional Dimensions of Growth

Category	Structural Dimension	Functional Dimension
Domains	• Physical • Cognitive • Personality	• Faith • Social • Moral • Vocational
Continuum of Possibilities	Less choice Nature: inherited capabilities at birth	More choice Nurture: goals for maturity

Issue	How do we fully utilize what we have inherited?	How do we respond to:
		  a. Themes of maturity (chap. 3)?
		  b. Quests of humanity (chap. 4)?

Bible stories. Yet their comprehension of those stories is largely based on childlike levels of thinking. Yes, they can recite verses and provide perfect definitions of key doctrines; but as adults, they may be unable to verbally defend their faith using Scripture. Furthermore, their lifestyle may exhibit little evidence of these divine truths.

Application to Ministry

A significant implication of cognitive development research is that the church must help its members upgrade their biblical comprehension at each new mental stage. This task is especially critical during the teen and young adult years. Throughout high school and college, young people are often forced to think about their faith from an adult perspective. The church must prepare them for this challenge.

Another implication of cognitive development theory pertains to Bible versions. Selection of a Bible version should be based on relative reading levels.

Think about It

Can you accurately discern various reading levels? Daily newspapers are geared at about an eighth-grade reading level. Table 5.5 lists translations of Romans 12:16 from Bible versions commonly used by evangelicals.

Table 5.5

Translations of Romans 12:16

A. Be of the same mind toward one another; do not be haughty in mind, but associate with the lowly. Do not be wise in your own estimation.

B. Live together in peace with each other. Do not be proud, but make friends with those who seem unimportant. Do not think how smart you are.

C. Be of the same mind one toward another. Mind not high things, but condescend to men of low estate. Be not wise in your own conceits.

D. Be of the same mind toward one another. Do not set your mind on high things, but associate with the humble. Do not be wise in your own opinion.

E. Live in harmony with one another. Do not be proud, but be willing to associate with people of low position. Do not be conceited.

1. See if you can guess (a) the reading level of each translation and (b) which Bible version is represented.

   Clue 1: Reading levels range from third to twelfth grade.

   Clue 2: The following six Bible versions are represented, listed here in alphabetical order: International Children's Version (ICV), King James Version (KJV), New American Standard Version (NASV), New International Version (NIV), New King James Version (NKJV).[18]

2. Which Bible translation would you recommend for the public reading of Scripture? Why?

3. Which Bible translation would you recommend as best for:

   (a) Youth? Why?

   (b) Children who can read? Why?

A prominent contribution of the Protestant Reformers was their unswerving support of Bible translations in commonly spoken languages.[19] Today there are many excellent Bible versions suited to the varying mental abilities of children, youth, and adults.

Personality Growth

"Personality" is a global concept referring to all of the characteristics that uniquely make up a person. The literature identifies at least two basic components of personality: temperament and identity.

Temperament

Temperament is made up of the dispositions that significantly influence how a person feels and acts. Rothbart (in Goldsmith et al. 1987) suggests that temperament involves reactivity or intensity of emotional arousal[20] and self-regulation or level of activity and inhibition.[21] Combinations of

these factors yield the variety of personality types we observe in our family and friends.[22]

Since we can observe characteristic traits in young infants (Goldsmith 1983), is temperament given to human beings at birth?[23] If God assigns natural talents to all and spiritual gifts to believers, he may also provide all persons with their unique temperaments. Although temperament may be largely grounded in our nature, how we express temperament is influenced by environmental factors and how well we "keep in step with the Spirit" (Gal. 5:25).

Identity

"Who am I?" Whether explicitly or implicitly, we constantly confront this question as we pass from childhood to adolescence to adulthood. A famous wood carver was once asked how he knew what to cut from the wood block, as he carved a life-sized statue. He testified that he cut away whatever did *not* belong and left what *did*. Throughout our lives, we attempt to determine what should belong to our personality and what should not.

We enter life as "undifferentiated" infants; the world is an extension of ourselves. Personality growth involves a lifelong "differentiation" process, in which we strive to balance the competing tensions of hanging on to growing aspects of a mature sense of self and to healthy relationships, and letting go of immature and sinful aspects of self and unhealthy relationships.[24] Jesus alludes to such tensions: "If anyone would come after me, he must deny himself and take up his cross and follow me. For whoever wants to save his life shall lose it, but whoever loses his life for me and for the gospel will save it" (Mark 8:34–35).[25]

The essence of personality development, then, is creating a sense of identity distinct from those with whom we live, work, and play (parents, relatives, church members, teachers). A Christian view of personality development finds dual involvement in this process. We do not grow alone; each of us grows in a unique partnership with God: "I have been crucified with *Christ* and *I* no longer live, but *Christ* lives in *me*. The life *I* live in the body, *I* live by faith in the *Son of God* who loved *me* and gave himself for me" (Gal. 2:20). On the basis of this mysterious union with Christ, each believer lives and grows toward maturity.

As part of the structural dimension of our lives, our self-image plays a significant role. In developing a healthy self-image, Anthony Hoekema challenges us to avoid two extremes. "Man's self-image is sometimes inordinately high (in the form of sinful pride) or excessively low (in the form of feelings of shame or worthlessness)" (1986, p. 104). In response to the first extreme of sinful pride, God "helps us cultivate true humility. This includes, among other things, an honest awareness of both our strengths and weaknesses, so as to give us a realistic image of ourselves" (p. 106).

In response to the "worm theology" stemming from the second extreme, Hoekema suggests that a careful understanding of three important concepts provides a foundation for developing a positive self-image: divine forgiveness, our continuing growth through the sanctifying work of the Holy Spirit, and our status as new creatures, living in a new era of life. Finally Hoekema cautions: "The Christian self-image is never an end in itself. It is always a means to the end of living for God. . . . It delivers us from preoccupation with ourselves and releases us so that we may happily serve God and love others" (p. 111).

Progress over the Life Span

Erik Erikson (1963) posits that everyone confronts eight sets of psychosocial crises from infancy to old age (see Table 5.6).[26] According to Erikson, if one does not resolve each crisis in a positive manner, that particular issue will continue to hinder healthy personality growth and functioning.

Both therapists and educators utilize these Eriksonian concepts to help guide the growth of clients and students.[27] For exam-

Table 5.6

Erikson's Psychosocial Stages

Period	Psychosocial Crisis	Resulting Virtues or Vices
Infancy	Trust versus Mistrust	Hope versus Withdrawal
Toddlerhood	Autonomy versus Shame and Doubt	Will versus Compulsion
Preschool	Initiative versus Guilt	Purpose versus Inhibition
School Age	Industry versus Inferiority	Competence versus Inertia
Adolescence	Identity versus Identity Confusion	Fidelity versus Repudiation
Early Adulthood	Intimacy versus Isolation	Love versus Exclusivity
Middle Adulthood	Generativity versus Stagnation	Care versus Rejectivity
Later Adulthood	Integrity versus Despair	Wisdom versus Disdain

Source: Erikson (1963, 1982).

ple, the popular term "identity crisis" originates from the particular crisis that adolescents face. By understanding how central this crisis is for youth and college-aged young people, youth workers can be better prepared to assist them through this critical identity formation period. Likewise, when working with small children and infants, caregivers must nurture trust. Other theories of personality development[28] offer additional insight into this essential aspect of our human growth.

Conclusion

As Christians, we may not realize how significantly growth in physical, cognitive, and personality domains can affect our spiritual growth. Such structural growth may either help or hinder our potential for ministering to others.

Think about It

---

1. In a previous "Think about It" exercise in this chapter, we asked you to assess your own growth in the physical, cognitive, and personality domains. Now that you have more information about these three structural dimensions of human growth, which of your responses would you revise?
2. Consider some of the persons you may be discipling, especially those who give evidence of arrested growth in the cognitive or personality domains. How might this new information help you guide their development? What would you specifically do to help them take the next positive step toward growth?

For example, contemplate the theory of cognitive development. Imagine you are in-

volved in youth ministry. Remember that young people are radically changing how they think. They possess new high-technology equipment—the capability of "abstract" adult reasoning. They may claim they already know what you are teaching from the Bible. But be a little skeptical. At this time, it is important for you to guide teens to *transform* their biblical "childhood" data into "adult" data. Youth who have been reared in the church really do not need a lot of new information. They need:

- to be challenged to think for themselves.
- to reflect on the implications of their Bible knowledge.
- to dialogue with peers and adults to crystalize their views.
- to act out their "adult" beliefs.

In this chapter we have described normal patterns of development for the *structural* dimension: physical, cognitive, and personality growth. Inhibited cognitive growth is evident in learning disabilities and shallow thinking. Likewise, arrested growth in personality and emotional development can severely restrict corresponding growth in the functional domain, such as faith or moral development. As Christian leaders, we must encourage believers to move beyond the sometimes painful barriers that so easily limit our full potential as ambassadors for Christ. A holistic concept of Christian maturity must give consideration to these structural domains of growth. As the superstructure of our human nature, the *structural* dimension provides the essential framework for growth in the *functional* dimension—faith, social, moral, and vocational development. In the next chapter, we take a closer look at these inner domains of human nature.

6 Patterns of Growth: The Functional Dimension

Introduction
Faith Development: Communion
Social Development: Community
Moral Development: Character
Vocational Development: Commission
What of Spiritual Growth?
Conclusion

Introduction

When a watch is working we hardly give it a second thought. It's almost like one of our appendages. This time piece signals us when to go to work, keep a sales appointment, meet friends for lunch or dinner, get to the ball game on time, and watch our favorite news program. In this very time-conscious culture, a chronometer gets us through the day. But we don't realize *how* dependent we are on a watch until it breaks. We become very disoriented.

What do we do when a watch stops working? If it has a broken mainspring, we take it to a watchmaker to get it fixed. If it's a digital watch, we replace the battery. Or, we may even replace it with a newer model. Why do we expend so much effort to remedy

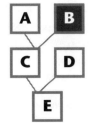

the problem? Because a watch is useless if it can't tell time. Without a working *structure,* there can be no *function.* A broken watch cannot fulfill its primary purpose.

And so it is with people made in the image of God. Without the necessary human structure (physical, cognitive, and personality domains), we could not serve the function or purpose for which we have been created: to glorify God (1 Cor. 10:31).

But, an exclusive focus on the *structural* dimension would present only a partial picture of humanity. Of greater importance in a Christian worldview is the *functional* dimension of human growth: faith, social, moral, and vocational development (see Figure 6.1). "God is now retrieving from the fallen world a people to share his fellowship, values, and work" (Lewis and Demarest 1990, p. 103).

Figure 6.1

An Integrated View of Personhood

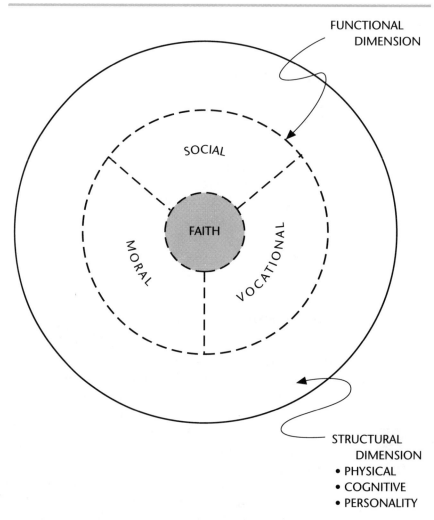

Note: The dotted lines indicate interaction within the four "functional" domains, as well as between the functional and structural dimensions.

As presented in Chapter 3, Scripture addresses the four related themes of Christian maturity, each of which can be aligned with four functional domains. We will first address the central arena of faith development. Then the subsidiary domains of social, moral, and vocational development will be featured.

Faith Development: Communion

"Where is your faith?" (Luke 8:25). Our Lord's most vigorous rebukes to his disciples arose from their lack of faith in God. At the heart of any relationship is trust. In Erikson's psychosocial theory of personality development, the concept of trust (versus mistrust) stands as the basic issue that everyone faces. At the heart of our relationship with God is our growing faith in him.[1]

Faith versus Sight

We can either rely on what God has promised in his Word, or we can trust our "sight"—what we see and believe about our circumstances in this physical world. "Now faith is being sure of what we hope for and certain of what we do not see" (Heb. 11:1). Our Lord honored such faith in his reply to Thomas' lack of faith: "Because you have seen me, you have believed; blessed are those who have not seen and yet have believed" (John 20:29). Believers must place more credibility in spiritual reality than in material reality (2 Kings 6:16; Matt. 14:30). Such faith is not a leap in the dark; it is based on the trustworthiness of God (Heb. 11:6). In fixing our eyes on the unseen (2 Cor. 4:18), we march to the drum of kingdom priorities (Matt. 6:31–34).

Progress in Faith

Though we initially placed our faith in God at the moment of salvation, we have much room in which to grow. The disciples urged Jesus, "Increase our faith!" (Luke 17:5). How does our faith in God develop?[2] Bruce Powers (1982) suggests one outline of how faith grows from childhood to adulthood. These five stages stem from his own faith pilgrimage and that of others, and are based on a number of interviews.

0–6 years	Nurture	Feeling cared for and loved
7–18 years	Indoctrination	Mastering the content of faith
19–27 years	Reality Testing	Identifying inconsistencies and establishing a faith separate from that of parents and other childhood influences
28–35 years	Making Choices	Taking responsibility for one's own choices; attempting to resolve the inconsistencies
36 years +	Active Devotion	Effectively living with one's convictions

---

Think about It

How does your pilgrimage compare with Powers' faith stages? What similarities and differences have you experienced? (If you didn't grow up in a church, ignore the age ranges. Focus on the various stages.)

Another view of faith development is presented by John Westerhoff (1976). He compares faith to the growth rings of a tree. The first ring at the core of the tree is our initial, childlike *experienced faith.* If the proper nurturing environment is available, additional rings of faith may grow: *affiliative faith,* the faith of one's family, group, or church (early adolescence); *searching faith,* when faith is questioned and one begins to accept responsibility for one's own interpretation; and *owned faith,* the culmination of growth in a trusting commitment to the call of God.

If the proper environment or interactions are lacking, we will be arrested in our faith development. Expanding to another ring of faith is a very slow process. It takes time; it cannot be rushed. Like the growth of a tree, no one can see the expansion, but we do see the results. No rings of faith are eliminated. Each new style is added to previous ones. We do not lose a style of faith, nor do we outgrow one.[3]

As finite creatures, we continually grow to know God more intimately and to trust him more, both in this life and the next life. The essence of eternal life is knowing God (John 17:3) as he makes his permanent dwelling with redeemed humankind (Rev. 21:3). Faith development is synonymous with our life-long task of Communion.

Social Development: Community

"A new commandment I give you: Love one another. As I have loved you, so you must love one another. All men will know that you are my disciples if you love one another" (John 13:34–35). The mark of the church is people actively caring for each other. "Family" is the predominant metaphor that distinguishes our relationships. We actually assume the roles of family members: "Do not rebuke an older man harshly, but exhort him as if he were your father. Treat younger men as brothers, older women as mothers, and younger women as sisters, with absolute purity" (1 Tim. 5:1–2; see also Matt. 12:48–50). This second area of growth points to the Community theme of Christian education.

Within the structural domain of personality growth, we slowly develop a healthy sense of *self*; in the functional domain of social development, we generate a healthy sense of *others*. It is difficult to genuinely love others until we recognize and value the different perspectives that they hold and the individual needs they have.[4]

To sincerely love, we must be empathetic. We have to walk in others' shoes—a process of social perspective or role taking. Picture a mother resting on the sofa, suffering an escalating headache. Young Juan enters the room, vigorously beating the drum he received for his recent birthday. Juan's mother tells Juan that she has a headache, and asks him to stop playing immediately. Trying to relieve his mother's pain, the four-year-old proudly suggests that he play her a "pretty song." Her response is even more forbidding. Obediently, the youngster stops. Yet Juan fails to understand why his mother doesn't enjoy the drum as much as he does. He leaves the room bewildered.

The more an individual can take the role of others, the quicker that person will accept others' perspectives. Summarizing research literature, Martin Hoffman (1977) proposes four phases of social development during which the "sense of other" emerges (notice the close connection with Piaget's theory in terms of similar concepts and approximate age ranges).

1. At birth: Babies view the world as extensions of themselves. Self and others are conceptually inseparable.
2. During infancy: Toddlers begin to recognize that others exist on a permanent basis, separate from themselves.
3. During the childhood years: Children start to realize that other persons have their own thoughts, feelings, and values, distinct from their own.
4. During adolescence: Youth recognize that each person's thoughts, feelings, and other internal states are influenced by unique personal circumstances.

Although adults have the potential to reach fourth-level maturity, some habitually function at only the third or second level. These adults assume that others generally think as they do. They believe that others solve problems the way they do. Since we are commissioned to share God's love, we must not underestimate our need to be "other-oriented." To fail to do so may result in forfeiture of genuine ministry to others.

As a case in point, we may presume that what a troubled friend needs is our advice. In reality, what she needs is a listening, sympathetic ear. Similarly, a husband may attempt to show love to his wife by buying her something special. After all, he reasons, that is how he feels when he receives a gift. But his wife may prefer a special dinner and quiet conversation, attending a play, or seeing a movie. We cannot assume that what meets *our* needs will necessarily meet the needs of others.

In America ethnocentrism (cultural self-centeredness) is intense. For example, we basically need only one language, English, to adequately communicate with almost everyone. In many parts of the world, people must know two or three languages or dialects in order to speak with others in a neighboring city. Communicating in a foreign language forces individuals to think in thought forms that are unlike one's own mother tongue.

A major goal of Christian education centers on gaining a divine perspective—to look at life the way God sees it. God's perspective includes the widest vantage point of all perspectives. By increasing our role-taking ability to be as empathetic as possible, we begin to live more compassionately in a sinful world. The incarnation of Christ represents God's ultimate role-taking posture. In love, he became one of us. Through this strategy, Jesus became our sympathetic High Priest whom we can boldly approach (Heb. 4:15).

We grow in our social-thinking ability the more we experience and accept perspectives different from our own. Therefore, in our educational ministry, we should promote activities that facilitate mature social thinking: role-playing exercises; developing friendships with those of another socioeconomic status; going to locations that provide diverse cross-cultural contexts; learning a foreign language; sharing our faith with persons of different religious backgrounds.[5]

Think about It

Listed in Table 6.1 are some of the "one another" verses from the New Testament.

1. Think back over your experiences this past month. For each passage, can you think of one specific instance where you encountered the verse's command? Identify a name or incident with each passage.
2. Pick one or two verses for which you lack significant background and skill. Ask God to provide you with helpful experiences in which you can observe the application of the passage.

Table 6.1

Selected "One Another" Verses

Accept one another, then, just as Christ accepted you, in order to bring praise to God. (Rom. 15:7)

Admonish one another with all wisdom. (Col. 3:16)

And let us consider how we may spur one another on toward love and good deeds. (Heb. 10:24)

Be devoted to one another in brotherly love. Honor one another above yourselves. (Rom. 12:10)

Be kind and compassionate to one another, forgiving each one, just as in Christ God forgave you. (Eph. 4:32)

Be patient, bearing with one another in love. (Eph. 4:2)

Carry each other's burdens, and in this way you will fulfill the law of Christ. (Gal. 6:2)

Do not slander one another. (James 4:11)

Offer hospitality to one another without grumbling. (1 Pet. 4:9)

Therefore, confess your sins to each other and pray for each other so that you may be healed. (James 5:16)

Moral Development: Character

Can genuine moral development or thinking exist apart from regeneration? The classic example is the rich young ruler (Luke 18:18–23). He had a respectable track record of moral behavior, a record that Jesus never challenged. This case affirms that observance of the Law's "horizontal" (or moral) requirements does not necessarily mean that "vertical" (or faith) obligations to God have been satisfied. In other words "moral" does not equal "faith."

Moral maturity, even for the non-Christian, results from God's common grace. We all possess his gracious gift of conscience (Rom. 2:15), a moral capacity to sense right and wrong. How, then, should we treat others? How do we grow in moral character? As believers, our "new self" has been "created to be like God in true righteousness and holiness" (Eph. 4:24). Yet Paul also warns us that it will take great effort to pursue this godliness (1 Tim. 4:7b–8). But it is not a task to be done alone. Empowered by the Holy Spirit (Gal. 5:22, 25), we should grow in righteousness in the company of others on the same pilgrimage (2 Tim. 2:22). For the Christian a theology of Character must highlight, among other aspects, two central lifelong activities that contribute to such growth:

1. *A focus on conscience* (Ps. 119:11).
   a. Educating, evaluating, and responding to a sensitive conscience, the seat of our standards of morality (Rom. 14:22–23; James 1:22–25).
   b. Improving our moral reasoning and decision making, conscience being the locus of arbitration regarding moral decisions (Heb. 5:14).
2. *A focus on lifestyle habits*—Developing and maintaining our self-control and participation in moral actions through personal habits and spiritual disciplines (e.g., 1 Cor. 9:24–27).[6]

Content and Rationale

In discussions of Christian morality in the church, we have tended to focus exclusively on right answers with little concern for the reasoning behind those answers. Yet, Scripture affirms that *why* we do (rationale) *what* we do (content) is just as significant (Matt. 6:1–18). How people make choices about moral matters continues to interest social science researchers.[7] Kohlberg's (Kohlberg, Levine, and Hewer 1983) research into the psychology of moral judgments suggests that as we mature physically from childhood to adulthood, the reasons for our actions must also mature.[8] The difference between these two concepts of "content" and "rationale" can be illustrated through the following interview responses:

Interviewer: Ashley, should people tell lies to each other?
Ashley (age 6): No. (*content:* lying is wrong)
Interviewer: Why is it wrong to tell a lie?
Ashley: Because if I get caught telling a lie, my parents will punish me. (*rationale*)

Interviewer: Galen, should people tell lies to each other?

Galen (age 26): No. (the same *content* as Ashley's response)

Interviewer: Why is it wrong to tell a lie?

Galen: Because if I get caught telling a lie, my parents will punish me. (same *rationale*).

Galen's response to the first question is appropriate. But his second response seems out of place for a twenty-six-year-old. As we grow, although our beliefs and values (content, e.g., "Do not lie") may not change much, our reasons why these beliefs and values are true *do need to change* (rationale). When teens and adults continue to use child-appropriate reasons they significantly hinder their moral growth.

Aligning Spheres of Concerns

What are appropriate reasons in moral decision making at each stage of development? Young children tend to consider exclusively their own needs and concerns.[9] Then, in late childhood and the early teen years, in addition to concern for themselves, adolescents begin to attend to the approval of their peers. Finally, in adulthood, an additional third lens of concern emerges:

being able to consider and live by abstract moral principles. Thus, with each new stage of growth, we can increase the number of factors we consider in evaluating moral issues we encounter. But only with the complex cognitive capabilities of adulthood are we able to keep in mind all three lenses of concerns in moral decision making.[10] Figure 6.2 outlines the development of these emerging lenses from childhood through adulthood. The mature believer should have an appropriate concern for self, others, and moral principles, with all three lenses being viewed within a divine perspective.

Teens and adults encounter problems when they focus exclusively on the concerns of "self" and "others" without regard for moral principles. For example, how might the "Golden Rule" be understood when consideration is restricted to a few lenses of concern? Table 6.2 lists these restricted perspectives followed by scriptural cases that illustrate each view. Remember, it is normal for children and young teens to focus exclusively on self and others due to their limited

Figure 6.2

Lenses of Moral Growth

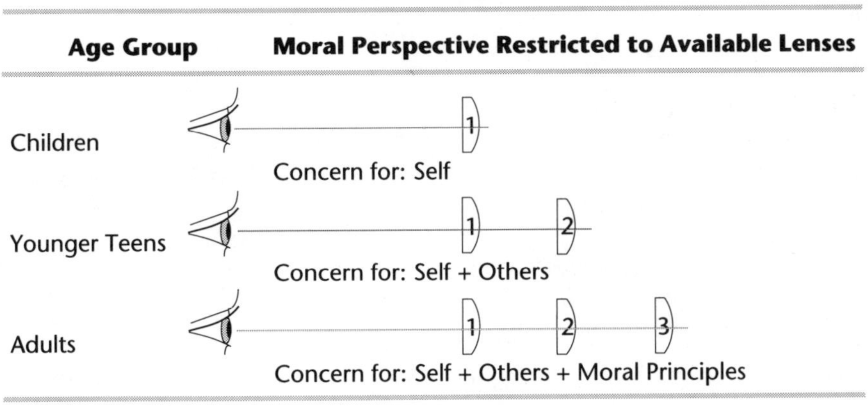

Age Group	Moral Perspective Restricted to Available Lenses

Children — Concern for: Self

Younger Teens — Concern for: Self + Others

Adults — Concern for: Self + Others + Moral Principles

Note: 1. With each new life phase, a new lens capability emerges.

2. Christian workers must customize God's truth so it can be understood within the students' lens capability.

Sources: Adapted from Kohlberg (1981); Lickona (1983); Ward (1989).

cognitive capabilities. But these restrictions do not apply to mature teens and adults.

Table 6.2

Lenses of Moral Growth Focusing on "Self" and "Others"

Exclusive Focus on Me

Perspectives appropriate for children:

"I will do what I like to do since everyone else would do the same thing if they were in my shoes."

"Let's make a deal: I will do this for you if you do this for me."

Scriptural cases of inappropriate adult perspectives:

John 12:3–8: Judas claimed that the money used to purchase expensive perfume should have been given to the poor. He wasn't concerned about the poor but about the disciples' treasury since he regularly stole money from it.

Mark 7:9–13: Jesus castigated the religious leaders for the deceptive practice of "dedicating" their possessions to God ("Corban") so they could set up a life estate for themselves while avoiding the obligation to provide for the needs for their aged parents (dedicated property could not be used for secular purposes) (cf. also 1 Tim. 5:8).

Exclusive Focus on Self and Others

Perspectives appropriate for younger teens:

"If everybody in the group does it, then I will do it too."

"I try to put myself in your shoes and do what would be best for you—whether the action itself is right or wrong."

Scriptural cases of inappropriate adult perspectives:

Matt 6:2: Jesus claimed that the religious leaders gave to the poor, not to please God, but to show off and to build up a reputation among the people.

Acts 4:36–5:11: Ananias and Sapphira, apparently in order to copy the example of Barnabas and to gain the acclaim of the early church, pretended to give the full proceeds of a sale, when they had actually kept back a part.

The examples in Table 6.2 indicate that although actions can be perceived by others as being good, what may be an appropriate rationale for a child may be totally inappropriate for a teen or adult. Another implication: The number of lenses of concerns we regularly consider in our decision making affects our interpretation of Bible passages and understanding of moral messages. For example, a pastor may preach a sermon on the "Golden Rule," but members of the congregation will comprehend the message within their own thinking patterns, as illustrated in Table 6.2

Our goal as educators, then, is to help teen and adult believers consider and align all *three* lenses of concerns as they make moral decisions.[11] Table 6.3 provides some examples related to finances. Ideally, harmony is possible among the three lenses because God's truth is not ultimately opposed to our concerns for ourselves, for others, or for moral principles. Even in difficult situations, we can experience the harmony of God's truth among the three lenses. Compare the example of Daniel's three companions (Dan. 3) and Peter and John (Acts 4:1–31). Just as an optometrist aligns various lenses to help us see clearly, so must we align all three lenses of concern to gain a clear perspective of God's truth.

Table 6.3

Aligning Three Lenses of Moral Growth with God's Truth

Peter claimed that Ananias and Sapphira were free to keep their money or give it for the needs of the saints, but by claiming to give more than they actually did they lied to the Holy Spirit (Acts 5:3–5).

Believers who benefit from those teaching God's Word should financially support these teachers (Gal. 6:6; 1 Tim. 5:17–18).

"Do not be deceived: God cannot be mocked. A man reaps what he sows." "Whoever sows sparingly will also reap sparingly, and whoever sows generously, will also reap generously" (Gal. 6:7; 2 Cor. 9:6).

God's grace was manifest in the sacrificial giving of the (mostly Gentile) Macedonian believers (Philippi, Thessalonica, and Berea); despite their poverty, they made a generous contribution for the poor in Jerusalem (2 Cor. 8:1–5; cf. Rom. 15:26; Acts 24:17).

Based on Christ's example of gracious selfless giving, Paul urges the (mostly Gentile) Corinthian believers to complete the generous commitment they had previously made to collect additional money for the poor in Jerusalem. In the future, these Jewish saints may be able to help the Corinthians in their need (2 Cor. 8:6–15; 9:5; cf. Rom. 15:26; Acts 24:17).

God loves cheerful givers (2 Cor. 9:7).

Vocational Development: Commission

The purpose of our existence is to serve God: "For we are God's workmanship, created in Christ Jesus to do good works, which God prepared in advance for us to do" (Eph. 2:10). We have been given life and we are gifted for service. In light of our life task, we must restore the full meaning of the term "vocation," which is based on the Latin *vocatio,* "to call." For centuries Christians have used the phrase "a calling from God." Unfortunately, we now restrict the meaning of the phrase to full-time religious work.

In God's eyes, *all* of life is holy—dedicated to him. For Christians, there is no dichotomy of the sacred and secular. God has made each of us stewards of his grace and gifts, and he will hold us accountable for our time, talents, and treasures (Luke 12:42–48). The parable of the talents in Matthew 25:14–30 stands as a prominent reminder of this comprehensive view of Commission. Growth in vocation involves competence and confidence in being stewards of our God-given opportunities and capabilities.[12] Ultimately, we will reign with God and serve him for ever (Rev. 22:3–5).

One area of accountability is our spiritual gifts. Paul encourages Timothy to "fan into flame" his gift (2 Tim. 1:6). Although these divine gifts are fully operational when given, we need to learn how to use them responsibly. Those who have gone before us can guide us as we become more competent and confident.

Specific patterns of growth for each skill or task should be articulated.[13] As a general guide, leaders can assess levels of skill development based on two criteria: ability and willingness.[14]

Level 1: *Unable and unwilling*—People are not competent or confident in the skill or task. They may be insecure about what is expected of them. They may doubt that they can successfully grow in this area. The writer to the Hebrews addresses believers who fit this category. He accuses them of being "slow to learn" (5:11). Their choice to refrain from growing caused them to remain as infants in the faith. This consequence was unfortunate because they had ample time to become teachers.

Level 2: *Unable but willing*—They are confident, but lack the specific training in the required skills. Although he was not able to feed the large crowd that had been listening, a boy was willing to share his lunch of five barley loaves and two fish (John 6:9).

Level 3: *Able but unwilling*—They may be insecure about some aspect of the skill or task. They are reluctant for a number of reasons, including lack of dedication. Probably the story of Jonah the prophet may come to mind. In an unusual manner God forced Jonah to reconsider his attitude and actions about preaching God's message to the citizens of Nineveh.

Level 4: *Able and willing*—They are ready and equipped to serve. They probably require a minimum amount of supervision. Once Moses had received the plans from God, Bezalel, Oholiab, and the other skilled craftsmen who were willing began to build the tabernacle in the wilderness (Exod. 36:2).

Think about It

1. Think of a couple of colleagues in ministry or those to whom you are currently ministering. Do you sense a reluctance on their part to get involved in a certain task? Use the above four-part framework to help diagnose the specific barrier. Is the problem based in lack of ability and training (e.g., Level 1 or 2) or willingness and commitment (e.g., Level 1 or 3)? Evaluate what you know about the situation and make a preliminary diagnosis of the main problem (either Level 1, 2, or 3). Then develop a strategy to help this colleague face the central issue and to grow in this particular area.

2. How about yourself? Do you need to grow in any areas of ministry? What specifically has been holding you back?[15]

What of Spiritual Growth?

We have traversed the territory of human development and have yet to address "spiritual" growth. This direction has been intentional. It is our view that the substance and process of human development are basically universal. Most marks of maturity hold true for the believer and not-yet-believer alike. Yet *optimal* human development is available only to the Christian.[16] Paul provides accurate, distinguishing terminology. In 1 Corinthians 2–3 he stresses that nonbelievers are identified by natural human development criteria while believers require a *spiritual* evaluative framework. In this way we honor both of God's creative acts: the original creation of humanity

(now fallen from grace) and the *re-creation* of humanity in grace (2 Cor. 5:17). Regeneration does not produce something other than human. In Christ, we have the potential to become fully human—we are now fully alive (Eph. 2:5)!

In our view, no separate domain of spirituality exists. Our "spiritual" nature represents the totality of our human nature made alive in Christ. At the moment of rebirth, a new believer does not automatically receive an extra measure of physical agility, intelligence, or moral character. Theologically speaking, we are released from enslavement to sin. And, on the positive side, we are empowered to become Christ-like. From a human development perspective, born-again people have the power to utilize all the potential of human life. They are not supermen or superwomen. But they are set free from the limitations brought on by spiritual death and are now empowered to live the abundant life.[17] So, for example, we have the opportunity to know God (Eph. 2:1–10). We can grow in our love for each other (1 Thess. 3:12). We can manifest a greater measure of all the Spirit's fruit (Gal. 5:22–23).

A theology of "spiritual" human development must address at least four central issues:

1. *Initiation Process:* How are persons initiated into the status of being "spiritual" persons, as differentiated from "natural" persons? What divine elements are involved and what human elements are necessary? How does our human development affect this initiation process? For example, what about children who grow up in a believing community? Is the initiation process the same for children as it is for adults? Or are there any differences due to growth factors such as cognitive

development? What about those who are mentally incompetent? What about infants who die at a very young age?

2. *Essential Nature:* What is the nature of spiritual persons? What are the constituent elements that make up a Christian believer? What are the common elements shared by both "natural" and "spiritual" persons? What are the unique aspects of spiritual persons? In the eternal state, what elements will be retained, what elements will be changed, and what elements will be new?

3. *Growth Maintenance:*

   a. What empowers and facilitates spiritual growth? What divine resources and what human resources are available? When spiritual growth occurs, what part is divine and what part is due to human efforts? What role do individual and corporate human aspects play? For example, what aspects of spiritual growth are out of our control and what aspects are under our control?

   b. What is the normal path of spiritual growth? Is it always "upward" and "positive"? Are there periods of regression or backsliding? Are there any recognizable stages that all believers will experience or is each pilgrimage unique? What outward evidences, if any, can be assessed to indicate that growth has taken place?

   c. What supernatural and natural hindrances exist? When relapses take place, who or what could be the cause? For example, do we hold two believers equally accountable for growth, if one of them comes from an abused background?

   d. Must Christians grow and evidence Christ-like qualities? What are the various legitimate reasons that should motivate Christians to pursue growth in this earthly life? What are the benefits of undertaking this pursuit? What are the liabilities for failing to make the effort?

4. *Final Goal:* What are the characteristics of Christian maturity? What should the ideal Christian be like? What characteristics should be common to all believers? Is there freedom for divergent manifestations of spiritual maturity? Will there be any kind of growth or learning in the eternal state?

Scripture seems to provide milestones of global, "spiritual" growth. Analogies to human development supply one type of illustration. In 1 Corinthians 3:1–3, Paul refers to believers in their initial phase of faith as "infants in Christ." Characteristics that are normal for this stage include an ability to accept only the "milk" of the Word instead of "solid food," and a lifestyle of "worldly" habits, very much like those of nonbelievers. Paul expects the Corinthians to grow up so they can digest more challenging truths.

In addition to this two-part view of spiritual growth, 1 John 2:12–14 introduces a third category. John refers to his audience as "children," "young men," and "fathers." Stott explains that "He is indicating not their physical ages, as some have thought, but stages in their spiritual development, for God's family, like every human family, has members of different maturity. . . . The little children are those newborn in Christ; the young men are more developed Christians, strong and victorious in spiritual warfare; while the fathers possess the depth and stability of ripe Christian experience"

(1964, p. 96). The identification of such biblical phases seems to offer a promising way to delineate the maturation process within believers. But more study is needed of these and related passages,[18] if we desire to recognize critical milestones of growth in our Christian pilgrimage.[19]

Think about It

---

1. How can you tell that you have grown spiritually? Can you offer any outward evidences of growth? What kind of outward evidences should Christian leaders use to assess if church members are making progress in their spiritual growth? In which of the four functional domains would you place evidences of growth? Should Christian leaders attempt to assess if church members are growing?
2. Do you think that there are any common milestones or global stages that all believers will pass through, something like those in physical development (child, youth, adult)?

Conclusion

God has fashioned us as complex beings. It shouldn't surprise us that we grow in very complex ways. As we suggested in the previous chapter, identify *one* major concept in the chapter. Ponder ministry implications of this single idea. Incorporate the concept in your teaching ministry. Experiment with the concept yourself. Then proceed to the other functional domains of development.

For example, in the moral domain, we highlighted the need to focus on lifestyle habits. Consider Olympic athletes. We marvel at the self-discipline they evidence in their training. Now think about one aspect of the Spirit's work: "self-control" (Gal. 5:23). How can the "natural" Olympic athlete muster such self-control without the special working of the Spirit? And why don't more Christians manifest a higher level of self-control than Olympic athletes demonstrate—even when believers have a supernatural resource?

Paul sets the pace for us:

> Do you not know that in a race all the runners run, but only one gets the prize? Run in such a way as to get the prize. Everyone who competes in the games goes into strict training. They do it to get a crown that will not last; but we do it to get a crown that will last forever. Therefore, I do not run like a man running aimlessly; I do not fight like a man beating the air. No, I beat my body and make it my slave so that after I have preached to others, I myself will not be disqualified for the prize. (1 Cor. 9:24–27)

Jesus' penetrating question must goad us into serious thought and action, if we desire to live up to our name as Christians: "Why do you call me 'Lord, Lord' and do not do what I say?" (Luke 6:46).

7

Aspects of Learning

Theory and Practice
What Is Learning?
Conclusion

Theory and Practice

Why worry about how people learn? Shouldn't we just teach and let the Holy Spirit work within people? These questions represent fundamental concerns for educational ministry in the church. To deal with these issues, we will take a trip back into medical history.

Medical Theory and Practice

Bloodletting was one of the more peculiar techniques utilized by doctors. The early Greeks practiced it. In America, the general practice continued until the nineteenth century.[1] The word means just what it says: letting blood drain out of the body. The blood was discarded after a patient was bled.[2]

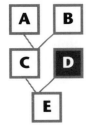

Doctors perpetuated this practice because of medical theory. Before modern science, it was assumed that the body contained four basic fluids (called "humors"): (1) blood, the chief fluid, (2) phlegm, (3) choler or yellow bile, and (4) melancholy or black bile.[3] A healthy body, it was believed, possessed a balance of these humors. Thus, all disease stemmed from imbalance. Diagnosis of disease was simple. Accurate diagnosis determined the imbalance among the humors. Bloodletting was the most direct way to normalize the blood humors, since all four were interconnected. Drawing off one area would drain off the other, and a healthy ratio would be reestablished.

What's the point of the history lesson? Simply this axiom: What we *do* is always based on what we *think*. To rephrase it: *Theory drives practice.* The practice of medicine is based on assumptions or theories of how the body functions. The practice of teaching has its own set of theories. As the physician works within God's design of the human body to facilitate healing, so the teacher works within God's design of the mind and heart to facilitate learning.[4] Effective physicians and instructors master their respective disciplines in harmony with God's purposes.

There is another application from this historical sketch: Faulty assumptions about physical processes lead to faulty *practice*. Sometimes our instructional practices in the church contain "faulty theories" comparable to "humoral theory."

crease its learning value for the student.

The purpose of this and the next chapter is to gain a greater clarity about the psychology of learning.[5] We intend to outline the basic theories of learning in order to make teaching practice more effective. As a result of your comprehension of the material, we anticipate the development of two skills: (1) that you can explain why any particular teaching method "works," why it contributes to learning; and (2) that you can make an accurate diagnosis of certain educational problems to facilitate greater learning.

In the following section we examine common beliefs about educational psychology. Whether our views are accurate or not, our understanding of the learning process will control our practice of teaching. If we hold to faulty learning principles, we may actually hinder our students from learning.

Think about It

All effective teaching methods emerge from one or more sound learning principles. Three common teaching methods are lectures, group discussions, and quizzes/tests.

1. Why does each method work? What specific factors give each method its "learning value" for the student?

2. Suggest one way that each method could be improved in order to in-

---

Think about It

Imagine that this fictitious principle of learning were true: "Students who run one lap around a track tend to learn better than those who don't." How might this particular learning theory affect the practice of education in a college or seminary? Perhaps the faculty would require students to run a lap before the school day begins or before each class! What might two laps do?

State at least two other related implications of this particular learning theory:

1.
2.

Now, try it in a church context. For example, how might this particular learning principle affect

(a) the Sunday school?
(b) the preaching portion of the Sunday worship service?
(c) a home Bible study group?

Give two different implications of one of these three areas:

1.
2.

Now let's come back to reality. We know that our teaching *practice* expresses what we believe about learning *theory*. Let's critique a few misunderstandings that tend to be alive and well among believers today.

Who Is Responsible for Effective Learning?

What if teachers in our churches held the following "theory" about learning?

"Learning among believers results *solely* from the work of God."

What would teachers be required to do? First, teachers would not take great pains in preparation. The cause for student learning originates and remains with the Creator. Second, teachers would not need to have any training at all. Since it doesn't matter what the teacher does, training (or lack of training) is irrelevant. Third, we would not even need human teachers. If God is the *sole* worker in the lives of believers, the argument goes, he is all we need. Human efforts are unnecessary.

But we know—both experientially and biblically—that there *is* a human role in education that is Christian. God has bestowed a variety of gifts to activate believers for ministry. One of these gifts is teaching (Rom. 12:7; 1 Cor. 12:28; Eph. 4:11).

Human effort in Christian education, therefore, cannot be discounted.[6] To the contrary, such gifts imply responsibility and accountability. But how much responsibility?

Imagine that teachers held another "theory" about learning:

"Learning among believers results *solely* from human effort."

If this were true, then learning for Christians would not be unique; learning would be no different for Christians or non-Christians. Thus, we would need to extract "Christian" out of "Christian education." Only educational psychology and empirical research about the learning process would be important to comprehend. There would be no need to pray for our students' mastery of the material.

This faulty view obviously gives the teacher too much responsibility. It presumptuously leaves God out of the picture. We need to realize that the Divine Teacher works both within and alongside of the human teacher. In fact, one name for the Spirit, the Paraclete, means "One who counsels alongside us."

It's clear that these two extreme theories of learning are faulty. Neither divine nor human teachers can be ignored. To repeat an earlier analogy with the medical profession: The Christian teacher works within God's design of the mind and "heart" to facilitate learning.

The Most Popular Teaching Method

Imagine another "theory" about learning—another common misunderstanding:

"Christian students have a *total comprehension* of whatever they hear."

What implications does this theory have for teaching practice? Colleges and seminaries would require only large lecture halls. Teachers would just present the facts. They would never review any material. Instructors wouldn't need to answer any student questions. Any student-teacher dialogue would be unnecessary. In fact, students could listen to an audio cassette or view a video cassette in their home and never set foot in a school. Best of all, there would be no need for pop quizzes or exams!

This erroneous theory provides the impetus for an exclusive dependence on the lecture method. We may well ask why lecturing is still the most popular teaching method. We understand its exclusive practice *before* the invention of the printing press—a time when the lecture was the primary means of transmitting knowledge in an expeditious manner. But the printing press radically changed how information was disseminated.[7] Today, in the age of high technology, we have added both *audio media* (records, cassette tapes, compact discs) and *visual media* (overhead projectors, films, video tapes) to aid us specifically in knowledge transmission. Coupled with photocopying and computer technology, we can disseminate information in a more efficient and permanent manner than through the lecture method.[8]

Misconceptions about Learning and Teaching

Learning, like breathing, occurs every minute of every day. Because it is so natural, it often goes unnoticed. Since learning is such a common experience, we overlook its complexity. Misunderstandings about learning and teaching prevail in formal educational settings as well. Until we recognize *and* correct these particular misconceptions, we fail to fully learn and teach. We fail to utilize all of God's revelation. We fail to accurately employ the gift of teaching. Consider three persistent fallacies that create formidable barriers to learning.

"To Teach Is to Tell"

This misconception equates teaching with facts. Instruction occurs, the myth states, when information is imparted to students. But two related deceptions appear. First, subject mastery is falsely viewed as the teacher's sole responsibility.[9] In this case, minimal concern (if any) is given to the learner. For example, why is it that some students have an extremely difficult time with certain content? Too often it is assumed that if the teacher understands the material, then the student does too.

Excellent teaching does require great skill in mastering the subject matter. But it also takes skill to know how students best learn the material. Mark 4:33 offers relevant insight into the Master Teacher's balanced strategy: "With many similar parables Jesus *spoke the word* to them, *as much as they could understand.*" We evangelicals value the first part of the Lord's example (i.e., teaching "the word"). Yet many of us lack skills for the second half: the need to know our students so well that we, like Christ, know their limits. The "lesson" must be balanced by the students' "lives."

The second deception involves a reductionistic fallacy: It falsely assumes that one of the parts of teaching (in this case, the prominent activity of lecturing) can be substituted for the whole concept. The "teaching = telling" misconception, therefore, reduces to a very simplistic formula. At best, we are left with a superficial view of teaching.

"To Tell Is to Know"

The second misconception assumes that a student will correctly and fully comprehend everything spoken by the teacher. This misleading view of learning is humorously portrayed in the following example: "The Sunday School teacher had told her class of kindergartners about God's decision to destroy Sodom and Gomorrah. As the teacher explained, 'God wanted to spare

Lot, so He told him to take his wife and flee.' With that, the teacher sat back and watched the silence of comprehension take over the faces of each class member. Finally, one little guy ventured a question. 'What happened to the flea?'" (Schimmels 1989, pp. 19–20).

Sometimes, even instructional intentions go awry, as illustrated in the following episode. Using a demonstration and an object lesson, a teacher wished to communicate the dangers of alcohol to her sixth-grade class.

> She filled one beaker with water and another with alcohol. She dropped a worm into the beaker filled with water; and the worm frolicked around in obvious joy. She then fished the lively worm out and dropped him into the beaker filled with alcohol. Immediately, the worm sank to the bottom, dead.
>
> "Now," the teacher asked in her finest teacher voice, "what have you just learned from this lesson?"
>
> The silence which followed suggested that the students were working on an answer. Finally, one young man proposed a possibility. "I think I know," he said seriously. "People who drink don't have worms." (Schimmels 1989, p. 226)

In both examples what was *intended* and what was *learned* were worlds apart. In these cases, we recognize the discrepancy only because the teachers provided an opportunity for student feedback. When such feedback is not available, how many other cases of *miseducation* could be cited?

"To Know Is to Do"

The final misconception assumes that students will automatically change their conduct once they acquire new information. Such a "student-proof" view of teaching is ludicrous. It neglects the "inner factors" of students noted by LeBar (1958/

1989): the sin nature, motivation, the response to the Spirit, and the complexities of making choices and persevering in those choices. Information and understanding are necessary components of growth. But several other factors deserve consideration.

What Is Learning?

A proper understanding of the learning process includes five factors:

Levels of learning—What do we learn?

Extent of learning—How well did we learn?

Avenues of learning—In what ways do we learn?

Readiness for learning—Are we prepared to learn?

Nature of learning—What is learning?

The remaining part of this chapter provides an overview of each factor.[10]

Levels of Learning

What kinds of learning are possible? Even from a single lesson, various learning outcomes appear. Three major domains of learning outcomes are identified in the educational literature. Specifically, learners can increase or improve their:

1. Knowledge (cognition)
2. Attitudes, values, and emotions (conviction)
3. Physical skills and habits (competence)[11]

Although we separate these domains for analysis, it is difficult to separate them in practice.[12]

Knowledge (Cognition)

The most recognized form of learning is the acquisition of information. We associate this category with the primary purpose of formal education. Acquisition of facts, however, also includes the cultivation of thinking skills—the ability to process facts (e.g., solving a problem, interpreting a Bible passage, speaking a foreign language). No doubt God is concerned about what believers understand and think (see 2 Cor. 10:5; Phil. 4:8). But there is much more to learning.

Attitudes, Values, and Emotions (Conviction)

The Christian life necessitates love for others: being compassionate, kind, humble, and gentle (Col. 3:12–14). God desires "willing hearts" who serve him (Exod. 35:5; 36:5–6). These virtues take time to mature since they are more "caught than taught." Analogous to gardening, convictions require patience to cultivate. Motivation, emotions, and attitudes are also learned. Some people like math, some dislike economics; some look forward to Bible study,

some avoid witnessing for Christ. In every educational situation, students develop personal, effective responses to the teacher, the subject matter, and the classroom. These attitudes, in turn, affect future learning.

Physical Skills and Habits (Competence)

Whether it's serving a tennis ball, operating a printing press, sewing clothes, or driving a car, we have all mastered numerous skills. Even activities like praying or evangelizing include learned competencies. Learning good habits and persevering in the routines of our lifestyle contribute to the development of Christian character (1 Tim. 4:7b–8).

All three of these levels of learning were evoked within those who heard Peter's sermon (Acts 2). Notice the synthesized domains that Luke records: "When the people *heard* [cognition] this, they were cut to the *heart* [conviction] and said to Peter and the other apostles, 'Brothers, what shall we *do?'*" (v. 37). Their ensuing repentance, baptism, witness, and fellowship speak of the competencies found in the early church (see vv. 38–47).

Extent of Learning

How well have we learned? Is our learning relatively simple or more sophisticated? For example, in the domain of knowledge or cognition (the first "level"), facts can be comprehended within differing degrees of mastery: (1) *awareness* (being conscious of something); (2) *understanding* (having a better perception of its meaning); and (3) *wisdom* (consistently using that fact in making an important decision).[13] So, we can know that the earth is a round globe (awareness). Also, we can deduce that, if it's a globe, someone could travel around the world and eventually return to the starting point (understanding). Furthermore, we can decide whether it would be good judgment to actually take a trip around the world (wisdom).[14] For the cognitive domain of learning, Benjamin Bloom and his colleagues (1956) developed a standard taxonomy of educational objectives.[15] This taxonomy identifies six degrees of cognitive functioning. To illustrate these various degrees, consider the subject of bicycles.[16]

Awareness

Imagine your initial introduction to bicycles. You hear about them for the first time. After brief instruction, you are able to identify what a bicycle is. You select a picture of a bike from among several pictures, which include a car, a shopping cart, and a skateboard. Awareness signifies that a mental concept is associated with some object.

Comprehension

Here, you demonstrate a basic understanding by drawing your own picture of a bicycle. Your picture exhibits the essential features of a bike. It portrays the appropriate relationship of those parts (although perhaps not to scale). This task requires you to express the concept based on your own understanding. In contrast to "awareness," the picture originates from *inside* you, rather than from external sources.

Application or Transfer of Learning

Assume you don't know what a unicycle or a tricycle is, but you do understand what a bicycle is. You are presented with pictures of all three objects; again you recognize only one. Reasoning from the two-wheeled bicycle, you ask yourself: "If we call this a 'bicycle,' what should these other two be called?" You may not use the exact term, but you could use your understanding of "bi" and "cycle" to name the remaining objects. You apply or transfer known principles to a new situation involving some unknown factors.

Analysis or Problem Solving

This category requires the learner to understand the operational parts of a concept and their relationship to each other. To test for mastery, you might be presented with a broken bicycle that needs repairs. Or, you might be given a box of bicycle parts to assemble.

Synthesis or Creating

Could you gather all known parts and rearrange them into a new form? That's the challenge of this category. Try your hand at this task. Using the basic parts of a bicycle (e.g., seat, handle bars, wheels, pedals), design a different sort of "pedaled" nonmotorized mode of transportation on land. Options might include a reclining bicycle or a tandem bicycle.

Evaluation

The final category requires the learner to make a judgment about the object, based on a set of criteria. We may ask, for instance, "Of the following modes of transportation, which one is the best?"

- 10-speed touring bicycle
- 18-speed mountain bicycle
- tricycle
- tandem bicycle (two-seater)
- unicycle

Your answer, of course, depends on the standards you use. For what purpose and in what situation will this vehicle be used? Who will use it? Does the rider possess the necessary skills?

LeRoy Ford (1978) groups five of these cognitive learning categories under the heading "understanding" to distinguish them from the elemental category of "awareness." Table 7.1 provides a summary of these five categories of critical thinking.

The taxonomy is an effective guide to assessing the diverse cognitive tasks we require of our students.[17] For instance, are we challenging them to analyze or synthesize concepts? Or are we interested only in comprehension or awareness? Sample discussion questions for each category are also presented in Table 7.1.

Besides the domain of cognition, there are also degrees of mastery in learning attitudes[18] and skills,[19] the other two "levels" of learning. For purposes of illustration, Table 7.2 outlines degrees of "extent" according to each level. For ease of communication, the table assumes one-dimensional scaling along three degrees of mastery.[20]

Avenues of Learning

In what ways do we actually learn? Every teacher makes assumptions and judgments about specific learning processes. We regularly employ teaching methods that we think will best help students to learn: small group discussions to encourage interaction and decision making; projects to facilitate deeper understanding and personal application. Each method is undergirded by particular learning principles.

In his review of learning theories for *Harper's Encyclopedia of Religious Education,* Craig Dykstra (1990) identifies three major learning families: behavioristic approaches, cognitive approaches, and social learning theory. Due to their importance for teaching, a more detailed explanation of these learning families is featured in the next chapter.

Readiness for Learning

We all remember playing games in our childhood: "Ready . . . set . . . GO!" In the classroom, the teacher is ready to teach—but are the students ready to learn? For effective growth to occur, students must be

Table 7.1

Categories of Critical Thinking

Category/Meaning	Relevant Verbs	Relevant Activities/Questions
Comprehension To integrate new data with existing information	Interpret Paraphrase Translate Illustrate	In your own words, summarize Moses' thoughts and anxieties during the burning bush experience (Exod. 3).
Application or Transfer of Learning To use information in new situations	Construct Demonstrate Implement	Conduct an "interview" with one of the servants who saw Moses' confrontation with Pharaoh during the plagues.
Analysis or Problem Solving To distinguish facts in their relationships	Categorize Diagram Outline	How was Moses' burning bush experience similar to and different than Paul's Damascus road experience?
Synthesis or Creating To reorganize or integrate facts into a new whole	Design Develop Plan	Create a two-minute-spot radio newscast script, using the sea-crossing event in Exodus 14.
Evaluation To judge facts using a specified standard	Appraise Rank Rate	Read Exodus 15:1–21. Now read verses 22–24. Assess your feelings as if you had experienced this situation as Moses did. What if you had been Miriam?

Source: Unknown.

Table 7.2

Mastery in Learning

Level of Learning	Extent of Learning		
	Degree 1	Degree 2	Degree 3
COGNITION (Knowledge)	Awareness	Understanding	Wisdom
CONVICTION (Attitudes/ Values/Emotions)	Expressed by sensitivity to others	Expressed by empathy	Expressed by compassion in action
COMPETENCE (Skills/ Habits)	Accomplished with some difficulty	Accomplished with ease	Accomplished with improvisation

both *able* and *willing* to learn. In the case of the Corinthian believers, Paul was discouraged that they were not prepared to advance toward the next step of maturity: "I gave you milk, not solid food, for you were not yet ready for it. Indeed, you are still not ready" (1 Cor. 3:2; cf. Heb. 5:11–12).

Ability

Ability includes maturational development, a topic treated in the two previous chapters. What happens when a teacher falsely assumes that each student has "normal" mental and physical functioning? Learning-disabled students or physically handicapped learners require alternative teaching strategies that attend to "ability" concerns.

Another element of ability is prior learning. For instance, it is impossible to teach people how to study the Bible until they can read. Once a person has learned one foreign language, it becomes easier to learn another one. As teachers, do we have an accurate understanding of what our students know? Are we correct in our assumptions of their experiences? Do we know what they have accomplished? This factor of prior learning expresses one dimension of how teaching must be geared to the level of capability of the child, youth, or adult.

Willingness

This concept refers to student motivation and the desire to expend effort to learn.

Factors inside the learner refer to the way they feel about the whole situation. Because of their past experiences with this class or other classes, were the learners eager to come to class today . . . ? Do they enter heartily into group work, are they indifferent toward the group, or do they bestir themselves to invent their own interests? . . . Are their personal psychological needs for security, affection, recognition, new experiences, freedom from guilt, being met by the class? (LeBar 1989/1958, p. 34)

Students develop positive and negative attitudes about the subject being taught, teaching methods, the teacher, and the classroom. Consequently, their willingness to participate is directly affected. In cases where learning does not occur, student motivation is often the reason. The teacher's task is to gain and sustain student interest in learning. A variety of factors contribute to student motivation. Within certain factors, teachers possess significant control: teacher competence and enthusiasm; relevance of the topic; how the topic is taught; teacher expectations of students; and teacher-student relationships. As Howard Hendricks says, "It is a sin to bore people with the truth."[21] If we want our teaching to be effective, we should assess our students' readiness: How willing and how able are they?

Nature of Learning

"To learn is to change! Learning is changing!" (Leypoldt 1971, p. 27). When the term "change" is employed as the essence of learning, we need to eliminate those changes that do not fit. We know that any change based on maturation (natural processes of growth, such as physical development) does not equal learning.

Put simply, learning is something that occurs through our experiences and interactions. Yet, this description even includes counterproductive changes: "Did you learn that repulsive habit from your friends?!" In this case, "learning" is one step forward and two steps backward. Consequently, it is imperative that we educators focus on biblical aims. We must adhere to standards from God's revelation. We should be attentive to divine patterns for growth that alert us to such counterproductive learning. In terminology used by James, "listeners" of the word are not true learners; "doers" of the word are (James 1:22–25).

Conclusion

Within a Christian worldview, learning is both natural and supernatural. Christian education involves changing toward conformity to Christ, a process involving human effort and the work of the Holy Spirit (2 Cor. 3:17–18). Learning for Christians is change that is facilitated through deliberate or incidental experience, under the supervision of the Holy Spirit, and in which one acquires and regularly integrates age-appropriate knowledge, attitudes, values, emotions, skills, and habits into an increasingly Christ-like lifestyle.[22]

Think about It

To review, we have outlined five basic features that comprise learning:

Levels of learning—What do we learn?

Extent of learning—How well did we learn?

Avenues of learning—In what ways do we learn?

Readiness for learning—Are we prepared to learn?

Nature of learning—What is learning?

Identify which words in the summary statement above relate to each of the five features. Circle words in the summary, adding the respective *letter* of the acrostic "LEARN" to each word.[23]

A more comprehensive understanding of learning provides a helpful analytical framework for diagnosing learning difficulties. For example, imagine that, at a Backyard Bible Club, you have just asked young Bobby to explain a verse he can easily recite from memory. "I don't know," responds the third-grader. Your remedy to this problem depends on your diagnosis. Here are some possibilities.

1. *Level of learning.* Tone of voice: scornful. Bobby is *bored* (conviction level of learning). He knows what the verse means, but he won't tell. He hasn't been challenged by the activities and has developed a "bad attitude" toward the program. But his mother requires him to attend. Some positive attitudes need to be developed.

2. *Extent of learning.* Tone of voice: sincere. Bobby really doesn't have a clue. Bobby may only have an *awareness* degree of knowledge of the verse. He now needs to build on this basic foundation to the next degree of comprehension.

3. *Readiness for learning.* Tone of voice: hesitant. Bobby is *fearful* of giving the wrong answer (willingness/motivation). He has a good idea what the verse means, but doesn't want to risk being embarrassed. He needs to be accepted and his confidence strengthened.

With an increased understanding of learning, teachers have more options with which to accurately remedy learning problems. Once the diagnosis is made, how do we help them take the next step in their learning? The next chapter provides the details. It is an intensive look at the basic ways that people learn.

Avenues of Learning

The Evil Eye

Imagine that you are a health worker in a Third World rural community. You want to help impoverished parents prevent their babies from getting diarrhea. Diarrhea among infants is widespread in Third World nations due largely to the use of unclean baby bottles. Helping the mothers return to breast feeding as a more hygienic practice sounds easy. But you become very frustrated when you learn why these parents are not easily persuaded by your logic. They believe that the cause of diarrhea is the "evil eye" (Rogers 1983, p. 102). Any person's glance at a healthy infant brings dire effects. In order to prevent evil eye, mothers tie various charms around their baby's neck or wrist. And, of course, they hide their precious infants from public view to avert such lethal glances. No compliments about a healthy baby are welcome.

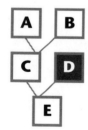

Our ideas and beliefs directly affect our actions. This holds true whether we live in a rural village in a Third World country or in a metropolitan city in America, whether our ideas are right or wrong. As stated in the previous chapter, our practice of teaching is affected by our ideas about how people learn. We addressed various misconceptions about the learning process: "to teach is to tell," "to tell is to know," and "to know is to do." Our practice of teaching will improve in proportion to the adjustments we make in our view of the learning process.

In this chapter we focus on the ways that we learn: the *avenues* of learning. Too often, an analysis of educational psychology seems overly complicated. Little appears applicable to teaching practice. A helpful assessment of the problem comes from a Stanford University education professor: "A finger of blame must be pointed at both the mystifiers [educational psychologists] and the mystified [teachers], at the former for spreading confusion and at the latter for tolerating it" (Jackson 1986, pp. 37–38). In our attempt to "demystify" the subject, six avenues of learning are suggested. They represent the substance of each of the three learning "families" summarized by Dykstra (1990): cognitive or Information-Processing Learning theory;[1] behavioral or Conditional Learning theory; and Social Learning theory. Each learning family contains a pair of contrasting avenues. These half-dozen categories are *not* mutually exclusive; each shares characteristics with other avenues. Figure 8.1 presents the six avenues

Figure 8.1
Learning Families and Related Avenues of Learning

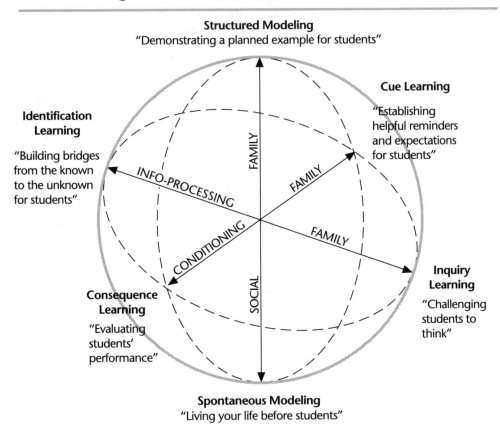

Structured Modeling
"Demonstrating a planned example for students"

Cue Learning
"Establishing helpful reminders and expectations for students"

Identification Learning
"Building bridges from the known to the unknown for students"

INFO-PROCESSING

FAMILY

FAMILY

FAMILY

CONDITIONING

SOCIAL

Inquiry Learning
"Challenging students to think"

Consequence Learning
"Evaluating students' performance"

Spontaneous Modeling
"Living your life before students"

of learning in relation to the three major learning families.

Jesus consistently displayed sound principles of instruction. The Master Teacher provided superb guidelines for emulation. One of his teaching episodes—the miraculous feeding of the five thousand—demonstrates the effective use of each of the learning avenues.

Information-Processing Learning Family

Information-Processing theories assume an active role for the learner's intellect. Specifically, the learner calculates, classifies, coordinates, contemplates, and criticizes information. Identification Learning and Inquiry Learning represent two major cognitive avenues.

Identification Learning

Remember the setting for the feeding of the five thousand? The twelve disciples were anxious about the crowd's needs. The multitude had followed Jesus all day. They were hungry. No food was available in the immediate vicinity (Luke 9:12). Jesus empathetically responded to these needs. But he did so in an unexpected way.

Physical needs were confronted in concert with spiritual necessities. The next day following the miracle, in a discourse to the same crowd, Jesus referred to himself as the "bread of life" (John 6:35). This metaphorical imagery was a specific reference to the miraculous feeding of the previous day (John 6:26). It paralleled God's provision of manna for the Israelites in the wilderness (John 6:31).

Identification Learning attempts to locate some meaningful connection with the student's life situation and uses that information as the medium to teach new information. This "life-to-lesson" approach moves from the known to the unknown. It builds bridges, so to speak, from the student's present understanding to new concepts. For example, to explain how the human conscience functions, a teacher may suggest several real-life comparisons: a fire bell clanging at a fire station; a flashing red warning light on a car dashboard indicating engine trouble; or a smoke alarm sounding off to awaken a sleeping family. We often use familiar objects to introduce students to new ideas. But such word pictures are very culture-specific; they depend on and assume a common experience-base between teacher and student.

A more elaborately structured analogy uses a "picture within a picture." A simple metaphor might explain prayer as a phone conversation with God. Wanting to stress that God is always attentive to our supplications, a mother explained to her third-grader: "No, you don't have to wait for a dial tone to talk to God. There are no busy signals. And no need for a call-waiting service."

The foremost biblical example of Identification Learning was the incarnation. "The Word became flesh and made his dwelling among us" (John 1:14). In addition to becoming "one of us," Christ's teachings overflowed with relevant life illustrations. He often made reference to culturally appropriate analogies, such as shepherds and vineyards. Metaphors are utilized in the New Testament to explain Christ and his relationship to the church: the head and the body (1 Cor. 12; Eph. 1), the cornerstone and the stones of a building (Eph. 2; 1 Pet. 2), and the bridegroom and his bride (Rev. 19:7). The Christian life is pictured as a military battle (Eph. 6), a foot race (1 Cor. 9; Heb. 12), a boxing match (1 Cor. 9; 1 Tim. 6), and sowing and harvesting a field (2 Cor. 9).[2]

You may recall an earlier reference to an example of Identification Learning in

Chapter 4. Jesus intended to convey to Nicodemus the reality of the Spirit's work in regeneration. He cited a simple parallel from nature: "The wind blows wherever it pleases. You hear its sound, but you cannot tell where it comes from or where it is going. So it is with everyone born of the Spirit" (John 3:8). Not only did Jesus proceed from the known to the unknown, but he included an excellent tool for memory retention. He constructed a play on words. The Greek word *pneuma* is translated as both "spirit" and "wind." Since spiritual realities are typically unseen, they must be comprehended in terms that make sense to the hearer. Such analogies must relate to pressing needs.[3]

Inquiry Learning

Just before Jesus performed his miracle, he posed the "problem" of feeding the hungry crowd of five thousand to the Twelve (John 6:5–6). Philip claimed the task was impossible (John 6:7). But Andrew, in faith, attempted to deal with the problem by presenting a boy's small lunch (John 6:8–9). Inquiry Learning occurs when difficult situations are faced, when perplexing questions are raised. In such cases, learners seek solutions for themselves.

Contemplate a contemporary example. Someone who doesn't feel confident about buying a car may seek advice from others, read a pertinent magazine, or engage in a comparative study of potential vehicles.

This learning situation transforms into a teachable moment. God intended Israel's routine ceremonies and family habits to encourage children to ask questions—to create such teachable moments. This afforded adults the opportunity to transmit their faith legacy to the next generation. We read about such intentional learning strategies as they pertain to the Passover meal (Exod. 12:23–27), the sacrifice of the firstfruits (Exod. 13:11–16), and the memorial stones of the Jordan River (Josh. 4:5–7).

Trials in our lives provide opportunities for us to think about, clarify, and integrate our theology and lifestyle. Learning gained through such deep wrestling in the crucible of life is learning not easily forgotten.

In the classroom, teachers prompt Inquiry Learning through critical questions, provocative statements, debates, case studies, puzzling events, and integrative homework assignments. Encouraging students to reflect on personal experiences stimulates lifelong critical thinking skills.[4]

In contrast to Identification Learning, which builds on the student's previous knowledge base, Inquiry Learning focuses on solving newly encountered problems. To put it another way, the former highlights issues that make sense and the latter matters that don't make sense. Table 8.1 suggests a few appropriate teaching methods for both Identification and Inquiry Learning.

Table 8.1

Teaching Methods for Identification and Inquiry Learning

Identification Learning	*Inquiry Learning*
"Building from the known to the unknown for students"	"Challenging students to think for themselves"
1. Graphic imagery: metaphors, analogies, parables	1. Good discussion questions, provocative statements
2. Advance organizers; organizational frameworks	2. Case studies, moral dilemmas
	3. Exploration of "live" puzzling events

Consider your own learning experiences through these two avenues of the Information-Processing family. Select one example of how you learned something through each particular avenue. Or, pick a concept you would like to teach others. Think of one way you could teach for each avenue. To help you get started, here are a couple of examples.

a. Identification Learning:
Recently, we heard a pastor preaching on forgiveness. He used the analogy that forgiveness was the lubricating oil of relationships. At the close of the sermon, we were challenged to check our oil level.

b. Inquiry Learning:
A man needed to sharpen the blades on his mower. The twin blades were so tight, a dilemma arose. To loosen them, should he unscrew the bolts in the normal pattern (i.e., rotate counterclockwise) or in the reverse pattern? If he chose the wrong way he might overtighten the bolts and possibly strip the threads. A call to the local shop helped solve the problem: normal threads. With more confidence and effort, the bolts easily came off.

Now it's your turn. Again, provide either a personal learning experience or an anticipated teaching illustration. Give one example for each avenue.

1. Identification Learning:

2. Inquiry Learning:

Conditioning Learning Family

Every learner is influenced, or "conditioned," by other people. The environment also shapes us. This truism expresses the primary contribution of the behavioral or Conditioning Learning family. Two major subcategories include Consequence Learning and Cue Learning.

Consequence Learning

The miraculous feeding of the five thousand had consequences. Despite the apostles' insistence that only a minimal supply of food was available (Mark 6:37–38), the crowd eventually had plenty to eat. In fact, the disciples collected twelve baskets of leftovers (John 6:12–13)! What an embarrassing—and enlightening—homework assignment! We can imagine how the disciples were convicted for their lack of faith in Jesus.

We experience consequences regularly. Largely based on this feedback, we either repeat or discontinue specific thoughts, feelings, words, or behaviors. Some consequences we judge as good; we feel encouraged to perform the action again. Or, we may determine consequences to be bad. We feel discouraged. Chances are we will curtail that behavior.

Virtually every activity carries a consequence. For instance, in conversation, a nod indicates agreement or approval while a frown suggests the opposite. Take another example. What happens when a key does not easily move into the tumblers of a door lock? Based on previous experience, we make quick judgments. The problem may be with the key or with the lock. The key may be upside down; it could even be the wrong key. The lock may be broken, or it may be "frozen." Consider one more example. When term papers are returned, students expectantly read the teacher's comments to find out how well they did. These are consequences in written form. Most students feel cheated if a significant number of remarks are not made. Such consequences reinforce what was done well. They also indicate needed improvement.

Encouragement is one appropriate way to offer a constructive "consequence" for believers. Paul modeled this educational strategy through his encouragement to the Thessalonians (see 1 Thess. 1:2–10). Admonishment also provides believers with feedback. Correction helps those veering away from God's principles (1 Thess. 5:14; James 5:19–20). Admonishment is the first phase of the process of reconciliation (Matt. 18:15–20). Since our self-concept is largely determined by feedback we receive from others, the kind of feedback we give should be carefully evaluated (Eph. 4:29–32). This consequence system of feedback represents one intentional plan among others that God has built into us.[5] He designed it for us to grow in our relationship with him and with each other.[6]

Cue Learning

In his earthly ministry, Jesus observed that people correctly interpreted the signs ("cues") of the weather, but failed to read the more significant signs of the Messiah (Matt. 16:1–4; Luke 11:29–32). In his Gospel, Luke portrays the feeding of the five thousand as the last event that confirmed Jesus as the Messiah (9:10–17).[7] This miracle offered the final sign or "cue" for the Twelve to come to this understanding.

Cue Learning establishes a mental link between an object and what that object represents. We are bombarded by stimuli daily. We attach meanings to many of these encounters and we rate their level of significance. For example, young Lita is riding in a car with her father. She asks him why the car suddenly stops. Her father points to the traffic signal. The red color, he explains, means the car must stop. Lita begins to realize that all drivers link red lights with stopping their cars. As she gets older, additional cues will be learned. Lita will comprehend, for instance, the meaning of a flashing red traffic light. Furthermore, she will learn to discern between a flashing red light at an intersection and the same light at a railroad crossing. Both meaning and significance are attributed to certain cues.

As cues are mastered, accompanying behavioral responses are learned. Habits are formed. Some eventually require very little thought.[8] The significance and distinctions we make about cues affect these habits. Some objects we learn to ignore; we may sleep through a blaring train horn at 4 A.M. Some objects we try hard not to ignore; we wake up to a clanging alarm clock at 6 A.M. The Cue Learning process is quite commonplace, yet it is often unconscious for both teacher and student.

Cue Learning focuses on that which *precedes* the activity; we see the red light (cue) so we step on the brakes to stop the car (response). In contrast, Consequence Learning centers on what *follows* our activity; we step on the brakes to stop for the red light (activity) or to avoid having an accident or receiving a traffic ticket (consequence).

Think about It

Creative reading and writing tasks represent one means of Cue Learning. Fashioning helpful links between word and reality, Christian teachers challenge students to develop effective communication skills. For example, what feelings emerge as you read the following "cues"?

It was warm and bright and the trees were in full color, magnificent, explosive, like permanent fireworks—reds and yellow, oranges, some so brilliant that Crayola never put them in crayons for fear the children would color outside the lines. (Keillor 1987, p. 133)

Jot down a couple of your responses.

Memory Aids

Cues—and the links we make—help us remember facts. Have you ever tied a string around your finger? The object and its associated message are like pairs—when you see one, the other comes to mind. Through repeated experiences, the first one becomes the cue for the second. Familiar links include these categories: personal names that evoke memorable people (e.g., Babe Ruth, Adolf Hitler); important passages in Scripture (e.g., John 3:16; Ps. 23); and physical or geographical locations with distinctive reputations (e.g., the White House, Las Vegas, Wall Street). Throughout America, various places are designated as significant historical sites (e.g., Abraham Lincoln's birthplace) or of commemorative significance (the Vietnam Memorial). Religious ceremonies and habits practiced by the Israelites were reminders of their special relationship with God. Recall the altar on the banks of the Jordan River. These stones were intended as a "witness" for the eastern tribes (Josh. 22:21–28). For the church, the Lord's Supper reminds believers of the Lord's earthly pilgrimage and suffering sacrifice. Furthermore, the ordinance also serves as a cue that he will return some day (Matt. 26:29).

Cue Learning is employed in various instructional systems. Some of us have been taught to use the word "homes" to remember the names of the five Great Lakes. Famous orators used comparable devices to recall the outline of a speech (Lorayne and Lucas 1974). These proven techniques have relevance for retrieving an array of facts.

Lists of Bible characters, telephone numbers, persons' names, and personal identification numbers (PIN) for automated tellers are but a few ways we utilize Cue Learning. These helpful memory devices save time. When used successfully, they also prevent embarrassing memory losses. Francis Bellezza (1981) provides an overview and categorization of helpful memory devices.

Attitudes in Learning

As significant as the recollection of facts is, certain cues also remind us of important feelings, emotions, and values. Note that attitudinal responses are initially developed through Consequence Learning. For example, a student is bored with a particular class session. If this feeling persists in subsequent class sessions, the course itself becomes a cue of boredom whenever the student enters the classroom. Just thinking about the course can evoke feelings of apathy.

Certain feelings and values emerge with particular cues. Even expectations arise. For instance, singing favorite hymns stirs earlier, moving moments of worship. Smells of favorite foods, reflections on family photo albums, the high-pitched sound of the dentist's drill become meaningful cues for us. They elicit earlier attitudes and experiences. Skilled teachers enable students to acquire and then associate positive attitudes with their teaching (Mager 1984a).

Take one summative example of Cue Learning. Through each of our senses, complementary cues can confirm a nearby fire: We *see* bright flames; we *smell* pungent smoke; we *touch* scorching heat; we *hear* crackling flames; and we *taste* hot ash filtering through the air. In addition, certain fears grip us and parallel behaviors become automatic, like running to safety. Each cue is learned at some point; such knowledge is not innate.[9] Table 8.2 offers teaching sug-

Table 8.2

Teaching Methods for Consequence and Cue Learning

Consequence Learning	Cue Learning

"Evaluating students' performance"
1. Verbal (spoken/written) (e.g., "good," "you can do better")
2. Nonverbal (e.g., smile, nod)
3. Rewarding achievements
   a. concrete reward (e.g., candy, free time)
   b. symbolic reward (e.g., points, grades)
	"Establishing helpful reminders and expectations for students"
	1. Use of the arts: music (singing, recorded); visual (posters)
	2. Classroom routines, "habits"
	3. Drill and practice in class
	4. Memory devices

gestions for the whole Conditioning Learning family.

Think about It

1. Think of some foods that you like and dislike. Can you explain what particularly attracts or repels you about these foods? Consider the five senses (taste, sight, smell, touch, sound) as a guide to your analysis. Can you remember how you initially came to like or dislike each? Dislike for the "fishy" taste of certain seafood may result from regular doses of cod liver oil during childhood. Some can't stand drinking orange juice because their juice was laced with cod liver oil. Can you explain the source of any of your likes or dislikes?

2. We tend to like and dislike certain subjects of study (e.g., theology, physical education, math, physics). What subjects do you like and dislike? Can you identify possible reasons for your feelings about these subjects?

3. As believers, we are attracted to or avoid certain Christian activities and spiritual disciplines (e.g., class socials, personal Bible study, witnessing, singing, prayer, fasting). Select a few Christian activities that you tend to practice and others that you tend not to practice as regularly. In light of Cue Learning theory, what insights can you gain about your own habits for the activities you selected?

Social Learning Family

By watching others we learn much. The phrase "like father, like son" points to the impact of social learning in the home, yet this principle applies to other environments too. An integration of Information-Processing and Conditioning components, Social Learning theory focuses on reflection and imitation. As others speak and act we observe. We analyze what we see. We make value judgments to follow or to avoid the same practice. If the former course is selected, we adapt the practice to our own setting.

Albert Bandura (1977, 1986) identifies three primary modes of Social Learning, also known as modeling. Direct modeling involves firsthand experience. Live action is visualized. Watching a parent hug a child, having someone greet you with a warm smile, or viewing two antagonists engaged in a heated argument depict direct modeling. Who hasn't looked to the host or hostess at a formal dinner to determine proper dining etiquette? Evaluation arises from such firsthand observation. In addition, the results of an action are pertinent to modeling. Noticing what kind of clothes a person wears, the type of car a person drives, or even the attractive appearance of a term paper portrays direct modeling.

Verbal modeling involves either written or spoken "how-to" explanations. Have you been compelled by a moving biography of a great Christian leader, or the public testimony of a respected believer? Then you've experienced verbal modeling. Direct and verbal modeling can be combined to increase learning potential. Demonstrating how to use a computer (direct) while also explaining how to use the computer (verbal) represents one application.

The visual mass media, like television, movies, video tapes, magazines, and newspapers, represents another powerful mode of modeling.[10] It, too, can be harnessed for beneficial educational use. For example, in the field of human resource management, training videos help salespersons perform their jobs more efficiently. This training guides managers in developing morale among employees.

The influential nature of being an example to others cannot be overrated. Many passages in Scripture point to this learning system. Luke records that a student "who is fully trained will be like his teacher" (6:40). No wonder James warned teachers about their stricter judgment (3:1)! When directed to the example of others in the epistles, one of three Greek word groups is used: *mimetes* ("imitator"), *tupos* ("example"), and *hupodeigma* ("example").[11] Paul acknowledges that Israel's failures are examples to avoid (1 Cor. 10:11). Each sphere of life has its heroes. In the business world, they are called "mentors." Sports enthusiasts have their superstars. Media buffs treasure television and movie idols. John exhorts us to be cau-

tious regarding which models we emulate (3 John 11).

Structured Modeling

The Twelve witnessed Jesus' personal life and ministry. His compassionate healing ministry became a normal feature of their daily agenda. Just prior to the miraculous feeding of the five thousand, the disciples once again saw the compassion of Jesus. Although Jesus was tired, he healed the sick (Matt. 14:14). He taught about the kingdom of God (Luke 9:11). Following the miracle, Jesus sought solitude for a time of prayer (Matt. 14:23), a prominent habit during his earthly pilgrimage (Luke 5:16).

Structured Modeling involves "planning your work, then working your plan." Examples include a lecture or sermon, a dramatic scene, or a full-length movie. Each of these forms suggests preparation (even rehearsal) before the final "performance." Routines and habits fall into this category. That is, a particular routine was either planned prior to the first instance, or thought to be worth repeating after the first instance. The explicit purpose of Structured Modeling is to provide a standard for emulation. Good teaching exemplifies Structured Modeling, for it requires invaluable planning. One benefit of such noble instruction is to uphold commendable features of quality education. Carefully prepared classroom activities, for instance, effectively advance student learning.

Films, television programs, and magazines also present divergent models to emulate. In its fullest expression, the mass media is a twentieth-century phenomenon within the modeling repertoire. Bandura notes the power of the mass media for the dissemination of ideas and values over large geographical areas:

Whereas previously modeling influences were largely confined to the behavior exhibited in one's immediate community, nowadays diverse styles of conduct are brought to people within the comfort of their homes through the vehicle of television. Both children and adults acquire attitudes, thought patterns, emotional bents, and new styles of conduct through symbolic modeling. In view of the efficacy of, and extensive public exposure to, televised modeling, the mass media play an influential role in shaping human thought and action. (1986, p. 70)

Think about It

Television and movies are basic features of our lives. Recall a particular television program or movie that significantly affected you in either a positive or a negative way.

1. Can you identify any specific influences it had on your life?

2. How do you think the show or movie prompted this? What specific aspects were involved?

Spontaneous Modeling

The miraculous feeding of the five thousand was prompted by a momentary need. In light of all the miracles Jesus had performed previously (e.g., healing the sick, the blind, the lame, and lepers; raising the dead), never had the Twelve asked Jesus to feed the masses. So special was this miracle for the disciples, that it confirmed for them that Jesus was the Messiah. So overwhelming was the miracle for the crowds, they wanted to make him king (John 6:15). Yet Jesus dismissed them and sent the disciples away (Matt. 14:22). It was not time for him

to establish his kingdom on earth. This example of Spontaneous Modeling must have perplexed the disciples.[12] Did Jesus not come to re-establish his reign on earth? Did he miss a golden opportunity to get the crowds behind him?

Spontaneous Modeling is not planned—it just happens. It is characteristic of how we live our lives before others. It expresses how we respond to others and the various circumstances of life. What do we say and how do we react to a flat tire, spilled coffee, or a "C" on a test or final exam? Deuteronomy 6:6–9 catches the spirit of this pervasive learning avenue: "These commandments that I give you today are to be upon your hearts. Impress them on your children. Talk about them when you sit at home and when you walk along the road, when you lie down and when you get up. Tie them as symbols on your hands and bind them on your foreheads. Write them on the doorframes of your houses and on your gates."

An intentional feature of Christian education exists in this command, akin to Structured Modeling. Because of the dynamic nature of life, however, much of our instruction is unplanned. Preparing for Spontaneous Modeling is not easy—it literally takes a lifetime. Our character is what is on display for people to view: in last-minute conversations prior to class, in unscheduled counseling sessions, in moments of unintended confrontation, in how we talk about and treat others of the opposite sex. "By this all men will know that you are my disciples, if you love one another" (John 13:35).

The contribution of Spontaneous Modeling to learning is that we can observe others' faith in life. We represent living "commentaries" of what we claim to be truth. We demonstrate the validity of what it means to be in intimate relationship with God. Spontaneous Modeling demands that we

Table 8.3

Teaching Methods for Structured and Spontaneous Modeling

Structured Modeling	*Spontaneous Modeling*
"Demonstrating a planned example for students"	"Living your life before students"
1. Live demonstrations	1. Open question and answer sessions; class discussions
2. Reading excerpts of biographies	2. Classroom "town hall" meetings
3. Viewing training video tapes	3. Field trips

attend to the development of our private lives, since, in our actions, our character becomes public domain to those around us.

Isn't it contradictory to say we can teach students to "plan" for "Spontaneous Modeling"? Take, for example, standard times of questions and answers. As teachers, how are our characters exhibited in such moments? Do we become defensive when students ask questions? Do we use our status as teachers to intimidate? Can we honestly admit that we don't have an answer to a particular question? Is our nonverbal communication consistent with our verbal feedback? Are both expressive of the John 13:35 litmus test? Question and answer times are not interruptions in the lesson. They provide a distinctive opportunity, in class, to view the real you.[13]

Table 8.3 summarizes teaching methods that fit the Social Learning family.

The decision for us believers is not *whether* we learn from the example of others, but *which* behavior we decide is most appropriate to emulate. Conversely, it is not a question of *whether* we'll be models, but rather, *what kind* of models we will be.

Six Avenues for Productive Learning

We've observed that the feeding of the five thousand was an important learning opportunity for the Twelve. Table 8.4 presents the learning avenues that were operative in this educational experience. The

Master Teacher knew that when several approaches to learning are involved, a greater potential for growth exists.[14]

Table 8.4

Avenues of Learning and the Feeding of the Five Thousand

INFORMATION-PROCESSING LEARNING FAMILY

Identification Learning: The disciples were naturally concerned for the hungry crowd. Jesus responded to their concern and dealt with the crowd's hunger. What Christ did "made sense." The miracle *identified* with their concerns. In a subsequent discourse, Jesus called himself the bread of life. Thus, he moved from the known to the unknown. His reference incorporated both the previous miracle and the manna given to the Israelites in the wilderness.

Inquiry Learning: When Jesus performed the miracle, he did so in an unexpected way. Jesus asked the disciples to participate in the miracle. He asked them to help solve the food problem. By discussing the crowd's limited food resources with the Twelve, what Christ did initially "did not make sense." It encouraged mental reflection and probing.

CONDITIONING LEARNING FAMILY

Consequence Learning: The disciples also participated by collecting twelve baskets of leftover food—more than what they started with. Simple arithmetic prompted convicting thoughts about their lack of faith in God.

Cue Learning: This miracle ignited subsequent insight for the disciples. It provided a significant, additional memory link to confirm Jesus was the Messiah.

SOCIAL LEARNING FAMILY

Structured Modeling: Jesus was compassionate. He routinely and faithfully taught the crowds and cared for them. Perhaps even Christ's prayer during this miracle followed a standard form similar to the Lord's Prayer.

Spontaneous Modeling: Although Jesus had certain planned (i.e., structured) approaches to ministry, he also responded to impromptu needs. This miracle indicates that, in contrast to the Pharisees, Jesus was thoroughly consistent in his lifestyle.

Although all avenues are operative in almost every learning situation, some avenues tend to be more effective in achieving specific learning levels. The arrangement (in Table 8.5) between learning levels and avenues suggests distinctive contributions for instructional approaches. Our learning goals help us select appropriate avenues to employ. These avenues, in turn, allow us to select appropriate teaching methods and learning activities.

In standard teaching situations, what avenues of learning tend to be most common? Table 8.6 outlines the use (or lack of use) of all six avenues within three distinct educational settings: (1) a Sunday morning sermon[15] or adult Sunday school lecture, (2) a traditional lecture-oriented college or seminary class, and (3) an adult class involving a variety of learning activities. If our teaching purpose is to develop initial awareness or to convey new information quickly, then a session-long lecture may be a viable method. But if our complete goal is to nurture holistic growth, then we must use comprehensive teaching methods. Employing several avenues promotes lifelong learning and retention.

Conclusion

Think about It

1. Now that you have a better understanding of the learning avenues, identify the appropriate avenues for the teaching methods you analyzed in the first "Think about It" section of this chapter.
   a. Lecture:
   b. Group Discussion:
   c. Quiz/Test:
2. What would you do to improve the use of each method? How can you fully tap its learning potential?
   a. Lecture:
   b. Group Discussion:
   c. Quiz/Test:
   Compare your responses here with the responses you gave earlier in the chapter.[16]
3. All good teaching methods utilize one or more avenues of learning. Analyze additional teaching practices and identify the major learning avenues

Table 8.5

Levels and Avenues of Learning

Level	Prominent Avenues
Cognition (Knowledge)	Inquiry, Identification, Consequence
Conviction (Attitudes, Values, Feelings)	Cue, Consequence, Spontaneous Modeling
Competence (Skills and Habits)	Structured Modeling, Consequence, Cue

Table 8.6

Educational Settings and the Avenues of Learning

Good sermon or Sunday school lecture	**Significant Use:** • Identification: illustrations, familiar words, stories, humor • Cue: attitudes and expectations about the pastor, church, Bible, and God; note-taking outline **Some Use:** • Structured modeling: sharing personal examples, practical "how to" instructions from presentation or Bible **Little or No Use:** • Consequences (how well they learned) • Inquiry (figuring it out for themselves) • Spontaneous modeling
Traditional lecture class (college or seminary)	**Significant Use:** • Identification: illustrations, stories, familiar vocabulary • Inquiry: exams, raising questions in class, out-of-class assignments and reading • Consequences: comments on assignments, course grades, answers to questions in class • Cue: attitudes about teacher, subject, course, repeated concepts, summary outline of subject; taking notes **Some Use:** • Structured modeling: practical "how to" instructions from class or reading • Spontaneous modeling: answering student questions
Adult class using variety of teaching methods	**Significant Use:** • Identification: illustrations, stories, familiar vocabulary • Inquiry: in-class individual or group tasks (case study, problem solving) • Consequence: teacher evaluation of in-class small group work, answers to questions in class • Cue: attitudes about teacher, subject, course, repeated concepts, advanced organizer: summary outline of subject, taking notes • Structured modeling: videotape, practical "how to" instructions from class or reading • Spontaneous modeling: role play

that support the effectiveness of each method.

4. Complete the following sentence: "To encourage student learning, the next time I teach I will be sure to . . ."

"Good news" and "bad news" come with a broader definition of learning. The good news is a greater appreciation for its breadth and depth. This assumption yields the potential for more precise learning assessment. No longer can we be satisfied with just one degree of cognitive mastery or just one level of learning. More complex thinking, attitudes (conviction), and skills (competence) can be expected.

These benefits ironically represent the "bad news" of broader perspectives of learning. That is, the learning process becomes quite complicated. Its sophistication may deflate the motivation of even the most enthusiastic instructors. Moreover, this reality is especially harsh for those who want simplistic answers to tough educational problems. To repeat James' warning to unqualified instructors: "Not many of you should presume to be teachers" (3:1). Inadequate and presumptive teaching—based, in part, on simplistic notions—results in devastating consequences for teacher and student alike. This complex understanding of educational ministry should not ultimately discourage believers. Rather, this knowledge should elicit proper respect for learning and teaching.

Part 2

Educational Ministry Practice

9 Components of Teaching, Part 1

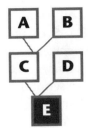

Part 1 of this book emphasizes the *foundations* of teaching in educational ministry. Part 2, which begins with this chapter, stresses the *practice* of teaching.[1] Specifically, this chapter and the next outline the essential factors that comprise teaching.[2] Subsequent chapters suggest features of teaching that are relevant for differing age groups (adults, youth, and children). Then, in Chapters 17 and 18, a composite picture of the church's educational ministry is presented. The focus is on leadership and coordination of multiple age-level ministries. Helpful ideas for administrative decision-making tasks are offered.

One Sunday Morning . . .

Mixed messages circulate in the Mariner's Sunday school room, some familiar, some unfamiliar. The young adults are well-acquainted with the aromatic smell of brewing coffee. Well-known also is the tantalizing display of fruit slices and Danish rolls. Not-so-familiar sights include an unusual furniture arrangement. It sends a message of uncertainty to several class members. The neatly configured chairs are visibly absent; in fact, chairs are nowhere to be found. The feeling of uncertainty reminds these young adults of earlier school days, when the teacher was ill, when the person in charge forgot to prepare the day's lesson.

Five minutes before the start of class, the clanging of folding chairs resounds above the noise of lively conversation. But it's not the noise that interrupts conversations. Eyes are glued on Pastor Snyder, Associate Pastor Jungker, and Marshall Troyer, chair of the church board. The three men feverishly set up chairs for class. Some members attempt to join in, but the trio persuade them to return to their refreshments. The threesome arrange the chairs in a large circle.

Gaining the Class's Attention

Mariner's teacher, Carl Rowntree, writes two phrases on the chalkboard: "Winning Through Intimidation" and "Looking Out for #1." He invites everyone to be seated. "Anybody recognize these phrases?" Carl queries. A few heads nod. One person comments that the terms were popular phrases in business during the past decade.[3] Rowntree confirms this observation. He describes some intimidation strategies used to gain a psychological edge. For instance, Carl refers to the positioning of office furniture. "Intimidators place their desks near the door, so that more office space is located behind them than in front of the desk. Visitors feel

disadvantaged from the start. Furthermore, the positioning of the visitor's chair is important. Visitors," Carl suggests, "should face the window, forcing them to squint." Laughs are heard and smiles surface across the class. Jerry, a successful salesperson, testifies that he visits such offices. "Concentrating on my presentation is next to impossible," he confides.

Cynthia expands the concept. A friend of hers, an avid tennis player, taught her a few tactics. "When you enter the tennis court, choose the court nearest you," Cynthia recollects. "That forces your opponent to walk to the far side. It gives the impression you're in control." Other class members offer examples of intimidation. These initial responses signal a relevant topic for class members.

What Does the Bible Say?

Returning to the chalkboard, Carl crosses out the word "Intimidation" and writes "Humility" just above it. "Today, we'll be looking at a passage that teaches the *real* key to getting ahead. It's not 'Winning Through Intimidation,' but, 'Winning Through Humility.'" A Scripture reference is scribbled next to the revised phrase. Carl invites the class to investigate John 13:1–17. Class members locate the passage in their Bibles while the teacher reviews the message of the Fourth Gospel: "Jesus is the Son of God." Also reviewed is the three-part outline of the book: seven miracles (chaps. 1–12); upper room teaching (chaps. 13–17); final miracle (chaps. 18–21). As members identify the outline with matching chapters, their teacher nods his affirmation.

Carl then reads John 13:1–5. He provides a brief background of the chronology preceding the upper room discourse. To gain a better understanding of the scriptural context, he challenges his class to determine the expectations that Jesus and the Twelve brought to that eventful meeting. Four perspectives will be studied. In small groups of three to five people, class members are asked to identify the attitudes of Peter, Judas, Jesus, and the disciples as a whole.[4]

After ten minutes, Carl elicits each group's responses and summarizes the findings on the chalkboard. Some of the group's responses include: Peter's claim that though every other disciple would fall away, he would fearlessly stand by Jesus (Mark 14:29); Judas' betrayal of his teacher and friend, Jesus, for money; and the disciples' debate about which one of them was the greatest (Luke 33:23–30). He concludes this part of the study, indicating that the disciples were generally more concerned about themselves than Jesus' needs.

A contrasting attitude is displayed by Jesus. In the upper room he provides an unexpected and graphic lesson about humble servanthood. He washes the disciples' feet. The Twelve, especially Peter, are embarrassed. (This object lesson subsequently yields the ultimate example of humble service: Christ's sacrificial death on the cross.) Carl briefly explains the cultural custom of foot washing, necessitated by dusty roads and sandals. Foot washing was a sign of hospitality. Typically this humble act was performed by the lowest servant in the household.

Indicating that the class will study verses 6–11 next week, Carl reads aloud the key verses (vv. 13–14). Sheets of paper are distributed. "At this time I want you to paraphrase verses 13 and 14. What do these verses really mean?" he asks. After a few minutes, individual compositions are read. Carl summarizes the recurring focus of these paraphrases. He jots down the biblical equation: "Humble service = No task is too menial."

The Implications of the Passage for Today

Words appear on the overhead projector screen: "Learn how to jump-start a life." Carl quizzes the class as to the ad's sponsor. "The Red Cross," someone yells. The organization is offering courses on CPR (cardiopulmonary resuscitation). "Advertisers know their audience," Carl states. "And the successful ones communicate their message in pictures that make sense to their audience." He then sings a ditty: "Plop, plop, fizz, fizz. Oh, what a relief it is." Smiles indicate the recollection of the old Alka-Seltzer jingle.

Then Carl directs: "Please rearrange yourselves back into groups of three to five persons. Imagine that each group represents a successful advertising agency. Your job is to create an ad that accentuates the message of humble servanthood for today's world. You can either (1) make a billboard ad using about five to seven words, (2) adapt a popular radio jingle and put new words to music, or (3) create a thirty-second television commercial. The leader of each group is the person whose first name begins with the letter closest to the letter 'Z.' Several types of magazines are stacked around the room to stimulate your ideas. Large sheets of paper and marking pens are available at the front of the room." Slowly, group brainstorming begins. The decibel level rises accordingly.

After fifteen minutes, Carl invites the groups to present their ads. One group spokesperson exhibits newsprint with the billboard phrase: "Reach for the Mop and not the Top!" Chuckles are heard. The newsprint is taped to an adjacent wall.

Another group leader describes their television commercial: "The ad begins with a close-up shot of a T-bone steak sizzling on a grill. The picture fades, but the sizzling sound remains throughout the whole commercial. A small square appears in the middle of the screen. It shows a dentist treating an Ethiopian child. This square relocates to the upper left corner of the screen. A new square appears center screen with a group of people refurbishing old homes. This shot moves to the screen's upper right. The new scene in the middle is a feeding line at a Union Gospel shelter. As with the others, it shifts to the lower right corner. The fourth middle square shows a person comforting an AIDS patient in a hospital bed. This picture is transferred to the lower left. Finally, a black square in the middle appears, highlighting these words: 'Well done, good and faithful servant.' The sizzling sound fades to silence. The small black square, with the phrase, grows and fills the whole screen. End of ad."[5] A round of applause breaks out, as the group leader sits down. Other group leaders present their ads and jingles.

Carl congratulates the class for their thought-provoking projects. He writes the following captions across the top of the board: "At Home," "At Work," "At Church Gatherings," "In the Neighborhood," "While Driving." Pointing to the five headings, Carl asks, "What are some specific and practical ways that Christians serve the needs of others in these spheres? Think specifically of menial tasks."

Taking a Personal and Responsible Step of Action

One class member distributes blank 3 by 5 cards. On the chalkboard, Carl writes the open-ended sentence: "This week, I will . . ." Once again, he reads John 13:13–14. "Select one of these five categories we've just discussed," he begins, "and, on a 3 by 5 card, jot down some menial service you will perform this week. Take this card with you and post it in some prominent place as a reminder. Next week, we'll share the results of your projects." As Carl closes the lesson, he shares the story of how one prominent person performed a menial task to serve others.

"The key to winning," he reminds them, "is not through intimidation, but through humility."

Following the singing of a chorus about servanthood, Carl directs the class to read out loud the earlier equation: "Humble service = No task is too menial." He then rereads John 13:13–14. Finally Carl offers a closing prayer that God will help each person serve others this week.

Think about It

Although you weren't actually in Carl's class, you were a distant observer. Reflect on the five categories of application:

Home	Work	Church	Neighborhood	Driving

What particular form of menial service might the Spirit be prompting you to perform this week?

Seven Components of Teaching

Teaching is a high calling, a ministry requiring a sober perspective, as James reminds us (James 3:1). One main responsibility of church leaders (as elders) includes teaching (1 Tim. 5:17). Of all the gifts Christ has given to equip the saints for ministry, the teaching gift plays a prominent role (Rom. 12:7; 1 Cor. 12:28; Eph. 4:11–12).

What does it mean to be a teacher? Since teaching and learning are so commonly experienced, the question may initially seem simple. Just a little probing, however, reveals that the concept of teaching is quite complex. Do you envision the teacher as one who typically stands behind a lectern and does most of the talking? Do you assume that the teacher is the one who knows the most about the subject?

How we think about teaching—our understanding of what teaching is—significantly affects how we teach: "A person setting out to teach needs to clarify his concept of teaching because the concept he holds directly influences the activities he will engage in" (Hyman 1974, p. 35). Some un-necessarily distinguish teaching from discipleship[6] or preaching.[7] But to advance the church's educational ministry, it seems best to outline common factors of effective edification, regardless of the various forms that edification takes.[8]

Any conception of teaching incorporates at least seven comprehensive components.[9] These broad categories permit analysis of

Figure 9.1

The Components of Teaching

Scene A

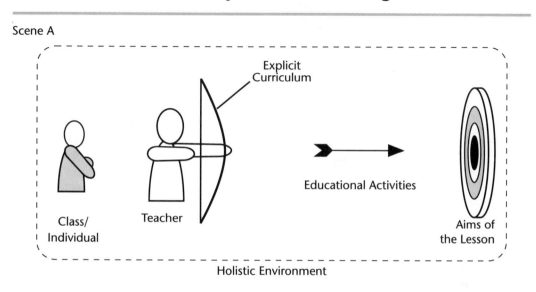

Scene B

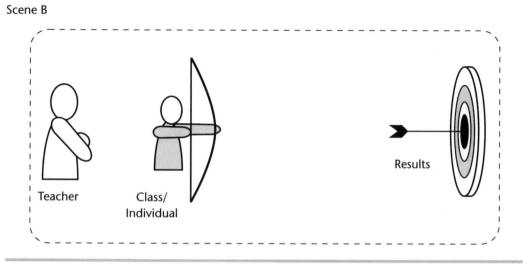

any instructional situation, for *every* teaching episode involves all seven.

Teacher
Explicit Curriculum
Aims of the Lesson
Class and Individual Learner
Holistic Environment
Educational Activities
Results of Teaching

Figure 9.1 graphically portrays these seven interrelated concepts. An investigation of all components follows. The first three are discussed in this chapter; the remaining four in the next chapter. Notice how each feature is discrete, yet connected to the others.

The Teacher

Education that is Christian demands attentiveness to both divine and human teachers. The Holy Spirit wrote the Scriptures, and he is constantly involved in teaching the Word to all believers (John 14:26). Some Christian educators view teaching as the sole responsibility of the Spirit. Yet, God chooses to use human instruments to accomplish his will. He provides some of us with the supernatural ability to instruct the church.

The Spiritual Gift of Teaching

Controversy exists over whether spiritual gifts are synonymous with "natural" talents.[10] The Holy Spirit sovereignly distributes gifts and natural talents to believers. All spiritual gifts and talents, therefore, are gracious endowments of God. To be sure, particular distinctions do exist. Minimally, a spiritual gift has (1) a special *purpose* (to benefit the church and build God's kingdom; 1 Cor. 12:7; 14:26b; 1 Pet. 4:10) and

(2) a special *power* through the Holy Spirit (1 Cor. 12:6, 11).[11]

In spite of its divine origin, the gift of teaching must be developed and used regularly by the recipient. Paul exhorts Timothy, "For this reason I remind you to fan into flame the gift of God which is in you through the laying on of my hands" (2 Tim. 1:6–7). This inspired reminder is given, in part, because spiritual gifts can be abused. Believers may use their gifts for the wrong purposes. The Corinthians' misuse prompted Paul to address this topic in 1 Corinthians 12–14. Spiritual gift inventories provide some guidance for Christians who want to serve faithfully. Yet giftedness can best be discerned through regular use and through confirmation within the body.

Not all believers have the gift of teaching (1 Cor. 12:29), but all saints are called to the disciple-making/teaching ministry. The Bible says that, without saying a word, we can teach and influence others by our life example (1 Pet. 3:1–2). Thus, whether gifted for teaching or not, we must all attempt to become better teachers. We must be empowered by and work with the Divine Teacher.[12]

What Most Teachers Know?

Exceptional competence in teaching is rare. Outstanding instructors pay attention to four significant domains. First, teachers must know the Divine Teacher. In education that is Christian, the human teacher and Divine Teacher work in harmony for the sake of students. Ultimately, regardless of our particular subject matter, we are discipling believers to know God. The more we know him, the better able we are to help our students work toward this essential goal. Deuteronomy 6:4–9 provides insight into the correct instructional sequence. Here it particularly relates to parents as teachers. Parents must *first* know and love God themselves and *then* teach their children to know and love God. We can impart only what we ourselves possess.

Next, teachers must know whom they are teaching. Consider the Master Teacher's knowledge of the Twelve: "With many similar parables Jesus spoke the word to them, *as much as they could understand*" (Mark 4:33). To meet our students' specific needs, we must know them well. What are their strengths and weaknesses? What are their most pressing problems? What expecta-

tions do we have for them, based on their capabilities and potential? In-class and out-of-class contact with students is non-negotiable.

Third, competent instructors must know what they teach. Mastery of subject, personal conviction, and enthusiasm all reflect this skill. The Gospels show that the crowds sought Jesus for his teaching. What he said attracted attention. To the masses, he didn't teach as the scribes taught. He taught with authority. Figure 9.2 presents Joseph Low-

Figure 9.2
Subject Mastery and Interpersonal Skills

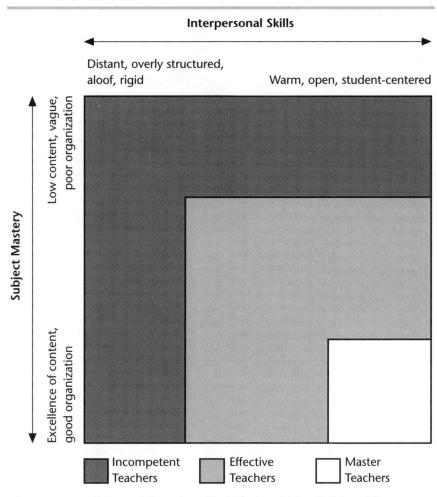

Source: Lowman (1984, p. 20) as adapted by Wilhoit and Ryken (1988, p. 65).

man's (1984) summary of good teaching. A strong relationship exists between subject mastery and interpersonal skills. Neither is sacrificed for the other.

Finally, exceptional teachers know how to teach. As previously mentioned, teaching involves more than "telling." Skillful instructors know how best to help students learn and how to guide students in their learning. What unique contribution do teachers make to the instructional encounter? (Since more effective means are available for imparting new information today, that task no longer comprises the teacher's preeminent or sole function.) Using the six avenues of learning, Table 9.1 presents several important teacher responsibilities.[13] Ezra's example of good teaching challenges us still today. Note the order: "For Ezra had devoted himself to the *study* and *observance* of the law of the Lord, and to *teaching* its decrees and laws in Israel" (Ezra 7:10).[14]

Table 9.1

The Teacher's Responsibilities

Identification Learning:
1. To help students see the big picture by providing a meaningful summary outline and synthesis of the subject; to demonstrate to students, at regular intervals, how the various parts relate to the whole.
2. To present the subject in such a way as to make sense to students by building bridges with what students already know, by using vocabulary, illustrations, examples, and the like, which relate to their experience and background; to relate the subject to the particular goals and needs of students.

Inquiry Learning:
3. To help students progressively think more deeply and broadly about the subject; to challenge and probe students' thinking so they move beyond a simplistic and superficial understanding of the subject.

Consequence Learning:
4. To provide, at regular intervals, appropriate individual feedback and encouragement regarding each student's progress in learning the subject in an holistic manner; to identify areas of strength and areas needing improvement with relevant and helpful suggestions.

Cue Learning:
5. To nurture in students positive and receptive attitudes about the subject; to excite students to want to grow and learn more about the subject, even after the class is over.
6. To believe in the student; to set appropriate expectations for the abilities and progress of each student for learning about the subject.
7. To provide helpful means for students to remember the significant factors and concepts of the subject using a variety of senses.

Structured Modeling:
8. To present to students the best examples and demonstrations of the theoretical foundations and practical outworking of the subject, using appropriate teaching activities and audio/visual aids.

Spontaneous Modeling:
9. To "incarnate" the subject in your demeanor in class and in your general lifestyle; to exhibit, in a consistent and integrated manner, the personal value of the subject.

Think about It

Study the nine items in Table 9.1.

1. Identify one or two for which you do well in your teaching. Give an example from a recent teaching experience for each one.

2. Identify one of the nine items in which you need to make significant improvement. What practical steps can you take in your next teaching experience to work on this area?

An Explicit Curriculum

Every teacher teaches something. That "something" we call subject matter, content, or curriculum. A perennial educational question is: *"What* knowledge is most worthy to teach?" For Christians, the answer is obvious: We want to know God and his Word. We want to obey him. What we teach (i.e., our subject) and what we want to accomplish (i.e., our aim) converge at this foundational level.

Teaching That Facilitates
Christian Maturity

The heart of Christianity revolves around relationships—with God, self, others, and creation. In Chapter 2, we presented a model of Christian maturity, a common goal for all believers. Central to that Reconciliation Model is our Communion with God. Our fellowship with the Creator is like any other maturing relationship. We never fully achieve a finished status. We continue to open up new vistas of growth. James promises, "Come near to God and he will come near to you" (4:8).

As we continue to commune with God, we become like him in at least three ways. We mature in our Community and love for other believers. The family of God becomes more important to us. We derive a new corporate sense of identity as "fellow heirs" in Christ. Also, we grow in Christian Character. Lifestyle patterns of integrity should mirror our righteousness and holiness. Our moral obligation to all individuals should reflect our vertical alliance. Third, we faithfully use our God-given gifts and abilities. In so doing, we attend to our Commission. The explicit curriculum of every church should direct learners toward these reconciling purposes. A balanced emphasis should be struck in all four subthemes.

Planning the Course

"Curriculum" comes from the Latin word meaning "race course." In education, it implies a course of study.[15] Church leaders must ask, "Have we developed a 'course' or overall plan for nurturing believers to maturity?" A rationale should be developed for the selection and arrangement of subject matter. Otherwise, decisions about subject matter tend to be made on an expedient, week-by-week basis.

In the training of the Twelve, we observe Jesus focusing on common elements throughout their training as well as unique emphases for different stages of mastery. For example, he emphasized the central theme of Communion and faith development, and he regularly rebuked the disciples for their lack of faith in God. He also exemplified a life of prayer to God and regularly taught about prayer.

To prepare the disciples for their specific roles as apostles of the church and witnesses to the world—the theme of Commission and vocational development—three distinct phases of training were uniquely designed for them. Each phase focused on a different goal, providing the basis for the next step in their training. Table 9.2 provides an overview of these phases.[16] Our Lord's example encourages us to attend to these matters of curriculum planning.

Table 9.2

Jesus' Training of the Twelve

Phase One:

Teaching Focus: "I am the Messiah" (implicit in Gospels)

Conclusion of Phase: Peter's confession and the transfiguration (Matt. 16:13–20; Mark 8:27–30; Luke 9:18–21)

Phase Two:

Teaching Focus: "The Messiah must suffer, die, and rise again" (Matt. 16:21–26; Mark 8:31–37; Luke 9:22–25)

135

Conclusion of Phase: Final days before Christ's ascension (Luke 24:44–49; Acts 1:3–5)

Phase Three:

Teaching Focus: "You are my witnesses to all nations" (Acts 1:6–8)

Conclusion of Phase: Jerusalem Council (Acts 15:1–35)

Sunday school curriculum publishers reveal their complete course of study in "scope and sequence" charts. These charts describe what particular *topics* will be taught (scope) and in which *order* (sequence). The teacher's manual for the quarter usually provides teaching plans for twelve or thirteen sequential lessons, arranged by the overall plan. Publishers typically cover Bible books and major theological themes in two-, three-, or four-year cycles.[17] Lessons in subsequent cycles of coverage might explore the same topic at more sophisticated levels.[18]

Curriculum Decision Making

Who should create policies and make decisions about subject matter selection?[19] In most cases, more than one person or group contributes. For example, whether for Sunday school, home Bible study groups, or Christian higher education, major decision makers often include: (1) curriculum committees or boards (whether in the church, denomination, school, or other parachurch agency); (2) curriculum and textbook publishers; (3) teachers who follow the objectives in their manual or their own idea of what is best;[20] and (4) students (if there is little or no attendance, the class may be cancelled). Not all of these parties have an equal role in the decision-making process. Yet, we fool ourselves if we ignore any category. Each group does influence, in some way, what subject matter is taught.[21]

The Hidden Curriculum

If we think that only planned curriculum is taught to students, we deceive ourselves.

Unplanned (or implicit) lessons are communicated in every teaching scenario. Most implicit or "hidden" curriculum goes unnoticed; it also goes unevaluated. In its extreme form, this hidden teaching may contradict explicit subject matter. That is, what we *don't* say may speak more forcibly than what we *do* say.[22] Our unspoken attitudes toward the curriculum may be counterproductive. Furthermore, negative feelings we harbor toward our students may hinder a healthy relationship with God. Understanding the potency of this concept, Carl Rowntree purposefully arranged his classroom chairs in a large circle, to encourage face-to-face participant dialogue. He intentionally created an environment that facilitated his objectives. His nonverbal and verbal communication were aligned. Moreover the menial ministry that the three church leaders performed modeled the explicit subject of "winning through humility."

Consider some beneficial instances of the "hidden curriculum." What "lessons" do they convey to *you?* Notice how ordinary they might appear to the untrained eye.

1. When the pastor consistently preaches from a particular version of the Bible, what implicit teaching about translations is communicated?
2. At a church wedding, when the solemn vows of the bride and groom are purposefully emphasized by the pastor, what is implicitly taught to the attending married partners concerning their own commitments?
3. At a funeral service of a believer, what implicit instruction is taught to the entire gathering when the pastor preaches on the brevity of life along with the Christian hope of the deceased?

1. When a single person attends a church whose marquis reads, "We study the Bible as a family," what message is being communicated to that individual?

2. What other hidden curriculum have you been "taught" in an educational setting? Give one or two examples that are either *complementary* or *contradictory* to what was explicitly intended.

If church leaders became aware of even the most rudimentary implications of hidden curriculum, significant congregational events like communion and baptism could teach more compellingly.[23]

Aims of the Lesson

Teaching is an intentional activity. Teachers want students to learn. Every teaching situation involves explicit and implicit aims. An aim represents a value statement—it prescribes what ought to be. In teaching that is Christian, the broader aim of every teacher is that students grow to full maturity in Christ. To the extent that instructors understand this overarching aim—an image of the ideal Christian—they more easily focus their teaching practice.

Aims and Lesson Planning

Our ministry as teachers shows students how to take the necessary steps toward growth. As fellow pilgrims we facilitate their primary reconciliation with God and others, in concert with particular age-appropriate subject matter. Achieving such a goal requires planning. We develop lesson plans for more than just the *content*. Our plans should also guide our *practice* of teaching. We outline the "product" as well as the "process."

Planning a lesson is like planning an expedition. The travel guide knows the ultimate destination. The guide identifies several worthwhile points of interest along the way. This travel leader realizes the travelers' responsibilities and limitations. So also, the teacher acknowledges ends, means, and student involvement. Extending the trip analogy, the interests and needs of fellow-travelers must be considered. Whether developed by the teacher alone or in concert with students, writing a statement of aims clarifies teaching purposes. These procedures assure that instruction is challenging yet achievable.

Teachers have traditionally tended to specify only the *subject* to be taught. "To present the elements of an aim statement" is an example of such a written aim. Yet other factors are just as important to articulate. One theoretical model for aim statement construction employs the acrostic "AIM." The model includes three elements:

Achievement level of student learning
Indicator of student learning or **I**nvestigation planned
Main subject being taught

To repeat, the specific lesson topic is designated in the main subject, the third element. The achievement level specifies the particular "level" and "extent" of learning to be reached.[24] Are we only interested, for example, in the student's awareness of the topic? Or is it understanding that we seek? Do we desire the student to consistently apply a concept in a decision-making strategy? Our targeted achievement level affects the total aim. Too often, our teaching practice only expects from students a low-level cognitive functioning. Challenging students to think more deeply takes greater planning.

Indicators or Investigations?

The most difficult part of an aim statement to articulate is the "I" element. Whether you specify an "indicator" or an "investigation" in your aim statement depends on the learning outcomes you intend. Indicators typically match outcomes that are *convergent* in nature, when either one or very few correct answers is permissible. Investigations pair up with *divergent* ends, when many solutions pertain.[25]

An indicator expresses the teacher's educated guess of how students will need to demonstrate their learning in relation to the identified achievement level. As noted above, limited categories of assessment are used. Using a medical analogy, physicians look for "indicators" of good or poor health. They check various vital signs of normal bodily functioning: blood pressure, temperature, pupils, breathing, and reflexes. In business, managers look at the bottom lines of revenue and expenditures to detect the "health" of their enterprise.

When Spanish Jews were required to become Catholic Christians or face death in the fourteenth century, many did so in name only. At home, they followed their Jewish religious customs as before. Spain's chief inquisitor became aware of an indicator of their false conversion. Peering over the Jewish quarter in Seville one Saturday afternoon, he commented to his assistant, "You see how cold it is yet how few chimneys have smoke coming from them?" He reasoned that lighting a fire for practicing Jews would be considered breaking the Sabbath.[26]

God gave Gideon two sets of indicators to identify the three hundred soldiers who should go to battle against the Midianites (Judges 7:1–8). First, only those soldiers who weren't fearful should be chosen (v. 3). Second, only those who drank water with their hands (while on their knees) were selected (vv. 5–6). In other words, if they evidenced these two indicators, they passed the test. In teaching, we would say they scored 100 percent on their final exam, for they demonstrated learning and maturity.[27]

In contrast with medical and business practice, standard indicators for Christian growth are quite complex. No common list of exhaustive factors can be compiled. Therefore, a teacher in Christian education selects a few representative indicators from many possibilities. In formal academic settings, typical "vital signs" are measured through (1) written forms (e.g., exams, quizzes, term papers, and written responses to the reading); (2) verbal forms (e.g., class presentations, questions or comments given in class); and (3) nonverbal forms (e.g., puzzled looks and nodding heads). Such student responses help a teacher gauge the extent of student learning. In school settings, most interpretations of student learning are based on written indicators. Yet in most nonacademic settings, like a Sunday school class, verbal and nonverbal forms are utilized. All three forms make a contribution to student evaluations. Similarly, all three pose different types of problems when it comes to interpreting learner responses. For instance, most teachers realize the limitations of true-false exams, as well as uncertainties of nonverbal student eye contact.

Combining these three elements in an AIM statement yields the following formula for the teaching aim construction:

> "The student shall demonstrate a(n) [achievement level] of the [main subject] by [indicator] ."

For example, a simple aim statement in the knowledge or cognitive domain is:

"The student shall demonstrate an_[A] understanding of the [M] elements of an AIM statement by [I] supplying one example for each of the three categories: A, I, M."

This indicator still allows variety in expression. Students can write their answers on the board or provide oral responses in a question-answer format, to name two possibilities.[28] Whether or not a teacher states an aim exactly this way is immaterial. What *is* important is for instructors to think through these three main concepts in the planning process. If teaching that is Christian intends to bring about comprehensive student *learning,* then comprehensive *planning* is non-negotiable. Table 9.3 offers examples of various indicators for a lesson on John 13, some of which Carl Rowntree used in his class.

Think about It

Reflect on a recent class or Bible study group you have taught. Imagine that you were required to give a letter grade to each participant in your class or group. Select some of your better students.

1. What grade would you give them: a "C," "B," or "A"?

2. Why? Identify specific reasons for assigning each grade. On what basis did they earn their grade?

Think about the qualities you identified. These factors represent your implicit "indicators" of student learning.

Table 9.3

Sample "Indicators" for a Lesson on John 13

Main Subject: "Humbly Serving One Another"

Achievement Level	Possible Indicators
KNOWLEDGE	[For the most part, these can be easily included in a classroom setting.]
Awareness	Identify the theme of John 13 as humility and serving. Recall a memorized phrase defining humble service.
Understanding	Provide an example of humble service. Write a summary statement of the main point(s) of John 13:1–17.
ATTITUDES, VALUES, AND EMOTIONS	[For the most part, these indicators will be based on observing students' actions outside of class, especially the patterns of behavior.] Regularly picking up trash around the church, campus, or neighborhood Regularly saying a kind, encouraging word to at least one person each day Regularly choosing to watch less television and using this time to help a family member or friend who has a need
PHYSICAL SKILLS AND HABITS	Improved capability in the skill of: a. saying encouraging words to others b. providing first aid c. being an usher

Investigations to Promote Student Learning

Indicators match convergent lesson aims when outcomes are determined with some certainty and when lower achievement levels of cognition (knowledge) and competence (skills) are addressed. Conversely, when outcomes are not as clear, then an investigation element in your aim statement is appropriate. Divergent ends are anticipated. It is difficult, for example, to identify precise indicators when you are aiming at higher degrees of cognition or competence. The same is true when you are aiming at conviction outcomes (attitudes, values, or emotions).

Elliot Eisner (1985) suggests that learning that is divergent cannot be reduced to defining specific indicators. If you ask your students to solve a problem, analyze a case study, or watch a video, you have some general ideas of what you want them to experience. But you can't be too specific in your learning expectations. Thus, in your aim statement, you identify the investigation or divergent task in which your students will participate. Consider Table 9.4. Notice the potential investigations for teaching a lesson on John 13. Compare these more divergent suggestions with the more specific indicators of Table 9.3

Contemplate the subject of evangelism. If they were quizzed, most evangelical leaders would be able to detail common (convergent) essentials of the gospel message. Yet multiple (divergent) strategies of evangelism would also surface. Or consider Christian ethics. It can't be covered in a three-part sermon series. The topic of Christian parenting cannot be exhausted and reduced to pocket-sized pamphlets. The complex topic of discovering God's will cannot be resolved in a couple of counseling sessions. There are certain general "knowns" of our faith (e.g., avoiding temptation, walking in the Spirit). But there are far more "unknowns," as they are applied to specific real-life cases.[29]

Table 9.4

Possible "Investigations" for a Lesson on John 13

Achievement Level	Possible Investigations
KNOWLEDGE	
Understanding	Identify situations in which Christians need to be more humble in their service to others. Suggest various expressions that humble service could take.
	Identify situations in which humble service may be difficult or impossible to perform.
	Provide Christian solutions to a hypothetical case study.
Wisdom	Identify and provide Christian solutions to one personal problem where humble service is lacking. What perspectives of life or habits need to be changed in conjunction with these new-found insights?
ATTITUDES, VALUES, AND EMOTIONS	Watch a movie in which humble service is portrayed as a primary intent. Discuss the movie and share individual reflections. Were any personal attitudes or convictions altered or reaffirmed? Why?

Flexibility in Planning Aims

Like pilgrim adventures, not all experiences in the classroom are similar. Certain teaching-learning scenarios are more convergent. For instance, either students know how to recite John 3:16 or not. Either they can explain the meaning of the Great Commission or not. In these cases, written indicators in aim statements are most conducive. Broader outcomes are not as easy to determine ahead of time. In these cases, written investigations are more appropriate.

On occasion, you will need to adjust your lesson aims. For example, your students may not be as ready as you want them to be. Jesus had that experience with the disciples (Matt. 16:5–12) and Paul with the Corinthian believers (1 Cor. 3:2). Or some special event or tragedy may preempt your lesson. What if you discover that a local high school student has committed suicide? What if you learn this news one hour before the senior high Bible study that you lead? Would it make any difference in your teaching plans? How would a digressive look at death and Christian hope help?

Lesson aims are like road maps. You know your destination. Although there are many ways to reach that point, you have to select a particular route you think is best. But, along the way, you may need to take a few detours or add a few extra side trips in light of student interest and need. If you know where you are eventually going, it's easy to get back on course. But with no final destination point and no planned itinerary, you may end up traveling in circles with little student learning as a result.[30]

Conclusion

Think about It

Fill in the blanks with the appropriate responses. In the first column, fill in the name of the component. In the second, write two questions that come to mind about that component. Your questions may request clarification of points in the chapter. Or, they may probe points not covered in the chapter.

Component: Questions:

T _____   1. _____

   2. _____

E_____   1. _____

   2. _____

A _____   1. _____

   2. _____

In the Gospels, Jesus is referred to as "teacher" forty-two times. "The fact that Jesus was so frequently called Teacher is sometimes obscured by the rendering Master in the King James Version. As Lewis J. Sherrill has pointed out, 'When the Bible was being translated into these earlier versions, Master (Latin: *Magister*) denoted a *schoolmaster*, but the word has now lost that meaning in ordinary speech, and some of the recent versions use the word Teacher to translate *Didaskolos*'" (Coleman 1984, p. 16). Ronald Allen (1985, pp. 59–60) suggests that we should recognize Jesus as occupying the office of Teacher:

> In classical Protestant theology we have been encouraged to think of Jesus Christ as having three principal offices. These are Prophet, Priest and King. That is, as Prophet, Jesus is superior to Moses. As Priest, he is grander than Aaron. As King, he is more excellent than David. It

is time to add to our understanding of the offices of Christ. There is a neglected office of Christ. *He is also Teacher.* Y'shua is the Wise whose wisdom surpasses Solomon. Jesus is the Sage whose wisdom was anticipated by the imagery of Lady Wisdom in Proverbs 1–9. Jesus is the great Rabbi, the master teacher of the ages, who came to explain very God.

Teaching is a high calling. The Master Teacher has given us an example to follow. We must pursue excellence in Christian instruction.

10 Components of Teaching, Part 2

Introduction

Think about It

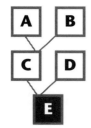

Traditionally we have understood that the teacher bears the brunt of responsibility for student learning. If this perspective is correct, then what portion of responsibility should the student have in the teaching-learning process?

a. 0 percent student—100 percent teacher?
b. 10 percent student—90 percent teacher?

c. 25 percent student—75 percent teacher?

d. ____ percent student—____ percent teacher? (fill in the blanks with your own estimate)

Before we discuss this issue, let's review the TEACHER concept introduced in the previous chapter. Every teaching episode includes the following seven components:

Teacher

Explicit Curriculum

Aims of the Lesson

Class and Individual Learner

Holistic Environment

Educational Activities

Results of Teaching

In the previous chapter we looked at three of these components. The remaining four are treated in this chapter. Let's return to the issue of student responsibility raised in the "Think about It" section.

Class and Individual Learner

Most treatments of educational accountability place the weight of responsibility for student learning fully on the teacher's shoulders. Our theology, however, informs us that all persons are accountable to the Creator. Student life represents one sphere of stewardship.

> The student, of course, is also accountable for whether or not he learns, a fact that many contemporary educators are not willing to admit. "If the student doesn't learn," it is said, "the teacher hasn't taught." That may or may not be true in a given situation. It is certainly not axiomatic. As a responsible being [before God], the student must give an account of his stewardship in carrying out academic tasks. He must choose to study. It is not

> something he will do automatically [even] if properly motivated by the teacher. (Harper 1981, p. 21)

In education that is Christian, appropriate levels of accountability must be shared by students, regardless of their age.[1]

As mentioned in the previous chapter, effective teachers must know *whom* they are teaching. Teachers should plan their lessons based on an assessment (or assumption) of the students' entry characteristics (their current status of both maturation and learning). Knowledge of normal developmental growth patterns and age-appropriate capabilities offers teachers a framework from which to encourage greater growth as well as to spot any abnormalities.

Also, an understanding of the learning process is essential for effective teaching. For example, knowledge of group dynamics can be used to encourage individual learning. Some students may avoid speaking in class, but will freely discuss class matters with a smaller circle of peers. To summarize, informed teachers tend to make better lesson plans; responsible students tend to apply greater effort to the learning opportunity.

Holistic Environment

When teachers and students interact, they do so in some setting: a classroom, a living room, a coffee shop, a camp. Factors in each location either build bridges or barriers to learning. Helpful factors include comfortable seating, good lighting, and useful teaching aids, such as a chalkboard or an overhead projector. Barriers to learning include a variety of distractions: a room situated near a street, with noisy traffic or construction work; a location with an annoying fly or a barking dog; a room that is too hot or too cold.

Other issues beyond physical factors are also important (Elias 1983; Bronfenbrenner

1979). Table 10.1 summarizes a holistic conception of the environment, involving five major aspects: physical, organizational, relational,[2] cultural, and historical.

Table 10.1

Holistic Environment in Teaching

P – Physical factors

comfortable temperature, good seating arrangement, unobstructed visibility and adequate lighting, good acoustics, good ventilation, size of room, available teaching aids

O – Organizational factors

mode of education (formal or nonformal), curriculum and administrative policies and practices, financing and budget, facilities and available support staff, institutional norms, availability of published texts and curriculum materials, course plan and syllabus, teacher-student agreements about the nature of the class and the individualizing of instruction, classroom management/discipline procedures, other classroom norms and habits

R – Relational factors

teacher-student relationships, student-student relationships in and out of class, respect, trust, caring, opportunity for student input in decision making, degree of formality, out-of-class availability of teacher, class morale

C – Cultural factors

mode of national government (e.g., democratic, totalitarian), roles and expectations for the teacher and the student, community value placed on education, socioeconomic status of the community and related values, diversity of

Table 10.2

Threes Modes of Education

Dominant Features	Example	In Christian Education
Formal Education Goal: to gain a credential (i.e., theoretical orientation; academic advancement) Subject matter: selected by teachers/administrators Learning: structured Attendance: required Societal role: conserving/stabilizing	Foreign language course in school	Christian day schools Christian higher education
Nonformal Education Goal: to gain competency (i.e., functional orientation; life skill need-based) Subject matter: selected by teacher and students Learning: structured Attendance: voluntary Societal role: change-oriented	Private tutoring in language for a business trip Conversation class sponsored by a club	Seminars/workshops Sunday school program Small group programs Parent education Leadership development Home-schooling
Informal Education Goal: to pass on culture and basic life skills (i.e., socialization; functional orientation) Subject matter: selected by circumstances Learning: unstructured Attendance: required Societal role: conserving/stabilizing	Learning language in a bilingual home Living overseas	Socialized by: people (family, friends, church, community), media (television, movies)

Source: Adapted from Ward (n.d.).

languages and dialects, view of women's roles in society

H – *Historical factors*

previous class sessions that may have been influential (positive or negative) in learning

One organizational factor needs more explanation. Because we are so familiar with the schooling (or formal) mode of education, we falsely assume that all approaches to education must adopt typical schoolroom characteristics. Besides formal education (FE), two additional modes exist: informal education (IE; i.e., socialization in life) and nonformal education (NFE; i.e., structured learning experiences related to life skills) (see Table 10.2).

Formal and nonformal education share some characteristics (e.g., both are structured and staffed), but they also differ significantly (e.g., FE is more *theoretically* oriented while NFE is more *functionally* oriented).[3] Sometimes those of us schooled in formal education do not shift our thinking in appropriate ways when we teach various age groups in the church (i.e., in a setting that fits the nonformal education mode). Our teaching style leans more toward formal education. We instruct in a more "academic" mode, rather than an NFE "adult continuing education/workshop" mode.

Educational Activities

In every teaching situation, some method is chosen to enable the teacher and student to interact with the subject. Key questions for the teacher in method selection include: What is the main purpose of this particular class session? How can I best use the time to facilitate student learning? What skills do my students possess? Which activities motivate them?

Picture in your mind a carpenter building kitchen cabinets. The only tool available is a hammer. Imagine that, besides its intended function, the carpenter uses that hammer to level the cabinets, to secure the screws, to measure and cut wood, and to apply the paint. This would be absurd! Yet we teachers emulate a similar pattern. Too often, we assume that the exclusive instructional purpose is to impart new information. Therefore, we're convinced that the best method is lecturing. Why do we repeatedly use this method? Listen to one seasoned veteran's explanation:

> "We teach the way we were taught," the old adage assures or warns us, depending on your perspective. We may want to protest and rebel a bit, but I'm convinced that there is more truth here than most of us wish to admit. The way we learned something, the way we got our mind around it, the way we first came to understand it becomes *more than a method of learning,* but it becomes *a part of what we have learned as well.* Not only is this important for teachers to understand about themselves, but it is also important for parents to understand as well.
>
> Most of us make educational decisions and evaluations based on a standard I call the "glorified I." We say, "I remember how I learned, and since I am almost perfect, everyone else must learn the same way." This may help to explain why schools [and church classrooms] don't change all that much. (Schimmels 1989, p. 123)

Appropriate Uses of Lecture

A number of studies present the advantages and disadvantages of the lecture method (as summarized by Gage and Berliner 1988, p. 401). The lecture method is appropriate when:

• the material is not available elsewhere

- the material must be organized and presented in a particular way for a specific group
- it is necessary to arouse interest in the subject
- students need to remember the material for only a short time
- it is necessary to provide an introduction to an area (or direction for a learning task) that is going to be taught through some other teaching method

Lecturing is *not appropriate* when:

- objectives other than acquisition of information are sought
- long-term retention is necessary
- the material is complex, detailed, or abstract
- learner participation is essential to achievement of objectives
- higher-level cognitive objectives (analysis, synthesis, evaluation) are the purpose of instruction

---

Think about It

One primary reason why so many teachers use lectures is because they want students to become acquainted with new information.

1. List two realistic alternatives to lecturing that teachers could use to help their students become aware of new information.
   a.
   b.
2. For your own learning, do you favor the lecture for this purpose of awareness, or do you prefer a method you have listed above? Explain your reasons.

3. When have you, as a student, found it appropriate for the teacher to use the lecture method?

Just as an array of custom-made carpentry tools is employed for their specified intent, so a variety of teaching methods must be chosen according to their purposes.[4] As teachers gain the skills for multiple activities, their confidence grows. Also, their increased wisdom fosters selection of the most appropriate method, given the lesson's aim.

Teaching activities can be organized according to:

- age-appropriateness of the activity
- the form of the activity (e.g., written, visual media)
- the responsible participant (e.g., whether it is mostly a "teacher" or a "student" activity)
- the learning principle undergirding the activity (e.g., arranged by the six avenues of learning)
- the function of the activity (e.g., based on expected student outcomes)

Table 10.3 identifies the particular avenues of learning that Carl Rowntree used in the lesson described in the opening case study in the previous chapter. Table 10.4 presents a three-category functional outline with a list of exemplary teaching activities for each category.[5] Table 10.5 focuses on the conviction level of learning. Methods are listed according to the six avenues of learning.

Guidelines for Selecting Methods

Generally speaking, methods should be selected because they facilitate (1) students' *motivation* to participate in learning and/or

Table 10.3
Rowntree's Teaching Methods

Information-Processing Learning Family

Identification Learning
(makes sense)
- Lecture on foot-washing custom
- Group project: Advertisement
- Board list: Relevant menial tasks

Inquiry Learning
(does not make sense)
- Group study of disciples
- Paraphrase verses 13–14
- Group project: Advertisement
- Brainstorm ways of serving
- Select application project

Conditioning Learning Family

Consequence Learning
(follows experience)
- Encouragement for correct responses
- Follow-up of response during next lesson

Cue Learning
(precedes experience)
- Review of Gospel's purpose
- Use of the response card as a reminder
- Singing: "Make Me a Servant"

Social Learning Family

Structured Modeling
(planned examples)
- Direct: Chairs set up by pastors
- Verbal: Jesus washing feet

Spontaneous Modeling
(unplanned examples)
- Modeling sensitivity in accepting impromptu responses during brainstorming

Table 10.4
A Functional Outline of Teaching Activities

Critical Thinking

Primary function: to develop students' knowledge of concepts as well as evaluative thinking skills.

Examples: expository teaching or lecture, advance organizers, memory devices, inquiry, case studies, listening teams, Scripture search, question and answer, interview

Cooperation

Primary function: to facilitate interpersonal efforts of learning among students; to encourage students to seek solutions as a group; to develop social skills

Examples: debate, role play, drama, panel discussion, neighbor nudge, buzz group, small group discussion, simulations, group projects

Contemplation and Expression

Primary function: to encourage students to understand themselves; to develop greater independence and self-control; to reach beyond past experiences and present levels of ability; to elicit change in people and social structures

Examples: creative writing, art or music, classroom "town hall" meeting, individual projects, reflection exercises, movies, story-telling, field trips, mission services

Source: Categories and teaching methods adapted from Joyce and Weil (1986); some of the teaching methods come from Gangel (1974); LeFever (1985); and Leypoldt (1967).

Table 10.5

Guidelines for Teaching Convictions

Information-Processing Learning Family

Identification Learning
- Provide ways for learners to have meaningful emotional experiences (e.g., display pictures, explain feelings, view a film, take field trips). [5]

Inquiry Learning
- Provide opportunities for learners to analyze their own values—to practice making decisions on moral and ethical problems (e.g., case studies, simulation games, role plays). [7]
- Lead learners to take a positive action. Many of these activities will require out-of-classroom experiences (e.g., write a report about a field trip, do volunteer work, survey needs of people, write letters to members of Congress). [6]

Conditioning Learning Family

Consequence Learning
- Provide ways for learners to reflect upon their life experiences in the light of God's Word. [8]
- Arrange for learners to share insights with others in a climate of freedom, acceptance, and caring (i.e., small group). [9] (also *Spontaneous Modeling*)

Cue Learning
- Help learners to identify and specify attitudes and values and learn what they mean (e.g., select appropriate attitudes and values from a given list, make up stories that illustrate them, write synonyms and antonyms). [4] (also *Inquiry Learning*)

Social Learning Family

Structured Modeling
- Arrange for learners to read or hear about others who exemplify the attitude or value (e.g., biographies, films). [2]
- Expose learners to authoritative sources—sources that students consider authoritative (e.g., the Bible, listen to or interview experts, read authoritative writings). [3]

Spontaneous Modeling
- Encourage learners to observe persons in everyday life who set the right examples, who exemplify the attitude or value (e.g., your life, guest speakers, field trips to meet others). [1]

Source: Adapted from Ford (1978).
Note: Bracketed numbers represent Ford's order of principles.

(2) students' *actual learning* of the subject. Table 10.6 expands these basic factors of method selection.

When planning an instructional sequence, assess the place of "psychological" ordering, as well as "logical" ordering (i.e., item 7c in Table 10.6). "Logical" ordering proceeds from foundational matters to particular concerns, from theory to practice.

For instance, an instructor might begin a study of the Book of Jonah by surveying the history of the Assyrian nation and the role of Israel's prophets. Then, the sequential story of Jonah would be investigated. Chapters 1 to 4 would be detailed in an ordered progression.

By contrast, consider the value of "psychological" instructional ordering. This ap-

Table 10.6

Guidelines for Preparing a Bible Lesson

A. What are the major "Givens" of your teaching situation?

1. *Explicit Curriculum:* What is the overall curriculum plan that your church or agency is following to guide students toward balanced living in the four themes of Christian maturity: Communion, Community, Character, and Commission?
2. *Holistic Environment:* What factors provide basic boundaries for the teaching situation?
   a. Physical (e.g., classroom size); b. Organizational (e.g., time of meeting); c. Relational (e.g., how well students know each other and you); d. Cultural (e.g., role of teacher and student); and e. Historical (e.g., previous class sessions)
3. *Class and Individual Learners (Main Subject):* In what specific areas do the students need to grow? What is the "next" step your students must take to grow in this area?
4. *Teacher:*
   a. Holy Spirit: What particular Bible passages are relevant to the topic(s) identified in #3? Do a thorough study to gain God's perspective on this.
   b. Human Teacher: How are you applying these truths in your life? What strengths and weaknesses as a teacher do you bring to the class? How have you personally prepared yourself to teach this class?

B. What is the main purpose of your lesson?

5. *Aims of the Lesson:* Within your understanding of items outlined in "A" above
   a. To what degree can you help your students gain (Achievement Level):
      (1) a better awareness or understanding of the subject?
      (2) appropriate attitudes, values, or feelings about the subject?
      (3) relevant life skills based on the subject?
   b. What kind of response *(Results of Learning)* from your students are you expecting on a:
      (1) long-term basis?
      (2) short-term basis (i.e., during the class session [Indicator or Investigation])?

proach contemplates the best ways to secure and sustain student motivation. For example, the teacher might delay a treatment of Assyrian history until the second or third session. Perhaps it could be covered at the end of the series. In the first session, students could be confronted with the basic message of the book: developing godly compassion for those outside of the kingdom of God. The teacher may actually begin with the key issue of the last chapter: "Have you ever been angry? Have you ever been angry *at God?*" This technique of lesson ordering challenges students to identify with the prophet Jonah as the entry point to studying the book's significant message. Relevant information about Assyria, the Old Testament prophets, and Jonah subsequently arises through a more inductive study of the text.[6]

One widely used psychological ordering framework is the "Hook, Book, Look, Took" approach (Richards 1970). Every lesson or lesson series should have these four basic components. The *Hook* segment helps students focus on the lesson topic in some interesting and pertinent manner. That is, the point of departure is with the learner.

Table 10.6 continued.

C. Which particular *Educational Activities* will you use in your lesson, in light of items outlined in "A" and "B"?

6. *For the sake of student learning:* (Six Avenues of Learning)

   a. How will you relate the subject to their experience and present knowledge base? Is there a graphic analogy or story you can use? How can you move from their known to the unknown? (Identification Learning)

   b. How will you prompt students to think about the subject at a deeper level, according to their cognitive ability, especially from God's perspective? (Inquiry Learning)

   c. How will you give them feedback about their progress in learning, during class? between classes? (Consequence Learning)

   d. How will you help them remember the main points? What particular student expectations are you encouraging? (Cue Learning)

   e. How will you provide examples and demonstrations of the subject? (Structured Modeling)

   f. How will you provide occasions in which students set the agenda and you respond to their direction? (Spontaneous Modeling)

7. *For the sake of student motivation:*

   a. Teacher-Student Relationship: How will you relate to your students so that they will want to learn about the subject and to grow toward Christian maturity (e.g., to love God more deeply)? What kind of atmosphere will you create in the classroom?

   b. How will you attempt to incorporate their particular interests and preferences in the lesson? (e.g., ARCS model of motivation: Attention, Relevance, Confidence, Satisfaction [see Footnote 21, page 381]; Kolb's and Dunn and Dunn's learning style theories [see Appendix D])

   c. How will you use psychological ordering (instead of logical ordering) in sequencing the material and educational activities to enhance student interest and learning? How will you organize the lesson so that you move from the students' experiences to the subject of the lesson and then back to life application (e.g., Richards: Hook, Book, Look, Took)?

Carl Rowntree's class discussed how businesspersons attempt to win by intimidating others, for example.

In the *Book* section, the main subject is investigated and explained. The Mariner class studied the expectations Jesus and the Twelve brought to the upper room. Carl cited Jesus' foot-washing example of humble service. Then, each student paraphrased verses 13 and 14.

Next, the application of the subject is broadly explored in the *Look* segment of the lesson. What are the general implications for today? Carl had groups of students create a contemporary advertisement to communicate the truth of the lesson's slogan. Later, they developed a list of various menial services.

Finally, the lesson theme is privately addressed in the *Took* segment. "What will *I* personally choose to do?" Here, Carl's students filled in response cards. They committed themselves to a specific form of humble service in the coming week.[7]

Figure 10.1 presents a number of options for meaningful method selection.[8] Figure 10.2 visually portrays the general movement of this four-part framework.

Figure 10.1

Selecting Teaching Methods for a Lesson

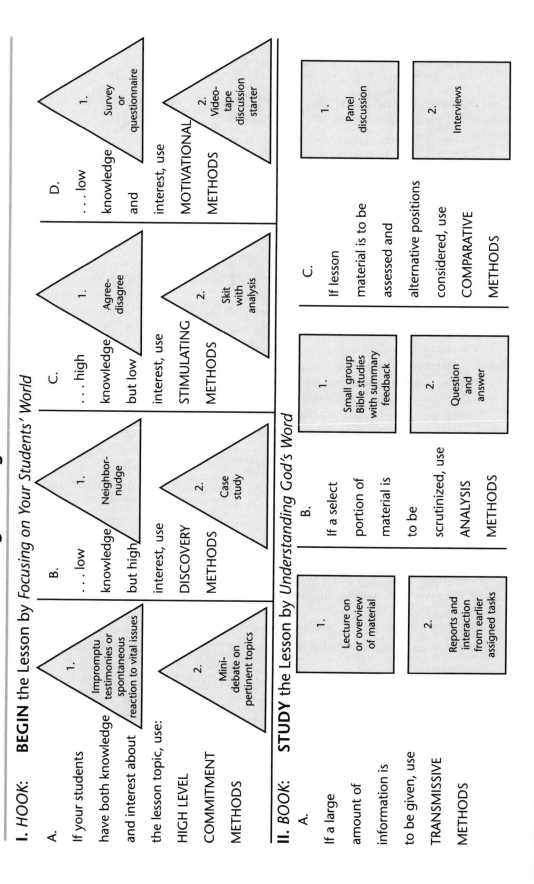

I. HOOK: **BEGIN** the Lesson by *Focusing on Your Students' World*

A.
If your students have both knowledge and interest about the lesson topic, use:
HIGH LEVEL
COMMITMENT
METHODS

1. Impromptu testimonies or spontaneous reaction to vital issues

2. Mini-debate on pertinent topics

B.
. . . low knowledge but high interest, use
DISCOVERY
METHODS

1. Neighbor-nudge

2. Case study

C.
. . . high knowledge but low interest, use
STIMULATING
METHODS

1. Agree-disagree

2. Skit with analysis

D.
. . . low knowledge and interest, use
MOTIVATIONAL
METHODS

1. Survey or questionnaire

2. Video-tape discussion starter

II. BOOK: **STUDY** the Lesson by *Understanding God's Word*

A.
If a large amount of information is to be given, use
TRANSMISSIVE
METHODS

1. Lecture on or overview of material

2. Reports and interaction from earlier assigned tasks

B.
If a select portion of material is to be scrutinized, use
ANALYSIS
METHODS

1. Small group Bible studies with summary feedback

2. Question and answer

C.
If lesson material is to be assessed and alternative positions considered, use
COMPARATIVE
METHODS

1. Panel discussion

2. Interviews

III. LOOK: PONDER the Lesson by *Examining Multiple Areas of Potential Application*

A.

If the lesson emphasizes long-range issues, use PLANNING METHODS

1. Develop possible goal-setting strategies

2. Draft some creedal or position statements

B.

If the lesson centers on immediate concerns, use SUMMARIZATION METHODS

1. Identify many fill-in-the-blank responses

2. Create a few slogans or paraphrases of the lesson

C.

If the lesson is not necessarily limited to short- or long-range themes, use BRAINSTORM METHODS

1. Group listing of all possible ways to apply God's truth

2. Individual listing of possible applications and group reporting

IV. TOOK: CONCLUDE the Lesson with *Appropriate Implementation*

A.

If the lesson lends itself to an individual response, use PERSONALIZED METHODS

1. Write a brief poem

2. Provide a pledge/promise on a 3 x 5 card

3. Private prayer

B.

If the lesson lends itself to a group response, use CORPORATE METHODS

1. Prayer in groups of 2 or 3

2. Accountability partners for special interest areas

3. Realistic projects, voluntarily chosen and customized

Source: Adapted from Presseau (1982, p. 62).

Figure 10.2
Movement of a Lesson

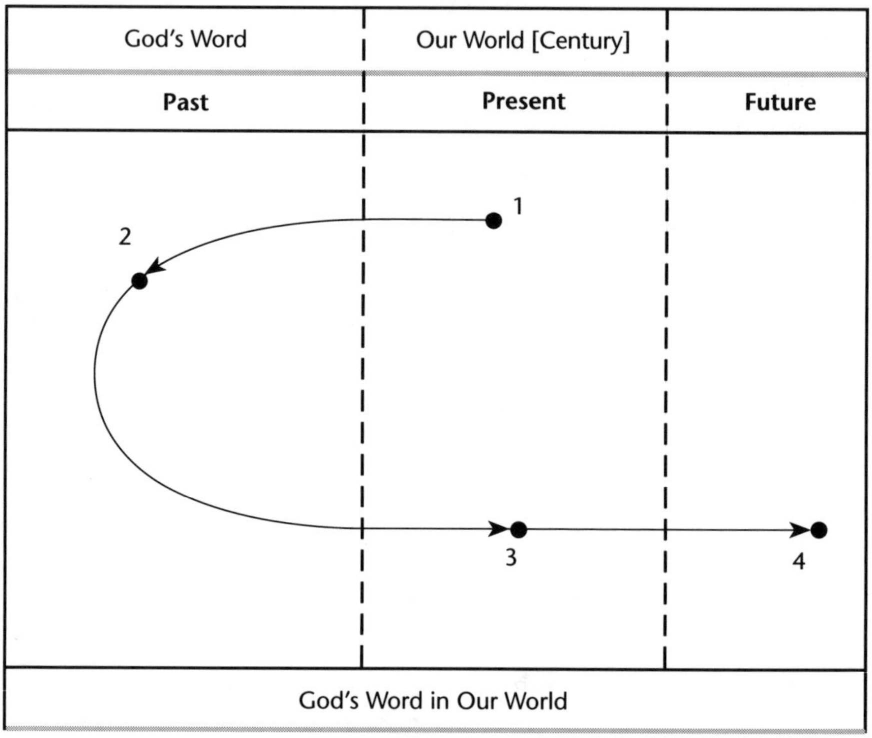

God's Word	Our World [Century]	
Past	Present	Future

God's Word in Our World

1 Hook: Popular Subject
2 Book: Pertinent Scripture
3 Look: Possible Strategies
4 Took: Personal Steps

Results of Teaching

The "result" component identifies any and every change in students. Such changes occur both during and subsequent to the lesson. Effective teachers initially encounter this component when they plan for *anticipated* outcomes in designing the aims of the lesson. They follow up this aspect when *actual* results of learning are evaluated.

To help teachers discern between the categories of "anticipated" and "actual," we include a discussion of Robert Stake's (1967) elementary theory.[9] The Stake model has two halves. The left half identifies the teacher's thoughts about the lesson *before* teaching the class. Three subsections comprise this preclass planning. From top to bottom (on the left side) these categories are:

Anticipated Preliminaries: what you assume will be true about the students and the teaching situation *before* you start teaching (including student motivation, their knowledge and other entry characteristics, your motivation and preparation as the teacher, etc.)

Anticipated Plans: what you assume will be the sequence of educational activities and methods *during* the session in light of the aim(s)

Anticipated Performances: what you as-sume will be achieved *after* this educa-tional experience; what you hope your students will learn regarding cogni-tion, convictions, and competence

The right half of the Stake model uses the same three categories, but with one impor-tant twist. Whereas the *left* half focuses on "anticipated" or desired factors, the *right* half focuses on "actual" factors—what really happened. Since the dynamics of ac-tual instruction alter the content of these three right-sided categories every time, *no teaching experience is ever the same.*

Helpful evaluation questions from Stake's theory prompt instructional im-provement. Such improvement is neces-sary, since one of the most neglected tasks in Christian education is thorough evalua-tion of learning outcomes. When we *do* as-sess what was learned, we tend to make judgments on weak indicators of learning. We rely too much on what is easily mea-sured (e.g., student responses like atten-dance and raised hands). When evaluating the effectiveness of teaching for student out-comes, some general principles should be kept in mind:

1. Use a variety of evaluation strategies (e.g., self-report evaluation form, writ-ten quizzes, role play, interview, group discussion, class presentation, live demonstration, research project).
2. Make many assessments. Don't base your judgment on just one or two eval-uations.
3. Pursue observations over a longer pe-riod of time. Some learning takes a while to manifest itself. The Christian life is not a one-hundred-yard dash; it's a marathon.
4. Make evaluations in a variety of set-tings and contexts. Signs of growth in the classroom do not guarantee that the student can effectively teach the Bible, resist personal temptations, or demonstrate faithfulness in marriage.
5. Several mature leaders should be in-volved in the evaluation process. Scripture refers to the importance of having two or three witnesses verify an interpersonal judgment (Deut. 19:15; Matt. 18:16).

Using the three categories in Table 10.7, we can devise strategies to evaluate student

Table 10.7

Criteria for Assessing Results of Learning

1. *Purpose* (Explicit Curriculum and Aims)
   a. Intended outcomes: To what degree was the lesson aim achieved?
   b. Unintended outcomes: What other changes took place in students' lives (either due to the lesson or to other causes)?
   c. Reconciliation Model of Christian maturity: How do student outcomes compare to biblical ideals (Communion, Community, Character, and Commission)?
2. *Domain* (three "levels" of learning)
   a. Cognition (knowledge)
   b. Conviction (attitudes, values, and emotions)
   c. Competence (skills and habits)
3. *Mastery* ("Extent" of learning)
   a. Degree of sophistication (e.g., knowledge level: awareness or understanding or wisdom?)
   b. Degree of retention (short-term, long-term?)
   c. Effect: What percentage of the students in class gained a minimum degree of mastery?

learning. These categories range from *direct* ways (e.g., test responses or personal testimonies of real-life experiences) to *indirect* means (e.g., find out how many people checked out certain Christian biographies from the church library in the past year). To the degree that it is possible to verify results, our judgment must derive from accurate and reliable indicators.[10] Remember that some outcomes are not readily observable. They may be latent and surface later in the student's life. They may be quite private for good reasons (Matt. 6:1–6) or poor ones (Matt. 23:3). Some outcomes are known only to God; they are unknown to both teacher and student until the effects become evident much later (1 Tim. 5:24–25).

Scriptural principles regarding outcomes for Christians are cited by our Lord: "Make a tree good and its fruit will be good, or make a tree bad and its fruit will be bad, for a tree is recognized by its fruit. . . . For out of the overflow of the heart the mouth speaks. The good man brings good things out of the good stored up in him" (Matt. 12:33–35).[11] No matter what curriculum we teach, we must nurture our students toward full, spiritual maturity. To be reconciled to God and others is our overarching teaching aim. In the end, all outcomes should feature this goal. Sometimes we get so caught up in the minuscule details of our subject that we neglect the weightier matters. We lose sight of our target when this occurs. Results, the last of seven teaching components, keep our aim accurate.[12]

Think about It

---

1. Remember the students you were asked to grade in the previous chapter? In light of these new suggestions for evaluating learning results, list three ways to improve your "grading" of their learning.

a.

b.

c.

2. If you were being evaluated as a potential deacon or elder in your church, what evaluation strategies would you hope the committee would use? In order for them to assess you accurately, write down three specific (and diverse) evaluation strategies that you could recommend to them.

a.

b.

c.

Teaching Various Age Groups: A Preview

Effective teaching is done *in light of,* not *despite,* the needs and characteristics of our students. For example, raising pertinent questions about faith poses a never-ending task of spiritual growth. But what is pertinent for a child will often be irrelevant for an adolescent or adult. We need age-appropriate guidelines for teaching adults, youth, and children.

Differences in Teaching a Bible Lesson

One of the implications from cognitive development theory is that children think differently than adults. How might this apply in preparing a Bible lesson? What differences exist between teaching teens and adults? As general guidelines, we suggest the following emphases for each age group.

Children

Limit your explanations and vocabulary to the concrete experiences of the children. Use objects that are familiar to them (e.g., illustrations about riding a bicycle rather than driving a car). They tend to be literalistic in their understanding of words. Expand their experience-based knowledge by having them do new things, by showing them new things, by taking them on field trips. Emphasize "hands-on" learning.

Youth

Help adolescents realize the potential of formal adult reasoning. Pose relevant dilemmas. Make them think. Challenge them to transform their "child-developed" faith into fully mature "adult" faith. Allow them room to experiment with their views, to try out new theories. Remember that part of experimentation is failure. Help them realize their inconsistencies and integrate truth, including all relevant factors.

Adults

Direct adults' abilities to comprehend scriptural principles as a means of solving their own life problems. Use their wealth of experience. Be sensitive to the tough problems they face at home, in the neighborhood, and at work. Encourage them to focus scriptural light on their specific life situa-tions, to root out inconsistencies and un-healthy habits.

Differences in Heightened Learning Potential

As a general rule of thumb, all three learning families and related avenues pertain to each age group. As we scrutinize teaching strategies that are age-appropriate, however, a more discriminating look is necessary. In light of developmental needs, we have matched each age division with one learning family. Again, although the remaining two categories are permissible to use, one learning family best correlates with each age group. These pairings are based on comparative consideration of developmental theories. Figure 10.3 portrays our proposed combinations.

These matched sets primarily derive from implications of moral reasoning theory, as developed by Lawrence Kohlberg (1981,

Figure 10.3

Age Groups and Learning Families Emphases

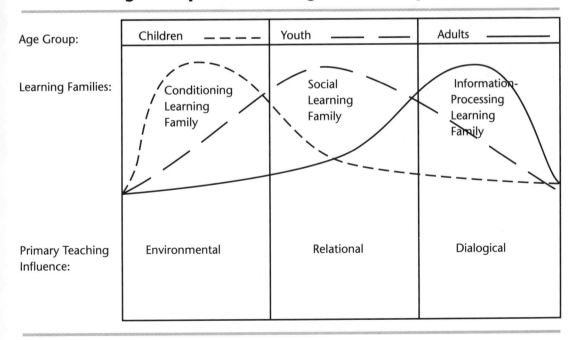

Source: Adapted from Kohlberg (1981, 1984) and Ward (1989, p. 94).

1984) and adapted by Ted Ward (1989, p. 94). For example, children (Kohlberg's Level I) are basically motivated by rewards and punishment. These reinforcements represent the basic features of the Conditioning Learning family. Mature youth (Level II) are morally persuaded by societal rules and role models. Social Learning theory exhibits a parallel perspective. Finally, mature adults (Level III) are motivated by dialogue and interpersonal transactions. Information-Processing Learning theory fits here, since growth is seen to be generated by sophisticated thought and interpersonal interaction.

Remember: These pairings between age groups and learning families only indicate *heightened tendencies, not exclusive associations,* as depicted in Figure 10.3. Given this reminder, consider some practical implications of such pairings via the six avenues (see Table 10.8).

Conclusion

Think about It

How would you react in these scenarios?

1. You are filling your car at a local service station. Suddenly, a car screeches to a halt near you. A man sits behind the wheel. At his side, a very pregnant woman is in severe distress. The driver calls out to you, frantically seeking directions to the nearest hospital. How do you respond? What attitude do you take to this "educational" opportunity? How do you "teach"?

2. Now, consider the same situation, but pretend the person asking directions is an adolescent who just started driving. How do you react to this "teaching" situation? What would you do differently, compared with the first case?

Table 10.8

Learning Families and Age Group Teaching Strategies

Age Group	Learning Family and Avenues	Strategies
Adults INFORMATION-PROCESSING FAMILY	Identification	• Study subjects based on needs and interests (e.g., finances)
	Inquiry	• Organize learning according to thought-provoking ends (e.g., case studies, dilemmas)
Youth SOCIAL LEARNING FAMILY	Structured Modeling	• Select good media (music, magazines, television, movies/videos, books) • Evaluate heroes/heroines
	Spontaneous Modeling	• Provide role models (i.e., friends, youth leaders, adult sponsors) • Offer opportunities for varied experiences and examples (e.g., cross-cultural trips)
Children CONDITIONING LEARNING FAMILY	Consequence and Cue	• Develop godly attitudes (e.g., love, joy, peace, patience) • Foster godly habits/lifestyle (e.g., daily Bible reading, prayer, conflict resolution)

3. Finally, envision the same setting, but the one confronting you is a person who speaks very little English. How do you feel? What "teaching" approach will you take this time?[13]

To review, this case study illustrates that competent instruction includes at least seven teaching components.

Teacher: In every instance, your role as the resource person is invaluable.

Explicit Curriculum: In each case, the location of the hospital and the directions to the hospital remain the same.

Aims of the Lesson: Although not exactly identical for each scenario, the aim involves helping the driver comprehend the instructions.

Class and Individual Learner: The student in each of the three examples represents diverse learner needs. (Contrast their peculiar features.)

Holistic Environment: You are in a familiar location at the time and you have a clear idea where the hospital is. But what if you were in unfamiliar territory? For that matter, you are not certain how well your "students" are acquainted with the environment—all the way from the service station to the hospital.

Educational Activities: Needless to say, your anticipated instructional strategies would vary. For instance, would it be wise to ask the driver to repeat your directions? Would it be useful to draw a map in the third case? Would you tell them to follow you?

Results of Teaching: Finally, student learning would be difficult to fully evaluate unless you followed the couple to the hospital in your car. You may decide to take the "student" in your car to the hospital. By the way, notice how taking your car completely alters the aim. The outcome may be more satisfactory, yet activities, too, have been significantly modified.

Aspiring to be a good instructor constitutes a challenging task. It represents a labor-intensive journey.[14] The teaching ministry is not meant for the faint-hearted. Nor is it for those easily satisfied with tokens of student accomplishment. Teaching that is Christian involves complex gifts, skills, and judgments. It is influenced by conscious, value-laden goals. Moreover, our pursuit of excellence in teaching must be done with the power and the guidance of the Holy Spirit.

11 Teaching Adults

A Century-Old Lesson
"Trees" of Dissimilarity
Questions as Solutions
"Forest" of Reconciliation Themes
Conclusion

A Century-Old Lesson

One day in the late 1860s, an Iowa farmer left his fields for an hour to watch the construction of the transcontinental railroad near his farm. He watched the track being laid. A few minutes later a steam locomotive came through. The farmer went back to his fields and thought, "So that's what railroading is all about: tracks and trains." What didn't the farmer see about the railroad's possibilities? He didn't see that he could get his products to market much more quickly, that he could get them to many new markets, and that once there they would have to compete against products from many more places. He didn't see the rise of Chicago, Kansas City, Denver, and San Francisco, and the development of intercontinental trade. He didn't see that it would be possible to go across country in less than a week, and that people's perspective on distance and time would change.[1]

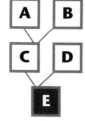

The farmer saw the locomotive and the steel rail, but he failed to see the big picture. He saw the parts, not the whole. His limited perspective might prove harmless initially. But long-term naiveté could cost him his livelihood.

Occasionally when we contemplate Christian education, we restrict our thinking to weekly programs. Like the farmer, we see only the rails. We ignore the larger issues. Specifically, when we consider age-level ministry, we fail to differentiate among particular groups within the church. What makes them different? What does a bird's-eye view show us?

Think about It

Pretend you are organizing the adult ministry in your local congregation. What "big picture" concerns of adults do you want to keep in mind? List some *age-distinctive needs* of adults. (Some ideas are provided to get you started.)

1. Adults typically have job-related needs.
2. Adults are often concerned about family responsibilities (e.g., children and aging parents).
3. _____
4. _____
5. _____
6. _____

Another way to read the Iowa farmer story is to recall the familiar "trees and forest" analogy. The farmer's problem was that *he couldn't see the forest for the trees.* He failed to comprehend the total picture. And that's a serious problem. Many Christian educators mimic this pattern.

But it's also counterproductive to overlook the trees. Since the "forest" portrays the overall picture of adult ministry, "trees" represent the details of adult work. We dare not lose sight of the particulars. Impoverished is the professional who can't "*do* ministry.*" The world-renowned philosopher Goethe said that "To put your ideas into action is the most difficult thing in the world."

"Trees" of Dissimilarity

Both features—"trees" and "forest"—are important.[2] In fact, all successful ministries require the incorporation of both, for one complements the other. Our day-to-day educational activities—the particulars—should evidence signs of restoration and peace. Our aerial view of the forest—the universals—must rivet us to the same, relentless cause of reconciliation.

Dissimilar Life Span Concerns

Review the entries you made in the last "Think about It" assignment. What unique lifelong needs of adults did you list? What makes these needs different from those of children and youth? Was there a sequence or pattern to your ideas?

Sometimes, what differentiates a good teacher of adults from a great one is the ability to understand and to meet age-specific needs. As this knowledge is transformed into curricular objectives and strategies, adult learners mature. Jerry M. Stubblefield suggests nineteen teachable moments throughout the full range of adult life (see Table 11.1).[3] Teachable moments arise when age-specific needs are confronted.[4] As these concerns are attended to, motivation for learning escalates. Moreover, learning retention increases. Conversely, as these age-specific needs go unattended, educational plans become irrelevant.

Various resources[5] containing goals[6] of adult work exist. Suggestions that correlate specific adult needs with particular ministries appear in this literature.[7] Scriptural in-

Table 11.1

Teachable Moments in Adult Life

Establishing independent living arrangements
Entering the work world
Deciding whether or not to marry
Deciding whether or not to be parents
Being a good citizen
Selecting the right friends
Being a community leader
Living with teenagers
Living within your income
Choosing leisure activities
Living with one's spouse
Accepting physiological changes
Adjusting to aging parents
Coping with personal age
Accepting reduced income in retirement
Adjusting to the loss of one's spouse
Living with one's peers
Being a good friend and a good citizen
Relocating living arrangements

Source: Modified from Stubblefield (1986a, pp. 239–55).

junctions for holistic growth must be heeded if we intend to abide by biblical designs.[8]

Dissimilar Adult Learning

We have noted in the previous chapter that, as a general rule of thumb, all three learning families and six avenues function within every age group. Yet for each age division, one learning family is inherently more appropriate than the other two. The Conditioning Learning family is more conducive to childhood. Children learn primarily through reinforcement and by the shaping of their environment. The Social Learning family works well with adolescents. Youth learn fundamentally via modeling and peer influence. The Information-Processing Learning family typifies adult growth patterns. Adults basically learn by problem solving and critical thinking.

Dissimilar Adult Growth

Hebrews 5:11–6:3 identifies three key phases of Christian growth and describes some unique features of adult development. Hebrews 6:1 advances the ultimate aim of Christian instruction: "Therefore let us . . . go on to maturity." Next, three practical guidelines are suggested for discipling adults.[9]

Truth-Believing

First, something must be trusted. Trust necessitates cognitive as well as affective commitment. Adults in churches should be firmly anchored to truth. Which truths? Hebrews 6:1–2 groups six doctrines into three couplets: (1) repentance and faith (v. 1) speak of *soteriology*; (2) baptisms (possibly referring to ceremonial washings) and commissioning of believers ("laying on of hands") (v. 2a) refer to *ecclesiology*; and (3) resurrection and judgment address *eschatology*. Again, the point is that some foundational truth must be trusted.[10] It is safe to assume that these basic adult doctrines are far too abstract for children;[11] many youth would likewise fail to comprehend them. Thus, this first of three guidelines for growth affirms unique adult development schemes from Scripture.[12]

Truth-Behaving

Scripture verifies that maturity can never be restricted to private, ascetic aims. Hebrews 5:14a describes growing adult believers in two ways: (1) they apply truth to their lives "by constant use." That is, appropriation of God's revelation is never-ending. And (2) by using truth, they "train themselves." Genuine believing is connected with sincere behaving. Truth accepted equals truth enacted. We should not be satisfied with adult education that remains in the classroom. We should not propose plans for adult nurture that reside solely in creeds or memory lists. Teaching that is Christian brings life-change. Daily routines are altered; motives and attitudes are transformed. Again, it is the issue of persistence that makes this second guideline for growth unique to adults. As subsequent chapters on youth show, adolescent maturity—at best—is an on-again, off-again reality. Children are even less consistent. In contrast, growing adults can be expected to regularly display congruent patterns of godly living.

Truth-Becoming

Hebrews 5:14b infers that the extensive application of truth to life yields the ability "to distinguish good from evil." We label this scriptural synonym "wisdom," a virtue rarely found in Christian novices. Wisdom comes from steadfastness and consistency. We must expose the myth of instant maturity, for education that is Christian knows no quick fix. Few children or youth demonstrate the virtue of wisdom; they can't be expected to show it. That's because "becoming" truth is a character quality reserved for adulthood.[13]

A succinct reference to this unique, three-part growth sequence is based on the most common descriptor of New Testament believers. More often than not, early Christians were known as followers of "the Way" (Acts 9:2; 19:9). No doubt, this title extended from Christ's claim in John 14:6. But it is Paul who makes more direct reference. In his testimony before Felix, he discloses details of this renowned "sect" (as the Jews described Christians).

Think about It

Read Paul's testimony in Acts 24:14–16. Where are the three phases of adult growth? Provide the verse and a couple of words used in Scripture to describe each growth phase:

1. *"Truth-Believing"*— _____

2. *"Truth-Behaving"*— _____
3. *"Truth-Becoming"*— _____

Compare your answers with our recommendations.[14]

Dissimilar Experiences among Adults

So far, we have investigated the unique aspects of adult life and ministry. We have analyzed the ways adults differ from children and youth in terms of their needs, their predominant learning mode, and their biblical patterns of maturity. In this section, we will focus on how adults differ from one another. Obviously, we leaders can not completely fashion our ministries to each individual. But we can become more sensitive to meaningful experiences that set one adult apart from another.

One way to comprehend adult differences is to look at two basic factors: *life-events* and *times during life*. Life-events are adult challenges, happenings, and accomplishments. Times during life are particular moments in adult experience. For example, one of us has three daughters, ages thirteen, nine, and five. A professional colleague of the same age has a five-year-old son. In some ways, both sets of parents presently face similar "life-event" concerns (e.g., aging parents). Yet the colleague's family will soon face—for the first time—the challenges of sending their only child off to school. Our family already faced that issue eight years ago. This second example represents differences of "time during life." Moreover, in some ways, our middle-aged colleague is addressing a "life-event" more often associated with young adult "time."

Consider just one educational implication of this scenario. What happens when this same colleague, along with his wife, are inadvertently shuffled off to a middle adults' Sunday school class (because of *their* age)?[15] In certain areas, aren't they really better suited for the young adults' class? Isn't this young adults' class even more appropriate if both classes are studying family-related topics?[16] Table 11.2 graphically suggests the complexity of similar and dissimilar adult experiential combinations.[17]

"Assembly markers" represent certainties. They are unquestioned realities—in both event and date. There are generally few exceptions.[18] "Milestone markers" are expected experiences, but times do vary in some cases.[19] "Momentous markers" feature known dates, but unknown participants. They are drawn from two calendars: the church calendar and the "Hallmark" calendar (e.g., Mother's Day). The question in this third quadrant becomes one of personal applicability, for the date of public recognition is sure. For instance, in some churches every quarter of the year, the standard query is raised: "Who is prepared for baptism this time?" Occasionally leaders are inundated with candidates; at other times, the baptismal service must be cancelled or postponed because no candidates are available. Every second Sunday in May, the leadership must ask: "How many women in our congregation are mothers?" Pastors who seasonally preach about the virtues of motherhood must raise questions about other implicit messages.[20]

"Private markers" denote the uncertainty of experienced events as well as timing. Typically, the fourth event-time quadrant depicts the most difficult of all combinations in Table 11.2 when it comes to ministry effectiveness. It's hard to recognize unique experiences of adults. It takes time. It requires sacrifice and demanding communication skills. Yet, to serve a significant number of people, we leaders must be "private marker" servants. We must sympa-

Table 11.2
"Markers" of Adult Life

Times During Life

Life-Events		Similar	Dissimilar
	Similar	"Assembly Markers" (e.g., Sunday school picnic, Christmas program, the Lord's Supper)	"Milestone Markers" (e.g., high school graduation, learning to drive, retirement)
		Explanation: Event occurs for *all*, on *expected* dates.	Explanation: Event occurs for virtually *all* at *unexpected* times.
	Dissimilar	"Momentous Markers" (e.g., anticipated "calendar" experiences like baptism, Mother's Day)	"Private Markers" (e.g., divorce/remarriage, promotion, career changes)
		Explanation: Event occurs for *some*, on *expected* dates.	Explanation: Event occurs for *some*, at *unexpected* times.

thize with diverse adult challenges and accomplishments.

Anderson (1990) expresses a parallel concern for the diverse experiences of adults. He approaches this topic from the perspective of generational differences. For instance, "baby boomers" and "baby busters" have divergent backgrounds. Their parents' experiences were even more dissimilar. He summarizes (p. 65): "Shared (or unshared) experiences bond generations together. This is often such a powerful phenomenon that many individuals are completely unable to see the perspective of another generation; therefore there can be no dialogue. This can be very damaging for families, communities, businesses, and churches, which all need to operate intergenerationally. Recognizing this enables us to see why certain patterns develop in the church."

Think about It

Try your hand at the diagram in Table 11.2. Provide at least one more example for each of the four quadrants.

"Assembly Markers"_____
"Milestone Markers"_____
"Momentous Markers" _____
"Private Markers" _____

If you can, give one personal illustration of a "private marker"—particularly one where you felt that fellow believers were insensitive to your individual needs. (*Note:* If you are unable to provide a personal illustration, write down one instance you've heard from another adult's life.)

_____
_____
_____

Questions as Solutions

How do we effectively minister to adults? How do we take into consideration their life-cycle needs, as well as their age-appropriate learning "family"? How do we value their unique experiences as adults?

A simple, though significant, strategy for teaching adults in any setting is to ask questions, skillfully.

In particular, three sets of interrogative methods assist us. They complement the assertion that adults learn best through the Information-Processing family. Each inquiry set provokes thinking skills in varying degrees. Each set values adult needs, growth, and experiences. These specific methods include: (1) questions seeking answers; (2) questions requiring discussion; and (3) questions posing problems. By definition, this sequence moves from *convergent* query methods to *divergent* ones. In other words, "questions seeking answers" project a limited range of correct responses. "Questions requiring discussion" allow wider, acceptable solutions. "Questions posing problems" encourage the broadest feedback. Actually, the last classification cannot be strictly limited to one single method; it represents several related strategies (e.g., questions about problems can generate case studies, interviews, and research/reporting). The phrase "problem posing" was chosen to ensure these many optional strategies, as well as multiple learner responses.

Having identified this complementary set of interrogative methods, it is imperative to note the similarity found in these three questioning patterns. Each affirms critical thinking skills. And, if mature believers are to "always be prepared to give an answer . . . [for] the reason for [their] hope" (1 Pet. 3:15), we must begin with such teaching-learning tools. Ownership of convictions emerges when adults wrestle with the life-long question: "What is it that *I* believe?"

Questions Seeking Answers

Francis Bacon concluded that "The skillful question is the half of knowledge." Christ skillfully employed questions, verifying his title of Master Teacher. Notice just two ways the Lord used questions in the Gospel of Mark.[21]

In an unusual teaching episode, Jesus, pressed by the crowd advancing to Jairus' home, suddenly stopped. "Who touched my clothes?" he demanded (Mark 5:30). The disciples, again demonstrating their humanness, responded (in the vernacular): "You're joking, aren't you? A mob encircles you, and you want to know who touched you?"

But Jesus, as always, proceeded with his intentional instruction. Ignoring the Twelve, he continued his search. The woman, healed from a dozen years of hemorrhaging, eventually stepped forward.

Jesus' *question*—which sought a particular *answer*—was exercised deliberately. Christ determined, by one inquiry, to elicit personal responsibility.

A pair of simple questions are likewise raised in Mark 8. They focus on the miraculous feeding of the four thousand. Christ again employed the Information-Processing Learning family for his strategy. Prior to the miracle, Jesus listened carefully to his disciples. They logically stated the predicament of the masses: "But where in this remote place can anyone get enough bread to feed them?" (v. 4).

Jesus' Identification Learning query struck a harmonious cord with their assessment. "How many loaves do you have?" (v. 5) seemingly confirmed their predicament. They readily answered, "Seven." And it appeared that Jesus proved their point: The challenge for nourishment was humanly impossible to meet.

Of course, every Sunday school child knows how the merciful miracle subse-

quently occurred. But what they're not told is that Jesus simultaneously posed an *Inquiry-oriented* question: "Be careful . . . for the yeast of the Pharisees and that of Herod" (v. 15). Christ commenced his symbolic warning to the Twelve. Then, he offered his problem, in a related pop quiz: "And when I broke the seven loaves of the four thousand, how many basketfuls of pieces did you pick up?" (v. 20).

"Seven," the disciples repeated. To which Jesus countered: "Do you still not understand?" (v. 21).

Through his *pre-* and *post*questioning, Jesus determined to verify his miracle. Furthermore, he intended to contrast his truth with his enemies' false messages.

At least three types of questions seeking answers exist. In keeping with this book's valuing of tensions, this trio is arranged in bipolar fashion:[22]

1. *Open-ended* versus *closed-ended* questions. "Explain your convictions about how to discern God's will" portrays the former. "How many spies investigated the promised land?" typifies the latter. The issue at stake in this first category resides with the *range of acceptable responses*.

2. *Directed* versus *generic* questions. The first type of inquiry includes a particular student's name along with the question (e.g., "Ann, what discoveries did you make from the assignment?"). The second type of inquiry encourages any class member's feedback. The issue signals the *range of intended respondents*.

3. *Loaded* versus *hypothetical* questions. Loaded questions tend to limit interaction, while hypothetical ones have the opposite effect. The focus is the *range of desired responsiveness*. A question like: "Nobody here believes in infant

baptism, do they?" silences participants. In contrast, a question facilitating input is: "What if you believed in
infant baptism? What biblical concepts or passages would you embrace
to support that position?" Typically,
"What if" inquiries set the tone for
greater responsiveness.

Questions Requiring Discussion

A second interrogative method from the
Information-Processing Learning family
emphasizes extended dialogue. Contrasting
the former category, this method registers a
difference of quantity and quality. First,
more people are potentially included.
Meaningful discussion with adults does not
restrict conversation to the teacher and a
single learner (quantity). Productive discussion often occurs among learners, with only
minimal input from the leader. Moreover,
discussion fosters potential for comprehensive subject analysis. More details can be
examined, fuller conclusions can be drawn
(quality). To phrase it differently, discussion
has an advantage over questions and answers in terms of both *breadth* and *depth*.[23]

For the times we successfully ignite discussion, we need to know how to keep it
going. A word of caution: We must also discover how to keep it from blowing up in our
face. Em Griffin (1982, pp. 101–5) suggests
a half-dozen dos and don'ts he has found
helpful: (1) *Don't judge.* If you ask for opinions, keep the focus assessment-free. (2)
Don't preach. This approach tends to
squelch the contributions of others. (3)
Avoid the detached stance of the scholar. Nonverbal (as well as verbal) communication
indicates whether the leader genuinely accepts group members' ideas. (4) *Plan ahead.*
Preparation doesn't rule out spontaneous,
on-the-spot discussion ideas; neither does
spontaneity overlook the value of preliminary study time. (5) *Use humor.* Let the

funny side of life come out naturally, to encourage leader transparency. Avoid caustic
sarcasm or inappropriate humor. (6) *Seek
balanced participation.* Involve silent members, while controlling monopolizers.

The Master Teacher modeled techniques
of adult discussion for the church. We
teachers can benefit from three of his examples. In Mark 8:27–30 a classic discussion
surfaces concerning Jesus' identity. Christ
uses *discussion to distinguish rumor from truth.*
His two questions move from broad to narrow: "Who do people say I am?" (v. 27) "But
what about you? . . . Who do you say I am?"
(v. 29).

In Mark 11:27–33 Christ's authority is
challenged. He answers his rivals' questions
of authority (v. 28) with his own question:
"John's baptism—was it from heaven, or
from men?" (v. 30). The Lord's enemies respond indecisively. Christ uses *discussion to
check allegiances.*

In Mark 12:13–17 the controversy of paying taxes arises. Introducing a denarius as
an object lesson, Christ quizzes: "Whose
portrait is this? And whose inscription?" (v.
16). His purpose is to use *discussion to acknowledge both earthly and heavenly obligations.*

In summary, two precepts of the group
discussion method surface. Each precept
features a tension. A specific subject is addressed and a particular benefit unfolds.

First, diversity is valued within dependent relationships. Multiple opinions are
prized; even tangential questions are respected. Otherwise, there is no need for
more than one group member or viewpoint.
Conversely, interpersonal ties remain, or
there is no justification for group function.
These features ensure the best balances of
discussion contributions and commitments.

Second, acknowledged departure points
preside, along with destination points. That
is, facilitative group discussion commences

with certain ground rules, assumptions, and terms (e.g., "What respect do we show toward other group members?"). Furthermore, recognized ends endorse productive means. This feature establishes discussion cohesiveness from start to finish. "What is it," each group member regularly asks, "that we are analyzing? What is our aim?"

Questions Posing Problems

Herman H. Horne provides (1982, pp. 33–34) a useful summary of problems that Jesus introduced to his hearers. Among other reasons, Christ posed problems to induce contemplative thought. He prompted individuals to ask: "What do I *really* believe about this subject?" We teachers cannot do less.[24]

Which of the problems in Table 11.3 catch your attention? For the most part, they represent the Master Teacher's problem-posing instructional approach.

Think about It

Jot down one or two responses to these questions:

1. Which problem-posing incidents in Table 11.3 caught your eye? Why?

   _____

   _____

Table 11.3

Jesus' Problem-Posing Strategies

Persons	Their Problems
The scribes (2:7)	Who can forgive sins?
The scribes and Pharisees (2:16)	Jesus' association with publicans and sinners
The Pharisees (2:24)	Sabbath observance
The scribes (3:22)	How Jesus cast out demons
His fellow-townspeople (6:2, 3)	The sources of Jesus' power
The scribes and Pharisees (7:5)	Why the disciples did not observe traditions
The Pharisees (8:11)	They wanted a sign
Peter, James, and John (9:11)	The coming of Elijah
The disciples (9:34)	"Who is the greatest?"
John and others (9:38)	Tolerance of other workers
The Pharisees (10:2)	Divorce
The rich young ruler (10:17)	Inheriting eternal life
James and John (10:37)	Sitting on his right and left hand
The Sadducees (12:23)	The resurrection
A scribe (12:29)	The first commandment
Peter, James, John, and Andrew (13:4)	"When shall these things be?"
Some at Simon's dinner (14:4)	The waste of ointment
The high priest (14:61)	Whether Jesus claimed to be the Christ

Source: Modified from Horne (1982, pp. 33–34).

2. What additional dilemmas did Jesus raise (not in Table 11.3) that posed problems?

_____

_____

3. Select any one of these problems that Christ used. Speculate how you would have reacted, if you were part of the crowd. _____

_____

_____

How do we Christian educators introduce useful problems to adult students? Partly, this happens as we share relevant struggles from our own pilgrimage experiences. Partly, problem posing springs from knowledge of local and world affairs, by selecting dilemmas that speak to the twenty-first-century church.

Take the subject of war. Note how Em Griffin (1982, p. 102) utilizes this topic to get to the debated ethical issues: "A gentle probing works wonders—never challenging but in a friendly spirit of curiosity, exploring the depths of what another is saying. If a girl states that she is against war, I try to find out what war? Vietnam? Israel's six-day preemptive strike against Egypt? The Allies' resistance to Hitler and Tojo in World War 2? It may turn out that there are some conflicts she'll regretfully support."

Scrutinize another dilemma that Griffin has examined within a group. This problem-posing controversy finds direct correlation with a Bible character: "If a fellow announces categorically that God would never have us lie, I'll mention Rahab the prostitute who lied about the spies she was hiding in the attic. In Hebrews 11 she's praised for her faith. I won't push the point. And there are any number of objections to my example. But chances are my question-

ing will be an impetus for others to plunge into the discussion" (Griffin 1982, p. 102).

To update an earlier comparison: Problem posing plots a more complex educational route than the discussion method. Indeed, the former may start out the same as discussion, but multiple "spin-off" strategies raise the level of instructional sophistication. Again, options include interviews, buzz groups, and research/reporting. For instance, using the Rahab example above or a more current dilemma from Corrie Ten Boom's life, a case study could be easily constructed for adult instruction. "When Lying Is Right" would make a provocative title.

To conclude by way of application, consider three useful categories that classify problems. In Table 11.4, we have added some practical suggestions for adult problem-posing activities.

Table 11.4

Problem Classification

Category #1: Fact

Problems of fact focus on *information*. For instance: "What does the Book of Hebrews say about angels?" Inductive Bible study provides facts about this inquiry.

Category #2: Value

Problems of value focus on *moral standards* and judgment. For example: "What are the obligations of believers, when they disagree on gray areas of faith?" Besides facts, wrongs and rights must be determined; the difference between descriptive and prescriptive statements must be appreciated. Believers in every subculture must decide on gray areas.

Category #3: Policy

Problems of policy focus on *implementation of facts and values:* the decision-making procedures. "How can the local church apply Paul's principles in Romans 14?" represents one illustration of policy. For instance, in the late 1960s and early 1970s many church and parachurch organizations created policies prohibiting male members from having long hair. In the 1990s this policy represents antiquated ideas for most groups. With every new generation, the church must reapply Paul's principles. Which issues are cultural? Which are timeless?

Source: Modified from Potter and Andersen (1976, pp. 118–21).

In virtually every Christian education setting—home, church, community—believers especially voice their concern about "policy" matters, pertinent to the volatile "gray areas" of faith. We must learn how to get along with Christians who hold convictions different than ours.[25] Dialogue gets us started on this objective.

Guidelines for effective problem posing are critical. Without them, education that is Christian becomes counterproductive. Adult instructors, consequently, must adhere to a few basic directives:

- Select a *significant* problem
- Select a *relevant* problem
- Select a *thought-provoking* problem
- Select a *properly worded* problem
  - stated in question form
  - stated to encourage probing
  - stated to promote ownership
  - stated as a manageable topic
  - stated unambiguously
  - stated impartially
  - stated briefly[26]

"Forest" of Reconciliation Themes

Ministry to any age group starts with the four themes identified in Chapter 3. We instructors require an evaluative grid, to assure that our instructional strategies are biblical, that we're shooting at appropriate targets. Every age group, for instance, must confront the topic of *Communion*. How do we assist learners in their relationship with the Creator? The *Community* theme satisfies belonging needs. We want students to know the privileges and responsibilities of Christian fellowship. Also, every age must address the subject of *Character*. What is it that God wants us to be as individuals? How we relate to the world around us involves *Commission*. Subcategories of this theme include evangelism, stewardship, advocacy, and ecological issues.

It is imperative to remember that these four themes precisely match the four universal quests, as noted in Chapter 4. Specifically, the quest for Immortality pairs with Communion; our lifelong question, "What is ultimate reality?" expresses human belief needs. The quest for Intimacy equals Community. We continually ask, "How should I relate to others?" Belonging needs are featured. Integrity and Character are synonymous. Being needs prompt the query: "Who am I morally?" And Industry parallels Commission. "What must I accomplish?" points to behavior concerns.

The following section briefly reviews the connection between quests and themes, with adults specifically highlighted. Various social scientists and religious educators recognize this association.[27] Erich Fromm (1955, pp. 27–66) points out, for example, five human needs that are "the same for man in all ages and all cultures" (p. 69).[28] Research shows that all adult subgroups gravitate toward these human quests. Gail Sheehey (1976, p. 32) notes how young adults face these universal queries. She describes the deep-seated search of her "Trying Twenties" in this way: "The Trying Twenties confront us with the question of how to take hold in the adult world. Our focus shifts from the interior turmoils of late adolescence—'Who am I?' 'What is truth?'—and we become almost totally preoccupied with working out the externals. 'How do I put my aspirations into effect?' 'What is the best way to start?' 'Where do I go?' 'Who can help me?' 'How did *you* do it?'"[29]

As with their younger counterparts, middle-aged adults also confront human quests. Sheehey (1976, p. 36) calls them the "Deadline Decade," those thirty-five to forty-five years old. The authenticity crisis (the author's term) that middle adults often feel is that "this is my last chance"—typically referring to vocational (or Commission) crises. Sheehey explains (p. 36): "To come through this authenticity crisis, we must reexamine our purposes and reevaluate how to spend our resources from now on. 'Why am I doing all this? What do I really believe in?' No matter what we have been doing, there will be parts of ourselves that have been suppressed and now need to find expression. 'Bad' feelings will demand acknowledgment along with the good."

Older adults also encounter the quests, albeit from yet another angle. Elbert C. Cole (1981, p. 265) deduces that the elderly ask two questions of society and of life in general: (1) "How can I maintain my life?" (2) "What gives [life] meaning and purpose?" Cole concludes that "Both questions have religious implications and the community of faith needs to be aggressive in responding." Stepping back for a wider perspective, Martin J. Heinecken (1981) suggests that the critical factor is how society collectively responds to the needs of the elderly. He (p. 78) rephrases the quests in this manner: "The general attitude of a culture toward its aged is determined by its predominant view of human life, its values and its destiny."

Conclusion

How, then, do we orchestrate adult development? What strategies do we employ to this end? Certainly, no magic formulas exist. In *The Spirit of Disciplines* (1988), Dallas Willard provides some meaningful guidelines. His fifteen disciplines of life are listed in Table 11.5. We've paired the related reconciliation themes. The match-ups represent a synthesis of "trees" and "forest" for adult ministry.

Table 11.5

Life Disciplines

THEMES	DISCIPLINES
Communion	solitude; silence; study; worship; prayer
Community	celebration; fellowship; submission; confession
Character	fasting; frugality; chastity; sacrifice
Commission	service; secrecy

Source: Willard (1988, chap. 8).

In the end, we realize that serving adults is beyond our human capabilities. God's grace sustains us, ultimately. Even the questions we raise—the quests—are not fully resolved by human discovery and verification. Attention to the four themes is not a one-sided affair. Our heavenly Father, who initiated the themes, is also at work. His attempts at reconciliation will not fail. This is why the theme of Communion reflects our focal point. From this place of origin, all other themes receive attention. Heinecken (1981, p. 77) sums it up concisely: "We human beings are derived beings, thus unless the relationship to the Creator to whom we owe our being is right, our relationship to ourselves and to each other and the created world cannot be right either."

12

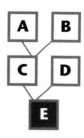

Commendable Adult Curriculum

A Realistic Appraisal
Commendable Curriculum
Evaluating Published Curriculum
Conclusion

A Realistic Appraisal

It is foolhardy to believe that every adult is *ready* to grow. It is equally foolish to think that all adults *want* to mature.[1] The prudent instructor discerns the difference between these learning roadblocks. It is unwise to assume that even the best teaching strategies work in all educational settings. One group of adults that faced Kenneth Gangel (1974, p. 36) represented a not-so-atypical class:

About 10 years ago, I was conducting a Christian Education Conference in a church in downstate Illinois. At the last minute I was asked to teach a young adult Sunday School class. I decided to attempt dialogical approach, just to see what would happen. My first question, "What have you been studying this quarter?" brought no response whatever from the 20 young adults. I then asked, "Is it in the Old Testament or the New Testament?" I still got no response. After two or three more questions a lady in the back row timidly raised her hand and volunteered a piece of information.

That class was communicating to me their ideas of what Sunday School ought to be. It was clearly a place where the students sat and listened while the teacher spoke. Classes like this do not change their attitudes easily nor quickly.

Think about It

Several reasons could be suggested for why Gangel's class failed to respond to even the simplest questions. Besides the input from the illustration, give five of your own educated hunches:

1. _____
2. _____
3. _____
4. _____
5. _____

Gangel's conclusion is quite accurate: "Classes like this do not change their attitude easily nor quickly." Pretend you have the opportunity to teach this same class for one year. Your aim is to encourage more class participation. Provide three practical ideas to hit this target.

Idea 1 _____
Idea 2 _____
Idea 3 _____

Commendable Curriculum

Which published materials provide excellent teaching resources? What curriculum is exemplary? Using the parameters of the reconciliation themes, we will look at commendable materials for effective adult ministry.[2] Since we've suggested in Chapter 10 that adults are best matched with the Infor-

mation-Processing Learning family, much of what is analyzed in this section emphasizes critical thinking skills. We must teach adults both the *what* and *why* of their faith.

All referenced curriculum in this section comes from Serendipity's *I Corinthians— Mastering the Basics* by Lyman Coleman and Richard Peace. In every instance, material is featured from the student's guide. (An accompanying pastor/teacher commentary, published as a separate textbook, is also available from Serendipity.[3])

Curriculum for Communion/Character

The Christian classic *Your God Is Too Small* pinpoints many of our rudimentary faith problems. J. B. Phillips' half-century-old insights remain relevant for adult Christian instruction. His bottom-line argument (concerning our deficient perspectives) is that we've pigeonholed the Creator of the universe. We have theologized, categorized, and galvanized so many classifications of God that we've restricted his work.

In Mark 6:1–6a, Jesus' hometown crowd did the very same thing. Pigeonholed as "Mary's son" as well as "the brother of James, Joseph, Judas and Simon" (v. 3), Christ's hands were figuratively tied. The Son of God "could not do any miracles there, except lay his hands on a few sick people and heal them" (v. 5). Such a vivid testimony of boxing God up! Limiting the Holy One! Just note what the last verse in this passage says about Christ's personal reaction: "And he was amazed at their lack of faith" (v. 6a). Their disbelief shocked the Lord! We do the same thing every time we fix boundaries around God. We limit God's work in our lives when we misunderstand who he is. David A. Seamonds (1991, p. 9) notes: "I have come to the position that I honestly think about three-fourths of the emotional problems and personality hang-ups in Christians come from wrong, distorted concepts of God, how they feel about God, and how God feels about them."

With slight modifications from Phillips (1956, pp. 9–64), ponder some of our self-limiting classifications of God (Table 12.1). Do you find yourself affirming any of these false views of God?

Table 12.1

Self-Limiting Views of God

1. Heavenly Policeman—God exists only to enforce broken laws.
2. Celestial Parent—Psychological guilt and fears are projected from earthly guardians onto God.
3. Bearded Grandfather—The Sovereign One is not only visualized as old but old-fashioned and weak.
4. Meek-and-Mild—God, through distorted images of Jesus, is pictured as soft and sentimental.
5. Absolute Perfection—God cannot accept anything less than 100 percent perfection from people.
6. Blissful Escape—Serving God takes the form of spiritual thumb sucking, providing a way to evade life's responsibilities.
7. God-in-a-Box—Idiosyncrasies of believers claim to cage the Creator (e.g., denominational exclusivity).
8. Transcendent Commander-in-Chief—When compared to the universe's vastness, it is preposterous to believe that God cares about individuals.
9. Media-mutilated Being—Most of the lies people are told about God are colorized by misrepresentations in the media.
10. Perennial Disappointment—Whether through unanswered prayer or undeserved disaster, he is the One who lets people down.
11. Pale Galilean—God is primarily a negative force in the lives of believers; they reduce spirituality to legalistic restrictions.
12. God-in-Our-Image—God is merely an extension of private expectations: God hates things that "others" do, yet he overlooks personal transgressions.

13. Time-Server—Like a hurried executive, the Father is driven by the clock.
14. Eternal Elitist—God is a respecter of persons, favoring the privileged.
15. Sinai Superior—Old Testament commandments are valued over New Testament principles; the God of works over the God of grace.
16. Impersonal Power—God actually represents ultimate values; an enlightened form of rationalism.
17. Gods of Other Names—The Creator is linked with "gods" of fame, fortune, and success.

Source: Modified from Phillips (1956, pp. 9–64).

Think about It

What additional titles can you add to Table 12.1, which limit God's work? List one or two phrases that come to mind, along with an explanation._____

_____

In particular, how do these titles *negatively* affect the theme of Communion, as you understand it? _____

_____

The combined themes of Communion and Character[4] are disclosed in Illustration 12.1, our first example of exemplary adult material. All three methodological families are found in Illustration 12.1. The half-dozen avenues are noticeable, too. For instance, prominent teaching strategies affirm the Information-Processing family, as most of the "Study" section demonstrates. Basic inductive Bible skills are required. When adult students make sense of Scripture, Identification Learning techniques pertain. The "Apply" section promotes Inquiry Learning by calling for deductive understanding of "wisdom."

Conditioning Learning family methods exist in several places, especially in the "Group Agenda" section. In particular, Cue Learning arises in the "To Close" portion through the second question: "When in your spiritual journey did the 'mind of Christ' start to make a difference in your values, choices and decisions?" This question precedes an additional focus on the theology of renewed thinking. Consequence Learning also appears in the question, "What evidence can you point to this past year in which the 'mind of Christ' has given you spiritual understanding?" (see "To Close"). This year-in-review exercise offers reinforcement for a relevant faith.

A couple of Social Learning examples are explicitly stressed in the "To Begin" portion. Influential and wise people are recalled, plus those characterized by spiritual understanding. These personalized recollections are contrasted with the subsequent hypothetical case study (see "To Go Deeper"). The former represents Spontaneous Modeling, the latter Structured Modeling.

Table 12.2 summarizes the above paragraphs. It graphically shows the curricular examples for all six learning families from Illustration 12.1.

Curriculum for Community/Character

Imagine a tribe of people cut off from the rest of the world by a dense rain forest. Highly organized taboos and rules govern every part of their life. Religious practices quench some fears, arouse others. Rituals and beliefs are enforced: if a member fails without reason to show up for a ceremonial dance, he may be punished or ostracized for a time. Shame and ridicule make everyone conform.

Suppose an ostracized member wanders around until, finding himself at the edge of the thick jungle, an opening allures him. He stumbles upon another tribe with practices he has never seen before. They do not perform the same rituals, yet they still prosper. They eat foods he was told would poison, but no harm comes to them.

Formerly, he had thought his tribe's rules were the only right ones (i.e., absolute) and were for all (i.e., universal). If he found more tribes with different views, would he not begin to doubt the universal and absolute nature not only of his tribal ways but those of any tribe? Would relativism seize control of his thinking? How would he feel? What values and rules would he now choose to live by?

Were he to return to his home, what would happen? He could not keep quiet about the wasteful and useless practices of his people. The authorities would reject him in order to protect their homeland's beliefs and customs, and he would probably be punished or banished. He would suffer because he would still yearn for the

Table 12.2

Adult Curriculum for Communion and Character

Information-Processing Family	Identification Learning	Inductive Bible study questions
	Inquiry Learning	Deductive questions pertaining to the comprehension of "wisdom"
Conditioning Family	Cue Learning	Reflection upon the relevance of the "mind of Christ" in personal, spiritual pilgrimages
	Consequence Learning	Year-in-review exercise that locates "evidence" of the "mind of Christ" in daily life
Social Family	Spontaneous Modeling	Recollection of personal models who were influential
	Structured Modeling	A hypothetical case study of modeling

Illustration 12.1

UNIT 4—Wisdom From the Spirit/1 Corinthians 2:6-16

TEXT

Wisdom from the Spirit

⁶We do, however, speak a message of wisdom among the mature, but not the wisdom of this age or of the rulers of this age, who are coming to nothing. ⁷No, we speak of God's secret wisdom, a wisdom that has been hidden and that God destined for our glory before time began. ⁸None of the rulers of this age understood it, for if they had, they would not have crucified the Lord of glory. ⁹However, as it is written:

"No eye has seen,
no ear has heard,
no mind has conceived
what God has prepared for those who love him"ᵃ —

¹⁰but God has revealed it to us by his Spirit.

The Spirit searches all things, even the deep things of God. ¹¹For who among men knows the thoughts of a man except the man's spirit within him? In the same way no one knows the thoughts of God except the Spirit of God. ¹²We have not received the spirit of the world but the Spirit who is from God, that we may understand what God has freely given us. ¹³This is what we speak, not in words taught us by human wisdom but in words taught by the Spirit, expressing spiritual truths in spiritual words.ᵇ ¹⁴The man without the Spirit does not accept the things that come from the Spirit of God, for they are foolishness to him, and he cannot understand them, because they are spiritually discerned. ¹⁵The spiritual man makes judgments about all things, but he himself is not subject to any man's judgment:

¹⁶"For who has known the mind of the Lord that he may instruct him?"ᶜ

But we have the mind of Christ.

ᵃ9 Isaiah 64:4   ᵇ13 Or Spirit, interpreting spiritual truths to spiritual men   ᶜ16 Isaiah 40:13

STUDY

READ

First Reading/First Impressions
What's going on here? (Check two) □ Preaching □ Teaching □ Warning □ Comforting □ Pleading □ Defending □ Other _____

Second Reading/Big Idea
What's the main point or topic? (Fill in the box)

SEARCH

1. What two phrases does Paul use to describe what God's wisdom is not? (v. 6)

2. What two words does Paul use to describe where God's wisdom has been kept? (v. 7)

3. Why? (v. 7)

4. Why did all the rulers of the world from the beginning of time not respond to God's wisdom? (vv. 8-10)

5. Who finally came to understand God's wisdom? (v. 10)

6. Who makes possible the understanding of spiritual things? (v. 10)

---

warm, emotional attachment and the sense of belonging he had with his family and community. But his intellectual awakening has cut him off.

He might return, conform to the tribe's ways, but at the cost of denying himself. Or he might become embittered, cynical about society and truth and turn wholly inward.

He would have no one to trust, nothing to believe in, but himself.⁵

Think about It

1. Jot down a personal experience similar to that of the ostracized tribal wanderer. When your perceptions, knowledge, or values came under scrutiny, how was your faith affected? _____

_____

2. What tensions did you find between "personal" convictions and "interpersonal"

7. What explanation does Paul give for "lowly," ignorant people understanding spiritual things that wise people did not understand? (vv. 10-11)

8. What else does the Spirit bring besides spiritual understanding? (vv. 12-13)

9. How does a person who does not possess the Spirit of God look upon spiritual truth? (v. 14) Why?

10. What does the Spirit enable the believer to do? (vv. 15-16)

APPLY

Make a study of the word "wisdom" in this passage. First, jot down the verse reference and any information in this verse on the word "wisdom." Then put together a 25 word summary at the close.

FOR EXAMPLE
v.6   There are two kinds of wisdom . . . .

SUMMARY/25 words or less.

GROUP AGENDA

Divide into groups of 4 before you start to share and follow the time recommendations.

TO BEGIN/10 Minutes (Choose 1 or 2)

☐ Who do you consider one of the wisest people living today? Why did you choose this person? ☐ Who do you look up to for spiritual understanding and wisdom? ☐ How well did you keep secrets when you were a child? Who was one person in your life you enjoyed sharing secrets with? ☐ What did you jot down under READ?

TO GO DEEPER/20 Minutes (Choose 2 or 3)

☐ Share the SEARCH portion of the Bible study, one question at a time. ☐ What do you think was going on in the church in Corinth to require this response from Paul? ☐ Read Romans 1:20. What is it about God that can be clearly understood and what requires his own Spirit to understand? ☐ How would you summarize the nature of God's wisdom in this passage? ☐ Case History: Your friend has gotten into "meditation" through her interest in karate. Her teacher is into Tai Quandu, an Oriental religion that seeks to bring the mind and the body together through meditation. As a Christian, what do you say to your friend?

TO CLOSE/5-20 Minutes (Choose 1 or 2)

☐ What did you do in your word study on "wisdom"? ☐ When in your spiritual journey did the "mind of Christ" start to make a difference in your values, choices and decisions? ☐ What is a particular instance in which your outlook on life has changed since becoming a Christian? ☐ In practical terms, what does it mean to you to have the "mind of Christ"? What evidence can you point to this past year in which the "mind of Christ" has given you spiritual understanding?

expectations—between Character and Community? _____

3. What strategy did you follow, given these tensions? What resolutions (or partial resolutions) did you experience, if any?

_____

_____

4. If someone, who had an experience similar to yours approached you for advice,

what would you say?_____

_____

We teachers regularly and effectively confront the combined Community-Character theme through meaningful class discussion.[6] Successful facilitators know the necessary balance between personal and interpersonal dimensions of the dialogue method. In fact, as Stephen Brookfield (1990, pp. 201–2)

Illustration 12.2

UNIT 14—Warnings from Israel's History/1 Corinthians 10:1-13

TEXT

Warnings from Israel's History

10 For I do not want you to be ignorant of the fact, brothers, that our forefathers were all under the cloud and that they all passed through the sea. ²They were all baptized into Moses in the cloud and in the sea. ³They all ate the same spiritual food ⁴and drank the same spiritual drink; for they drank from the spiritual rock that accompanied them, and that rock was Christ. ⁵Nevertheless, God was not pleased with most of them; their bodies were scattered over the desert.

⁶Now these things occurred as examples,ᵃ to keep us from setting our hearts on evil things as they did. ⁷Do not be idolaters, as some of them were; as it is written: "The people sat down to eat and drink and got up to indulge in pagan revelry."ᵇ ⁸We should not commit sexual immorality, as some of them did—and in one day twenty-three thousand of them died. ⁹We should not test the Lord, as some of them did—and were killed by snakes. ¹⁰And do not grumble, as some of them did—and were killed by the destroying angel.

¹¹These things happened to them as examples and were written down as warnings for us, on whom the fulfillment of the ages has come. ¹²So, if you think you are standing firm, be careful that you don't fall! ¹³No temptation has seized you except what is common to man. And God is faithful; he will not let you be tempted beyond what you can bear. But when you are tempted, he will also provide a way out so that you can stand up under it.

ᵃ6 Or *types*; also in verse 11   ᵇ7 Exodus 32:6

STUDY

READ

First Reading/First Impressions

What's going on here? (Check two) □ Preaching □ Teaching □ Warning □ Comforting □ Pleading □ Defending □ Other _____

Second Reading/Big Idea

What's the main point or topic? (Fill in the box)

SEARCH

1. What does Paul do to warn against willful disobedience on the part of some people in the church at Corinth? (v. 1)

2. What five things does Paul cite that showed the privileged position of the children of Israel? (vv. 1-4)

3. Did such "sacraments" protect the Israelites? (v. 5) Why not?

4. Why has Paul recounted this lesson from history? (v. 6)

aptly summarizes, the fine art of leading discussion is nothing but balance—especially a balance of *others* and *self*:

> Discussion facilitation is essentially a question of balance. . . . Balance between accepting the contributions of confident and articulate group members, and arranging exercises which provide silent members with the chance to speak. . . . Balance between making sure every member's contri-

butions are respected and making clear that racism and bigotry are unacceptable. Balance between facilitators expressing their own opinions honestly and openly, and keeping these private so as not to give messages to participants regarding "approved" or "acceptable" views. Balance between emphasizing the connections of discussion themes to the immediate circumstances and concerns of adults' lives, and prompting learners to consider ideas and explore perspectives which they had

5. What four problems in the church at Corinth are warned against? (vv. 7-10) What happened to the children of Israel when they engaged in these activities?

6. Why does Paul warn the Corinthians in particular? (v. 11)

7. How does Paul encourage them "not to fall"? (v. 12)

8. What are four principles or statements Paul makes about temptation? (v. 13)

APPLY

Here is another one of those promises in the Scripture that you should commit to memory if you have not already. Photocopy the verse or write it out on a 3 X 5 card and place it on the dashboard or over the kitchen sink for constant reference. See if you can commit to memory this verse before your next group meeting.

"No temptation has seized you except what is common to man. And God is faithful; he will not let you be tempted beyond what you can bear. But when you are tempted, he will also provide a way out so that you can stand up under it."
1 Corinthians 10:13 NIV

GROUP AGENDA

Divide into groups of 4 before you start to share and follow the time recommendations.

TO BEGIN/10 Minutes (Choose 1 or 2)
□ What are two things you remember about your grandfather? □ Who is the big "storyteller" in your family—who keeps alive the stories of your family heritage? □ What did you jot down under READ?

TO GO DEEPER/20 Minutes (Choose 2 or 3)

□ Share the SEARCH portion of the Bible study, one person answering the first question, the next person the second question, etc. □ To what events in Israel's history is Paul referring in verses 1-5? (See Exodus 13-17) In what way are these events parallel to events in a Christian's journey today? □ What is the spiritual principle or lesson you get from this passage? What is the warning? What is the great promise? □ Case History: Your roommate grew up in a strong Christian home, went to a great church, and committed himself to Christ early in life. But something happened when he went away to college. He forgot about his spiritual roots, made fun of his "old fashioned" church, and delighted in "pushing the limits" against God. Last night, he asked if you minded if he brought his girlfriend to the room for the weekend. What do you say?

TO CLOSE/5-20 Minutes (Choose 1 or 2)

□ Check to see if everyone can repeat the Scripture verse word perfect. Encourage one another in this project. □ What kind of spiritual heritage did your forefathers leave you? What would you like to pass on to your kids? □ From your own experience, could you verify the promise in verse 13? How? □ What is one of the struggles you are dealing with now? What does God say to you about this struggle from verse 13?

---

previously rejected as being of no immediate relevance to them. Balance between meeting the declared felt needs of learners, and asking them to engage in activities which they initially resist. And balance between learners feeling enlivened by the joy of learning and being ready to face the anxiety and painful self-scrutiny sometimes involved in critical thinking.

Chet Meyers (1986, pp. 61–65) suggests five keys to creating and maintaining an interactive classroom: (1) begin every class with a controversial issue;[7] (2) use silence to stimulate reflection on problems; (3) arrange the classroom to encourage discussion; (4) whenever possible, extend class dialogue;[8] (5) create an inviting, hospitable environment. Whatever the method is called,[9] class dialogue is not without its benefits[10] as well as its risks.[11]

How do we Christian educators squarely confront Community-Character in the church? Illustration 12.2 provides one exemplary model. This material balances the "individual-among-the-group" needs of these twin themes. It encourages our adult learners to keep focused on both.

The historical study of the Old Testament provides invaluable lessons for contemporary believers. The essence of Paul's entire analogy derives from the Social Learning family. In particular, he portrays Israel as an ungodly model, a negative example to be avoided. Even though the chosen nation reflects the dark side of life, the teaching approach is just as effective as a positive image. Question 5 in the Bible study "Search" expresses one example of the Structured Modeling strategy: "What four problems in the church at Corinth are warned against (vv. 7–10)? What happened to the children of Israel when they engaged in those activities?" That is, Paul's case study of erring Israel represents an immoral lifestyle to forsake. The complementary issues of emulation and legacy continue throughout the lesson, as the last series of inquiries indicates: "What kind of spiritual heritage did your forefathers leave you? What would you like to pass on to your kids?" (see "To Close"). The latter question, in particular, features Spontaneous Modeling techniques. It causes the respondent to assess personal, firsthand accounts of familial faith-in-life.

Another predominant method highlights Information-Processing Learning. Numerous questions in the Bible analysis ("Read" and "Search") reveal this fact. Specifically, the first half points to the need for synthesis (i.e., "What's the main point or topic?"); the second part encourages analytical thought (e.g., Question 8: "What are the four principles or statements Paul makes about temptation? [v. 13]"). These questions support Inquiry Learning. In an adjoining curriculum article by John White (*not* located in Illustration 12.2), the topic of temptation is further analyzed. White chooses a musical analogy to explain his subject. In so doing, Identification Learning is addressed, as the reader is enabled to make more sense of temptation.

The Conditioning Learning family is also noticeable. In the "Apply" portion students are requested to write out 1 Corinthians 10:13 on a 3 by 5 card. The exercise, as well as the objective to memorize this verse, points to Consequence Learning. Where the card is placed—"on the dashboard or over the kitchen sink for constant reference"—recognizes the value of Cue Learning. The verse on temptation is now associated with everyday life settings.

Table 12.3 packages the above information about Illustration 12.2 in diagram form. Again, the learning families and respective avenues provide the necessary organizational grid.

Curriculum for Character

How do we encourage adults to assess and develop their true selves? How do we help them to evaluate inner struggles as well as victories? Ponder the following personal testimony of Charles Swindoll:[12]

> The longer I live, the less I know *for sure.* That sounds like 50% heresy . . . but it's 100% honesty. In my younger years I had a lot more answers than I do now. Things were absolutely black and white, right or wrong, yes or no, in or out, but a lot of that is beginning to change. The more I travel and read and wrestle and think, the less simplistic things seem. I now find myself uncomfortable with sweeping generalities . . . with neat little categories and well-defined classifications. Take people, for example. They cannot be squeezed into pigeon holes. People and situations are far more complex than most of us are willing to admit.

Table 12.3

Adult Curriculum for Community and Character

Information-Processing Family	Identification Learning	John White's article on temptation, associated with a musical analogy
	Inquiry Learning	Several Bible study questions that relate to the topic of temptation
Conditioning Family	Cue Learning	Daily reminders of the lesson verse on temptation, which have been written on a card and set in a noticeable place
	Consequence Learning	Writing out the lesson verse (1 Cor. 10:13) and committing it to memory
Social Family	Spontaneous Modeling	Contemplating and discussing how students plan to pass on their spiritual legacy to family members
	Structured Modeling	Studying the ungodly model of Israel in Paul's letter to Corinth

- Not all Episcopalians are liberal.
- Not all athletes are thickheaded.
- Not all Republicans are Christian good guys.
- Not all collegians are rebels.
- Not all artists are kooks.
- Not all movies are questionable.
- Not all questions are answerable.
- Not all verses are clear.
- Not all problems are easily solved.
- Not all deaths are explainable.

Maybe the list comes with a jolt. Great! Jolts are fine if they make you think. We evangelicals are good at building rigid walls out of dogmatic stones . . . cemented together by the mortar of tradition. We erect these walls in systematic circles—then place within each our over-simplified, ultra-inflexible "position." . . . Occasionally, however, a strange thing happens—a little restlessness springs up *within* the walls. A few ideas are challenged. Questions are entertained. Alternative options are then released. Talk about threat! Suddenly our overprotected, cliche-ridden answers don't cut it. Our simplified package offers no solution. The stones start to shift as the mortar cracks.

Think about It

Swindoll concludes that whereas we *all* encounter "cracks," none of us engage the same cracks. Which challenge to Character have you faced? What major changes in your views of life resulted? What has altered your perceptions of faith? It might help to replay a crisis or difficult experience. Jot down at least one personalized "crack" below. (We've provided a "crack" that we've experienced as professional educators to get you started.)

Our example: "Not all students with high GPAs are effective in Christian ministry."

Your Example: _____

_____

_____

Besides having different cracks, Swindoll (1983, pp. 320–21, emphasis added) adds that *we all respond to our experiences in diverse ways.* Contemplate his insights:

Two common reactions are available to us. *One:* We can maintain the status quo "position" and patch the wall by resisting change with rigidity. *Two:* We can openly admit *"I do not know,"* as the wall crumbles. *Then we can do some new thinking by facing the facts as they actually are.*[13] . . . No longer can we offer tried, trite statements that are as stiff and tasteless as last year's gum beneath the pew. *The thinking person deserves an intelligent, sensible answer.* He is weary of oversimplified bromides mouthed by insensitive robots within the walls. . . . If you've stopped thinking and started going through unexamined motions, you've really stopped living and started existing.

So, how do we proceed? How do we help adults confront Character? How do we enable them to be what God wants? Foundationally, we must facilitate critical thinking—specifically, critical thinking about their adult faith. We must call for adult convictions that are not surrogate.[14]

Many resources assist the serious and diligent Christian educator who is concerned about the theme of Character. Numerous human development studies point out the significance of critical thinking as it pertains to personal choice. Gail Sheehey (1976), for instance, speaks about the continuous tension of choices and commitment over against the desire for freedom.[15] The issue of choices permeates the research of Daniel J. Levinson (1978). He advances the theory that, throughout life, two prominent phases of maturity interact. One is the transitional (or structure-changing) period. But the other is the stable (or structure-building) period. It is in this latter category, Levinson contends, that we make key choices. These choices include relevant goals and values.[16]

Several other materials could be cited.[17] Yet, we will note just three outstanding resources that specifically value critical thinking aims for adults. Stephen Brookfield's (1987) contribution is germane to this instructional intent. Among other subtopics, Brook-

field describes the nature and components of critical thinking. Five phases in the process emerge: *a trigger event* (i.e., something that prompts a need to learn or grow); *appraisal* (of current conditions, including self-examination); *exploration* (i.e., searching for new ways to explain life's discrepancies or discomforts); *developing alternative perspectives;* and *integration* (i.e., determining which resolutions best meet needs and how they are woven into life). In addition, Brookfield offers ten useful strategies that elicit critical thinking.

A second text that captures the essence of reflective and critical thought is Thomas H. Groome's *Christian Religious Education* (1980). Besides necessary reflection and critique, his "shared praxis" concept prompts well-placed dialogue between teacher and student. As Groome shows, this educative approach parallels Christ's instruction on the road to Emmaus (see Luke 24).[18]

Sharon Parks' *The Critical Years* (1986) also provides an insightful look into the necessary cognitive skill development of adults. Building on the classic work of William G. Perry (1968), Parks condenses Perry's nine categories of cognition into four. She combines the adult's locus (or center) of authority with forms of faith (among other combinations). For instance, Parks (pp. 70–71) explains how an "authority-bound" brand of cognition—one that produces a dependent, others-oriented faith—might see God almost exclusively as a loving Parent "who cares for me and guides me." What's helpful about Parks' conceptualization is that it allows instructors to understand correlations among thinking patterns, emotional/social schemes, and faith modes.

In sum, these three texts permit Christian educators to visualize fuller dimensions of critical thinking. This trio respectively captures the nature, process, and associative forms found within the cognitive challenges of adult education.

One painless way to further cognitive skill development is presented below. Try out your inductive and deductive thinking abilities—and don't be afraid to have some fun in the process!

Think about It

Each of the First Church staff members eagerly plan to attend the annual Conference meetings. But lagging budget funds prohibit one of the three members from going. Dr. Ellison, the head pastor, can choose only two staff to accompany him. To complicate matters, some of the staff have been at odds with the other leaders; some have identified members that they refuse to attend with. Which two men finally went to the Conference?

List the two men that Dr. Ellison selected. Give their first and last names, and their staff responsibility.

1. Mickey refused to go with Mr. Newberry.
2. Mr. Sikes refused to go with the senior adult pastor.
3. Don refused to go with the youth pastor.
4. Tom is not Mr. Sikes.
5. Mr. Bautista is not the youth pastor.
6. The children's pastor is not Don.[19]

Curriculum for Commission/Character

A refreshing way to view this last theme investigates the meaning of "vocation."[20] One new-found synonym for the word, which Fowler suggests, is "partnership with God." Accordingly, several practical implications of Commission for adult ministry unfold. Fowler, for instance, offers at least six basic attitudes and habits that would be altered as "consequences of understanding our lives in terms of vocation":[21]

- People realize that their vocational callings are unique. Competition with others is reduced.
- We are freed from the anxiety that someone else might fulfill our particular calling.
- We rejoice in God's grace and favor in others, and are not threatened by them.
- We are freed from the false guilt to be "all things to all people." We find comfort in God's plan that we *each* have a task to perform. Nothing more; nothing less; nothing to sidetrack us.
- We are released from self-vindicating thoughts and behavior. We don't need to prove our worth. We seek the balance of time and energy in all of life's responsibilities (family, culture, and church).
- The tyranny of time itself no longer incarcerates us. We are given God's grace in life—and even in death.

Commission is never dull. It is sovereignly altered by changes in our lives. The configuration of our fourth theme responsibilities adjusts it in kaleidoscopic fashion. Fowler (p. 105) concludes that "A Christian view of the human vocation suggests that *partnership with the action of God* may be the single most fruitful way to finding a principle to orchestrate our changing adult life structures."

Think about It

---

1. Which of the six tenets above help you comprehend Commission better? Why? _____
   _____
   _____

2. Which statement(s) encourages you to more consciously engage this theme? Explain your response. _____
   _____
   _____

Illustration 12.3

UNIT 21—Love/1 Corinthians 13:1-13

TEXT

Love

And now I will show you the most excellent way.

13 If I speak in the tongues of men and of angels, but have not love, I am only a resounding gong or a clanging cymbal. [2]If I have the gift of prophecy and can fathom all mysteries and all knowledge, and if I have a faith that can move mountains, but have not love, I am nothing. [3]If I give all I possess to the poor and surrender my body to the flames, but have not love, I gain nothing.

[4]Love is patient, love is kind. It does not envy, it does not boast, it is not proud. [5]It is not rude, it is not self-seeking, it is not easily angered, it keeps no record of wrongs. [6]Love does not delight in evil but rejoices with the truth. [7]It always protects, always trusts, always hopes, always perseveres.

[8]Love never fails. But where there are prophecies, they will cease; where there are tongues, they will be stilled; where there is knowledge, it will pass away. [9]For we know in part and we prophesy in part, [10]but when perfection comes, the imperfect disappears. [11]When I was a child, I talked like a child, I thought like a child, I reasoned like a child. When I became a man, I put childish ways behind me. [12]Now we see but a poor reflection; then we shall see face to face. Now I know in part; then I shall know fully, even as I am fully known.

[13]And now these three remain: faith, hope and love. But the greatest of these is love.

[a]1 Or *languages*   [b]3 Some early manuscripts *body that I may boast*

STUDY

READ

First Reading/First Impressions

What's going on here? (Check two) ☐ Preaching ☐ Teaching ☐ Warning ☐ Comforting ☐ Pleading ☐ Defending ☐ Other _____

Second Reading/Big Idea

What's the main point or topic? (Fill in the box)

SEARCH

1. What are three "spiritual gifts" that Paul compares in importance to love, and how does each compare to love? (vv. 1-3)

2. What is his point?

3. What is love? List the 8 characteristics that love "is" and the 7 characteristics that love "is not." (vv. 4-7)

LOVE IS	LOVE IS NOT

---

3. What other deductions can you draw from these half-dozen ideas? Write one or two more expanded statements about Commission that could be added to this list. _____

_____

_____

Besides traditional forms of outreach, one refreshing example of Commission stresses a comprehensive focus on the church's work in the world. "The Shepherd's Center" model[22] is neither a "program" nor a "place." It's a ministry to (and with) older adults,[23] "a process that grows out of the needs of persons in a specific population base; it would seek to work with those persons to enable them to remain independent as long as feasible and

GROUP AGENDA

4. What contrast does Paul make in verses 8-12?

5. Why will spiritual gifts cease to be relevant? (vv. 11-12)

6. What three things carry over into the new age? (v. 13)

APPLY

Take the first phrase of verse 4: *"Love is patient,"* and rewrite this phrase in your own everyday speech . . . putting into your own translation what this *really* means at home, school, work, etc.

Love will not blow its top when things go wrong — even though my kid borrows my screwdriver for the fifth time in a week and loses it — love will not take out its anger on my kid.

Be honest to the verse, whether you are this way or not!

Then take the next phrase: *"Love is kind,"* and rewrite this, etc. When you are through, you should have verse 4 in your own everyday language and everyday situation. "Love is patient, love is kind. It does not envy, it does not boast, it is not proud."

Divide into groups of 4 before you start to share. And follow the time recommendations.

TO BEGIN/10 Minutes (Choose 1 or 2)

☐ When you were a child, who did you feel loved you the most? ☐ What is the most important quality to you in a loving relationship? ☐ Outside of your family, who made an indelible impression on your life because of their unconditional love for you? ☐ What did you jot down after reading this passage on your study sheet?

TO GO DEEPER/20 Minutes (Choose 2 or 3)

☐ Share the SEARCH portion of the Bible study, one person sharing question 1, the next person number 2, etc. ☐ One Bible scholar has said that Paul was able to write eloquently about love because of his own struggle to be a loving person. How do you feel about this? Do you think that certain people are naturally more loving than others? What is the difference between being "naturally loving" and the love that Paul is talking about? ☐ Case history: Tony Compolla, a sociologist, says that the average person will fall in and out of love seven times before getting married, and seven times after marriage. Your friend has just gone through one of those cycles and comes to you in tears. How would you counsel this person from your own experience?

TO CLOSE/5-20 Minutes (Choose 1 or 2)

☐ Share your paraphrase of verse 4 from APPLY. ☐ When, if ever, have you been burned in a "love relationship"? What went wrong? How was the love in that relationship different from the love Paul is talking about? ☐ What have you learned about love in the past six months? ☐ How would you paraphrase the last verse in your own words?

---

to find meaning and purpose in their later years" (Vogel 1984, p. 146).

Four overarching objectives, or areas of direction, are described by Elbert C. Cole (1981, pp. 264–65), one of the center's early influential guides: (1) life maintenance ministry—servicing basic physical needs; (2) life enrichment ministry—servicing an array of educational interests and human talents; (3) life reconstruction ministry—servicing life change and crisis needs; and (4) life transcending ministry—servicing ultimate issues of legacy and eternal hope.[24]

As Linda Jane Vogel (1984, p. 147) notes, the theological assumption that undergirds the Shepherd's Center rings clear. In brief, the spiritual axiom that is upheld "is that the Judeo-Christian traditions can be the source for finding meaning and purpose in life. Faith communities are called to nurture and sustain persons because of their views about God and persons." Vogel (pp. 144–45) correctly observes that we Christian educators must be aware of every premise that shapes our ministries. To do less shows poor stewardship. She poses ten superb suggestions for consideration.[25]

To correlate with the Character theme, Commission necessitates personal choice. We leaders must encourage adults to become intentionally involved in outreach, without falling into typical extremes.[26] Again, Commission means "partnership with God." Therefore, we must help people feel compelled to serve—but not out of guilt, or pressure, or even tradition and precedent. "What is it," we should enable adults to ponder, "that I—and I alone—can do for the kingdom, by God's grace?"[27]

One of the most specific applications of this challenge for teachers is raised by Guy Rice Doud, former National Teacher of the Year. Doud (1990) implements the truth of Matthew 25 in the classroom. He cites the fundamental need for instructors to love the unlovely, to help all learners visualize their particular life purpose. As this is done, the gospel is explicitly proclaimed.

Commendable curriculum for Commission (integrated with Character) is featured in Illustration 12.3. What evidence of each "family" method can you locate?

A good example of the Information-Processing family, once again, surfaces in the Bible study "Search." For instance, Question 3 sets up a contrast of what love is and what it is not (i.e., Inquiry Learning). A complementary article by Lewis B. Smedes (*not* found in Illustration 12.3) uses many life analogies to explain Paul's well-known treatise about love. Thus, Identification Learning relationships are drawn.

Social Learning is promoted at the lesson's start. Examples of human love are favorably recalled by students (see "To Begin"). This is yet another instance of Spontaneous Modeling. A case history (see "To Go Deeper") proposes one more exercise in Social Learning (via Structured Modeling of a hypothetical situation). The final

Table 12.4
Adult Curriculum for Commission and Character

Information-Processing Family	Identification Learning	Lewis B. Smedes' article of life analogies, pertaining to the "love" chapter (1 Cor. 13).
	Inquiry Learning	Identification of what Christian love is and is not.
Conditioning Family	Cue Learning	Linking the student's social experiences with Scripture. In addition, learners paraphrase 1 Cor. 13:4.
	Consequence Learning	Students are encouraged to share their paraphrase of 1 Cor. 13:4.
Social Family	Spontaneous Modeling	Students recall personal, affirming examples of human love.
	Structured Modeling	Students participate in a case study. The final question, "How would you counsel this person from your own experience?" identifies intentional approaches to modeling.

question ("How would you counsel this person . . . ?") points to planned approaches of modeling.

Cue and Consequence Learning (Conditioning family) both find representation in the "To Close" section. First, a reflective evaluation links individual experience with Scripture: "When, if ever, have you been burned in a 'love relationship'? What went wrong? How was the love in that relationship different from the love Paul is talking about?" These helpful "cues" personalize the passage. Also, students paraphrase 1 Corinthians 13:4. Second, Consequence Learning appears in the last assignment, where students are requested to share their paraphrase.

Table 12.4 summarizes the previous paragraphs in chart form. All six learning families are featured, as the themes of Commission and Character are addressed.

Evaluating Published Curriculum

We cannot afford to make false assumptions about adult students' readiness or willingness to learn. Neither can we jump to untested conclusions about professionally prepared curriculum. For our own good, we must raise constructively critical issues: Should we teachers always use professionally written material? Should we write our own? Do we try a combination of these two alternatives?

Advantages and disadvantages accompany the choice to use professionally written materials. There are many benefits. We receive well-constructed lessons, typically written by age-level specialists. We inherit a cohesive teaching plan, usually organized in units. Topical as well as biblical subject options abound. A consistent instructional model is followed, indicating strategies and methods. We can count on additional helps, such as student guides and audiovisual material. Also, costs and services are reasonable for these teaching tools.

The major disadvantage is that we tend to become too dependent on this curriculum. Whether we know it or not, our creative ideas dry up. There's a tendency to think that professionally written material is "teacher-proof." We put so much faith in it, we forget our personal responsibility. "The curriculum can almost teach, by itself," we think. We neglect specific needs of our particular class. We play down preparation time. "Since it contains everything from the experts," we rationalize, "what do *I* have to contribute that's worthwhile?" Subconsciously, we give in to the notion that purchased curriculum can stand on its own.

It would seem that, in most cases, a combination of *curriculum-dependent* and *curriculum-independent* strategies yields the best teaching results. The instructor begins with independent factors, asking basic (yet particular) questions like: (1) What is *my* specific purpose? (2) Who are *my* learners (e.g., their needs, motivations, spiritual gifts, etc.)? (3) What setting do *I* anticipate (e.g., location, time allotted, facilities, etc.)? When we fail to create an evaluative grid that is personalized—and independent—we become too easily swayed by professionally written materials. For example, if we reverse the process and get too excited by an excellent, published simulation game that we read—before assessing our own setting—we might forget we have only half the students the game requires. Also, we may overlook the time needed to debrief such an exercise. For that matter, we may neglect the fact that our adult students have never participated in such an exercise. They may lack the necessary skills and, perhaps, interest. Only when our particular plans have been preliminarily sketched should we employ professionally written material. Still, at that point, we must regularly make adjustments—even during the instruction time—for a correct fit between purchased curriculum, our ideas, and our class.

Customizing purchased curriculum to our individual setting, then, diminishes our dependency. Stated positively, we are prone to meet specific needs of the particular students we know, as we adapt professional curriculum.

Moving from Dependency

Certain elements of comprehensive instruction must be noted, then, if we want to correlate meaningful learning with adult teachable moments. Specifically, a trio of balanced concepts advance effective instruction:[28]

- Adult education that is Christian is not just *cognitive* but *affective*.
- Adult education that is Christian is not just *personal* but *interpersonal*.
- Adult education that is Christian is not just *formal* but *informal*.

Often, when we uncritically utilize published materials, we inadvertently accommodate the first aspects of this threesome, without the second. In practice, we may end up unconsciously adopting an educational philosophy that—when investigated—we don't fully accept. To correct this imbalance, we must recall our own past. How did *we* learn? What personal memories can *we* remember? Perhaps to our surprise, we'll find that *our* meaningful learning included: (1) emotional, volitional, and value-laden experiences (i.e., "affective"); (2) memorable times with other people (i.e., "interpersonal"); and (3) educative moments beyond the four walls of any classroom (i.e., "informal"). Certainly the cognitive, personal, and formal components of adult instruction yield rich rewards; but these features never

exhaust comprehensive biblical teaching and learning.

With this balanced trio of concepts in mind, then, the following hypothetical scenario moves us away from prepublished curriculum dependency. It concentrates on a plan for adult leadership training, by minimizing a detailed prescriptive design. Conversely, it values spontaneous participant input. This scenario pictures the initial stages of instruction for a local congregation. Although the details are purposefully sketchy, the plan adheres to our earlier noted advice: To reduce curriculum dependency, we must start with *our* customized purposes. We must draft a scheme that reflects *our* people, *our* convictions, and *our* needs. Then, and only then, must published curriculum be entertained. Throughout the planning process (and even *during* the instructional time itself) *our* team must retain *our* personalized concerns.

Four factors shape this educational plan for adult leadership instruction:

Setting: A camp or retreat facility is selected to meet the (unheralded) affective, interpersonal, and informal needs of church leadership development.

Staff: All new and experienced church officers are invited to attend the retreat. Also, interested members are encouraged to come.

Season: The training is scheduled on a weekend, soon after church officers and personnel have been elected or appointed.

Strategy: Four problem-related phases of leadership training[29] frame the weekend training agenda. Subsequent instruction, offered throughout the year, expands the insights raised from this weekend.

Phase 1: "Walk and Talk." Retreat participants ponder: What godly leaders have I observed in my life? How did they approach their leadership tasks and still remain aware of me, as a person? Participants recall exemplary believers. Cognitive and affective domains converge. This contemplative task is assigned to clusters of two or three people. Group members walk around the campgrounds or locate a quiet spot at the retreat. They identify particular leadership character qualities, along with one actual illustration for each quality. Insights are eventually reported to and then compiled for the entire group. This concludes the first phase and provides a smooth transition to the second.

Phase 2: "Check It Out." Participants conduct small group Bible studies on "What is a godly leader?" Study options include character sketches, character traits, or godly versus ungodly contrasts. Participants choose their area of preference.[30] Again, small group discoveries are ultimately relayed to the entire assembly. Notice that the Social Learning family is featured in Phases 1 and 2. Specifically, the former points to Spontaneous Modeling, the latter to Structured Modeling in Scripture.

Using the Information-Processing Learning family method, biblical findings from Phase 2 are correlated with Phase 1 comments. Certain aspects are singled out and examined as they pertain to specific local church concerns. For example, drawing from a familiar passage, participants are asked: "What does it matter that David was 'a man after [God's] own heart' (1 Sam. 13:14)? How should this truth affect leadership training at *our* church? From personal examples you have recalled (Phase 1), what do you think David's virtue would actually look like in real, twenty-first-century life?" Identification Learning (i.e., use of a familiar passage) merges with Inquiry Learning (i.e., discerning the correlation between David's testimony and modern-day training).

Phase 3: "Brainstorm Possible Processes." To this point, we have helped retreat participants reflect on influential leaders from their past and study what Scripture says leadership looks like. Now, we must investigate the possible ways we get from here to there. What potential processes exist for leadership development? What steps are necessary (e.g., should we use an apprenticeship plan?) What administrative styles might be employed in these processes? What do we want all leaders-in-training to experience? How does Scripture shed light on "process"? Remember: This phase is *not* evaluative. In brainstorming procedures, numerous suggestions should be encouraged.

Think about It

Read Matthew 17:24–27. Matthew discloses just one of many times that Jesus intentionally instructed his disciples for leadership. List as many suggestions from this leadership training process as you can find in these four verses. What did the Master Teacher *do* with Peter to encourage his growth and responsibility? _____

_____

_____

Compare your insights with some of our ideas.[31]

Again, Phase 3 brainstorms all possibilities. Options are wide open. Divergent thinking occurs. Closure comes only in the final phase.

Phase 4: "The Game Plan." Fairly detailed ideals have been identified so far. Moving from "what is" to "what should be" is never easy. Yet the descriptive-to-prescriptive thinking about leadership training deserves attention. "What do we do now?" is asked. The final step relies on responsible planning.

First, follow up on Phases 2 and 3. Small groups select one or two of the "process" statements they want to investigate (any one of the eight factors in Endnote 31 could be analyzed). They ask "Which ideas best serve *my* interpretation of biblical training for *our* church?" Related questions include: What meaningful and relevant plans frame my view of leadership development? Are our training tasks specific and realistic? Are our people matched with leadership chores, according to their giftedness? What forms of accountability exist in our plans?

After one or two of these process statements are selected for study in small groups, details of the "game plan" are organized. For instance, if an Inquiry Learning approach to training is valued, then specific learning strategies are employed. Several methodological routes could be employed. Retreat leaders could use a case study to stimulate discussion.

To summarize, this entire educational plan for adult leadership development reduces dependency on published curriculum. By observing a basic, four-part instructional sequence, retreat coordinators can achieve their customized purposes. This represents a significant accomplishment. Professionally prepared material may offer helpful, though supplemental, assistance.

Conclusion

In Herman Melville's *White Jacket,* we see what Christian educators should *never* do in adult ministry.[32] Unfortunately, it's what often occurs. Dr. Cuticle, Melville's ship surgeon, diagnoses a crew member's ailment. He then prescribes a radical leg amputation. He fashions an ignoble medical team from among the shipmates to assist in the operation. The eccentric Dr. Cuticle then becomes so enamored of the surgery itself, *he forgets about the patient.*[33] At one point, the ship surgeon gets so wound up in his lecture that his assistant pulls Dr. Cuticle aside to hand him his synthetic teeth![34] But the exclusive focus on the operation continues. During the infrequent times that the doctor does pay attention to the patient, he patronizes or criticizes him.[35] It comes as no surprise that, in the end, the patient dies long before the surgery is complete. The surgeon's staff, well-aware of this fact for some time, fail to interrupt Dr. Cuticle's monologue, out of respect for authority!

We need to take a kinder approach to our "patients." We need dedicated teachers who are not myopically focused on the "operation" of instruction.

By *no* means does this diminish skills of exegesis and lesson preparation. By *every* means, this urgent plea heightens our broader task. We must, like the Master Teacher, have command of the truth and show sensitivity to individual adults. On the Emmaus Road (Luke 24) Jesus never traded one ability for the other. Before he customized God's revelation to the two disciples, he first comprehended their particular needs. He "read" their nonverbal behavior, their despair. He listened intently to their understanding—yes, even their misbeliefs—concerning the Messiah. Then, *and only then,* did he explain God's truth to them. He illustrated where and how they misrepresented the prophet's insights. He restored their hope.

To avoid "Cuticle catastrophes" in Christian education, we need to recapture Christ's insightful Emmaus strategy. As wise servants, we must maintain the balance between prepared, *anticipated* plans and resources (including published curriculum) and *actual* strategies that we use (including the Holy Spirit's guidance during the lesson).[36]

13 Teaching Youth

Nature, Culture, and Fable
Dominating Forces
Strategies
Conclusion

Nature, Culture, and Fable

Chameleons possess the uncanny ability to alter their skin color—from brown to green, from green to brown. Some chameleons even remain partly brown and partly green because of the contrasting colors on which they crawl.

When it comes to identity formation, youth are much like chameleons. They're fickle. They'll change allegiances instantaneously. They will even identify with two different worlds simultaneously.

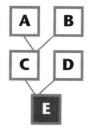

Besides skin color, chameleons adapt to their environment in other ways. If their tail is snapped off, it grows back. Also, they take full advantage of their independently moveable eyeballs. Their name literally means "lion on the ground." And, although they don't possess many of the attributes of the jungle king, chameleons do master their environment. Versatility and resilience are characteristic of a chameleon.

Robert J. Lifton, a Yale psychiatrist, pioneered studies of persons who adapted to large-scale crisis events (such as the survivors of Hiroshima and Nagasaki). Patterns of coping strategies gradually emerged, although the varying crisis situations were unrelated. Lifton noted certain internal skills of adaptability. Searching for an analogy in Greek mythology, Lifton rediscovered Proteus, a sea god capable of assuming different forms. More versatile than the chameleon, Proteus could become a dragon or a lion or even a flash flood. But Proteus' strength was, likewise, his weakness. He could become other forms easier than he could become himself. "What [Proteus] did find difficult," Lifton (1971, p. 319) explains, "and would not do unless seized and chained, was to commit himself to a single form, a form most his own."

Youth often succumb to their internal weaknesses, like Proteus, when determining their own identity. At times, they appear to be least like their true self.

James W. Fowler draws upon the mythological analogy of Proteus, too. He contrasts it with the static "tepee model" of human development theory. In so doing, he introduces the external dimension of identity formation that youth face. The tepee model refers to societies that powerfully influence their members. These societies institute strict cultural traditions that shape personal values. For instance, a society might directly affect a participant's religious choice, economic standards, and social obligations. These norms are mostly rigid and non-negotiable. They portray predetermined, self-standing structures.

Proteus found it most difficult to become his true self. Internal strength failed him in the end. Tepee model societies inhibit character formation for a different reason. They indiscriminately bypass the

individual's search for personhood. Personal perspectives are circumvented. By imposing prescribed roles and rules, members face external pressure regarding identity concerns. Fowler (1984, p. 14) suggests that these two dominant caricatures of human development and culture represent extreme points of a continuum. Fluidity and uncertainty are positioned over against stability and static qualities.

> I believe that the tepee and the Protean models depict, in polar tension, two yearnings and realities that pull powerfully at one another in the hearts of each of us and in the culture of which we are a part. These yearnings and realities— the experience of relentless change and the longing for continuity and stability— persist and conflict in the midst of the shifting tectonic plates of values and convictions underlying our societal and cultural life.

In one way, Proteus parallels Lewis Carroll's Mock Turtle in *Alice in Wonderland*. Neither character knew who they were. Both responded dysfunctionally to reality. When initially approached by Alice, the Mock Turtle exhibited despair, "sighing as if his heart would break." Alice asked why the Mock Turtle was sad. She was informed that his emotions were all contrived. "It's all his fancy, that; he hasn't got no sorrow, you know," she was told. Like Proteus, teenagers fashion themselves according to diverse circumstances. They grope for identity. Their most difficult challenge is to determine who they are, who God created them to be. Like the Mock Turtle, adolescents also grapple with their actual and imagined worlds. What is real? What is illusionary? What is contrived?

Contemplate your own adolescent years. Which were the toughest choices you had to make? What embarrassing moments did you experience? Which human development issues bothered you the most? What kinds of pressure did you feel from other youth? What expectations from adults surfaced?

From your responses to these questions, provide two specific, personal illustrations for each category below:

1. Give examples of *internal* turmoil from your youth.
   a._____
   _____
   b._____
   _____

2. Give examples of *external* challenges you faced.
   a._____
   _____
   b._____
   _____

Dominating Forces

There are two prominent influences in the adolescent's struggle for identity formation: *internal* and *external forces*.[1] The former focus on developmental realities; the latter highlight societal and cultural issues.

Internal Forces

In *Five Cries of Youth* (1974), Merton Strommen ascertains that the preeminent adolescent need is due to self-hatred. His study of seven thousand high schoolers reveals that self-hatred results from low self-regard, distress over personal faults, and lack of self-confidence. Robert Laurent (1988), obtaining similar findings from his smaller (four hundred teens) survey, notes the significance of low self-esteem. Laurent's research intentions were to decipher the top ten causes for teenage rejection of religion. Poor self-image came in fourth place. The specific chapter title, which details his findings in one phrase, says it all: "If Ugly Was a Crime, I'd Have Been Born in Jail."

Internal Thoughts about Self

David Elkind's work permits us to comprehend some of the complicated reasons behind a young person's low self-perception. He outlines three myths (or misbeliefs) that teens adopt to persuade themselves.[2] Myth 1 is *"Everybody's watching me."* Teens think abstractly. We've analyzed this phenomenon already. With this newly inherited ability comes "good news" and "bad news." The good news is that they are no longer limited by childlike reasoning patterns.[3] The bad news is that they refocus their highly critical thoughts inward. Youth possess a knack for recognizing phonies. Using the same evaluative patterns, they turn on themselves. Overly self-conscious, they become their own worst enemy.[4] They become increasingly oriented to self. Pimples and fashion take on new significance.

If these pressures weren't enough, a powerful mental shift in social perspective comes full cycle. It includes a more sophisticated view of others. Teens not only believe that everybody's looking at them. They believe that everyone knows that *they* know that *others* are observing *them!*

Elkind (1984, p. 33) calls this first myth the imaginary audience. Youth think they're on stage, and the whole world is watching. Whereas adults slip in and out of this mindset—sometimes as major, sometimes as minor players—young people are not afforded such luxury. To carry through the analogy, teens incessantly view themselves as lead (versus supporting) actors/actresses. They always occupy center stage.

Myth 2 is *"I'm the only one."* Extending the consequences of self-consciousness, adolescents are prone to extreme selfishness. "Egocentrism" is the technical term. A girl might have a crush on her youth pastor, because she's certain he likes her more than other group members (even though he doesn't express it). A young teen might exclaim, "Nobody knows how I feel!" He might say this when receiving a low grade in school or being unable to find a best friend. He alleges his predicament is unprecedented. Taken to another extreme, an adolescent might believe *she* could never die of cancer; *she* would never go hungry; *she* would never be the cause of a divorce. Elkind (1984, p. 36) labels this second assumption the personal fable.

Again, adults also tend to retain greater or lesser degrees of this self-talk. We tell ourselves, "I'm special." Taken in moderation and grounded on a biblical foundation, such intrapersonal communication is healthy. Anyone who reads Psalm 8 recognizes there exists a noble expression of self-identity, rooted in our creation. Adults may propagate their own brand of misbeliefs with statements like: "Others may have rebellious children who leave the church, but I won't." Or "Other people might not discover God's will, but I'll find it." It boils down to misunderstanding our special-ness—somehow believing we are immune or exempt from the mainstream of life. Youth distort this reality exceptionally well.

Myth 3 is *"I've done my part."* The first myth depicts self-consciousness; the second self-centeredness. This last myth features self-accomplishments. Following the first two, this perspective is also significantly warped.

One advantage of formal operational thought is that youth can determine an insightful answer to a difficult problem. The downside is that they are often unable to follow through on long-term plans that match their ideals. Zeal is short-lived. Their short-sightedness should be anticipated by us adult leaders. Long-term commitments made by youth must be prudently weighed in this light.

One of us organized some local church teens with the intention of firsthand missions education. We went to a city rescue mission, had a tour, and listened to the director speak. During two consecutive weekly meetings, the teens took on the project of painting the mission facility. For some of the youth, a subsequent hunger for more missions' participation evolved. They opted for a three-month evangelistic challenge. For the majority, however, a grave danger emerged: They believed they had done enough. Following their two-week stint, "missions" could be checked off their "to do" list. They had accomplished their part.

Internal Need for Others

Adolescents rivet themselves to heros and heroines. It's the rare youth who is not totally committed (at least for *this* week) to a musician, television character, sports star, or the like. (This is precisely why Social Learning theory expresses a commendable strategy for teen instruction.) Teenagers expend much time, energy, and money with friends and media (music, television, magazines, movies, etc.). They desire leaders. They seek worthy causes. They affiliate with those who share their allegiances.

Besides their innate drive for models, young people continue to mature in their cognitive abilities. They are able to hypothesize, scrutinize, and speculate with their new reasoning powers. The combination of these two qualities (modeling needs and reasoning abilities) signals a dangerous mix. Like old Western movies in which prospectors painstakingly carted nitroglycerine across the Rockies in buckboard wagons, adult workers must proceed cautiously with adolescent ministries. The infamous cry of teens, "Hypocrites!" reflects just one example of this potent combination. They are now developmentally equipped to comprehend what the *perfect* parent, pastor, and teacher should be like. They tenaciously grasp—and expose—the glaring differences between the ideal and the real.

External Forces

Structured Modeling

The explosive potential of youth is exacerbated by the media, in general, and by television, in particular. Neil Postman (1985) offers an exceptional and concise critique of this latter point. He claims that television replaces facts with emotions and opinions; that commercials portray all problems as easily solvable; that television implies "being sold solutions is better than being confronted with questions about problems" (p. 131); and that present-centeredness is valued above historic contributions or the call to prepare for the future. In brief, television teaches teens that theirs is a quick-fix world. Postman states that the media, which advance such life perspectives, affect us all. But

> One can hardly overestimate the damage that such juxtapositions do to our sense of the world as a serious place. *The damage is especially massive to youthful viewers who depend so much on television for their clues as to how to respond to the world. In watching television news, they, more than any other segment of the audience,* are drawn into an epistemology based on the assumption that all reports of cruelty and death are greatly exaggerated and, in any case, not to be taken seriously or responded to sanely.
>
> I should go so far as to say that embedded in the surrealistic frame of a television news show is a *theory of anticommunication,* featuring a type of discourse that abandons logic, reason, sequence and rules of contradiction. In aesthetics, I believe the name given to this theory is Dadaism; in philosophy, nihilism; in psychiatry, schizophrenia. In the parlance of the theater, it is known as vaudeville. (p. 105)

Spontaneous Modeling

Vernon and Carlos loved basketball. The church team provided an outlet for their passion. Carlos was a very responsible thirteen-year-old. He was punctual. He was disciplined. He gave everything he had. It came as no surprise, therefore, that Pastor Mike (the youth worker, who doubled as coach) could count on Carlos. In practice, Carlos complied with every instruction. He ran laps with gusto. He dribbled with both hands, as he was told. He followed shooting drills precisely, and paid full attention when Mike blew the whistle. When scrimmages were called, Carlos came in his complete uniform, pressed and tucked in.

Everything that Carlos was, Vernon was not. Marching to the beat of a different drummer, Vernon cut corners on his laps and dribbled only with his right hand. Following the whistle, Vernon would always take one last shot.

Oh, one more fact: Carlos was 4'8" and Vernon was a well-developed six-footer.

Finally, after endless practices, the evening of the first league game arrived. Parents and friends gathered in the small gym. Like clockwork, Carlos was there twenty minutes early, uniform pressed and tucked in. Carlos anxiously awaited the coach's pep talk.

When the coach arrived, however, it wasn't Carlos he noticed. It was Vernon, standing there in street clothes. The six-footer had forgotten his uniform. Scolding by the coach served only as temporary coping strategies; it elicited embarrassing grins from Vernon. In the hastily made decisions that followed, .it was Carlos, not Vernon, who found himself in shock. At the coach's command, the smaller boy mechanically peeled off his jersey and handed it to his irresponsible teammate. Carlos was consigned to an obscure end of the player's bench. "Keep the stats," he was told. Feelings numbed, Carlos obediently complied, once again.[5]

Think about It

Provide brief answers to the following inquiries.

1. What did Carlos "learn" from this basketball experience?_____

_____

_____

2. Describe what Vernon might have been "taught."_____

_____

_____

3. How will this encounter affect the way that Carlos and Vernon interact?

_____

_____

4. What will Carlos now hear the next time Pastor Mike teaches about fairness and justice in Sunday school?

_____

_____

Whether they knew it or not, Vernon and Carlos had just been educated. Mike served as youth pastor, coach, *and teacher*. Formal curriculum was absent. In fact, there were no textbooks or homework assignments. Nevertheless both young men were instructed in formidable fashion. They were taught lessons not soon forgotten. Most significant, perhaps, was that Vernon and Carlos were left alone to discern what lessons they had mastered. Nobody debriefed their instruction.

Among other lessons learned, Vernon and Carlos were introduced (or reintroduced) to *external* challenges in their lives. The youth leader/coach taught that hard work *doesn't* always pay off; if you're a six-foot teen you've got it made. Life *isn't* fair. The boys learned about adult priorities, too. The value of "win-at-all-costs" competition was communicated.[6] Possibly the most tragic lesson of all was that the teens' stature—something they had absolutely no control over—was highly prized. They learned lessons through Spontaneous Modeling.

Internal and External Forces

James Marcia (1966) identifies certain factors that generate "cracks" in human development. Building on the work of Erikson and others, Marcia studied phases of identity formation in older youth and college-age adults.[7] He discovered four distinct categories.

Identity diffusion signals a state of noncommitment. Few, if any, personal beliefs are found in these people. Friendships are superficial and often quickly abandoned. *Identity foreclosure* means that cues that help determine personhood are other-directed, not inner-directed. Pastors, parents, employers, and friends provide all answers to questions about self. Symbolically, a "closed" sign hangs in the window of the soul. *Identity moratorium* appears to look like "diffusion" to an outsider; few commitments are evident. Yet, the real difference is substantive: "Moratorium" holds off on personal decisions that matter, in order to test and contemplate alternatives. *Identity achievement* speaks of struggles like personal crisis and confrontation, yielding commitment. Ownership of ideas surfaces, refined in the fires of diverse life experiences, value conflicts, and meaningful decision making.

We teachers should assist youth to comprehend who they are and who God is helping them to become. Only as they reach

Marcia's "identity achievement" stage will they be able to constructively address three related themes of reconciliation. James W. Fowler (1987, p. 87) issues a sobering conclusion here. His extensive research findings merit serious consideration for Christian ministry: "It seems clear to me after a number of years of observation that we cannot be more intimate *with others* than we are ready to be *with ourselves*. Similarly, we cannot be more intimate *with God* than we are prepared to be with ourselves and others."

Strategies

If the church is to be effective in nurturing its young people, it must constructively confront the teens' potent combination of critical thinking and models. Leaders must blow the whistle on unjust external pressures. Biblical principles concerning adolescent culture must be analyzed and biblical solutions implemented. Implications of Postman's "theory of anticommunication" must also be addressed. Three particular strategies of effective youth work surface at this juncture.

Formal and Nonformal Instruction

One way to accomplish the objectives of youth ministry is assessment of the music videos, soaps, commercials, and sitcoms that adolescents witness.[8] This approach intentionally confronts Structured Modeling influences. Table 13.1 offers guidelines for teen workers who desire youth participation in such formal media critiques.[9]

Youth require much more than formal, four-walled classroom training. They demand flesh-and-blood representations of faith. For this reason, we turn our attention to pertinent details about Spontaneous Modeling.[10]

One of the most beneficial summaries of effective modeling principles has been compiled by Larry Richards. Drawn from the behavioral science literature, Richards' study affirms theological directives as well. Our modification of his seven points (see Table 13.2) sets us on track to provide youth with the nonformal instruction they require.

Think about It

1. In your opinion, which of Richards' seven principles are central to successful youth ministry? Select two concepts that you consider most crucial:

   a._____

   b._____

2. Briefly explain your selections. Why did you choose these two? _____

   _____

3. Which of Richards' seven principles do you believe is the most abused or neglected in youth work? What leads you to this conclusion? _____

   _____

Jerome Kagan (1972, p. 103) reminds us of the importance of peers to youth: "The earliest adolescent wants many friends, for he needs peers to help him sculpt his beliefs, verify his new conclusions, test his new attitudes against an alien set to evaluate their hardiness, and obtain support for his new set of fragile assumptions."

Ralph Keyes (1976, p. 183) in his insightful text, *Is There Life After High School?* refers to the "especially impressionable stage" of adolescence. He reverses one traditional view that teens are strongly influenced by adult values. Keyes claims that "adult values grow directly out of high school" (p. 182). Mike Yaconelli and Jim Burns (1986) report on the impact of peer pressure and social groupings. Curriculum materials consistently attest to the significance of social ties for teens.[11]

Table 13.1

Guidelines for a Biblical Critique of Media

1. To encourage a silent member in discussion:
   "Teresa, from your perspective as a senior, how do you interpret this biblical imperative, as it pertains to the sitcom you observed?"

2. To support expression of feelings and Christian values:
   "How does this Scripture passage challenge one typical way our culture views this moral controversy?"

3. To call attention to issues that have not been raised:
   "Is something missing here? If you take an alternative perspective to what has already been stated, what do you come up with?"

4. To foster reflective skills and statements of personal experience:
   "In two minutes, I will ask for each of your responses to this topic. So, jot down one or two relevant examples you can share about this question: 'How does this video exaggerate—even lie—about what you know to be true?'"

5. To maintain the focus of the discussion topic:
   "That's interesting, Sid. Now, how do we bring these comments to bear on our subject?"

6. To utilize conflict constructively:
   "Since we can't seem to come to a conclusion on this theme, can we move on to the next point? Perhaps further information will clarify the issues at stake."

7. To suggest that additional information is needed to continue productive discussion:
   "Look carefully at the context of this passage. Notice what the author says just before and after our Scripture. Does this new information shed any light on what's been said?"

8. To cite the source of information:
   "Okay, that's a good caution to remember, Ted! Can someone other than Ted tell us where in the Bible this warning is found?"

9. To check the degree of acceptance for a particular viewpoint:
   "Some of the commentators agree with that perspective; some don't. By raising your hands, how many here agree?"

10. To concentrate on the subject rather than on distracting personalities or groups that might be connected:
    "Are we placing too much attention and emotion on secondary topics here? Perhaps we're overreacting or being uncritical of heros and heroines we have."

11. To prevent a few monopolizers from dominating the conversation:
    "Excuse me, Yvonne. Before you continue, may we hear from someone who hasn't expressed an opinion?"

12. To raise the need to make a procedural decision:
    "Now, we've spent about ten minutes on this particular subject. Earlier we planned to discuss two more, related themes. Do you want to continue with our present topic or discuss the other two?"

13. To state the need to close the discussion:
    "May we have two or three more final remarks as we close tonight?"

14. To address the matter of follow-up:
    "In review, what have we all decided to do in preparation for our next Bible study session?

Source: Adapted from Potter and Andersen (1976, pp. 51–52).

In the end, it comes down to modeling. It's not a question of *whether* youth will emulate others; it's a question of *whom*. Who will be their heros and heroines? The church has the responsibility to provide alternatives to worldly leaders through two sources: godly peers and godly adults. Ya-conelli and Burns (1986, p. 107) advance constructive suggestions for the former category.[12] Technically, this group influence is called "peer ministry."

1. Adolescents should not just *go* to youth group; they should be allowed

Table 13.2

Principles of Effective Modeling

1. Youth need to have frequent, long-term contact with the model(s).
2. Youth must experience a warm, loving relationship with the model(s).
3. Youth should be exposed to the inner values and emotions of the model(s).
4. Model(s) for youth need to be observed in a variety of life settings and situations.
5. Model(s) need to exhibit consistency and clarity in behavior and values.
6. There must be compatibility between the behavior of the model(s) and the beliefs and standards of the model's larger community (e.g., the parachurch group).
7. There should be explanations of the model's lifestyle, along with accompanying life demonstrations.

Source: Modified from Richards (1975, pp. 84–85).

to *do* the youth group. Kids should have the opportunity to use their gifts in your youth ministry program, not just to occupy a seat and watch.

2. Provide lots of small group activities in which kids (without adults or with silent adults) discuss the lesson and come up with their own conclusions. Small group activities are the primary source of peer ministry opportunities. Too many youth groups either don't have small groups, or, when they do, use them to accomplish some activity rather than share with each other.
3. Keeping a journal and letter writing provide great opportunities for peer ministry.
4. Service projects are another great environment for peer ministry.

When it comes to the complementary need for godly adults, a team is required. Les Christie cautions against the Lone Ranger mentality. This attitude prevails not only in megachurch youth ministries but in small teen groups as well. Christie advises youth pastors to recognize the value of an adult team and to foster a variety of adult models.[13] He (1987, pp. 17–18) delineates a helpful rationale:

> Maybe you're wondering, *Why do I need other adults working beside me? I can handle these few kids on my own.* Even if I had only a handful of kids in my group, I would still recruit other adults to work with me—not because of *my* needs, but because of the kids' needs. Kids need a variety of adult models.
>
> Any adult who will interact with kids regularly becomes a model to them. In recruiting a team of adults, look for a variety of role models: married couples, singles, young adults, older folks. Youth will respond differently to different people. Kids need to see the quiet adults, the thinkers, the huggers, the zanies, the serious, the jocks, and the nerds. They need to see the deeply religious and experienced as well as the recently committed Christian.

Finally, Doug Stevens (1985, pp. 127–28) provides very practical means by which adult team members can get to know their young people. Remember: Intentionality lies at the heart of effective youth work. Table 13.3 expresses a modified version of Stevens' ideas.[14]

Table 13.3

Practical Ways to Strengthen Relationships with Youth

Get to know your teens as you:

Go to a school athletic event.

Take a teen along on one of your errands (driving time in a car facilitates conversation).

Play miniature golf.

Go to a worthwhile movie.

Go to the beach or lake.

Go out for ice cream.

Work on or fix something.

Loan a teen a good Christian book or CD and discuss it later.

Make a casual telephone call.

Attend a school play or musical.

Drive a teen home after school.

Watch a television show together.

Arrange to meet a teen during the lunch hour.

Drive a teen home after a youth-group event.

Meet for breakfast before school.

Have a girls' slumber party or a guys' overnight (based on the leader's gender).

Help a teen with homework.

Write a letter, note, or card.

Following an activity, go out to eat on the way home, to talk.

Play games like ping-pong, basketball, or chess.

Take a walk or go hiking.

Drop by with one of their friends.

Begin this relationship-building process as you:

Develop a roster of the youth group.

Make a note to yourself of teens to see and call.

Call them up.

Make an appointment at the youth-group meeting.

Volunteer to pick them up.

Ask their good friends to bring them.

Call to confirm just ahead of time.

Source: Modified from Stevens (1985, pp. 127–28).

Anticipated and Actual Instruction

Adolescents learn much about life and faith outside the classroom. This comes as no surprise. Teens are regularly influenced beyond the four walls of any formal setting—where published curriculum rarely extends. Yet only prudent instructors recognize that such out-of-class influences significantly affect in-class instruction. Youth bring their unique convictions, moods, perceptions, understandings, experiences, questions, and values into every formal setting. Consequently, curriculum publishers can only make educated guesses about the teenagers who will come into classes. Pro-

fessionally written material, at best, *anticipates* what *actually* happens.

A profoundly simple theory, which helps teachers distinguish these categories of "anticipated" and "actual," was constructed by Robert Stake (1967). This theory was briefly discussed in Chapter 10. We now consider it in greater detail for the purpose of practical classroom use. A modified version of the Stake model is presented in Table 13.4.[15]

Table 13.4

A Modified Overview of Stake's Curriculum Model

PROFESSIONALLY WRITTEN IDEAS FOR *ALL* CLASSROOMS	INSTRUCTION ACTUALLY ACHIEVED *PER* CLASSROOM
Anticipated Preliminaries	Actual Preliminaries
Anticipated Plans	Actual Plans
Anticipated Performances	Actual Performances

Source: Adapted from Stake (1967).

The left half of Stake's model, in top-down vertical sequence, identifies: (1) all anticipated factors *before* instruction, including motivations and experiences of students and teacher; (2) all hoped-for interaction *during* instruction, including student with teacher, environment, God, and other students; and (3) all intended results *after* instruction, including revised attitudes, new-found knowledge, and life application.

The right side of the Stake model repeats the same before-during-after categories, but details what *actually* happened. To repeat what was said earlier, because of these various and uniquely functioning classroom dynamics, *no teaching experience is ever the same.*

Using the *Stake* model as a point of departure, then, several valuable questions can be raised to encourage effective teaching and learning. Table 13.5 provides a representative list of such inquiries.[16]

An added bonus of the *Stake* model surfaces when educational evaluation is conducted. If quality control is taken seriously, at least a half-dozen inquiries must be raised, following each teaching opportunity. Figure 13.1 reflects these sample questions.

What does the *Stake* model look like in action? How does it assist conscientious teachers who want to facilitate growth in their adolescents? Suppose you planned a summer-long youth discipleship training program. *Anticipated preliminaries* reveal that you plan to hold Friday night Bible studies from 7:00 to 8:30 P.M. at the church. The intended size is a dozen high schoolers who show interest and promise. *Anticipated plans* include a brief time of prayer and singing, along with an extensive, exegetical study of Romans. Youth are expected to be faithful in attendance and to participate by taking notes. Completion of weekly home-

Table 13.5

Implications of Stake's Curriculum Model

CURRICULUM IDEAS	ACTUAL TEACHING
BEFORE: Anticipated Factors Preceding Class 1. Will you have the full time you are expecting? 2. Can you expect a blackboard? 3. What extra materials will you need for the youth? 4. Will the room be properly heated or cooled?	*BEFORE:* Actual Factors Preceding Class 1. Did my time get cut short or was it extended? 2. Did someone take the blackboard? Was chalk available? 3. Did I have enough pencils, pictures, and handouts? 4. Did the heating/cooling system work as I anticipated?
DURING: Anticipated Class Experiences 1. How should you begin in a way that will get teens interested in the Bible? 2. What passage of the Bible will you teach? 3. Should you lecture, do an inductive Bible study, hold a class discussion, or use diagrams on the board? 4. How many adolescents do you anticipate? 5. Which youth will bring Bibles?	*DURING:* Actual Class Experiences 1. Did the lesson introduction begin well? Did it interest my young people? 2. Did I actually finish the whole passage? 3. Did I use the methods I was planning to use or did an alternate method arise? 4. Did all youth come that I expected? 5. Did my expectations match the number of Bibles brought? Were they used, like I expected?
AFTER: Anticipated Results from Class 1. What life issues would you like the youth to struggle with, as a result of a deeper understanding of Scripture? 2. What characteristics of a Christ-like life would you like to see more consistently evidenced in your youth? 3. What changes in habits would indicate that students actually learned?	*AFTER:* Actual Results from Class 1. What hints do I have that these issues were dealt with by students? Did I have a realistic understanding of their prior Bible knowledge? 2. What indications do I have that my teens are struggling to evidence these characteristics? 3. What habit changes do they talk about, or have I seen?

Note: The left-hand and right-hand column questions are matched horizontally. This is indicated by similar Arabic numerals.

Figure 13.1

Evaluative Questions Based on the Stake Model

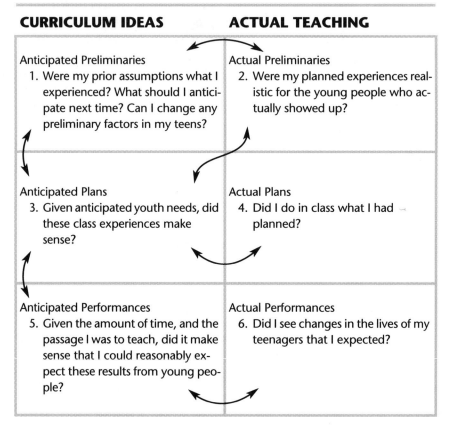

CURRICULUM IDEAS

Anticipated Preliminaries
1. Were my prior assumptions what I experienced? What should I anticipate next time? Can I change any preliminary factors in my teens?

Anticipated Plans
3. Given anticipated youth needs, did these class experiences make sense?

Anticipated Performances
5. Given the amount of time, and the passage I was to teach, did it make sense that I could reasonably expect these results from young people?

ACTUAL TEACHING

Actual Preliminaries
2. Were my planned experiences realistic for the young people who actually showed up?

Actual Plans
4. Did I do in class what I had planned?

Actual Performances
6. Did I see changes in the lives of my teenagers that I expected?

work assignments portrays one *anticipated performance.* Scripture memory and genuine enthusiasm for God's Word are among other expected outcomes.

Actual preliminaries, however, make you more conscious of reality. Only eight youth attend, because of summer jobs and other commitments. Also, you discover that the last two weeks of August are reserved for vacation Bible school—a church ministry that invariably requires teenage workers. By way of impact, the summer discipleship program is reduced to two-thirds size and is dropped from twelve to ten weeks. *Actual plans* show that teens take careful notes, but they want more from the program. They also want an applicable missions project. So for the final half of the summer, they implement their particular study by adapting the Roman Road[17] method of evangelism. *Actual performances,* consequently, are dramatically altered. The eight teens enthusiastically witness in a city park for five consecutive Saturdays. Their prayer time at the Bible study takes on a new focus; their singing is more authentic; discussion questions emerge with renewed spirit. All these instructional "plans" are directly affected by "performances" and vice versa. Furthermore, "preliminaries" shift weekly. The youth who began the summer training are not the teens of mid-August. A transformation has occurred in their lives.

A. Review Figure 13.1. In your opinion, which of the six questions provide particular insight into more effective youth instruction? Why? _____

_____

_____

B. Pretend you are leading a teacher's training workshop for adults who work with youth. State three specific pieces of information (or advice) that you would share with these adults based on the Stake model.

Item 1 _____

_____

Item 2 _____

_____

Item 3 _____

_____

_____

The Stake model reminds us that professionally written curriculum, at best, provides only half of a teaching lesson (i.e., the left side). We educators must supply the other half, in the classroom.

Teaching Reconciliation

The first two strategies for youth education focus on contrasting tensions: (1) we need to teach adolescents via formal as well as nonformal means; and (2) we must concentrate on anticipated as well as actual details of teaching. The third strategy represents the overarching instructional aim for *all* age groups. It expresses the four themes of the Reconciliation Model. Although these themes should characterize all of Christian education, we leaders must be sensitive to age-specific peculiarities. Teens' needs nec-

essarily dictate the way we approach the themes for youth.

Conclusion

Among other significant topics in this chapter, we've stressed the value of teamwork. Peer ministry and adult workers[18] portray two conceptual examples. Besides the pragmatic value of teamwork, biblical references also lend support to this view. The Lone Ranger syndrome runs contrary to biblical motifs of accountability and the wisdom derived from group counsel. Also, this "me-against-the-world" mindset results in pain and burnout.

Through the following light-hearted parable, these detrimental features of soloing are identified. The tale is based on a health insurance claim. The policyholder, a bricklayer, filed a claim concerning a job-related accident. In response, the insurance company requested more information on the disability claim. Here's the laborer's second letter:[19]

I am writing in response to your request for clarification of the information I supplied in block *number eleven* on the insurance form, which asked for the cause of my injury. I answered, *"Trying to do the job alone."* I trust the following explanation will be sufficient.

I am a bricklayer by trade. On the date of the injury, I was working alone, laying brick around the top of a three-story building. When I finished the job, I had 500 lbs. of brick left over. Rather than carry the bricks down by hand, I put them into a barrel and lowered them by a pulley, fastened to the top of the building.

I secured the end of the rope at ground level, went back to the top of the building, loaded the bricks into the barrel, and pushed it over the side. I then went back to the ground and untied the rope, holding it securely to insure the slow descent of the barrel. As you note on block *number six* of the form, I weigh 145 lbs. At the shock of being jerked off the ground so swiftly by the 500 lbs of bricks in the barrel, I lost my presence of mind—and forgot to let go of the rope.

Between the 2nd and 3rd floors I met the barrel. This accounts for the bruises and lacerations on my upper body. Fortunately, I retained enough presence of mind to maintain my tight hold on the rope and proceeded rapidly up the side of the building, not stopping until my right hand was jammed in the pulley. This accounts for my broken thumb (see block *number four*). Despite the pain, I continued to hold tightly to the rope. Unfortunately, at the same time the barrel hit the ground, the bottom fell out of the barrel. Devoid of the weight of the bricks, the barrel now weighed 50 lbs. I again refer you to block *number six,* where my weight is listed. I began a rapid descent.

In the vicinity of the 2nd floor, I met the barrel coming up. This explains the injury to my legs and lower body. Slowed only slightly, I continued my descent, landing on the pile of bricks. Fortunately, my back was only sprained. I am sorry to report, however, that I again lost my presence of mind—and let go of the rope.

I trust this answers your concern. *Please note that I am finished trying to do the job alone.*

Effective youth ministry calls for team response. Teens need other teens. Teens mature through multiple adult models. At best, this team strategy expresses the body of Christ at work.

14 Commendable Youth Curriculum

Protestant Cats?
Basketball Flashback
Curriculum for Reconciliation
Conclusion

Protestant Cats?

No doubt about it, youth are different than any other age group. We can't expect them to demonstrate adult faith and life; but neither should we settle for childhood expressions. David Elkind (1984, p. 33) contrasts the child's thought processes with the teen's new reasoning powers:

> Formal operations make it possible for young people to think about thinking. Children think, but they don't think about thinking. For example, in a study I conducted on children's conception of their religious denomination, I asked, "Can a dog or a cat be Protestant (or Catholic or Jew, depending upon the denomination of the child)?" Regardless of religious denomination, children said that a dog or a cat could not be Protestant, Catholic, or Jew because the minister, priest, or rabbi would not allow the animal in the church or the synagogue. "They would make noise and run around!" one child explained.

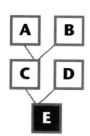

Teenagers, on the other hand, uniformly offered a different answer: "They are not intelligent; they would not understand religion." Others said, "They don't believe in God." Concepts like "intelligence" or "understanding" or "belief" are ideas about thinking that children rarely use but teenagers use with increasing frequency. Teenagers can think about thinking, about what goes on in their heads and what goes on in the heads of others.

Think about It

Few Christian educators have bothered to think through implications of the teen's new-found reasoning abilities. Try these questions yourself:

1. Based on their maturing intellect, what new types of truth can we now teach youth (i.e., things we cannot teach to children)? _____

   _____

2. Reflect on Elkind's closing sentence: "Teenagers can think about thinking, about what goes on in their heads and what goes on in the heads of others."
   a. List one specific, positive implication for youth education (i.e., What subjects should we teach, knowing this fact?). _____

   _____

   b. Provide one negative implication from this quote (i.e., based on new anxieties within youth). _____

   _____

Basketball Flashback

Whether we know it or not, we teach youth every single time we encounter them. Our instruction may not be intentional or even conscious, but it is just as real. Contemplate your own adolescent experiences.

Remember the time you were pleasantly surprised by a teacher in your teen years—an instructor who held the door for you, or gave you a word of encouragement, or exhibited mercy for a late assignment. How about the teacher who let you down—who embarrassed you in public, who displayed a poor witness for Christ? Every time we teach, we make a deposit into a teen's "bank of memorable instruction." Learning involves both credit and debit accounts.

Reconsider Carlos and Vernon. This time, evaluate the scenario according to the four themes. What were Carlos and Vernon taught about *Character?* How did the coach react to Carlos' admirable quality of self-discipline? How about *Community?* What lessons of competition were stressed? What effect do you anticipate that this theme had on the two boys as they gathered for other church youth functions? What values of *Commission* permeated this educational experience? What personal contributions were prized? Do you think Vernon sensed any guilt from being rewarded with Carlos' game jersey? Finally, what did Pastor Mike teach the young adolescents about *Communion?* How did this unjust setting affect the boys' relationship with God? What deductions might Carlos draw about other areas of his spiritual walk?

The questions we adult leaders should regularly raise include: How are our youth taught the themes of reconciliation? What is being neglected? Are we doing anything that is counterproductive to these intended aims?

Curriculum for Reconciliation

If we plan to teach comprehensive Christian education to youth, then we must faithfully attend to all four themes of reconciliation. This chapter features detailed illustrations of each theme from commendable youth curriculum. Two particular publications are examined throughout,[1] although other material could also be analyzed.[2] Since Social Learning theory expresses a formidable instructional strategy for teens, the theme of Community is particularly emphasized in the subsequent section.

Communion

Stephen D. Jones describes patterns of spiritual formation. He provides special insight into how youth grow close to God. Childhood up through half of midteen life is labeled "affiliation" years by Jones. Children through middle adolescence primarily come to their faith by intimate social groups. They accept spiritual realities, for instance, because their parents want it that way or because it pleases their grandparents. The latter half of high school to mid-twenties are the "personalizing" years. More ownership of faith is anticipated. Adhering to another organizational scheme, Jones elsewhere delineates three chronological categories relevant to adolescent growth (see Table 14.1). Specific descriptions by Jones (1987, p. 54) advance the serious challenges of youth Communion needs.

One beneficial feature of Jones' theory is that he offers directives to adults who want to help youth mature. Teen ministry workers, as well as parents, should be trained to confront seven particular formation tasks (see Table 14.2). According to Jones, these seven aims precisely correlate with the adolescent's sequential trials of faith.[3]

For teens and adults alike, Task 6 in Table 14.2 represents the most difficult challenge. It's not easy to watch young peo-

Table 14.1

Adolescent Faith Development

LATE CHILDHOOD AND EARLY TEEN YEARS (junior and junior high years)

- Taking first steps beyond parental or societal expectations of faith
- Living with intense conflicts between internal and external belief systems
- Beginning to understand and assert personal values, perspectives, and needs regarding faith
- Affiliating with one's faith community via "a personal decision," such as confirmation or baptism

MID-TEEN YEARS (high school years)

- Increasing tension between inherited and personalized faith
- Lessening of parental faith influence; heightened influence from other adults and peers
- Asserting individuality and identity, venturing beyond previous limits
- Being authentic to one's own chosen faith
- Experiencing diverse range of faith activity

LATE TEEN YEARS AND EARLY TWENTIES (post-high school, college, early career)

- Experimenting with novel ideas of faith; showing signs of restlessness
- Formulating the most important life directions amidst erratic faith growth
- Rebelling against parental influence and separating from one's own heritage of faith
- Coping with adult independence; recognizing the challenges and limits of one's own faith shaping

Source: Adapted from Jones (1987, p. 54).

Table 14.2

Adult's Tasks for Teen's Faith Trials

Teen's Trials of Faith	Adult's Faith-Shaping Tasks
#1 – EXPERIENCING *Youth encounter spiritual feelings*	Be receptive to multiple emotions. Do not judge too quickly. Encourage feelings that lead to fuller expression of self. Allow youth to express themselves openly. Build memorable experiences. Model your own feelings. Do not stop with feelings. As teens are ready, encourage them to move to the next challenge.
#2 – CATEGORIZING *Youth sort out feelings, values, and experiences*	Study Christian ideas and values together. Involve teens. Do not focus on particular answers; provide a broad framework. Develop character, as a person who can be trusted. Never ridicule ideas, no matter how ludicrous they appear. Be accepting. Do not take everything too seriously. Be affirming. Provide honest feedback. Do not agree dishonestly with everything uttered.
#3 – CHOOSING *Youth decide what is true for them*	Encourage youth to think. Challenge them! Model your own values and choices. Focus discussion on beliefs that can be discerned and selected. Teach youth how to doubt constructively, to arrive at more authentic beliefs. Take advantage of their increasing ability to think abstractly and critically. Employ case studies and real-life dilemmas.
#4 – CLAIMING *Youth determine to which truths they will be loyal*	Plan many invitations to faith commitment in a variety of settings. Talk to youth individually and intimately about their own decisions of loyalty. Create appropriate times of celebration when "claiming" occurs. Be certain to provide follow-up support after such decisions. Do not treat claiming as an end in itself but as one step in a lifelong process. Teach youth how to pray for divine wisdom and open themselves to spiritual transformation.

ple struggling through this phase of spiritual development. Yet James promises that "the testing of your faith develops perseverance" (1:3). To this biblical axiom we add that scrutinizing—even separating from—faith often yields deeper commitment. David Elkind (1984, p. 43) gives parallel advice to adults who want to nurture youth, commenting that they should "provide opportunities for the social interaction and discussion of values, beliefs, and actions that young people need to discover who and what they really are."

Dewey Bertolini (1989) suggests that one fundamental approach to Communion is to cultivate a "heart" for youth ministry, to be genuine. Specifically, he believes that as adults grow in their love for God, they'll love youth more fully. Adults who model this vertical dimension of faith nourish themselves in the Word (1 Tim. 4:6) and "relentlessly avoid error" (1 Tim. 4:7a). Jim

Table 14.2 Continued.

Teen's Trials of Faith	Adult's Faith-Shaping Tasks
#5 – DEEPENING *Youth mature in their active faith*	For youth who are ready, provide appropriate intellectual stimulus (e.g., an apologetic study of the cults). Develop realistic expectations. Share the depth of your faith, your struggles, your questions, your growing edge. Be a helping and enabling person. Let them know that you undergird them with your prayers and support.
#6 – SEPARATING *Youth question and/or set aside faith for a time*	Do not be disappointed or worry unnecessarily as this occurs. Express honest reactions, but give freedom and respect to separated youth. Never let this trial sever relationships. Open and trusting communication is the key. Keep in touch! Work together with parents and other adults who have been affected by their own sense of guilt, despair, or failure. Help everyone to see the purpose of this phase. Celebrate new growth as it occurs.
#7 – RESPONDING *Youth commit to God's will for them*	Encourage this response when the person is ready. Initiate only with great sensitivity. Portray callings as personal, noble, and dynamic. Study gifts and prayer/meditation with youth. Always affirm a teen's gifts, abilities, and talents. Provide a warm, positive atmosphere for youth to experiment with their own mission and purpose in life.

Source: Adapted from Jones (1987, pp. 60–61).

Burns (1988, p. 104) interjects the value of intentionally focusing on worship. He observes that when adolescents "have developed the skills to worship God, then young people can have a regular and meaningful worship experience even in the confines of a more traditional church."[4]

Two particular aspects of Communion require attention: *public* and *private* domains. We often think in terms of corporate gatherings only. But "private time" or "devotions" are critical to youth ministry, too. David Lynn and Mike Yaconelli (1985) supply suggestions for private worship and growth.[5] Using a journal to report signs of growth, this resource is more than a fill-in-the-blank approach to spirituality. Along similar lines, Bertolini (1989, p. 20) offers guidelines for maturity from Psalm 119. Table 14.3 displays how leaders and teens should revere Scripture. Bertolini's chart portrays a helpful representation of confronting Communion through God's Word.

Public worship complements private worship. Active involvement by *all* participants is the key. Leaders should, therefore, be reluctant to quickly and uncritically accept the teen's cry that worship services are always irrelevant. Burns (1988, pp. 104–5) gives this insightful advice: "When kids say the worship service is boring, we shouldn't apologize because it didn't meet their need. We must first help them understand for themselves whether in fact it really wasn't

Table 14.3

A Personal Inventory of Private Worship

Look at Psalm 119. Its 176 verses express in clear terms the psalmist's heartfelt commitment to the truth of the Word of God. Does your heart echo these same thoughts? "How blessed are those who observe His testimonies, who seek Him with all their heart. They also do no unrighteousness; they walk in His ways" (vv. 2–3). God's ways, as expressed in his Word, are:

- to be rejoiced and delighted in (vv. 14, 16)
- filled with wondrous things (v. 18)
- a reviving force and strengthening power (vv. 25, 28)
- to be cleaved to and trusted in (vv. 31, 42)
- to be kept continually forever and ever (v. 44)
- to be loved (v. 48)
- our comfort (v. 50)
- righteous judgments (v. 62)
- better than thousands of gold and silver pieces (v. 72)
- trustworthy and eternal (vv. 86, 89)
- never to be forgotten (v. 93)
- making us wiser than our enemies (v. 98)
- giving us more insight than our teachers (v. 99)
- giving us more understanding than the aged (v. 100)
- sweeter than honey to our mouths (v. 103)
- a lamp to our feet and a light for our paths (v. 105)
- the joy of our hearts (v. 111)
- our hope (v. 114)
- wonderful and longed for (vv. 129, 131)
- thoroughly tested (v. 140)
- truth (v. 151)
- founded by God forever (v. 152)
- awesome (v. 161)
- the songs of our tongues (v. 172)

Source: Modified from Bertolini (1989, p. 20).

relevant or whether they simply came with low expectations (which were then met). Since worship is an active response, we must help the young people understand why and how they can and should participate."

Portions of Gospel Light's *The Complete Junior High Bible Study* (also titled "Light Force") series and Rick Bundschuh's (1989) *On-Site* have been selected as commendable youth material. Like the professionally written lessons in Chapter 12, these samples were chosen for two reasons: (1) each lesson addresses at least one of the themes of Christian maturity; and (2) each lesson demonstrates one or more of the three families of learning.

The first selection, "Jesus Makes It Possible," typifies exemplary material appropriate to Communion (see Illustration 14.1). Junior high students discover the vibrant, vertical dimension of faith that only the Lord provides.

In this first example, the Conditioning family appears in the following ways. *Cue Learning* is recognized (1) as the students' curiosity is aroused by the suspense of an unopened letter (see "Creative Alternative"); and (2) as the students' interest is piqued through a class game. Hidden clue cards foster this interest (see "Bible Exploration," Step 2). In short, these methods subtly affirm that "learning Bible truths can be fun."

Consequence Learning includes: (1) the pleasure of enjoying a Coke with the teacher, if unopened letters are faithfully returned to class (see "Creative Alternative"); (2) a contest, promoting "a small reward" (see "Bible Exploration," Step 2); and (3) the creation of three slogans that point to a relationship with God (see "Bible Exploration," Step 3). Notice that the instructions for this slogan exercise reinforce a superb definition of *Communion:* "These slogans should help people see how God has reached out to establish a relationship with us, and what we have to do or don't have to do to gain that relationship."

Illustration 14.1

Jesus Makes It Possible SESSION 2

WHAT THE SESSION IS ABOUT

Christ is the One who makes a relationship with God possible.

SCRIPTURE STUDIED

Ephesians 2:1-10

KEY PASSAGE

"For it is by grace you have been saved, through faith—and this not from yourselves, it is the gift of God—not by works, so that no one can boast." Ephesians 2:8,9

AIMS OF THE SESSION

During this session your learners will:

1. Examine how God through the ultimate gesture of love restored humanity's relationship with Him;
2. Write slogans about the relationship God wants to have with them;
3. Consider their personal relationship to Christ and their need to begin or renew that relationship.

INSIGHTS FOR THE LEADER

God created us as special people: as people who have worth and value, as people with whom He wants to have a relationship. Last week's session focused on this truth.

In this session you and your class are going to look at the barrier that stands in the way of the relationship that God wants to have with us, and at what He did to remove that obstacle in order to enable us to have that relationship.

Dead in Your Transgressions

Ephesians 2:1-10 is the Scripture for the session. Paul begins the passage by reminding the believers of how they used to live. Students who have been raised in the warm environment of a godly home and who have had great input from the Scripture may find it difficult to identify with the life-style Paul describes. Some young people even feel that they have missed something in their conversion experience if they didn't have to crawl out of the "pit of sin" or didn't get saved from something tangible and dramatic like drugs, crime or immorality.

Actually no one has to look very far to get a good dose of "the ways of the world" described by Paul. The apostle has not provided a list of specific sinful acts. He has instead put his finger on the root of all problems: willful disobedience against God caused by a sinful, selfish nature that seeks to satisfy its own desires. That old self-centered nature still

clings to even the most devout saint. It is not necessary to go out and prove that you have it. A careful self-examination will reveal much more than we usually admit. It is this rebellion against God and His rule that shattered the connection between God and humanity, leaving people physically alive, but literally dead towards God and His benefits.

Sin has done more than just add some flaws to otherwise nice people. It has destroyed any capacity to win back a relationship with God. Dead men tell no tales, nor do they repair the damage that killed them. Therefore, humanity's only hope is for God to take action.

Alive with Christ

Paul says, "But because of his great love for us, God, who is rich in mercy, made us alive with Christ even when we were dead in transgressions" (Eph. 2:4,5). God wants a relationship with the people He created. Christ is the arm of God reaching out to reverse the damage caused by sin.

Although the passage does not speak specifically about Christ's sacrifice for our sin, there is obvious allusion to it. Your more mature Christians will quickly discern this.

The magnificence of Christ's work on our behalf dramatically emphasizes that there is nothing that we can do through our own efforts to earn this relationship with God. It is only by trust in and reliance on Jesus Christ that anyone comes to know the Creator. "For it is by grace [favor you don't deserve] you have been saved [rescued], through faith [trust, reliance on God]—and this not from yourselves, it is the gift of God—not by works [your own effort, goodness and striving], so that no one can boast (Eph. 2:8,9, with explanations). Just as God created people originally, with no human advice or assistance, so He now re-creates us "in Christ Jesus," by His grace and power. Good works can never create new life in the spiritually dead. But once we are alive in Christ, good works are the result God seeks, evidence that He has changed us from the self-centered, rebellious people we were before.

The passage clearly shows helpless humanity being rescued by a loving and caring God through a huge sacrifice on His part. Some of your students may have heard this many times, and the session will be a review for them. But perhaps there are several in your class who are new or who come from backgrounds where the gospel message is a strange language. Perhaps there are some who just recently have developed "ears to hear," and the truth that they have heard over and over again has finally sunk in. Others may now, for the first time, be developing a true appreciation for God's understanding love for them.

God wants to have a relationship with you and each member of your class. He sent His Son in order to make that relationship possible. What should you and your students do? There are many ways to respond to the truths that your class will examine in this session. Some may want to get to know God for the first time, to take advantage of the offer of a relationship with Christ. Others, who already have that relationship, may want to thank Him for what He did in reaching out to them, or to share that message with others. Some may wish to become more serious about their faith and/or about some Christian discipline that they need to strengthen.

Some of your students may not be ready for a relationship with God at the present time. They may realize that such a relationship will cost them something in terms of their friendships or activities. They may need to wrestle with God some more before they are ready to receive Him and enjoy His love.

In the Conclusion of this session your students will have an opportunity to respond to Christ. Some may wish to have further dialogue with you before making a decision, so make sure to contact those who have so indicated. Pray for those who have expressed needs and doubts. Be available to offer support to your learners in the spiritual struggles that they may face.

NOTES

NOTES

SESSION PLAN

BEFORE CLASS BEGINS: Photocopy the Gateway student worksheet and Fun Page take-home paper. See the CREATIVE ALTERNATIVE under the ATTENTION GRABBER for important instructions and materials required. The EXPLORATION also requires special preparation.

Attention Grabber

ATTENTION GRABBER (3-5 minutes)

Distribute paper and pencils. Have each student write a paragraph about a time that he or she came *close* to winning or achieving something good. After your class has finished ask, **What are some of the times that you have come close to winning or achieving something good?**

Allow a few students to share, then wrap up with something like this: **We have been talking about coming close to achieving something but yet missing it. The Bible tells us that this is the same kind of situation that everyone faces in having a relationship with God. You see, God is perfect. Imperfection cannot come into His presence, just as light cannot exist alongside darkness. Turn on a light and the darkness ceases. People are not perfect. If you doubt that, just look around. But God wants a relationship with us anyway. Today we are going to see what God has done in order to initiate that relationship with you that He wants to have.**

CREATIVE ALTERNATIVE (2-3 minutes)

Materials needed: Paper, envelopes, stamps, mailing list or addresses of class members (for a letter to be sent in advance of the class session).

Preparation: The week before this class session write a letter that says something like this: "Thank you for being a part of my class. As a reward for bringing this letter to class unopened, I want to invite you to have a Coke with me this week." (You can make the reward anything you like.) Make a copy of the letter for every student in your class. Fold the letter so that it cannot be read through the envelope if held up to a bright light. In bold letters on both the front and the back of the envelope write, "Bring this letter to class with you UNOPENED this Sunday morning." Send the letter so that it arrives early in the week before class.

When students arrive with their letters, ask, **How many of you can honestly say that you did not open your letter? How many of you tried to read your letter by holding it up to the light? How many of you tried to steam open your letter?**

After the class has responded, let them open the letters. Record the names of those who will be entitled to enjoy the reward. (Make sure you follow up on this.)

Tell your class, **You may be wondering what the point of this stunt was. I wanted to demonstrate to you how difficult it is for people to follow certain kinds of commandments. Most of you wanted to open the letter all the more just because it said not to, whereas if it were a piece of junk mail you might not have bothered to open it at all.**

If we had to please God with our own efforts in order to have a relationship with Him, we would have to follow His commands to the letter because God is perfect and can not allow imperfection into His presence. As you can tell from our experiment, it is very hard to obey even very simple commands. In fact, Jesus went so far as to say that if you even want to do something wrong it is the same, in the sense of rebellion, as if you had done it (although it may not have the same social consequences). It is this tendency to disobey, to do our own thing, that leads us to disobey God—to sin.

I think that this object lesson can help us see something about our own sinful nature. Today we are going to see what God did for us because of that sinful nature, how He went to the greatest lengths of love to establish a relationship with us.

Bible Exploration

EXPLORATION (25-35 minutes)

Before class begins, cut apart the 9 questions on the Teaching Resource page. Tape them in various places around the room—under chairs, on the ceiling, in the door jamb—any place that will be fun to locate.

Step 1 (1-2 minutes): Move students into groups of three to five and tell them, **Let's read Ephesians 2:1-10. In a few minutes you will be asked to answer nine questions about this passage.** Read the passage aloud (or have several volunteers read portions).

Step 2 (10-15 minutes): Say, **We are going to have a little contest that will be just for fun.** (If you think it will motivate your students more, offer a small reward.)

On your Gateway worksheet you will find the numbers one through nine. When I say go, I want you to search the classroom for a card with a question. Work as a group to answer it. (You may have to carry your Bible around with your finger in the passage we've just read.) **Then locate** another question hidden somewhere in the room and answer it. Remember to write full and complete answers on your worksheet, because we will be asking you to share them later. The object is to locate and correctly answer all the questions before we run out of time. Ready, set, go!

Keep track of the time and the progress of each group of students. If students are having a difficult time finding the answers, let them know they may not have time to complete all nine questions. If your class is streaking through the assignment, you may gain some extra time for Step 3. Be the timekeeper and periodically announce the time remaining.

When the time is up, have your students report their answers to the questions. If an answer is incorrect, ask the group to indicate where in the passage they got their response. Stimulate discussion on some answers by asking questions such as these: **How would most of the people you know respond to that statement? Which**

part of the passage is the most difficult for people to understand? How would your school be different if all your friends understood and believed this passage? Comment as necessary, using material from INSIGHTS FOR THE LEADER.

Step 3 (12-15 minutes): Tell students, **Now, each group should come up with at least three slogans that could be developed from the verses that you've just read. These slogans should help people see how God has reached out to establish a relationship with us, and what we have to do or don't have to do to gain that relationship.**

(If your students have a hard time comprehending what you mean, give them an example from a secular company that has a slogan that summarizes what they want to do for the customer. Then give them an example from the text, like, "You don't deserve a break today—but God will give you one anyway." Remind them that the slogan doesn't have to be fancy or catchy but needs to communicate what God is doing to establish a relationship with us.)

Step 4 (3-4 minutes): Ask groups to share the slogans that they have created; write them on a sheet of newsprint or on the chalkboard as they are reported.

Conclusion and Decision

CONCLUSION (5-8 minutes)

Wrap up the lesson by saying something like this: **We have been looking at how God made possible a relationship with us through Christ. We have seen that there is nothing that we could do to help ourselves or to earn this relationship with Christ. I'd like you to take a look at "The Tie That Binds" section of the Gateway worksheet and prayerfully fill out that section. Then I'd like you to fold your Gateway worksheet in half and give it to me before you leave this morning.**

After your students have completed their worksheets, close in prayer. Collect the students' papers as they are going out the door. Distribute the Fun Page take-home paper.

This week, make sure to follow up on those who have indicated a desire for you to do so.

THE GATEWAY

Session 2

> "For it is by grace you have been saved, through faith—and this not from yourselves, it is the gift of God—not by works, so that no one can boast."
> Ephesians 2:8,9

Nine Questions   You may need to use extra paper for your answers.

1.

2.

3.

4.

5.

6.

7.

8.

9.

The Tie That Binds

Please check the box that best describes your present relationship with Christ:

☐ I know Him . . . but we don't speak much.
☐ I've known Him for a long time but I'm starting to get doubts.
☐ I know the Lord and our relationship is great!
☐ I really don't understand much about all of this.
☐ I know all about Him, but I don't know Him.
☐ Other:

☐ I'd like to talk more about my relationship with God. (Write your name and phone number.)

Name _____ Phone _____

☐ I'm not ready to deal with this yet.

Teaching Resource page

Cut the questions apart along the lines and hide them in your classroom as instructed in the EXPLORATION.

1. What is the description of the kind of spiritual life that we had when we followed the ways of the world?	2. Who did we follow before we were Christians? What is that another name for?	3. What was our inner nature before Christ changed us?
4. What did God do to show His love for us? Why was that a demonstration of His love?	5. What do you think the word grace means? (The Bible doesn't define it here but it gives lots of clues.)	6. From what you can figure out from this passage, who made the first move towards establishing a relationship between God and man? What was that move?
7. How does this passage say that we receive God's love, salvation and forgiveness?	8. What does this passage say about working our way towards salvation?	9. What were we created to do?

The Sleuth

The Nicodemus File

Case #John 3:1-16

It was a dark and scary night. I witnessed the religious Pharisee Nicodemus approach the Lord Jesus. I watched the following incident while I concealed myself behind a sleeping camel . . .

Jesus told Nicodemus that a person must be spiritually reborn in order to reach heaven.

REBORN? BORN TWICE? HOW CAN THESE THINGS BE?

Jesus told him that whoever believes fully in the Son may have eternal life. Made sense to me.

FOR GOD SO LOVED THE WORLD, THAT HE GAVE HIS ONLY BEGOTTEN SON, THAT WHOEVER BELIEVES IN HIM SHOULD NOT PERISH, BUT HAVE ETERNAL LIFE!

ULP!

Sleuth's comment:

All the clues in this case lead to this conviction: Anyone who truly believes and trusts in Jesus the Son will have ETERNAL LIFE with God in heaven!

HOT THOT

"For it is by grace you have been saved, through faith—and this not from yourselves, it is the gift of God—not by works, so that no one can boast."
Ephesians 2:8,9

Mug shot # 09309

suspect: Nicodemus

Aliases: Nick the Pharisee; Lefty.

right thumb

THE COMPLETE JUNIOR HIGH BIBLE STUDY RESOURCE BOOK #5

© 1988 GL/LIGHT FORCE, VENTURA, CA 93006

THEME: Christ brings us to God.

Session 2

BIBLE STUDY OUTLINE

Read John 3:1-18 to your listeners. Make the following remarks as time permits.

Introductory remarks: Nicodemus was a man who looked like he had it all together. He was a religious leader, a man who should have been at peace with God and with himself. But he came to Jesus looking for answers. This is his story.

Verses 1-3: Perhaps Nicodemus came to Jesus at night because Jesus was such a busy man, or maybe because Nicodemus was nervous about being seen with the Lord. Jesus was a dynamic and controversial figure. Nicodemus knew He was a great teacher and a miracle worker. In response to Nicodemus's greeting, Jesus brought up an unexpected subject: being born again.

Jesus was able to go straight to the heart of Nicodemus's problem. Nick wasn't born again. He didn't even know what it meant.

Verses 4-8: Jesus explained by connecting the Holy Spirit to salvation. No one can enter heaven without a spiritual rebirth.

Each person is spiritually dead because of sin (see Rom. 6:23). That was Nick's problem, and that's our problem.

Verse 9: Nicodemus didn't understand what Jesus was talking about.

Verses 10-15: Nicodemus didn't understand that Jesus had come from heaven and that He must die so that all could have eternal life.

Verses 16-18: These verses describe the way to be born again.

(Now tell the True Story.)

TRUE STORY: STRANGE BIRTH

(This story of a strange birth is presented to help illustrate the fact that there is only one way to be born into God's family. We do not condone all the procedures described.)

On September 28, 1987, Pat Anthony became the first woman in the world to give birth to her own grandchildren. When Pat's daughter was unable to have children through natural childbirth, Pat volunteered to act as a surrogate mother. So the daughter's eggs were mixed with the husband's sperm in a laboratory. The fertilized eggs were implanted in Pat's womb—and months later she gave birth to her daughter and son-in-law's triplets! Pat was 48 years old.

Modern science has enabled natural birth to be occasionally supplanted by so-called "test tube" births. Natural birth is also aided by medications designed to make the woman more fertile. Caesarean section operations allow the baby to be delivered through a cut in the mother's abdomen. All of these procedures allow babies to be born who never could have been born by natural birth.

But when it comes to being reborn—born again as Jesus said—there is only one way. Jesus is our Savior. There is no other way to reach eternal life. (Conclude by describing the need to be reborn and the best way to get started in the Christian life.)

DISCUSSION QUESTIONS

1. **Why wasn't Nicodemus good enough to reach heaven on his own?**

2. **In John 3:2, Nicodemus declares that he knows Jesus is from God. Why do you suppose this wasn't enough in Jesus' view to qualify for saving faith?**

3. **Who is the Holy Spirit and how are we related to Him?**

4. **Why did Jesus have to die?**

5. **What are some ways we can demonstrate our faith in God?**

Well, the Nicodemus File on the other side of this paper tells us that Jesus Christ is the way to God and heaven. Most people already know that. But is there a way to heaven OTHER than Jesus?

Let's find out in this tongue-in-cheek look at the

Heavenly Maze

The object of the maze is to reach heaven (up in the clouds, of course). Even though there are several paths to take at the bottom of the maze, one and only one leads to heaven! Can you find it? (If you can't . . . well, you're not too sharp today!)

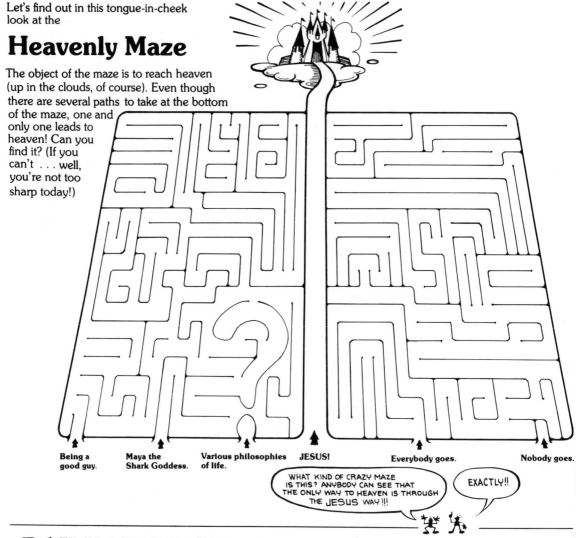

Being a good guy.   Maya the Shark Goddess.   Various philosophies of life.   JESUS!   Everybody goes.   Nobody goes.

WHAT KIND OF CRAZY MAZE IS THIS? ANYBODY CAN SEE THAT THE ONLY WAY TO HEAVEN IS THROUGH THE JESUS WAY !!!

EXACTLY!!

DAILY NUGGETS Wisdom from God's Word for you to read each day.

Day 1 Read Ephesians 2:11-18. What has Jesus done, according to this passage? What does this mean for you personally?

Day 2 Romans 5:1. How is a person justified? What is one benefit faith brings?

Day 3 Ephesians 1:13,14. What happens as a result of one's believing the gospel message? What role of the Holy Spirit is described in these verses?

Day 4 1 John 1:9. When we confess our sins, what will the Lord do for us? If there is a particular sin in your life that you haven't yet told the Lord about, why not do so now in prayer?

Day 5 John 11:25. When we believe in Jesus, what does He give us?

Day 6 James 5:14-16. What is the Lord's response to those who have committed sin? How should we approach Jesus with our sins (vv. 15,16)?

The Social Learning family emerges in Illustration 14.1 too. Locate the "PopSheet" at the back of this lesson. The reading of the Word of God (John 3:1–18) emphasizes *Structured Modeling. Spontaneous Modeling* occurs through "Bible Exploration." For instance, class members study the Scripture in groups of "three to five." Topics from the teen's world, as well as the Bible, are discussed. Life examples from the young people and the teacher are held up for emulation.

Finally, the Information-Processing family is given attention. *Identification Learning* surfaces in "The Nicodemus File." Here, bridges from the known to the unknown are constructed through contemporary art work and the relevant contents of Nicodemus' biography. The "Heavenly Maze" provides graphic imagery that Jesus Christ is the only way to heaven. *Inquiry Learning* recognizes that students must be challenged to think through their faith. This happens with the five discussion questions (see "Pop-Sheet") and "The Tie That Binds" (see "Conclusion and Decision"). It is significant to notice that this final learning strategy requires students to assess their "personal relationship with Christ" in a noncoercive fashion. For example, two of the responses that teens may check include "I'm starting to get doubts" and "I'm not ready to deal with this yet." Allowing for (and respecting) free choice, at this juncture, illustrates Stephen D. Jones' earlier advice to adults who nurture youth.

Table 14.4 consolidates the information from the previous paragraphs. Accordingly, the entire lesson, "Jesus Makes It Possible," is viewed at a glance, per learning family.

Rich Bundschuh's *On-Site* features at least two lessons on Communion for youth.[6] Illustration 14.2 challenges teens to experience tree sitting. The purpose is to simulate Zacchaeus' experience when he encountered Christ. The lesson focus, from Luke 19:1–10, causes youth to realize that "Jesus comes to us while we are still sinners." The "Plugging into Daily Life" section encourages relevant application of the passage.

Table 14.4

Youth Curriculum on Communion

Conditioning Family	Cue Learning	1. curiosity from students' unopened letter 2. challenge of class game, involving hidden clue cards
	Consequence Learning	1. reward if unopened letters are brought to class 2. a contest, featuring a "small reward" 3. small group project to create slogans
Social Family	Structured Modeling	1. reading John 3:1–18 2. news story about surrogate birth
	Spontaneous Modeling	1. small group Bible study in which members share testimony by way of example
Information-Processing Family	Identification Learning	1. the "Nicodemus File" 2. the "Heavenly Maze"
	Inquiry Learning	1. discussion questions 2. the "Tie That Binds"

Illustration 14.2

ON-SITE UP IN A TREE

Sitting in the branches of a large strong tree is a perfect way to bring home to your students the story of Zacchaeus, the tax collector.

Naturally, you'll want to choose a tree that will sustain the weight of your class. Bring a ladder with you to help the kids who are not part monkey.

Being up in a tree will limit what you can hold in your hand or work on. The best idea is to so familiarize yourself with the Scripture that you can simply tell the story while sitting in the tree.

A tree isn't the cleanest environment. Warn your students before the trip to wear clothing for the outdoors.

Focus: Jesus comes to us while we are still sinners.
Bible passage to share and discuss: Luke 19:1–10.

Getting Started

After you're securely lodged up in the tree ask your students to describe to the group the best seats for an event (such as sports or concert) that they have ever had. Tie that into the lesson by saying that a seat similar to the ones you now occupy was the best seat that a guy named Zacchaeus could get when he tried to see the event of the year in Jericho: Jesus coming to town.

Looking in the Word

In the tree, retell the story of Zacchaeus and his encounter with Christ. Do a little background investigation so that you can explain the significance of a tax collector to the Jewish people. Prepare some discussion questions. For example:

1. What would be your response if a total stranger invited himself to dinner at your house?

2. What indications did Zacchaeus give that he had genuinely changed his way?

3. Why did the people mutter against Jesus eating with Zacchaeus?

Plugging into Daily Life

Ask your students to discuss:

1. What are modern equivalents of tax collectors?

2. What do you think shows that we have a genuine faith in Christ?

3. What should our actions and attitude be toward today's "tax collectors"?

4. Do you think people who become Christians should make some sort of restitution to people they've cheated before they were Christians? Why or Why not?

Adding It All Up

Ask your class to spend a few moments in silent prayer for a friend who doesn't know about Christ. Have them ask God to give them an opportunity to show them the depth of their faith by their kind deeds and actions.

Illustration 14.3 nudges youth groups toward hands-on participation. The lesson, "Upper Room," reenacts the Last Supper. Teens experience this provocative, historical moment. By celebrating Jesus' death for them, young people gain new appreciation for his sacrifice. They are reminded that "Christ shed his blood to pay for our sins." As the teens read various Scripture excerpts, they reflect on the disciples' thoughts and feelings. In order to personally identify with the Last Supper, each adolescent is asked to "write down a sin that they have committed this week that Christ's blood removed." These pieces of paper are then torn up and discarded, signifying the practical power of confession and forgiveness.

Community

Paul said, "Follow my example, as I follow the example of Christ" (1 Cor. 11:1). Modeling expresses a critical component of Community. This is especially so within youth culture. Imagine yourself as the young person in the scenario below. Sense the eroding confidence in adults that you experience.

> When I was to enter senior high school, our Sunday church school teacher was very popular with the youth. His class was always crowded with youth who appreciated the questions that he allowed and the free-wheeling discussion that often veered away from "the quarterlies" (the curriculum books). One of the important role-model couples got wind of the unorthodox approach of this teacher and used their influence to have him dismissed. The teacher left the church at the beginning of the fall when I was to enter his class. Some months later when my older sister told me the whole story, a huge crack [in my faith] broke open for me. For the first time adults appeared more defensive and less trustworthy, as if they had something to hide that my questions might uncover.[7]

Think about It

Jot down a brief response to these questions:

1. What does this story tell you about the difficulties of teaching Community?

   _____

2. Provide one "crack" in Community that you have personally experienced (i.e., an example of faith disillusionment because of other believers).

   _____

   _____

A useful distinction that Lawrence O. Richards makes at this point is the difference between *telling* and faithful *living*. It's one thing, he says, to make verbal claims concerning faith in God. It's quite another thing to back words with action. To incarnate personal beliefs consistently is both more difficult and more necessary for genuine Community.

Pretend you are outside. It's January. You're up North, and snow flurries swirl around you and some youngsters, who stand by a lake.

> In Michigan the cold winters bring ice skating. When I was a young child, I would often stand on the shore of our local lake and wonder if the ice was thick enough yet. Sometimes I or one of my friends would gingerly put one foot on the ice, and try our weight. Often the ice creaked frighteningly, and we were afraid to go out.
>
> But imagine an adult who . . . [tells] us, "Go on out, kids. The ice is safe." If we know him well, we might even get beyond the creaking ice at the edge. We might take the risk. But there's a better way. He can walk out on that ice himself, turn to

Illustration 14.3

UPPER ROOM

ON-SITE IN AN

To bring a new dimension to the Lord's Supper, try taking your class to an upper room all set up for dining.

The closer you can come to the original scene the better. Try having the kids sit on the floor around a low table, wash each other's feet, and have a genuine meal celebrating Christ's death for us.

Focus: Christ shed his blood to pay for our sins.
Bible passages to share or discuss: John 13:1–17, Luke 22:7–22.

Getting Started

Well in advance of your lesson, find an attic, a loft, or some other "upper room" that you can bring a class to.

About a week before your lesson, send out invitations to all your students, giving them the time and location of the class at the upper room. (Be sure to post the information on the door of your classroom at church in case anyone shows up who is not on your mailing list.)

Have the room set up in advance, and the elements waiting for your group members when they get there.

Try having your students remove their shoes and socks before they enter the room; then, before they are seated, wash each of your students' feet.

Try to keep a solemn atmosphere and say as little as possible to your students as you perform the foot washing. (Note: the reaction of your group to foot washing can vary, but most kids catch on pretty quickly if the environment is sober and serious.)

After your students have been seated, ask them how they felt about having their feet washed.

Looking in the Word

Divide your chosen passage of Scripture into short, readable sections; assign those sections to several members of the class who are strong readers. Let them take turns reading to the whole class.

Ask your students to describe what the disciples might have been feeling and thinking during the Last Supper.

Plugging into Daily Life

Distribute slips of paper and ask your students to write down a sin that they have committed this week that Christ's blood removed. Ask them to tear up the paper to signify their confession and repentance of the sin and God's faithfulness to forgive it.

Adding It All Up

Close your lesson by having your students celebrate the Lord's Supper together. But make it a real meal as the early church did. Sing a hymn or praise song and then dismiss.

us, and say, "*Come* on out, kids. The ice is safe. See, it holds me!"[8]

Richards concludes that the difference between the first adult response and the second compares to the difference between "telling" and "living" the Christian faith. How does this example translate into youth education that is Christian? Quite simply, successful teachers are those who intentionally develop quality relationships with their students; teachers who are sensitive to the needs and dreams of youth; teachers who exhibit genuine interest in and care for youth; teachers who "walk their talk." This is how Community is best taught. Experienced youth workers strike a balance between one-to-one relationships and group skills. Successful youth workers are faithful in their scheduled formal meetings, but they're also available for informal times with adolescents throughout the week. These adults are genuine when they ask young people: "How's it going? Have you seen any progress in the problem we discussed a few days ago?" No, successful youth workers are not superhuman. But they possess the ability to make teens feel comfortable in relationships.

Don Kimball (1987, p. 12) believes that Community consists of three relationship levels: (1) one-to-one ties; (2) the small group; and (3) large group associations. Most people typically feel comfortable at one of these levels, but not necessarily at all three. (Kimball confesses that he personally enjoys larger groups.[9]) David Lynn's creative book, *One-to-One,* effectively addresses Kimball's first category.[10]

Small group Community building (the second category) takes different shapes also. Most youth are members of at least one small group.[11] No individual adult can effectively minister to every type of group. Jim Burns (1988, p. 44) sketches a superb

example of how adults must sensitively recognize and serve within the peculiar confines of teen small groups:

> In 1980, I started a new youth ministry at a church in Newport Beach, California. Six freshmen came to my first Bible study—three guys and three girls. The next day I took the three guys out for a Coke after school to get acquainted. I tried every possible way I could, but I couldn't get these young men to talk. Finally I asked them "What do you do here in the summer?" They all shouted at once, "We fish!" Immediately the conversation opened up as we talked about fishing. . . . Their social group and influence centered around their mutual love for fishing. I had to adjust my youth ministry programming to include fishing trips.

Extending the principles of his small group experiences, Burns (1988) combines the second guideline above with the earlier stated demand for one-to-one relationships. Since no adult can attend to all teen group needs, why not match every adult worker with a handful of youth? Why not create friendships with each teenager individually? His ninety-minute plan has contributed greatly to the maturity of his young people.[12]

Community building within large groups is often an overwhelming task. Frequently, two extreme conditions prevail: Either a "rules-dominated" youth group setting leads to lifeless regimentation and legalism or an "anything goes" view of Community promotes hostility, strife, and division.

Think about It

The following nine statements are from a "Youth Club" members' list of responsibilities.[13] As you read them, what first impressions do you get about this high school group?

1. To be on time every week and to stay for the entire program.
2. To participate in all aspects of the Youth Club program, that is, crafts, singing, games, study, service, dinner, vespers. To participate in the extra activities if I am able to do so.
3. To observe good manners and seemly conduct at all times.
4. To show respect for the church building and program supplies.
5. To clear away my place at the dinner table and return to the table until I am excused by an adult.
6. To clean the dining room when my table is assigned that job.
7. To show respect for all adults and teachers present and to try to get to know them as my friends.
8. To try to be a special friend to all other Youth Club members—"We are one in the Spirit, we are one in the Lord . . . And they'll know we are Christians by our love."
9. To share our faith with our friends inside and outside the church and bring them as guests to Youth Club. Guests come one week for free. Members are responsible for their guests. Be sure to tell them what to do and introduce them to others.

This nine-point pact, Stevens tells us, is then co-signed by youth and parents alike. Now, ask yourself: What subtle messages are communicated by this list? What disturbs you?[14] _____

_____

Needless to say, this scenario portrays one negative extreme of large group Com-

munity. As Doug Stevens correctly observes, "warmth and closeness" are *all but impossible* to experience in this youth club. In contrast, Wayne Rice (1989, p. 9) graphically portrays the "anything goes" opposite side of Community. Do these confrontations sound familiar to you?

• Donnie, Shane, and Steve are ninth graders who are close friends, but not with Jeremy, so they tease him about being short.
• Janine and Amber are upset because several other girls in the group have been spreading rumors about them.
• Alicia has stopped coming because some of the boys call her "Tubbs."
• None of the kids from Roosevelt High will sit next to anyone from Central.
• Jason started dating Kim, which means that he and his former girlfriend, Chris, aren't talking to each other.
• Jessica is the new girl who has been coming to the youth group now for three weeks but still hasn't made any friends.

How are we leaders to promote genuine Community among our teens? How do we help Jeremy realize that he's needed, that he's important?[15] What means do we employ to strengthen Alicia's identity? What must be known about youth value systems and adolescent struggles?[16] How can we meet the friendship needs of Jessica?[17] Is it possible to know the heros of our youth, to better comprehend their unique lifestyles?[18]

Rice (1989) maintains that we must begin with certain prerequisites for Community building. Then, we should determine specific strategies. Unless we proceed in this order, we'll misinterpret the meaning of Community. Rice's seven-point list (pp. 14–17) of prerequisites show: (1) the need for intentionality; (2) the willingness to make a long-term commitment to Community building; (3) a design to limit groups to about fifteen people; (4) the aim of respecting and satisfying individual member's needs; (5) an environment that encourages Community; (6) an inclusive (versus exclusive) spirit toward all teens; and (7) a Christ-centered focus.

Rice then posits nine strategies for Community building (pp. 20–25); among these are the needs to learn and to worship together; to affirm and to minister to each other; and to spend significant time together.

In Illustration 14.4, the Conditioning family finds expression through its two subcategories. *Cue Learning* includes (1) the key verse (1 Cor. 12:27) reminders in both of the "Attention Grabbers"; (2) the anticipated teen curiosity in both of these activities; and (3) the object lesson found in "Balanced Diet." This last method provides visual images of the instructional aim (see "Pop-Sheet"); that is, by using our senses of sight and touch (possibly smell and taste as well), the analogy of Christ's body is better understood.

Consequence Learning emerges at several points. It can be seen in the revealed answer to the coded Bible verse, as well as the explanation of the jigsaw puzzle exercise (see both "Attention Grabbers"). Also, classroom response is expected through discussion questions and the eight inquiries on 1 Corinthians 12:12–21.

Creative approaches that are faithful to the Social Learning family also arise within this curricular illustration. *Structured Modeling* incorporates the tape recordings of church staff members. As participants summarize their job descriptions in riddle form, another dimension of this teaching strategy is emphasized (see "Bible Exploration," Step 4). *Spontaneous Modeling* occurs

in at least three areas: (1) the small group interaction throughout the "Bible Exploration" section; (2) the subsequent "live" interview with the church youth minister ("Bible Exploration," Step 5); and (3) the class creation of a letter directed to one of the staff members.[19]

Identification Learning devices in the Information-Processing family are exposed, as links are made between the known and the unknown. "The Brick Pile File" offers one example. Both the content (Rick the Brick doesn't feel like he fits in) and the graphics (cartoon format) supply relevant learning transitions. Inquiry tactics appear as students are encouraged to resolve different issues. It was earlier noted (under Cue Learning) that arousing curiosity in teens (see both "Attention Grabbers") verified that particular learning avenue. Specifically, a coded verse and a mailed puzzle piece built positive attitudes for learning receptivity. The *resolution* of both of these introductory tasks, however, calls for inquiry thinking.[20] In similar fashion, the "I'd Like to Help (I Think)" section points to this method of problem solving.

Table 14.5 offers a concise overview of the information from the previous paragraphs.

On-Site, again, complements the *Light Force* curriculum. Youth are challenged to think of God's protection for them, both individually and corporately (see Illustration 14.5). Riding in an armored vehicle simulates God's protection. Personalizing Bible verses from the psalms provides truth about God's care. Drawing on the resources of Community, teens are challenged to jointly create a jingle for an advertisement slogan that will remind them of God's security. Illustration 14.5 offers additional information.

Church Life

WHAT THE SESSION IS ABOUT

The junior high student is an important part of the Body of Christ.

SCRIPTURE STUDIED

1 Corinthians 12:12-27

KEY PASSAGE

"Now you are the body of Christ, and each one of you is a part of it."
1 Corinthians 12:27

AIMS OF THE SESSION

During this session your learners will:

1. Discover that the Bible says that each Christian is an essential member of the Body of Christ;

2. Discuss ways their age group can contribute to the church;

3. Choose ways to join more fully in the church's life.

INSIGHTS FOR THE LEADER

On the day of Pentecost, when the Holy Spirit came upon the apostles, Peter stood up and boldly announced that here was the fulfillment of Joel's prophecy: "In the last days, God says, I will pour out my Spirit on all people. Your sons and daughters will prophesy, your young men will see visions, your old men will dream dreams. Even on my servants, both men and women, I will pour out my Spirit in those days, and they will prophesy" (Acts 2:17,18). Joel's words, quoted by Peter (see Joel 2:28,29), describe God's Spirit coming upon people of all ages, enabling them to be used by God.

Jesus promised the Holy Spirit to anyone, young or old, who receives Him as Savior (see John 14:16,17). Your junior highers are included in His promise just as surely as elders or deacons or your pastor are included. Your learners have their place in the Body of Christ right now. Depending on your church's policy, they may or may not be enrolled as members. But regardless of whether they are on the membership roll, your students have an important place among Christ's people!

Today's Scripture from 1 Corinthians 12 is about the unity and diversity of the Body of Christ: its "oneness" and its "many-ness." Like the human body, the Body of Christ is one organism. It may be harder for believers to visualize this oneness of the Christian Body than it is to understand the oneness of the

human body because the Body of Christ appears to be quite diverse. But in God's eyes and in the reality of spiritual truth, the Body is one. The members are as closely related to one another as the members of an individual human body.

Yet Christ's Body does have its "many-ness," right alongside its oneness, just as the human body does. Our earthly bodies have hands and feet, eyes and ears, hearts and lungs and stomachs. All look different and serve different purposes. Yet each is vitally necessary to the functioning of the whole body. None of us would want to try to live without some part of his or her body. Nor can any part of each of our bodies claim that it doesn't need the other parts.

Similarly, it is a mistake for any Christian to think he or she has no rightful place in the Body: "If the foot should say, 'Because I am not a hand, I do not belong to the body,' it would not for that reason cease to be part of the body" (1 Cor. 12:15). It is equally a mistake for any Christian to imagine that he or she is all-important: "The eye cannot say to the hand, 'I don't need you!'" (12:21).

It is important to remember that God is the one who chooses the arrangement of the members of the Body of Christ, just as He chose the arrangement of our human bodies (see v. 18). Not everybody can be a hand or an eye. All the parts are needed, even those parts that seem insignificant or "less honorable" (see vv. 22-25). One cannot look down on another's position. And no one should feel inferior about his or her own role either, but should remember that God has assigned that role and intends to use that person through it.

Anyone who has hurt a bodily part or lost one because of injury or disease will have a particular appreciation for the importance of the body's members to one another. When one part of the body is hurting, the rest of the body tends to favor that part. A person who has had abdominal surgery discovers that even taking a deep breath can make the incision hurt. So the brain tells the rest of the body to be careful, and the other muscles move very cautiously when they move at all, because the whole body tries to avoid the pain that can come from disturbing the injured part.

Similarly, the Lord expects the members of the Church to "have equal concern for each other. If one part suffers, every part suffers with it; if one part is honored, every part rejoices with it" (vv. 25,26). This is the ideal toward which we are all to grow, under the headship of Jesus Christ. No one is to feel self-sufficient and independent of the Body. No one is to feel unneeded and inferior.

Your junior highers probably lean toward the "inferior" side. Perhaps they consider themselves "on hold" in the church until they grow up. They may not see that they have any place in the church right now. It is fair to say that some churches do better than others in making junior highers feel like a part of the Body of Christ.

It will be good, before you teach this session, to talk over with your pastor (or someone else in charge of your church's program) some way your junior highers can participate more fully in the life of your church. It may be a one-time project or a new, continuing activity.

Some Suggestions

Make a banner or other worship aid for the sanctuary.

Form or join church choirs. (Ask your choir director about the minimum age for the "adult" choir; in some churches anyone past sixth grade is welcome.)

Meet people of other age groups (this one takes some work to get kids past the stage of mumbling and looking at their shoes).

Serve a refreshment after a church function.

Serve at a church dinner.

Participate in a church work day.

Read Scripture and offer prayers in worship services.

Plan and present an entire worship service of their own, or a portion of a regular service.

Assist teachers of younger children, or even teach, in Bible schools and Bible clubs.

Visit retirement homes and nursing homes.

Pitch in with someone in the church who needs help with a special project: cleaning up a lawn or shoveling snow for a disabled person, helping with farm work in a rural area. (Yes, that's helping the church, because the church is the people!)

Present a drama illustrating a biblical story or a principle of Christian living.

When adults are giving testimonies or asking for prayer, junior highers can count themselves in by voicing their own testimony or concern, even if it's only a few words. The adults will listen and be proud of their junior highers. They will also be flattered that junior highers trust them.

Pray for adults in the church during your class or other meetings for junior highers.

As you look for ways to involve your students in the total life of the church, try to keep a variety of activities available. Avoid building a total youth program around one type of involvement (such as youth choir), since kids who don't enjoy that activity may become shut off from the rest of the group, and those who are involved may grow up with a very limited concept of ministry.

NOTES

SESSION PLAN

BEFORE CLASS BEGINS: See the ALTERNATE ATTENTION GRABBER for special instructions. Photocopy the Gateway and the Fun Page. Step 4 of the EXPLORATION describes a tape recording you are to make before the class begins.

Attention Grabber

ATTENTION GRABBER (3-5 minutes)

Distribute the Gateway and have the students individually decipher the coded Bible verse. Ask students to silently raise their hands when they think they have the answer. The correct solution is 1 Corinthians 12:27: "Now you are the body of Christ, and each one of you is a part of it." After several students have raised their hands, ask one to give the answer and how he or she found it. (The verse is not scrambled; the letters are in proper order but the words break in the wrong spots.)

Thank your students and say something like, **This verse, 1 Corinthians 12:27, tells us that each one of us is a member of Christ's Body here on earth. We will spend the rest of our session today learning what that means and how you can be involved in important ways.**

ALTERNATE ATTENTION GRABBER (5-8 minutes)

Write the words to 1 Corinthians 12:27 on a large sheet of card stock or poster board. Cut the cardboard into jigsaw puzzle-like pieces, enough pieces for each of your regular attenders to have one. A few days before class time, mail the pieces to your students, one per student. Enclose a note in each envelope that says something like, "Please bring this with you to this week's Bible study."

When students arrive for class, ask them to assemble the pieces into a complete puzzle. Some of the pieces will probably be missing because some students are absent or forgot to bring their piece of the puzzle.

Make a transition to the EXPLORATION by saying, **The puzzle isn't complete because some pieces are missing. Each piece has an important part in the puzzle. In the same way, you and I are important parts of Christ's Body, the Church. The Church isn't quite whole until each person is doing his or her part as a Christian.** (Read 1 Corinthians 12:27 to the class.)

Bible Exploration

EXPLORATION (30-40 minutes)

Step 1 (10-12 minutes): Read 1 Corinthians 12:12-21 aloud (or have volunteers read segments). Direct learners' attention to the Bible study in their Gateways titled "Fitting into the Body of Christ." Have students work together in threes or fours to complete the study. (Or lead a discussion.)

Step 2 (3-5 minutes): Reassemble the class and ask for reports. Discuss the answers learners have found in the Scriptures.

Step 3 (5-6 minutes): Briefly review 1 Corinthians 12:22-27, pointing out the concern the members of the Body should have for one another. (Use INSIGHTS FOR THE LEADER as needed.) As you move into Steps 4 and 5 and the Conclusion, students need to understand the reasons why believers should be involved in the work of the Church.

Step 4 (5-8 minutes): As noted in BEFORE CLASS BEGINS, you are to make a tape recording to play to your class. During the week, interview as many of the church staff members as is convenient. Each staff member should record a one or two sentence description of his or her job. For extra fun, have the staffers disguise their voices and put their job descriptions in a riddle form. For example, the senior pastor could say, "I shepherd the flock. Who am I?" The building maintenance manager could say, "I keep the place looking great. Guess who I am before it's too late."

Play the recording to your learners, stopping the tape as necessary to allow students to guess the identities of the staff members. Discuss each person's place in the Body of Christ. Be careful to note that some jobs may seem more important than others, but each is essential to the proper functioning of your local church.

Step 5 (8-10 minutes): Now introduce your church's youth minister (if he or she is someone other than yourself). Allow the youth minister to describe many important areas of need in which your students can be involved. (Areas such as inviting friends to church, setting up meeting rooms, leading songs, providing homes for Bible studies and socials, running the sound system and so on.) Allow students to contribute their own ideas. List all suggestions on the chalkboard. Use INSIGHTS FOR THE LEADER for additional thoughts.

Make a transition to the CONCLUSION of the session by saying, **Scripture says that every one of you has an important place in the Church right now, not just years from now when you're an adult. Let's do some work on finding specific ways you can get personally involved.**

Conclusion and Decision

CONCLUSION (3-5 minutes)

Direct attention to the "I'd Like to Help" section of the Gateway and say, **Check your answer thoughtfully. I'm going to ask you to hand in your Gateway when you're done so I can see**

NOTES

Note: You'll need at least one candy bar for the next session's (Session 12) ATTENTION GRABBER. See page 149 for more information.

what you have said.

Let students work. Then close in prayer and ask students to give you their Gateway sheets. Distribute the Fun Page take-home paper.

After class, read through the Gateway sheets turned in by students. Find ways to use the students who want to serve. Organize a project in which a number of students expressed similar interest. Pass on names of other interested students to church staff and volunteer helpers so they can put the junior highers to work in their areas of interest.

ALTERNATE CONCLUSION (10-15 minutes)

Tell students, **We're going to work together to plan a letter to a staff member in our fellowship.** (Specify the appropriate person.) **In our letter we will express how you feel as a group about your role in our church. Also, we will offer to do our part as members of the Body of Christ in the specific ways which we have thought of in our groups. We'll all work together to figure out how to word the letter, and then one of us will copy it onto paper and someone else will deliver it.**

Use the chalkboard to record students' ideas until a final form is decided upon. Then select a student with good handwriting to copy the letter onto paper. Also select a volunteer to deliver the finished letter to the appropriate staff member.

Help students remember that the point of the letter is to express to your church's leadership the idea that their junior highers have something to give.

Close in prayer, asking for God's guidance and wisdom in being the part of the Body of Christ He wants your junior highers to be.

Distribute the Fun Page.

For the class member who is to deliver the letter to the appropriate leader, provide assistance in preparing an explanation of the letter's purpose.

THE GATEWAY

> "Now you are the body of Christ, and each one of you is a part of it."
> 1 Corinthians 12:27

Decode This Message:

"NO WYO UARETH EBO DY OFCH RISTA NDEACHO NEOFY OUISA PAR TO FIT."

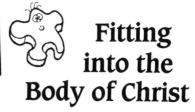

Fitting into the Body of Christ

=== **Read 1 Corinthians 12:12-21 and answer these questions.** ===

1. This passage of Scripture is about:

2. Verses 15 and 16 are talking about people who:

3. What do you think the answers are to the questions in verse 17?

4. Who puts the parts of the body where they belong?

5. Why are they put in the places they are?

6. Verse 21 is talking about people who:

7. In one sentence describe the message of this whole Bible passage.

8. You have a part to play in this church right now. ☐ True ☐ False ☐ I'm not sure

I'd Like to Help (I Think)

=== **Check the box that best speaks for you.** ===

☐ I'd like to help my church by giving my services for things I can do.

☐ Not interested, maybe in a couple of years.

☐ Um, I'm new here and uh . . . well . . . um.

☐ I think that I could serve the people (or a person) in my church by:

☐ You can call me or pass on my name to a person who is organizing for a project.

NAME _____

ADDRESS _____

PHONE _____

I'm usually available on _____

HoT THoT

"Now you are the body of Christ, and each one of you is a part of it."

1 Corinthians 12:27

The Brick Pile File:

Case #1 Corinthians 12:27

Here's the way it happened. There was a brick wall, see. It was huge! Biggest stone bricks I ever saw. But wait until you hear what happened!

These are the true facts in the case:

The wall held back the pounding ocean surf.

Every brick fit together perfectly to form the mighty wall. Each brick was vitally important to keep that wall strong!

But Rick the Brick felt otherwise . . .

I'M JUST A BRICK... I DON'T **FIT IN !!**

So, feeling sorry for himself, Rick the Brick left the wall . . .

SNIFF!

BAM!

Sleuth's comment:

Some Christian people may feel the way Rick the Brick felt about himself: useless, not up to par, not someone that God would want or need! But the Bible indicates that each Christian is an important and necessary part of the "wall," the Christian Body. (See 1 Corinthians chapter 12.)

So don't be a brickhead! God loves you!

WANTED:

Rick the Brick.

Suspect wanted for questioning in connection with: Being an important, involved member of the Christian body.

 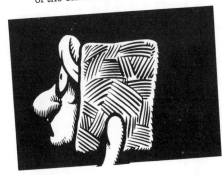

Description: Can have any appearance: young, old, short, tall, fat, thin, girl, boy ... in fact, anybody can be and should be a contributing and important member of Christ's body!

Distinguishing marks: Loves the Lord, wants to help other Christians, willing to give of self for others.

Aliases: Can have any name imaginable, from John Smith to Penelope Q. Thudgeeker.

Previous record: Before becoming a Christian the suspect was just another blob in the crowd, but now he has purpose in life and joy in his heart!

Convictions: The suspect has several convictions:
1. Believes in Jesus as Lord and Savior.
2. Desires to serve the Lord any way he can.
3. Knows that every Christian has the same privilege and responsibility he has: to serve the Lord by serving others!

◼ DAILY NUGGETS ◼

Day 1 Read 1 Corinthians 12:4-6. Who is the same through all the "differences" mentioned in these verses?

Day 2 1 Corinthians 12:12,13. Write a summary statement explaining what is said in these verses.

Day 3 1 Corinthians 12:14-19. Create a list of various "parts" or rules that people might be fulfilling in your church.

Day 4 1 Corinthians 12:15-26. How should different people in the church treat each other?

Day 5 1 Corinthians 12:27-31. Who is the "body" of Christ? List some abilities that God has given to people in His Body.

Day 6 1 Corinthians 13:1-3. What is the ultimate gift one Christian can give to another Christian?

POP SHEET

Session 11

THEME: Areas of service in the youth group.

BIBLE STUDY OUTLINE

Read Acts 2:42-47. Make the following remarks as time permits.

Introductory remarks: This passage describes the early church, right after Jesus ascended into heaven. From it, we can learn a bit about our own group here.

Verse 42: The early Christians were students. They listened to the apostle's teachings, which are now recorded for us in the Bible. They fellowshipped, which means they hung out together and cared for each other. They shared their meals and spent time together in prayer. The key word in this verse is *devoted*. The early Christians were healthy spiritually because they were sold out to Jesus Christ and to each other. Every individual was in some way involved in the local group. That's the key to a healthy church. When each member is contributing, our own youth group is strong.

Verse 43: The Spirit of God was obviously present. When people believe in God and expect Him to work in miraculous ways, He does. His presence is necessary to our group's spiritual health. Notice that God was doing His work through people. God wants to use each of us today.

Verses 44-46: The early Christians were excited about God. They honored Him by meeting together, sharing, meeting each other's needs and eating together. That sort of experience lasted a relatively short time in the early church—soon God spread them around the world to spread the gospel. Today our group exists because of their success at spreading the gospel. These things they did are also things that we can be involved in.

Verse 47: They continued to praise the Lord and they enjoyed the favor of the people in the area. And why not? Good things were happening, and they were happening because each individual was devoted to serving God by service to others. Because of their attitude and devotion, people were joining the group in large numbers.

OBJECT LESSON: BALANCED DIET

Bring in some canned or packaged foods that together represent a good balanced diet: meats, vegetables, fruit, cereals, liquids and so on. Point out (or ask your listeners to explain) what would happen to someone who continually left any of the important food groups out of his or her diet. That person would be unhealthy.

Explain that when all the members of the youth group are actively involved with God and with the group, the group is like a healthy, well-balanced meal. But if some of the members aren't contributing properly, the group suffers. Everyone must be involved, that's the way God wants it to be.

DISCUSSION QUESTIONS

1. What are some areas of service or experiences our youth group provides for its members?

2. What additional opportunities should we provide?

3. How can we motivate more members to come to the meetings? How can we help everyone develop a closer relationship with God and with each other?

4. Why do you suppose the early Christians were so excited about God? How can we become more like them?

Table 14.5

Youth Curriculum on Community

Conditioning Family	Cue Learning	1. the key verse (1 Cor. 12:27) reminders 2. curiosity about these reminders 3. the object lesson
	Consequence Learning	1. answer provided for coded Bible verse 2. explanation of the jigsaw puzzle 3. discussion questions 4. questions about 1 Cor. 12
Social Family	Structured Modeling	1. tape recordings of insights from church staff members
	Spontaneous Modeling	1. small group Bible study 2. interview with the youth pastor 3. class letter, written for and sent to a staff member
Information-Processing Family	Identification Learning	1. the "Brick Pile File"
	Inquiry Learning	1. resolution of the coded verse and puzzle 2. "I'd Like to Help (I Think)" section, at the lesson's conclusion

Character[21]

Daily, on their way home from school, four teens would stop at the mall. One particular store caught their eyes—and ears. Loudspeakers at "The House of Mirrors" blared: "Give us a chance, and we'll change your life." Many shoppers balked at the invitation. Some ventured in.

"Let's check it out," Lisa and Stephanie urged. Juanita and Michelle tagged along.

"Hey, what wild displays!" Juanita commented, noticing her multiple reflections in the merchandise. "I didn't know there were so many ways to make a mirror."

Every mirror imaginable was featured. There were concave and convex mirrors. Minute and enormous ones were displayed. With the aid of lighting and angles, visitors saw something about themselves they had never seen before. For some, their discovery occurred instantly. Perseverance was required for others. Certain people liked what they saw; the mirrors complemented them.

But the majority found personal flaws. They left, shaking their heads or making up some excuse.

The foursome represented the second category. Lisa took off in a huff. "I don't need this grief," she blurted out and was gone. "Same here," Stephanie signaled.

Juanita, lingering a few minutes longer, was also visibly shaken. "Catch ya tomorrow," she promised Michelle, and headed for the exit.

Admittedly, Michelle wasn't crazy about reminders of personal flaws. Who would be? But the resounding message of the loudspeakers convinced Michelle to take a chance. Although her three friends refused to return, Michelle gazed into the mirrors daily. The first couple of weeks, Michelle removed some blotchy makeup; she put stray hairs back into place; she coordinated her wardrobe after noticing particular hues didn't match. By the end of the first month,

Illustration 14.5

ARMORED CAR

This is one *On-Site* activity that everyone looks forward to—especially junior highers: a lesson taught from the safety of an armored car.

To get the use of an armored car, it helps to have connections—but you might be surprised at what a simple request can accomplish. Keep in mind that a small group is much better for this activity.

If you can arrange it, have a driver cruise you around town while you teach your lesson.

If you live near a military base, you might be able to get permission to use a mothballed tank or personnel carrier. Both would work well for this activity. Talk to the base commander or chaplain.

Focus: God is our shield against Satan's attack.

Bible passages to share and discuss: Ephesians 6:16, Psalm 5:12, 18:30, 33:20, 84:11.

Getting Started

Have your host explain to you the workings of the armored car, what it will protect against, and how thick the walls and glass are. Encourage your students to ask questions.

Looking in the Word

Distribute printed copies of the passages of Scripture you want to use to each student. Ask them to draw comparisons between the armored car and the verses of Scripture:

1. Do you feel safer in this vehicle than in a regular car?

2. What does God keep us safe from?

3. What might we do that would jeopardize God's protection?

Plugging into Daily Life

Have each of your students take one of the verses and personalize it with his or her name and an incident from life. For example, Psalm 5:12 might sound like: "For surely, O Lord, you will bless John if he is righteous, you will surround him with your favor during times of disappointment for not making the team as you would with a shield."

Have your kids share their rewritten verses with each other.

Adding It All Up

Ask your students to create a jingle for an ad slogan that would represent the protection that God offers those who seek him.

Michelle started making more important changes. She smiled more.

By chance, one day, the four girls ran into each other at the mall. "You've really changed!" Juanita exclaimed. "Yeah, what's gotten into you?" echoed Lisa. "It's the mirrors . . ." Michelle began. "But we were *all* in that store," Stephanie impatiently interrupted. "How come we never changed?"

Michelle confessed: "I guess it's because I did something about what I saw."

This modern-day parable confronts adolescents with the relevance of Character. Four phases of instruction[22] might utilize the parable as follows.

In Phase 1, the story is read to prompt curiosity and encourage involvement. The story identifies a significant subject within the teens' world. It features realistic learner needs using palatable language.

The second phase of the lesson highlights God's truth. What does the Bible have to say about teen Character? The relevance of Scripture is stressed. Teens might be asked if they recall a biblical message that supports the parable. James 1:21–27 represents a complementary Scripture. The following kinds of questions are introduced to teens for Bible study: How is the Word of God described in this passage? Using James' analogy, how should believers respond to the Bible? What promises are offered to the "doer of the Word"?

The third phase of instruction weaves the first two sections together. The purpose here is to contemplate how principles of the Word inform needs in the world. One of several ways that this teaching phase is accomplished is to brainstorm with teens about the question: What are some ways God is inviting you to be a "doer of the Word"? Divergent responses are encouraged.

Finally, personal response is a must. The last phase of teaching seeks student ac-countability, without coercion. Individual feedback is encouraged, not forced. Each student might be asked which of the four girls represents their own life. "What is your personal response," a youth leader could ask, "to seeing yourself in the mirror of God's Word today? What personal flaw is he prompting you to correct?"

At another level of experienced youth education, *On-Site* offers a couple lessons on Character formation. First, youth are challenged to have God's priorities in "Cancer Ward" (Illustration 14.6). Teens are asked to contemplate their greatest fear. Looking at verses like Matthew 6:33 helps focus attention on "heavenly things." Taking adolescents to a cancer center—or even sitting on the grass at the center—evokes powerful feelings. It helps youth concentrate on what's really important. By way of debriefing, youth are led to draft a two-column chart. On one side, they describe what people usually live for; on the other, they list how people would act if they faced pending disaster. Finally, based on the second-column task, young people compose a letter to their family. They detail what is most meaningful in life to them.

Helping teens resolve the "leaven" of hypocrisy in their own lives represents another *On-Site* lesson of Character. Illustration 14.7 suggests that young people visit a bakery to investigate how yeast works. As in the earlier curriculum about mirrors, the adolescent moves from the "Look" phase to the "Took" phase of learning. "Plugging into Daily Life" encourages youth to "come up with a number of areas where Christians might practice hypocrisy." This phase enumerates various possible applications for the lesson subject (this expresses Richards' "Look" phase of teaching). Then, "Adding It All Up" shifts to the "Took" phase. Students select one of the brainstormed possibilities that pertains to them. They narrow the field

Illustration 14.6

ON-SITE IN A CANCER WARD

Certain kinds of realities are hard for the average kid to grasp—especially in the area of godly priorities or values. Most of the people in this world have their priorities backwards. Often, it takes a brush with death to make a person reevaluate what is important. Taking kids to a cancer clinic can help spark that reevaluation.

Consider combining your lesson with some sort of service project in the hospital. Ask the nurses for ideas; they often know what would be the most welcome. Obviously, you'll need to clear your plans with hospital officials.

Be sure to explain to your students what type of behavior you expect from them. Ask them to try to put themselves in the place of the patients.

If you can't take your students into the hospital itself, just sitting on the grass outside the hospital can still have an impact.

Focus: We must bring our priorities in line with God's way of thinking.
Bible passages to share and discuss: Matthew 6:33, Hebrews 9:27.

Getting Started

Before leaving for your destination (and before you have informed your students where you are going) ask your group, "If you just had a physical examination and the doctor said 'There is something I need to talk to you about,' what would be your greatest fear?" Their responses may be wide and varied, but very likely someone will mention a disease that has the potential to be terminal. When they've completed their responses, explain where you're going and the purpose of the lesson.

Looking in the Word

Begin your lesson by sharing the idea that many people, when faced with a potentially fatal illness, reevaluate what is really important in life. Have your students examine the passages you select and then create a list of priorities in life that are dictated by Scripture.

Plugging into Daily Life

Ask your students to help create a double list: on one side, what people usually live for and what they might live for if they were faced with pending disaster. Contrast the values represented in the two columns.

Adding It All Up

Ask your students to imagine that they were diagnosed as having cancer, and that they knew they had only a short while to live. Have them write letters to their friends and families, expressing what would be important to them if they really faced imminent death.

Illustration 14.7

BAKERY
ON-SITE IN A

Some ideas in Scripture are difficult for students to visualize, especially ideas that are tied in with a custom no longer practiced within view of the ordinary kid. One such idea is Christ's teaching about the leaven or yeast of the Pharisees. Most of today's kids have no idea of what leaven was (or is). They think bread magically shows up at the grocery store each night.

A great way to bring this teaching to life is to show kids around a bakery so that they can watch bread in preparation. (It's especially nice if you can acquire some warm bread or donuts as part of the event.)

Focus: Don't be a hypocrite or a phony.

Bible passage to share or discuss: Matthew 16:5–12, Luke 12:1–2.

Getting Started

Ask your students whether they can define "leaven." If they can't, ask them to explain what "yeast" is. (Yeast is a fungi used in fermentation or baking.)

Looking in the Word

Provide each student with a clipboard, pencil, and paper. Before visiting the bakery, ask them to read the passage assigned and to write down in their own words what they think Jesus was saying.

Plugging into Daily Life

After the visit, ask your students, "Since Jesus warns us not to be involved in the same kind of sin as the Pharisees, can you come up with a number of areas where Christians might practice hypocrisy?" Write down what your students suggest.

Adding It All Up

Ask your students to identify at least one area from the list you have created in which they may be prone to hypocrisy. Have a time of silent prayer to ask God's help in strengthening those areas.

of ideas. They personalize an area where "*they* may be prone to hypocrisy." Silent prayer is raised for these areas of recognized weakness.

Commission

Every believer has a spiritual gift, something to offer to the church. So, too, each Christian has a calling, something to offer the world. Walter Brueggemann suggests that the standard question of identity formation—"Who am I?"—is the wrong question. "*Whose* am I?" shifts the focus from self to Savior, from creature to Creator. This shift, Brueggemann claims, "transposes all identity questions into vocational questions."[23]

The term "vocation," as we saw in Chapters 11 and 12, is not restricted to the words "job," "work," or "profession." It's not limited to the hours of 9 A.M. to 5 P.M. It represents our call or calling from God, what we were meant to do in life. Brueggemann explains vocation as "a purpose for being in the world that is related to the purposes of God."[24] James W. Fowler (1984, p. 95) similarly defines vocation as "the response a person makes with his or her total self to the address of God and to the calling of partnership."

This liberating view of partnership is all-inclusive. Neither children nor the elderly are left out.[25] There is no bias toward the weak or unskilled. Gender, race, ethnicity, or religion sets no restrictive guidelines when it comes to vocation. All have been commissioned by God.

In short, vocation (Commission) means *partnership with God.* Youth today especially need to hear this challenge. Shifting their focus from self to "partnership with God" commences healing from spiritual blindness. Myopic sight is removed and God's broad vision is implanted. Completing the analogy, sensitive Christian leaders must associate each searching teen with blind Bartimaeus. He pleaded for divine mercy, even though the crowd rebuked him. Subsequent to divine healing, he "followed Jesus along the road" (Mark 10:52). But that wasn't all. Everyone in Christ's company immediately headed to Jerusalem for the triumphal entry (see Mark 11). Recall the connection in Scripture. Once Bartimaeus' eyes were opened, once his focus was readjusted by God, his life purpose shifted dramatically. He turned from serving self to serving the Savior. Picture a former blind man who no longer gropes in darkness. Is there any doubt what Bartimaeus did, as he joined the jubilant crowd who spread their cloaks on the road? Is there any question that he enthusiastically engaged in the very first Palm Sunday service? Can't you see him united with the chorus of voices, exclaiming "Hosanna! Blessed is he who comes in the name of the Lord!" (Mark 11:9)?

And it all started with a fundamental re-orientation. New vision brought new purpose. Bartimaeus' Commission came alive when he discovered three truths: (1) who Christ was; (2) who he was;[26] and (3) what he was called to do with God's help.[27]

This last feature, service, represents a critical element of healthy adolescent development.[28] Dean Borgman (1987, p. 73) notes the resurgence of the Peace Corps and other service organizations in the late 1980s. He concludes: "The strongest youth groups are those including a strong program for serving. Work-study-celebration programs bond a group in vital community so longed for and needed by adolescents."[29]

Youth Commission projects come in all shapes and sizes. Table 14.6 specifies a number of opportunities, modified from Cheryl Enderlein (1989) in Pioneer Clubs' *Searching Together* curriculum.[30]

Table 14.6

Youth Commission Projects

"Adopt a Grandparent." Have members adopt an elderly person from church or a nearby nursing home as their grandparent. Plan a get-acquainted party. Encourage members to see, call, or write to their grandparents. Continue to provide opportunities for members to share what they are doing and learning.

Bake Sale. Members bake cakes, cookies, muffins, and so on. Sell the items, and send the money to a missions group.

Big Brother/Big Sister. Members become big brothers or sisters to younger children in the church or community. Plan a party to get things started; then encourage members to stay in touch by asking how things are working out.

Booth at a Mall. Set up a booth at a local mall and distribute Christian literature. Another option is to distribute information on world hunger.

Bowling for Missions. Have members get sponsors to donate a specific amount of money for each pin they knock down during three games of bowling. Funds may be donated to a special missions project.

Care Packages. Make care packages for students attending college, people in the hospital, missionary children in foreign countries, and so on.

Eyeglass Collection. Collect used eyeglasses. You could go door-to-door or set up a collection box at the church. Send the glasses to an agency that sends them to people in needy countries.

Free Car Wash. Give people something for nothing. Sponsor a free car wash for your community. To advertise: make posters, ask local papers for free ad space, put an announcement in the church bulletin, print flyers to put on neighborhood cars.

Help the Elderly. Set up a job service to help elderly people. Members could shovel snow, clean windows, mow lawns, or plant flowers.

Heroes of Our Faith Celebration. Do research on some of the older members in your congregation. Hold a "This Is Your Life" type of recognition service for them.

Hospital Visits. Make arrangements with a hospital for your group to visit patients who do not have regular visitors. Have your pastor or a nurse talk with members so they know what to expect.

Nursing Home Visits. Plan a worship service or talent show for residents of a nursing home. You could do this quarterly.

Pen Pals. Begin corresponding with junior high missionary children. Learn about the countries they live in. Send cards on holidays and their birthdays. Find out something they really like but are unable to buy in their country, and ship it to them.

Toys for Tots. Collect toys for young children in a hospital or orphanage. Wrap the toys before you give them away.

Tutoring Service. Arrange for members to help younger children with their homework. Ask a teacher to talk with members about tutoring. Schedule a regular time and place for the tutoring.

Source: Modified from Enderlein (1989, pp. 12–13).

Think about It

Using Enderlein's examples to get you started, create at least two more projects for the teen's Commission task. Be specific. (*Optional:* Develop your three projects within a range—low, moderate, and high degrees of challenge.)

1. _____
   _____

2. _____
   _____

Once again, Gospel Light's *Light Force* and Rick Bundschuh's *On-Site* (1989) curriculum advance commendable material for Commission. "The Light from Your House" lesson provides one superb illustration of the former. Specifically, "Bible Exploration" (Step 1) attends to who we are ("light[s] of the world") and how we became lights. Step 3 underscores Commission since it explicitly deals with how we should live as "light"; three real-life case studies in Step 3 are provided for this purpose (see "The Parchment").

Cue Learning (of the Conditioning family) is featured in the crossword puzzle (as a reminder of the lesson's key verse), and in the subsequent "Daily Nuggets" section.

The Light From Your House
Session 4

INSIGHTS FOR THE LEADER

The topic for this session is Jesus' statement to His disciples, "You are the light of the world" (Matt. 5:14). This is an example of "parabolic sayings" used by Jesus to make a point. A parabolic saying makes use of everyday facts well-known by the audience.

When Jesus told His disciples that they were the light of the world, He did so knowing that God is light (see 1 John 1:5; Jas. 1:17) and that He Himself, the Son, was sent forth to be "the light of the world" (see Matt. 4:16; John 1:4,9; 8:12; 9:4,5; 12:35,36).

Light comes from its own source, or from a reflection of a source. The reason we as Christ's followers can be like lights to the world is that God has given us the capacity to receive light from Him through Christ. We reflect and project God's light much as the moon or the planets shine by the light of the sun. Because Christ is in us, we receive God's transmission of light, and we are to beam that light as would a bright lamp on a tall lampstand.

Make sure students understand that the Christian's light is a derived light. It is God's light with which others must be dazzled. The glory must go to Him. The lamp is not to be the center of focus. You don't turn on a lamp in your room in order to look at and admire the lamp; you turn it on so that you can see by its light. Similarly, Christians are to provide the light that will help others "see" the way to God. Light causes darkness to vanish. In much

the same way the very presence and nature of God simply repels sin. Obviously the more light we have, the less darkness. Likewise, the more we take on God's nature the less room sin has to grow in us.

The function of light is to enable us to see where we are going and to know clearly what we are doing in the spiritual realm. This process also reveals some unpleasant truths about ourselves and our surroundings. It is clear that by showering us with His light He is not attempting to limit us, but to help us see what is really there, hidden in the cloak of darkness.

Jesus said, "Neither do people light a lamp and put it under a bowl. Instead they put it on its stand, and it gives light to everyone in the house" (Matt. 5:15). The reason for turning on a lamp is to let the light shine. God puts Christians into the world to be lights. We are to reflect His light to others so that they will praise Him.

There are sometimes barriers thrown around our light that keep it from doing the job it was meant to do. Poor choice of friends, lack of self-control, poor devotional habits, bad attitudes, selfishness and many other diversions can throw a dark shade on our light to the world.

As we free ourselves from the barriers blocking our light we can find many opportunities to reflect Christ in an accurate way. Young people can shine for Jesus at home, at school,

WHAT THE SESSION IS ABOUT

Christians' lives should reflect God's working in us.

SCRIPTURE STUDIED

Matthew 5:14-16.

KEY PASSAGE

"In the same way, let your light shine before men, that they may see your good deeds and praise your Father in heaven." Matthew 5:16

AIMS OF THE SESSION

During this session your learners will:

1. Define the meaning of "light of the world";
2. Explain how to be a "light" to other people;
3. List situations in which they can be better reflections of Christ.

in their free-time activities, in church programs—in fact, wherever they go. A "shining light" Christian at home will be cooperative, obedient to parents, kind to brothers and sisters. At school the Christian will be courteous to others and will exclude no one from his or her friendship. This "shining light" will try to do his or her best in studies and will cooperate with teachers and coaches. The same attitudes of love, kindness and caring for the rights and needs of others will be manifested in clubs, sports and just "hanging around" with friends. Christians who let their lights shine will attract others to the light who is Jesus.

SESSION PLAN

BEFORE CLASS BEGINS: Photocopy enough Parchment worksheets for each student to have one. Follow the instructions on the Teaching Resource page which immediately follows the Parchment. See the CREATIVE ALTERNATIVE to the ATTENTION GRABBER for special materials required.

Attention Grabber

ATTENTION GRABBER (2-3 minutes)

Materials needed: The Teaching Resource page, cut apart as described on the page.

As students enter the classroom, give each student one of the slips you've cut from the Teaching Resource page. Tell students that they are to solve the riddle on the slips, and that there are a total of three different kinds of slips. Instruct your learners to mill around until they've each had a chance to read all three slips. The first student to give the correct answer is the winner. The answer is "light."

Make a transition to the EXPLORATION by commenting on the importance of light for daily activities; explain that this session will explore something Jesus said about His followers being light.

CREATIVE ALTERNATIVE (5-10 minutes)

Materials needed: Scarves or bandannas to serve as blindfolds; candy bar or other edible reward.

Explain, **We're going to have a race to see who can be the first to get across the room blindfolded and find the candy bar I'll place on the other side.** Show the candy bar to students and continue, **The first one to find it can keep it. Some of you will be blindfolded and will have to move across the room without being able to see. The rest of you will stand on the sidelines. The spectators can call directions to the blindfolded people.** (You may want to warn the superintendent about this one.) **But you who are blindfolded won't know whether the other people are giving you good instructions or are trying to confuse you. You won't really know whom to believe.**

NOTES

Select students to be blindfolded by choosing those whose birthday is nearest to today. Make sure the blindfold is 100 percent effective. After the students are blindfolded, place the candy bar opposite them in plain sight. If you like, spin the players to make them slightly dizzy. Move the other students to the sides of the room and let the "race" begin. End the activity when one student has found the candy bar. If five minutes have elapsed and no one has found it, end the activity without a winner, and give the reward to the closest person.

Make a transition to the next part of the session by commenting on the obvious difference between darkness and light, and how light helps us avoid confusion and shows us the right path. Explain that this session will focus on something Jesus said about His followers being light.

Bible Exploration

EXPLORATION: (20-25 minutes)

Step 1 (5-7 minutes): One person in the class should read Matthew 5:14-16 aloud while the rest follow in their own Bibles. Ask the following questions, jotting students' responses on your chalkboard.

1. **What do you think Jesus meant by saying, "You are the light of the world"?**
2. **Who is the true light?**
3. **How do you think we become lights ourselves?**

Commend and underscore thoughtful and appropriate answers. Correct any inaccurate ideas, using material from INSIGHTS FOR THE LEADER. *Step 2* (6-8 minutes): Erase your chalkboard if necessary, and write on it these three headings: Sources of Light; Things that Block Light; Things that Prevent Christians from Shining.

Explain, **In the left column let's list all the possible sources of light that we can think of. Then in the middle column I want you to tell me all the things you can think of that could block that light. In the last column I want you to tell me what prevents a Christian from shedding the light that he or she has.**

Allow students to share their thoughts. Ask, **What are some ways that we can prevent our "light" from being blocked?** Let volunteers respond.

Step 3 (7-10 minutes): Tell students to look at their Parchment worksheets. Read Situation 1 to your class, and lead a discussion based on the situation and the questions that follow it on the worksheet. Do this for all three situations, or for as many as time allows.

CONCLUSION (2-3 minutes)

Direct attention to the section of the Parchment titled, "I Need to Shine For." Instruct students, **Think about people who need to see Christ in your life. They may be family members, people at school, people on your team or in your club. Write the names of three of them. Then pray silently that our Lord will help you do a better job of reflecting His light to these people.**

Close in a brief audible prayer.
Distribute the Fun Page.

Your students may wish to see this solution to the Fun Page Puzzle.

(If you like, write the solution on an extra copy of the Fun Page and pin it to your classroom bulletin board.)

Note: See "BEFORE CLASS BEGINS" on page 59.

The Parchment

Let Your Light Shine

About half the kids in your youth group are really trying to be the Christians Jesus wants them to be. But the rest of the kids are just "fakin' it." They are there for the fun events and games. They don't care about Jesus at all.

Situation 1:

1. How do the things Jesus said about the light relate to this situation?

2. What could you do to help one or two of these "fakin' it" kids?

Situation 2:

Your big sister has been blowing it: she's been sneaking out the window at night to go see her boyfriend. You're not only concerned about her deception, but about what she may be doing with her boyfriend.

1. How do you think Jesus would deal with your sister if He could talk to her face to face?

2. What do you think He would want *you* to do for your sister?

3. What could you do if your sister did not respond to you?

Situation 3:

During lunch in the school cafeteria, a kid trips and splashes a chocolate shake all over your friend sitting next to you. Your friend goes bananas, screaming and swearing at the kid who tripped.

1. Name something you could do or say immediately that would "shine some light" into the situation.

2. What could you do later in a quiet moment that would help your friend?

I Need to Shine for:

Write the names of three people who need to see Jesus in your life. Then write some simple things you could do to let His light shine in their lives.

Teaching Resource 4   Instructions: Cut apart all the slips on this page (if you expect more than twelve students in your class, make enough photocopies of this page for each student to have one slip.)

Solve this riddle: "Part of the time I come for free, the rest of the time you pay for me. What am I?"	**Solve this riddle:** "I am faster than the fastest thing, but if I run into you, you'll feel no sting. What am I?"	**Solve this riddle:** "Here's a tough one— I come in waves, but I'm not the ocean. What am I?"
Solve this riddle: "Part of the time I come for free, the rest of the time you pay for me. What am I?"	**Solve this riddle:** "I am faster than the fastest thing, but if I run into you, you'll feel no sting. What am I?"	**Solve this riddle:** "Here's a tough one— I come in waves, but I'm not the ocean. What am I?"
Solve this riddle: "Part of the time I come for free, the rest of the time you pay for me. What am I?"	**Solve this riddle:** "I am faster than the fastest thing, but if I run into you, you'll feel no sting. What am I?"	**Solve this riddle:** "Here's a tough one— I come in waves, but I'm not the ocean. What am I?"
Solve this riddle: "Part of the time I come for free, the rest of the time you pay for me. What am I?"	**Solve this riddle:** "I am faster than the fastest thing, but if I run into you, you'll feel no sting. What am I?"	**Solve this riddle:** "Here's a tough one— I come in waves, but I'm not the ocean. What am I?"

**The Bible says that we should let our light shine (Matt. 5:16).
In order to help drive this home, we've come up with this
lighthearted, light-headed lightweight crossword puzzle about
—you guessed it—LIGHT! Most of the answers relate somehow
to light. The person who gave you this page has the solution.**

Session 4

ACROSS

1. When Jesus says, "You are the light of the world" (Matt. 5:14), who does He mean?
6. Comes after day.
9. 3.14159.
12. Short for "identity."
13. "You are the light _____ world." (Matt. 5:14. Two words.)
16. "Turn on the _____."
17. A color in the rainbow.
19. The garden of _____ (Gen. 2:8).
21. Finish
22. A shining light _____ the subject.
28. We are to be the light of the _____ (Matt. 5:14).
32. What a sinner commits.
33. "What _____?"
34. Short for "each."
35. A device for turning the lights down.
37. In boxing, when a fighter "punches your lights out," it's a _____.
38. _____, what, where, when, why.
40. The opposite of "dim."
42. In electrical terms; a unit of current (abbreviated form).
43. To destroy, or an ancient damaged site.
47. The Gospel of _____.
48. Not your pa, but your _____.
50. One less than twice.

51. If your window has these, you can adjust the light.
53. A truth.
55. _____ of light: the sun, light bulbs, fire, etc.
57. "I have _____ the light!"
58. A city mentioned in Joshua 7:2.
59. You generally look up _____ see the sun.
60. Happens just before night.
62. Happens about 12 hours after 60 across.
64. Your sister's daughter is your _____.
65. Short for "Police Dept."
66. An old-fashioned name for the sun.
67. Opposite of "no."

DOWN

1. A sound doves make.
2. If your life is routine and boring, you're in a _____.
3. Your eyes need light to _____.
4. The sun doesn't shine _____ night.
5. What the sun does during the day.
6. When someone understands something, you might say, "That's it! You've hit it on the _____!"
7. In many versions of the Bible, Matt. 5:16 says we are to let our light shine so people will see our _____ (two words).
8. A drink similar to coffee.
9. An animal mentioned in the Bible.
10. If a light bulb appears over your head, it means you have a bright _____.
11. Who, what, where, when, _____.
14. In a storm, sailors look for a light _____.
15. When Daniel was put in it, it was probably dark in the lions' _____, (Dan. 6:16)
16. An old song: "This little light of mine, I'm gonna _____ it shine."
18. A word meaning "nothing" or "of no effect."
20. "Light has come into the world, but men loved _____ instead of light" (John 3:19, NASB).
23. "Your word is a _____ to my feet" (Psalm 119:105).
24. You look at your reflection in this.
25. "But if we walk _____ the light . . ." (1 John 1:7).
26. Past tense of "see."
27. Spanish for 44 down.
29. If you want to hide something in the darkness, you could sweep it under the _____.
30. This is what a detective does.
31. These two were the original people in the garden of Eden: _____ and _____.
36. Short for "I am a."
39. Plural of 14 down.
40. If you come too close to fire, you may suffer _____.
41. Short for "in other words," in Latin that is.
44. Your father's brother is your _____.
45. Frozen water.
46. Persons who cannot see are _____.
47. A boy's name.
49. The opposite of "stop."
52. The president says no to a bill.
53. This will burn you.
54. You probably have five of these on your foot.
55. Jesus is the _____ of God.
56. To "employ" something. For example, a hammer.
58. "_____ and all."
61. Opposite of down.
63. "Who _____ it?"

DAILY NUGGETS

Day 1 Read Luke 11:33-36. What part of the body is the lamp? What happens when it is good?

Day 2 Ephesians 5:8-14. How should we walk as children of the light?

Day 3 Philippians 2:14,15. How should we do things? What should we become?

Day 4 1 Timothy 4:12. In what ways are young Christians to be examples? How could you be a good example this week?

Day 5 1 Peter 2:9. What does Peter say Christians are? What are they to do? Are you doing this?

Day 6 Matthew 5:14. How will you be a light to someone this week?

HOT THOT

"In the same way, let your light shine before men, that they may see your good deeds and praise your Father in heaven." Matthew 5:16

POP SHEET

Session 4

THEME: Christians' lives should reflect God's light.

BIBLE STUDY OUTLINE

Read John 8:12 to your listeners. Stress the fact that Christians have Jesus in their lives, and therefore have His light. Describe the nature of light (it illuminates, reveals, exposes, brings to attention) and compare it to the spiritual light that Christians have.
Now read Philippians 2:14,15. Make the following points:

• We are to be blameless and pure, two things that are seemingly rare in our time. And we are to be without fault in a crooked and perverse generation. In other words, we are to stand out like sore thumbs! Or as the Bible puts it, we are to shine "like stars in the universe." It is never easy to take a stand against the majority of people. It's not easy to say to a good friend, "No, I won't do that because I'm a Christian," or "I want to be like this and do this good thing because I am a Christian." But that's what Christ calls us to do. We are to be different. We are to shine like lights. Christ's light is to shine through us. *(Now go to the OBJECT LESSON.)*

OBJECT LESSON: SIN SACKS

Materials needed: A table lamp with the shade removed to expose the bare light bulb; extension cord if needed; several paper lunch sacks; a felt marker. Note: This object lesson works best in a darkened room.

Plug in and turn on the lamp for all to see. Again talk about the nature of the light it casts; how it illuminates, helps us see, and so on. Now hold up one of the sacks. Say, **This sack represents sin.** Label a common sin on the sack with the marker, such as "Bad Language." **When I place this sin sack over the light, see what happens. It dims the light and makes it much harder to see.** Leave the sack on the light bulb. Take another sack and again label it with another common sin (ask the crowd to make suggestions). Cover the first sack with the second. Do this several times until the light is completely blocked. Discuss the nature of sin and the way it can block a Christian's effectiveness and purpose. Talk about confession and forgiveness of sin, removing the sacks one by one as you do.

Wrap up the message by describing how a person who shines with God's light can make a positive and important impact in the lives of other people.

DISCUSSION QUESTIONS

1. **What do the words *blameless* and *pure* mean? How can we be that way?**

2. **In what ways is our generation crooked and perverse?**

3. **Name several practical ways a Christian can shine God's light on friends or family.**

4. **How can we help each other when we find it hard to shine or stay blameless and pure?**

NOTES

This second activity encourages the habit of daily devotional reading. Passages pertinent to the lesson, as well as useful life application questions, promote receptivity of this devotional routine.

Consequence Learning is introduced in the "Creative Alternative" through a blindfold exercise. One simple reward includes a candy bar for the winner. A more sophisticated reward pertains to the search for correct information; blindfolded youth try to discern good from bad advice given by spectators on the sidelines. The purpose illustrates how spiritual darkness yields confusion through worldly perceptions. The "Bible Exploration" time offers helpful feedback: Step 1 (a group study of Matt. 5:14–16), Step 2 (a group brainstorming session), and Step 3 (the previously cited case studies). Each supplies teacher and student responses. Curriculum guidelines for the instructor stress this feedback method: "Commend and underscore thoughtful and appropriate answers. Correct any inaccurate ideas, using material from Insights for the Leader."

Structured Modeling occurs in the reading and contemplation of Scripture. But this lesson provides one additional (albeit somewhat negative) example of modeling, through the case studies (see "The Parchment"). For instance, consider Situation 2: "Your big sister has been blowing it: she's been sneaking out the window at night to go see her boyfriend." This real-life scenario lends credibility to the lesson. This believable story takes advantage of teachable moments and encourages effective, interpersonal learning.

Spontaneous Modeling is exceptionally replicated in the blindfold race, as spectators shout both correct and incorrect directions to participants. Very much like teen life itself, peer pressure is simulated by spectator involvement. As the curriculum writer reminds the teacher: "[The] blindfolded won't know whether the other people are giving you good instructions or are trying to confuse you. You won't really know whom to believe." Thus, the Social Learning family receives substantial visibility. It portrays the teen's actual world.

Finally, Identification Learning extends from the Information-Processing family throughout the entire lesson. That is, the lightness-darkness motif stands out as both an advance organizer (framing the entire subject matter at the outset) and as a graphic metaphor-picture. The object lesson, "Sin Snacks," draws out analogies concerning the nature of light.

Inquiry Learning ranges from a provocative riddle exercise (see "Attention Grabber") to standard discussion questions (see "PopSheet"). "The Parchment" raises thoughtful faith dilemmas through cases. The conclusion of these dilemmas challenges the youth to personal life change. The concluding portion of the case studies requests: "Write the names of three people who need to see Jesus in your life. Then write some simple things you could do to let His light shine in their lives." A problem is coupled with the challenge of life response.

Table 14.7 supplies a visual review of these previous paragraphs.

On-Site's "Fish Pond" extends a more traditional interpretation of Commission: "God wants us to actively win others to Christ." The lesson objectives are straightforward. The familiar picture, "fishers of men," is analyzed (see Illustration 14.9).

By contrast, Illustration 14.10 demonstrates a nontraditional view of Commission. "Old Folks' Home" questions teens regarding their respect for the oldest generation. "What kind of treatment do you think the Bible suggests for older people?" represents this lesson's focus. Following their experiential exercise, teens create

Table 14.7

Youth Curriculum on Commission

Conditioning Family	Cue Learning	1. the crossword puzzle, using the key verse 2. the challenge to develop a daily devotional life
	Consequence Learning	1. the blindfold game 2. the Bible Exploration
Social Family	Structured Modeling	1. the reading and study of Scripture 2. the case studies
	Spontaneous Modeling	1. the blindfold game, especially the real-life "advice" of sideline spectators
Information-Processing Family	Identification Learning	1. the lightness-darkness motif as both: (a) an advanced organizer; and (b) a helpful metaphor 2. the object lesson "Sin Snacks" develops this motif, too
	Inquiry Learning	1. the riddle exercise 2. the discussion questions 3. the conclusion of the case studies

"ten commandments" that reflect their personal obligations to the elderly. Individual accountability surfaces as youth write to older people, seeking advice on various issues.

Conclusion

Scrutinize the following testimony of a teenager who experienced a workcamp.[31] Try to identify all four themes of Christian maturity:

My greatest fear was being alone in a crowd. I had always been shy around strangers, and my greatest fear revealed my low self-esteem. Then came the summer of our workcamp. . . . The first night, I talked with a youth pastor I didn't even know. I was amazed at the ease with which I talked with this stranger. This was the "new me" coming out—a stronger, self-assured individual. During the week, I worked with five other participants from different churches. Our assignment was to build a cinder-block wall behind the house

of Sonny and Carol. My group was apprehensive about meeting these strangers, but the excitement of helping quickly grew on us. . . . At the workcamp, I found strength inside me I never thought I possessed. I learned to do things independently. I found the confidence I had always lacked. Now I am prepared to meet the challenges of going to college and facing new experiences with new people. The workcamp convinced me I can handle my greatest fear and live with confidence.

Think about It

1. What themes did you find in this case study?_____

_____

2. Notice the integration of the themes—how each is affected by the other. If you were asked to provide one word of advice to youth leaders concerning theme integration, what would you say?_____

_____

Illustration 14.9

FISH POND

Sometimes combining fun and a lesson can help create a connection to Scripture that will never be forgotten. One way to do this is to create a lesson about being "fishers of men" combined with a fishing trip.

Of course, you will need to bring bait, fishing poles , clean equipment, and a charcoal grill (if you plan on eating your catch). Kids can learn a lot from the comparisons of winning a fish for supper and winning another person to faith in the Lord!

Focus: God wants us to actively win others to Christ
Bible passage to share and discuss: Mark 1:14–20.

Getting Started

At the fishing hole discuss what kind of fish you're going after and what kind of bait they like. Show kids how to bait their hook and to cast without scaring away the fish.

Looking in the Word

Distribute preprinted copies of the Scripture to all of your students. Ask them to memorize verses 16–18 as they sit waiting for a fish to bite.

Plugging into Daily Life

As you wrap up your short fishing trip ask your students:

1. If we are to be "fishers of men" what kind of "bait" do you think would be attractive to people who don't know Christ?

2. What is the significance of Andrew and Simon Peter leaving their nets behind to follow Christ?

3. What things of our old life might we have to leave behind when we decide to become "fishers of men"?

4. What would you say is the single most important way to effectively be a witness for Christ in a school like yours?

Adding It All Up

Ask students to think of one friend that they know who is not a Christian. Ask them to consider an action that they could take this week that would make coming to Christ more interesting to this person. Close by having each student silently pray for the person they have thought of.

Illustration 14.10

ON-SITE IN AN OLD FOLKS' HOME

his lesson can be combined with a service project directed to the senior citizens in your community or to people in retirement homes or convalescent hospitals.

With the exception of Grandma and Grandpa, many kids seldom get a chance to interact with people of the oldest generation. Putting kids in contact with old people (especially those who are still vital) can teach them a valuable lesson in respect, compassion, understanding, and dignity. The Bible clearly teaches that old people have a wealth of wisdom and experience to learn from.

Note: If your group is to visit people who are sick, handicapped, or very weak, it may be good to take an older person with you who is in the peak of health, so that kids can see that old age is not automatically the same as incapacitation.

Focus: Old people have great worth, value and wisdom
Bible passages to share and discuss: Job 12:12, Proverbs 16:31, Psalm 92:12–15.

Getting Started

Ask:

1. How old would you like to live to?

2. What is something that do you do now that you plan to still be able to do when you are eighty?

3. What do you find most interesting about old people?

Looking in the Word

Ask your students to read the passage and then to help you create a list of attributes that come with a life of godly living.

Ask: What kind of treatment do you think the Bible suggests for older people?

Plugging into Daily Life

With your students create "ten commandments" we should consider in order to show respect to old folks and a willingness to learn from them. Hang your ten commandments on the wall of your classroom.

Adding It All Up

Distribute pencils, paper, envelopes, and stamps to your students. Ask each of them to write a letter to an old person they know, asking for advice and insight on a number of issues. (You may wish to brainstorm some issues with the students before distributing the paper.)

Adolescence is an especially impressionable age. Some have compared it to a replay of childhood.[32] Others speak of the potential for powerful memory building.[33] Consequently, we youth leaders must design pertinent ministries that might develop maturity. We must coordinate the complementary challenges of the four themes. We must move teens beyond themselves, consciously "apathy busting" in the process. When young people discover their potential, and have opportunities to utilize that potential, their views about God, the Christian faith, and themselves can be revolutionized.[34]

Camps and missions projects tend to feature effective instructional ingredients of productive youth programming.[35] Burns (1988, p. 92) testifies of an often-experienced consequence of teen camps and retreats:

A 27-year-old man came up to me recently at a restaurant and said, "In 1977 (ten years prior) we went on a week long houseboat trip together. It was the greatest week of my entire life. Seldom does a day go by without me thinking about that significant week. Until recently I've strayed from God, but the memory of that single week on the houseboat with our church group has drawn me back to God." To be honest, I had almost forgotten the trip and barely recognized the man. Yet that one-week trip had created a lifelong memory for him.

Burns believes that one of the best results of meaningful retreats is tradition building. Youth begin to anticipate the annual ski weekend or service project. The positive memory both prepares them for subsequent experiences and anchors their faith in times of turbulence. This experienced youth leader advises: "Never overlook the power of creating healthy lifelong memories and traditions."

Paul Borthwick affirms this assessment of camps and mission projects. His conclusions (1988, p. 169) lay the foundation for ministries with adolescents. When older teens apply for college, he says, "many of our students list the youth missionary teams as *the most important and memorable experience* of their high school life. That kind of testimony encourages us to make these teams a priority in the youth ministry."

Such projects increase our dependency on God (Communion) and on others (Community). Challenges concerning self (Character) are also voiced. And, certainly, outreach (Commission) is evident. For the sake of integrity and obedience to Scripture, we leaders must boldly assess traditional patterns of youth work. We must constantly question: "What does it take to produce healthy signs of growth in my teens?"

15 Teaching Children: Classroom Situations

A Biblical View of Childhood

Children *do* need to "learn about God." But what do we need to learn about *children*? How are they special, even unique? What must we understand about children and their world?

Insights from Paul's Childhood

Paul provides a provocative reflection from his own childhood in 1 Corinthians 13:11. Contemplate this well-known verse, as though you have never read it before. Consider what the author *is* saying and what he is *not* saying: "When I was a child, I thought like a child, I reasoned like a child. When I became a man I put childish ways behind me."

1. What do you think is the major point of this verse in relation to childhood?

2. What is Paul *not* saying about childhood?

3. What do you think he is affirming about adulthood?

4. Write your own paraphrase of the verse.

First, Paul speaks of the similarities children have with all people: They talk and they think, for example. Remember the human growth model presented in Chapters 5 and 6? Like adults children possess the structural dimension of life (physical, cognitive, and personality development) and the functional dimension (faith, moral, social, and vocational development).

Second, Paul lists the dissimilarities of childhood: Young children stand apart from other age groups. Three times he uses the phrase "like a child" to denote this differentiation. He claims, by way of example, that there is something distinctive about a child's speech and thought patterns.

Third, childhood is not to be negatively contrasted with adolescence or adulthood. In fact, in certain categories childhood can never be compared with other phases of life. It stands on its own. Children are not incomplete or miniature adults, but neither are they sub-par youth. Read between the lines of Paul's confession. In fact, insert this parenthetical phrase between his two main propositions: "And it was appropriate to act this way when I was a child." The inserted commentary provides the real meaning of

Paul's personal testimony: "Being a child" should not cause guilt feelings.

Finally, 1 Corinthians 13:11 discerns the difference between child-*likeness* and child-*ishness*. The former term verifies the previous point: "Being a child" is proper and acceptable when you are a child. The latter term is judgmental. It condemns an adult's behavior as "childish," when actions fail to proceed from that infant state (cf. 1 Cor. 3:1–3).[1]

Some believers consider children to be an inconvenience when it comes to ministry. We must put up with them, they contend. Their reasoning includes such comments as:

"Children aren't full participants in church life. They only receive; they don't give."

"They have no meaningful function in ministry. They can't serve as teachers. They can't help in the kitchen or drive a car. They can't even help pay the costs of church ministry."

"Young ones are more of a nuisance to ministry. They cry and act silly. Children distract others who want to learn and grow. As long as we keep them out of the way and keep them quiet, everyone will be happy."

"Let's get on with the more important ministry to adults (and, maybe youth)."[2]

Reflect on these questions about childhood:

1. Why does God have all humans begin life as babies instead of adults?

2. Why do several years of growth precede adulthood? Why didn't God

make this period of time much shorter, like he did for animals?

3. When he came to earth, why was Jesus born as a baby? Why didn't he just appear as an adult, and save all that time?

Childhood as a Biblical Metaphor

What else can we learn about children from God's revealed truth? Scripture exhorts us to observe and to learn from children. The New Testament often focuses on children as spiritual object lessons. Examples of both the good and the bad appear. Consider some representative verses about childhood in Table 15.1. Each illustration prompts us to comprehend a certain dimension of our earlier years. Thus, if only for the sake of our spiritual benefit, we *must* understand children.

Table 15.1

New Testament Metaphors of Children

- "And do not think you can say to yourselves, 'We have Abraham as our father.' I tell you that out of these stones God can raise up children for Abraham." (Matt. 3:9; par. Luke 3:8; cf. John 8:39)
- "She begged Jesus to drive the demon out of her daughter. 'First let the children eat all they want,' he told her, 'for it is not right to take the children's bread and toss it to their dogs.'" (Mark 7:26–27)
- "The disciples were amazed at his words. But Jesus said again, 'Children, how hard it is to enter the kingdom of God!'" (Mark 10:24; cf. John 13:33)
- "To what, then, can I compare the people of this generation? What are they like? They are like children sitting in the marketplace and calling out to each other: 'We played the flute for you, and you did not dance; we sang a dirge, and you did not cry.'" (Luke 7:31–32)
- "Yet to all who received him, to those who believed in his name, he gave the right to become children of God . . . born of God." (John 1:12–13; cf. Rom. 8:16; 9:8)
- "So also, when we were children, we were in slavery under the basic principles of the world." (Gal. 4:3)
- "Then we will no longer be infants, tossed back and forth by the waves, and blown here and there by every wind of teaching and by cunning and craftiness of men in their deceitful scheming." (Eph. 4:14)
- "For you were once darkness, but now you are light in the Lord. Live as children of light." (Eph. 5:8; cf. Phil. 2:15)
- "As obedient children, do not conform to the evil desires you had when you lived in ignorance." (1 Pet. 1:14)
- "You are her [Sarah's] daughters if you do what is right and do not give way to fear." (1 Pet. 3:6b)
- "This is how we know who the children of God are and who the children of the devil are: Anyone who does not do what is right is not a child of God; nor is anyone who does not love his brother." (1 John 3:10)

Building on these metaphorical references as a whole, the Bible offers particular insights into growing patterns. Ponder these questions: What are the needs of new believers? How do we meet these special needs? In 1 John 2:12–14, John refers to a helpful model of nurture, using the family metaphor of "children," "young men," and "fathers." Paul (1 Cor. 3:1–2) uses the common metaphor of "baby milk" in contrast with "solid food." This comparison depicts diverse levels of growth toward maturity. Thus, references to human relationships and to physical qualities of growth parallel spiritual realities.

Moreover, what Christ says about young ones demands our consideration. How he honors them bears repetition: "'Let the little children come to me, and do not hinder them, for the kingdom of God belongs to such as these. I tell you the truth, anyone who will not receive the kingdom of God like a little child will never enter it.' And he took the children in his arms, put his hands on them and blessed them" (Mark 10:14–16).[3] Do we bless children in our various settings? Or do we curse them? How is Christ's model emulated or ignored in our contemporary environments? For instance, according to current estimates, two-thirds of believers in America come to a saving knowledge of Jesus Christ before they reach the age of eighteen (Barna 1990, p. 119). This fact alone requires that we seriously attend to the needs of young ones. Children's work must not be relegated to a lowly status in the church's educational ministry. Whoever "welcomes a little child" in Christ's name welcomes Christ himself (Matt. 18:5).

A Focus on Conditioning Learning

Children enter life helpless. Other people make choices for them. They cannot look after themselves; they must receive constant care. Although they are helpless, children possess an innate, God-given capacity to learn. During these early years, we leaders guide their growth by various means. For instance, as adult caregivers, we are role models for our children (Social Learning family). Furthermore, we stimulate their cognitive abilities (Information-Processing family). But our primary responsibility is shaping Christ-like attitudes and habits. Such nurturing strategies express the essence of the Conditioning Learning family.

As a reader, you might react negatively to this match of children and Conditioning theory. Part of your response, however, may stem from a limited notion of behaviorism. Far more than a system of rewards and punishments, Conditioning Learning af-

fects our thinking, attitudes, values, and skills. Such learning often occurs through what is known as "socialization." Patterns of child rearing outlined in the Old Testament point to this informal mode of education. In the Jewish home of that day, all the experiences of the young child's life—both the common and the special, the unplanned and the routine—became potential learning opportunities (Deut. 6:5–9). Children experienced multiple activities of family and cultural life (e.g., Sabbaths, the Passover, and other annual feasts). Initially, young ones were taught these customary practices. Later, interpretation and meaning were imparted (Exod. 12:24–27). Since life patterns developed without significant mediation of language and thought, even attitudes of small children were purposefully shaped. These formative years provided a critical opportunity to lay the foundation for godly dispositions and virtues.[4]

Through the Conditioning avenues of Consequence Learning (e.g., an adult saying "good girl" in response to a child's appropriate action) and Cue Learning (e.g., bedtime habits of prayer and singing), we help cultivate our children's acquisition of Christian values. Self-image in young ones results exclusively from environmental feedback. How others respond to children fashion the opinions they initially hold about themselves. As adult caregivers, we should soberly assess this image-shaping influence of children. We must monitor both explicit and implicit communication with youngsters so that God-honoring self-perceptions emerge.[5]

Some Christian educators and leaders falsely assume that the ultimate objective of children's ministry is to foster total autonomy in their young ones. Part of this faulty thinking originates from our Western ideal of rugged individualism—the "Lone Ranger" mentality. Biblical maturity represents a

Figure 15.1

Moving from Dependence to Interdependence

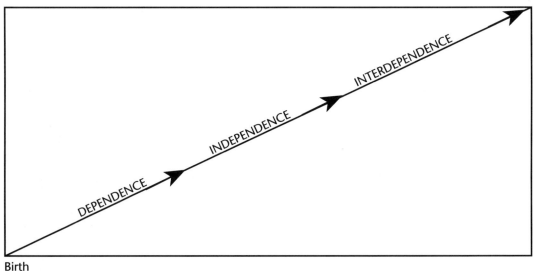

Adult Maturity

INTERDEPENDENCE

INDEPENDENCE

DEPENDENCE

Birth

healthier alternative. We don't seek, on the one hand, *dependence* as our aim. This robs us of personal choice and responsibility. Nor do we desire *independence;* this steals away interpersonal duties and accountability. Living a balanced life with others requires *interdependence.*

Recall John Mark (Acts 13:13)? His desertion showed his immaturity. He exhibited evidence of independence—freedom from all personal obligations—which led to his bankrupt, ineffective ministry. Had it not been for Barnabas' patient discipleship, John Mark may have never reversed his counterproductive direction. His ministry potential could have been in jeopardy. Providentially, in the end, this relative of Barnabas matured. Remember Paul's eventual petition for John Mark's services? It stands as a tribute to God's work through Barnabas and also as a concise statement of our *interdependent* aim: "Get Mark and

bring him with you, because he is helpful to me in my ministry" (2 Tim. 4:11).

Figure 15.1 suggests a visual way of understanding this important growth process. At first, all childhood abilities represent only potentials. These at-birth endowments are latent, but not fully usable. As evidence of maturity appears, we parents and leaders begin the process of "letting our children go." We launch them toward interdependent roles. Our prayer is for them, eventually, to serve as co-laborers with us.

Our facilitative task in the child's growth acknowledges two polarized duties: to provide both a *safe* and a *stimulating* environment. Most Christian leaders recognize the value of the former, and focus on physical and spiritual safety. Yet, problems arise when we foster an overly dependent condition. This may be perpetrated consciously or unconsciously. The consequence is identical: retarded growth. Because of potential negative effects outside the church and

Figure 15.2
Retarding Growth in Children

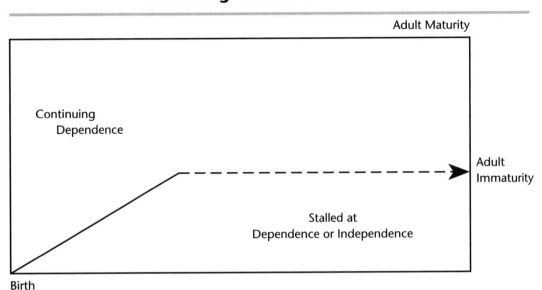

home, we may overprotect our children, shelter them inordinately from the world's influence. Such overprotection, ironically, hinders their growth. Either unhealthy dependence or extreme, rebellious independence results (see Figure 15.2).

Equally important to promoting safety—and sometimes diametrically opposed—we must also *stimulate* their growth. "No pain, no gain" often typifies this principle. Risk is involved, on our part and theirs. In large measure, this comes down to children encountering diverse experiences and making personal choices, within limits. Opting for these challenging strategies—even ones that lead to failure—frequently yields growth. "Guided failure," with the safety net of adult supervision, serves as one realistic principle to encourage interdependence.

Guidelines for Children's Programs

Before we detail issues related to classroom concerns, certain general consider-

ations deserve attention. Four rules of thumb should govern our stewardship of children's programs.

Parents must be involved in some way. Some programs ignore parents; others make parental involvement optional; still others require parental involvement. If the church takes seriously its task of equipping parents, church-home links are intentionally established. Sadly, some children's programs usurp parents' responsibility to nurture their children in godliness. Levels of involvement should take into consideration parents' needs, abilities, and limitations.

Target "at risk" children for special attention. Most congregations serve children with a variety of backgrounds: from healthy, spiritually vibrant settings to non-Christian, dysfunctional homes. Treating all children with the same curriculum intent will place the latter group at a significant disadvantage.

Learning activities should be age-appropriate. In Chapters 5 and 6 we looked at how children change as they grow. For instance, the difference in thinking capacity is not just one of *quantity*. Children are not restricted by an insufficient amount of information. Rather, they think in a *qualitatively* different manner than adults do. Their cognitive structures are restricted to a different type of logic. They can make mental references only to their own concrete experiences. Consider a seminarian's reflection about his childhood understanding of prayer:

> When I was quite small, I heard that God answered prayer. In my little head, that translated to "I ask God for things, and He gives them to me." Whatever I wanted I thought God would give me. Soon I found myself asking for some things that I never got. This caused a dissonance in my mind—God gives me what I ask for, but I ask for things that He doesn't give me. I could have responded with avoidance—ignoring or denying the presence of unanswered prayer. Another response could have been [assimilation]—"customizing" the new data to fit into my pre-existing framework. In this way, I might have said, "Ah, I didn't *really* want it anyway." A third response, and the most constructive, would be resolution [accommodation]—a working through of the discrepancy, modifying my thoughts to more accurately reflect reality. In my case, that would lead to a deep understanding of prayer and how God answers it.[6]

To effectively teach children, workers require a good sense of what is appropriate. Workers must not only understand children, but they must know what skills can be successfully performed in class. To use a clothing analogy, there must be a custom-fit of child and classroom activity—no tight apparel, no baggy garments.[7]

Carefully monitor the selection and training of children's workers. Since children are significantly influenced by their adult caregivers, the highest qualifications should be required of those who teach our children. It seems that, of all those who serve in the church, the lowest visibility and least honor are given to children's teachers and workers. Yet Paul exhorts that we should "treat with special honor" those parts of the body we tend to think are less honorable (1 Cor. 12:23).[8] We will come back to the topic of qualifications at the end of this chapter.

Teaching Young Children[9]

The operative principle for this age group is "guided play." For children, "play" compares to adult "work." Make no mistake about it: Play is serious business. It's God's way for them to grow. Therefore, prepare the nursery, toddler, and preschool environments with multiple resources and "learning centers." These centers (tables or areas of the room) can be organized around a particular segment of the lesson theme. Typically, teachers utilize several learning centers per lesson, including block building (wood or cardboard), housekeeping, library or book corner, music or listening post, puzzle rack, God's "wonder table" (science, including animals and insects), and art.

Teachers shouldn't be preoccupied about time. Let the children's curiosity, ability, and interest carry them through each planned learning opportunity. Instructors may limit the number of children per learning center, but the critical component rests in their intrinsic motivation. Play with children, using "guided conversation" to teach them about God and his world. Provide affirming comments to focus play, such as: "You like to use your hands. God made our hands" or "I like your smile. It makes me happy, too." Physical touch and eye contact complement verbal instruction. Wes Haystead (1989, pp. 16–17) suggests six methods for communicating Bible truths to young children:

1. Focus on relationships between teacher and child.
2. Provide firsthand experiences.
3. Look for teachable moments.
4. Add descriptive conversation.
5. Ask questions related to activity.
6. Answer questions.

Nursery Programs

The instructional objective for teaching in the nursery remains the same. As we noted earlier, the goal is to provide a *safe* and *stimulating* environment. Safety includes cleanliness of the room, sheets, and toys. Infants and toddlers must be prevented from unintentionally hurting each other. Remember that each child has notably different needs. They require distinct resources to stimulate growth.[10]

Think about It

Imagine that you are visiting a church for the first time. Also imagine you are a new parent. Standing at the nursery door, you are about to drop off your child. For each of the following aspects of the nursery, identify one characteristic that would make you feel *secure* in leaving your child in the nursery, or *anxious* about leaving your child:

(a) Nursery facilities
   (1) Secure:
   (2) Anxious:
(b) Nursery staff (e.g., their actions, their words)
   (1) Secure:
   (2) Anxious:
(c) Nursery policies or procedures
   (1) Secure:
   (2) Anxious:

Preschool Programs

Programs for preschoolers require more planning for educational activities. Guided conversation during play is a significant teaching mode. Conversation should be age-appropriate. Words must be limited to the child's experience. With evidence of the preschooler's growth, the potential for instructional techniques broadens.[11]

Teaching Older Children

Children in later childhood possess even greater potential. They raise tougher questions, hold deeper convictions, and present new challenges. As they mature, our goal is not just to impart information about God, but to help them become lifelong disciples of the Way. Effective work with older children involves balancing the four "Rs": relationship, responsibility, recognition, and remediation.

Relationship

Children need to be unconditionally accepted, to feel loved. This is communicated in classroom demeanor by kind, affirming words and personal interest in their lives. Yet, a deeper level of relationship requires out-of-class involvement as well. Doug, a sixth-grade Sunday school teacher, became convinced of this out-of-class potential. He discovered the positive difference in classroom behavior of Jim, a rambunctious child of a church family. Doug invited Jim and another Sunday

Illustration 15.1

4 Good News, Bad News

The bad news is . . .

Read 1 John 1:8. Whether we want to admit it or not, we all have sinned (even since we became Christians). Circle what you think sin is.

Sin is disobeying God.

Sin is ignoring God and not thinking about him.

Sin is getting mad and fighting.

Sin is being mean.

Sin is stealing and lying.

Sin is cheating on a test.

Sin is doing bad things like calling someone names.

Our sin keeps us from being friends with God. That's *bad* news.

The good news is . . .

Read I John 1:9. God loves us so much that he wants to forgive our sins. On a piece of paper, write a sin you need God to forgive. Pray and ask him to forgive you and help you do better.

Now tear up the paper, and throw it away. Because God has forgiven you, your sin is gone—just like the piece of paper. When God forgives us, we can be friends with him again. That's really *good* news!

5 New Life Is a Free Gift

When we become Christians, God gives us many free gifts. He makes us part of his family, he forgives us, and he gives us a new life. Read II Corinthians 5:17.

This blank page is like your new life in Christ. In each section, write or draw one way you want to show you have a new life in Christ.

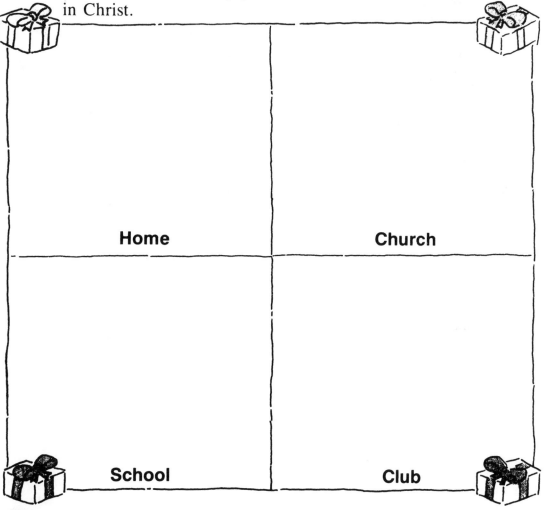

Home	**Church**
School	**Club**

6 Memory Verses

____ Romans 1:19

____ Romans 5:6

____ Acts 13:38

school classmate to play golf with him one Saturday. The special time together opened up new opportunities for trust and communication.

Responsibility

What expectations do we have of our older children? Do we offer them activities appropriate to their ability? Some children prefer to write new words to an old tune. Others want to play the role of a news reporter, interviewing a Bible character. Still others enjoy making billboard posters or bumper stickers. Children need "hands-on" experiences while studying God's Word. Much of class time can be devoted to such diverse activities.[12] If we regularly communicate positive expectations, children will eagerly attain our hopes for them.[13]

Recognition

We fail our children when we do not honor and appreciate the times they act appropriately ("Thank you for paying attention, Marla. That means a lot to me" or "I appreciate how hard you are working on your project, Jason"). Instead, we tend to emphasize negative behaviors ("Sit down, Joshua!"). Viewing our long-term teaching goal, we desire to help children become self-disciplined, mature adults. Attention to positive character traits is a necessity. In keeping with the Conditioning Learning's heightened emphasis, we must employ various modes of recognition: tangible honors (e.g., earning points for meaningful prizes) or more intangible rewards (e.g., compliments, hugs). This feedback encourages children's interest and effort to learn.[14] Without consistent and explicit indicators of progress (i.e., rewards), children will be ignorant of treasured Christian virtues.

Remediation

Dealing with inappropriate behavior represents a "Catch-22" dilemma: Nobody likes to do it, but if nothing happens, behavior usually gets worse. Surprisingly, many of the "behavior problems" of children in class frequently stem from teacher error: lack of good lesson planning; poor pacing of lessons ("dead time" between activities); or meaningless or irrelevant activities. Furthermore, our discipline strategy assumes that a strong foundation was established in the first three "R" guidelines: If we have not given attention to close *relationships,* failed to identify meaningful *responsibilities* or infrequently *recognized* growth, then we have not earned the right to correct behavior. Effective classroom management strategies utilize recognition (reward) *and* remediation (punishment) efforts in two directions: at *individual* levels (e.g., extra points; a "time out" corner) and *group* levels (e.g., earning or losing class privileges such as playing a favorite group game).[15]

Commendable Curriculum

In relation to the four themes of the Reconciliation Model of Christian maturity, every age must confront the topic of Communion. How do we teachers assist children to grow in relationship with their Creator? Community emphasizes belonging needs. We want children to experience the privileges and responsibilities of Christian fellowship. Also, every age must address the subject of Character. "What is it," we challenge each child, "that God wants you to be as an individual?" How we relate to the world around us brings up Commission concerns. Just two of the subcategories in this final category include evangelism and stewardship. The following section illustrates these four basic themes as they appear in one curriculum. These pages come from a booklet that each child studies and then brings to class.[16]

Table 15.2

Children's Curriculum on Communion

Information-Processing Learning Family

Identification Learning:	Picture of school scene
	Terms used: good news, bad news
	Examples of sin listed
	Torn paper exercise illustrating forgiveness
	Drawing activity of familiar settings
Inquiry Learning:	Identifying what student thinks is sin
	List own sins on paper
	Drawing exercise

Conditioning Learning Family

Consequence Learning:	Bible content: We are sinners, God forgives our sin
Cue Learning:	What "sin" is and that it separates us from God
	Memorizing Bible verse
	Associating "forgiveness" with torn paper

Social Learning Family

Structured Modeling:	Content of Bible verses
	Text explanation of sin and forgiveness
Spontaneous Modeling:	What student draws in each square

Communion

In Illustration 15.1, Section 4, the "bad news" highlights personal sin via Inquiry Learning. Children are asked to think about sin by circling statements. The "good news" instructs children to move from their general definition to particular sins. As they write out one personal sin on paper—and then tear it up, in light of God's 1 John 1:9 promise—a meaningful analogy develops between their action and God's forgiveness. Inquiry methodology continues in Section 5. There children create specific, deductive implications of new life in Christ through four familiar settings. These implications are affirmed (Consequence and Cue Learning) through a written account or drawings.

Table 15.2 summarizes the relevant avenues and activities.

Community

Section 1 encourages youngsters to understand the church. They are invited to tour their church facilities. They think and talk about "what happens in the rooms" they visit on the tour. Role models are provided by church members, who explain their leadership responsibilities. This hands-on tour helps children develop associations between function and facility (Cue Learning).

Section 2 continues an inquiry into "What Happens in Church?" with a study of Psalm 100:1–2 and worship. Discussion

All about Church

To earn this award, do the things listed and check off each one.

1 What's Your Church Like?

Go on a tour of your church. Go with your family or club. Talk about what happens in the rooms you visit. If you can, meet 1 or 2 church leaders. Find out what they do.

2 What Happens in Church?

Read or listen to Psalm 100:1-2. Talk with a grown-up about what it means to go to church to worship God. Circle the pictures that show ways you can worship God. Then pick one of those ways, and worship him right now.

3 How Can You Help Church Friends?

Do 2 of these things to encourage some of your church friends. That means to help them or cheer them up.

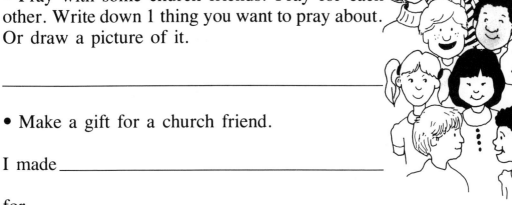

• Pray with some church friends. Pray for each other. Write down 1 thing you want to pray about. Or draw a picture of it.

_____

• Make a gift for a church friend.

I made _____

for _____.

• Visit someone from church who is sick. Or call

him or her on the telephone.

I talked to _____.

• Help fix some food for a meal at church.

I helped fix _____.

• Do something else you think of. Write it here.

_____

Table 15.3

Children's Curriculum on Community

Information-Processing Learning Family

Identification Learning:	Tour of church building with family or club
Inquiry Learning:	Tour: Talking about what happens in church Circle pictures relating to worship Pick one way to worship to practice now Pick two of four options to encourage a friend

Conditioning Learning Family

Consequence Learning:	Earning a reward for doing the activities Conversation with family or club on tour Bible content: Ps. 100:1–2 Discussion with group about worship Recording what activities were done
Cue Learning:	Tour: Purpose of each room in church building Pictures that do and do not show worship "Encourage" means various activities listed

Social Learning Family

Structured Modeling:	Tour: Church building architecture Bible verses Text explanation of worship and encouragement activities Pictures of worship
Spontaneous Modeling:	Tour: Conversation with club or family Interview adult about worship in church Interview with church leader Pray with a friend Write down what to pray about

with grownups fosters Spontaneous Modeling. Associations are reinforced by picture selection and personal worship experience (Consequence Learning). Children are challenged to serve another church member through prayer, a gift, or a visit in Section 3. Table 15.3 summarizes these avenues and activities.

Character

Children are told to ponder real-life scenarios in Section 4. They are asked: "Do these remind you of situations you've been in?" This Inquiry method prompts learners to draw on individualized analogies and conclusions. Follow-up discussion "with your club or with an adult you trust" provides for peer support and adult affirmation of a drug-free lifestyle. Section 5 allows students to reflect on Romans 12:1–2 and then to "help your friends say no, too." Finally, the project of creating a television commercial with friends fosters values through

4 You, Your Friends, and Drugs

Today was awful. The police came to our school and questioned a couple of girls who had gotten sick on drugs.

Jimmy and Al asked me to come to their secret party this afternoon. Jimmy said his brother could get us some beer. I wasn't sure what to say. . . .

We were playing at Tricia's house when we found these lying out. They were her mom's, but she wasn't home. We thought it might be fun to try just one. . . .

Most people face times like these sooner or later. Do these remind you of situations you've been in? Get together with your club or with an adult you trust and discuss how drugs can affect kids.

5 And Now, an Important Message . . .

You can be part of drug abuse prevention! How? First, say no to drugs yourself. (Romans 12:1-2 gives some good reasons.) Second, help your friends say no, too.

With your club or a group of friends, come up with a television commercial that encourages kids to say no to drugs. Act it out as if it were being filmed for television.

6 Who, Me? Afraid?

We've all got fears. Some are big and terrible. Some are little and silly, but real all the same. No matter what you're afraid of, the first step in overcoming a fear is admitting you have it.

What is your biggest fear? _____

What Bible verses can help you with this fear?

Circle the ones that apply:

Deuteronomy 31:6

Philippians 4:6-7

Philippians 4:13

I John 2:17

other: _____

What are some things you can *do* when you feel afraid?

_____

_____

7 Memory Verses

____ Philippians 4:8

____ Psalm 98:1

____ Romans 12:1

Table 15.4

Children's Curriculum on Character

Information-Processing Learning Family

Identification Learning:	Pictures and descriptions of various scenes: drugs, beer, smoking Exercise about television commercial
Inquiry Learning:	Exercise about television commercial to say no to drugs Identify biggest fear and how to deal with it

Conditioning Learning Family

Consequence Learning:	Bible content: Do not be conformed to world system How to deal with fears
Cue Learning:	Reminder: Saying no to drugs Memorizing Bible verse

Social Learning Family

Structured Modeling:	Picture scenes: drugs, beer, smoking Content of Bible verses Text explanation: Saying no to drugs Encourage friends to say no Dealing with fears
Spontaneous Modeling:	Discussion with club or adult about drugs Working on television commercial together

Spontaneous Modeling of peers. Table 15.4 summarizes these avenues and activities.

Commission

For clarification of this final theme, we offer two sets of commendable curriculum examples. First, students are stimulated to consider the vital subject of sharing Christ in their own world (Section 2). Activities include practicing what to say when witnessing (Section 3) and living a godly life before peers (Section 4). A personal project to encourage missionaries rounds out the lesson. Table 15.5 summarizes the avenues and activities.

In the second sample, emphasis centers on being good stewards of the earth. Children are asked to complete a specific stew-ardship project (Section 4). Finally, they are to contemplate creation's God-ward reflections from Psalm 19:1 (Section 6). Table 15.6 summarizes the avenues and activities.

Selecting Bible Versions

A common activity of most published curriculum involves Bible reading and memory. Church leaders are often asked, "Which Bible is best for my child?" Given the developmental nature of a child's mental growth, it makes sense to direct parents to versions that are most appropriate for children. For instance, which version contains vocabulary most familiar to youngsters?[17]

The main difficulty in changing version as children grow up is that Bible memoriza-

Sharing My Faith

To earn this award, complete and check off each requirement.

▷1 Your Mission

You are God's special agent! Read the memo to find out your mission.

MEMO

TO: Special Agent # _____

(Pick a code number and write it here.)

YOUR MISSION: To tell others about God.
(Read I Chronicles 16:23-24.)

Draw lines to connect the first part of each sentence with the best middle part and the best ending. Then read the sentences to find some ways to tell others about God.

Tell	someone	in club.
Invite	what God	to church or Sunday school.
Explain	the person	has done for you.
Bring	what happens	to club.

2 Go and Tell

Where does God want you to carry out your mission? In Brazil? In Outer Mongolia? Well, maybe someday that would be possible! But for now, God wants you to tell people about him right where you live. Use the symbols to draw a map of where you live.

Symbols

Where you live	
Where a friend lives	
School	
Playground	
Park	
Church	

Now think about each place that you drew. Could you tell someone there about God? If so, draw a person beside that place.

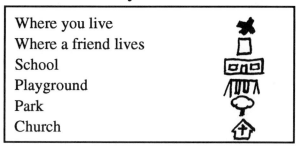

▷ 3 Practice Telling Others

What would you say if someone said one of these things to you? Practice your answer with a friend, or write it in the speech balloon.

> I don't believe in Jesus. Why do you?

> Maybe I'll come to your club next week. What do you do there?

▷ 4 Show God to Others

Besides telling people about God, you can also *show* them what he's like! How? By acting more like him. (Read I Thessalonians 1:6–7.) Think of what God is like—patient, truthful, helpful, and so on. In the wheel, write one way you can be more like him at home, at school, and while playing with friends.

Then put a star by one of the things you wrote, and practice it this week.

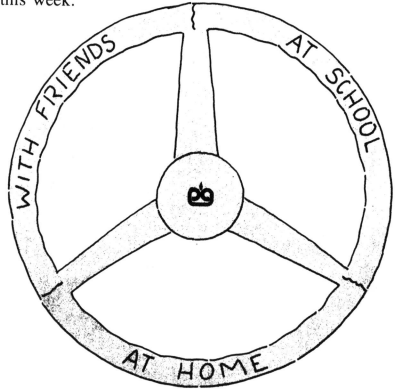

▷ 5 Help a Missionary

Read II Thessalonians 3:1 and Philippians 4:15-18, and find two ways to help missionaries. (Paul, one of the very first missionaries, wrote these verses.) 1. _____

2. _____

Find out about a missionary. (Your pastor, a club leader, or a parent can help.) What does the missionary do? What are his or her needs?

☐ Pray for the missionary's needs.

☐ Do one of the following projects. Check with a grown-up before you do it.

• *Give encouragement.* Mail a letter to the missionary. Write it or tape-record it. You could tell things about yourself and your family. Tell what is happening in club or church. Show that you are interested in the missionary's work. Say you prayed for him or her.

• *Give some money.* Find a way to raise money, such as raking lawns or walking dogs or washing cars. Donate what you earn to the missionary.

• *Your choice* _____

▷ 6 Memory Verses

_____ I Chronicles 16:23

_____ Romans 1:16

_____ II Corinthians 3:18

Table 15.5

Children's Curriculum on Commission

Information-Processing Learning Family

Identification Learning:	Map of neighborhood exercise Three contexts on wheel: friends, school, home
Inquiry Learning:	Drawing map of neighborhood Identify with stick figure persons to tell about God Responses to questions in #3 Ways to be like God in three contexts in the wheel Bible study on helping missionaries Select project to help missionary

Conditioning Learning Family

Consequence Learning:	Bible content Information from missionaries from others
Cue Learning:	Stick figures and those to tell about God What "missionary" means Memorizing Bible verse

Social Learning Family

Structured Modeling:	Bible verses Text explanation
Spontaneous Modeling:	Inquiry about missionary from others

tion becomes confusing. If just one version had to be selected for the entire life-span, we recommend the New International Version. Children below Grade 7 could use another version for reading and study, but memorize verses from the NIV. Difficult words could be explained to youngsters in the early elementary years, to minimize rote study.[18]

To help us become better teachers, a variety of written and media resources is available. These materials can help us use various teaching methods, understand children's needs, arrange class time effectively, and deal with discipline problems.[19]

Conclusion

Think about It

1. In this chapter you have become acquainted with a variety of ways to teach children. Now it's your turn. Imagine preparing a lesson for Grades 3–4. The lesson comes from Ephesians 4:11–16. The aim is to explain that everyone contributes to the church's growth. Pick one or two categories below, and design two Bible learning activities for each category. That is, what would you have children do, in order to communicate your aim?

Illustration 15.5

4 Preservation Plan

God wants *you* to help take care of his creation. There are lots of ways to preserve nature right where you live! Think of one thing you can do in the next week. In the leaf below, write out your plan.

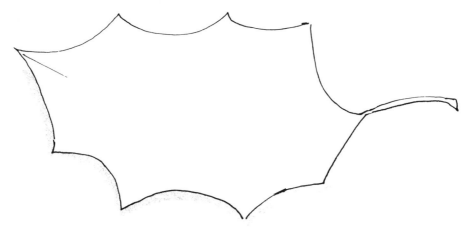

Date I carried out my plan: _____

5 What Do You Like?

What is your favorite thing to do? Illustrate it in the space below by drawing a picture or design.

What could someone tell about you just by looking at what you drew?

_____

_____

_____

6 Eh, What Did You Say?

Use your imagination to fill in what these parts of nature might be
saying about God.

As a caption under the cartoon, write in today's memory verse,
Psalm 19:1.

Psalm 19:1

Table 15.6

Children's Curriculum on Commission

Information-Processing Learning Family

Identification Learning:	Favorite activity
	Familiar elements of nature
Inquiry Learning:	Selecting ways to preserve nature
	Selecting and drawing favorite activity
	Response about this drawing
	Filling in the bubbles

Conditioning Learning Family

Consequence Learning:	Bible content
Cue Learning:	Concept and activity: "preserving nature"
	Memorizing Bible verse

Social Learning Family

Structured Modeling:	Bible verses
	Text explanation
Spontaneous Modeling:	What student writes and draws

Art   Drama   Music
Oral communication
Creative writing   Service projects
Bible games   Research

---

2. Earlier in the chapter we suggested that great care be given to the selection of children's workers. In light of the particular demands of this ministry as outlined in the chapter, identify what you think are five essential characteristics required for ministering to children.

(1)
(2)
(3)
(4)
(5)

We have emphasized, in this chapter, the use of copyrighted material. The church would be severely hampered if it weren't for these published resources. We need the expertise and assistance that curriculum companies provide. But there's a flip side to this view. We teachers who are "in the trenches" know our particular setting better than anyone: We know our students best; we know our own abilities (and limitations) best; and we know our learning environment best. Consequently, we must customize professionally written curriculum to our specific needs. We don't need to be geniuses or creative artists. But we should adapt these published materials to increase our effectiveness.

This adaptive process starts with personal conviction. We instructors must analyze why we teach in the first place. In this book

Table 15.7

Goals of Teaching Children

COMMUNION	COMMUNITY	CHARACTER	COMMISSION
Knowing God	*Serving One Another*	*Becoming Like Jesus*	*Serving the World*
1. Develop habits: Prayer Confession Scripture memory 2. Understanding God 3. Worshiping God (celebration) 4. Singing 5. Rejoicing in the Lord 6. Learning about baptism and the Lord's Supper	1. Show hospitality 2. Sharing 3. Helping/serving 4. Thinking of others 5. Sharing testimony 6. Praising God 7. Treat others with re- spect 8. Make/keep friends 9. Relate to opposite sex positively 10. Realize importance of church "family"	1. Learning truth a. Read the Bible b. Memorization 2. Discern truth a. Teachable attitudes b. Appropriate deci- sions 3. Tell truth a. Honesty b. Thankfulness 4. Live truth a. Citizenship b. Self-control c. Self-image	1. Tithe/generosity 2. Use gifts/talents 3. Serve others 4. Develop a world vision 5. Learn a foreign language 6. Sharing Christ 7. Giving to meet others' needs

we have suggested, for example, four life-long themes of biblical Reconciliation: Communion, Community, Character, and Commission. Table 15.7 identifies specific indicators of each theme for children.[20] These indicators are not exhaustive, but representative signs of balanced growth. Dozens of additional indicators could be added. Whether these four themes are chosen (or another set of emphases), we teach-ers must constantly critique our ministries: Am I addressing my instructional goals? Am I utilizing appropriate educational strategies? With this basic filter system in mind, we confidently approach profession-ally written curriculum. Our attitude and our focus rest on what God leads *us* to do with *our particular* students. The curriculum becomes one means to an end, rather than the end itself.

16 Teaching Children: Corporate Strategies

An American missionary to China was speaking at a conference back in the United States. The missionary's wife and his three children listened attentively to his challenge. That night, at home, the youngest family member spoke to her father.

"I think you and Mommy should have another baby. We need four kids in our house," said the kindergartner. Before the father could respond, the youngster added: "And the next child should be Chinese."

The startled father tried to explain how difficult that request would be. But the young girl interrupted. "No, you could do it, because you said so in the meeting tonight."

"When did I say that?" the father asked, confused.

"You said that one out of four babies born in the world today is Chinese."

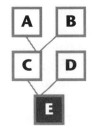

We enjoy listening to little children talk. They represent a world of innocence—a world removed from our cares and worries. It brings to mind some of the simple experiences we remember having as children. But our romantic notions do not represent contemporary reality as we approach the threshold of the twenty-first century. Reports of child abuse, child pornography, and child prostitutes appear regularly in the newspaper. As we mentioned in the previous chapter, children enter this life in a helpless state. They are very dependent on adult caregivers. In response to the disciples' question about greatness, Jesus asked a child to stand among them (Matt. 18:2). After making an initial, figurative comparison between the characteristics of children and true greatness, our Lord then directs the apostles' attention to children *themselves*. His words still resound with ominous judgment: "But if anyone causes one of these little ones who believe in me to sin, it would be better for him to have a large millstone hung around his neck and to be drowned in the depths of the sea" (Matt. 18:6). Such harsh words connote the seriousness of our responsibility to protect and guide our children.

How can we adults help children grow up to love and know God and to become spiritually mature adults? We must first understand what major forces affect the growth of our children. To this end, we provide a brief overview of the various contexts in which our children must live. In light of these pervasive influences, we suggest a five-pronged, practical strategy for nurturing children to Christ-likeness.

Influential Worlds of the Child

We no longer live in the agrarian society of Laura Ingalls Wilder's *Little House on the Prairie*. Life on a farm, for most, is about as familiar as Star Trek life on Captain Kirk's *U.S.S. Enterprise*. In addition, the growing percentage of a child's waking hours are taken up by nonhome influences.

Figure 16.1 identifies the major "worlds" that daily influence our children: (1) the home, (2) the extended family, (3) the church, (4) the marketplace, (5) the neighborhood, and (6) the state.

Family Communities: Home, Extended Family, and Church

Three related social structures are divinely appointed as the preeminent vehicles for nurturing children. First, there is the child's immediate family. What a marvelous and unique privilege of God's design for parents: to participate in the creation of life! Children are gifts from the Lord.

But the nuclear family is not left alone in the difficult task of child nurturing. In addition to *immediate* family members, there are *extended* relations of aunts, uncles, and grandparents. Moreover, for children within the church, the family of God represents a significant third resource. Debates over whether the earthly family or the church family is more important for the child are generally futile. Both communities are essential. Both cultivate the potential maturity of a child. Only when these groups cooperate with each other do children reach full, spiritual adulthood.[1]

Cultural Contexts: Marketplace, Neighborhood, and State

Besides family communities, our culture also has a significant influence. For example, in a capitalistic system, the marketplace eagerly vies for our children's attention and devotion. Merchandising efforts are ever-present. The siren call of advertisers beckons all who hear to spend dollars at their shrines. Increasingly, media efforts are coordinated to increase childhood markets. Whether it's Barbie dolls or Teenage Mu-

Figure 16.1

The Worlds of the Child

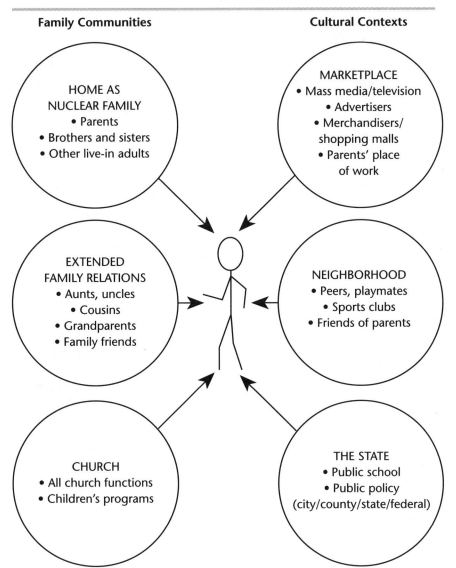

Family Communities   Cultural Contexts

HOME AS
NUCLEAR FAMILY
• Parents
• Brothers and sisters
• Other live-in adults

MARKETPLACE
• Mass media/television
• Advertisers
• Merchandisers/
shopping malls
• Parents' place
of work

EXTENDED
FAMILY RELATIONS
• Aunts, uncles
• Cousins
• Grandparents
• Family friends

NEIGHBORHOOD
• Peers, playmates
• Sports clubs
• Friends of parents

CHURCH
• All church functions
• Children's programs

THE STATE
• Public school
• Public policy
(city/county/state/federal)

tant Ninja Turtles, toy manufacturing companies do not limit their influence to our pocketbooks.[2] Although subtle, perhaps unintentional at times, the marketplace challenges our values and lifestyle.

The neighborhood symbolizes a second cultural context, which includes childhood playmates and peers. Value systems in this sphere may affirm or oppose Christian

mores. Examples of neighborhood settings range from staying overnight at a friend's home to week-long sports camps; from Girl Scouts to Little League; from science clubs to piano lessons. All possess the potential to affect a child's character for good or for ill.

The state's influence on children comes primarily through government-sponsored elementary school (to a lesser degree, at private school or a home school, depending on relevant laws and regulations). In addition, public policy about children affects how we might view or value children. This includes such diverse policies as child-related income tax deductions, the legal age of minors, the removal of children from homes suspected of child abuse, and the support of abortions.

Think about It

Reflect on your own childhood years. Consider the cultural influences that affected you. Identify one positive and one negative influence on your life, associated with each of these "worlds."

	Marketplace	Neighbor-hood	State
Positive			
Negative			

A Broad-Based Approach

Stanley Hauerwas implores the church to support the Christian marriages of its members. His plea is no less relevant to Christian families as a whole: "The character necessary to sustain the life of marriage . . . is not formed by the family but by the church. . . . Indeed that is why marriage is only possible if it is sustained by a community more significant than the marriage itself" (1985, pp. 280, 282). The local church sets the pace and the priorities for a discipleship ministry to children. Since children are significantly shaped by their surroundings, we must answer some basic questions. Whom do we want as the primary instructors of our children? Who should teach them their values? If we take stock of our children's daily routines, we discover that, oftentimes, other children influence our children. Whether it's within diverse experiences of school,

neighborhood play, or play with siblings, children are largely found in the company of their peers. Yet, biblical patterns indicate that *mature adults* should primarily socialize children (Deut. 6:4–9).

Consequently, as we consider the church's comprehensive ministry, we must think beyond traditional programming for children.[3] Attention should be centered on a wider arena—one that encourages generous exposure to many mature adult role models within the church family. We offer five specific focal points. Each requires concentration for balanced, successful children's work. An acrostic, "CHILD," is employed as a memory device. The strategies are set within three broader spheres, in order of priority:

1. Life Patterns	C –	Church life of the child
	H –	Home life of the child
2. Specific Programs	I –	Intergenerational programs
	L –	Learning programs for children
3. Arenas beyond	D –	Development of public policy about children

Church Life of the Child

Every organization has a mission, a reason for its existence. Furthermore, every organization has a regular gathering time in which to set the tone for its mission. For example, businesses schedule weekly staff meetings. Schools have faculty conferences. Smaller cities hold town hall meetings. The church's primary gathering centers on weekly worship.

The Worship Service
The regular worship service represents a strategic time for the whole church to meet together. When children are absent—attending a separate program—what are they missing from this church family

time?[4] Picture a rural church of thirty-eight members at their worship service with small children in attendance.

John, two-and-a-half years old, and Catherine, four months old, came to worship with their parents. Catherine was asleep in her father's arms, and there were many offers to share his burden. There was a portable baby swing at the back of the sanctuary for Catherine in case she started to fuss.

John brought paper, crayons, a stuffed dog, and a blanket. He settled himself and his belongings along the pew beside his parents. He did not remain there long. He was free to sit beside anyone in his wandering, but he attracted no special attention. During the sermon and prayers he was treated with a kind of benign neglect—helped, hugged, or ignored without much fuss or concentration.

John joined in singing his version of the hymns and actually approximated the words of the Doxology. Once his hymn lasted longer than the congregation's. He copied the bowed heads in prayer for as long as five seconds. He stood by the end of the pew and placed his gift in the offering plate, then accompanied the usher to the front of the church.

At the close of the service John stood by the minister and shook hands with people for a few minutes, then joined two older children who rolled a ball with him while his parents visited. Catherine, now awake, was admired and held. About half the congregation went home to John's house for iced tea. (Ng and Thomas 1981, p. 10)

Think about It

Reflect on the above account. What do you think John "learned" about the community of God's people as they worshiped? Identify ways that he sensed affirmation and support from church members.

Churches use a variety of approaches to include children in the worship service:

- having children make periodic visits to the "adult" worship service (e.g., once every month or two), which may include participation (such as singing in a children's choir)
- having children visit for part of the worship service (until the sermon is preached), then attend children's church
- having children attend the whole worship service every other week; for the alternate weeks, children go to children's church just before the sermon begins
- having children attend the entire worship service every Sunday

In addition to these general options, differing "cut-off" grades are used for churches providing children's church.[5] For example, the upper limit for attendance may be restricted to children attending sixth grade, third grade, or kindergarten.

When children attend the worship service, due to their limited attention span and differing interests, they often are involved in activities other than listening directly to the sermon. But don't assume that learning isn't taking place. "Pew art" often gives testimony that much more is going on in the child's mind than just frivolous doodling:

A friend was sitting beside a small girl who was attending worship with her mother. During the sermon the small girl took a stewardship envelope and drew upon it. The mother who was engrossed in the sermon did not notice what her daughter was doing. During the last hymn, the mother caught a glimpse of her daughter's handiwork on the back of the envelope. Without looking at it, she reprimanded her daughter for drawing in church. "You should

Illustration 16.1

An Example of "Pew Art" from Ruth, Aged 4

have been paying attention," she growled as she hurried her daughter out of the pew. The piece of art was left crumpled on the seat. My friend uncrumpled it. The small girl had drawn a decorated heart shape. Inside its borders she had written "Jesus loves me." (Stewart 1987, p. 61).

During one worship time, one of our daughters, at the age of four, drew the picture displayed in Illustration 16.1. Her "canvas" was the back of a missionary letter inserted in the church bulletin. The picture depicts our family going to church. All of us are carrying a Bible, except for little Ruth. Since her Bible was just a "picture" Bible and not a "real Bible with just words,"

perhaps she excluded it. This is just one instance of a child's indirect learning through community worship. Children must regularly experience the entire church fulfilling its significant mission: worshiping God together.[6]

Corporately Nurturing Faith in Children

Churches rarely highlight, in a public manner, their children's progress in the faith. Only during infant dedication or baptismal ceremonies do we typically observe pastors and children together. Some churches feature a children's sermon, but often the presentation is poor or inconsistent. Since our Lord openly welcomed children, and encouraged other adults to do the same, greater corporate involvement with children is needed.

More thought needs to be given to our theological understanding of the child's salvation experience. The evangelical church's standard has been the adult "crisis" conversion model, when a mature person shifts dramatically from a secular to a Christian culture. We employ this model because it is exclusively presented in the New Testament. Virtually no guidelines exist for how children—who grow up in the church—should come to faith. The experience of Timothy, reared in a Jewish home, is the only explicit biblical reference to an individual who received childhood nurture (2 Tim. 1:5; 3:14–15).

Although children must make a conscious decision to place their faith in God, the ideal is for children to grow up developing "Christian" character *before* and *after* a personal decision is made for salvation in Jesus Christ.[7] Such a conversion model suggests that we view salvation as encompassing many phases over time. In that sense, it is not just a "one-time" decision. Rather, like any significant commitment, there is a point of origin and several, subsequent affirmations. Given age-level differences, these subsequent decisions represent, in some sense, fresh and independent choices.[8]

Listen to the concerns of one mother as she anticipates the road ahead for her two children who have just received Jesus Christ as their personal Savior. Her daughter is five and her son is three:

> While I was as touched as any mother would be at this momentous occurrence, doubts cast a shadow on the delight of my joy. *They're so young. Will this decision stick? When she's twelve, will she even remember this moment? When he hits sixteen, will he pull away in defiance, negating the reality of what happened here?* How could I help

them recall this moment with the sincerity and unswerving commitment only a child could bring to it? (Morgan 1991)

The immediate family is not alone in this responsibility. The earthly family and the church family must work together in supporting this important journey. By corporately nurturing faith in children, we can encourage our children's faith to mature, eventually, to "adult" faith. Table 16.1 suggests several occasions when children might be publicly recognized.[9] In this way, we can provide them with spiritual milestones so that their faith journey does not become stagnant.[10] Positively stated, these growth markers express respect for developmental distinctives.

Table 16.1

Corporately Nurturing Faith from Childhood to Adulthood

Phase One: "Family *Reception* [during first year of life]

Part 1: Parent-Child dedication/baptism

• Preparation classes for parents (and grandparents)
– Church ceremony of dedication/baptism that focuses primarily on the nuclear family. It secondarily focuses on the congregation's responsibility.

Part 2: Salvation decision by child

• Church leader(s) interviews the child and parents following the time when the child consciously chooses to receive Jesus as personal Savior. They ascertain the genuineness of the decision.
– A white carnation, symbolizing the second birth, is set on the pulpit or platform announcing this joyous occasion to the congregation.

Phase Two: "Family" *Presentation* [minimum age: start of elementary school]

• Preparation classes for child and parent
– Baptism; participates in first Lord's Supper.

Phase Three: "Family" *Affirmation* [minimum age: start of high school]

• Preparation/catechism classes for youth
– Public testimony

Phase Four: "Family" *Commissioning* [minimum age: start of college/career]

• Preparation classes for young adult
– Optional commissioning ceremony: voluntary response to God's call; serving God in vocation.

Note: Although minimum ages are given, progression through these phases is dependent on the initiative of the child/teen.

Four major life phases are linked with five public ceremonies. Each phase relates to significant times of spiritual commitment. Each phase includes a preparation class for instruction. The teacher's purpose is twofold: (1) to help participants realize their respective *private* commitments; and (2) to help them understand the aims and events of the *public* ceremony. The latter includes roles for the church leadership, parents, and children. Even the congregation plays an important part.

In Phase 1, *"Family" Reception,* the child is initially received by the church family for corporate nurture.[11] At the ceremony, the congregation is challenged to encourage and support the parents as they commit themselves to disciple their child. This life phase concludes when the child personally accepts Jesus Christ as Savior.[12] A white carnation is set on the pulpit or platform complementing the red rose for physical birth. The second birth of the child is thus symbolized.

"Family" Reception is the motif of Phase 2. Following a preparation class for family members, the child is presented to the church "family" in a special way. The spiritual milestone here is indicated by two im-portant events: (1) the child's baptism—the initiatory rite, and (2) the child's first participation in the Lord's Supper—the family meal.[13] Following the ceremony, the child is encouraged to become involved in ministry and to begin exercising spiritual gift(s).

Phase 3, taking place sometime in mid-adolescence, focuses on *"Family" Affirmation.* In preparation for this milestone, teens are challenged to transform their "childhood" understanding of basic doctrine into "adult" levels of comprehension. At this special ceremony, they publicly indicate their faith in God through personal testimony. Continuing responsible ministry involvement is encouraged.

The necessity for some kind of "affirmation" of faith during adolescence stems from the new cognitive capacity (formal operations) now available—the ability for full adult thinking. For example, some churches withhold key responsibilities of membership from children (particularly voting privileges) until the mid-teen years for related reasons. Why not formalize this important rite of passage and link it with a special period of instruction?

Phase 4 is optional. Here, young adults may wish to commit themselves, in a public manner, to serving the Lord, regardless of vocational pursuit. Diligent study of God's truth and intentional personal reflection precede this *"Family" Commissioning for Service* ceremony.[14] Each of these corporate services yields blessings for the entire membership. Not only are first-time participants challenged to grow, but every ceremony offers an occasion of faith reaffirmation for each member.[15]

Example of Church Leaders

Children learn much more than their Sunday school lessons at church. They carefully observe interactions among adults; they watch associations between adults and children. Children appreciate it when adults talk with them at their level. They know which adults are friendly and which adults are not. Perhaps this is one reason the Spirit included this important qualification for church leaders: "He must manage his own family well and see that his children obey him with proper respect. (If anyone does not know how to manage his own family, how can he take care of God's church?)" (1 Tim. 3:4–5). Those who have reared their children well are more sensitive to their development. They are aware of how children are shaped by the broader scope of the church's ministry. Such leaders also set a good example for adults and teens. As they accept children as part of Christ's body, they model godly behavior and values to others.

Home Life of the Child

Donald Joy calls the home God's "first curriculum" for children (1986, p. 11). Young children spend far more time at home than with the church body. It only makes sense that church leaders invest significant time and resources into parent training strategies.[16]

The Bible makes one thing very clear: Parents play a critical and fundamental role in their children's growth (Deut. 6:5–9; Eph. 6:4). "Faithful marital relationships generally tend to produce children, and the *parent-child relationship* is crucial in God's management of the world for the upbringing of the coming generation. God gives parents not only the privileges and joys of parenthood but also its responsibilities" (Lewis and Demarest 1990, p. 98).[17] Yet, C. Nelson Ellis suggests,

Rather than turning religious education over to the parents exclusively, we must recognize that the parents are also under judgment and need their Christian understanding expanded and clarified while they fulfill their role as parents. Therefore, we must give *first attention* to the continued training of adults who are parents, so that they may grow "in the grace and knowledge" and then, as part of their training, help them better to perform their role as parents and teachers in the home. (1971, p. 209, emphasis added)

The role of church leadership is facilitation: "to prepare God's people for works of service, so that the body of Christ may be built up" (Eph. 4:12). A scriptural focus and sequence emerge from this verse. The church concentrates on parental instruction. Parents then attend to childhood instruction. This pattern does not portray an exclusive relationship, for the church also pursues direct ministries with children. Yet, this pattern does emphasize a *primary* relationship; the first level of accountability links parent with child.[18]

For these family and parenting demands, a wealth of resources exists.[19] A helpful training plan is called for which identifies, organizes, and promotes such resources. The aim to address transitional

Table 16.2

Family Life Transitions

1. Getting married
2. First child (becoming parents)
3. First child to attend school
4. First adolescent
5. First child to leave home
6. First child to get married (becoming parents-in-law)
7. First grandchild (becoming grandparents)

Source: Adapted from Guernsey (1982).

family needs presents a related challenge. That is, to suggest useful resources is one thing; to recommend resources for parents *when they are most ready to use them* is an altogether different matter. Predictable times of parent need correlate with the critical transitions within the child's maturation process. Each transition represents a window of opportunity for teaching parents. Table 16.2 identifies seven of these major shifts in family life.

As a case in point, listen to this report of one mother's anxious thoughts regarding school-age transition:

> Last August, I heard a sad story. This lady I know, the mother of one, had just sent her child away to the first grade. For the past six years, these two people had been almost inseparable. They were constantly together, learning, walking, going to the library, and shopping. And now the son had gone away to the first grade.
>
> Each morning, after the bus came, the mother cried for several minutes. For one thing, there was the mystery of it all. Her son had disappeared into the mysterious world called school and she really didn't have any idea of where he was or what he was doing. But she was also lonely. Instead of filling her days with all the exciting things she had often thought of doing, visiting friends, cleaning the house, planting flowers, she just sat around being lonely. But then, she reminded herself that this schooling experience was going to last at least thirteen more years, and she was really sad.
>
> Yes, this was indeed a sad story. But I wasn't sad because of the mother. I was sad for the boy. If the mother thought she had to make adjustments, she should have been in her son's shoes; but at a time when her son needed her the most, this mother was so wrapped up in her own problem that she did not have any feelings left to help her son with. That is what makes this a sad story. (Schimmels 1989, pp. 210–11)

Parents should be targeted for extra church support both preceding and shortly following each growth phase. For example, a list of relevant written materials or useful video tapes (available in the church library) might be distributed to parents in transition. If there are sufficient numbers and interest, a Sunday school elective class or a mid-week support group could confront particular concerns of these life shifts.

Think about It

Pick one of the life transitions in Table 16.2. Pretend you are designing a Saturday morning workshop for parents going through that particular hurdle. What concepts, attitudes, or skills would you think are important to teach?

Besides personal assistance, parents require guidance in helping their children. As children grow, they face concerns related to each of the earlier noted "worlds": home, extended family, church, the marketplace, the neighborhood, and the state. For example, church education programs can assist parents in the regular evaluation of children's habits within the home. Which practices foster growth and which tend to hinder development? Viable instructional activities in the home range from dinner conversation to family recreation, and from discipline practices to conflict management.[20]

One of the most simple, albeit significant, strategies parents can engage in is reading aloud to their children. In this endeavor, a parent gives undivided attention to the youngster. Nurture is further advanced via closeness and physical touch. Communication skills develop. The child is introduced to new vocabulary and new worlds. Reading the Bible, Bible story books, and books with moral truths greatly benefit the child. Bonding is enhanced. Godly values are generated.[21]

Obviously, scores of educational needs exist in the home: time spent with playmates; how much time and what is being viewed on television;[22] what toys should be available or avoided; and how to work with teachers and principals to get the most out of school.[23] To summarize, church leaders could provide a synthesis of biblical and common-sense guidelines for the aims and practices of parenting.[24] The purpose of this home education is not to indoctrinate, but to serve families and to rear godly children.

But providing information is not enough. Parent education classes are not sufficient. Many caregivers, due to pressures, problems, and expectations, do not give their children the attention they require. To complicate matters, many children live in single-parent homes.[25] Whatever the reasons, the church must especially minister in homes with "at risk" children.[26] We must lend a helping hand to express the genuine love of Christ.[27]

Intergenerational Programs

Since children learn from many life experiences, the church can't be satisfied with worship and home instruction alone. Complementing these educational strategies will yield greater learning experiences for children. Many churches sponsor regular Sunday school or mid-week classes in which people of all ages join together to learn about God. "The first major program goal of IGRE [Inter-Generational Religious Education], then, is to respond creatively to this problem [isolation and insulation of age-restricted programming] by helping people relate to one another qualitatively across generations" (White 1988, p. 177). Such intergenerational learning benefits not only children, but people of all ages. It values both the similarities and the dissimilarities of age groups. It strikes a balance in education that is Christian.

What does such a program look like?

In an *ideal* IGRE program, all four of the patterns of relationship will be enacted. People come together and have [1] an in-common experience. Then they break to separately investigate the common subject at a level appropriate for their highest learning abilities [2—parallel learning]. They come back together to present their insights and works in a shared program [3—contributive occasions]. Then different generations might finally interact with one another, giving and receiving in the exchanges [4—interactive sharing]. (White 1988, pp. 29–30)

In a composite gathering of children, youth, and adults, there are educational times when each age group learns God's Word among peers; at other times, they learn across generations. Besides offering an elective Sunday school class, how are these opportunities to be organized? What would they look like? James W. White (1988) lists a variety of options for intergenerational growth and challenge: (1) family cluster groups/extended spiritual families; (2) one-day workshops; (3) special events, primarily associated with major holidays; (4) worship service and related activities; and (5) annual family camps.[28]

Learning Programs for Children

When someone speaks of children's ministry activities, "standard age-appropriage programs" typically come to mind: Sunday school, vacation Bible school, and mid-week club organizations. These mental reactions are expected—and acceptable. As presented in this chapter, such programs represent only a portion of the potential ministry.

Development of Public Policy about Children

The final aspect of our five-pronged strategy may seem too political for some. But, minimally, we must become aware of policies that directly or indirectly affect our children. A sampling of such diverse policies include those which allow convenience abortions of unborn children,[29] permit toy manufacturers to sell unsafe toys, propose anti-Christian values in public school textbooks, or perpetuate unethical and immoral standards on commercial television programs for children. If we want to provide healthy environments for our children, we must pursue legal means to protect ("safety" criterion) and nurture ("stimulating" criterion) our children.[30]

Figure 16.2
The Abused Child's World

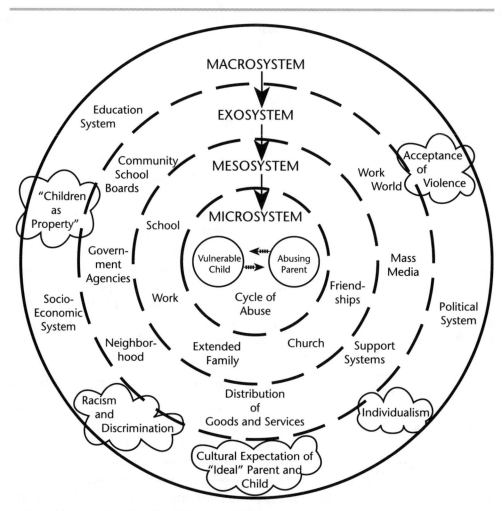

Source: Unknown; based on Bronfenbrenner (1979).

Urie Bronfenbrenner's (1979) ecological theory helps us identify various influences on children. Figure 16.2 provides one example of the environmental contexts that directly or indirectly affect a child within an abusive home. Related comments (per context) are worthy of Christian critique. Each comment warrants our best efforts to bring about change. Part of our Commission responsibility includes intentional designs to assess our culture and to transform it.[31]

Conclusion

"Go to your rooms and read Luke 19:28–49," a father asked his two eldest daughters one Easter season. "Tell me if anything sounds unusual to you. I think you're going to be surprised." The first- and fifth-graders scurried off to their rooms.

It wasn't long before they reappeared with eyes like saucers. In unison, they exclaimed, "The rocks could talk!"

"Oh really?" Their father played along. "Tell me about it." So the story of Jesus' triumphal entry—significantly paraphrased—was retold by the two elementary-aged children. Each had their personal insights to share as they went along.

"I'll tell you what," the father suggested at the end of their summaries. "Let's take a walk in our neighborhood and collect samples of things that God has created. Not Styrofoam cups or plastic wrappers. But pieces of God's nature, realizing that these things *could talk,* if God wanted them to."

The girls ran to the door leading to the garage. No need to ask them twice. "C'mon, Dad!" they shouted over their shoulders. "This is going to be great!" Both grabbed their bikes.

About a dozen items were collected in three and one-half minutes: twigs, leaves, small wild flowers, tree bark, and, of course, stones. The girls chose to put all their findings in the basket attached to Missy's bicycle. It gave the first-grader a sense of pride to carry the family's treasures.

"Okay, let's return home. I think we've got enough," said their dad. "I'll show you what to do when we get there."

Back home, the youngsters carefully unloaded each item and placed them on the stairway leading to the front porch. The oldest, Elizabeth, asked "Now what?" before every souvenir was transferred.

"Tell me again about the story from Luke 19. Tell me what happened," their father quizzed. This was accomplished in about twenty seconds, since excitement was still running high. "Now, we know about the possibility of talking stones—as well as other 'speaking' parts of nature. But what would each of *our* collected items actually *say,* if *they* would talk? Missy, you go first."

The girls were thankful that bark covers the tall oak and maple trees. Leaves were happy, they said, in the fall when they changed into gorgeous yellows, oranges, reds, and browns. The discussion lasted only a couple of minutes. But it was quite apparent that both girls had given serious attention to God's "speaking" creation.

"There's one more thing I want you to do, if you don't mind," their father said. "Take one of your objects and write on it just how it would praise God." The girls complied.

Four years have passed. Both sisters still talk enthusiastically about their Palm Sunday "lesson." Technically, they had studied ecological issues of faith, elements from the theme of Commission—our relationship to creation and creation's relationship to the Creator. Their father still has one of the artifacts. A half-pound rock sits as a paperweight on his office desk. Etched in black marker is the testimony "I'm special"; it is signed "Missy."

How will the home and the church respond to the eminent and imminent need to educate children? Only God knows. But parents who take seriously the summons to proclaim biblical reconciliation will fare best. Teachers who dare to implement practical strategies of God's comprehensive restoration plan will succeed. Growth and learning will result because, like faithful pilgrims, they steadfastly obey the Great Commission.

17

Focus on People: Working with Teachers

Leader as Completer
Getting Along with Your Teachers
Recruiting and Developing Your Teachers
Conclusion

In the previous chapters, we described age-specific issues and strategies for Christian instruction. In this chapter we will analyze an essential ingredient in effective educational ministry—teachers, leaders, and workers. The axiom rings true: A program is only as effective as its staff.

In one sense, this chapter and the next represent something of a synthesis for this book. They pull together practical applications of the four themes. Certainly, we want our ministry staff to be maturing men and women of God. We don't view them as objects; we value their growth experiences. Thus, Communion and Character are explicitly addressed. Naturally, these chapters raise Community concerns as well. How will they get along with other workers in God's kingdom? Finally, the Commission theme surfaces. How can we help our staff become effective laborers in educational service? What barriers prevent productive ministry? What about broader implications outside the local church? To these issues we now turn.

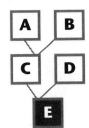

To live above, with the saints we love
 Oh . . . that will be glory!
But to live below, with the saints we know,
 Well . . . that's another story!

Take a moment to consider:

1. What kind of personality really rubs you the wrong way?

2. What is there in *your* personality that might rub others the wrong way?

Even in the New Testament, believers didn't always get along. Paul urged the church in Philippi to resolve a skirmish between two believers: "I plead with Euodia and I plead with Syntyche to agree with each other in the Lord" (Phil. 4:2–3). Because Christians will never agree 100 percent on everything, it is important to determine what prompts these disputes.

Some disagreements arise because of differing emphases. Take the Great Commission. Some believers focus on the *goal:* to reach the world for Christ. They organize programs and initiate projects to this end. Other Christians focus on *relational* elements of the Lord's command. They ask, "Are we discipling men and women to become Christ-like? Do we value their individual needs?" It comes down to what theorists label "task-oriented" versus "people-oriented" emphases.

Task as well as *people* concerns represent valid ministry perspectives. Their joint significance deserves consideration. This is especially true in our American culture, which overemphasizes busyness while it undervalues relationships. Such warped viewpoints spill over into the church. For many church leaders the bottom line of ministry is "getting the job done." Pure task orientation jeopardizes the dignity of people. God's Word fashions a radically different imperative: love *people* and use *things,* not vice versa.

It's fairly easy to "love one another" during the Sunday morning worship service. The church picnic fosters good feelings as well. But how do we act toward others in a committee meeting or at the annual church business session? Christian ministry insists on showing concern for those *whom* we serve, but also for those *with whom* we serve. The "one another" passages, presented in Table 17.1, tell us how we should conduct ourselves. It wasn't coincidental when Jesus stipulated that his followers should be characterized by mutual love (John 13:35).

Table 17.1

"One Another" Passages

Accept one another. (Rom. 15:7)

Be devoted to one another. (Rom. 12:10)

Be kind and compassionate to one another. (Eph. 4:32)

Be patient, bearing with one another. (Eph. 4:2; Col. 3:12–13)

Carry each other's burdens. (Gal. 6:2)

Clothe yourselves with humility toward one another. (1 Pet. 5:5)

Confess your sins to each other. (James 5:16)

Don't grumble against each other. (James 5:9)

Do not lie to each other. (Col. 3:9)

Do not slander one another. (James 4:11)

Do what leads to peace and mutual edification. (Rom. 14:19)

Encourage one another. (Eph. 4:32; 1 Thess. 4:18)

Forgive one another. (Eph. 4:32; Col. 3:13)

Have equal concern for each other. (1 Cor. 12:25)

Honor one another. (Rom. 12:10)

Live in harmony with one another. (Rom. 12:16; 15:5)

Love one another. (John 13:34)

Offer hospitality to one another. (1 Pet. 4:9)

Pray for each other. (James 5:16)

Serve one another. (Gal. 5:13)

Speak to one another with psalms, hymns, and spiritual songs. (Eph. 5:18–20; Col. 3:17)

Spur one another on toward love and good deeds. (Heb. 10:24)

Submit to one another. (Eph. 5:21)

Teach and admonish one another. (Col. 3:16; Rom. 15:14)

God commissioned the church to serve him. Moreover, he provided the necessary resources to get the job done via gifted believers.[1] Each member in Christ's body possesses at least one spiritual gift (1 Cor. 12:7). Thus, each believer potentially makes some contribution. Indeed, we are *expected* to help the body build itself up (Eph. 4:16; 1 Pet. 4:10). Therefore, how should we utilize these "people" resources for ministry (a task concern) without abusing them in the process (a people concern)? Continual management of this tension provides the healthiest alternative. Specifically, a balance between task and people orientation emerges from our leadership style, how we relate to others, how we recruit and develop teachers, and how we design and organize ministry programs.

Leader as Completer

Since some believers assume church leadership roles, responsible Christians ask, "Who is qualified to lead? What indicators point out giftedness in this particular area?"[2] The Bible presents comprehensive criteria for leadership selection:

- willingness and interest in being a leader (1 Tim. 3:1)
- mature Christian character and convictions (1 Tim. 3:2–3, 9; Titus 1:7–8)
- good management of home life (1 Tim. 3:4–5, 12; Titus 1:6)

- some length of time as a believer (1 Tim. 3:6)
- a proven track record of ministry (1 Tim. 3:10)
- good reputation with non-Christians (1 Tim. 3:7)
- sound understanding of and ability to use Scripture (Titus 1:9)
- recognizable spiritual gifts (Eph. 4:11; 1 Pet. 4:10–11)

No one excels in all of these categories. Yet, concerted efforts should be praised; substantive evidence of growth should be recognized in every potential leader.

Besides busyness and superficial relationships, another problem in the church is rivalry (see Matt. 20:21; Luke 9:46; 22:24). We leaders jostle among ourselves. Who is on top? Who possesses the most power? But Jesus vividly contrasts the world's approach to leadership with his own: "You know that the rulers of the Gentiles lord it over them, and their high officials exercise authority over them. Not so with you. Instead, whoever wants to become great among you must be your servant, and whoever wants to be first must be your slave—just as the Son of Man did not come to be served, but to serve, and to give his life as a ransom for many" (Matt. 20:25–28).

It was Peter, the leader of the Twelve, who eventually learned what it took to differentiate between these two managerial approaches. In life's school of hard knocks, this rugged fisherman was slowly transformed into a godly leader. Incidents like Christ's foot washing (John 13:1–17) finally made sense. Peter affirms this upside-down view of Christian leadership: "To the elders among you, I appeal as a fellow elder . . . Be shepherds of God's flock . . . not lording it over [same word used in Matthew] those entrusted to you, but being examples to the flock" (1 Pet. 5:1–3). The "lord it over" mode typifies worldly leadership. Daily we experience this brand of governance, whether at home, school, or work.

How do we break the cycle? How do we alter this natural inclination to control others? How does a servant-leader function? One way to get a handle on this challenge is to think of the *leader as completer* (Brilhart and Galanes 1989, p. 194): "Each member supplies those services he or she does best, with the designated leader providing what others cannot." Thus, leaders help members grow by providing opportunities for them to use their gifts. Moreover, leaders fill in where others are yet unable to serve.

In his definition of management, Myron Rush provides another way to clarify the servant-leader role: "Management is meeting the needs of people as they work at accomplishing their jobs" (1983, p. 13). In other words, the leader is an *equipper* (Eph. 4:11–12).

Getting Along with Your Teachers

Bill Cranfield, Sunday school superintendent at First Church, submits his annual fall report to the Christian education committee. Among his written comments he highlights the teaching staff's response to recent growth. For some, this growth has brought pain. Bill assesses the staff's reaction to a particular growing pain: the need to move some classes around due to space problems.

The second Sunday in October is the target date, and that's only two weeks away. Mark and Sue Wong, the seventh and eighth grade teachers, are looking forward to having more room. They've been really crowded for a whole year. Julie Porter, the ninth grade teacher, wasn't very excited about the move, but she realizes that we sometimes have to sacrifice a little for the good of the whole Sunday school program. She'll miss the nice carpet and large win-

dows, but she likes the larger wall space in the new classroom. She was also disappointed that she didn't hear about the move a little earlier. Then there's Jerry Abrams, our young adult teacher. He's putting up a real fuss. He doesn't like leaving the classroom he's had for three years now. He says he doesn't agree that there is a real space shortage. He thinks the decision was made without really talking to the teachers. As it is now he'd rather quit teaching than move. And of course, George Mayberry, another adult teacher, is dragging his feet again. He's certain I railroaded this decision through.

How do we deal with disagreements and conflict in the church? Are there effective ways to handle tensions among believers?

Think about It

Compare a few conflict resolution approaches:

- attack opponents as trouble-makers
- defend your viewpoint at all costs and force your plan through
- withdraw completely from the conflict or quit your position
- give in to an opponent's demands on the "outside," but seethe on the "inside"

Does one of these strategies predominantly fit your approach to leadership? If so, why do you think you tend to use this strategy? Have you attempted alternate means?

An inevitable characteristic of ministry is that *change will occur.*[3] Whether it's moving into a new classroom facility, starting a new outreach strategy, or calling a new pastor, change will come. But this truism doesn't make adjustment to change any easier. With changes, conflict and tensions also arise. Some conflicts result from selfish attitudes. Other conflicts arise because change is handled poorly. Why not minimize these latter problems? It's possible to prevent many unnecessary conflicts. As change is contemplated, make the most of two key factors: empathy and participation (Kirkpatrick 1986).[4]

Empathy: Put Yourself in Their Shoes

Do you like being ousted from familiar settings? Jerry Abrams has a legitimate complaint. As leaders we tend to see just one side of change—we trumpet all the *benefits*. But change involves a *loss* for one or more persons. Jerry Abrams loses his custom-designed classroom. Julie Porter loses attractive furnishings and sunlight. As we understand our teachers' feelings, we no longer ignore their perspectives. For instance, as time and budget permit, we could organize a work team to help Jerry fix up his new classroom. We could renovate Julie's room by putting in a window or by adding a skylight.

Dealing with Personality Conflicts

Bill Cranfield and George Mayberry just don't see eye to eye. George thinks Bill doesn't listen, and that he decides much too quickly. Bill thinks that George doesn't stand up for his convictions; he's too sensitive to people's opinions. Whenever there's a need to do something, George insists on convening a task force to study the issue first. Bill thinks committees are a waste of time, that "committee accomplishment" is an oxymoron. From this single case we see how particular conflicts among believers can run deep. Dispositions and personalities clash.

Paul and Barnabas had a serious disagreement (Acts 15). John Mark represented the point of contention. Paul thought John Mark was unqualified for their second missionary journey. The mission team would enter new regions on this next trip, potentially facing more adversity than before. Paul felt they shouldn't risk having someone who gave up so easily on the former journey (Acts 13:13). On the other hand, Barnabas saw potential in Mark. (He had spotted the same potential in Paul earlier; Acts 9:26–27.) For Barnabas, John Mark was well worth the risk.

Who was right? In such cases, conflict portrays a direct consequence of alternate perspectives. Neither right nor wrong exists. Besides perspectives, spiritual gifts play a part in such struggles. Paul's gifts were more task-oriented and Barnabas' were more people-oriented. These men resolved this stressful dispute by organizing *two* missionary teams. They agreed to disagree, and to get on with God's work.

Various personality or social style instruments are available to help us comprehend our basic orientations to tasks and people.[5] These inventories are used widely, both in business circles and among church organizations. They represent a means of uncovering strengths—and potential conflict areas—among staff workers and leaders. In addition to task and people orientations, some of us tend to have more of a "take charge" manner ("tellers"), while others prefer to ask the tough questions ("askers"). Four basic patterns emerge: analytical (beaver), driver (lion), expressive (otter), and amiable (golden retriever). These are outlined in Table 17.2.[6]

It's a Real Zoo!

This four-part grid explains why Bill Cranfield (a strong "lion") tends to offend his teachers. People like Bill focus on *what* needs to be done. They tend to dominate any kind of opposition to finish the job. We need these people to move us into action.

Table 17.2

Motivational Patterns of Behavior

Emphasis on Task

	Emphasis on Task		
"Asks" Slower Pace	BEAVER ANALYTICAL How?	LION DRIVER What?	"Tells" Faster Pace
	GOLDEN RETRIEVER AMIABLE Why?	OTTER EXPRESSIVE Who?	

Emphasis on Relationships

Source: Adapted from Phillips (1989).

Their ability to make quick decisions is especially critical in times of emergency.

Amiable "golden retrievers" like George Mayberry exhibit the exact opposite motivation. They sensitively determine *why* we do the job we do; they make sure all opinions are considered; they are cooperative and loyal. These people model good teamwork for us. But, in conflict, they would rather switch than confront.

Expressive "otters" are more alert to *who* is involved. They like to be with people. They are great motivators. They encourage us. We need their kind words, their hopeful spirits, and their helpful affirmation. One downside is that they let important details fall through the cracks.

Analytical "beavers" want to know *how* the job will get done. They are critical thinkers who ask the tough questions. We need their quality-control emphasis. But they tend to be too critical and very slow to make decisions.

Figure 17.1 suggests the distinctive emphases that leaders from each style contribute. Ultimately, we need the benefit of all styles, providing balanced leadership. If we understand our own tendencies, it is easier

to explain our interpersonal frustrations. We also head off unnecessary conflicts by realizing how our words and actions are often misunderstood. Furthermore, as we understand the personalities of others, we put ourselves in their shoes. We are able to look beyond our individual gifts and private viewpoints. By checking our selfish reactions, we begin the reconciling process of working toward mutually agreeable solutions.

Think about It

Review the four inappropriate ways to resolve conflict and match them with related behavior style:

1. Attack opponents as trouble-makers.
2. Defend your viewpoint at all costs and force your plan through.
3. Withdraw completely from the conflict or quit your position.
4. Give in to an opponent's demands on the "outside," but seethe on the "inside."

_____ Beavers—Analyticals?
_____ Golden retrievers—Amiables?
_____ Lions—Drivers?
_____ Otters—Expressives?[7]

Participation: Involving Them in Decision Making

Jerry Abrams felt left out. He felt he had no say in the decision to rearrange classrooms. When people are permitted some degree of participation in decisions, potential conflict diminishes. This principle expresses the second key ingredient for sidestepping interpersonal trouble. People should have the privilege to make suggestions about issues that affect them.[8]

Figure 17.1

Complementary Leadership Styles

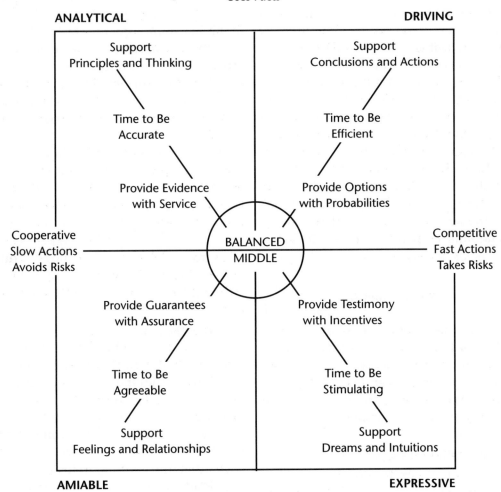

Cool, Independent, Uncommunicative (Guarded)
Disciplined about Time
Uses Facts

ANALYTICAL   DRIVING

Support   Support
Principles and Thinking   Conclusions and Actions

Time to Be   Time to Be
Accurate   Efficient

Provide Evidence   Provide Options
with Service   with Probabilities

Cooperative   Competitive
Slow Actions   BALANCED MIDDLE   Fast Actions
Avoids Risks   Takes Risks

Provide Guarantees   Provide Testimony
with Assurance   with Incentives

Time to Be   Time to Be
Agreeable   Stimulating

Support   Support
Feelings and Relationships   Dreams and Intuitions

AMIABLE   EXPRESSIVE

Warm, Approachable, Communicative (Open)
Undisciplined about Time
Uses Opinions

Source: Gangel (1989, p. 24).

Keeping Communication Channels Open

The Christian education committee hasn't convinced Jerry Abrams that a lack of facility space exists at First Church. He doesn't accept their conclusions. The proposed changes, for him, are unnecessary. Was Jerry notified about the classroom change through a letter that circulated in September? For that matter, was Jerry invited by the committee in early summer to ex-

311

plain his ideas about the proposed change? What about that gathering several months before? Was Jerry encouraged to attend the informal session that first identified the problem of growing pains? Did this young adult teacher help brainstorm possible solutions? *How* and *when* we communicate is just as important as *what* we communicate.

As soon as it is feasible, leaders must inform teachers and staff about issues that could affect them. If they procrastinate, misunderstandings may lead to anger and resistance. Some information may need to be kept confidential. Yet, since ownership of ideas is crucial, workers should be brought into the decision-making process at strategic points. Jerry Abrams received a letter about the classroom changes. But "telling" is not the same as "creating understanding" and gaining support for an idea. In fact, it often yields the opposite end.

Think about It

Various means of input are available to encourage participation. They range from simple to more complex possibilities. Which means have been helpful to you in the past? Which have permitted you to satisfactorily express your opinions?

- the traditional suggestion box
- regular teachers' meetings
- church leaders entertaining members in their home for a dinner discussion
- task force participation to investigate particular concerns
- formal presentations to the church board or a business meeting
- other _____

Some congregations hold annual all-church gatherings to identify past blessings and to plan for the future. One fellowship set aside four Sunday evenings in May for this purpose. People were divided into groups of about ten. Each group was led by a church board member and met for about forty-five minutes. In the first meeting, all groups listed what ministries and procedures were going well. They thanked God for his blessings. Also, they briefly described why these ministries should continue. In other words, participants were indirectly asked to assess the objectives and functions of the body. Were specific evidences of healthy progress toward reconciliation found?

During the second gathering, members listed major problems or obstacles that hindered the church's mission. Then, in the third and fourth meetings, each group concentrated their efforts on two of these problems. Their task was to suggest realistic ways to remedy the difficulties. Church leaders then evaluated all group work, determining particular strategies for the future.

Deciding How to Decide

The selected method for decision making can actually foster conflict. Em Griffin (1982) notes that making good decisions is not the only goal committees should keep in mind: "You want the group to reach a quality solution that all are committed to in a short amount of time while still liking each other and learning in the process" (p. 67). Besides employing the common method of majority vote, issues can also be settled by consensus, by using an expert (or a group of experts), or by ranking and voting on items. The last method allows committees to narrow the options before arriving at the best solution. In Table 17.4, Griffin evaluates each of these four methods by means of the factors identified in Table 17.3. Each method has advantages and disadvantages. Wise leaders select methods that balance task and people con-

Table 17.3

Factors in Decision Making

Quality: How consistent is the decision-making strategy with Scripture: Does it complement or contradict additional criteria established (e.g., denominational positions)?

Time: What length of time does the decision-making process take?

Commitment to solution: To what degree are people willing to personally follow through on what is decided?

Attraction to group: How will decisions affect group cohesiveness? To what degree are members willing to work together after the decision has been made?

Learning: To what degree does the decision-making process encourage learning about the subject of the decision, as well as the whole decision-making process?

Source: Adapted from Griffin (1982).

cerns.[9] Exercising empathy and participation provides the incentive for better relationships.[10]

Recruiting and Developing Your Teachers[11]

Just when staffing needs in one educational program are filled, vacancies pop up in another. Consider a variation in the old proverb for church ministry: The only certainties in life are taxes, death, and *recruiting volunteers.* Even Jesus acknowledged staffing problems: "The harvest is plentiful, but the laborers are few" (Luke 10:2). How do we encourage believers to become involved—then to *stay* involved—in educational ministries?

It may seem backward, but think about it: Longevity requires that needs of *present* workers are met. Retaining workers alleviates much of the demand for additional personnel. In short, the best recruiting strategy is a satisfied customer—the current staff. This principle permeates the first five of the seven guidelines below. The last two guidelines pertain to *potential* workers.[12] "RECRUIT" provides an acrostic for these seven foundational concepts.

Table 17.4

Options in Decision-Making

Option	Quality	Time	Commitment to Solution	Attraction to Group	Learning Value
1. Voting	+	+	+/–	–	+
2. Using an Expert	?	++	–	0	–
3. Voting and Ranking	+	++	– –	0	–
4. Consensus	++	– –	++	++	+

++ major advantage   + advantage   0 neutral   – drawback   – – major drawback

Source: Griffin (1982, p. 85).

Research	
Encourage	
Communicate	(for *present* workers)
Review	
Upgrade	
Identify	(for *potential* workers)
Train	

Research

The word "research" might elicit negative attitudes. It may connote term papers or study projects. Actually, it means "being aware" of individuals and the opportunities for service.

Research Your People

"Congratulations! You're gifted!" Without exception, this significant message must be communicated to believers. A gift unused is a gift abused. As we "research" people, determining their giftedness signals our initial task. This is accomplished in several ways, including prayer for wisdom, self-evaluation,[13] feedback from others (regarding past ministries), and various assessment inventories.[14] With perseverance, every believer can effectively narrow the options of service.

Each gift from God is quite complex. Two believers may have the same spiritual gift, but the manifestation of that gift may differ (1 Cor. 12:4–6). Distinctiveness exists, in part, because of a special burden (or ministry focus) that God lays on each heart.[15] For example, one "exhorter" concentrates on helping young mothers cope with parenthood; another directs efforts to raise Christian consciousness about issues like abortion. One "helper" prepares food for socials or shut-ins, while another welcomes new believers by befriending them. Still another helper deals with the material needs within the community. A personal ministry burden, when confirmed by others, motivates a believer despite difficulties.[16] We leaders have a responsibility to help people find ministries in which they can utilize their giftedness to best serve Christ.

Research Your Ministry Opportunities

For each ministry position, a specific job description is required. Include the position's purpose, responsibility, authority, and specific length of commitment. When matching people with particular ministry positions, be flexible. In this way the position is custom-fitted to the individual.[17] Sensitive church leaders, therefore, accomplish two purposes: On the one hand, existing ministries are adjusted in light of the staff's gifts and burdens; on the other hand, new ministries are created in response to the Spirit's work within each person.[18]

Encourage

All of us are susceptible to weariness in ministry. Even Paul was discouraged at times (Gal. 4:11, 19–20; 1 Thess. 3:5). Sometimes we wonder: Is our effort really worth it? Are needs really being met? Are believers growing in their faith? Are they making the right decisions? Are those outside the family of God becoming more sensitive to spiritual things? As leaders of teachers, we must encourage them to "stand firm. Let nothing move you. Always give yourselves fully to the work of the Lord, because you know that your labor in the Lord is not in vain" (1 Cor. 15:58). Encouragement, like a birthday present, can be packaged many ways: a kind word of gratitude, a written note of thanks, a helping hand, an arm around the shoulder, a public testimony of praise, an appreciation dinner, a special award. The concept of encouragement includes more than just honoring faithful workers. Common sense and a little empathy go a long way.

Communicate

A rule of thumb for healthy ministry relationships: "If you have to err, err by *over-*

communicating rather than *under*communicating." It's better to repeat yourself than to assume a single conversation was fully understood. Two distinct groups call for attention when it comes to information exchange.

Communicate to Your Staff

We all like to know what's going on. Even surprise birthday parties can unsettle some of us. Up-to-date information is especially desired if it affects our sphere of ministry. Topics of communication include issues like future directions, board decisions, new workers, recent purchases, equipment needs, prayer requests of workers, special training events, testimonies of praise. Two-way communication is best. As previously noted, dialogue evokes the empathy of leaders for their staff. Furthermore, it encourages teachers to participate in administrative decisions concerning program change.

Communicate to the Whole Church

From time to time, the entire local fellowship must be reminded of its comprehensive ministries. Education that is Christian encompasses the whole body. Consequently, churchwide knowledge leads to churchwide commitment, prayer, counsel, participation, and financial help. Multiple communication channels inform a congregation: church bulletin inserts, public prayer requests, the Christian education annual report, monthly newsletter articles, the church telephone chain, bulletin board notices. Prayer partners might be recruited for each worker. Alternating lists of staff members' names, printed in the bulletin, heighten awareness of ministry needs and visibility. One church scheduled an open house; each ministry sponsored an exhibit booth. Light refreshments were provided. As church members toured the exhibit hall,

workers introduced themselves and reviewed their ministry's accomplishments. Some of these were on display. Future goals were also featured.

Review

Periodically, workers require feedback. People need to know how well they are meeting stated goals and policies. Each believer needs to know: "What significant part am I playing in building up the body of Christ?" To use a sports analogy, athletes gain confidence and drive as they contribute to a winning team. Such evaluation may pinpoint special areas of need. For example, a Sunday school teacher may be effectively meeting so many students' needs that her class is bursting at the seams. The suggestion to divide her class into two sections is the simplest and most logical response. Yet, corollary decisions (like additional staffing and extra rooms) illustrate the review procedure.

The review process itself takes any number of options. Minimally, workers complete self-evaluation forms. They assess the program itself and their own ministry. A subsequent step could involve a private meeting with the program leader, in which written self-evaluation remarks are discussed. Another level of assessment might include a corporate evaluation of workers from the same ministry. For example, all primary Sunday school teachers might gather together for a special group critique of their department.[19]

It is beneficial to combine personnel review and program evaluation. Both ministries and workers alike gain from such assessments. We leaders should exercise spiritual discernment to guide the development of our staff. In this way we keep our ministries on track.

1. Recall some ministries in which you have participated. How often was your ministry evaluated? What kind of feedback did you receive from leaders? Was it planned or impromptu?

2. What specific kinds of feedback help you the most? To what forms do you react negatively?

3. If you are currently in a supervisory position, what review system do you use to provide constructive feedback to workers?

Upgrade

To the Thessalonian believers, Paul wrote, "we request and exhort you in the Lord Jesus . . . that you may excel still more [in pleasing God]" (1 Thess. 4:1). To "excel still more" involves upgrading. It means improving ministry skills. Starting with self-evaluation forms (and other aspects of the review process), workers must be encouraged to set annual personal growth goals. "How can I be my very best for God?" represents the undergirding inquiry. Educational opportunities supply one means of improvement. These range from in-house church seminars to regional conferences and workshops. Further training includes self-instructional materials and group study programs.[20] Groups of workers (such as senior high workers) might be persuaded to make firsthand observations of innovative ministries at other churches. Creative ideas within parachurch organizations might be studied. Leaders of such groups could be in-terviewed, or consultation services might be sought.[21]

Identify

Every organization needs to standardize ways to locate and contact potential workers. Without one person or committee supervising this objective, chaos results. A "first come, first served" mentality is guaranteed. Without a coordinated plan, potential recruits are barraged with ministry opportunities.

Supervision of recruiting efforts extends beyond the staffing needs of Christian education. Similar needs exist for diverse church ministries, including worship, music, finances, maintenance, missions, and outreach. A churchwide "ministry placement committee" best matches *all* workers with the host of ministry possibilities. Committee members consist of caring people who share a common burden: to see believers effectively serving God, the church, and the community.

Although one committee represents the clearinghouse, every leader and worker seeks potential workers. The recruiting process often starts in the new members' class. Here, participants are introduced to the church's total outreach. A ministry interest/involvement questionnaire is completed. Personal contact follows. Some churches conduct an annual membership survey of abilities and previous ministry experiences. The process permits them to update their records.[22]

Train

Once prospective workers are identified, the important step of new staff development begins. Short-term schemes are alluring. But leaders must resist the urge to move newcomers into ministry too quickly. Sink or swim training strategies produce too many fatalities. Filling urgent staffing needs is not the ultimate aim; long-term ministry effectiveness is. The following three-part plan provides a framework for training in a graduated manner.

Phase 1: Observation and Orientation

Two safe assumptions about most potential workers are: (1) they possess little or no knowledge of the particular church ministry under consideration; and (2) their understanding of age group needs is probably minimal. Consequently, future staff members require orientation to program goals. By attending planning meetings with current workers, new staff become acclimated to colleagues and to ministry objectives. This action initiates their on-the-job training. Also, as new staff read program materials, their understanding is supplemented.

Leaders may require prospects to take a specific training course. Some churches offer training sessions during the Sunday school hour or at a mid-week program. Encourage future staff to study a few pertinent magazine articles related to their learners' age group. Allow sufficient time for prospective workers to observe the program in operation. Also, the prospect could visit with the regular teacher while planning a weekly lesson. That way, the prospect develops an experiential link between planning and teaching.

Phase 2: Planning the Lesson

The next level of training involves extensive experience. After a couple weeks of the Phase 1 strategy, limited program assignments are given to the prospective worker. Gradually, responsibilities increase. The current teacher and the prospect plan the lesson together. Feedback is given to the trainee following each ministry event. Eventually, the prospect teaches the entire lesson, with the current teacher observing and offering advice.

Phase 3: Evaluation and Follow-up

The entire training period represents an inquiry process. After sufficient time, the trainee and program leader mutually decide if a good match has been struck. Should the prospect continue in this program? If so, a regular ministry position is assigned; if not, the prospective worker begins Phase 1 in another ministry. Unsatisfactory matches should never be viewed as failures. In fact, this intentional design *prevents* future frustration and failure. This three-part plan fine tunes a recognition of giftedness, individual burden, and place of ministry.

Fruitful, long-term recruiting strategies keep two goals in mind: (1) to utilize the full giftedness of believers; and (2) to meet the staffing needs of existing programs. In other words, church leaders must be sensitive to *people* and *task*. Attending to both goals lays a strong foundation for effective education that is Christian.

Think about It

Can you name the seven concepts of the recruiting process? For each concept, list one corresponding principle of action. To get you started, the first line is completed.

Concept	Principle of Action
R esearch	Help my staff understand their strengths.
E	
C	
R	
U	
I	
T	

Conclusion

Our Calling: To Serve One Another

Jesus Christ epitomized a life of service: "For even the Son of Man did not come to be served, but to serve, and to give His life a ransom for many" (Mark 10:45). On the anguishing night of his betrayal, Jesus served his disciples by washing their feet. "Now that I, your Lord and Teacher, have washed your feet, you also should wash one another's feet. I have set you an example that you should do as I have done for you" (John 13:14–15).

Sacrificial involvement in ministry is not optional. It does not matter if our service is public (teaching a class, or singing a solo) or behind the scenes (making phone calls, cooking for others, or assembling mailings). Believers fulfill their purpose when they are obedient to the design for which they were created: to serve one another by doing good works (Gal. 5:13; Eph. 2:10).

Our Confidence:
To Recall God's Work Through Us

Whenever human effort is involved, believers must remember that God is sovereign. Every detail of our lives is under his control. We have the privilege of being his ambassadors (2 Cor. 5:20). God does not actually *need* our help, but works his will through our efforts (Phil. 2:12–13).

When Israel crossed the Jordan River, only as the priests, carrying the ark of the covenant, touched their feet to the water did God perform a miracle. Then—and only then—did the chosen nation cross over on dry ground (Josh. 3:13–17). Had the priests hesitated to extend their feet over the water, the Israelites may never have entered the Promised Land! Mature believers exhibit full reliance on God without shrinking from personal obligation.

Our Challenge: To Pray and Invite
Other Workers to Join Us

Remember when Nehemiah and the Jews were rebuilding the walls around Jerusalem? Their task was not easy. Moreover, they received hostile threats from the surrounding regions (Neh. 5:8). Their response? "But we prayed to our God, and because of them we set up a guard against them day and night" (Neh. 5:9). Notice the balance: They prayed for protection *and* they set a twenty-four-hour watch. These actions were not mutually exclusive; sovereignty was coupled with service. Similarly, we must *both* pray for more laborers *and* enlist other believers in kingdom building.

Jesus' personal challenge to the church is to "beseech the Lord of the harvest to send out laborers into His harvest" (Luke 10:2). Such petitions cannot negate hands-on involvement. Conversely, work never diminishes the need for prayer.

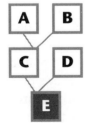

18 Focus on Task: Designing Ministry Programs

Introduction
Inner Factors
Outer Factors
Conclusion

Introduction

Often we do things out of habit, without knowing why. This problem poses a particular hazard when passing on important religious traditions. For example, the Pharisees thought that keeping their cups and kettles clean was an essential task of religious leaders (Mark 7:1–15). They perpetuated such traditions, which had been passed down to them. But Jesus criticized their false interpretation. He reminded them that *external* traditions were only a secondary means of acknowledging primary ends: a holy *inner* life.

Confusing Means with Ends

In the church's educational ministry, we similarly confuse the *main purpose* of an activity with its associated *cultural practice*. Traditions frequently sidetrack us. For instance, we expend much effort to set new attendance records in Sunday school. Yet we need constant reminders that attendance represents only a *means.* Our real *goal* is to help every attender obey God's message of reconciliation.

Throughout the course of Bible history, basic ministry *goals* remain, while ministry *forms* alter. For example, one recurring goal identifies loving care for widows (e.g., Deut. 10:18; James 1:27). Yet approaches to this end were diverse. Table 18.1 displays various forms that served widows' material needs. As evangelicals we affirm that, although basic goals do *not* change, the ways we confront these goals—the form of the program—will change. Gene Getz (1974) warns us about our tendency toward institutionalism: "We have allowed nonabsolutes to become absolute. This way of thinking is the most subtle of all in leading the church into institutionalism. That which is meant to be a *means* to an end, becomes an *end* in itself. We allow ourselves to get locked in to patterns and structures that are no longer relevant and adequate, to help us minister to the people who live in our contemporary culture" (p. 209). The particular shape of our ministries must not become frozen in some historical time warp, becoming irrelevant museum pieces to the modern world.[1]

Table 18.1

Ministry to Widows in the Bible

Old Testament
- Widows were allowed to glean in the fields (Deut. 24:19–22; Ruth 2:2–3).
- Widows received portions of a third-year tithe (Deut. 14:28–29; 26:12–13).

New Testament
- Food was distributed to widows by the apostles (Acts 6:1–4).
- Food was distributed to widows by a select group of men (Acts 6:1–6).
- Widows who met certain qualifications were placed on an official list to receive church support (1 Tim. 5:3–16).

Cultivating Our Ministries

Healthy ministries, like healthy gardens, never stop growing. Yet sometimes growth becomes unwieldy, like an untended vegetable patch. How do we facilitate a healthiness that complements biblical purposes? When should we initiate new ministries? At what point do we adjust program structure or staff? How do we assess whether ministries accomplish their purposes?

Leaders wrestle with a host of issues in growing the church's educational ministries. We will analyze significant strategies that propagate healthy ministries. We can set these features as components of a wheel design. The "Educational Planning Wheel" suggests a dynamic process. Task and people emphases are balanced. We've chosen a wheel design because, in practice, no planning process is linear. Factors are simultaneously considered. Sequence of events varies. Church leaders recognize that cultivating growing ministries is a complex process that defies simplistic formulas. For ease of description, we display the features of a wheel in a logical progression (see Figure 18.1).[2]

Inner Factors

In Acts 6, Hellenistic-Jewish believers started complaining when their widows were neglected in daily food distributions. They voiced their displeasure to Hebraic Jews. Due to the burgeoning number of disciples, the meal program lost its effectiveness. Outmoded ministry methods required modification. Initially this ministry to widows rested on the apostles' shoulders.[3] But growing pains forced these primary leaders to reassess their direct participation. It is worthy to note that this passage portrays a critical insight into the early church's pilgrimage. After evaluating their priorities,

Figure 18.1
The Educational Planning Wheel

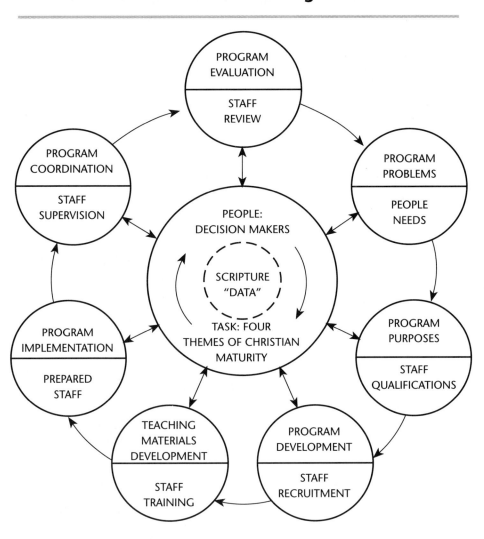

Source: Adapted from models used by LeBar (1968) and Gangel (1989).

the apostles reestablished their foundational purpose.

The Twelve intentionally restricted their focus "to prayer and the ministry of the word" (Acts 6:4b). Emphasis rightly centered on Communion with God. Other ministries proceeded from that point.

The apostles proposed the formation of a committee of seven men to serve widows be-

cause they valued Community. They used a justifiable rationale: "It would not be right for us . . . to wait on tables" (v. 2b). The Twelve never intended this assignment to reflect a menial task—they had been in charge of the program before the complaints. Rather, it was simply not meant *for them.* Spiritual gifts and calling figured into their decisions.

The theme of Character likewise appears here. The apostles wouldn't settle for a random selection of seven individuals. The chosen had to be "from among" the group, "known" by all (v. 3a). Reputation was non-negotiable. Also, these men had to possess the fullness of the "Spirit and wisdom" (v. 3b). Perhaps the impotence of contemporary Christianity stems from, in part, a neglect of such Character. Finally, Commission surfaces in the text. Following the body's affirmation of the seven, believers obediently testify of Christ. Luke specifically records that a large number of priests were converted (v. 7).

By way of application to the "Educational Planning Wheel," the hub (or inner circle) includes three crucial elements:

- as central, the Scriptures—the *data* from which we develop a Christian worldview
- the four themes outlining a Reconciliation Model of Christian maturity—the *task* to which we have been called
- the *decision makers*—the persons who study the data and influence believers' efforts, in various ways, toward task accomplishment

This hub of the wheel provides balance and perspective to the whole planning process. As evangelicals, we affirm that our *theology* of ministry must drive our *practice* of ministry. The inner circle reminds us that each ministry or program is centered in an overall view of ministry. At the heart of ministry is the need for God's people to think in God's way.[4] Accurately interpreting Scripture and developing a Christian worldview are incumbent on *each* believer, not just church leaders, since anyone can influence, or hinder, the church's maturation. Believers must regularly study Scripture to develop deeper understandings of the four

themes: Communion, Community, Character, and Commission. Yet these conceptions and their implications for practice must not be regarded as final conclusions. Rather a dynamic process is envisioned. These understandings must be continually refined as church leaders and members grow to know God better.

"Decision makers" are those who exert an influence on a particular ministry. At the formal level, this means official members of boards and committees, program leaders, and staff. Informal decision makers don't claim any official capacity, but their influence is just as potent.[5] For example, if individuals from the latter category do not attend a church event, they have "voted with their feet." Their absence might communicate that the event is not relevant or that other priorities are more important. In Acts 6, five groups, including formal and informal decision makers, participated in setting a new direction for the meal distribution program: the Grecian-Jewish widows, the Hebraic-Jewish widows, the Twelve, the Seven, and the sum total of believers.

The rounded arrows of the inner circle symbolize the never-ending process of decision making fashioned by the truth. Ideally, it captures the reality of believers' constructive responses to the themes of Christian maturity. It portrays, essentially, the evaluative grid through which all educational planning is scrutinized. Particular assessment of *each* planning factor is reflected in Figure 18.1 by the arrows' reciprocal movement between inner and outer circles.

Outer Factors

In every factor of the outer wheel complementary features regarding both task (or program) and people (or staff) are respectively addressed. Within this balanced tension, effective leadership emerges.

When is it time to initiate a new program or to make changes in an existing one? Complaints may indicate that change is necessary. We begin our discussion of the outer wheel with the first component evident in the Acts 6 case study. This New Testament case will be followed to illustrate each of the various features of the outer circle.

Program Evaluation and Staff Review

Sometimes, leaders take a *reactive* posture. They wait for an informal evaluation. For example, in Acts 6 Hellenistic-Jewish believers complained to Hebraic Jews that their widows were neglected (v. 1). Or, leaders may opt for a more *proactive* stance and regularly assess programs. Regardless of the choice, the underlying issue is the same: "Are programs accomplishing their purposes?" Like the apostles, leaders may be unaware of the ineffectiveness within human-made programs and structures.

As we make such evaluations, we also must review our staff and teachers. While modifying the meal program, the apostles also reassessed their own ministry role (vv. 2, 4). Various approaches enable leaders to take the pulse beat of programs and people: from personal observations to detailed inspections, and from casual conversations to group feedback. A commonly used method is the survey. Table 18.2 offers one means by which to evaluate the fellowship climate of a church or a particular class.[6]

Program Problems and People Needs

In Acts 6, the growing number of disciples prevented the meal program from meeting some important needs. The apostles realized they could no longer administer the program. When we clearly identify all the parts of the problem, we are well on the way to providing an effective solution. Too many times, once the difficulty is recognized, our tendency is to attend to that need

Table 18.2

Group Atmosphere Survey

On a scale of "excellent" to "very poor," mark the degree of satisfaction you experience on each item. In the blank space following each item, give specific experiences, perceptions, or other information that prompted you to mark the instrument as you did.

1. An Environment of Active People:
   I felt that I was personally involved in the learning process, and significantly involved in the decision-making process.
   ☐ excellent   ☐ very good   ☐ good   ☐ average   ☐ fair   ☐ poor   ☐ very poor

2. A Climate of Respect:
   I felt a high value was placed on individual worth and dignity; a sense of caring prevailed.
   ☐ excellent   ☐ very good   ☐ good   ☐ average   ☐ fair   ☐ poor   ☐ very poor

3. A Climate of Acceptance:
   I felt I could believe and act the way I wanted to (I was not manipulated).
   ☐ excellent   ☐ very good   ☐ good   ☐ average   ☐ fair   ☐ poor   ☐ very poor

4. A Climate of Self-Discovery:
   I felt that we were helped to identify and meet our own needs rather than having our needs dictated to us.
   ☐ excellent   ☐ very good   ☐ good   ☐ average   ☐ fair   ☐ poor   ☐ very poor

Source: Adapted from a survey developed by Dr. Don Moore.

as quickly as possible. But should we attempt to meet *every* need in this manner?

A stranger approaches you and asks for $50.00. Imagine that you have the money to give.

1. Would you oblige, if the person wanted to:

   Person 1: buy alcoholic beverages?

   Person 2: eat a meal at an expensive restaurant?

   Person 3: buy groceries for their family?

   Person 4: pay utility bills?

2. Let's call these above items the *presented* need. In contrast, identify one related *primary* need pertinent to each situation. For example, maybe Person 1 needs money for professional help and moral support to kick the drinking habit.

As we confront the concerns of our people, we must constantly evaluate whether we're providing the *best* ministry for *appropriate* needs. Although two responses may initially appear to satisfy similar needs with the same effectiveness, further analysis might prove otherwise. Consider the case above: Both Person 2 and Person 3 express the legitimate need for food. But obliging the former shows indiscretion.

Parents of teens often want churches to sponsor exciting, recreation-oriented youth activities. Meeting these *presented* needs of

parents may develop trust in and credibility for church leaders. But the *primary* needs within these families must also be recognized, such as fostering healthy communication in the home. Church leaders should plan for both the presented and the basic needs of the body.

Program Purposes and Staff Qualifications

As they responded to complaints about the food program, the Twelve reminded the church of their chief purpose as apostles. To maintain effectiveness they were forced to limit their focus. They could not minimize their Communion aim. Programs should be need-*based,* not need-*driven.* As educational aims are formulated by local congregations, summative purpose statements provide guidelines for all programs. One church developed a helpful statement of purpose for its children's ministry, summarized this way: "That, by the sixth grade, the children of our church should evidence a meaningful, functional and growing relationship with Jesus Christ." Such a goal values traditional Bible memory programs. But it also encourages children to develop the habit of daily prayer. Such broader goals require cooperative efforts with parents.

After defining ministry purposes, we must determine what kind of people we need to accomplish them. These two factors are inseparable. The apostles set the following qualifications for new "table waiters":[7] "Brothers, choose seven men from among you who are known to be full of the Spirit and wisdom" (Acts 6:3). In brief, they were to be believers, of sufficient number, from the local fellowship, reputable and known for their spiritual maturity.[8] It only makes sense. Unless we get the type of people who represent—and embody—our purposes, we're only asking for trouble. Inappropriate selections yield counterproductive results.

Program Development and Staff Recruitment

In Acts 6, a long-standing ministry of serving tables was modified in response to a genuine need judged by the apostles to fall within the scope of the church's purpose. Ministry programs (like this modified one) are meant to accomplish purposes in contemporary ways. As noted earlier, foundational ministry goals don't change, but specific means will. For instance, we are challenged to encourage one another (Heb. 3:13), to build up one another (Rom. 14:19), and to meet the needs of one another (Titus 3:14). But how we attend to these interpersonal tasks are not given exhaustive treatment in Scripture. Diverse patterns of ministry are evident in Scripture as illustrated in the previously cited references to the care of widows.

Consider this principle from another angle. Two prominent subpoints comprise this fourth wheel component: function and form. *Function* in ministry is universal and permanent; *form* is cultural and temporal. One of our students from the Far East recently attended a national youth conference in the United States. She assessed that the seminars helped her because they stressed universal concerns in youth work (function). However, she was quite disappointed by all the "fun and games." For her, these particular activities precluded more intensive Bible studies. In her culture, youth are sufficiently motivated to get into the Word without so many activities (form).

Besides major questions about foundational purposes, several other questions confront us as we develop a specific program for ministry.

Where?　Should we meet at the church building, a home, or a restaurant? Besides the class time, should we plan other activities, such as a retreat or a social?

When?　How often will we meet? Daily, weekly, monthly? Should we meet for an hour, or for a longer time?

How?　Should students study before coming to the meeting or do no preparation at all? Should the meeting primarily focus on imparting new information or should time be spent on comprehending previously known concepts?

These decisions must be made in light of available resources and environmental constraints: finances, facilities and equipment, and cultural expectations. Rather than start from scratch, leaders can identify key features of existing programs and adapt these features to their context.[9]

As we are in the early stages of designing the new ministry, we also want to recruit the leadership and staff. Since this group will carry on the ministry, their early involvement can foster personal commitment to the program. Here we ask questions such as who meets the qualifications for carrying out the program, how many staff members we need, what specific steps of recruitment we should follow (e.g., planning a calendar for program publicity and potential worker interviews).

We see in Acts 6 that program and personnel issues were confronted simultaneously. Sometimes we need to "grow" our own staff to meet specific program qualifications. Jesus' training of the Twelve typifies this model of simultaneous accomplishment.

Teaching Materials Development and Staff Training

Once the basic program structure is decided and new staff are secured, materials and methods are addressed.[10] When published programs are selected (like Pioneer Clubs or AWANA), often the program comes as a complete package. Purposes, structures, personnel qualifications, curriculum—even training opportunities—are included. But each church situation is a bit different. Leaders often need to make specific modifications of the prestructured program.[11]

Beyond the task of materials development, the ministry staff require training to perform various roles. For existing programs (or when only slight modifications are planned), the training schedule outlined in the previous chapter applies. When certain new programs are implemented a modified approach follows. Staff may need to observe the program in operation at another church. Sometimes the training timeline needs to be extended to ensure competent program leaders. For example, First Church decides to launch a small group ministry. Effectiveness in this particular ministry depends on well-trained group leaders. Besides reading and classroom instruction, the best preparation for leading a small group is to be a member of a healthy small group. Thus, the initial small group ministry would involve only groups of potential leaders. Following this training period, the actual program would begin.[12]

Program Implementation with Prepared Staff

Good ideas on paper don't always get carried out. Many details compete for our attention; any one of these can snag a top-flight plan. Questions related to implementation include:

1. How do we tell the whole church about new or modified programs?
2. Do we have enough money to cover expenses?
3. Are there sufficient facilities (e.g., chairs or tables) for the program?
4. Do we need to train more staff than first anticipated?
5. Will any of these issues postpone our planned date of implementation?

More important, we forget that change doesn't come easy to any of us. All teachers must collectively adjust to new procedures. We leaders must exercise patience, discretion, and flexibility.

Table 18.3

Resistance to Change

1. Lack of Perceived Need to Change:
   a. A perception that disavows change (e.g., statements like: "We've always done it this way," or lack of imagination/creativity; lack of motivation; lack of vision; lack of flexibility; laziness)
   b. A general perception that change produces more harm than good ("If it's not broken, don't fix it.")
   c. A specific perception of personal criticism (e.g., usually it comes from those who created the existing system—they do not want others tampering with it.)
2. Lack of Participation in Decision Making:
   a. No input allowed regarding the change
   b. Lack of understanding about the change
   c. Objectionable manner in which persons heard of the change (e.g., receiving second-hand information rather than directly from the appropriate source)
   d. Objectionable manner in which change was introduced (e.g., authoritarian, top-down approach)
3. Anticipation of Subsequent Loss and/or Extra Work:
   a. Personal loss (possibly due to a vested interest) (e.g., security; friends and important contacts; visibility; freedom; responsibility; good working conditions; status; threat or fear of the unknown)
   b. Related consequences of change (e.g., it can yield confusion and mistakes, retraining needs)
   c. Bad timing for some individuals (e.g., experiencing personal or domestic problems; working on another educational degree or at an additional part-time job)
4. Preexisting Negative Attitudes (no matter what change is proposed)

a. Lack of respect for certain person(s) leading the change process

b. General negative attitudes about the church/parachurch and/or its leadership

c. Pride: a personal challenge to any authority (e.g., "Regardless of what happens, *I'm* not changing.")

Source: Adapted from Kirkpatrick (1986, chap. 4).

For many reasons, we resist change. Table 18.3 outlines four broad categories of resistance. By giving reasonable consideration to such concerns, leaders facilitate long-lasting change in ministry.

Think about It

Each of the four categories given in Table 18.3 are listed below. Next, two brief case studies provide particular strategies that deal with resistance to change. Each case study uses strategies pertinent to at least one of the four categories. Identify which category (or categories) is addressed per case:

(1) Lack of perceived need to change

(2) Lack of participation in decision making

(3) Anticipation of subsequent loss and/ or extra work

(4) Preexisting negative attitudes

Case A: You are a youth pastor who initiates a new Bible study format during the summer months. Then, in September, all those who are involved (youth, adult leaders, and parents) evaluate its effectiveness. As a group you ask, "Was the new format helpful? What could be used from this experiment on a more permanent basis?"

Which category (or categories) is addressed: 1, 2, 3, or 4?

Case B: You are a singles adult leader who complains that your classroom is too small. It's inadequate for the needs of single adults. You invite committee members to attend the fellowship portion of your mid-week meeting. The overly crowded room convinces the committee to take your complaints more seriously.

Which category (or categories) is addressed: 1, 2, 3, or 4?[13]

Program Coordination and Staff Supervision

If someone (or a committee) does not monitor the progress of change, frustrations may arise. Even worse, some may gravitate back to the "old way" of doing things. Lack of habit or guidance could prompt this regression. Most changes require modifications and final adjustments once implemented, including extra staff, more financial or material resources, additional staff training, and policy clarification. As new programs are added, open communication lines must be intentionally maintained. This final component of the Educational Planning Wheel requires constant monitoring. Progress as well as problems must be checked; coordination of efforts should be assessed regularly.

Lines of Cooperation

A potential roadblock to fruitful ministry is directly related to organization: How are boards and committees linked together? Inadequate board structure often perpetuates a subtle lack of empathy if it impedes communication. In some churches, no official (or formal) tie exists among standing committees.

One board with several committees elicits productive feedback. This organizational design provides one main policy-making board with as many committees as needed.

Every committee has direct access to the board, for each is officially tied to it through a personnel link. This concept opens communication channels. It clarifies lines of responsibility. It avoids competition or negligence. A related truism applies: The better people understand each other, the better they work together. For purposes of illustration, Figure 18.2 details one congregation's creative structure. In this church, both elders and deacons serve as leaders (churches using other leadership roles could adapt this concept).[14]

In this illustration, the main board (consisting of elders) creates and regulates the church's overall ministry. Each board member is given a specific responsibility.[15] To assist board members with their specific tasks,

Figure 18.2
Creative Church Structure

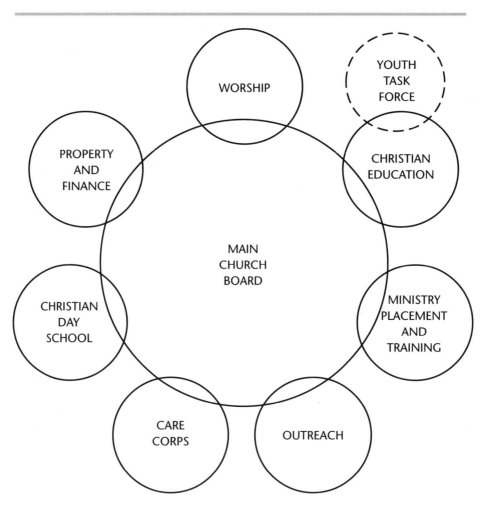

Source: Adapted from a model developed by Don Weaver and Klaus Issler, pastors of Grace Church, June 1985. (See Appendix I for further description.)

two or three qualified deacons team up with an elder per area. No separate board of deacons exists. Rather, several committees (or subgroups) of deacons provide leadership per specified area. The assigned elder chairs the respective committee. For small churches, perhaps only one elder is assigned to an area. Larger churches may assign two or three elders to certain ministry tasks.[16] This structure encourages wise judgments based on group decision making as recommended in Proverbs 15:22. Furthermore, coordination of efforts enables ministry continuity, even when pastoral staff changes occur.

Board and committee members are responsible to recruit their own staff (with the help of the ministry placement committee). For special concerns, a temporary task force forms. For example, a general policy matter about youth ministry is first studied by a youth task force (see Figure 18.2). Then, the leader of the youth task force (also a Christian education committee member) passes their suggestions on to the CE committee. After discussion in that committee, the policy is taken by the Christian education committee chairperson, an elder, to the board for consideration. If the policy matter is approved, decisions to implement the policy are made at the lowest organizational level (in this case, by the youth task force). The goal of building trust at each structural level is accomplished. Moreover, decision ownership is realized at each level.[17]

Supervising Staff

Leadership/supervision style raises yet another potential source of unnecessary conflict. For instance, one associate pastor delegated responsibility for the children's Christmas program to an inexperienced worker in October. He naively left the worker alone to fulfill her assignment. By early December, the Christmas program was still only a vague idea. So, the associate pastor had to step in. The worker's ability (or her willingness) to direct the program was misunderstood. In this case, the associate pastor used the wrong level of supervision. What leadership style would have been more appropriate? What approach would have been less embarrassing and more fruitful?

Contrary to the claims of some advertisers, one style of supervision does not fit all. For example, at First Church, Maria Lopez desires more of a free rein in leading her ninth-grade Sunday school class. Whether it's developing creative ideas or dealing with discipline problems, Maria is a self-assured instructor. Timothy and Janet Park are relatively new teachers; they don't feel as confident as Maria. They require encouragement and guidance from a more experienced teacher. Marianne Rawlinson, a public school teacher, provides this leadership. Marianne serves as youth department superintendent. She calls Timothy and Janet weekly, offering counsel on a variety of matters. What if Marianne used the same leadership style with Maria?

Think about It

What about you? What style of supervision do you prefer as a teacher on a church staff?

The Situational Leadership Model developed by Paul Hersey and Ken Blanchard (1982) provides a useful diagnostic tool for church leaders. It suggests ways to adjust our management style in light of the occasion (see Figure 18.3). Emphasis on *task* runs along the horizontal axis; concern for *relationship* describes the vertical axis. Four specific leadership styles emerge:

Telling (S1): Provide specific instructions and supervise performance closely.

Figure 18.3
Situational Leadership Model

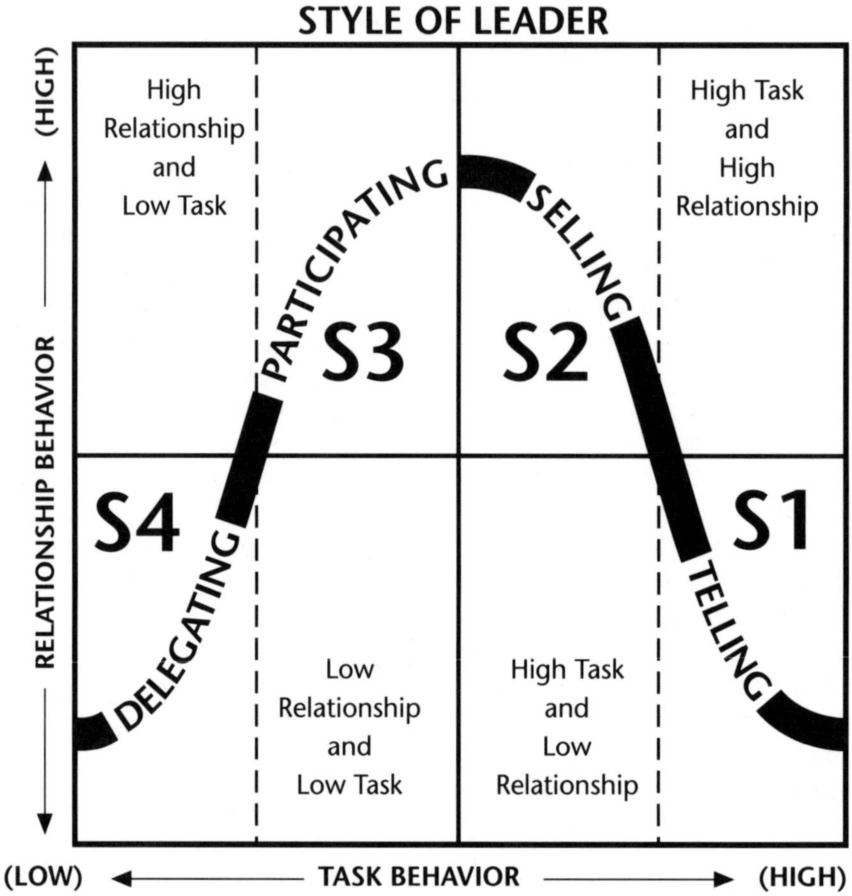

Source: Hersey and Blanchard (1982, p. 152).

Selling (S2): Explain decisions, provide opportunity for clarification; don't supervise closely.

Participating (S3): Share ideas, facilitate in decision making, and leave sufficient freedom of choice.

Delegating (S4): Turn over responsibility for decisions and implementation to the person.

The associate pastor in the scenario described above initially assumed that a "delegating (S4)" style was appropriate. But the worker desired a "selling (S2)" or "participating (S3)" style of supervision. She really needed more guidance and support.

In the other scenario outlined above, Sunday school teachers Timothy and Janet Park required a "telling (S1)" style, whereas Maria Lopez preferred a "delegating (S4)" mode. Our inclination, as leaders, is to use the same style of leadership for everyone. But that's often when conflicts brew.[18]

Conclusion

Our survey of the Educational Planning Wheel with its inner and outer components is completed. The seven outer factors serve as a checklist for what to anticipate in program development or modification. Whether new ministries are created or existing ones are revised, this wheel design offers helpful input. Note that whenever one aspect of these seven components is changed, then adjustments may be required in related, outer circle components. For instance, when a staff person leaves, others must assume additional responsibilities. Or a new worker must be identified and trained. Changing Sunday school curriculum may involve such things as adjustments in the stated departmental goals, retraining of teachers in light of new views about the learning process, or the reorganization of supplementary teaching materials in the resource files. A comprehensive view of these critical factors of the planning process helps leaders anticipate potential difficulties arising from planned or unplanned change.

Think about It

To review the components of the *outer* circle of the Educational Planning Wheel:

1. See if you can match each of the seven *task* components with its related *people* component. We matched the middle one for you. Try the rest.

Task Components   **People Components**

____ Teaching Materials   A. Prepared Staff
Development

____ Program   B. Staff Qualifications
Coordination

____ Program   C. Staff Recruitment
Development

_D_ Program Evaluation   D. Staff Review

____ Program   E. Staff Supervision
Implementation

____ Program Problems   F. Staff Training

____ Program Purposes   G. People Needs[19]

2. Now try to place the matched components in the logical sequence, in the order discussed in the text. We'll fill in the first one for you.

(1) <u>Program Evaluation & Staff Review</u>
(2) _____
(3) _____
(4) _____
(5) _____
(6) _____
(7)[20] _____

To review, the Educational Planning Wheel values both *task* and *people* concerns when our ministry programs are designed. Each of the seven factors of the outer circle is affected by inner circle features that are in dynamic refinement: Scripture directs decision makers as they pursue the four themes of Christian maturity. The clockwise movement of the outer circle need not be viewed linearly; as illustrated in Acts 6, several factors are often dealt with simultaneously. What is more important than a prescribed sequence is the nature of the factors themselves. Each point of the outer circle *must* be addressed, at some time, in all productive educational ministries.

19 At a Crossroad

Looking Back at Our Journey
Our Continuing Journey
The End of Our Journey

Looking Back at Our Journey

Pretend you're in your inaugural year as youth minister of First Church. With the encouragement of the leadership, you begin to plan a summer teen missions trip. This is an unprecedented challenge at First Church. You ask yourself how the puzzle pieces should come together. Who should be involved in the task? What should be intentionally planned, and what should be left to spontaneity?

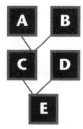

Frankena's analytical outline of educational philosophy has been used to organize this book (see Figure 19.1). We introduced this model in the first chapter. Succeeding chapters addressed issues within each of his five-box categories. This chapter affirms the usefulness of the entire Frankena model. Specifically, the model is helpful in both evaluating ministry and guiding instructional planning. Our final glance at this theory reveals two sets of tensions or polarities.

Figure 19.1

Summary of Concepts within the Frankena Model

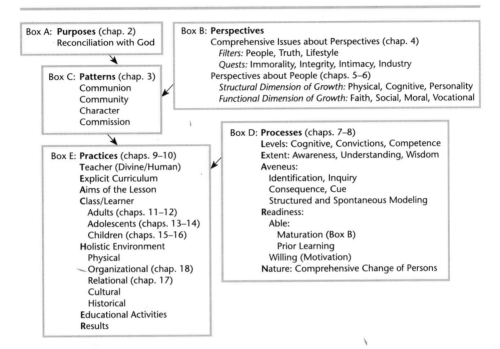

Box A: **Purposes** (chap. 2)
Reconciliation with God

Box B: **Perspectives**
Comprehensive Issues about Perspectives (chap. 4)
Filters: People, Truth, Lifestyle
Quests: Immorality, Integrity, Intimacy, Industry
Perspectives about People (chaps. 5–6)
Structural Dimension of Growth: Physical, Cognitive, Personality
Functional Dimension of Growth: Faith, Social, Moral, Vocational

Box C: **Patterns** (chap. 3)
Communion
Community
Character
Commission

Box D: **Processes** (chaps. 7–8)
Levels: Cognitive, Convictions, Competence
Extent: Awareness, Understanding, Wisdom
Avenues:
Identification, Inquiry
Consequence, Cue
Structured and Spontaneous Modeling
Readiness:
Able:
Maturation (Box B)
Prior Learning
Willing (Motivation)
Nature: Comprehensive Change of Persons

Box E: **Practices** (chaps. 9–10)
Teacher (Divine/Human)
Explicit Curriculum
Aims of the Lesson
Class/Learner
Adults (chaps. 11–12)
Adolescents (chaps. 13–14)
Children (chaps. 15–16)
Holistic Environment
Physical
Organizational (chap. 18)
Relational (chap. 17)
Cultural
Historical
Educational Activities
Results

A Foundational and Practical Polarity

In the first polarity, the complementary halves of the five-box framework represent the tension between theory and practice. Boxes A through D emphasize the theoretical or *foundational* component of the Frankena model. Chapters 2–8 addressed these four connected categories. The *practical* dimension of Frankena's theory arises in Box E. Chapters 9–18 offered specific insights for this second half. To see how this first polarity becomes a useful guide for ministry, return to the illustration at the beginning of this chapter. Depending on your understanding of both the theoretical issues and practical matters of educational ministry, the mode of planning for the summer missions trip will vary. Table 19.1 identifies the various approaches that are taken by four persons.

Case #1: Allen. A college sophomore in Bible college, Allen represents learners who

Table 19.1

Approaches to Educational Ministry Planning

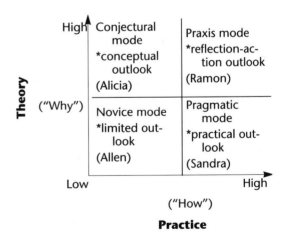

hold a novice mode of planning youth missions trips. This twenty-year-old has little theory and little practical know-how. He needs to confront both the "why" and the "what" of teen outreach. Because of his broad educational task, Allen's formal learning is restricted to a cursory glance at a detailed subject; that is, the curricular objectives for Allen's second-year youth courses must retain an introductory status. The sophomore is restricted to a limited outlook on planning for summer outreach.

Case #2: Alicia. This thoughtful seminarian is majoring in youth work. Based on her thorough studies, Alicia shows a good grasp of the theological and the human development issues pertinent to adolescence. For instance, she is well acquainted with the history, contributions, and shortcomings of various parachurch youth agencies. But she has limited hands-on experience in teen ministry. Her previous work has primarily been with the children of First Church. She typifies the conjectural mode of planning youth missions trips—high on "theory" but "low" on experience. She develops a second-hand plan for the summer missions trip. Alicia necessarily takes an indirect and conceptual outlook on her task.

Case #3: Sandra. A former elementary school teacher, this third potential youth minister has recently joined the First Church staff. In her prior church work, Sandra served as a junior high sponsor and Sunday school teacher. She has led several missions trips to Mexico and Haiti. Sandra approaches her pending summer outreach in a pragmatic mode. Her view of ministry arises from her extensive nuts-and-bolts experience with adolescents. Sandra holds a practical outlook on teen work. Yet she needs to augment her practitioner's strength with pertinent theory and theology. Sandra must construct a foundation for "why" she does "what" she does.

Case #4: Ramon. The last person of four possible scenarios is a thirty-eight-year-old professional within a parachurch youth organization. Ramon's Christian liberal arts training has provided him with useful foundational ideas for ministry. His dozen years of parachurch work have supplied meaningful experiences. Ramon's education and vocation have taught this youth worker both to think critically as well as to perform constructively. He has wrestled with the "why" and "what" of teen ministry.

Now, Ramon faces a mid-life change—from parachurch to local church service at First Church. His twelve years of previous youth work included administration, recruiting and training of volunteers; teaching; counseling and outreach. If there is one area where he feels ill-equipped for the First Church position, Ramon knows it is outreach. His earlier evangelism tasks focused exclusively on local high school and neighborhood clubs. How will these experiences help him prepare for a summer missions trip? Employing the balance between theory and practice, Ramon takes a praxis mode of learning to his youth ministry planning. That is, he assumes a reflection-action outlook to his challenge of cross-cultural outreach.

In review, each of these four cases holds something in common: They express complementary scenarios of what a youth minister at First Church might look like. This foursome likewise poses diverse approaches to the challenge of teen evangelism. Now, it's time for a reversal. Instead of looking at this educational puzzle from the *learner's* perspective, picture the *teacher's* perspective. By employing the Frankena model, how would you instruct Allen, Alicia, Sandra, and Ramon?

Consider the first case. The person who teaches Allen's sophomore youth courses needs to take a bird's eye-view. That is, the teacher would intentionally structure a general overview of youth and missions, balancing the "theory" of Boxes A–D with the "practice" of Box E. Assignments would necessarily feature basic content with limited experiences. Students like Allen may increase their low levels of theory and practice by viewing videos of missions, participating in an inner-city outreach field trip, and writing integrative papers that reflect on experiences as well as theological and developmental concerns. Instruction of students who are like Allen must value the novice mode of learning.

Think about It

Now, it's your turn. How would you teach each of the remaining three students?

1. What assignments should you provide for Alicia, who employs a conjectural mode of learning? _____
   _____
   _____
   _____

2. Pretend that Sandra has enrolled as a part-time student in a Christian liberal arts graduate school. How would you teach an experienced student like her? Would your educational strategies be similar to those used with Allen or Alicia, or altogether different? Provide one instructional idea below, along with your rationale.
   _____
   _____
   _____

3. Imagine you are a colleague of Ramon. You share professional staff responsibilities with him at First Church. He has come to you for assistance regarding his summer planning concerns. What specific reflection-action assignments do you suggest? Why do you advise these strategies?
   _____
   _____
   _____

Alicia's seminary professor must realize that she has historically taken a theoretical approach to the Frankena model. That is, Alicia knows helpful facts about foundational issues (Boxes A–D). She also conceptually knows what a fruitful youth missions ministry "should look like." This student has an educational philosophy, but has created it second-hand, by repeating what others say about youth missions.

To complement Alicia's training, the professor employs a range of less direct, first-hand activities (like debates) to more direct course assignments (like on-sight observations and interviews). In brief, the teacher uses Frankena-in-reverse. For instance, Alicia might be assigned to interview members of a youth team who experienced a recent missions trip (i.e., in retrospect, how Box E appeared to this youth team). Then, Alicia might be asked to prepare a paper, using both inductive and deductive thinking: (1) inductively, she would collect and rearrange the interview data; also, she would make comparative statements, relying on her understanding of relevant theology and adolescent theory; and (2) deductively, she would draw implications from her data. For example, she would ask: "What were the implied intermediate aims of this trip [Box C]?" Again, the Frankena model is used in reverse order—a bottom-up approach—for Alicia's seminary course tasks.[1] Beyond these traditional assignments, more extensive first-hand experiences would prove invaluable to Alicia. A closely supervised internship, for instance, could provide the necessary balanced education this learner needs.[2]

In many respects, Sandra portrays the educational flip-side of Alicia. Sandra's pragmatic mode of learning contrasts with her counterpart's conjectural perspective. Sandra, in comparison to peers in her graduate school course, possesses an unparalleled practical knowledge of teen missions. Her questions and comments in class demonstrate this fact. How could Sandra's experience in youth work be valued in class? Perhaps Sandra might be requested to address the class in her area of specialty. But what about her own development? To complement previous learning, Sandra's professor motivates her to contemplate foundational questions underlying her practical accomplishments. For instance, has she inadvertently accepted an exclusive behaviorist or humanist theory of learning, based on her involvement in previous summer projects? Does she want to fully retain such limited perspectives? If so, what could be the consequences? Has she implicitly valued other aspects of these theories that may be unbiblical? In short, a top-down approach to Frankena should be taken by Sandra's instructor. Pertinent theory and theology (from Boxes A–D) need to undergird the learner's weaknesses.

As a colleague in the final scenario, you should complement Ramon's praxis mode of learning. He is able to integrate his valuable experiences with his critical thinking skills. As a facilitator, you must encourage this ability. For example, Ramon might recall an earlier ministry experience when he was insensitive to an adolescent. He penalized a teen who did not participate in "required" fund-raising activities for an outreach campaign. To his embarrassment, Ramon discovered later that this teen failed to participate because of family obligations. In short, Ramon's reflection causes him to be more aware of learner needs. He realizes how certain policies may actually result in counterproductive ends. With these critiques in mind, Ramon reconstructs a better design for future fund-raising strategies.

To state this instructional position in Frankena terms, the colleague-instructor helps Ramon take a both-ends-against-the-middle approach. Foundations are balanced by practical plans. In the end, Ramon's interactive education prepares him well for his first cross-cultural youth work. Additional praxis assignments, like keeping a journal during and after the trip, will fine-tune his future outreach.[3]

Table 19.2 summarizes these four instructional approaches.

Table 19.2

Teaching Approaches to the Frankena Model

Teaching Approach to Frankena		Four Case Studies
Bird's-eye-view/simple overview	A–D / E	Allen: *Novice* learning mode
Bottom-up (reverse order)	A–D ↑ E	Alicia: *Conjectural* learning mode
Top-down	A–D ↓ E	Sandra: *Pragmatic* learning mode
Both-ends-against-the-middle	A–D ↕ E	Ramon: *Praxis* learning mode

A Prescriptive and Descriptive Polarity

In addition to the foundations-practice tension, a second helpful polarity comes from the Frankena model. Boxes A, C, and E center on *prescriptive* issues (see Figure 19.1). What "ought" to guide our thinking and practice? What does God's Word say? Furthermore, Boxes B and D stress *descriptive* matters. What is our world like? What do our senses, our reasoning, our empirical research, and our personal experiences tell us about people and how they learn?

It's an understatement to say that balancing the prescriptive dimension with the descriptive dimension of our instruction is difficult. We must take our cue from the people of Issachar in the Old Testament: they *"understood the times* and knew what Israel *should do"* (1 Chron. 12:32). There was no compromise between their skills of description and prescription. They were sensitive to their surroundings, yet maintained their principles and beliefs. The Issacharites were commendable scientists. They were careful observers of their times. They reasoned inductively, putting ideas together. In other words, they possessed important skills of description. Likewise, their commitments to prescriptive truths pointed them toward what had to be done.[4]

Evangelicals tend to be experts of prescription. We know what God says and what we ought to do. But we also tend to be ignorant about descriptive concerns. We lack knowledge about the people to whom we are ministering. In the classroom, we need to become adept at finding common ground, appropriate points of contact with our students. Table 19.3 outlines points of contact used by Jesus, Peter, Stephen, and Paul. Each example complements its respective setting.[5]

Let's analyze the fourth example in Table 19.3 more closely. Paul's outreach strategy at the Areopagus initially shows his descriptive abilities.[6] Certainly the prescriptive message is evident in Acts 17:16–34, but the "ought" is framed by descriptions of Paul's Greek audience.[7] Paul begins his sermon by describing the altar to the unknown god. But we usually fail to recall what precedes that familiar citation. First, Paul spent significant time with his audience. He intentionally "walked around" the area. He studied his hearers, with great detail and compassion. Second, Paul didn't adhere to a routine sermon. His message was not "canned." Third, he had his eyes open. He testified "I *see* that. . . ." Paul was a watchful observer, a good scientist. He admitted "I . . . *looked carefully* at your objects of worship." Can't you see Paul (with his poor eyesight) stooping to read the fine print on those altars? Finally, he drew valid

Table 19.3

Points of Contact in Teaching

Passage	John 4	Acts 2	Acts 7	Acts 17
Teacher	Jesus	Peter	Stephen	Paul
Audience	Samaritan woman	Religious Jews at Pentecost feast	Sanhedrin	Greek philosophers
Point of Contact	Water to living water	Old Testament quotes	Moses, the lawgiver	"An Unknown God"; Paul quotes a pagan philosopher

conclusions. He determined that "in every way" the Athenians were interested in religious matters. Paul employed inductive and deductive reasoning.[8]

The church must emulate the ministries of Jesus, Peter, Stephen, and Paul. We must teach teachers to "read" their audience; to know their particular setting.[9] We must help instructors realize how complex each learning scenario really is, because learners themselves are complex.[10]

Our Continuing Journey

Our obvious task as teachers is to facilitate growth and learning in our students. Our not-so-obvious task (although no less important) is to grow as teachers. We need to mature in our personal and our professional lives. To this end, Ted Ward (n.d.)

presents one helpful model of teacher growth. It particularly focuses on the changing relationships between teacher and student. Three important transitions surface (see Figure 19.2).

Phase 1: Teacher as Content Expert

"For many, the original motivation to become a teacher arises out of the love of a particular subject matter, content area or skill" (Ward n.d., p. 2). The tendency is for the beginning teacher to focus on content mastery. Students must become acquainted with certain, prearranged materials. Yet, at times students often express a lack of interest in or appreciation for the subject. Such feedback frustrates the instructor. Their reciprocal response is typical: "Teachers are thus apt to sharply divide students into two categories: good (highly motivated) and

Figure 19.2

Turning Points in the
Teacher-Student Relationship

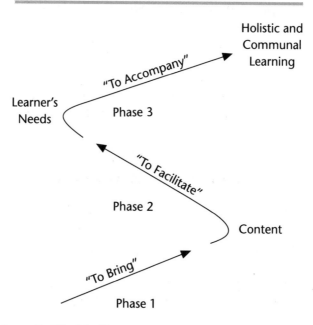

Source: Ted Ward (n.d.).

bad (lacking motivation) students" (p. 3). Phase 1 teachers experience success with students who have great enthusiasm for the content.

Phase 2: Teacher as Counselor

Due to some students' lack of appreciation for the subject, educators may probe beyond learner disinterest. "As teachers gain experience this deeper problem can be recognized and identified: the students, individual and as a group, have needs that the content is not meeting" (p. 3). With this new insight, certain teachers begin to study the particular need of their students, with the same eagerness that they pursue their own discipline. A new corner is turned. "The importance of content is not rejected, but it is subordinated to a higher value: the facilitation of the meeting of needs" (p. 4). In addition, teachers may expand the definition of their discipline. The importance of meeting students' needs takes on a greater dimension. However, these responsibilities still take place within the context of the learner's encounter with the planned subject. The burden of caring for many students' needs consequently becomes an overwhelming challenge. This may prompt yet another turning of the corner.

Phase 3: Teacher as Colleague

Here, neither the significance of the content nor the importance of the learner's needs are rejected. This third phase "represents a different sort of relationship—one in which the teacher becomes a full participant in the life-walk of the student" (p. 5). A new commitment of learning together emerges. It is a phase where "the common-ground sharing of teacher needs and learner needs becomes the basis for fulfillment of human development" (p. 4). Within this dynamic relationship, an emphasis is placed on the mutual growth of learner and teacher. Informal (as well as formal) settings are treasured. The teacher and students prize a commitment to shared values and ideals, as exemplified in the relationship of Jesus and the Twelve.

Models such as Ward's provide challenging insights to help us mark our own progress as educators. Whatever approach to teacher development is taken, we cannot be satisfied with business as usual. As Christian instructors, we must learn and grow along with our students.

Think about It

Your journey in this book is about over. As a result, you now stand at a crossroad. How will you respond to the concepts and principles about the teaching ministry in this book? Since learning involves change, what specific changes have you made (or do you plan to make) in your teaching? Make note of at least one significant change below.

The End of Our Journey

Albert Einstein once advised, "Everything should be as simple as possible, but not simpler."[11] It has been our purpose to offer a new design for Christian education. Our intention was to make it simple, but not to oversimplify it. We have suggested the Reconciliation Model as portraying God's view of his plan of renewal. Through Christ, every relationship should comply with divine standards of restoration and peace. This includes recognized associations with family and neighbors. Yet this garden-instituted plan also incorporates less-emphasized themes within our ministry—advocacy for the needy, concern for our planet and its resources, peace within ourselves.

We have especially singled out four essential components of God's reconciliation: Communion, Community, Character, and

Commission. These themes provide a comprehensive framework for our lifelong task.

> And he has committed to us the message of reconciliation. We are therefore Christ's ambassadors, as though God were making his appeal through us. We implore you on Christ's behalf: Be reconciled to God. (2 Cor. 5:18b–20)

APPENDIX

 Protestant Christian Education Introductory Texts Since 1930

The changing face of Christian education is easily discernible in its literature. The "introductory" textbook represents one significant record of this field. Such texts address a spectrum of relevant topics—matters of both foundations and practice in the educational ministry of the church. Beyond these general parameters, survey texts typically include chapters on ministry to children, youth, and adults, as well as on leadership and organizational factors.

The texts listed here are comprehensive in nature. "Comprehensive" is understood as: (1) breadth of subject coverage as indicated by the guidelines stated above; (2) at least 170 pages in length; and (3) significant bibliographical information. These criteria eliminated works that primarily focus on just teaching or administration, the twin themes of Christian education, works that were lacking in size, or works that were more popularly written, lacking significant bibliographical substantiation. Three authors (Mason, LeBar, and Gangel) wrote or edited books which, if combined, would constitute a comprehensive introductory text. These six works were included with their respective emphases (noted in Table A.1 as TE = teaching and AD = administration). Also included were three books, though primarily geared to the Christian day school context, providing helpful coverage of topics relevant to Christian education (Jaarsma, Byrne, Harper; noted as CS = Christian school).

In the 1930s, two significant comprehensive Christian education texts were published: one edited and written by evangelical Protestant authors (Price et al.) and one edited and written by mainline Protestant authors (Lotz and Crawford). These publications set the arbitrary starting point for our list. Although we have limited ourselves to Protestant authors for the sake of space, we do not intend to diminish the significant contribution of non-Protestant scholarship. Helpful insights from scholars such as James Michael Lee and Thomas Groome are cited elsewhere in the book.

Table A.1 presents a chronological list of names of editors/authors and dates of publication. Two main columns represent the broad divisions of evangelical and mainline authors. Within each division, edited works and single author books are identified. In cases where three (Daniel et al.) or four (Price et al.) authors each wrote several chapters, the book was placed in the single author category. The list includes references to 49 first edition books, ranging from 172 to 702 pages and from 7 to 35 chapters. Publication dates are placed in parentheses for those books that were reissued or revised.

Anthony, Michael J., ed. 1992. *Foundations of ministry: An introduction to Christian education for a new generation*. Wheaton, Ill.: Victor. [400 pp., 25 chapters; written by the Christian education faculty at Talbot School of Theology, Biola University]

Bryan, C. Doug. 1990. *Relationship learning: A primer for Christian education*. Nashville: Broadman. [253 pp., 8 chapters]

Table A.1

Protestant Christian Education Introductory Texts Since 1930

Evangelical Protestant Authors		Mainline Protestant Authors	
Edited work	**Single author**	**Edited work**	**Single author**
1932 Price et al.	1939 DeBlois	1931 Lotz/Crawford	1933 Munro
			1939 Harner
	1940 Price et al.	1947 Vieth	
	1943 Murch		
1953 Jaarsma CS	1955 Mason TE	1950 Lotz	1954 Schisler
	1958 LeBar TE		1954 Smart
	1958 Person		1955 Wyckoff
	(1958) Murch		1956 Miller, R.C.
	(1959) Price et al.		1956 Munro
			1958 Cully
1960 Wymore	1960 Mason AD	1960 Taylor	1960 Fallaw
1964 Hakes	1961 Byrne CS	1966 Taylor	1962 Butler
	1963 Byrne		1962 Shinn
	1968 LeBar AD		(1963) Miller, R. C.
			(1965) Cully
			1967 Lentz et al.
1978 Sanner	1970 Gangel AD	1976 Taylor	(1971) Smart
1978 Sisemore	(1973) Byrne		
	1975 Richards		
	(1977) Byrne CS		
1981 Graendorf	1980 Daniel et al.	1984 Taylor	1987 Miller, D. E.
1988 Gangel/Hendricks TE	1981 Harper CS	1987 Roloff	1989 Johnson
	(1981) Gangel AD		
	(1981) LeBar TE		
	(1987) Daniel et al.		
	(1989) LeBar TE		
	(1989) Richards		
1991 Clark et al.	1990 Bryan	1990 Foltz	
1992 Anthony	1992 Habermas/Issler		

Butler, J. Donald. 1962. *Religious education: The foundations and practice of nurture*. New York: Harper and Row. [321 pp., 18 chapters]

Byrne, Herbert W. 1961. *A Christian approach to education: Educational theory and practice*. Grand Rapids: Zondervan. [372 pp., 13 chapters; reissued by Mott Media, Milford, Mich., 1977]

_____. 1963. *Christian education for the local church: An evangelical and functional approach*. Grand Rapids: Zondervan. [355 pp., 9 chapters; revised edition, 1973, 379 pp., 9 chapters]

Clark, Robert E., Lin Johnson, and Allyn K. Sloat, eds. 1991. *Christian education: Foundations for the future*. Chicago: Moody. [636 pp., 40 chapters]

Cully, Iris. 1958. *The dynamics of Christian education*. Philadelphia: Westminster. [205 pp., 8 chapters; reissued 1965]

Daniel, Eleanor, John Wade, and Charles Gresham. 1980. *Introduction to Christian education*. Cincinnati, Ohio: Standard. [351 pp., 26 chapters; revised edition, 1987, 352 pp., 25 chapters]

DeBlois, Austen K., and Donald R. Gorham. 1939. *Christian religious education: Principles and practice*. New York: Fleming H. Revell. [385 pp., 18 chapters; DeBlois wrote the entire book using the outline developed by Gorham]

Fallaw, Wesner. 1960. *Church education for tomorrow*. Philadelphia: Westminster. [219 pp., 9 chapters]

Foltz, Nancy T., ed. 1990. *Religious education in the small membership church*. Birmingham, Ala.: Religious Education. [234 pp., 10 chapters]

Gangel, Kenneth O. 1970. *Leadership for church education*. Chicago: Moody. [392 pp., 30 chapters; revised and combined with *Competent to lead*, 1974, and retitled as *Building leaders for church education*, 1981, 428 pp., 35 chapters]

Gangel, Kenneth O., and Howard G. Hendricks, eds. 1988. *The Christian educator's handbook on teaching: A comprehensive resource on the distinctiveness of true Christian teaching*. Wheaton, Ill.: Victor. [358 pp., 21 chapters; written by the Christian education faculty at Dallas Theological Seminary]

Graendorf, Werner, ed. 1981. *Introduction to Biblical Christian education*. Chicago: Moody. [407 pp., 30 chapters]

Habermas, Ronald, and Klaus Issler. 1992. *Teaching for reconciliation: Foundations and practice of Christian educational ministry*. Grand Rapids: Baker. [421 pp., 19 chapters]

Hakes, J. Edward, ed. 1964. *An introduction to evangelical Christian education*. Chicago: Moody. [423 pp., 32 chapters]

Harner, Nevin C. 1939. *The educational work of the church*. New York: Abingdon-Cokesbury. [257 pp., 10 chapters]

Harper, Norman E. 1981. *Making disciples: The challenge of Christian education at the end of the 20th century*. Memphis, Tenn.: Christian Studies Center. [194 pp., 7 chapters]

Jaarsma, Cornelius, ed. 1953. *Fundamentals in Christian education: Theory and practice*. Grand Rapids: Eerdmans. [482 pp., 40 chapters]

Johnson, Susanne. 1989. *Spiritual formation in the church and classroom*. Nashville: Abingdon. [173 pp., 9 chapters]

LeBar, Lois E. 1959. *Education that is Christian*. Westwood, N.J.: Revell. [252 pp., 9 chapters; reissued 1981, 256 pp., 9 chapters; reissued 1989 by Victor, Wheaton, Ill., with notes by James E. Plueddemann, 314 pp., 9 chapters]

_____. 1968. *Focus on people in church education*. Westwood, N.J.: Revell. [256 pp., 7 chapters]

Lentz, Richard E., Paul H. Vieth, and Ray L. Henthorne. *Our teaching ministry*. St. Louis, Mo.: Christian Board of Publications, 1967. [224 pp. 11 chapters]

Lotz, Philip H., and L. W. Crawford, eds. 1931. *Studies in religious education*. Nashville: Cokesbury. [702 pp., 29 chapters]

Lotz, Philip H., ed. 1950. *Orientation in religious education*. New York: Abingdon-Cokesbury. [618 pp., 43 chapters]

Mason, Harold C. 1955. *Abiding values in Christian education*. Westwood, N.J.: Revell. [176 pp., 20 chapters]

_____. 1960. *The teaching task of the local church*. Winona Lake, Ind.: Light and Life. [214 pp., 14 chapters]

Miller, Donald E. 1987. *Story and context: An introduction to Christian education*. Nashville: Abingdon. [400 pp., 12 chapters]

Miller, Randolph Crump. 1956. *Education for Christian living*. Englewood Cliffs, N.J.: Prentice-Hall. [418 pp., 23 chapters; second edition, 1963]

Munro, Harry C. 1933. *Christian education in your church*. St. Louis, Mo.: Bethany. [240 pp., 11 chapters]

_____. 1956. *Protestant nurture: An introduction to Christian education*. Englewood Cliffs, N.J.: Prentice-Hall. [270 pp., 10 chapters]

Murch, James DeForest. 1943. *Christian education and the local church: History—principles—practice*. Cincinnati, Ohio: Standard. [416 pp., 35 chapters; revised edition, 1958, 345 pp., 35 chapters]

Person, Peter. 1958. *Introduction to Christian education*. Grand Rapids: Baker. [224 pp., 16 chapters]

Price, John M., L. L. Carpenter, and J. H. Chapman, eds. 1932. *Introduction to religious education: A comprehensive survey*. New York: Macmillan. [489 pp., 24 chapters]

Price, John M., James H. Chapman, A. E. Tibbs, and L. L. Carpenter. 1940. *A survey of religious education*. New York: Ronald. [333 pp., 24 chapters; second edition 1959, by John M. Price, James H. Chapman, L. L. Carpenter, and W. Forbes Yarborough, 466 pp., 24 chapters]

Richards, Lawrence O. 1975. *A theology of Christian education*. Grand Rapids: Zondervan, 1975. [324 pp., 28 chapters; discussion of adult and children's ministry is included; a separate book on youth ministry was published in 1972; reissued as *Christian education: Seeking to become like Jesus*, 1989, 336 pp., 28 chapters]

Roloff, Marvin, ed. 1987. *Education for Christian living: Strategies for nurture based on biblical and historical foundations*. Minneapolis: Augsburg. [236 pp., 12 chapters]

Sanner, A. Elwood, and A. F. Harper, eds. 1978. *Exploring Christian education*. Kansas City, Mo.: Beacon Hill. [503 pp., 19 chapters]

Schisler, John Q. 1954. *Christian teaching in the churches—Religious education today—Its nature, scope and purpose*. New York: Abingdon. [173 pp., 12 chapters]

Shinn, Roger L. 1962. *The educational mission of the church*. Boston: United Church. [176 pp., 14 chapters]

Sisemore, John T., ed. 1978. *The ministry of religious education*. Nashville: Broadman. [239 pp., 15 chapters]

Smart, James D. 1954. *The teaching ministry of the church: An examination of the basic principles of Christian education*. Philadelphia: Westminster. [207 pp., 10 chapters; reissued 1971]

Taylor, Marvin, ed. 1960. *Religious education: A comprehensive survey*. Nashville: Abingdon. [446 pp., 37 chapters]

_____. 1966. *An introduction to Christian education*. Nashville: Abingdon. [412 pp., 32 chapters]

_____. 1976. *Foundations for Christian education in an era of change*. Nashville: Abingdon. [288 pp., 21 chapters]

_____. 1984. *Changing patterns of religious education*. Nashville: Abingdon. [319 pp., 21 chapters]

Vieth, Paul, ed. 1947. *The church and Christian education*. St. Louis, Mo.: Bethany. [314 pp., 9 chapters]

Wyckoff, D. Campbell. 1955. *The task of Christian education*. Philadelphia: Westminster. [172 pp., 18 chapters; reissued 1965]

Wymore, Leonard D., ed. 1960. *Christian education handbook*. Cincinnati, Ohio: Standard. [176 pp., 9 chapters]

Multidisciplinary Evidences for Quests and Filters

Quests and Related Disciplines

Because the quest for Immortality represents the nucleus of the remaining three inquiries,[1] our initial commentary focuses on this point. Diverse resources from various disciplines are subsequently cited to support the existence of quests as a whole.

Philosophical Evidence

Bertrand Russell, the atheist philosopher, confessed: "The center of me is always and eternally a terrible pain—a curious wild pain—a *searching for something beyond what the world contains.*"[2]

We all seek reality outside the physical realm. Atheists and believers attest to this verity. It's what Augustine referred to as a void or vacuum within all people—a void satisfied only by the Creator's presence. Ecclesiastes 3:11 confirms this truth: "[God] has also set eternity in the hearts of men; yet they cannot fathom what God has done from beginning to end." C. S. Lewis (1975, p. 16) referred to this lifelong quest of Immortality as "our longing to be reunited with something in the universe from which we now feel cut off, to be on the inside of some door which we have always seen from the outside." Paul Tournier (1968, p. 37) liked to think of this common human desire as a "place." He contrasted this hope with the despairs of life: "I believe it is the place of perfection, which in fact does not exist in this world—a place that will give real security and protection from disappointment. It is our homesickness for Paradise. The place we are all looking for is the Paradise we have lost. The whole of humanity suffers from what we might call 'The Paradise Lost Complex.'" To put it simply, we all gravitate toward some form of belief. We all exercise commitment to a reality beyond ourselves. C. S. Lewis (1959) employed the analogies of Desire and Joy to portray this human longing. He claimed that the sincere search for God will be rewarded; if people genuinely attend to the quest for Immortality, God will answer their prayers. Lewis (1956, p. 165) maintained that "all find what they truly seek."[3] He coined the challenging phrase in his last book of the *Narnia Chronicles:* "Come further up, come further in!" (p. 171)—persevere in seeking God and his kingdom.[4]

To sum it up, this universal questioning about transcendent realities should affect our witness for Christ. Acknowledging our common spiritual need should enable us to better hear the world's cry, to express empathy and love. Having God's answer to this pervasive quest, we educators should satisfy our students' thirst with Christ's eternal hope.

Anthropological Discoveries

Years ago, international studies isolated certain "common denominators" of all people groups.[5] "Are there similar categories through which all individuals view reality?" researchers asked. A partial listing from one study was given by its author, anthropologist George Murdock (1945, p. 124). Some of the seventy-three categories common to all cultures included athletic sports, calendars, cosmology, dancing, education, eschatology, family, games, hair styles, joking, language, medicine, music, numerals, personal names, property rights, propitiation of supernatural beings, soul concepts, surgery, and weather control.

Robert Redfield (1953, p. 86) suggests that a composite of such categories represents a worldview. All cultures have a worldview. They all share certain frameworks of reality. When Redfield sifted through the data of anthropological studies, he recognized a provocative pattern. Every participant response could be synthesized into three broad categories: people, nature, and God. Redfield makes it clear that these primary factors have been around for some time. Even primitive civilizations showed evidence of the threefold pattern Redfield (1953, p. 103) elaborates: "Before there were cities, there was a view of God and nature and man himself."

Regrouping the above findings, essential features of the four quests are apparent: *Immortality* (e.g., Murdock's "propitiation of supernatural beings"), *Integrity* ("personal names" and "soul

concepts"), *Intimacy* ("family" and "property rights"), and *Industry* ("education" and "medicine").[6]

Stephen Grunlan and Marvin Mayers recognize the quests, based on their "theory of functional creation." They claim that the Genesis account of creation was not so much designed to explain "when" and "how" life begins, but "Who" created life and "why." In particular, Grunlan and Mayers (1979, p. 41) propose three major systems of reality: 1. The natural system consisting of the universe, the earth, plant and animal life—man's relationship with the environment; 2. The social system—man's relationship with man; 3. The spiritual system—man's relationship with God. Quests of Industry, Integrity/Intimacy, and Immortality are respectively endorsed. Furthermore, these two men introduce a helpful rationale for their theory of functional creation. In philosophical and theological circles, it's called the "teleological" argument; that is, nature itself reveals meaning and order. Grunlan and Mayers (1979, p. 41) explain: "The theory of functional creation sees all of God's creation as functional or purposeful. It also sees God's creation as orderly with underlying principles or 'laws.' While the natural sciences seek to discover God's order in the natural realm, the behavioral sciences seek to discover God's order in the realm of human behavior."

Empirical Research on Faith

James W. Fowler and others support the essence of human quests from another angle. Going well beyond the general "faith-choice" hypotheses of Knight, social scientists have studied how faith actually matures within individuals. Simplifying their findings, these researchers claim that we all attend to specific phases of faith development.

Of particular importance to the four quests, Fowler (1981, p. 17) offers a theoretical analysis of generic faith development within all societies. His model utilizes the symbols "s," "o," and "scvp." "S" refers to *self* (the individual) and "o" to *others*. Fowler contends that loyalty and trust reciprocally nurture these first two factors. *Shared center(s) of value and power* (scvp) identify the model's third factor; it represents realities pointing beyond people to the supernatural.[7] This last factor also sets a premium on loyalty. Consequently, Fowler (p. 17) concludes that both individuals and groups "rest their hearts upon" chosen transcendent powers.[8]

Missiological Proposals

A significant overlap appears between the triangular designs of Fowler and Redfield. David J. Hesselgrave expresses a comparable structure. Whether he assesses cultures adhering to a naturalist or a tribal worldview, a Chinese or a Hindu-Buddhistic perspective, Hesselgrave (1979, p. 80) repeatedly recognizes a triangular analysis. Furthermore, the lifelong quests are portrayed. Specific questions about Industry, Intimacy, and Immortality-Integrity are raised, respectively. Hesselgrave's rationale for his three-part structure emerges from biblical imperatives entrusted to the human race. First, "God gave man a *Cultural Mandate* which entailed certain rulership over his environment (Gen. 1:26–30)." Thus, Industry is affirmed. After God intervened through judgment by the flood, "Noah and his family received promises and a *Social Mandate* that was to apply to them and their progeny down through the generations (Gen. 8:21–9:17)." Intimacy is endorsed. Finally, as Hesselgrave points out, our primary relationship with God surpasses these basic responsibilities. But because of debilitating sin, only Christ can restore individuals to righteous fellowship with their Creator. Therefore, the *Gospel Mandate* of Matthew 18:18–20 expresses the last precept. Both Immortality and Integrity are featured.

John R. W. Stott (1988, p. 125) expresses his version of the universal human questions when he writes, "Modern men and women are engaged in a threefold quest . . . the quest for transcendence, the quest for significance, and the quest for community." Transcendence means "the search for ultimate reality beyond the material universe"; it is akin to Fowler's "shared center(s) of value and power." People might attempt to satisfy this quest through drugs or Eastern mysticism, Stott concludes. But the church must provide the alternative: authentic worship of an all-powerful, all-personal God.

Stott's quest for significance refers to personal identity, our search for dignity and direction. Stott determines that the church must propagate the intrinsic value of people. The twin doctrines of creation and redemption launch us into the right direction. Fashioned in the image of God— although rebellion has left us as fallen beings— we realize that all people are *both* sinful *and*

worth saving. God creates us. God wants to reconcile us.

The quest for community focuses on the never-ending need to love and to be loved. People need people. Believers provide sustenance for human belonging through genuine fellowship.

Based on the collective studies of related social science disciplines, one additional component must be added to Stott's threesome: the quest for contribution. Redfield (1953, p. 103) prefers the phrase, "an attitude of responsibility to that which man confronted." We search to know what to do with our lives.

Personality Theories

Erik Erikson designates the added "quest for contribution" as "Industry" and "Generativity." In fact, his theory of psychosocial stages corroborates several features of the four quests. The chart below provides approximated pairings between Erikson's eight crises and the four quests. The chart is modified from Erikson (1963/1982).

Age	Psychosocial Crisis	Quests
Infancy	Trust versus Mistrust	Immortality
Toddler	Autonomy versus Shame and Doubt	Integrity
Preschool	Initiative versus Guilt	Integrity
School Age	Industry versus Inferiority	Industry
Adolescence	Identity versus Identity Confusion	Immortality and Integrity
Early Adulthood	Intimacy versus Isolation	Intimacy
Middle Adulthood	Generativity versus Stagnation	Industry
Later Adulthood	Integrity versus Despair	Integrity and Immortality

The Value of Understanding Filters

Neil Postman and Charles Weingartner (1969, pp. 87f., emphasis added) masterfully describe the reality of private "filters" or perspectives. They draw upon a relatively unknown researcher, Adelbert Ames, Jr., to prove their point.

The following historical sketch identifies the potency of perspectives, as well:

> Beginning in 1938, Ames created a series of "demonstrations" designed to study the nature of perception. His "laboratory" included oddly shaped rooms, chairs, and other objects which seemed to "distort" reality when perceived by ordinary people. Perhaps his most impressive "demonstration" is the trapezoidal window which revolved in a 360 degree circle. The perceiver, however, observes that the window turns 180 degrees, stops, and then turns back 180 degrees. Some of the people who were shown the "demonstrations" were not convinced that they had any significance and labeled them "optical illusions." But a few thought otherwise, including Albert Einstein, Dewey, Hadley Cantril, and Earl Kelley. Dewey believed that Ames had provided empirical evidence for the "transactional psychology" he and Arthur Bentley had formulated in *Knowing and the Known*. This term was used by them to minimize the mechanistic oversimplification caused by the use of the term "interaction." The sense of *"transactional psychology"* is that what human beings are and what they make their environment into is a product of a mutually simultaneous, highly complex, and continuing "bargaining" process between what is *inside* their skins and *outside*. Dewey believed that Ames had provided substantial understanding of the nature of that bargaining process.

Postman and Weingartner (pp. 90–91) tabulate helpful information for educators regarding individual perceptions. Their half-dozen insights include:

1. "The first and most important fact uncovered by [Ames'] perception studies is that *we do not get our perceptions from the 'things' around us. Our perceptions come from us.* This does *not* mean that there is nothing outside of our skins. . . . 'reality' is a perception, located somewhere behind the eyes."
2. "What we perceive is largely a function of our previous experiences, our assumptions, and our purposes (i.e., needs)."
3. "We are unlikely to alter our perceptions until and unless we are frustrated in our attempts to do something based on them. If our actions seem to permit us to fulfill our purposes, we will not change our perceptions no matter how often we are told that they are 'wrong.'"
4. "Since our perceptions come from us and our past experience, it is obvious that each individual will perceive what is 'out there' in a unique way. We have no common world, and communication is possible only to the extent that two perceivers have similar purposes, assumptions, and experience. The process of becoming an effective social being is contingent upon seeing the other's point of view."
5. "Perception is, to a much greater extent than previously imagined, a function of the linguistic categories available to the perceiver. As we said, reality is a perception located somewhere behind the eyes. But 'behind the eyes' there is a language process. We know that 'nature' never repeats or standardizes. We do it. And how we do it depends on the categories and classifications of our language system. It is only a slight exaggeration to say we 'see' with our language."
6. "The meaning of a perception is how it causes us to *act*. If rain is falling from the sky, some people will head for shelter, others will enjoy walking in it. Their perceptions of 'what is happening' are different as reflected in the fact that they 'do' different things. The fact that both groups will agree to the sentence, 'It is raining' does not mean they perceive the 'event' in the same way."

Internal factors; experiences and assumptions; pragmatic resistance to change; uniqueness; linguistic capacities; and behavioral influence—these are the values of comprehending our filters.[9] As the Master Teacher, Jesus was well aware of individual perspectives. We've seen that he did his best to work *within* his audience's viewpoint.[10] Paul was also conscious of these worldview features.[11]

APPENDIX

Perspectives on Persons

A Slice of Life in the Classroom

The clock registers 10:14 A.M. at Berean Church. Jill Sinclair leads her second-grade Sunday school class through a craft activity. She attempts to show the children how God is with each of them every moment of the day. Robby, first to finish, attempts to help those near him as he often does. Marilyn looks out the window, oblivious to the classroom noise. Not even the bustle of voices or the rustle of paper and scissors interrupts her solitude. Scott, one of the youngest, is out of his chair for the tenth time. He runs around the table, tripping over the chair leg. While the class laughs at him (they have seen him do this before), Scott bursts into tears.

Jill becomes angry and discouraged. As a first-year teacher, she has spent hours of study and preparation for this class. For a split second, she secretly ridicules her own subject: "How can *I* sense God's presence in this chaos?" What should she do?

Jill's response to her predicament will depend on her expectations of the six- to eight-year old children and her understanding of each child's individual life situation. In addition, her reaction is contingent on her understanding of God and his dealings in her own life—the God whom she is helping her students understand.

Factors Affecting Growth and Learning

Meet three children from Jill's class. Scott suffers from minimal brain dysfunction (MBD), a disorder of behavioral and cognitive functioning. The condition is often characterized by a heightened level of

349

activity without detectable brain damage. It is commonly referred to as the "hyperactive child syndrome" (Elkind and Weiner 1978, p. 340). Scott's problem is due to a genetic shortcoming.

Marilyn experiences severe emotional stress due to her home life. Her mother, recently divorced, lives with a boyfriend who verbally berates Marilyn. Marilyn is also a latchkey child; after school, she is alone until her mother gets off work. To cope, Marilyn spends hours daydreaming. In a world of her own, she plays with her imaginary friends. Marilyn's problem stems from the adverse effects of absent nurture.

Both of Robby's conscientious parents are professional teachers. They provide a healthy learning environment in the home. For example, Robby loves to read. But it's no secret that Robby's father and mother have read to him since the day he was born. Because of his advanced reading skills, Robby approaches Jill's class with eagerness and confidence in his abilities.

Jill Sinclair, like the others, brings her own background to class. At thirty-two, she desires to serve God and the church as a single woman. Jill likes to be in control of her circumstances. Her class thwarts that desire. These personal trials raise soul-searching questions about her competence. Should she be in this kind of ministry? It may be that God, in his omniscience, is helping Jill develop patience and flexibility through Marilyn and Scott.

These personal vignettes highlight three critical, interacting factors present in any educational setting:

1. Heredity: "At birth" natural endowments (and limitations) related to human nature are featured here. This includes physical and psychological abilities. Supernatural realities include sin tendencies and (for believers) spiritual regeneration at conversion. These gifts are bestowed according to the sovereign plan of God.
2. History: Factors related to background and past experiences are emphasized. This includes previous learning and memories with people, places, and events. God's superintending activity with his creation is particularly valued.
3. Here and Now: Contemporary circumstances and contexts of learning are stressed. What God is presently accomplishing takes prominence, as seen from a Christian worldview.

The potential combinations of these factors alone should tell us that *each learner is unique.* Awareness of these basic categories can help educators diagnose teaching-learning difficulties and can provide a framework for educational planning. Each student comes to the classroom with a unique constellation of "entry characteristics." How well the teacher is able to build on the qualities depends on how well these characteristics are understood.

For example, if a child begins to disrupt a Sunday school class, a number of reasons may be offered as possible causes for misbehavior. Disruptive behavior may be due to:

1. Heredity (the child may have physical problems such as Scott's hyperactivity; or a very young child may be frustrated by the lack of physical coordination skills necessary to color a picture neatly within the lines)
2. History (the child may not have learned sufficient self-control habits; or, due to past abuse, the child may react to being touched by a classmate or the teacher)
3. Here and Now (a bee may be chasing the child, spiritual warfare may be evident, or a student may experience an exciting, teachable moment)

No matter what the circumstances, God's sovereign activity reminds us that he is in control. Through all circumstances, he will bring glory to himself and good to his people (see Paul's example of Job, Pharaoh, and the Israelites in Rom. 9:22–23). Romans 8:28 is the teacher's plumb line for keeping the bigger picture in perspective.

Successful educational planning requires an accurate diagnosis of students' entry characteristics. Chapters 7 and 8 of this book provide basic information about how we learn—whether that learning took place in the past (i.e., *history* factors) or is presently occurring (i.e., *here and now* factor). Chapters 5 and 6 on patterns of growth discuss more fully the *heredity* factor. A few additional matters now need mentioning.

Divine Endowments

Factors related to heredity significantly affect how and what we learn. "Heredity" refers to the capacities that God gives us at physical birth (or, later, at spiritual rebirth). Understanding these divine endowments helps us comprehend inherent possibilities and constraints of each individual learner. It would be foolish for us to pray that God would give us a third hand. It would be just as futile to request certain intellectual or spiritual giftedness that God did not intend us to have. Some of our human endowments have a common reference point with other creatures (e.g., eyes and limbs for mobility). Yet, other capacities are unique to humankind. For instance, being created in the image of God means that we have a conscience.

Stewardship

In the class scenario described earlier, Scott's brain functioning was slightly dysfunctional. Some individuals are born with "slightly damaged equipment" (congenital in nature, either genetic or stemming from problems during prenatal development). Others may have their physical and mental faculties adversely affected *after* birth through severe accidents or diseases (e.g., amputation of limbs, brain damage through drug abuse).

Some handicaps are more detrimental to human functioning than other handicaps. For Scott, medication would help him reduce his hyperactivity. In addition, early detection may prevent Scott from experiencing negative self-attitudes of failure and alienation resulting from his disruptive behavior. Other handicaps (such as extreme mental retardation) set more permanent limits on intellectual functioning.

All physical human bodies are subject to abnormalities in prenatal development, disease, aging, and eventual death and decomposition (Gen. 3:19; Rom. 5:12–14).[1] Our years on this earth are limited.[2] The debilitating consequences of the curse have significantly affected our structural capacities.

From a biblical perspective, having unmarred bodily and psychological operations is not an ultimate value. The critical issue is that, whatever our abilities, we should determine to bring glory to God. Although we may be limited by *structural* defects, we must strive to *functionally* demonstrate the dynamic work of God in our lives.

In a fallen world, God sovereignly allows a wide range of functional and dysfunctional bodily members for his own purposes (John 9:1–3). The whole physical creation groans and believers await expectantly for ultimate reconciliation (Rom. 8:19–23). Yet, regardless of the inequitable conditions of individual God-given capacities, each believer confronts stewardship responsibilities. The parable of the talents encourages believers to fully utilize what *has* been given, and not to dwell on that which has *not* been given or has been taken away (Matt. 25:14–30; John 21:21–22).

Unity in Diversity: Body and Soul

While humankind functions as a unitary being, Scripture uses a variety of terms that allude to differing aspects of essential human nature. The following terms come from Paul's writings (McDonald 1984, p. 678):

1. *pneuma* (used 146 times as "spirit")
2. *sarx* (used 91 times as "flesh")
3. *soma* (used 89 times as "body")[3]
4. *kardia* (used 52 times as "heart as the seat of life")
5. various Greek words translated as "mind"; the most common term is *nous,* used as such 21 times
6. *psyche* (used 11 times as "soul")

The question that confronts us is: Is a person essentially made up of constituent elements that interact in harmony but are distinct, or is a person an indivisible unit?

Basic to any understanding of person is the concept that humankind is created in the image of God (Gen. 1:26; James 3:9). As discussed earlier in the book, the image of God can be understood as encompassing both functional and structural aspects (Hoekema 1986). The *structural* aspect refers to our endowments and capacities (e.g., muscular mobility of body, conscience). *Functional* aspects relate to the proper use of these gifts according to God's purpose (e.g., speaking a blessing rather than a curse, James 3:9–12).

Historically, a biblical understanding of humanity's structure has yielded two basic categories: *material* (i.e., based in physiology—the "body") and *immaterial* (i.e., not based in physiology—typically termed the "soul").[4] Regarding the physical body, the most common term used in the New Testament is *sōma* ("body"). On occasion *sarx* ("flesh") is translated in a neutral sense as "body" (e.g., 2 Cor. 4:11), although this term is usually employed in more of an ethical sense (e.g., the flesh versus the spirit). Paul refers to the body once as the "outer man" (2 Cor. 4:16), once as a "house" (2 Cor. 5:1), and twice as an "earthly tent" (2 Cor. 5:1, 4).

Traditional evangelical theology has also postulated that, at death, the soul is separated from the physical body. Later the soul will be united with a resurrection body. Some contemporary evangelical authors are challenging this conception of personhood. How do we resolve the fact that persons function as holistic beings, yet, biblically, they are described as made up of body and soul? Diverse responses are offered to solve this age-old "mind-body" or monism-dualism" dilemma.

Why is the debate important? One's choice for ontological monism or dualism has implications for one's view of what takes place after physical death. The significance and nuances of the issue are analyzed by John W. Cooper (1989). A full review of the issue lies beyond the scope of this book. Briefly, the implications are as follows.

Ontological dualism holds that a person is made of body and soul (i.e., two constituent parts). After death, the soul continues to exist and is later united to a resurrection body. Thus, for a temporary period, persons are in a disembodied state. "Again, anthropological duality does not imply a metaphysical dualism according to which body or flesh is evil, but affirms that man is made up of two substances which belong together though they possess the capability of separation" (Gundry 1987, pp. 83–84).

Ontological monism sees a person as an indivisible unit (i.e., one constituent part). Thus, at death, the person ceases to exist. Then, immediately, or at a later time an individual is recreated as a glorified person. Thus, there is no continuity of existence.[5] "For MacKay, the quality of our earthly life is preserved in the memory of God and recreated, as a sequel to our present relationship with God, by an act of God" (Farnsworth 1985, p. 140).

It is important to note that one cannot mix and match views. They are mutually exclusive. If one holds to an intermediate state in which the soul exists after death, then one is an ontological dualist.[6]

Unity and Diversity: Male and Female

According to Genesis 1:26, God made humankind in his image. Thus male and female together constitute the fullness of humanity. Adam and Eve were both blessed by God and commanded to fill and to rule the earth (Gen. 1:28). And we are heirs together of life in Christ (Gal. 3:28) and God's grace (1 Pet. 3:7). Although we share certain physiological attributes, distinctive features are evident (e.g., reproductive glands, facial hair). We cannot be certain to what degree psychological differences result primarily from socialization or genetic structure (Van Leeuwen 1990).

Yet our growth toward maturity in Christ should seek to incorporate the fullest richness of our gender—not ignore it—for we have been created as male and female. Contemporary debate in the church revolves around appropriate roles for men and women in ministry. Among evangelicals, three main positions have emerged, arranged below from the least to the most restrictive position (Conservative Baptist Seminaries 1989, p. 5):[7]

Egalitarian Position—All ministries of the church are open to all qualified men and women. Gender is not a relevant distinction for excluding a person from any office.

Moderate Position—The office of elder alone is reserved for men. Women are to be encouraged to minister in any other office or ministry open to any other nonelder, assuming their qualifications and appropriate gifting.

Hierarchical (Traditional) Position—The office of elder and usually deacon is reserved for men. Women are excluded from any ministry that includes public teaching to the corporate body or the exercising of authority over men. As a pattern, men will be in authority over women and not vice versa.

Proponents of each view have marshaled biblical and theological facts as evidence for support.[8] We consider the issue of critical significance and commend a continuing study. But let us also persevere in our efforts to serve one another and to demonstrate the unity of the body.

Learning Styles

Through repeated learning experiences, we each gravitate to favored educational preferences. Some people like to discuss theories, while others would rather work with practical ideas. Some prefer to make an oral presentation on a subject, others would rather write a term paper. Certain learners prefer to study in a quiet room, while others are never bothered by background noise.

Educational research is helping us understand these individual "learning styles" (Dunn et al. 1989; Bonham 1988). The simpler models reduce options to four individual learning styles. Each style has its own optimum set of teaching methods. David Kolb (1984) suggests four quadrants with two perpendicular axes (concrete versus abstract, active versus reflective). The foursome, as adapted for the teacher by McCarthy (1987; Kolb's terms are in parentheses), includes:

1. *Imaginative Learner* (Diverger): emphasis on group activities to explore many ideas through a variety of means
2. *Analytical Learner* (Assimilator): emphasis on facts, logical soundness of ideas, and organized presentation of information
3. *Common Sense Learner* (Converger): emphasis on practical and relevant-to-life uses for ideas and theories
4. *Dynamic Learner* (Accommodator): emphasis on "hands-on," trial-and-error, and results-oriented experimentation in which learners are free to select activities from various options

To work with these particular student interests, McCarthy suggests that teachers rotate through a four-part cycle in their teaching, incorporating each of these four emphases. This permits students to learn in their most productive mode at least for a period of time.

Some learning style models include more variables. For example, Rita and Kenneth Dunn's model (1978; Dunn et al. 1988) involves five groupings of twenty-one categories that affect learning:

1. Environmental	sound, light, temperature, design
2. Emotional	motivation, persistence, responsibility, structure
3. Sociological	self, pair, peers, team, adult, varied
4. Physical	perceptual, intake, time, mobility
5. Psychological	global versus analytic, hemispherity, impulsive versus reflective

For instance, in the physical category, "visual" (perceptual) learners retain information best by picturing it, while "manipulative" (mobility) learners prefer more "hands-on" involvement. In the sociological category, "dyadic" (pair) learners work best with a partner, rather than alone (self) or in a group (team).

The main reason we include this subject is because teachers must also be concerned about student *motivation.* In Chapter 8, we explained the basic processes for how we all learn. Yet based on our personalities and experiences, we develop a certain *preference* for how we like to learn. Thus, learning styles research provides another helpful model for tapping into students' *willingness* to persist in a particular learning activity.

A helpful overview of learning styles, especially as it relates to multicultural education, can be found in Bennett (1990). The "Learning Style Inventory," based on Kolb's model, is available from McBer and Company, 137 Newbury Street, Boston, MA 02116. Learning style inventories based on Dunns' model are available for adults and those in Grades 3–12 from Price Systems, Box 1818, Lawrence, KS 66044.

Carl Rowntree's Lesson Plan for John 13

Location: Mariner's classroom

Time: 9:15–10:30 A.M.

Passage: John 13:1–17

Aim: To demonstrate an understanding of humble servanthood by designing a contemporary advertisement

Resources needed: Bibles, group instructions, paper and pens, overhead sheets and pen, butcher paper and marking pens, magazines, 3 by 5 cards

Before-class preparation: Remove chairs from the classroom; ask Pastor Snyder, Associate Pastor Jungker, and Marshall Troyer to set up chairs in a circle five minutes before class starts; check with Tim and Maria about refreshments

Five minutes before class:

Chairs are set up by three church leaders (a visible demonstration of servanthood for the whole class).

A. *Hook:* (2–4 min.)
   1. Write on board: "Winning through intimidation" and "Looking out for #1." Ask class if they recognize these phrases and listen to their responses. Describe an intimidation strategy.
   2. Transition: On board, cross out "intimidation" and substitute "humility." Today, we'll be looking at a passage that teaches the real key to getting ahead.
B. *Book* (25–30 min.)
   1. Write John 13:1–17 on the board; have class turn there; review theme and outline of book (see review sheet).

2. Read John 3:1–5, then review the chronology of events preceding this event (see notes).

3. Group exercise: What expectations did the disciples and Jesus have as they came to the upper room? Divide class into groups (three to five in each group; leader—first name closest to "A"); distribute handout assignments (10 min.; circulate among groups to help out if needed).

4. Group responses: Write four main headings on board (Peter, Judas, Jesus, and the Twelve); write responses under each heading; contrast disciples' expectations with Jesus'.

5. Minilecture: custom of foot washing (see notes).

6. Focus on John 13:13–14: (we'll study vv. 6–11 next week); read verses 13–14; ask class to individually paraphrase verses (distribute paper and pens; 3–5 min.).

7. Have some read paraphrases. Summarize on board "Humble service = No task is too menial."

C. *Look* (25 min.)

1. Transition: Write on overhead projector: "Learn how to jump-start a life"

   a. Who sponsored this ad? What are they promoting?

   b. Sing old Alka-seltzer jingle.

2. Group exercise: Have groups reconvene (leader name closest to "Z"); each group is a successful advertising agency; create a contemporary ad to communicate humble servanthood; options (15 min.):

   a. Design a five- to seven-word billboard phrase.

   b. Adapt a popular radio jingle with new words.

   c. Create a thirty-second television commercial.

   Available resources: magazines, butcher paper, and pens

3. Group sharing of ads.

4. Class brainstorming: under headings: At home; At work; At church gatherings; In the neighborhood; While driving. "What are some specific and practical ways that Christians serve the needs of others in these spheres?" Write responses on board.

D. *Took* (5–8 min.)

1. Distribute 3 by 5 cards; on board write: "This week, I will . . ." Read John 13:13–14. Ask members to select one category and one menial service to do this week; write this on their card and post the card prominently to remind you.

2. Illustration of Mr. Sheldon Livesay and menial service.

3. Closing song: "Make Me a Servant."

4. Have class read aloud: "Humble service = No task is too menial"; read John 13:13–14; close in prayer.

Class Activity for
John 13

Group Instructions

What were the expectations of the participants in the upper room? Describe your assigned participant's attitudes or preoccupations. The following sets of passages relate to the time before, during, and after the meeting in the upper room.

1. Judas:

   Before: John 12:4–8 (John 11:57); Luke 22:3–6 [parallel: Mark 14:10–11; Matt. 26:14–16]

   During: John 13:2, 27

   After: Matt. 27:3–5

2. Peter (and John):

   Before: Luke 22:8–9, 13

   During: John 13:37 [parallel: Luke 22:33]; John 13:8

   After: Matt. 26:33 [parallel: Mark 14:29] (probably at Mount of Olives)

3. The disciples:

   Before: (1) Mark 9:33–34 [parallel: Matt. 18:1; Luke 9:46]; (2) Matt. 20:20–24 [parallel: Mark 10:35–41]

   During: Luke 22:24

   After: Acts 1:6

4. Jesus:

   Before: (1) Mark 9:35 [parallel: Matt. 18:4; Luke 9:48]; (2) Matt. 20:25–28 [parallel: Mark 10:42–45]; (3) Matt. 23:11–12

   During: John 13:1, 21

   After: Luke 22:41–44 [parallel: Matt. 26:39; Mark 14:35–36]

Comparing Preaching and Teaching

How does preaching compare and contrast with teaching? Let's imagine that an informal poll of church members was conducted to determine possible viewpoints on this issue. Some of the following distinctions between these two terms might be raised:

	Preaching	Teaching
Volume	Loud, "prophetic" tone	Mild, conversational tone
Place/Time	Sanctuary at 11 A.M.	Classroom at 9:30 A.M.
Aim	Conviction	Comprehension
Qualifications	Must be ordained	Anyone can teach

Yet a thorough study of the New Testament indicates that such contrasts are more *cultural* than *biblical.* For instance, there are five passages where the primary words for preaching (Greek *kerusso*) and teaching (Greek *didasko*) are used in the same context: three in the Gospel of Matthew, one in Acts, and one in Romans. Careful analysis reveals that these two words are basically synonyms. Consider these passages:

"Jesus went throughout Galilee, *teaching* in their synagogues, *preaching* the good news of the kingdom, and healing every disease and sickness among the people" (Matt. 4:23; Matt. 9:35 is almost identical). "After Jesus had finished instructing his twelve disciples, he went from there to *teach* and *preach* in the towns of Galilee" (Matt. 11:1).

"Boldly and without hindrance he [Paul] *preached* the kingdom of God and *taught* about the Lord Jesus Christ" (Acts 28:31).

"An instructor of the foolish, a *teacher* of infants, because you have in the law the embodiment of knowledge and truth—you, then, who *teach* others, do you not *teach* yourself? You who *preach* against stealing, do you steal?" (Rom. 2:20–21).

The word "to teach" *(didasko)* is also used in combination with other Greek words that are translated as "to preach" or a related synonym. Thus, *didasko* is used with:

anangello (Acts 20:20)
euangelizo (Acts 5:42; 15:35)
laleo (Acts 18:25)
noutheteo (Col. 3:16)
parakaleo (1 Tim. 4:13; 6:2)
logos (1 Tim. 5:17)

The noun form of teacher *(didaskalos)* is placed in a close connection with the word "pastor" *(poimenas;* Eph. 4:11) and in the same context with the word "herald" *(kerux;* 2 Tim. 1:11).

Consider one historical metaphor of the word "preaching." In ancient times, this term paralleled the role of a king's herald, that is, someone who served as a Paul Revere-type messenger. The herald verbally spread the ruler's prescribed message quickly throughout the kingdom. In our understanding of *contemporary* preaching, though, the *form* of preaching is not the critical issue; rather the *function* is. Two main features of teaching God's Word favorably compare with the distinctive features of a "herald": (1) All heralds must be credible. Thus, Bible teachers should have high qualifications. Such qualifications are outlined for elders (including their tasks of *both* "preaching and teaching") in 1 Timothy 5:17 and Titus 1:9. (2) All must hear the message of the herald. Thus, preaching (or teaching) of the Word represents one of the premier purposes of the gathered church.

The most prominent form of *contemporary* preaching is, in educational terms, a lecture (sometimes called expository preaching or teaching). For example, principles regarding good lecturing are very similar to principles regarding good preaching. Yet the lecture form of preaching is not sacrosanct. Even fully costumed dramatic presentations (whether a monologue or involving many actors) have been accepted in the church.

A metaphor for the "herald" today might take the form of the presidential spokesperson who disseminates the president's message at a nationally televised press conference. Following the officially prepared remarks, the gathered reporters are given an opportunity to ask questions for clarification. Or, we may choose the metaphor of a major network anchor on the evening news. A brief presentation of each major event is accompanied by a caption, a related still picture, or a video report. Either of these two metaphors could be adapted to make our preaching relevant to an audience living on the threshold of the twenty-first century.

Major Curriculum Publishers and Children's Ministry Resources

Accent Publishers
P.O. Box 15337
Denver, CO 80215
Sunday school curriculum

American Bible Society
P.O. Box 5656
Grand Central Station
New York, NY 10017
Films, Bibles

Augsburg Publishing House
426 S. 5th Street, Box 1209
Minneapolis, MN 55440

AWANA
2301 Toilview Drive
Rolling Meadows, IL 60008
Mid-week club programs

Bible Club Movement, Inc.
237 Fairfield Avenue
Upper Dailey, PA 19082

Child Evangelism Fellowship
Warrenton, MO 63383
Home Bible clubs, teaching resources

Christian Education Publishers
P.O. Box 261129
San Diego, CA 92126

Christian Service Brigade
P.O. Box 150
Wheaton, IL 60189
Boys' programs

Concordia Publishing House
3558 South Jefferson Avenue
St. Louis, MO 63118
Sunday school curriculum

Convention Press
127 Ninth Avenue North
Nashville, TN 37203
Sunday school curriculum, teacher's resources

David C. Cook Publishers
850 N. Grove Avenue
Elgin, IL 60120
Sunday school and church time curriculum/
    teacher training

Evangelical Training Association
P.O. Box 327
Wheaton, IL 60189
Teaching training resources

Focus on the Family
P.O. Box 35500
Colorado Springs, CO 80935
Various resources for children and families

Gospel Light Publications
P.O. Box 3875
Ventura, CA 93006
Sunday school and church time curriculum/VBS
    material/teacher training

Pioneer Clubs
P.O. Box 788
Wheaton, IL 60189
Boys' and girls' programs

Regular Baptist Press
1300 North Meacham Road
Schaumburg, IL 60173
Sunday school curriculum

Scripture Press Publishers
1825 College Avenue
Wheaton, IL 60187
Sunday school and church time materials/
    teacher training

Standard Publishing Company
8121 Hamilton Avenue
Cincinnati, OH 45231
Sunday school curriculum

Success with Youth
P.O. Box 27028
Tempe, AZ 85282

The Train Depot
5015 Tampa West Boulevard
Tampa, FL 33634
Club programs/resources

Ventura Press
1626 Ventura Drive
Tempe, AZ 85281
Voyager clubs

Westminster Press
925 Chestnut Street
Philadelphia, PA 19107

Word of Life Clubs
8280 Green Hills Way
Roseville, CA 95678

Youth Specialties
1224 Greenfield Drive
El Cajon, CA 92021

A Position Description

Title: Create a clear and descriptive title indicating the general level of responsibility (e.g., director, coordinator, associate) and the particular area of responsibility.

• Associate Pastor for Christian Education

Purpose/Importance: Identify the main purpose of the position and how this position fits into the overall scheme of ministry within the church.

• To oversee the process of encouraging spiritual growth for each believer in the body

Scope: List the major items/areas/tasks of responsibility.

• Leadership development, growth groups, parent ministry, children's ministry, youth ministry, budget, personnel, facilities use, communication to the body

Responsibilities: Briefly describe each specific item of responsibility. Designate the general level of activity with the opening verb (e.g., train, formulate, submit, monitor, recruit, represent, provide, coordinate, schedule, maintain, develop, prepare, create, explore, collect, plan, assess, implement, direct, lead, promote, advise, guide, recommend, conduct, meet, report.

Decision-making authority: Indicate the kind of decision-making authority for each specific responsibility:

1. *Act upon approval* [A/U]: Refer the final decision to the individual to whom you report; after the decision has been made, you will be informed and then you can implement the decision.
2. *Act and inform* [A/I]: The decision is yours; you only need to inform the individual to whom you report.
3. *Act* [A]: The decision is solely yours.

Basis of evaluation: Indicate what kind of accountability is expected and how performance will be evaluated.

In addition include (a) any special instructions, procedures, or background information and (b) what resources are available and to whom the person can go for any assistance.

- Formulate a budget per instructions (refer to separate sheet of guidelines available from the finance elder) for all educational programs for the coming year. Submit the budget to the elders for approval by September 1. [Act]

Working Relationships: Indicate with whom the individual will be working.

I report to: (to whom is the individual responsible)

- Elders

Reporting directly to me: (who reports directly to the individual)

- Directors of leadership development, growth groups, parent ministry, children's ministry, and youth ministry.

I must coordinate with: (with whom or what groups must the individual coordinate planning, personnel recruitment, and use of facilities)

- Ministry involvement team elder (for personnel recruitment), Christian school elder and custodian (for use of facilities), director of childcare ministries (for nursery).

Time Requirements: Indicate approximate time involved in various tasks: supervising and training personnel, monitoring progress of programs and projects, research and development, informing, meetings.

Regular meetings: (Indicate membership with ongoing group meetings)

- Elders' meeting—each Wednesday evening, 8:15–9:45 P.M.
- Christian education council—second Monday evening of each month, 7:30–9:00 P.M.

Continuing Education Growth Goals: Provide guidelines and identify crucial resources to encourage the individual to keep abreast of current thinking and practice in the particular area of ministry. [You may also encourage some planning in the area of personal development.] Have the individual set some realistic goals to be accomplished within a certain period of time (e.g., quarter, six months, one year). Ideas include: Studying certain books of the Bible or Bible passages and relevant topics of theology; reflective reading of significant articles, chapters, or books; attendance at seminars and conferences; interviewing key resource persons.

Periodic Review of Progress: Indicate how often a periodic review will take place for the purpose of asking questions and receiving feedback related to:

(a) clarification and/or adjustment of responsibilities
(b) assessment of progress on tasks and working relationships
(c) guidance for improvement with the various responsibilities
(d) application to the ministry of insights gleaned from continuing education projects

For example, every three months, every six months.

Orientation and Initial Training: Outline the procedures for helping the individual become familiar with the new area of responsibility before the position officially begins (e.g., audio and/or video training; on-the-job apprenticeship; policy manuals and handbooks; meeting current personnel; attending planning meetings).

Qualifications: Outline special qualifications for this particular position. General qualifications for all ministry positions would be listed elsewhere.

Length of Commitment: Indicate the minimum term for this position (e.g., one quarter, one year, three years).

Date: Indicate the date of the most recent revision of the position description.

Source: Adapted from a model developed by Don Weaver and Klaus Issler, June 1985

Board and Committee Structures at Grace Church

Mission Statement: to glorify God by making disciples through winning and building people.

Worship: to facilitate a regular corporate celebration and worship of God.

- Sunday morning events, music (musicians, singing, ensemble), drama, seasonal specials (Christmas, Easter)
- Sunday morning coordinator and support personnel (sound, parking, ushers, greeters, physical arrangements, communion and baptism arrangements, etc.)

Christian education: to facilitate the spiritual growth and development of each believer in the body toward a mature faith in God with an accompanying Christ-like lifestyle.

- Adult ministry: Sunday evening classes; small groups; men's ministry; women's ministry; singles ministry
- Youth/parent ministry: Sunday school class; weekly Bible study; social and ministry events; parent meetings
- Child/parent: [from age 2 up to Grade 6] Sunday school classes; weekly children's club; parent meetings; parent-child workshop (formerly "children's church"); parent-child dedication classes
- Intergenerational discipleship events (e.g., family clusters groups)

Ministry placement and training: to facilitate a maturing, balanced participation by each believer in body-focused and outreach functions.

• Simple tracking system for all members; testing and periodic review of ministries and workers (e.g., DiSC inventory); up-to-date record of position descriptions and specific personnel needs for all official church functions
• Leadership development (elder and deacon growth): workshops; evaluation forms

Outreach: to facilitate each believer's participation in reaching out to those who have yet to place their faith in Jesus Christ.

• Four strategies are used:
(1) "Farming" a neighborhood
(2) Free community seminars (e.g., finance seminar)
(3) Large group events (e.g., annual Thanksgiving dinner)
(4) Small group events (evangelistic home Bible studies)
• Training in four strategies; visitor follow-up and tracking system; hospitality to newcomers; newcomers class
• Communication to the church

Care corps: to coordinate efforts to meet special needs of the body.

• Nursery (infants, crawlers and toddlers until "toilet-trained")

• General and crisis hospitality (e.g., meals, flowers, visitation, funerals, groceries, lawn care, etc.)
• Social functions and church events (picnics, suppers, weddings)

Christian day school: to provide formal Christian education for preschool and elementary age children, and, through this vehicle, to reach non-Christian parents for Jesus Christ.

• Set policies: for elementary and preschool; coordinate: writing of "Policy and Procedures Manual" (philosophy of education, job descriptions, use of facilities, etc.)
• Develop master plan for school
• Supervise scope and sequence plan for curriculum
• Child/family evangelism

Property and finance: to coordinate efforts to provide appropriate facilities and adequate funding, as faithful stewards of God's resources, so that the church is able to carry on its mission.

• Budget process and setting final budget; fund raising
• Facilities: maintenance, grounds keeping, remodeling; property acquisition

Source: Adapted from a model developed by Don Weaver and Klaus Issler, Grace Church, June 1985.

Practical Categories of Instructional Questions from Jesus' Ministry

Robert Delnay (1987, p. 65, emphasis added) declares: "Much of teaching seems designed to tell people *what* to think. It is harder to teach them *how* to think." And, with that viewpoint, Delnay proceeds to describe how Christ planted "time-delay charges" in his hearers' heads. Jesus prodded people to think, to scrutinize, to grapple with difficult questions. He would not settle for less. Delnay (pp. 74–83) cites seven specific ways that Christ raised challenging questions. (More often than not, Jesus' questions ultimately sought to bring people closer to God.[1]) Of particular benefit, the author also suggests how we instructors can emulate these seven qualities of the Master Teacher.[2]

Category 1: Use questions to "open a conversation." Jesus adhered to common-sense communication techniques. He proposed inquiries that naturally bridged his purposes.

- "Turning around, Jesus saw them following and asked, 'What do you want?'" (John 1:38).
- "When Jesus saw him lying there and learned that he had been in this condition for a long time, he asked him, 'Do you want to get well?'" (John 5:6).
- "Early in the morning, Jesus stood on the shore, but the disciples did not realize that it was Jesus. He called out to them, 'Friends, haven't you any fish?'" (John 21:4–5).

We can follow Christ's lead through "normal" conversation patterns. As we ask a few (sincere) questions of others, we'll become more aware of their conditions. Sample inquiries include: "What did you think of the television special last night?" "How's that overtime coming along on your job?" "Any more news about the family concern we discussed earlier?"

Category 2: Use questions that "prepare for instruction." In John 9:35, Jesus raised a significant question with the man who was being persecuted by the religious leaders; it took him beyond the issue of physical eyesight to spiritual vision: "Jesus heard that they had thrown him out [of the synagogue], and when he found him, he said, 'Do you believe in the Son of Man?'"[3] Relevant preinstruction questions for us might include: "How can a just God let guilty people off? Have you ever thought about that?"

Category 3: Use questions to "induce reflection." Delnay (p. 76) begins this third section with a cogent appeal:

> Probably every teacher can remember the times when his best insights came to him after he thought he had finished his lesson plan, not during the process. The work of preparation paid off in getting his mind to reflect, and the reflection paid off in deepened understanding and originality.
>
> Now if reflection enriches us, it is bound to enrich our students. How can we convey to them this wealth? It is not a commodity or a bag of coins that we can hand to them. It is more like a thirst that we can cause by salting their tongues. So how did Jesus do it?

One time Jesus prompted contemplation through a standard custom of his day: foot washing. Just before Christ's final Passover feast, John records: "When [Jesus] had finished washing their feet, he put on his clothes and returned to his place. 'Do you understand what I have done for you?' he asked them" (John 13:12). Of course, Jesus was speaking about much more than a traditional Jewish custom.

How do we do the same? First, by modeling. Our adult learners should observe our transparency, our ability to communicate personal, reflective moments. Second, our teaching assignments should value contemplation. Writing a journal, for instance, expresses one worthwhile technique. We can challenge adults to regularly record answers to prayer, signs of growth, and personal interaction with weekly lessons. Typically, reflective tasks begin with the question "Why?"

Category 4: Use questions to "pull hearers up short." Perhaps adult students are straying from the truth. Confrontation is necessary. Remember the story of Jesus and his disciples at sea? Recall how, in the midst of the storm, the Twelve awakened him, crying, "Teacher, don't you care if we drown?" The Lord, after calming the storm, disquieted their hearts with the inquiry "Why are you so afraid? Do you still have no faith?" (Mark 4:38, 40).[4] Of course, we human instructors must

humbly realize our own frailties. When we confront, we must act with love, in wisdom.

Category 5: Use questions to "probe for motives." Jesus tested the motives of both his enemies (Matt. 22:18) and his followers (Matt. 26:10). As relationships with our adults are strengthened, probing will be a sign of caring accountability, not intrusion. Valid questions include:

- "Why do you feel that way?"
- "Why do you want to succeed in that?"
- "Search your heart. Was that the real reason?"
- "Do you feel this is the best use of your gifts?"

Category 6: Use questions to "force an admission." Although these moments may be infrequent, we teachers must be prepared to initiate what some call a "spiritual gut check"—to help our adults abandon safe, secure positions of faith without manipulation.[5] Jesus powerfully drove home his point at the conclusion of the parable of the good Samaritan: "Which of these three do you think was a neighbor to the man who fell into the hands of robbers?" (Luke 10:36). We might raise a similar inquiry: "How are you fulfilling Paul's command to 'help the weak' (Acts 20:35)?[6] Give me specific examples."

Category 7: Use questions to "answer a question." As Jesus entered the temple court, the chief priests and elders quizzed him: "By what authority are you doing these things?" Instead of a direct response Jesus replied, "'I will also ask you one question. If you answer me, I will tell you by what authority I am doing these things'" (Matt. 21:23–24). The complementary subject of John the Baptist's ministry is then introduced. By answering a question with a question, the Master Teacher gets at the heart of the problem. The religious leaders' "don't-confuse-us-with-the-facts" mindset is revealed for what it is: hypocrisy.

In conclusion, Delnay (p. 82) suggests two basic interrogative responses to questions that we teachers can employ:

- "Why did you ask that question?"
- "What do you have in mind?"

Reactions to these questions may reveal matters more worthy of attention. These seven types of questions ultimately direct our thoughts toward God and toward the Communion theme.

Notes

Chapter 1: Boxes and Blind Men

1. See Harris (1987, pp. 49–50).
2. Foltz supplies a superb understanding of "religious education" (although we prefer the term "Christian education").
   Foltz (1990, p. 8, emphasis added) captures the purpose
   and dimension of this concept in a helpful definition:

   > The purpose of religious education is *to help persons re-*
   > *spond to God.* Religious educators are environmental
   > shapers and directors. We create environments, shape
   > them to teach and learn, and are shaped by them. At
   > our best we are environmental directors of religious ed-
   > ucation, creating environments that will teach who God
   > is. We offer individuals opportunities to interact, to pas-
   > sionately express their love for God and for one another.
   > Religious education is *not* about curriculum resource,
   > building, and position. Religious education is about
   > knowing that *we* are the curriculum; we are the design-
   > ers of space; and the ultimate issue is how we position
   > ourselves to God and others.
   >
   > Religious education is defined in our day-to-day inter-
   > personal interactions. *At its best, religious education is the*
   > *culmination of our expressed life. . . . The way we feel, think,*
   > *act, and most importantly live tells who we are.*

   See Foltz's earlier description (1988, pp. 174–75). Parallel-
   ing the need for foundational direction, see Appendix A for
   a comprehensive bibliography of Christian educational
   survey textbooks.
3. We are indebted to LeBar (1958, 1981) for this helpful
   phrase.
4. See Twain (1912, pp. 240–41).
5. Appreciating paradoxes (truths that seem to contradict
   each other) of our faith is a healthy activity, although often frustrating. Valuing paradoxes prevents us from artic-
   ulating neat, simple answers to complex questions. For
   instance, what potential paradoxical ideas surface when
   you compare and contrast the metaphor of "pilgrim" in 1
   Peter 2:11 with "soldier" in 2 Timothy 2:4? How about "servants" (Acts 16:17) and "sons of God" (Rom. 8:14)?

   Charles Dickens, in *A Tale of Two Cities,* penned perhaps
   the greatest description of real-life paradoxes. Notice how
   Dickens' classic tensions express what believers typically
   encounter today: "It was the best of times, it was the worst
   of times, it was the age of wisdom, it was the age of foolishness, it was the epoch of belief, it was the epoch of incredu-
   lity, it was the season of Light, it was the season of
   Darkness, it was the spring of hope, it was the winter of despair, we had everything before us, we had nothing before
   us."
6. Appreciation is expressed to Cheryl Sparks, one of our students, for suggesting this analogy.
7. See White (1984, pp. 162–66).
8. Certainly other factors also distinguish Christian education, like the work of the Holy Spirit. The chapters on teaching will analyze these comprehensive factors.
9. Hoekema (1986, p. 76) extends the fish analogy and its
   purposes: "Since man's relatedness to God is his primary
   relationship, all of his life is to be lived *coram Deo*—as before the face of God. Man is bound to God as a fish is bound
   to water. When a fish seeks to be free from the water, it loses both its freedom and its life. When we seek to be 'free'
   from God, we become slaves to sin."

10. This statement came from a private conversation with Ken Mulholland, dean of Columbia Biblical Seminary and Graduate School of Missions, Columbia, S.C.
11. Even though the order of our analysis here actually rearranges the chronology of this passage, the educational concept and the biblical meaning remain true to the author's intent.
12. See Chapter 12 for further analysis of the passage from Hebrews.
13. Several other Scripture passages could be cited as a biblical-theological grid for our educational philosophy of ministry. These might include:

- Deut. 6:1–25—Not only is the "core" of our belief system to love God completely, but specific challenges are raised for implementation within our Christian institutions.
- Ps. 8:1–9—The nature of God's creation, especially the intrinsic value of humanity, is highlighted—all of which should elicit praise to our Maker.
- Mic. 6:1–8—Understanding the Lord's intervention in our lives is featured here. Specific ethical living is required of us, by way of response.
- Acts 20:13–38—Principles and practices of theological education, from Paul's three-year work at Ephesus, emerge.
- Eph. 4:1–13—Dissemination of spiritual gifts to the church for the complementary tasks of ministry is stressed. Our overarching purpose is Christ-likeness.
- 2 Pet. 3:1–18—Christian educational aims (including "wholesome thinking") are derived from the inspired words of the prophets and our Savior. Challenges—"as reminders"—are given so that we might respond appropriately to the imminent day of the Lord.

14. A few Christian educators have utilized the Frankena theory to fashion helpful instructional models. Most recently, Carol and Jim Plueddemann (1990) follow this design.
15. For a brief overview of his theory, see Frankena (1965). Certain adjustments are made from the original model to meet the general needs of Christian education and the particular aims of this book.
16. All quotations in this section come from the introduction to Frankena's *Philosophy of Education* (1965, pp. 1–18).
17. Frankena equates "basic ends or principles of ethics" (p. 8) with Box A. He admits that "There may also be *metaphysical and epistemological doctrines* which are not so readily tested by the methods of experiment and observation" (p. 6). The operative word is "not." As we'll see, methods of experiment and observation are more appropriate for the content in Box B.
18. Frankena refers to Box B as dealing with the "premises" (or perspectives) "about human nature, life, and the world" (p. 8). For instance, in the political and economic realms, it is apparent that a capitalist would have totally different "premises" about people, truth, and life than a socialist (even though both may be using the same data and resources).

    Whether we know it or not, there are radically different premises (or perspectives) in evangelical Christian education too. If you don't believe it, ask a number of Christians what it means for believers to be the salt and light of the world. If you probe a bit deeper, intriguing "premises" will surface from the perspectives behind their comments.
19. Frankena (1965, p. 8) cites one way to distinguish Box A from Box C. He characterizes Box A as the "ultimate" ends or principles of education, and Box C as the "proximate" aims. That is, Box C fulfills, or satisfies, Box A. It describes the total, component parts of our overarching objectives.
20. Like Box B, Box D draws on scientific evidence; these two boxes are more empirically based (whereas Boxes A and C are more philosophically and theologically based). Frankena (1965, p. 7) therefore, declares that Box D should "appeal to the facts of psychology, sociology, and the science of education." Believers would add "and the facts within Scripture."
21. Again, diverse Christian philosophies of teaching parallel these differences. Evangelicals differ, sometimes significantly, with regard to numerous viewpoints: the essence and sources of truth; the integration of human development and experience with faith; the nature of people; human responsibility to society; and so on.
22. We have observed that there are two halves to the Frankena model. The theoretical and practical sections are held in tension with each other.

- Boxes A-B-C represent the *theoretical* portion.
- The "theoretical line of reasoning," as Frankena puts it, points out "what excellencies are to be cultivated."
- "What?" questions often clarify Boxes A-B-C, since they lead to statements about objectives.

- Boxes C-D-E represent the *practical* half of the model.
- The "practical line of thinking" balances theory with specific applications.
- "How?" and "When?" questions clarify Boxes C-D-E, since these often focus on ways to teach stated excellencies.

See Chapter 19 for summative tensions within the Frankena model.

23. The following story modifies the well-known poem, "The Blind Men and the Elephant," by John Godfrey Saxe (1953).

Chapter 2: Advancing Comprehensive Reconciliation

1. Ultimate directions from Scripture represent Box A in our modified Frankena model.
2. See Hoekema (1986, pp. 66–101).
3. Hoekema (1986, p. 75) notes his indebtedness to Hendrikus Berkhof for the interrelated concepts stated here.
4. Hoekema (p. 81, emphasis added) summarizes:

    We ought now to observe that no other creature lives in precisely the same threefold relationship. When we say that *human beings are responsible to God* and that their lives must be concisely directed toward him, we ascribe to man a relationship to God found in no other creatures except the angels. When we say that human beings are capable of conscious fellowship with their fellowmen and that *their lives are to be directed toward their neighbors,* we ascribe to man a relationship found in no other creatures, probably not even the angels, who are not bound to each other in the same way that human beings are. And when we say that *human beings have been appointed by God to rule over and to care for the earth,* we ascribe to man a relationship found in no other creatures, not even angels.

5. Paul summarizes Christ's lordship over creation in 1 Corinthians 15.
6. Miller (1956, p. 55, emphasis added).
7. Wolterstorff distinguishes between corporate and private human responsibilities; that is, between social duties ("his fellows") and personal duties ("his abilities"). This distinction becomes a significant factor in the pages that follow.
8. All quotations in this section come from Martin (1978, pp. 420–29).
9. One complementary theory of the church's ultimate purpose is *shalom*. Among others, this perspective is propagated by such Christian leaders as Snyder (1985, pp. 18–20) and Miller (1987, pp. 81–82). Quoting Douglas J. Harris' study, Snyder notes that the word *shalom* (usually translated "peace") occurs 350 times in the Old Testament. Peace permeates the New Testament revelation as well. In Snyder's (p. 20) mind, *shalom* equals reconciliation: "we see that to unite all things in Christ, to bring peace, and to reconcile are all different ways of saying the same thing. Reconciliation means making peace."

   But Snyder (p. 19) makes it clear that *shalom* is far more than "the absence of conflict and immensely more than 'inner peace' or 'peace of mind.'" In coming to this conclusion, Snyder implies the triangular design of worldviews noted earlier. The component of creation is especially highlighted: "In the Old Testament sense, *shalom* might be called an ecological concept. It carries the sense of harmony, right relationship and the proper functioning of all elements in the environment" (p. 19).
10. See "reconcile" in *The American Heritage Dictionary* (1971, p. 1089).
11. See "conciliate" in *The American Heritage Dictionary* (1971, p. 276). When employed within a theological context, the doctrine of God's reconciliation through Christ translates into these respective claims: (1) the Father has, once again, "brought together" a faithful remnant in his name; (2) he has "united," through the Son, all divine purposes for his people; and (3) he has "won over" those who were lost and imprisoned by sin.
12. Miller (1987) debunks the notion that reconciliation represents a passive doctrine. He denies that it is a static theological term. For him, the reconciling concept "is much more dynamic, active, outgoing, and energizing" (p. 81). In fact (using his preferred synonym, *shalom*), Miller suggests a half-dozen qualities of our overarching purpose in life (pp. 80–85). Notice how these six factors correlate with the foursome we've identified:

    1. Value of persons—correcting discrimination and oppression.
    2. Participation in creative change—realizing the risk of potentially destructive change.
    3. Care for world resources—offering a thought-provoking analogy, Miller says "to pollute nature is to destroy the human umbilical cord" (p. 82).
    4. Involvement in the network of communities—strengthening human interdependence.
    5. Appropriation of God's love and power—visioning and employing the Creator's virtues, including justice.
    6. Importance of productive, interpersonal conflict—David Augsburger's "carefrontation" provides a useful cross-reference point.

13. It is significant to note that the image of God was retained in *all* people, even following the sin of Adam and Eve. The next section (Act 2) explains this phenomenon.
14. Hoekema (1986, p. 71) lists partial capacities that uniquely portray ways we mirror our Creator:

    Man's rational powers, for example, reflect God's reason, and enable man now, in a sense, to think God's thoughts after him. Man's moral sensitivity reflects something of the moral nature of God, who is the supreme determiner of right and wrong. Our capacity for fellowshipping with God in worship reflects the fellowship that Father, Son, and Holy Spirit have with each other. Our ability to respond to God and to fellow human beings imitates God's ability and willingness to respond to us when we pray to him. Our ability to make decisions reflects in a small way the supreme directing power of him "who works out everything in conformity with the purpose of his will" (Eph. 1:11). Our sense of beauty is a feeble reflection of the God who scatters beauty profusely over snow-crowned peaks, lake-jeweled valleys, and awe-inspiring sunsets. Our gift of speech is an imitation of him who constantly speaks to us, both in his world and in his word. And our gift of song echoes the God who rejoices over us with singing (Zeph. 3:17).

15. The exception, of course, is the relationship between people and Satan. Rather than a broken relationship, an antagonistic one erupted.
16. Colossians 1:21 (which is studied in the next section) reveals that both internal and external evidences of sin emerged: "Once you were alienated from God and were enemies in *your minds* because of *your evil behavior.*"
17. Rush (1983) does a commendable job showing the value that God places on human relationships. First, he (pp. 10–11) identifies God's *reactive* stance: how the Creator responds to interpersonal sins:

    Our greatest danger is from ourselves. Apart from God's intervention, man threatens to extinguish himself from the face of the earth. We seem unable to live in harmony and to relate to each other as individuals and nations. Because we don't recognize our own imperfections, don't grasp that relationships depend on forgiveness, reconciliation, and serving each other's needs, we endanger our own existence.

    God is concerned about our alienation from one another. "There are six things the Lord hates, seven that are detestable to Him: haughty eyes, a lying tongue, hands that shed innocent blood, a heart that devises wicked schemes, feet that are quick to rush into evil, a false witness who pours out lies and a man who stirs up dissension among brothers" (Prov. 6:16–19).

    God hates all these things because they undermine and destroy relationships. God intended for us to have good relationships, and He hates the actions that damage relationships. He knows we can destroy ourselves and others through degenerating relationships.

    Rush proceeds to delineate God's *proactive* stance: how he initially designed for us to live through the Ten Commandments, as well as the implications of his plan: "Four of the Ten Commandments deal with our relationship with God. The remaining six deal with our relationships with each other. All the commandments, then, deal with relationships. This should tell us something of their importance in God's sight. It also suggests our need for training in how to relate effectively both to God and to our fellow human beings."

18. Schaeffer (1970, p. 67) furnishes helpful insights into these refracted consequences of sin. In so doing, he casts his affirmative vote for the earlier-stated triangular worldview:

> The Fall . . . not only separated man from God, but also caused other deep separations. It is interesting that almost the whole "curse" in Genesis 3 is centered upon the outward manifestations. It is the *earth* that is going to be cursed for man's sake. It is the woman's *body* that is involved in the greatly multiplied conception and pain in childbirth.
>
> So there are other divisions. Man was divided from God, first; and then, ever since the Fall, man is separated from himself. These are the psychological divisions. I am convinced that this is the basic psychosis: that the individual man is divided from himself as a result of the Fall.
>
> The next division is that man is divided from other men; these are the sociological divisions. And then man is divided from nature, and nature is divided from nature. So there are these multiple divisions, and one day, when Christ comes back, there is going to be a complete healing of all of them, on the basis of the "Blood of the Lamb."

19. Paul repeats the same message in Romans 5:10–11: "For if, when we were God's enemies, we *were reconciled* to him through the death of his Son, how much more, *having been reconciled,* shall we be saved through his life! Not only is this so, but we also rejoice in God through our Lord Jesus Christ, through whom we *have now received reconciliation.*"

20. Making an important distinction, Smedes (1970, p. 35) observes, "The world had come to an end—the old world of the former regime; the 'end of the ages' had arrived (1 Cor. 10:11). 'The old has passed away, behold the new has come,' said Paul (2 Cor. 5:17), referring not to the individual experience of people but to the turn of events in objective history." Consequently, we proclaim a cosmic fait accompli. The age-old warfare has been won; the finality of victory is just around the corner.

21. Smedes (1970, p. 105, emphasis added) summarizes:

> Paul's vision of reconciliation is not crippled by an atomistic individualism. Paul is not cabined by a narrow theology which counts as gospel only the possibility of individuals escaping hell. He does not shrink his soteriology to the rescue of isolated souls from a forsaken world, nor his expectations merely to a hope in moral development of the inner life of the soul. The *entire world* that God made, the world that God kept on loving, the world to which God gave His Son—this is the world reconciled through Christ. *Nothing less than the panoramic vision of a world recreated will capture Paul's vision of reconciliation.*

22. More specific commands highlight peaceful living within two particular institutions. In the home, Paul claims that reconciliation is to be prized by both husband and wife; peace is to be a joint objective for life-partners (see 1 Cor. 7:10–11). Through the institution of the church, it comes down to our common bond in the Lord. "Let the peace of Christ rule in your hearts, since as members of one body you were called to peace" (Col. 3:15; see also 2 Cor. 13:11; 1 Thess. 5:13).

23. Using more particular modern-day examples, Hybels (1987, p. 64) submits a contemporary test of Matthew 25:

> How would it feel to be handicapped, unable to stand up, walk, dress yourself, drive or even find a good seat in church because there is no room for your wheelchair?
>
> How would it feel to be unemployed, to have a mortgage and car payments you cannot make and to have children you cannot provide for?
>
> How would it feel to be Black in a White community that is not particularly sensitive to minorities?
>
> How would it feel to be divorced, to be widowed, to lose a child or parent?
>
> How would it feel to have cancer, multiple sclerosis, Alzheimer's disease or AIDS?

24. God shows his personal concern for creation in the Book of Jonah. The last verse of the book states God's rationale for withholding judgment on Nineveh. First, more than 120,000 people had repented. Second, the Creator wanted to spare "many cattle as well" (4:11).

Recently, a few Christian resources on ecology have been published. One adult study is Michael A. Bechtle and Jay Kesler, *Sharpening Your Everyday Ethics* (David C. Cook, 1991). Ecological themes are highlighted in a chapter entitled "How Much Care for the Earth?" where practical illustrations range from the use of disposable diapers to getting good gas mileage in a car. A resource in children's curriculum is Bev Gundersen and Linda Kondracki, *Junior Electives: Teaching Kids How to Live in Today's World* (David C. Cook, 1991). Four lessons, including service project ideas, are devoted to the environment.

25. The three scenes of reconciliation's Act 3 parallel what some theologians have historically referred to as positional, experiential, and eternal phases of salvation. For instance, almost a century ago, Strong (1907, p. 869) acknowledged that "Salvation is something past, something present, and something future; a past fact, justification; a present process, sanctification; a future consummation, redemption and glory." All three components must be kept in tension to fully grasp the comprehensive biblical meaning of God's plan for peace: *back then, now,* and *not yet.*

26. Buechner (1984, p. 38) comments on the "first and greatest commandment":

> Love God. We have heard the words so often that we no longer hear them. They are too loud to hear, too big to take in. We know the words so much *by* heart that we scarcely know them any longer as words spoken *to* the heart out of a mystery beyond all knowing. We take the words so much for granted that we hardly stop to wonder where they are seeking to take us. Above all else, the words say, *you shall love*—not, first your neighbor as yourself because that is second and comes later. On the contrary, it is God you shall love first before you love anything else, and you shall love him with all you are and all that you have it in you to become—whatever that means, whatever that involves. The words don't explain. They just proclaim and command.

27. Recall 2 Corinthians 5:17–6:1 in this light. We are to be reconcilers, because God first drew us to himself in Christ. The *message* of reconciliation has been committed to us; so has the *ministry* of reconciliation. As Christ's ambassadors, God makes his appeal for restoration through us. Utilizing the fullest meaning of the phrase, Paul's conclusion becomes ours: "We implore you on Christ's behalf: Be reconciled to God" (5:20).

Chapter 3: A Reconciliation Model of Christian Maturity

1. Since this chapter centers primarily on goals of maturity—or components of reconciliation—Frankena's Box C issues are addressed. It is pertinent to recognize that Box C is in a strategic and unique position. Box C serves as the only connecting link among all five boxes in the Frankena model. Employing Frankena's (1965, pp. 8–9) own analysis of normative philosophy, Box C combines the "philosophical and theoretical line of reasoning" (Boxes A-B-C) with the "scientific and practical line of reasoning" (Boxes C-D-E).

2. Edward V. Hill answers this question by breaking down the church's tasks into five units. See Pazmiño (1988, pp. 40–46). Notice how the concept of reconciliation is highlighted in Pazmiño's subsequent comments, using polarized tensions.

   Dobson (1982, pp. 45–46) has developed a checklist for spiritual training. Suggested as particular targets for ministry with children, Dobson's five goals include:

   Concept 1: "And thou shalt love the Lord thy God with all thy heart" (Mark 12:30 KJV).
   Concept 2: "Thou shalt love thy neighbour as thyself" (Mark 12:31 KJV).
   Concept 3: "Teach me to do thy will: for thou art my God" (Ps. 143:10 KJV).
   Concept 4: "Fear God, and keep his commandments: for this is the whole duty of man" (Eccles. 12:13 KJV).
   Concept 5: "But the fruit of the Spirit is . . . self control" (Gal. 5:22–23 RSV).

   Pazmiño has recently noted that human responsibility is twofold: (1) all people are accountable to God; and (2) all people are accountable to God's creation. This second category includes relationships with self, other people, and the created world. Combined, Pazmiño notes, "these responsibilities entail obligations, the fulfillment of which satisfies the deepest longings of the human heart" (*Principles and Practices of Christian Education: An Evangelical Perspective* [Grand Rapids: Baker, 1992], p. 36).

3. In the Frankena model, Box A directly affects Box C. Analyzing this connection, we say that Box A deals with the ultimate purpose, whereas Box C identifies intermediate (or subpoint) aims.

4. "Communion" is not to be confused with the Lord's Supper or Eucharist. Rather, this comprehensive term means "Communion *with God.*" It represents the central component of the themes.

   Eugene H. Peterson delineates three crucial "acts" that pastors perform. This trio of responsibilities, he claims, determines the shape of everything else in ministry. The threesome includes praying, reading Scripture, and giving spiritual direction.

Peterson (1987, pp. 2–3) prudently assesses three facts about these crucial duties: (1) they are "quiet"; nobody knows if they are addressed or not, because of their private nature; (2) they are never demanded; "nobody yells at us to engage in these acts"; and (3) they "suffer widespread neglect."

Peterson continues his comparison of this threesome, highlighting the focus on God:

> The three areas constitute acts of attention: prayer is an act in which I bring myself to attention before God; reading Scripture is an act of attending to God in his speech and action across two millennia in Israel and Christ; spiritual direction is an act of giving attention to what God is doing in the person who happens to be before me at any given moment. Always it is God to whom we are paying, or trying to pay, attention.

5. Nouwen (1989, pp. 35–39) criticizes the opposite of Community: the "Lone Ranger" mentality of contemporary church leadership. He likens it to Christ's second wilderness temptation to throw himself from the temple heights, to be spectacular. Nouwen dismisses such individualism. In fact, he backs his criticism by taking a personal stand. He left his teaching post at Harvard for the L'Arche community of handicapped people in eastern Canada. He witnessed Community. Nouwen's experiences radically challenged the prevailing tone of Christian individualism in leadership positions. Learning from his personal lessons of accountability, Nouwen summarizes:

> Not too many of us have a vast repertoire of skills to be proud of, but most of us still feel that, if we have anything at all to show, it is something we have to do solo. You could say that many of us feel like failed [leaders] who discovered that we did not have the power to draw thousands of people, that we could not make many conversions, that we did not have the talents to create beautiful liturgies, that we were not as popular with the youth, the young adults, or the elderly as we had hoped, and that we were not as able to respond to the needs of our people as we had expected. But most of us still feel that, ideally, we should have been able to do it all and do it successfully. Stardom and individual heroism, which are such obvious aspects of our competitive society, are not at all alien to the Church. There too the dominant image is that of the self-made man or woman who can do it all alone.

6. Justice (1980, p. 143) also correlates the two sides of God's forgiveness: "The reconciled man has not only accepted forgiveness from God, but he has also forgiven himself." This interpretation of Christian Character is diametrically opposed to Leo Tolstoy's assertion that "Man's whole life is a continual contradiction of what he knows to be his duty. In every department of life, he acts in defiant opposition to the dictates of his conscience and his common sense" (cited in Willard 1988, p. 263).

7. Gribbon (1990, p. 42) relates a pertinent anecdote for the Commission theme. His meaningful encounter with a Mennonite farmer revealed Christ's love, through the mundane experience of automobile repair:

> I was in the middle of nowhere and two flats. . . . He came out, took two brand new tires out of his garage,

took them to my car, jacked the car up—wouldn't let me touch it. He took the tires off and threw them in the back of the truck and we went to another farm, changed the tires, put his new tires on my rims, put them on for me. . . . Well, I wanted to give him my driver's license or my license plus a twenty-dollar bill just for the help, and he said, "No, no, when you get tires, you just bring them back."

Never knew me. Never seen me before in his life. Well, I didn't get back fast enough for me. He knew I'd be back. But he was open, he showed me what I was looking for, and I didn't know it at that time either. But he had, right there he was right in front of me, God's love was being showed to me right there. I'd driven by this church for years, and I always wondered, What's a Mennonite? Some kind of new truck or something?

8. Adams (1989, p. 54, emphasis added), commenting on Matthew 5:20–26, discusses the significant connection between Communion and Community:

> Two phrases stand out: "Go first" (v. 24) and "Quickly come to terms" (v. 25). *Both of these phrases stress the urgency of reconciliation.* The idea of "first" being reconciled before continuing an act of worship is striking. . . . God insists you must be on good terms with your brothers and sisters if you expect to remain on good terms with Him. Your worship, if you have wronged another and not made it right with him by confession and forgiveness, is unacceptable. First (don't miss the order of priority), before offering a gift to God, straighten matters out with your brother; *the gift God really wants is reconciliation* (Ps. 51:17).

9. Diehl (1991, p. 40) illustrates "competency" by citing the broader issue of vocation: that God calls people to a wide range of services, not just to "professional ministries" like the pastorate. Diehl highlights one particular case, when a woman (from so-called secular work) caught a vision of her Commission:

> In most cases they have an intellectual understanding of the point I am making. But on one occasion I happened to say this to a reporter who had left her church out of disillusionment. She was absolutely fascinated by this concept of ministry, and we talked for some time about it. Several years later we met by chance, and she reminded me of our conversation. "I want you to know," she said, "that when you told me that I had a ministry as a reporter, something clicked inside of me. I knew it was true, and I remind myself of it every time I do a story. I've gone back to my church. Things aren't much better there than when I left, but it doesn't matter anymore. I know I am witnessing to my faith by the quality of my work."

10. Narrow views of Commission should be dismissed. Paul sums up this term, illustrating advocacy of the destitute: "we must help the weak, remembering the words the Lord Jesus himself said: 'It is more blessed to give than to receive'" (Acts 20:35). C. S. Lewis (1950, p. 180) brought out a more creative angle to Commission in his *The Lion, the Witch and the Wardrobe.* His two heroes and two heroines eventually become the kings and queens of Narnia. Lewis describes their legacy as not only a reign of peace (i.e., rec-

onciliation), but he says that they "saved good trees from being unnecessarily cut down" (p. 180). Furthermore, these rulers intervened on behalf of the oppressed. With tongue in cheek, Lewis says that they "liberated young dwarfs and young satyrs from being sent to school . . . and encouraged ordinary people who wanted to live and let live" (p. 180).

11. Details of this section are elaborated in the subsequent chapter. Since Frankena's model shows a direct correlation between Box B (the content of the *next* chapter) and Box C (the content of *this* chapter), a brief reference to Box B issues is made here.

12. The false assumption of the *tabernacle temptation* resides in the belief that holiness equals complete separation from everything. The myth of *country club* is that "family" (as opposed to nonfamily) members represent the best metaphor of the church. The *tightrope walker*, a typically Western viewpoint, clings to the misconception that leadership (contrary to Jesus' warning) must be "top-down." Thus, isolated, autocratic leadership prevails in many Christian organizations. Finally, the *Martha syndrome* falsely presupposes that busyness equals maturity. Spirituality is defined by what a person does. Therefore, in these cases, Christian or church activities saturate our calendars.

13. Recall that Frankena coins these phrases, balancing *theoretical* and *practical.* See his direct quotation in note 1 above.

14. See also Habermas (1989). This article concisely depicts six age-appropriate phases of communication.

15. See Romans 12:18. Paul provides a twofold condition to this directive. He begins the verse with "If it is possible," then adds "as far as it depends on you." It's obvious that Paul experienced his share of "difficult-to-get-along-with" individuals!

Chapter 4: Universal Quests and Unique Filters

1. Adapted from von Oech (1986, pp. 97, 99).
2. Modified from "The Temporary Gospel," in *The Other Side* (November–December 1975).
3. See Kraft (1979, p. 53).
4. Postman and Weingartner (1969, pp. 82–83) likewise remind us that teaching perspectives are shaped by the pictures or metaphors that we retain:

> For example, there is the type of teacher who believes he is in the lighting business. We may call him the Lamplighter. When he is asked what he is trying to do with his students, his reply is something like this: "I want to *illuminate* their minds, to allow some light to penetrate the darkness." Then there is the Gardener. He says, "I want to *cultivate* their minds, to fertilize them, so that the seeds I plant will flourish." There is also the Personnel Manager, who wants nothing more than to keep his students' minds busy, to make them efficient and industrious. The Muscle Builder wants to strengthen flabby minds, and the Bucket Filler wants to fill them up. How should we talk about "the human mind" and our always imperfect attempts to do something to it?

5. Recall that Box B (the substance of this chapter) should draw on empirical data, according to Frankena. Research from the social sciences, in particular, is featured in the subsequent sections.

6. See Marcia (1980, especially p. 160). Cliff Schimmels collected data from his personal, year-long observation of schools. He visited more than two hundred classrooms in more than seventy-five different settings. Combining the topic of motivation with self-concept, Schimmels (1989, p. 9, emphasis added) introduces his book as follows: "There may be more controversial subjects to concern ourselves with, but there is none more important. There is *no single factor which has more influence* on how successful any student is or how successful the schooling process is *than what that individual student thinks of himself.*" Schimmels (p. 26) also confesses his bias toward lifelong identity struggles: "When you are young, self-image is a day-by-day and even moment-by-moment affair. (Actually, it may not be all that different when you are older.)"

7. See Erikson (1968, p. 94). In his later works, Erikson modified some of his terms and concepts. For instance, "industry" was changed to "mastery," although the essence of this phase remained intact.

8. These life segments are: school-age children, younger adulthood, and older adulthood.

9. As a case in point, Erikson's childhood task of "industry/mastery" may be expanded to include lifelong challenges of Christian stewardship. Historically, this concept has been called "vocation." Recent studies have traced this word to the Latin *vocare* ("to call") and *vocatio* ("call" or "calling"). Fowler (1987) provides an invaluable reference point for the church in this regard. His second and third chapters of *Faith Development and Pastoral Care* offer a useful look at the original meaning of vocation: "And more, in the tradition of *vocatio* there is the conviction that our place, our office, our vocation, is not merely a destiny to which God assigns us but a place of *creative partnership to which God calls us* and in which God chooses to meet us and bring our work to some significant contribution to the purposes of God" (p. 31, emphasis added).

10. The three "filters" virtually overlap the three major divisions of philosophy: (1) *people* represent metaphysics (the study of reality), since anthropology portrays a primary (although partial) component of this division; (2) *truth* correlates with epistemology (the study of what is true and validating sources); and (3) *lifestyle* reflects axiology (the study of values, especially ethics and aesthetics).

Through these "trifocals," Frankena's (1965, p. 8) own definition of Box B—"empirical and other premises about human nature, life and the world"—is suitably addressed.

Frankena's theory warrants the inclusion of diverse truth sources, including scientific discoveries as well as statements of faith. Frankena (1965, p. 9) broadly notes: "Much of the character of a philosophy of education depends on the nature and content of the statements it includes and makes use of in [Boxes] B and D. Whether it is scientific or unscientific, naturalistic or supernaturalistic, secular or religious . . . depends entirely on what propositions it puts into B and D and makes use of in order to reach the normative conclusion in C and E."

11. For another example of Christ's critique of "filters," read Luke 13:1–5. First, Jesus condemns the prideful "we-they" mentality of his audience (i.e., the filter of *people*). The crowd believes that, because they have been spared from two catastrophes, God has blessed them. They are superior individuals, they think. Simultaneously, Jesus judges their perception of fact (i.e., *truth*); they mistakenly believe that "misfortune equals judgment." The Master Teacher corrects this distortion of reality. Finally, the Lord tells them to "repent" (i.e., *lifestyle*) or they will "all perish."

Through his critique of *private filters* (many in the audience probably were amazed that Jesus knew their sinful hearts so well), Christ also addresses the *public* (or universal) *quests:* he acknowledges that humans do raise common questions (in this case) about immortality and integrity, even though their answers may be wrong.

12. Appendix B provides additional social science research featuring the quests and the filters.

13. See von Oech (1983, p. 25).

14. The controversial issue of psychological (versus logical) ordering of curriculum is analyzed in subsequent chapters.

15. In addition, Hiebert (1976/1983, p. 356) provides the following useful interpretation of worldview. Our trifocal categorization has been inserted, along with the technical philosophical divisions that Hiebert acknowledges:

> Behind the observable patterns of human cultures seem to lie certain assumptions about the way the world is put together . Some of these assumptions, called "existential postulates," deal with the nature of reality, the organization of the universe, and the ends and purposes of human life [i.e., a focus on metaphysics or *people*]. Others, values and norms, differentiate between good and evil, right and wrong [i.e., a focus on axiology or *lifestyle*]. Some of these assumptions are made explicit in the beliefs and myths of the people [i.e., a focus on epistemology or *truth*]. Others appear to the anthropologist to be implicit in people's behavior. Taken together, the assumptions the anthropologist uses to explain a people's total response to their universe are sometimes called a "worldview."

16. It is significant to realize—based, in part, on an understanding of Frankena's theory—that the universal quests that all people experience (Box B) are fully answered through God's themes (Box C). In other words, the four "Is" are resolved through the four "Cs."

Chapter 5: Patterns of Growth: The Structural Dimension

1. Responses are taken from interviews conducted by students of the EMS 503 Learning Process class at Western Seminary, 1990.

2. "In Jesus, for the first time a human being was developing under ideal conditions, unimpeded by heredity or acquired defects" (Thomas and Gundry 1988, p. 40).

Erickson (1985, p. 735) comments on the deity and humanity of Jesus:

> The union of the two natures meant that they did not function independently. . . . His [Jesus'] actions were always those of divinity-humanity. This is the key to understanding the functional limitations which the humanity imposed upon the divinity. For example, he still had the power to be everywhere (omnipresence). However, as an incarnate being, he was limited in the exercise of that power by possession of a human body. Similarly, he was still omniscient, but he possessed and exercised knowledge in connection with a human organism which grew gradually in terms of consciousness, whether of physical environment or eternal truths. Thus, only gradually did his limited human psyche be-

come aware of who he was and what he had come to accomplish. Yet this should not be considered a reduction of the power and capacities of the Second Person of the Trinity, but rather a circumstance-induced limitation on the exercise of his power and capacities.

3. For another example from Scripture regarding differences in reasoning ability, consider the concept of the "age of moral accountability." The idea assumes some kind of a demarcation in cognitive capacity, that moral accountability cannot be reckoned to those who are incapable of full cognizance of their actions, such as very small children and those who are severely mentally retarded. Deuteronomy 1:39 gives some support for such a concept: "And the little ones that you said would be taken captive, your children who do not yet know good from bad—they will enter the land. I will give it to them and they will take possession of it" (see also Isa. 7:15–16).

4. Additional information related to this subject can be found in Appendix C.

5. The Greek word group of *auxano* (here translated as "grow") takes its point of reference from the botanical sciences. "Behind the use of the simple form there plainly stands the thought of growth in creation, especially in the plant kingdom. . . . The combination with *karpophereo* (Col. 1:16 and 10) again shows that we have here an image from the plant kingdom" (Delling 1972, p. 518). The *auxano* word group, appearing twenty-five times in the New Testament, is used of lilies (Matt. 6:28), mustard trees (Matt. 13:32), and the body (Luke 1:80). Metaphorically, it points to the spiritual growth of the body of Christ (Col. 2:19). With reference to such figurative growth in believers, Scripture records the use of *auxano* with reference to (1) the ministry of God's Word (Acts 12:24; Col. 1:6); (2) believers (Eph. 4:15; 1 Pet. 2:2); and (3) specific factors such as faith (2 Cor. 10:15), the knowledge of God (Col. 1:10), and the grace of the Lord (2 Pet. 3:18).

Of significance in this botanical metaphor is that there must be a correspondence between the nature of the *seed* and the nature of the *mature plant* (James 3:12). The analogy of the seed conveys the appropriate imagery of our spiritual and human natures. We are complete, based on both *natural* birth and *spiritual* rebirth. As we obey and trust God, our human nature unfolds and matures (Phil. 2:12–13).

6. This summary of the aspects of human development provides a way to organize past research efforts as well as to guide future research efforts. Throughout this chapter, the work of social science researchers will be cited to clarify how humans tend to grow. Most of these social science researchers are not evangelical believers. Yet "all truth is God's truth" (Gaebelein 1954; Holmes 1977) no matter who uncovers the truth. Regardless of whether the researcher is a believer or not, conclusions drawn from empirical research studies must be held tentatively, because additional data may clarify an interpretation or even contradict it.

From a Christian perspective, a major problem of social science research is that the people being studied are in a fallen condition. Even subjects who are regenerated are not "fully" human. Only in our glorified state will we truly manifest God's full design of humanity. Coupled with this problem is that the social science researchers themselves succumb to this same limitation. And faulty viewpoints, whether of believers or nonbelievers, likewise pertain.

See Pazmiño (1988, chap. 6) for a discussion of the major views of integrating social science knowledge with Scripture. See Wilhoit (1991) for guidelines about how evangelicals can approach social science research. Also, as an example of its utility for educational ministry, Eugene Gibbs of Wheaton Graduate School regularly reviews relevant social science studies in the *Christian Education Journal*.

7. The study of human development can be approached in three main ways: (1) a *topical* approach traces the changes in one area of human growth as a person matures from childhood to adulthood (e.g., first cognitive growth; then social growth; then moral growth); (2) a *chronological* approach discusses all of the areas of human development, first, in childhood, then, in adolescence, and, finally, in adulthood; (3) a *theory* or *theorist* approach presents the major theories of human development (e.g., Erikson, Piaget). It discusses the advantages and limitations of each. In this chapter we take primarily a topical approach. For discussions of human development from a Christian perspective, see Sparkman (1983), Aleshire (1988), and Steele (1990).

8. God has placed within our bodies an internal developmental clock that regulates both the timing and sequence of the physical maturation process. We have baby teeth before we have adult teeth, for example. In addition, this clock regulates the outside boundaries of our physical members, such as height. A different "clock setting" is given to God's other creatures. For example, it takes approximately one to two years for horses to reach adult form.

9. J. Singh, who directed an orphanage in India, kept a journal of the progress of two young girls who had been reared by wolves (Singh and Zingg 1939). Both girls died before they reached adolescence. The second half of this book recounts other bizarre cases where children lived under extremely repressive conditions. More recently, the Associated Press reported a case in which a four-year-old had been kept in a pen with sixty dogs (*[Tacoma] News Tribune*, March 17, 1990). The newly assigned foster parents were astounded that "he ran wildly through the house, crashing into walls, and most of the time he ran on all fours. If he wanted attention, he would run up to us and paw at our bodies, rub his head on us and wimper" (p. 1).

10. The purely materialistic view of human nature reduces an understanding of persons to what can be scientifically measured: physical acts and brain states, a naturalistic monism. The Bible teaches a "conditioned" or "holistic" duality of the constituent elements of personhood. We are both body (material) *and* soul (immaterial). See Appendix C for further comments.

11. Additional material on physical development is presented in Appendix C. A fuller discussion of the physical domain is beyond the scope of this chapter. The reader can consult any standard textbook on human development for more information (see, e.g., Newman and Newman 1991; Dworetzky 1981).

12. Piaget (1896–1981) offered a theory of cognitive-structural development that has significantly influenced psychology and education. In testing the IQ of children in France, Piaget was puzzled about the wrong answers children supplied. Further assessment led him to postulate that children's reasoning ability moves through *qualitatively* different forms before achieving full adult capabilities (Piaget and Inhelder 1969).

13. The age ranges listed for each stage are suggestive and not prescriptive.

14. Reported by Larry Wood, one of our students.

15. The use of geometric shapes to portray the qualitative changes in cognitive development was suggested by J. T. Dillon, associate professor of education, University of California, Riverside.

16. Further refinements into eight general phases or stages have been suggested by Fisher and Silvern (1985). See Flavell and Markham (1983) for a general review of cognitive development. An alternate theory of cognitive development is offered by American behavioral psychologist Robert Gagne (1977). His "cumulative learning theory" attempts to explain the effects predicted by Piagetian theory without reference to any qualitative or structural stage changes. "Learning is cumulative then, because particular intellectual skills are transferable to a number of higher-order skills and to a variety of problems to be solved. . . . These cumulative effects of learning are the basis for observed increases of intellectual 'power' in developing human beings" (p. 145).

17. Ward (unpublished handout, n.d.) draws a parallel between Piaget's four stages and God's progressive dealings with his people throughout history.

•Sensorimotor   Adam–Noah

Leadership and communication are personal, active, and experiential.

•Preoperational   Babel–Exodus

Communication is through signs, events, and people used as examples and signs.

•Concrete Operations   Sinai–Christ

Abstractions are made specific in tables and codes of law with special emphasis on ritual and concrete symbols. God's Word is put into Scripture for the first time.

•Formal Operations   Christ–Present

Emphasis is transferred to the underlying and unifying principles; sacrifices are transferred to "living sacrifice."

"There is a parallel between the stages of cognitive development of a human being (as understood through the research of the Swiss psychologist Jean Piaget) and development of God's progressive revelations. It is not clear why the parallel exists." These are general parallels for the whole period as God's mode of communication. It does not signify that individual persons within that period operated only at that cognitive stage.

18. Answers for the reading level and Bible version quiz:

A. 11th grade	New American Standard Version
B. 3rd grade	International Children's Version
C. 14th grade	King James Version
D. 9th grade	New King James Version
E. 7th grade	New International Version

Reading levels are reported in Kohlenberger (1987, p. 6) based on an analysis of thirty-six passages using the Fog Reading Index. Kohlenberger discusses two main criteria to consider in selecting a Bible translation: accuracy and readability.

19. The Greek of the New Testament was not the literary or classical Greek, but the common (koine) Greek spoken in the marketplace. Up until the time of the Reformation, the most common Bible version in the Western church was Jerome's fourth-century Latin translation, the Vulgate.

20. Research on emotions has focused primarily on three main aspects: nonverbal expressive components, verbal components of emotional language, and physiological components (Hesse and Cicchetti 1982, p. 10). These components are typically treated in conjunction with the growth of the self, explaining both the cognitive and emotional aspects. See Cicchetti and Hesse (1982) for a discussion of theories of emotional development.

21. Buss and Plomin (1984) identify a third factor: sociability, or one's preference to be alone or with others. It may be better to view this factor as one aspect of our "self-regulation" tendencies.

22. One popular four-factor temperament theory, to be discussed in Chapter 17, suggests guidelines for improving our working relationships. Understanding the temperament patterns of others can steer us away from unnecessary conflict.

23. Research on identical twins may provide some answers. For example, one University of Minnesota study of 348 pairs of twins, including some reared in different homes, indicates that heredity has a stronger influence than environment on many central personality traits (Goleman 1986).

24. The technical term for this process and tension is "object relations," or more properly, "subject-object relations" (see Kegan 1982, chap. 3). Object relations theory suggests that healthy growth of the self takes place within good relationships. Steele (1990, pp. 107–8) briefly discusses this concept as one of five essential components in his understanding of Christian maturity. One central factor that we must integrate into a healthy sense of self is gender (see Van Leeuwen 1990).

25. See Thomas (1991) for a brief survey of this "death-life paradox" concept in the New Testament.

26. For a more extensive discussion of the theory and practice of Erikson's theory from a Christian perspective, see Steele (1990, Chapters 10–12) and Sparkman (1983). Steele's (p. 132) adaptation of the stages is listed below:

Infancy:	Nurturing versus Neglecting
Childhood:	Enculturating and Training versus Ignoring
Early Adolescence:	Belonging versus Alienating
Adolescence:	Searching versus Entrenching
Young Adulthood:	Consolidating versus Fragmenting
Middle Adulthood:	Reappraising versus Re-entrenching
Later Adulthood:	Anticipating versus Dreading

27. Despite the practical utility of the theory, the major criticism is that it has been difficult to substantiate empirically. Recent research suggests that some of Erikson's polarities may not actually be true polarities existing on eight separate continua, but rather contributing features of two major dimensions: positive factors and negative factors.

Ledbetter (1991) analyzed various proposals for understanding Erikson's theory as: a two-factor theory (positive and negative factors), a three-factor theory (positive, negative, and a third factor), an eight-factor theory (traditional view of Erikson's theory), and an eleven-factor theory (a combination of bipolar and unipolar factors). Ledbetter's study is based on the national sample data of the "Measures of Psychosocial Development" developed by Hawley (1988).

In our own understanding of Erikson's theory, we prefer to coordinate the various crises with the four lifespan themes of our Reconciliation Model of maturity (see Chapter 3). Thus, we believe the issues highlighted by Erikson are equally important throughout life.

28. Both Kegan (1982) and Loevinger (1976) outline such stage theories. Kegan, building on a Piagetian cognitive-structural base, outlines six stages. The first three are linked to the sensorimotor, preoperational, and concrete operational periods, respectively. The final three stages fit with the formal operations stage.

Chapter 6: Patterns of Growth: The Functional Dimension

1. Our faith in God is both a gift we *receive* from him (Eph. 2:8) and what we actively *place* in him (Heb. 11:6; see also Phil. 2:12–13). The content of our faith in God adjusts developmentally as we grow older. Consider the following suggestive outline.

   During infancy and early childhood, the content of what we know about God is based on the characteristics and lives of *persons:* our parents and other early caregivers.

   In childhood, we shift our focus to *Jesus of the Gospels*—God in the flesh, the immanent God we see in pictures. At this stage in our life, we need concrete images. To previous knowledge gained from our parents and others, we add the stories of Jesus.

   In adolescence and early adulthood, we begin to think about the transcendent God—*God the Father*. We are aware that there is a Trinity, but practically, we act as if there is only one person in the Godhead. It's much easier to get to know one person than three persons.

   Sometime in later adulthood (for some earlier) we may grow to know God as a being in fellowship—*the trinitarian God.*

   Authors such as Houston (1989) and Piper (1986) have challenged us to a deeper walk with God. Donald Joy (1985) asserts that "God's relationship with humans is one of intimate bonding, and that all human intimacies are 'rehearsals' for the ultimate reunion of humans with their creator" (p. ix).

2. In attempting to measure the progress of faith in believers we are caught in a double bind situation. One means of assessing faith development is to collect self-reports about one's relationship with God from a variety of individuals in different seasons of life. In our review, one example of this line of research is included. Similarly, we could study the reports of how one's awareness of and conception of God change. (For summaries of this line of research, see Godin, 1965; Ratcliff 1985; and Meier et al. 1991, pp. 249–50). Yet James 2:14–26 indicates such verbal expressions of faith are not very reliable indicators. Genuine faith must express itself in observable ways, since "faith without deeds is dead" (v. 26). Another means to study faith development would be to study the actions and personal habits of those who give evidence of great faith (cf. Willard 1988). Yet, in focusing on good deeds we encounter another problem. Jesus claimed that good deeds alone will not guarantee

that living faith exists (cf. Matt. 7:22–23). Thus, the more holistic picture we are able to glean, the more accurate will be our understanding of faith development. And, we should be cautious and tentative about investigations into faith development.

3. James Fowler (1981, 1986) has offered a theory of "faith" stages. This stage theory is significantly influenced by his former Harvard colleague, Kohlberg, and by Piaget. The thought of H. Richard Niebuhr provides theological foundations for Fowler's understanding of faith (Fowler's doctoral dissertation is an investigation of Niebuhr's theology). We would agree with Fowler's purpose for developing his theory: "Our restlessness for divine companionship, if denied, ignored, or distorted, dehumanizes us and we destroy each other. Recognized and nurtured, it brings us into that companionship with God which frees us for genuine partnership with our sisters and brothers, and for friendship with creation" (1986, p. 40). Yet, two foundational difficulties with Fowler's theory stand out for evangelical believers: (1) Fowler's understanding of "faith" is so broad and ecumenical that *all* persons have faith (i.e., there is no such thing as a "unbelief" or "unfaithfulness"); and (2) the most mature form of faith is defined not by some content or particular belief about God, but rather by one's capacities for perspective taking and reflection, whether or not one is a Christian, a Jew, or a Muslim. See Dykstra and Parks (1986) for a summary and critique of Fowler's theory. See Lee (1990) for helpful study of the concept of faith, primarily within the Christian tradition. For a review of research on faith and religion, see Steele (1989) and Maloney (1990).

4. One important interpersonal skill for believers to master is that of conflict resolution. In our litigious society, Americans use immature and destructive means to get their way. In response to the challenge of 1 Corinthians 5, the Christian Conciliation Service was formed as a means to help believers resolve large and small conflicts within the church (see Buzzard and Eck 1982).

5. For an introduction to cultural psychology, see Stigler et al. (1990). See Lingenfelter (and Mayer's, 1986; 1992) for a model of cross-cultural ministry.

6. Holmes (1991) presents a similar outline. He provides an eleven-step process of attaining Christian character:

Phase 1: Forming the Conscience
(1) consciousness-raising; (2) consciousness-sensitizing; (3) values analysis; (4) values clarification; (5) values criticism
Phase 2: Learning to Make Wise Decisions
(6) moral imagination; (7) ethical analysis; (8) moral decision making
Phase 3: Developing Character
(9) responsible agents; (10) virtue development; (11) moral identity

Space considerations limit a discussion of each area identified above. Additional practical insights can be gleaned from Wolterstorff (1980), Ward (1989), Willard (1988), Smedes (1986), and Toon (1984). For a helpful guide on how to go about developing new habits, see Watson and Tharp (1989). Parents will appreciate the many helpful hints offered by Lickona (1983).

7. Predominantly cognitively oriented social science researchers focus on conscience. They publish findings under the terms "moral development" and "moral education" (see Sapp 1986). Behavioral-oriented researchers focus on

lifestyle habits. They tend to use the term "prosocial behavior" to describe their work (see Staub et al. 1984; Bridgeman 1983). Kurtines and Gewirtz (1987) include various research traditions in their edited work. A few studies have investigated moral development at Christian colleges and Bible colleges (Shaver 1985, 1987; Rahn 1991) and seminaries (Issler and Ward 1989).

In an attempt to draw upon the findings of all schools of research about the subject Rest (1983, 1986) suggests that there are at least four components involved in taking a moral action: (1) moral sensitivity (being aware of and correctly interpreting a situation as involving a moral issue); (2) moral reasoning (making a decision as to the ideal course of action); (3) moral motives and values (considering extenuating factors that will affect the final course of action to be taken); and (4) moral character or courage (executing the plan of action, despite any countervailing forces). Rest then organizes various past research efforts under these four major headings.

8. Though aspects of Kohlberg's moral reasoning stage theory are useful in Christian education, evangelicals should be aware of his problematic assumptions: (1) a naturalistic-atheistic basis (morality can stand on its own apart from religion); (2) an anthropocentric view of moral autonomy (the highest stage of moral reasoning involves freedom from all outside influences, including divine authority; thus Christians and others holding to divine authority typically receive lower moral stage scores); (3) a narrow view of the essence of morality that focuses on justice and fairness, thus eliminating Christianity's important twin foundations of truth (including justice) *and* love; and (4) an overemphasis on the liberal agenda of individual rights and individualistic decision making, devaluing individual responsibility and ignoring the community as an important resource in decision making. For a recent summary of Kohlberg's contribution, see Kuhmerker (1991).

9. The following discussion is also based on Kohlberg's theory of stages of moral reasoning. Rather than focusing on six stages or three levels of hierarchical reasoning, we focus on the three lenses of concern identified in Kohlberg's three levels. This adaptation, though related to Kohlberg's theory, issues from a scriptural basis.

10. Kohlberg's theory suggests, and we would agree, that becoming an adult does not guarantee that one would regularly incorporate God's principles in decision making. Reaching adulthood only suggests that we are now *capable* of such thinking, not that we actually *use* it. Thus, we see the need to challenge teens and adults to more comprehensive patterns of thinking.

11. In 1974, Kohlberg began to study growth in both moral reasoning *and* moral behavior in what they labeled the "just community." Working with a few groups of high school students (in an on-campus alternative setting in which both students and staff participated by choice), they challenged students to deal with their own "real life" moral situations. Staff and students would agree on corporate solutions and actions regarding matters of school governance (related to both academic and student conduct issues). The central feature of the program involved a "town hall"-like meeting in which policy was debated and enacted and punishment was meted out to those who violated these policies. Based on this kind of research (especially studies completed in the last decade of his life), Kohlberg concluded that the most effective way for individuals to become people of justice and morality is to experi-

ence this within a democratically oriented "just community" (Power, Higgins, and Kohlberg 1989). Since the church aspires to be a community of holiness, this particular line of research offers potential implications for church leaders to consider.

12. In his discussion of the concept of vocation, Fowler (1984) first outlines what vocation is *not* (a job, profession, or career). He then proposes that "Vocation is the response a person makes with his or her total self to the address of God and to the calling of partnership. The shaping of vocation as total response of the self to the address of God involves the orchestration of our leisure, our relationships, our work, our private life, our public life, and of the resources we steward, so as to put it all at the disposal of God's purposes in the services of God" (pp. 94–95).

13. For example, in the last chapter of this book, Ted Ward's three-part developmental path for teachers is presented.

14. This grid is an application of the situational leadership model developed by Hersey and Blanchard (1982). The model will be discussed in Chapter 17.

15. Additional information on training others is presented in Chapters 17 and 18.

16. The phrase "optimal human development" is used by Steele (1990, p. 106).

17. Ward (1989, p. 18) suggests a different way for organizing the domains of human development. He uses the human hand to illustrate the relationship among the various aspects of human development.

The spiritual domain is not viewed as a separate sixth finger, but as the underlying, invisible foundation that sustains and interacts with more visible domains of human development.

18. Owen (1956–57) understands Hebrews 5:11–6:3 to articulate a three-stage growth outline, very similar to the three levels of 1 John 2. Stage 1 describes babes in Christ. Because of a lack of experience, they have not achieved a lifestyle in accord with a moral standard. They can receive only the milk of the Word. Stage 2 characterizes those who are in the process of developing a standard of moral righteousness through experiential training. Stage 3 is for those who are mature, having already developed their moral standard through practice. They are now able to receive the solid food of the Word.

Another passage requiring additional study is 2 Peter 1:5–9. Seven virtues grow sequentially from a foundation of faith. Commentators disagree whether Peter intended a *growth* progression or was simply using a literary device.

19. Systematic theologies also outline distinctive paths to maturity in the Christian life. Summary diagrams of various paths can be found in Ryrie (1969) and Richards (1987). A discussion of the similarities and differences in these paths, as found in Wesleyan, Reformed, Pentecostal, Keswick, and Dispensational theologies is available in Dieter et al. (1987). For example, one major difference between theologies of the sanctification process is whether or not believers must have a postsalvation blessing/dedication experience.

Chapter 7: Aspects of Learning

1. "In the eighteenth century and much of the nineteenth, phlebotomy [bloodletting] held a position in therapeutics comparable to that of antibiotics today. For inflammatory diseases, such as pneumonia, phlebotomy was the traditional and generally accepted method of treatment" (King 1991, p. 192). In a defense of this traditional practice, one nineteenth-century physician wrote: "the efficiency of bloodletting in the treatment of pneumonia, is not an error and a delusion; it has its foundation in nature and in truth . . . clear, intelligible, philosophical demonstration" (Bartlett 1848, p. 42).

2. Various methods were used to drain the blood, depending on the physician's training, skill, and background. Some doctors would cut a vein (called "phlebotomy") and let the blood pour into a bowl. Or they might heat a cup and then apply it to the cut to draw out the blood. There was the more "mechanical" method—applying leeches! With this method, the doctor had to be skilled in locating a vein. To drain the required amount of blood (about twenty ounces) took about twenty leeches. To conserve leeches, the doctor could use just one leech by cutting off a part of it so the leech would not become fully engorged. But then the leech would die and it could not be reused (Copeman 1960).

   Amazing as it may seem, leeches are still used in medicine today. When a small part of the body (e.g., an ear or a finger) is being reattached, the arteries can be repaired, but the veins are too small to suture. The reimplanted part becomes engorged with blood and may be lost. In such cases, leeches remove the blood, which decreases the swelling and allows the veins to heal (personal conversation, Dr. Mary Wilder, July 17, 1991). For further information about this modern practice, see Gonzales (1987).

3. In addition to the fluids, there were four basic properties: heat, cold, moisture, and dryness. The four temperaments, a combination of these properties, were labeled after the names of the four humors, apparently sharing similar characteristics: sanguine (hot and moist), phlegmatic (cold and moist), choleric (hot and dry), and melancholic (cold and dry) (Copeman 1960, pp. 87–88).

4. An older definition of Christian education affirms this particular orientation: "Christian education is a reverent attempt to discover the divinely ordained process by which individuals grow in Christlikeness, and to work with that process" (Harner 1939, p. 20).

5. This chapter represents Box D in our analytical model for educational ministry—the study of how we learn. This section analyzes pertinent biblical and research knowledge about educational psychology.

6. "For instance, in spite of its long history and its estimable list of supporters, the [exclusive] notion of 'God as Teacher' fails, since in the end, human teachers do the teaching and the role of the human teacher must be explicated. Is he a deluded puppet or merely a mechanical intermediary?" (Williamson 1970, p. 113).

7. In *The Disappearance of Childhood*, Neil Postman identifies how various technological inventions have irreversibly transformed the way we think. Significant implications arise from this book for Christian education.

8. The unique contemporary contributions of the lecture method will be discussed in Chapter 10, which deals with teaching methods.

9. This confusion is apparent in how we talk about teaching, as pointed out by these comments from three different teachers: "I teach math"; "I teach history"; "I teach *students*" (from Mager 1984a, p. 112).

10. The next chapter offers a more extensive look at the third category, "avenues" of learning. More space is devoted to this middle factor since it pertains to the essential aspect of Box D in our model—the theory by which we determine the means (Box E) to accomplish our goals (Box C).

11. In some Sunday school curricula, a general reference to these three domains appears in the instructional aims of each lesson as

Sunday school	Our terms	Educational terms
"to know"	Cognition	Cognitive domain
"to feel"	Conviction	Affective domain
"to do"	Competence	Psychomotor domain

12. Two additional domains are suggested by Lee (1985): "self-discipline" and "lifestyle." Lee (p. 30, n. 5) hypothesizes that self-discipline seems to be a discrete category but he judges the empirical data to be insufficient. We see this important aspect fitting into the psychomotor or competence domain. Lee's "lifestyle" domain is treated in Chapter 9 of his book. This domain focuses on a holistic integration of the discrete learning domains. We agree that the whole is greater than the sum of the parts. We have used the synthesis of "reconciliation" and the four themes to address this need for synthesis. More thought should be given to an integrative view of learning. See Steinaker and Bell (1979) for one attempt to integrate the various domains into one taxonomic guide for teaching practice.

13. This three-part continuum is suggested by Lee (1985, p. 159).

14. In the experience of the apostles, significant growth took place in their knowledge, values, and actions regarding the Great Commission. Initially, the commission was legitimately focused solely on the nation of Israel (Matt. 10:5–6). This Jewish exclusiveness continued to cloud the apostles' understanding even after they received Jesus' "universal" commission (Matt. 28:19–20; Acts 1:8), as indicated by their Jewish-only activity in subsequent chapters in Acts. Following Peter's encounter with Cornelius, he professes: "I now realize how true it is that God does not show favoritism but accepts men from every nation who fear him and do what is right" (Acts 10:34–35). Prompted by events during Paul and Barnabas' first missionary experience (Acts 13), the apostles and the church officially affirmed a universal commission to the whole world at the Jerusalem Council (Acts 15).

15. Since the cognitive aspects of learning are foundational to teaching in formal settings, we will devote more attention to a clarification of this particular domain. A detailed analysis of the cognitive domain is provided in a self-instructional text for Sunday school teachers developed by Ford (1978).

16. Dan Stevens, one of our colleagues, uses this bicycle illustration to explain the various categories of Bloom's taxonomy.

17. Williams and Haladyne (1982) developed an alternative taxonomy for the cognitive domain. Their typology was developed to provide more guidance for higher-order test item construction.

18. See Chapter 11, n. 13 for a brief description of Krathwohl's taxonomy for the affective domain. Due to the complexity

of relating such factors as emotions, attitudes, values, and motivation, it is difficult to create one holistic taxonomy. Mager (1984a) isolates "attitude" in learning.

19. No standard taxonomy of educational objectives has emerged as the dominant summary of the psychomotor domain; a few have been developed. See Simpson (1966); Harrow (1969); Kibler, Barker, and Miles (1970); and Jewett and Mullan (1977). Ford (1978) provides a brief introduction to this psychomotor domain and uses Simpson's categories:

Perception	Becoming aware of objects and their qualities through one or more of the senses
Set	The readiness to perform a particular action
Guided response	Performing under the guidance of a model
Mechanism	The ability to perform a task consistently with some degree of confidence and proficiency
Complex overt response	The ability to perform a task with a high degree of confidence and proficiency
Adaptation	Performing new but related tasks based on previously learned motor skills
Origination	From understanding, abilities, and skills developed in the psychomotor area, the student creates new performances

When teaching new skills, it is helpful, first, to perform a "task analysis" by which the various subskills are identified and then taught (see Davis, Alexander, and Yelon 1974).

Regarding the topic of lifestyle habits, a similar but more simple continuum may prove helpful. Before working on a habit, the particular behavior is largely in Phase 1 (see progression below). Through systematic effort, the behavior comes under the individual's control (Phase 2). As the behavior becomes routine, it becomes a "second nature" habit (Phase 3).

Phase 1: Uncontrolled (out of control) by self
Phase 2: Controlled by self
Phase 3: Automatically controlled by self

See Watson and Tharp (1989) for additional guidance on developing lifestyle habits.

20. Another relevant topic related to the "extent" component is short- and long-term retention—our ability to recall what we have learned. Research focusing on what inhibits this recall suggests two main theories of "forgetting": (1) *inactivity* ("what you don't use, you lose"); and (2) *interference* (either old learning prevents new learning or new learning "erases" or blocks out old learning).

"Forgetting" is a major hindrance for God's people (Deut. 4:9; 6:12; 8:11). Various strategies encourage better retrieval of learned information: overlearning, deeper understanding of concepts (versus rote learning), emphasis on meaningful learning, and memory devices. A discussion of short- and long-term memory functioning is beyond the scope of this book. Standard educational psychology textbooks such as Sprinthall and Sprinthall (1990) provide a useful introduction.

21. Hendricks' (1987) masterful book on teaching is packed with gems to inspire any teacher of God's Word. Keller's (1987) integrative ARCS model of motivation summarizes four basic motivational factors: attention, relevance, confidence, and satisfaction. These factors pinpoint motivational problems and help teachers select appropriate remedies. Since the latter three concepts overlap with the three "avenues" of learning discussed in the next chapter, only a brief review is included here.

Attention. Students fail to learn because they are not fully listening (i.e., attending) to what is being taught. The concentration span of individuals varies—some can remain at a task for hours; others give continued effort for only a short time span. For some, the classroom may be too warm; others may be distracted due to emotional pain (such as a recent argument with a close friend). Effective teachers capture and sustain students' curiosity through novel introductions, humor, interesting personal stories, puzzling questions, and captivating dilemmas.

Relevance. The lesson material, in competition with other pressing matters, may have little or no connection to learners' needs. Students often ask why a chosen topic is valuable and how it is applicable to their life. Practical examples, exercises geared to students' life situations, and explanations concerning topic use confront this second factor.

Confidence. Students may lack self-assurance, either in themselves or in their ability to meet classroom demands. Their negative perspective hinders their ability to learn. Accordingly, teacher expectations play an important role. Believe in your students' potential. Anticipate positive outcomes, through verbal and nonverbal communication. As Bruce Wilkinson challenges in his "Seven Laws of the Learner" seminars, teachers need to become "people blossomers."

Satisfaction. Some students stockpile too many dissatisfying learning experiences; these hurtful memories prevent future efforts to learn. Busywork, condescending behaviors, speaking over the heads of students, and uncomfortable physical settings contribute to such attitudes. Praising students' efforts and relating newly learned concepts to life situations help students experience a sense of satisfaction.

22. Since learning is, in large measure, an internal process, we can never fully see learning take place; we often notice only the *effects* of learning (see John 3:8).

23. Answer to the Think about It: "Learning for Christians is change [nature] which is facilitated through deliberate or incidental experience [avenues], under the supervision of the Holy Spirit [nature], and in which one acquires and regularly integrates [extent] age-appropriate [readiness] knowledge, attitudes, values, emotions, skills, and habits [levels] into an increasingly Christ-like lifestyle [nature]."

Chapter 8: Avenues of Learning

1. The term "Information-Processing" is used by Joyce et al. (1992) with reference to our "drive to make sense of the world by acquiring and organizing data, sensing problems and generating solutions to them, and developing concepts and language for conveying them" (p. 7).

2. Since such metaphors are culturally and historically specific, we must transform these biblical illustrations into contemporary ones. "Shepherds," "sheep," and "vineyards" are no longer relevant to many contemporary believers.

3. The concept of identification or "meaningful" learning is developed by Ausubel (1963, 1968). One instructional strategy introduced by Ausubel is the "advance organizer." Prior to the introduction of new material, the teacher first ("advance") presents a conceptual framework, indicating how the new concept fits in with the larger body of knowledge ("organizer"). For example, when teaching an Old Testament lesson, the teacher can help the student organize Old Testament history using this simple chart of three basic periods of time, revolving around the most well-known period of history, the period of the kings:

Prekingdom Period	Kingdom Period		Postkingdom Period
Individual Leaders	Judges	United Kingdom	Divided Kingdom	Exile Return

Some confuse this technique with the brief overview sometimes presented at the beginning of class when the teacher outlines the material to be covered in that session. This particular activity is helpful—it explains the lesson agenda—but it is not an advance organizer. The advance organizer attempts to fit new information within a *conceptual* outline of a broader knowledge base. For example, the acrostic "LEARN" is an advance organizer for the concept of learning.

4. The theoretical background for the inquiry category stems from Festinger's (1957) cognitive dissonance theory and Piaget's (1977) concept of equilibration. An introductory treatment of Piaget's cognitive development theory was provided in Chapter 5.

5. In addition, our conscience is designed to provide feedback regarding our thoughts and actions (Rom. 2:15). For helpful studies of conscience, see Toon (1984) and Issler (in press).

6. Consequence Learning is based on "operant" or "respondent" behavioral conditioning, as initially developed by Skinner (1953). A treatment of these concepts from a Christian perspective is provided by Bufford (1981).

7. Even though certain disciples were initially introduced to Jesus by John the Baptist as the Lamb of God (John 1:29), it took about two years for the disciples to fully recognize Jesus as the Messiah. Besides the resurrection, the feeding of the five thousand is the only miracle that is recorded by all four Gospel writers, signifying its importance.

8. Such diverse skills as learning a foreign language and playing the piano depend on Cue Learning. For example, in playing the piano, we make two major forms of linkages: (1) between the different dots on a page and the appropriate keys to play, and (2) habit patterns of playing each key in proper sequence with the result that our fingers just "flow" across the keyboard.

9. Cue Learning (or "classical" conditioning) with its basic concept of "conditioned reflex" was developed in America by Watson (1930). A brief, readable discussion of both Consequence and Cue Learning is found in Chapters 5–7 of Mager (1984a) and in Gagne (1977). Gagne discusses the concept of "chaining." He explains how habits are developed through the combination of Consequence (operant conditioning) and Cue (classical conditioning) Learning.

10. Bandura identifies this mode as "symbolic modeling."

11. See Philippians 3:17; 2 Thessalonians 3:7, 9. *Mimetes* is used eleven times. *Tupos* is used nine times with this meaning; the word group itself is used a total of seventeen times. *Hupodeigma* is used with this meaning six times; the word group itself is used a total of fifteen times.

12. It is difficult to call anything our Lord did "spontaneous," since he always knew what he was doing. From the disciples' perspective, new events, such as this miracle, were spontaneous to them as participants; and they are spontaneous to us as readers. Technically, such happenstance events are the essence of this avenue of modeling.

13. The "classroom meeting," an informal discussion where teacher and students evaluate the class, is another means of bringing Spontaneous Modeling into the classroom. The idea is to have a "town hall" meeting and to talk about how the class is progressing (Joyce and Weil 1986). An understanding of Spontaneous Modeling should encourage teachers to increase out-of-class contacts with students.

14. Issler (1990) uses some of the learning avenues to outline alternate strategies for nurturing healthy marriages and families in the church: Inquiry Learning ("seizing the teachable moment"), Consequence Learning ("providing meaningful feedback"), and Structured and Spontaneous Modeling ("modeling biblical norms").

15. In a typical worship service, other learning avenues are evident, such as in the reading of Scripture (Cue Learning and Structured Modeling) and congregational singing (Cue Learning).

16. *For Lecture:*
   a. Avenues:
      (1) Identification Learning—common vocabulary, examples, analogies
      (2) Structured Modeling—planned, edited, rehearsed
   b. Improvement:
      (1) Identification Learning—use humor and examples relevant to the lives of the students
      (2) Structured Modeling—express enthusiasm for the subject
      (3) Spontaneous Modeling—allow opportunity for questions and answers following the lecture
   For Group Discussion:
   a. Avenue: Inquiry Learning—"analysis" level of Bloom's taxonomy
   b. Improvement:
      (1) Identification Learning—use discussion topics relevant to students' lives
      (2) Inquiry Learning and Spontaneous Modeling—have students critique each others' comments
   For Quiz/Test:
   a. Avenue: Consequence Learning—feedback on learning progress
   b. Improvement:
      (1) Inquiry Learning—vary the difficulty of the questions according to Bloom's taxonomy
      (2) Cue Learning—make sure it tests facts and issues that are representative of course objectives and significant for students
      (3) Spontaneous Modeling—have students exchange quizzes and grade them in class

Chapter 9: Components of Teaching, Part 1

1. In relation to the five-box model from Chapter 1, Part 2 fits into Box E: the practical implications of teaching, based on Boxes A through D.
2. A major conceptual difference exists between a theory of learning and a theory of teaching: the former involves a *descriptive* task—describing how people tend to learn; the latter involves a *prescriptive* task based on learning theory—how should we teach.
3. These phrases are titles of books written by Ringer (1974, 1977).
4. An outline of this lesson plan and group activities is presented in Appendix E.
5. Appreciation for these two creative ads is expressed to the educational ministry students in the spring 1990 teaching process class at Western Seminary.
6. Those who contrast teaching and discipleship would suggest that "teaching" takes place in a classroom solely to impart knowledge to students. On the other hand, it is believed that "discipleship" involves dialogue. It requires discussions among people. It necessitates raising tough questions—questions that do not always have easy answers. Discipleship focuses on holistic needs. It yields changed lives, not just information transfer.

   The contrast, however, is too sharply defined. The Greek word *mathetēs* (from which we get the word "disciple") means "learner" or "student." Specifically, in the New Testament the term refers to persons who have trusted Jesus and are now following him. The New Testament writers used the term indiscriminately to refer to *all* believers—not just to a committed cadre of spiritual "marines."

   We all realize that a primary task of the church is to "make disciples." This involves going, baptizing, and *teaching* them to obey (Matt. 28:19–20). Therefore, fully adhering to all Great Commission directives demands a more comprehensive understanding of education that is Christian. Biblical teaching is never restricted to four walls. To state it simply, teaching *is* discipleship. For a thoroughly biblical study of discipleship, see Wilkins (1992).
7. See Appendix F for a brief discussion of preaching and teaching.
8. A full investigation of the New Testament concept of teaching includes the following topics:

   - The Holy Spirit as teacher
   - The spiritual gift of teaching
   - Elders as teachers
   - Women as teachers
   - Parents as teachers
   - Believers as teachers
   - The Word of God and teaching
   - Purposes/outcomes of teaching
   - False teachers

   Besides these explicit references, one could study the example of prominent teachers in the New Testament such as Jesus, Peter and the other apostles, and Paul.
9. These components are adapted from the "seven commonplaces of teaching" introduced by J. T. Dillon, associate professor of education at the University of California, Riverside, in a class in 1981. Dillon uses these commonplaces in his 1987 book.
10. For example, Ladd (1974, p. 535) divides the gifts into two groups: *charismatic gifts* (prophecy, miracles, healing, and tongues) and *natural talents* used by the Spirit (the remaining gifts listed).
11. See Zuck (1984) for a more complete discussion of the spiritual gift of teaching, especially as it pertains to the work of the Third Person of the Trinity.
12. In this regard, persons with the gift of teaching can make three specific contributions to the body of Christ:

    - Gifted teachers can aspire to be "master" teachers, modeling excellent teaching through the varied educational ministries of the church.
    - Gifted teachers can identify others who also have the gift of teaching ("it takes one to know one") and help nurture and train these persons to become master teachers.
    - Gifted teachers can help *all* believers (i.e., not "gifted" in teaching) improve their teaching-discipling skills (e.g., parents). The church needs to fully use every God-given resource to accomplish its mission.
13. Bruce Wilkinson, president of Walk Thru the Bible, in his "Seven Laws of the Learner" seminar, suggests that it is the responsibility of the teacher to provide meaningful memory aids for learning a subject. In effect, when students must develop their own memory aids or summary outlines for a subject, they are taking on a major part of the teaching task themselves. One of the great benefits of the Walk Thru the Bible Old Testament and New Testament seminars is the summary outline of Bible history that seminar participants easily learn through creative, participative activities.

    Gage and Berliner (1988, p. 400) make note of such student effort in relation to the difficulty of interpreting research results from studies on the effectiveness of different teaching methods:

    > Students who know they are going to take a final examination compensate for the inadequacies of the methods by which they were taught, whether lecture or discussion methods, reducing differences in the effects of the teaching methods on student achievement. McLeish called this the *equalization effect*: "Irrespective of differences due to the teaching methods used, the work which students do for themselves in preparation for an examination will tend to bring their scores close to equality." (1976, p. 271)
14. See Wilhoit and Ryken (1988) for characteristics of a good Bible teacher and sound Bible teaching.
15. Glatthorn (1987) speaks of several kinds of curriculum: (a) the written or planned curriculum; (b) the supported curriculum (i.e., what is regularly supported by the budget and other resources); (c) the taught curriculum; (d) the tested curriculum; and (e) the learned curriculum.
16. Regarding the crucial transition, which distinguishes Phase 1 from Phase 2, Ladd (1974, pp. 182–83) remarks,

    > The gospel record makes Peter's confession of Jesus' messiahship at Caesarea Philippi a turning point in his ministry. After Caesarea Philippi a new note entered Jesus' teaching, "He began to teach them that the Son of man must suffer many things, and be rejected by the elders and the chief priests and the scribes, and be killed, and after three days rise again" (Mk. 8:31). This instruction about his impending death became an important element in the teaching of the subsequent days (Mk. 9:12, 31; 10:33; Mt. 17:12; 20:18, 19; Lk. 17:25).

17. A variety of approaches to studying and teaching the Bible is evident among evangelicals:

- *Sectional* study (e.g., a book, chapter, segment, paragraph, or verse of Scripture)
- *Subject* study (e.g., what the Bible says about a topic such as prayer or God's sovereignty)
- *Story* study (e.g., looking at a certain event or series of events such as the birth of Jesus Christ, or doing a character study)
- *Supportive* study (e.g., investigating background information to better understand the Bible, such as first-century cultural practices, history of the ancient Near East, geography of the land of Palestine)
- *Springboard* study (e.g., taking biblical principles and then exploring their historical and contemporary application such as lessons on business ethics, finances, or parenting)

18. The following factors can be used to evaluate published curricula:

1. Theological and biblical accuracy
2. "Teacher-friendly"—ease of use by instructors
3. "Student-friendly"—ease of learning by pupils, incorporating age-appropriate educational strategies
4. Organizational matters
   a. Cycle of coverage for Bible content
   b. How students are grouped (e.g., by grade or department)
   c. Organizing principle (e.g., different topics chosen for each age group or all age groups study the same topic)
   d. Available teaching aids
   e. "Dating" (i.e., whether or not dates are assigned to each lesson, possibly limiting the reuse of material)
   f. Cost of the materials

See the Spring 1988 issue of *Foundations* magazine (pp. 70–72) for a chart comparing twenty different publishers of Sunday school curriculum on some of these factors.

19. In this chapter, we look at the broad components of decision making in educational ministry. A more comprehensive decision-making model is presented in Chapter 18.
20. In this category we include pastors. They usually determine the topics in their sermon series.
21. For further guidance in curriculum theory and development, see Tanner and Tanner (1980) and Posner and Rudnitsky (1989); for direction from a Christian perspective, see Wyckoff (1961) and Colson and Rigdon (1981).
22. See Habermas (1985) for a treatment of the concept of hidden curriculum as applied to Christian education.
23. The church could learn a lesson from Old Testament history. For example, during the Feast of Booths, the Israelites camped in tents to commemorate their nomadic wilderness experience. By way of application, local church leadership may wish to remind members of their early experiences as a local body. An annual worship service could be held in a rented hall or school building (with folding chairs, portable sound system, etc.), similar to the very first worship services the church experienced. Such a memorial gathering may remind members of early sacrifices, refocusing attention on the important matters of the church.

24. Chapter 7 outlined the three "levels" (or domains) of learning and suggested various degrees of "extent" of learning.
25. Our "indicators" relate to Eisner's (1985) "behavioral objectives." Our "investigations" relate to his "problem-solving objectives" and "expressive outcomes" (see Eisner's Chapter 6).
26. See Wernick (1987). Appreciation is expressed to Carl Gibbs for bringing this example to our attention.
27. Through the incarnation of our Lord, God gave us a unique indicator as to what he is like (John 1:14) and an exceptional indicator of what the Christian life is like (1 Pet. 2:21). Not that we must do *everything* he did, or do it *exactly* as he did it—but we get an idea of what is expected of us.

    Further information regarding indicators of learning is found in Mager (1984b) and Ford (1978).
28. A fully developed "indicator" has three characteristics: (a) *performance*—what the student will visibly do; (b) *precision*—how well the student should perform this action; and (c) *percentage*—how many students will achieve this level of precision. In most cases, it is assumed—often unrealistically—that *all* the material would be learned by *all* of the students. Therefore, the indicator in this paragraph of the text could be revised to state, "by 70 percent of the students providing a correct response for each blank."
29. Brookfield (1991) offers a helpful term for instructors who face the educational challenge of guiding students toward divergent outcomes. He calls it "grounded teaching." Based on the related concept of grounded theory, Brookfield counsels teachers to be flexible and adaptive; to interact with students about their learning; to gather data and to modify instruction along the way as necessary. In short, teachers must be sensitive travel guides. Brookfield claims that, too often, models and practices of teaching ironically omit a critical component: the student's own experience of the learning process.

    In contrast, "Grounded teachers make a systematic attempt to elicit from learners their perceptions of the learning process" (p. 35). Specifically, instructors are to record "what they [the students] remember as being of most significance to them (rather than to teachers) about educational events." Brookfield (p. 35) suggests that three particular resources can be used to shape the instructor's process-oriented grounded teaching:

- the students' own descriptive analysis of previous learning experiences
- journals written by the students
- documented educational accounts of the students

30. For an analysis of four teaching strategies (including teaching as "adventure"), see Habermas (1990).

Chapter 10: Components of Teaching, Part 2

1. To use percentages, at an ideal level we may express responsibility for teaching and learning this way: 100 percent for the teacher, 100 percent for the student, and 100 percent for the Holy Spirit.
2. Regarding the relational factor, our theology must set the tone in the classroom, not common secular practice. For example, Paul encouraged Philemon (a Roman slave owner) to receive Onesimus (his runaway slave) not as a slave,

but as a brother in the Lord. Christianity breaks through secular models of relationships. In teaching that is Christian, we do not adopt arbitrary, academic models of teacher-student relationships (which may tend toward a "master-slave" understanding). Scripture emphasizes a family or community metaphor—we are all brothers and sisters, who serve each other. The core of any teacher-student relationship is the servant-leader's heart (Matt. 20:26–28).

3. It is interesting to note that formal educational institutions also provide evidence both nonformal education practices (e.g., for Christian higher education, chapel services, and internships) and informal education practices (e.g., the perpetual socialization process).

4. It may be difficult for college or seminary students to understand the need for using a variety of teaching methods. Students may reason, "My [college or seminary] teacher primarily uses the lecture method and I am able to learn very well from it. Why can't the people I teach learn like I do?" What students fail to recognize is that academic education is a package deal and classroom time is only *one* element of that package. Other elements significantly contribute to the effectiveness of classroom lecturing. For example, professors assume that students are already *motivated* to learn the material since: (1) students are working toward a degree; (2) grades are being earned; and (3) tuition has been paid. Intensified *learning* results from these major elements: (1) students spend hours of out-of-class time reading a textbook and writing papers; (2) students spend hours preparing for quizzes and exams in which, sometimes, they must teach themselves material that did not make sense in class; and (3) students receive substantial feedback on their learning through graded papers and exams.

Students in a typical Sunday school class are in a very different situation. They are not as motivated and they don't do any out-of-class homework. Thus, within that one hour of class, Sunday school teachers must tap into student motivation *and* help students learn the material. Any "homework" assignments must actually be done during class time—thus, the need for a variety of teaching methods that involve student participation.

5. Table 10.4 is an adaptation of Joyce et al. (1992) four-part functional organizing framework, which identifies various categories or "families" of teaching methods: (a) information processing, (b) social, (c) personal, and (d) behavioral. Little (1983) presents a five-category adaptation of Joyce and Weil's framework: (1) information processing, (2) group interaction, (3) indirect communication, (4) personal development, and (5) action/reflection.

6. Lewis suggests a provocative psychological ordering approach in teaching basic reading skills:

Students' motivation to read can be stifled by the kinds of reading assignments commonly found on reading lists. Often material is of little interest and does not encourage reading as a life-long pastime. Students are usually required to read the "classics," which are someone else's idea of what is interesting. . . . It may be possible to help students read more and at the same time to pique their interest in the classics by suggesting that they read the works of Louis L'Amour [the famous Western novelist]. (1987, p. 261)

7. As Richards (1970) suggests, not every lesson has a "Took" segment. A series of lessons (e.g., with six sessions) may build toward one significant "Took" during the final session. Thus, the first couple of lessons may just include "Hook" and "Book" segments. Later lessons may include a "Hook," a brief review of the previous "Book" material, and more emphasis on "Look" implications. The sixth session may be totally taken up with "Look" and "Took" segments.

The Hook, Book, Look, Took theoretical framework is primarily useful for teaching youth and adults. Although the principles are applicable to children, the segments are not as discrete. Children's sessions use a variety of combinations of "Hook-Book" activities and "Look-Took" activities.

8. A lesson design format used widely in public education was developed by Hunter (1982). This model includes seven basic elements:

- anticipatory set (gaining student attention)
- objective and purpose of the lesson (what students will learn and why)
- input (new information needed)
- modeling (teacher activities to illustrate content or skill)
- guided practice (student activities to practice in class)
- checking for understanding (gauging level of student learning)
- independent practice (homework)

For additional information on designing lesson plans, see Posner and Rudnitsky (1989).

9. Further examination of the Stake model can be found in Chapter 13.

10. See Cook (1988) for a helpful overview of the subject of evaluation and measurement in Christian education.

11. Yet sometimes we give mixed signals. Note Jesus' observation in Luke 6:46.

12. Additional thoughts on pursuing excellence in teaching can be found in Issler (1987).

13. This three-part case study is adapted from Cornett (1983, p. 14).

14. Empirically researched studies of instructional effectiveness aid us in our task. Major summaries have been edited by Doyle (1990) and Wittrock (1986).

Chapter 11: Teaching Adults

1. Von Oech (1983, p. 37).

2. According to the Frankena model, Boxes A–D describe the "forest"; Box E points to "trees."

3. These nineteen topics are neither exhaustive nor applicable to all adult experiences (for that matter, experience does not guarantee a teachable moment). Most adults, however, will encounter a significant percentage of these life challenges.

4. For further study, review Chapters 5 and 6, concerning human developmental theories.

5. One excellent theoretical resource is Elias (1986). Among other topics in this encyclopedic work, social contexts, historical perspectives, organizational matters, and educational designs of Christian education are considered. Wickett (1991) identifies several provocative models for adult education. Koons and Anthony (1990) offer a helpful text on Christian adult singles, based on a national study.

6. For example, Stubblefield (1986b, pp. 185–87) cites five aims of adult discipleship training: (1) growth toward Christ-likeness; (2) comprehension and application of biblical doctrine; (3) implementation of Scripture principles to life; (4) knowledge of and participation in the church's ministry; and (5) facilitation of others' growth.

    Pazmiño (1988, pp. 218–21) prefers a more integrated objective for education that is Christian. Citing Titus 2, Pazmiño isolates several imperatives where Paul commands his spiritual son *to be* something in his witness (e.g, *to be* temperate, worthy of respect, etc.). Pazmiño describes his rationale for shifting from a conventional trio of emphases: "No doubt knowing, feeling and doing are implied in the call to be, but a concern for being implies a larger purpose, a larger vision. Titus was to be concerned with character formation" (p. 219). For Pazmiño, the balanced virtues of love and truth offer evaluative criteria to determine godly modeling.

7. Hershey (1986, p. 95) suggests a philosophy based on a young adult ministry in Thousand Oaks, California. Three focused areas are raised: (1) relevant, topical instruction; (2) small group gatherings; and (3) monthly social activities. These areas express broader ministry objectives. Hershey proceeds to note that these three areas tie directly into the young adult needs of loneliness; career goals; lifestyle choices; and spiritual direction.

8. An appropriate verse that speaks of thorough change is Acts 2:37. The crowd who heard Peter's message at Pentecost is radically converted—a 180 degree shift from an unregenerate state to a regenerate one: "When the people *heard* this, they were cut to the *heart* and said to Peter and the other apostles, 'Brothers, what shall we *do?*'"

    A head-heart-hands growth process is unveiled in this fashion:

    - "head" signifies cognitive understanding
    - "heart" indicates altered emotions and values
    - "hands" points to significant behavioral change

    A noteworthy portrayal of this three-part emphasis is found in Groome (1980, pp. 57–66), who views faith as *believing, trusting,* and *doing.*

9. Although these three components are somewhat sequential, they are not meant to express a lock-step design. Nor are they intended as a magic formula for spiritual growth.

10. The writer of Hebrews is quite disturbed that his readers must be retrained in the "elementary teachings" (6:1) of the Christian faith.

11. Paul's personal testimony in 1 Corinthians 13:11 reminds us that a child's knowledge is both quantitatively and qualitatively different from an adult's understanding.

12. Bruner's (1977, especially pp. 52–54) theory of "spiraling" tells, us, among other things, that children *may* learn certain basic truths that adults learn. But their knowledge will be much less sophisticated.

    For instance, based on Hebrews 6:1–2, older children are able to grasp elemental truths about salvation, the church, and the end times. Yet these truths are necessarily filtered through their limited concrete reasoning capabilities. The author of Hebrews claims that his audience must be retaught these categories of truth at a higher plane of thinking (for example, "spiraling" God's revelation of this truth to the abstract level of "laying on of hands").

13. By way of comparison, note that Krathwohl, Bloom, and Masia (1964) have created a taxonomy of educational objectives for the affective domain:

    1. Receiving—a willingness to pay attention to a particular viewpoint
    2. Responding—a desire for sustained consideration that brings satisfaction
    3. Valuing—accepting, preferring, and committing to a particular viewpoint
    4. Organizing—conceptualizing and rearranging one's life according to this viewpoint
    5. Identifying—being characterized by this viewpoint, following complete association with it

    Their third, fourth, and fifth taxonomy levels match the three adult growth components of the Hebrews passage: (3) "valuing" emphasizes choosing a set of perspectives over against all competing positions—much like a believer who accepts certain doctrinal tenets; (4) "organizing" rearranges individual lifestyles according to those newly accepted viewpoints—similar to the Hebrew believers who "trained themselves" by applying truth; and (5) "identifying" signals the incarnation of a specific truth—like the mature Christian who is reputed to be wise.

14. In Acts 24:14–16, *truth-believing* is evidenced by Paul's confession: "I believe everything that agrees with the Law and that is written in the Prophets" (v. 14b). *Truth-behaving* surfaces through his lifestyle: "worship [of] God of our fathers" (v. 14a). Finally, Paul's driving motivation to continually "keep my conscience clear before God and man" (v. 16) signifies a *truth-becoming* virtue.

15. This age grouping is "normal operating procedure" for many congregations.

16. Besides the "only-child-in-school" struggle, other relevant concerns for this middle-aged couple (which match them better with young adults) include parental discipline and age-appropriate home instruction matters.

17. "Similar" quadrants identify close (if not exact) experiences among adults; "dissimilar" quadrants reflect diverse experiences.

18. For instance, we leaders would not expect adults in our ministry to withdraw from the regularly scheduled Lord's Supper (Eucharist). We take this stance even though, on a rare occasion, this may be expedient (1 Cor. 11:27 warns of participation "in an unworthy manner").

19. It is not unusual for adults to receive their high school diplomas (or GED) later in life. Also, retirement dates differ.

20. "How do we deal with first-time mothers who lost their only child in delivery?" or "What are we saying when we honor mothers about the mothers of children born out of wedlock?" are two related questions.

21. Specific illustrations of Jesus' multiple use of questions (from the second Gospel) are featured in all three interrogative methods from this section.

22. This polarized set of three categories has been modified from Potter and Andersen (1976, pp. 50–51).

23. Dillon (1987) proposes that few teachers really encourage *student* questions. Most discussions arise from *teacher* questions. He raises stimulating concepts to elicit the former.

24. Bateman (1990) demonstrates how this inquiry process is created and sustained. Bateman encourages student ownership of personal ideas.

25. See Habermas (1987) concerning biblical principles for gray areas of faith. How can we learn to "agree to disagree" with other believers?

26. Based on Potter and Andersen (1976, pp. 119–21).

27. For instance, Fiske and Chiriboga (1990, pp. 242–57) analyze the fundamentally human concept of commitment. For them, this phrase helps unlock the study of people, because the realities undergirding "commitment" express an individual's self-perception and worldview, among other matters. Based on their research, Fiske and Chiriboga identify four basic components of commitment. This foursome relates to the four themes, in our understanding, as follows: (1) "moral commitment" and *Commission;* (2) "interpersonal commitment" and *Community;* (3) "commitment to self-concern" and *Character;* and (4) "commitment to mastery" and *Commission.*

Likewise, Hershey (1986, p. 93) locates representative, felt concerns of young adults (i.e., quests). We have matched our themes with his standard needs.

Felt Needs	Themes
1. Lack of purpose	
2. Desire for spiritual guidance	Communion
3. Ultimate questions of life	
4. Anger and pain from terminated relationships	
5. Loneliness	Community
6. Desire for confidant or mentor	
7. Moral decisions	
8. Desire for integrity and respect	Character
9. Ethical dilemmas	
10. Money problems	
11. Leisure opportunities	Commission
12. Civic responsibilities	

28. Fromm describes what a "sane society" (his book title) should look like. A solution, he says, is found in sound mental health. This state emerges as the following human needs are satisfied (we've supplied the matching themes):

Universal Needs	Themes
1. Relatedness (versus narcissism)	Community and Character
2. Transcendence (self-expression through creativity versus destructiveness)	Communion and Commission
3. Rootedness (brotherliness versus incest)	Community
4. Identity (individuality versus conformity)	Character
5. Sense of orientation and devotion (reason versus irrationality)	Character and Commission

29. Parks (1986), extending Erikson's call for "fidelity," suggests that young adults cultivate a new-found ability to trust. What's often called "ownership" in education pertains to faith as well, Parks says. She concludes (pp. 77–78, emphasis added):

I propose, then, that the threshold of young adulthood is marked by the capacity to take self-aware responsibility for choosing the path of one's own fidelity. A consequence of this awareness is the recognition that *one even must take responsibility for the faith one lives by.* This is sometimes a chilling recognition. Faith can now have a doubt of itself; it is no longer the simple adoption of the convictions of another. One becomes a young adult in faith when one begins to take self-conscious responsibility for one's own knowing, becoming, and moral action—even at the level of ultimate meaning-making. *. . . When this new self-aware, critical, yet struggling strength does emerge, I am persuaded that it is an adult strength and marks the threshold of adult faith.*

Chapter 12: Commendable Adult Curriculum

1. The former category ("ready to grow") speaks of developmental and experiential matters (i.e., Do students have the capacity or ability? Do they have the proper experiences?). The latter category ("want to mature") refers to inner volition and motivation. Students may have the capacity, but no desire. See the chapters on human development, learning, and teaching for more information.

2. Integration is a critical factor when it comes to superb curricular examples. Consequently, the theme of Character has been chosen to link the three other themes in this section. That is, Character will not be treated separately. Rather, this theme will be individually paired with Communion, Community, and Commission, and these three combined sets will be used to demonstrate commendable curriculum. The Communion-Character set represents our first sample.

3. For more information, contact Serendipity House, Box 1012, Littleton, CO 80160, 1-800-525-9563.

4. Recall that *Character* is used as an integrative agent. It is synthesized with all three remaining themes. Therefore, no separate curricular example is provided for Character.

5. See Sell (1985, pp. 89–90), as modified from Duska and Whelan (1975, pp. 71–72).

6. At this point, we're making relative recommendations. "Class discussion," as a means to address the Community-Character themes, represents a simple, *routine activity* of adult instruction. On a larger, comprehensive scale, we teachers must be conscious of more sophisticated responsibilities in the body of Christ. McKenzie reminds us of this latter duty. He speaks about experiencing the mystical wonder and awe of the Christian community during the Lord's Supper (Eucharist). Then, he expands the concept of the body to mean more than wine-and-bread celebration. In fact, our spiritual partnership goes well beyond the church walls. McKenzie (1982, p. 138, emphasis added) explains:

In a word, Christian community must be a profane (*profanum* = outside the temple) community as well as a sacred community. Community must be based on the everyday needs and concerns of the people. *Community means being together in the world, and this implies being together outside the walls of the temple as well as inside these walls. . . . The mission of the church is to make meaning available by announcing the Good News and the teachings of Jesus, by serving the people in their needs (secu-*

lar as well as sacred), and by forming community (profane as well as liturgical).

Heinecken (1981, p. 85) echoes McKenzie's plea to see the church incarnate Christ's love in its daily activities: "All the Church's assurances of God's love mean nothing if this love is not embodied in flesh and blood people who care. And if the Church is not a community of such caring love, it is not the church of Jesus, the Christ. Unfortunately, we must face up to the miserable failure of the institution of the Church in this respect."

7. Meyers (1986, pp. 62–63) specifically suggests the use of controversial newspaper or magazine clippings to prompt lively interaction. Even though his comments are directed primarily at college instructors, notice how his three examples pertain—in principle—to adult Christian educators:

> Here are a few examples showing how instructors can use articles to stimulate discussion.
> • To introduce a new concept
>   An economics teacher distributes a newspaper editorial on rising gasoline prices and uses it to introduce a discussion about common misunderstandings of supply-and-demand theory.
> • To reinforce previously introduced concepts
>   After a lecture and discussion on Maslow's hierarchy of needs, students in an introductory psychology class are asked to clip and bring to class an advertisement from a magazine or newspaper and to explain how that ad appeals specifically to one or more of the levels of Maslow's hierarchy.
> • To analyze and compare theoretical concepts
>   Students in a physical anthropology class are given an article from *Time* magazine describing the discovery in Asia of an ancient humanoid skull. They are asked to comment on this article in light of previously assigned reading detailing Richard Leakey's theory about the African origins of human beings.

8. Oftentimes, depending on church schedules and relationships among group members, meaningful discussions can continue over a cup of coffee at a nearby restaurant or at a mid-week appointment. Moreover, class dialogue can be extended when teachers provide a follow-up article to read or a Bible passage to study; in a subsequent meeting group members may discuss the topic further.

9. Galbraith (1991, pp. 1–32) prefers a synonymous term, "transactional process," which he (p. 2) defines as "a democratic and collaborative endeavor whereby facilitators and learners are engaged in a mutual act of challenge, critical reflection, sharing, support, and risk-taking. The essence of the transactional process is collaboration. Facilitators and learners are full partners in the learning experience."

10. Lowman (1984, p. 119) draws the following comparison:

> A useful classroom discussion, unlike a dormitory bull session, consists of students' comments separated by frequent probes and clarifications by the teacher that facilitate involvement and development of thinking by the whole group. Dynamic lecturers captivate a class by the virtuosity of their individual performances. Master discussion leaders accomplish the same end by skillful guidance of the group's collective thinking processes.

Lowman (pp. 120–21) continues his comparison with the well-used lecture method, making an even more poignant contrast:

> Discussions must be well planned in order to be effective, but their quality also depends greatly on how well the instructor performs. Leading an excellent discussion demands just as much stage presence, leadership, and energy as presenting a lecture—and considerably more interpersonal understanding and communication skill. Because of these additional requirements, some educators believe that leading an outstanding discussion is more difficult than giving a lecture of comparable quality.

11. Galbraith (1991, p. 5) identifies a trio of significant risks involved in transactional process:

> A true adult learning transactional process engenders three types of risk taking: the risk of commitment, the risk of confrontation, and the risk of independence. A commitment to the ideals and actions of a transactional process is a risk. To submit to the transactional process suggests that facilitators and learners run the risk of self-confrontation and change. It involves the extension of oneself into new dimensions and territories of involvement and action. If adult learners are committed to a collaborative and challenging educational encounter, facilitators must be willing to make the same commitment—a commitment that suggests they too will experience opportunities for change, growth, and new learning.

12. See Swindoll (1983, pp. 320–21).

13. Swindoll (pp. 320–21) continues, but discerning that:

> The first approach is the most popular. We are masters at rationalizing around our inflexible behavior. We imply that change always represents a departure from the truth of Scripture. Now some changes *do* pull us away from Scripture. They must definitely be avoided. But let's be absolutely certain that we are standing on scriptural rock, not traditional sand. We have a changeless message—Jesus Christ—but He must be proclaimed in a changing, challenging era. Such calls for a breakdown of stone walls and a breakthrough of fresh, keen thinking based on scriptural insights.

14. See Habermas (1987).

15. Sheehey (1976, p. 33) describes this tension: "Two impulses, as always, are at work. One is to build a firm, safe structure for the future by making strong commitments, to 'be set.' Yet people who slip into a ready-made form without much self-examination are likely to find themselves *locked in*." But early choices in life *do* matter. How we help adults to think and choose *does* make a difference, as Sheehey (p. 33, emphasis added) concludes:

> Although the choices of our twenties are not irrevocable, *they do set in motion a Life Pattern*. Some of us follow the locked-in pattern, others the transient pattern, the wunderkind pattern, the caregiver pattern, and there are a number of others. *Such patterns strongly influence the particular questions raised for each person during each*

passage, and so the most common patterns will also be traced throughout the book.

16. See Levinson (1978, p. 49). Other fundamental references to choices and decision making are found on pages 43–45, 52, 61. For Christian educators, Levinson's concluding insights (p. 200) on necessary adult choice should radically motivate us to build productive, critical thinking skills within our learners.

> Moreover, we need developmental transitions in adulthood partly because no life structure can permit the living out of all aspects of the self. To create a life structure, I must make choices and set priorities. In making a choice, I select one option and reject many others. Committing myself to a structure, I try over a span of time to enhance my life within it, to realize its potential, to bear the responsibilities and tolerate the costs it entails.

17. Powers (1986a, pp. 21–26) stresses the need for both deductive and inductive learning. Ericksen (1984, p. 96) emphasizes problem-solving tasks to promote independent thinking. Sanders (1990, Chapter 6) recognizes the "art of questioning" from an instructor's perspective.

    McKenzie (1982, p. 11) takes a stand for critical inquiry of faith over against a hand-me-down religion. Persistently, McKenzie (1986, pp. 10–13) resumes this posture, acknowledging that "We come into the world with question marks in our heads. . . . [they] are never fully erased" (p. 11). McKenzie, too, believes that an unexamined faith is not worth living. Accordingly, he reasons:

> If we look at our life experiences in terms of the religious tradition, we must also look at the religious tradition in terms of our life experiences. *It is only by means of critical reflection on and evaluation of one's religious commitment* that faith becomes truly personal and more than a mere submission to religious convention. The large numbers of adults who are only conventionally and nominally religious may be attributed to the fact that some religious leaders have stressed obedience to religious leadership over adult critical reflection. . . . As a result, many *adults* go through life equipped solely with the meaning framework they acquired in *childhood,* a meaning framework that is inadequate for the living of a personal adult faith. (1986, p. 12, emphasis added)

18. Vogel (1984, pp. 130–33) supplies a concise commentary on Groome's "shared praxis." She carefully delineates his five movements, and so aids Christian instructors in comprehending this vital theory. Groome's latest text (1991) applies the "shared praxis" model to several church educational contexts.

    On a related topic, Brookfield (1991, pp. 33–56) proposes an instructional model called "grounded teaching." Similar to praxis, grounded teaching intentionally charts the growth of individuals through educational sources like adult students' descriptive analyses of learning, personal journals, and documented accounts of learning.

19. The three staff, by age group, are: Tom Newberry, children's pastor; Mickey Sikes, youth pastor; and Don Bautista, senior adult pastor. Dr. Ellison chose Tom and Don. Our thanks to Ben Hamilton (1991, pp. 92, 100) for his brainteaser, which stimulated ours.

20. Among other helpful sources, see Fowler (1987, pp. 27–51). Eugene Peterson (1987, pp. 7–9) develops a similar approach to this subject by distinguishing "job" from "profession" or "craft."

21. The subsequent list is modified from Fowler (1984, pp. 103–5).

22. Vogel (1984, pp. 145–47) provides a brief historical sketch of the original Shepherd's Center outreach (today, about one hundred independently operated satellites minister across the nation):

> In 1972 a small group of church leaders came together because they believed there was a need for a church related retirement home in Kansas City. They were convinced that the needs of older persons could best be met by a comprehensive, intentional ministry.
>
> They set out to confirm this need, and so they hired a consulting firm to do a feasibility study. The results were somewhat disconcerting. Since only 5 percent of all persons sixty-five and over at any given time live in an institutional setting, the other 95 percent live in communities which are served by churches and synagogues. The issue became one of seeking, intentionally, to meet the needs of older adults who live independently in their houses and apartments. That small group of church leaders chose the name, "The Shepherd's Center," because it reflects the kind of caring support found in Psalm 23.

23. Vogel (1984, pp. 186–87) offers a splendid resource list on the topic of older adults (see especially her Endnotes 26 and 27). In addition, Vogel recommends excellent simulations to understand older adults. We've tried some of her ideas with our students. Here are a few of her (pp. 161–62) suggestions:

> One of the most effective ways to sensitize young people to the sensory losses and physical limitations which aging may bring is to simulate those losses.
>
> Have students wear a pair of work gloves (arthritis), put dampened cotton balls in their ears (hearing loss), and put two thicknesses of saran wrap over their eyes (glaucoma). Simulate stiff joints in some students by using an elastic bandage to secure a folded up newspaper behind their knees. Then proceed to deal with the topic of aging. Show a film and discuss it. Take a break and ask the students to make a telephone call, buy decaffeinated pop or coffee from a coin operated machine (they may not take off their gloves) and go to the bathroom. After the break, continue the simulation by having them write down their feelings. At this point end the simulation and spend time debriefing. I have found that real empathy emerges.

24. Vogel (1984, pp. 164–83) highlights basic, although not exhaustive, ministries, employing this fourfold objective. Notice references to all four themes in her listing: (1) life maintenance: consumer issues, health, housing, legal services, nutrition, social support services; (2) life enrichment: involvement in ministry, creative leisure activities, self-improvement classes; (3) life reconstruction: retirement, death, divorce, widowhood, institutionalization; (4) life transcendence: Bible study, exploring issues of concern, intergenerational study.

For a more specific understanding of how Shepherd's Centers might confront these fourfold objectives, see Vogel (1984, pp. 147–50).

25. Vogel's (1984, pp. 145–46) ten foundational premises provide a useful grid for planning and assessment of Commission. Notice how her Point 5 specifically delineates primary features of reconciliation: "Being whole means being in right relationship with self, others, and God."

26. Powers (1986b, p. 193) comments: "As persons get involved in this process, there often is a sense of being overwhelmed. Where can few people with limited resources make much of a difference for very long? The reaction then might be either one of despair, or of conviction that we *must* do it all. Either decision illustrates our finiteness; some never start, and others burn themselves out emotionally and physically."

27. Powers (1986b, p. 193, emphasis added) reminds us that "Everyone is *not* called to do everything all the time. But each *is* called to find needs to which he or she can seek to meet in the name of Christ. Just as there is a variety of needs, there is a variety of gifts. And *as we make choices* for Christian service, we will find that some ministries will call for individuals; others will be more suitable for a small group or the entire congregation."

28. See Habermas (1990). Although the principles in this article are detailed for adolescent growth, parallel truths can also be drawn with adult ministries.

29. Our version of Richards' "Hook, Book, Look, Took" organizes this educational plan. See the chapters on teaching for a fuller explanation of Richards' theory.

30. It is at this juncture that published curriculum is most helpful. Excellent resources can be found for any one of these three approaches to leadership study.

31. Christ's instructional *process* showed that leadership training should be:

- *Meaningful*—Jesus raised the disturbing ethical problem of taxes.
- *Dialogical*—Jesus interacted with Peter via discussion.
- *Practical*—Specific, realistic directions were given to Peter.
- *Reasonable*—Jesus asked Peter to use his fishing skills.
- *Enjoyable*—Peter probably liked the task, involving his former vocation.
- *Responsible*—Peter actively took an important role.
- *Mutual*—Paying the tax for both of them, Peter bonded their relationship.
- *Memorable*—Peter never forgot this training experience, when taxes came due again.

32. Peterson (1987, pp. 74–75) also utilizes this analogy of Melville. However, we prefer a slightly different twist to the story's application.

33. For instance, Melville (1983, p. 619) describes an opening scene in this fashion (notice how the *patient* is, at best, almost *an obstruction* to the surgery process and corresponding lecture):

"Bring up the patient, then," said Cuticle.

"Young gentlemen," he added, turning to the row of Assistant Surgeons, "seeing you here reminds me of the classes of students once under my instruction at the Philadelphia College of Physicians and Surgeons. Ah, those were happy days!" he sighed, applying the extreme corner of his handkerchief to his glass eye. "Ex-

cuse an old man's emotions, young gentlemen; but when I think of the numerous rare cases that then came under my treatment, I can not but give way to my feelings. . . . Take an old man's advice, and if the war now threatening between the States and Mexico should break out, exchange your Navy commissions for commissions in the army. From having no military marine herself, Mexico has always been backward in furnishing subjects for the amputation-tables of foreign navies. The cause of science has anguished in her hands. The army, young gentlemen, is your best school; depend upon it. You will hardly believe it, Surgeon Bandage," turning to that gentleman, "but this is my first important case of surgery in a nearly three years' cruise. I have been almost wholly confined in this ship to doctor's practice—prescribing for fevers and fluxes."

34. Dr. Cuticle's assistant reminds the surgeon that his teeth "will make your discourse more readily understood" (see Melville 1983, pp. 622–23).

35. For instance, Cuticle addresses the patient, saying, "I would advise perfect repose of your every limb, my man . . . the precision of an operation is often impaired by the inconsiderate restlessness of the patient" (Melville 1983, p. 621).

36. This statement should not pit "published curriculum" against "the Holy Spirit's guidance." Rather, the contrast is one of distinguishable properties and functions. A teacher is like a person wishing to build a customized house. Written (and generic) curriculum material, by nature, compares to a resource book of architectural designs. The drawings are static and fixed, even though there are many options within the manual. On the other hand, the work of the Spirit can be related to last-minute changes that the individual makes, which are appropriate for various occasions of construction. They are dynamic, even often spontaneous. Both factors are indispensable. They're complementary.

Chapter 13: Teaching Youth

1. For those who want to pursue background studies that define adolescence historically, culturally, psychologically, and organizationally, see Koteskey (1987, especially pp. 11–24); Borgman (1987, pp. 61–74); and Richter (1982, pp. 1–53).

2. See Elkind (1984). Only three of his helpful research findings are isolated for discussion here. In Elkind's earlier work (1978), two of these three findings were discussed: the personal fable and the imaginary audience.

3. Recall that the adjective "childlike" describes normal behavioral patterns for children. This phrase is contrasted with "childish," which is reserved for youth or adults who act like children. The former word upholds the inherently valuable period of childhood; that is, children are not miniature adults or pint-sized youth.

4. Schimmels (1984, p. 40, emphasis added) offers beneficial advice to parents who want to help their young teens employ abstract, formal operations thinking in productive ways:

If you promise not to tell, I'll share my secret weapon, which I save for my children when they are struggling through these critical periods of re-identification. I find a vacant parking lot somewhere, and I teach them how to drive. You would be amazed how much thirty minutes at the wheel in an isolated parking lot can do for a thirteen-year-old's morale. I haven't resolved the problem. He isn't any more socially accepted, although he may brag about his driving skills all over school. But I have given him *a glimpse of what life is going to be like* once he gets through this time, and that seems to help. *Or at least I have helped him romanticize the next plateau of development.*

5. Adapted from Schimmels (1984, pp. 25–27).
6. Competition, in and of itself, is amoral. It may be employed for good or bad purposes. Paul often alluded to positive athletic illustrations of Christianity. Unfortunately, the church has done little to demonstrate how our faith *should* shape our views here. We need to create a theology of competition. Then, we must embody it, so that believers can mend the detrimental witness of our all-too-typical recreational performances.
7. Sprinthall and Sprinthall (1990, pp. 158–59) identify Marcia's trio of interview questions that he used for his research on identity formation. We've added cross-referencing of the four universal quests:

- Questions concerning *religious ideology,* such as "Are there any times you have doubted any of your religious beliefs?" (similar to the quests of Immortality and Integrity)
- Questions concerning *occupation,* such as "How much have you become interested in these careers?" (similar to the quest of Industry)
- Questions concerning *worldview,* such as "How would you compare your own political views with your parents' views?" (similar to the quests of Integrity and Intimacy)

In addition, Stevens (1985, pp. 56–57) usefully condenses the valuable theory of Marcia. (Notice that the *order* in which Stevens prefers to review Marcia's theory is reversed from the order in the text section below.)

Identity Achieved. The individual has wrestled with the alternatives and made personal commitment to an integrated identity. This may require time and may not be fully accomplished until the adolescent moves away from home. . . . Marcia discovered that although girls start out in adolescence ahead of boys, they take longer to achieve an adult identity (a girl's positive identification with an independent mother seems to help). Finally, high-identity status is often the result of less parental control, more praise, and growing up with a "masculine" father.
Identity Moratorium. This person is in the midst of weighing and actively struggling with the alternatives in anticipation and making binding decisions. He or she can be volatile and somewhat insecure but is probably on the necessary pathway to an independent identity. This person desires encouragement and space to maneuver. Marcia notes that moratorium types experience an ambivalent disengagement from their mothers.
Identity Foreclosure. A person in this state will often be mistaken for an identity achiever. Because they are well-behaved and submissive to authority, they usually create no disturbance—unlike the moratorium type. But the foreclosed individual has never grappled with the issues of identity; they have simply accepted the identity attributed to them. Foreclosure types tend to have active, coercive fathers.
Identity Diffusion. This person is wary of struggle; the quest for selfhood has been stymied in the past. He or she has no real sense of identity, and tends to be confused, withdrawn, feeling uncomfortable and out of place. Fantasy and flight are the tactics of retreat preferred by this type. These dejected individuals have inactive fathers.

8. A youth program that deals with music is *Hot Topics: Youth Electives* (Elgin, Ill.: David C. Cook, 1989). Among other emphases, this curriculum helps youth analyze lyrics, discuss absolute standards, and evaluate related ideas like album cover graphics and artists' lifestyles. Student interaction sheets include such items as the effect that music has on us though commercials, as well as through clothes, hairstyles, habits, and thought life.
9. Along similar lines, Lickona (1983, p. 274) advances a domestic model of problem solving. Specifically, he suggests a ten-step plan (based on three parts) for conflict resolution between parent and teen. This "sit-down fairness discussion"—contrary to earlier stated results of television—promotes logic and reason:

Part 1: Achieving Mutual Understanding
(1) State the purpose of the discussion (to solve the problem fairly). (2) State your intent to get both points of view out on the table. (3) Describe the problem as you see it. (4) Ask for your teen's feelings about the problem. (5) Paraphrase your teen's feelings to show understanding. (6) Ask your teen to paraphrase your feelings.

Part 2: Solving the Problem
(7) Make a list of possible solutions to the problem. (8) Write an agreement stating the solutions you both think are fair. (9) Plan a follow-up discussion to see how your agreement is working.

Part 3: Following Through
(10) Have a follow-up discussion to evaluate your plan.

Leman (1987) also provides a useful, *proactive* (versus reactive) model of healthy parent-youth relationships. In contrast to Lickona (who is directing his ideas to the parents of teens), Leman speaks from the youth's perspective. He specifically offers "A Teenager's Ten Commandments to Parents" (p. 146):

1. Please don't give me everything I say I want. Saying no shows me you care. I appreciate guidelines.
2. Don't treat me as a little kid. Even though you know what's "right," I need to discover some things for myself.
3. Respect my need for privacy. Often I need to be alone to sort things out and daydream.
4. Never say, "In my day . . ." That's an immediate turn off. Besides, the pressures and responsibilities of my world are more complicated.
5. I don't pick your friends or clothes, please don't criticize mine. We can disagree and still respect each other's choices.
6. Refrain from always rescuing me; I learn most from my mistakes. Hold me accountable for the decisions I make in my life, it's the only way I'll learn to be responsible.

7. Be brave enough to share your disappointments, thoughts and feelings with me. I'm never too old to be told I'm loved.

8. Don't talk in volumes. I've had years of good instruction, now trust me with the wisdom you have shared.

9. I respect you when you ask me for forgiveness for a thoughtless deed on your part. It proves that neither of us is perfect.

10. Set a good example for me as God intended you to do; I pay more attention to your actions than your words.

10. Two inaccurate notions must be identified, regarding our earlier pairing of Social Learning and youth work. First, Social Learning is not to be equated with "mindless mentoring." This concept was stressed in the chapters on teaching. Second, Social Learning is not limited to passive, implicit educational practices. We leaders should be intentional about "modeling" critical thinking skills. We should desire our teens to emulate our confrontation with the world—how we interact with reality and how we integrate faith and life.

11. See Dockrey (1989) for twelve practical lessons on teen relationships.

12. Yaconelli and Burns (1986, p. 107) further explain their rationale for peer ministry:

> Today's youth worker has no excuse for not using his best programming resource—the kids in the youth group. Kids can participate in almost any aspect of the program, often more effectively than an adult. *They aren't always* more effective. The kids may do worse or they may botch a program, but then, failure is one of the best ways to learn. And youth groups always seem to be able to accept the failure of their peers. High-school students are much less critical of other high-school students than they are of adults. Peer ministry is credible exactly because it is not professional.

These authors cite two helpful resources: Brian Reynolds, *A Chance to Serve* (Winona, Minn.: St. Mary's, 1983); Barbara B. Varenhorst, *Real Friends* (Harper and Row, 1983).

Burns (1988, pp. 114–17) explains how a peer ministry can be developed. Among other convincing facts, Burns cites a study based on the work of the Institute of American Church Growth, Pasadena, California, on why people become Christians and join the church. What is the attraction? The advantages of friendship contact are overwhelming:

They just walk in	2–3%
A particular program	3–4%
The pastor	3–5%
A special need	2–3%
Visitation results	1%
Sunday school	3–5%
Crusade	.001%
Friend/Relative	70–90%

13. Christie (1987, p. 18) suggests two overarching purposes for an adult group of youth workers:

There are two goals for your diverse ministry team. One is to model, among yourselves, many of the relationships (such as marriage, friendship, older Christian with younger Christian, and so on) in which your youth group members will eventually find themselves. The second goal is to have at least one advisor on your staff with whom each adolescent can feel some identification. Grandmothers and grandfathers make great youth workers, but you would not want an entire team of senior saints. The same is true of college students, who tend to be energetic and lively, but often lack stability, experience, and maturity. We need an intergenerational youth ministry team.

14. For further study of youth and learning theories of modeling, see Muus (1988). The third chapter in this book includes Erikson's and Marcia's views of identity formation. Chapter 11 considers Selman's theory of role taking. Elkind's model of adolescent egocentrism is analyzed in Chapter 12. Chapter 13 details broad contributions of Social Learning theory. Chapter 14 highlights friendship patterns and peer influences using the ecological position of Bronfenbrenner and others.

15. The Stake model is not limited to a particular age level. It is analyzed in this chapter on youth, however, because the complexities (and hidden components) of adolescent culture are respected and confronted by this curricular theory design.

16. Our appreciation is extended to Jim Plueddemann for his contributions to Table 13.5 and Figure 13.1. His work has been adapted to address youth ministry concerns.

17. That is, the gospel presentation using, in sequence, Romans 3:23, 6:23, 5:12, and 10:9–10.

18. We have provided just a couple of references to the importance of parental involvement in youth ministry. For further study of this area, see Burns (1988); Leman (1982); and Yaconelli and Burns (1986).

19. Adapted from a message presented by Oswald Hoffman at Billy Graham Evangelistic Training Seminar, Anaheim, California, July 1985. Cited in Christie (1987, p. 11).

Chapter 14: Commendable Youth Curriculum

1. Curricular references in this chapter are taken from either Gospel Light's *The Complete Junior High Bible Study* Light Force series (1988), or from Rick Bundschuh's *On-Site* (Zondervan, 1989). The former is more detailed. The latter offers forty on-location youth programs for young teens; it is especially appropriate since, by design, it emphasizes Social Learning theory through direct life observations.

2. For instance, see Yaconelli and Burns (1986). A helpful index is included. Their "Creative Learning Strategies" address all four themes: (1) the "Worship" section centers on *Communion;* (2) the "Building Community" and "Church" sections confront *Community;* (3) the "Ethics, Values, Morality" portion points to *Character;* and (4) the "Mission and Service" section notes seventeen activities for *Commission*. All contributions in the final part of their book come from the *Ideas* library, published by Youth Specialties, Inc. (El Cajon, Calif.), or from Campolo (1983).

3. Adapted from Jones (1987, pp. 60–61). This pattern does not express a normative design for every teen, but it portrays the author's impression of several valuable movements toward adolescent faith development.

4. Benson (1985) suggests worship services that are especially geared to youth groups. His book contains several excellent suggestions. At the back of his text, fifteen complete worship services are provided (e.g., worship at a youth work camp site).
5. "Grow for It!" workshops have been sponsored by Youth Specialties (El Cajon, Calif.) as a regionally based training program that encourages worship and growth.
6. Recall that every lesson by Bundschuh (1989) offers on-location instruction. Again, this highlights Social Learning theory for youth, through direct observation techniques.
7. Jones (1987, pp. 16–17).
8. Richards (1982, pp. 84–85).
9. Kimball (1987, p. 12) adds:

> All of these levels involve personal relationships, some with individuals and some with groups. A full relational life means that a person can interact effectively and lovingly on all three levels. To be honest, though, I think we probably enjoy one level more than we do the others. But that shouldn't make us avoid the other two levels of interaction. For example, I've always felt most comfortable in front of a large group. In small groups, I feel fairly comfortable with the give and take, but in my one to one relationships, I have had to grow the most. I still don't think I'm very good on that level, but I'm getting better. I've noticed, though, that the more relaxed I am in one to one relationships, the better I feel in groups, so it all seems to interconnect.

10. Lynn's purpose is to intentionally create pairs of youth who alternate as "speaker" and "listener" using a series of prepared questions. Spiral-bound, the book opens up like an A-frame house and sits between the communicating partners. These interpersonal exchanges can be used as ice-breakers or for more serious fun in a teaching lesson.
11. Burns (1988, pp. 43–44) recognizes various school cliques—what he calls "friendship clusters." He notes that each group can be identified by virtue of where they sit in the cafeteria. Members of certain groups are permitted "dual membership" in others; some groups completely clash with others. Burns lists these small groups as the "brains," cowboys, surfers, ethnic minorities, preppies, jocks, band, and Christians. Each group has its own language, dress, walk, and standards.
12. Burns (1988, p. 67) elaborates:

> For years I have had the audacity to ask my adult volunteers for an extra hour-and-a-half of ministry each week. I've always felt that the more ministry involvement which adults have, the longer they will stay as volunteers. I ask them for one hour a week of meeting with a student to study a growthbook together. During this time, they will study the word of God, but they will also talk and build a relationship. I then ask the adults for 15 minutes of phone calls to students a week. One week they may only talk to one student; the next week they may reach five students. I figure they will average around three calls a week. Lastly, I challenge them to take 15 minutes a week and write a positive, affirming note to three students. You can write three short notes, address the envelopes, and put them in the mailbox in 15 minutes. Within an hour-and-a-half your volunteers have had a significant influence in the lives of seven students.

90-Minute Influence

1 hour in growthbook	1 student
15 minutes for phone calls	3 students
15 minutes for notes	3 students
	7 students total

13. Taken from Stevens (1985, pp. 130–31).
14. Stevens (1985, p. 131) comments:

> I cannot decide whether this list of requirements would be more appropriate for a junior scout troop or a juvenile detention center. The tone is offensively condescending. It displays not even the barest appreciation for the special sensitivities of teenagers. Rules three, four, and five are particularly galling—as if little children were being addressed. And rule seven poses an impossible contradiction: a demand for a show of respect in conjunction with an invitation to warmth and closeness.

15. A church in Kitchner, Ontario, held a worship service to celebrate Christian education. The pastor read a portion of a letter penned by Darrien Ouellette, a new believer: "Jesus is here in this church," Darrien testified, "and he's so easy to find" (from *Teacher Touch* [Fall, 1991] published by David C. Cook). How do we enable the Jeremy in our youth group to experience *that* type of Community?
16. Posterski (1985) suggests a "value ladder," based on his study of Canadian youth and their priorities: Ninety-one percent ranked friendship on the top rung of their value ladder. (Nine out of ten high school students ranked friendship as their highest value.) Eighty-seven percent ranked being loved next on the value ladder (looking for friends and family who will love them). Cited in Burns (1988, p. 74).
17. Burns (1988, p. 74) comments on Posterski's findings:

> Rather surprisingly, only 21 percent considered being popular as very important on their ladder of values. General popularity has been replaced by being accepted in a friendship cluster.
>
> The bottom line for your youth ministry program is that if your students don't make friends in the group, they won't stay in the group. As we develop a relational evangelism ministry, we can never stray very far from the idea of the friendship cluster.

18. Stevens (1985, pp. 66, 91) provides thought-provoking comparison charts of adolescent culture over the past four decades. Understanding such trends enables us to be more effective as leaders, for Stevens (p. 65) assesses: "My own observations lead me to suspect that the church is pathetically out of touch with teenagers and, furthermore, blithely ignores or smugly denounces all that the youth may be up to. The church is often years behind in its understanding of the setting and problems of this age group. This ahistorical and otherworldly approach to youth ministry leads to a misreading of their circumstances and the accoutrements of their lifestyle." A modified and abbreviated version of Stevens' charts shows these comparisons of youth culture:

	The Fifties	The Sixties	The Seventies	The Eighties
Their representative heroes	Ike, Mickey Mantle, Mickey Mouse, Elvis Presley	JFK, Martin Luther King, the Beatles revolutionaries	Superheroes, Ali, Kiss, Charlie's Angels	computers, E.T., Harrison Ford, Matt Dillon, John Paul II, Ronald Reagan
Their attributes	safe, bland, conservative	colorful, controversial	fantasy, unreal	cool, nervy, adventuresome
They identified with	the "in group" country, school, fraternity	the world: the global village	the individual	"my own kind"
They believed in	technology (materialistic)	humankind (humanistic)	myself (atomistic)	my own abilities, allied with high tech

19. A point of clarification: The give-and-take dynamic of this third exercise portrays "spontaneous" expression—live, firsthand experiences. The letter itself typifies the "structured" modeling category—that is, organized, staged, and prepared strategies, in contrast to unrehearsed instruction. (See "Alternate Conclusion.")

20. This one example, among many that could be cited, depicts the close associations often found among learning families.

21. A different approach to the theme of Character appears here. For a change of pace—and to remind ourselves of the necessary balance explained in earlier chapters—a sample of *independent* curriculum is offered as a commendable design for teens. Whereas the theme of Communion is likewise cited in this example, it is the *changed Character* that is emphasized.

22. Richards' Hook, Book, Look, Took model frames this youth lesson. In summary, this four-part teaching model comes down to:

Phase 1—*HOOK*—The focus on a contemporary need of students.

Phase 2—*BOOK*—The connection of a relevant principle from the Word.

Phase 3—*LOOK*—A synthesis of Hook and Book; identifying numerous ways that the Word principle affects student need.

Phase 4—*TOOK*—The challenge to each student: "Now what will *you* do?"

23. See Brueggemann, *Interpretation* 33(2): 115–29.

24. Ibid., p. 126.

25. See Barth (1961, p. 599).

26. Five simple but profound truths about the Christian's self-image are presented in Burns (1988, pp. 213–14): (1) God loves us unconditionally; (2) we are created in God's image; (3) we are re-created in Christ to perform "good works" as his "workmanship" (Eph. 2:10); (4) we are children of God; and (5) we are forgiven by God. (*Note:* Burns combines the second and third points into one.)

27. Burns (1988, pp. 210–13) also connects the ideas of new vision and new purpose, as it pertains to the teen's self-image. Notice how Commission—what the youth *experiences* and becomes *involved in*—plays a significant part in this perceptual readjustment. Seven practical means of a healthy self-image include: (1) establish positive relationships; (2) have a proper "attitude focus" in spite of difficult circumstances; (3) check physical warning signs; (4) provide success experiences, using youth's talents; (5) practice thankfulness; (6) realize the benefits of professional counseling; and (7) challenge teens to serve others, to get "outside themselves."

28. Serving others as short-term missionaries offers realistic challenges for youth. On the one hand, it utilizes their idealistic zeal and trailblazer spirit. On the other hand, it respects the limitations of their impermanence and erratic commitment.

29. See Campolo's (1983) excellent suggestions for service opportunities, ranging from simple to sophisticated projects.

30. Enderlein (1989, p. 12) explains:

Each of the twelve units in *Searching Together* recommends one service project be completed during the four week unit. Service opportunities are very important for junior highers. Service opportunities provide members with experiences that will assist them in forming positive Christian values. Adolescents show signs of a growing need for responsibility and meaningful work. Young adolescents should have structured opportunities to make decisions and to engage in tasks that adults consider important. Leaders can help junior highers meet their rising needs for responsibility and industry by engaging them in meaningful projects aimed at communal issues, oriented to the well-being of others.

31. Shaw (1987, pp. 9–10). Shaw (p. 9) provides a general definition of a workcamp: "the workcamp experience is an organized mission project in which young people and their adult leaders combine their skills and enthusiasm to repair, refurbish and renew homes of needy people. Workcamps usually span a week or two in the summer. Youth groups often travel to other states than their own to participate in either a workcamp organized by themselves or by others (e.g., denominations, Group, etc.)." In Chapter 22 Shaw lists the diverse benefits of workcamps: benefits for the teens actually involved; benefits for the youth group as a whole; and benefits to residents, communities, and local churches.

32. Keyes (1976, pp. 182–83).

33. Smalley's (1984, pp. 162–63) research of "successful" families shows close ties were developed when family members "did a lot of things together." Specifically, Smalley's separate interviews of husbands/fathers, wives/mothers, and children indicated that camping was found to be an important activity among these satisfied families. In part, three educational strategies that are implicit within camping might account for these powerful and pleasant memories (see Habermas' [1990] article in *Youthworker*).

34. From "Breaking Through the 'Me' Barrier—Programs to Expand Your Kids' World," in *Youthworker*, Summer 1985, p. 34.

35. John Westerhoff makes the bold claim that "If we really wanted to be effective in Christian education, we would eliminate Sunday schools and use the money that we spent on them for camps and retreats. If you could get everyone

in your church away for two weekend retreats a year, you would have more and better Christian education than a whole year's worth of one-hour Sunday School classes" (cited in Burns 1988, p. 91).

Chapter 15: Teaching Children: Classroom Situations

1. The purpose of 1 Corinthians 13:11 in Paul's argument in verses 8–12 is to provide a human example of two different perspectives: one that is limited (our current *earthly* viewpoint—"now I know in part") and one that is full (our future *heavenly* viewpoint—"then I shall know fully").

2. Forty years ago a Philadelphia congregation watched as three nine-year-old boys were baptized and joined the church. Not long after, unable to continue with its dwindling membership, the church sold the building and disbanded. One of those boys was Dr. Tony Campolo, Christian sociologist at Eastern College, Pennsylvania. "Years later when I was doing some research in the archives of our denomination," Tony said, "I decided to look up the church report for the year of my baptism. There was my name, and Dick White's. He's now a missionary. Bert Newman, now a professor of theology at an African seminary, was also there. Then I read the church report for *my* year:

   'It has not been a good year for our church. We have lost 27 members. Three joined and they were only children.' Only children! Give children a few years of Christian nurture and those 'only children' will change our world." (LeFever 1991, p. 1)

3. Too often we assume that movement is in only one direction: that children must grow up to be adults. Here, Jesus provokes us to consider how adults must "grow up" to be like children! For a discussion of the implications of this passage for the status of children before God, see Cragoe (1987).

4. Levin (1990, pp. 113–14) affirms:

   Moral behavior is the product of training, not reflection. As Aristotle stressed thousands of years ago you get a good adult by habituating a good child to doing the right thing. Praise for truth-telling and sanctions for fibbing will, in time, make him "naturally" honest.

   Abstract knowledge of right and wrong no more contributes to character than knowledge of physics contributes to bicycling. Bicyclists don't have to think about which way to lean, and honest people don't have to think how to answer under oath.

5. See Dobson (1974) for ways to help children develop a positive self-image.

6. Reported by Jon Robertson, learning process class, Western Seminary, Fall 1990. The concepts of "assimilation" and "accommodation" are basic to Piaget's theory of cognitive development. Jon goes on to state: "By the way, teachers should realize that [inquiry] learning is potentially destructive—if the learner is faced with too great a discrepancy, he will be tempted to resolve the conflict by abandoning his previous beliefs. In my case, I might have decided to abandon my belief in God if the discrepancy had seemed insurmountable."

7. See Bolton et al. (1987) and Haystead (1989) for teaching methods and learning activities appropriate to various ages of children.

8. Schaller (1977) offers provocative insights on the issue of honor. His fourth chapter, "Silver Beavers or Dead Rats?" is intended to remind church leaders of this important task.

9. Appreciation is expressed to Anne Sandoval, one of our former colleagues, for her insights about ministry to younger and older children and for her assistance in compiling Appendix G.

10. Being toilet-trained is one easily identifiable marker to know when a toddler is ready for "graduation" to the preschool program. This occurs anywhere between 1-1/2 and 3-1/2 years of age.

11. Language skills, in particular, emerge. See Habermas (1989) for six phases of communication that enable parents to more effectively converse with their developing child. Helpful resources for church teachers of preschoolers include Haystead (1989), Ratcliff (1988), and Barber (1981).

12. During the first part of the session, children should be busily involved in a Bible learning activity, related either to art, drama, music, oral communication, creative writing, service projects, Bible games, or research. Then, they should be given an opportunity to present their findings in a group time of sharing, application to life, and singing. Bolton et al. (1987) explain how to effectively use such Bible learning activities.

13. In the *Little House on the Prairie* series, Laura Ingalls Wilder writes of Almonzo Wilder (her future husband) training his own oxen team at age ten and then, during the winter, using his team to haul timber. With the passing of the agrarian mode of life, many family responsibilities that children carried out have disappeared. Teachers might assign classroom responsibilities to each child on a monthly rotating basis. These assignments should not be just busywork, but involve important aspects of classroom life.

14. As adults, we fail to notice the underlying motivations of our own actions. A measure of self-interest is involved in almost every one of our activities. We receive *some* personal benefit (e.g., that we please God, that we have done our best) for what we do. Applying this concept to children means that we tap into children's motivation to give effort to the learning task—whether that motivation is based on tangible or intangible rewards. A "reward" is truly a reward if it encourages a child to persist in the task. We need to learn from our children what interests them and use this interest to motivate them for learning.

    The difference between "rewards" and "bribery": A *bribe* encourages a child to act in a certain way primarily for *our* benefit (e.g., to keep the child quiet so the teacher can present the lesson). A *reward* encourages a child to act in a certain way primarily for personal benefit—for which *both* the reward (e.g., points toward a pizza party) and the *means* to that goal (e.g., memorizing a Bible verse) are ethical.

15. Sprinthall and Sprinthall (1990, chap. 20) outline a developmentally appropriate classroom management strategy based on Kohlberg's moral reasoning theory.

16. For the sake of illustration, teaching material from only one representative children's organization is highlighted: Pioneer Clubs. Specifically, three workbooks for children are analyzed: *Voyager Handbook* (for Grades 1–2), *Pathfinder Handbook* (for Grades 3–4), and the *Trailblazer Handbook* (for Grades 5–7).

17. Kohlenberger (1987, p. 61) cites the reading levels for each of the following Bible versions:

International Children's Version (ICV)	3.9
New International Version (NIV)	7.8
Living Bible (LB)	8.3
New King James Version (NKJV)	9.1
Revised Standard Version (RSV)	10.4
New American Standard Version (NASV)	11.3
King James Version (KJV)	14.0

For those children who cannot read or who are just beginning to read, David C. Cook's *Picture Bible* offers an excellent way to survey the Bible. A cartoon format is used.

18. One sound approach to memorization consists of: Recite, Restate, and Review. After a verse is recalled from memory, the parent or teacher asks the child to explain its meaning. Initially, adults will have to assist the child. Later, the child will become more familiar with the interpretation task. Finally, subsequent review of memory verses reinforces the objective of helping children meditate on God's Word.

19. Basic reference sources for teachers in local church children's ministries are Clark et al. (1986), Brown (1986), and Richards (1983a). Since most sources attend to Sunday school concerns, a pertinent caution is raised: We must not assume that, once we select a particular Sunday school curriculum, we are assured of prescribed results. Many factors affect the curriculum's intended purposes.

Some teachers do not know how to effectively use the material provided; a few teachers choose not to use the agreed-upon materials—they develop their own goals and lessons or use lessons and material from other publishers. When a substitute is called in at the last minute, another lesson may be taught if the curriculum is not available for preparation.

Seasonal and holiday emphases (e.g., New Year's, Easter) and special events (e.g., missionary speaker, Sunday school promotion) will preempt the regular lesson.

Children miss class due to sickness and vacations. Children may be distracted and inattentive during the lesson; also, it is difficult to retain a child's regular attendance for the entire length of curriculum cycle.

A directory of publishers of major curriculum and club programs for children is provided in Appendix G.

20. The list is adapted from one developed by the Children's Task Force of Grace Community Church, Portland, Oregon.

Chapter 16: Teaching Children: Corporate Strategies

1. Any dysfunction within the home, the extended family, or the church hinders expected progress toward maturity.
2. Note the "Teenage Mutant Ninja Turtles" marketing strategy: first, a successful television cartoon series, then a major motion picture, then, a computer video game, then an expansive line of Ninja-related toys.
3. The focus of the remaining portion of this chapter will be practical. It advances a biblically based and culturally relevant strategy for holistic education to children. The reader who wishes to have more specific information about appropriate teaching methods should consult the resources cited in the chapter. For an extensive list of age-group characteristics of children, see Choun (1988, pp. 109–17).

4. We would think it ludicrous if parents required their children to eat in a separate room apart from older family members. Yet some churches adhere to a similar practice by excluding children from the main worship service.
5. Major publishers offer church time materials. Some produce curriculum coordinated with their Sunday school material—reinforcing the same aims, but using different activities.
6. Helpful practical advice on encouraging children's attendance in the main worship hour can be found in Stewart (1987). Pioneer Clubs' devotional material for children, *Daily Watch* (1990), combining Bible study and fun activities, could easily be used in the pew during the morning service.
7. In the words of Horace Bushnell, "that the child is to grow up a Christian, and never know himself as being otherwise" (1916, p. 4).
8. Further reading on the evangelism and salvation of children is available from Jeschke (1983); Hayes (1986, chap. 23); Richards (1983a, chap. 20); Downs (1983); Ingle (1970); Yoder (1959); and Cragoe (1987).
9. Church leaders should adapt these practices to fit their own ecclesiastical tradition. See Sparkman (1983, Appendix 5) for a detailed outline of words and music that could accompany such ceremonies.
10. Yoder (1955) identifies a crucial blind spot in church ministry—one that could ruin the health of the church:

> Throughout Mennonite history, a major cause of spiritual decline in times of tolerance, apart from the possession of wealth, has been the *too-easy integration of the children of Christians into the Church*. As long as persecution continued, it was clear to everyone what was involved in confessing one's faith, and the request for baptism retained its character of dangerous and conscious commitment to break with the world. With persecution gone it became easier for a young person to stay in the church community, which was also his family, than to leave it. Baptism became an act of conformity rather than a break with the world, and young people, ever so serious and well-meaning, could not really know what commitment was involved. Two generations of such practice, coupled with a lack of discipline, suffice to render any church *lukewarm*. (p. 29, emphasis added)

Periodic intensive instructional classes and public ceremonies for children and teens may help to address this blind spot.

11. One church presented parents with a candle, which was to be lit every year on the anniversary date of this occasion. Thus, with the lighting of the candle, parents were to rehearse, with the child, the story of the dedication, including any visual reminders of the ceremony, such as a written covenant, pictures, and videos.
12. Hayes (1986, p. 409) suggests these general guidelines for inviting children to respond to a gospel presentation:

    1. Ask children to respond "inside" before asking for an outward response.
    2. Make the invitation clear.
    3. Use natural situations to talk to children about receiving Christ.
    4. Avoid making the invitation so easy that acceptance is not genuine.
    5. Avoid group decisions with the young.

For additional suggestions for teaching children about God, see Haystead (1974).

13. For a scholarly treatment of baptismal practices in the early church, see Jewett (1978).

14. Westerhoff argues that the current practice of confirmation in mainline denominations should become an adult rite. It should be understood as "calling forth the Holy Spirit to 'ordain' adults for their ministry in church and society" (1982, pp. 114–15).

15. A potential problem with such church ceremonies would arise if children or teens are made to pass through these experiences at a *required* age, regardless of their *personal* response to God. As suggested here, movement through the phases is dependent on the *initiative and qualification of the individual*—no designated age should be legislated as a maximum; *minimal* age ranges may be appropriate. Although children or teens attend group classes, readiness for the public commitment of the ceremony is based on *individual* assessment. These general phases could be used, in a modified way, for new adult converts, as was the practice in the early church's form of Christian education, the catechumenal schools. See Gangel and Benson (1983, pp. 88–90) for more information about the catechumenal schools.

16. Sell (1981) provides helpful direction for family ministry on a variety of issues.

17. Lewis and Demarest go on to state that "In spite of the home-shattering moral, economic, and educational pressures of recent years, the faithful, loving husband-wife and parent-child relationships serve as God's established means for providentially accomplishing in the home the ends of peace and justice. Then as children mature and leave home, they should carry these values with them" (p. 99).

18. For children coming from homes of non-Christian parents, mature adults in the church could serve as "spiritual parents."

19. For example: guidance on using teachable moments (Pelfrey 1988); practical activities for preschoolers (Hadidian et al. 1989); a Bible study series for eight- to twelve-year-olds (Rinehart 1988–89); and a cassette tape series that puts Scripture to music (see King Communications' "G.T. and the Halo Express").

20. See Anderson and Guernsey (1985, chap. 10) for a discussion of parenting styles and their impact on children.

21. For helpful resources on selecting books, see Larrick (1975) and Hunt (1978), the latter written from a Christian perspective. Contact Focus on the Family, P.O. Box 35500, Colorado Springs, CO 80935, for information regarding Christian magazines, video tapes, and radio programs for children.

22. Herx and Zaza (1988) provide evaluative summaries on 7,500 movies distributed by the major studios. This handbook was sponsored by the U.S. Catholic Conference.

23. For information regarding schooling options for Christians, whether public school, private Christian school, or home school, see House (1988) and the April 1991 issue of *Focus on the Family* magazine. The January 1991 issue of *Phi Delta Kappan*, a teacher's magazine, focuses on parental involvement.

24. Diverse resources for parents are available. Contact Focus on the Family for suggestions. Lickona's book (1983), although not particularly addressed to Christians, provides guidelines for nurturing morality in children. Fine (1988) provides an academic introduction to the field of parent education.

An extensive series of nationwide studies of family strengths sponsored by the University of Nebraska yielded these six major qualities (see Stinnett and DeFrain 1985, p. 14). Members of strong families:

1. are dedicated to promoting each other's welfare and happiness—they value the unity of the family.
2. show appreciation for each other.
3. have good communication skills and spend a lot of time talking with each other.
4. spend quality time in large quantities with each other.
5. have a sense of a greater good or power in life, and that belief gives them strength and purpose, whether they go to formal religious services or not.
6. are able to view stress or crises as an opportunity to grow.

Based on her extensive survey of family life professionals, Curran (1983) found that healthy families: (1) communicate and listen; (2) affirm and support one another; (3) teach respect for others; (4) develop a sense of trust; (5) have a sense of play and humor; (6) exhibit a sense of shared responsibility; (7) teach a sense of right and wrong; (8) have a sense of family in which rituals and traditions abound; (9) have a balance of interaction among members; (10) have a shared religious core; (11) respect the privacy of one another; (12) value service to others; (13) foster family table time and conversation; (14) share leisure time; and (15) admit to and seek help with problems. Both a video tape (Curran 1987) and a study guide (1988) have been developed to give greater insight on these fifteen key traits.

25. Estimates vary on what percentage of children live in single-parent homes (from 25 to 50 percent). But whatever the exact amount, the impact on children is significant. The New Testament concept of "widows who are really in need" (1 Tim. 5:3) may have a contemporary application to single mothers. It is noteworthy that Scripture highlights the particular needs of "broken home" individuals. James states that "religion that God our Father accepts as pure and faultless is this: to look after orphans and widows in their distress" (1:27).

26. Some children are more "at risk" than others. In addition to children of single parents, we could include children of blended families, of non-Christian parents, and of those having a history of abuse. In our church strategy to minister to children, we will need to target these "at risk" children for special attention.

27. Parents may need counseling. Families may need mediation to resolve disputes. The church may need to intervene and monitor dysfunctional and abusive family practices until marked changes take place. If the church doesn't go the extra mile in such difficult situations, then the state (with its various social agencies) will intervene. Due to the intense pressures on the family, church leaders must take extra measures to help "empower" parents to fulfill parental responsibilities. See Issler (1990) for suggestions to help families evaluate their habits and practices as the first step in making changes.

28. See Miles (1990), McGinnis (1986), and Sell (1981, chaps. 18–20) for additional resources on intergenerational activities and curriculum ideas.

29. See Moreland and Geisler (1990, chaps. 2–3) for a readable philosophical analysis of the common arguments posed "for" and "against" abortion and infanticide.

30. For example, many states require all passengers in a car, including children, to wear a seat belt. On a related issue, the minivan is replacing the station wagon as the primary mode of family transportation. Parents may not be aware that minivans are classified as "trucks" and thus do not need to pass the rigorous safety standards required of "passenger vehicles."

31. For further reflection on this topic, see Brown (1977), Noll et al. (1983), and Niebuhr (1951). *The Citizen* keeps the Christian informed about American public policy and the family. It is available monthly from Focus on the Family. One significant ministry related to the public school is "Moms in Touch," a voluntary program that brings mothers together to pray for their local schools (P.O. Box 1120, Poway, CA 92074).

Chapter 17: Focus on People: Working with Teachers

1. The term "giftedness" includes both spiritual gifts and natural abilities. Both are given by God for his glory (Col. 3:17; James 1:17).

2. Since one of the major functions of church leadership is leading ("direct" NIV, "rule" NASB; 1 Tim. 5:16), what appropriate divine resources are available? Romans 12:8 speaks of a gift of "leadership" (NIV). The word used here occurs in 1 Timothy 3:5 ("If anyone does not know how to *manage* his own family, how can he take care of [parallel thought] God's church?") and in 1 Timothy 5:17 ("The elders who *direct the affairs* of the church well are worthy of double honor"). We find the phrase "gifts of administration" (NIV) used in 1 Corinthians 12:28. The word for "administration" is not used elsewhere in the Greek New Testament, although a related word is used in Acts 27:11 for the pilot of a ship. If two distinct gifts are intended, then it may be that the "leadership" gift involves supervising and caring for people. The "administration" gift may deal more with technical and logistical expertise.

3. The Christian worldview sustains a healthy skepticism of culture, leading to an openness to change:

> Herbert Schneidau [1976] argues that the openness of Western civilization to change, its refusal to accept institutions or ideas as eternal, the very spirit of critical inquiry nourished by our intellectual heritage, is due directly to the influence of the Bible. Mythological cultures, says Schneidau, are fully integrated and sanctioned by their religious systems. . . . There is not even the concept of a transcendent moral law by which to judge the kings and his laws.
>
> Such societies are remarkably resistant to change when left to themselves. Certain tribes of New Guinea are still today practicing the ways of their Stone-Age ancestors. . . . In contrast, our Western culture has changed enormously in a mere two thousand years, in a mere century, in a decade. The reason, says Schneidau, is the Bible. For societies touched by the Bible, it is impossible to believe that the government is sacred, that the society is holy. Human institutions may not pass themselves off as divine. There is a moral law that transcends the social system. Even the king must obey the Law of God. The one God alone is eternal and holy. Everything else, being transitory, changes; and when it conflicts with the Law of God, it must be changed. (Veith 1987, pp. 70–71)

4. Kirkpatrick's third concept, "communication—creating understanding," is included in the treatment of "participation."

5. Each of the following inventories are based on a similar four-factor view of style: The *Personal Profile System* (DiSC), a twenty-page, self-scored interpretive booklet from Carlson Learning Company, is distributed through the Charles E. Fuller Institute of Evangelism and Church Growth, P.O. Box 91990, Pasadena, CA 91109, (800) C-FULLER. *Social Styles,* a PC-scored inventory, can be purchased through University Associates, 8517 Production Avenue, San Diego, CA 92121, (619) 578-5900. The *Social Style Profile,* a computer-scored inventory, is available from Tracom Corp., 3773 Cherry Creek North Drive, West Tower, Suite 950, Denver, CO 80209, (800) 221-2321.

6. For additional information about these four behavioral patterns, see Merrill and Reid (1981); Bolton and Bolton (1984); written from a Christian perspective, see Phillips (1989); Voges and Braund (1989); Smalley and Trent (1990); and Perkins and Cooper (1989). Smalley and Trent use the four animal names. To identify which style best matches your own perspective, complete the simple test found in Chapter 2 of Phillips' (1989) book.

7. Answers: Beaver (3); Golden Retriever (4); Lion (2); Otter (1). Understanding this four-part framework can guide teachers as one model for knowing what elements different learners need to keep their attention. For example, the driver needs to know what the main purpose of the lesson is (early in the lesson) as well as how the lesson fits in with their goals; the expressive relishes stories and illustrations; the amiable appreciates personal remarks about the teacher's own experience; and the analytic requires appropriate factual substantiation for general statements or principles.

8. The opinions of church members (versus nonmembers) must be seriously considered, although not exclusively. Even nonmembers can provide valuable insights into church problems, as well as potential areas of need.

9. This prudence was demonstrated in the church council meeting recorded in Acts 15. All viewpoints were aired (e.g., the believing Pharisees and the Gentile believers' views as relayed by Paul). The council meeting involved the testimony of experts respected by the Jerusalem church (e.g., Barnabas and James) as well as the expert testimony of relevant Scripture. Finally, the apostles, elders, and church reached a consensus about the matter. The Antioch church was informed about the agreement through a letter (i.e., task element) that was delivered by leading individuals, respected by both the Jerusalem and Antioch churches (i.e., relational element).

10. For practical discussions of how pastoral staff minister together within a multiple staff setting, see Schaller (1980); and Westing (1985).

11. This section is a revision of a previously published article (Issler 1989).

12. Even the first five guidelines have important implications for potential workers. Implementation of the first five guidelines helps potential workers realize what support and resources are available and what is expected of them.

13. "Believe it or not, one of the easiest ways to identify a person's giftedness is to examine what he or she criticizes!" (George 1982, p. 84; cited in Gangel 1989, p. 318).

14. "Spiritual gift" inventories are available from the Charles E. Fuller Institute of Evangelism and Church Growth, P.O. Box 91990, Pasadena, CA 91109. Call toll-free 1-800-C-

FULLER. A fifty-four-item natural talent inventory, "The Talent Discovery Guide," is available from IDAK, 7931 N.E. Halsey, Portland, OR 97213, (503) 252-3495.

15. Richards and Martin (1981) develop this concept in their Chapters 8 and 12.

16. When a believer fails to heed the counsel and confirmation of others, God may speak through the reproofs of life. See the story of Harvey in Richards and Martin (1981, pp. 274–75).

17. Appendix H provides an example of what a ministry position document looks like.

18. This concept of "unleashing the church" is developed by Tillapaugh (1982). Certain basic and necessary ministries, such as a church nursery, are not able to be fully "unleashed." Yet innovative outreach emphases of the nursery could implement this concept.

19. For an extended treatment of this topic, see Rush (1983, chap. 12).

20. For example, LeRoy Ford's *Design for Teaching and Training: A Self-Study Guide to Lesson Planning* (Nashville: Broadman, 1978) is designed especially for Sunday school teachers. Walk Thru the Bible Ministries sponsors two seminars that provide a memorable survey of the history of either the Old or New Testament (61 Perimeter Park, N.E., Atlanta, GA 30341, [404] 458-9300).

21. One helpful consultation service for youth work is Sonlife, a parachurch youth organization. Their ministry statement details their burden: "to train this generation of younger leadership in a biblical strategy of evangelism and discipleship." Following ten years of direct ties with Moody Bible Institute, Sonlife has recently chosen to broaden its focus. At the time of this writing, eleven major denominations have secured a special affiliation with Sonlife. Within this working partnership, Sonlife develops a long-range plan for leadership training and mobilization per denomination. Each year a three-year vision statement is critiqued and implemented via specific goals. For further information, write: Sonlife, 1119 Wheaton Oaks Court, Wheaton, IL 60187.

22. Several books outline a number of creative strategies for identifying potential workers. See Senter (1990).

Chapter 18: Focus on Task: Designing Ministry Programs

1. A related challenge: We must refrain from judging creative and culturally relevant methodologies.

2. Our wheel design is an adaptation of a traditional understanding of the planning process. This approach is utilized by evangelical educators ("the educational cycle"; see LeBar 1968, p. 27; Getz 1974, p. 250; Gangel 1989, p. 38). Appreciation is expressed to Robert Radcliffe (one of LeBar's former students) for noting the utility of these concepts in contemporary practice.

3. Initially believers brought their monetary gifts to the apostles for distribution to the needy (see Acts 4:34–35, 37; 5:2).

4. Gangel recognizes the need for Christian teachers to develop such a Christian worldview:

The premise of this book rests on a twofold presupposition: that the Christian teacher is our best hope for rationality in an irrational age; and, that those Christian teachers must have highly developed and thoroughly consecrated minds in order to meet the challenge of leadership in such an age. Such minds are tuned to the process of constant biblical integration of faith and learning, a spiritual and academic commitment which stretches far beyond the boundaries of content transmission. (1988, p. 74)

5. The concept of working with decision makers is developed by Patton (1978).

6. This particular survey was adapted from one developed by Don Moore. See Sudman and Bradburn (1982) and Gorden (1980) for additional information on how to conduct surveys and interviews. For information regarding educational evaluation guidelines, see Worthen and Sanders (1987).

7. Our English word "deacon" is basically a transliteration of the Greek verb meaning "to wait on tables" (*diakoneō;* Acts 6:2); compare the use of the noun form in Luke 22:27.

8. Throughout Scripture, we see God initiating new forms of ministry by first identifying people with the right qualifications (e.g., Moses and the judges in Exod. 18:17–23; tabernacle craftsmen in Exod. 31:1–6; levitical priests in Lev. 21–22; and church elders in 1 Tim. 3; Titus 1).

9. For additional information about principles of program and course design, see Posner and Rudnitsky (1989). For a resource written from a Christian perspective, see Colson and Rigdon (1981). The educational ministry of the church usually takes a nonformal education mode, since it focuses on life-skill, functional emphases.

10. Some choose to use the term "curriculum development" for the particular task of this phase. Those having a broader view of the term use it to describe this phase *and* the previous two: program purposes, program development, *and* materials development.

11. Various kinds of teaching materials serving differing purposes are available. Some curriculums follow a basic "textbook" or content-centered approach. They predominantly act as an informational resource tool, somewhat like an encyclopedia. Others are "student-friendly," providing specific assistance for learning (e.g., a student's workbook). Still other materials are more "teacher-friendly." These resources offer suggestions for effective teaching. They do so through a series of detailed lesson plans (e.g., the teacher's or leader's guide). In addition to these materials, teachers select from a number of instructional methods.

12. For a helpful guide to training small group leaders, see McBride (1990).

13. Strategy A uses Categories 2 and 3; Strategy B deals with Categories 1 and possibly 2.

14. A description of the various ministries and responsibilities from Figure 18.2 are provided in Appendix I.

15. First Timothy 5:17 suggests that all elders have a managing function ("ruling"), whereas only some elders participate in the teaching ministry.

16. How do full-time vocational pastoral staff fit into this structure? In a two-tiered system of elders and deacons, pastoral staff qualify either as main board members (e.g., elders) or as committee members (e.g., deacons), depending on their qualifications and ministry background. For example, an experienced pastor could be the elder responsible for worship and preaching. A youth pastor, as recent seminary graduate, may first serve as a deacon with other deacons in the youth ministry. Eventually, this youth pastor may qualify to become an elder and a member of the main board.

17. Regarding the composition of most Christian education committees, two primary options exist: (1) the traditional

representational committee, on which each leader of the major educational programs serves (e.g., Sunday school superintendent, nursery director, children's club leader, youth club leader, church librarian, etc.); and (2) the *policy-making* committee, in which members, not program leaders, supervise larger areas of ministry (e.g., early childhood coordinator, childhood coordinator, youth coordinator, and adult coordinator). The *representational* committee allows immediate communication among program leaders, but discussion tends to focus on program specifics and not on larger policy issues. Also, "the squeakiest wheel gets the most oil." The *policy-making* committee gives its attention to the broader concerns of educational ministry. Specific problem solving for each program is resolved by the respective committee member and that program leader.

18. A discussion of the concepts of "willingness" and "ability" (used by Hersey and Blanchard 1982) is found in our "Vocational Development" section in Chapter 6. For additional information about supervising teachers, see Glickman (1985).

19. Your answers should be, in order, vertically: F, E, C, D, A, G, B.

20. The correct sequence is: (1) program evaluation and staff review, (2) program problems and people needs, (3) program purposes and staff qualifications, (4) program development and staff recruitment, (5) teaching materials development and staff training, (6) program implementation with prepared staff, and (7) program coordination and staff supervision. See Figure 18.1.

Chapter 19: At a Crossroad

1. There are several ways to create a balanced approach to theory and practice, even within a traditional instructional setting. For example, consider a course in youth ministry. Students could be assigned a project that includes spending a half-day in a local high school. They could experience activities like gym, lunch, hallway encounters, and classes. They could critique their "practice" through course readings on pertinent theologies and theories about young people.

2. Ten real-life alternatives to Alicia's education are cited in Ferris' (1990) study of innovative Christian higher education models.

3. Consider the following, additional case studies, with slight modifications from Grunlan and Mayers (1979, p. 247):

> Mary sits under a swaying palm tree on the beach overlooking the Pacific Ocean as it rolls up on a Malayan island. Next to her sits a young mother feeding her baby and sharing with Mary some of the traditions of her people.

> Harold sits at a table in the broiling sun outside a hut in Kenya, Africa. Equipped with a piece of paper and pencil, he asks an African youth to draw a picture of a person.

> Philip takes note of who's absent in his Chicago class. Throughout the day, as always, he mentally records nonverbal behavior. He observes other signs, too, including social interaction and quality of homework assignments. Three of his best students appear to be very troubled this week.

> Carl sits at the edge of a clearing in a tropical rain forest watching an Indian wedding ceremony. He carefully notes who sits where and who speaks with whom.

What do Mary, Harold, Philip, Carl, and Linda have in common? "They are all involved in anthropological research," according to Grunlan and Mayers (1979, p. 247). They all show sensitivity to the particular elements of their environments. This research is invaluable to a comprehensive educational philosophy. It tends to demonstrate matters pertinent to praxis learning.

4. We should communicate a relevant gospel. But we can't address diverse, demanding needs unless we possess the appropriate tools. We must be trained to be good observers. We must know our particular audience. Lewis (1970, p. 94, emphasis added) summarized it this way: "We must learn the language of our audience. And let me say at the outset that it is no use at all laying down *a priori* what the 'plain man' does not understand. *You have to find out by experience.*"

Anderson (1990, p. 134) offers practical advice, based on Lewis' principle to adapt the gospel to subculture needs: "If Christians and the church are to become effective in reaching modern pagans, we will need to go to them. In other words, we need to change the starting point of evangelism. We need to start where they are instead of where we are."

5. Appreciation is expressed to Tom Mosely, one of our pastors, for pointing out this fourfold comparison.

6. Appreciation is expressed to Mark Sandberg, one of our students, for his helpful insights here.

7. On a related matter, isn't it remarkable how cross-references to the Old Testament are noticeably absent from Paul's lengthy sermon? Conversely, Paul refers to pagan Greek writings for the purpose of authenticating his message!

Accordingly, Bruce (1959, p. 11, emphasis added) concludes that "while Jesus remains the *same,* and the gospel is unchanging, the *means* adopted to defend the faith may vary according to the situation in which the apologist finds himself and the public with which he is confronted."

8. Barclay (1970, p. 166, emphasis added) contributes a fifth feature of Paul's descriptive skills, as he comments on several of Paul's sermons:

> For Paul, missionary preaching was *not a monologue but a dialogue.* True, it was proclamation, but it was not take-it-or-leave-it proclamation. It was proclamation plus explanation and defence. The characteristic word of Paul's missionary preaching in the synagogue is the word *argued.* In Damascus, in Thessalonica, in Athens, in Corinth, in Ephesus Paul argued in the synagogue (Acts 9:22; 17:2, 17; 18:4; 19:8). The faith was proclaimed and defended at the same time. Acceptance of it was not given on a wave of emotion; from the beginning the *mind* had to be satisfied as well as the *heart.*

9. For example, read Luke 16:1–13, the Parable of the Shrewd Manager. Ask yourself the following questions: (1) What did Jesus mean when he said, "For the people of this world are more shrewd in dealing with their own kind than are the people of the light" (v. 8b)? (2) What should we believers *learn*—and *not learn*—to replicate from the shrewd manager? (3) Extending Christ's use of this particular truth, what does it mean to *learn from* "the people of this world?"

10. See Bowman (1990, pp. 9–10) for a realistic portrayal of education's complexity. He particularly focuses on the inner thought processes and reactions of three fictitious students in a Christian education setting. He concludes: "All this inner responding, from these alert class members, is racing along at a rate of about 450 words a minute. The teacher, meanwhile, having spoken four summary sentences of great importance, would do well to stop and provide illustrations. And each illustrative section, in turn, will prompt more reflections by learners" (p. 10). The alert reader may remember that the advice to use illustrations is supported by Identification Learning, one of the six avenues of learning.

11. Cited in the prologue of Minsky (1986, p. 17).

Appendix B: Multidisciplinary Evidences for Quests and Filters

1. Recall that the corresponding theme, Communion with God, is central to the presentation in Chapter 3.

2. Cited in Yancey (1988, p. 253, emphasis added).

3. This truth parallels Cornelius' conversion in Acts 11. Luke calls this centurion a "devout and God-fearing" man, who "prayed to God regularly" (v. 2). Later, at the moment of Cornelius' salvation experience, Peter acknowledges that "[God] accepts men from every nation who fear him and do what is right" (v. 35).

4. Anderson (1950/1975, p. 236) confronts the question of God's gracious work through other religions. He speaks of the quest of Immortality which is fully resolved in Christ alone: "It is not through other religions as 'saving structures,' as I see it, but rather through the basic fact of God's general revelation, vouchsafed in nature and in all that is true (including, of course, the truth there is in other religions), and the equally fundamental fact of our common humanity, that the Spirit of God, or the 'cosmic Christ,' brings home to men and women something of their need."

In his presentation, Anderson also cites Newbigin (1969, p. 59, emphasis added) regarding those who believe in Christ after other religious experiences. Newbigin discusses the "element of continuity" that is "confirmed in the experience of many who have become converts to Christianity from other religions. Even though this conversion involves a radical discontinuity, yet there is often the strong conviction afterwards that *it was the living and true God who was dealing with them in the days of their pre-Christian wrestlings*."

5. See Murdock (1945).

6. Smart (1969, pp. 6–11) identifies similar features within all religions. Smart cites six dimensions: ritual, mythological, doctrinal, ethical, social, and experiential. Kraft (1979, pp. 84–89) designates four major areas of human experience and need. These include such factors as Maslow's (1954/1970) physiological and psychological concerns. Kraft labels his foursome as biological, psychological, sociocultural, and spiritual human needs.

7. A comprehensive study of adult faith development discovered that the concept of transcendence was a remarkably significant factor in growth. [See *Faith Development in the Adult Life Cycle*, (1987), Part 3, Module 2, p. 46]: "About 35% talked about experiencing a sense of the holy or other transcendent moments when the ordinary becomes extraordinary. These were unexpected but moving moments when a person felt connected to a power or source beyond the self. These often occurred while one was close to nature or through experience with music and art. Both men and women had these experiences."

8. Paul's experience at the Areopagus professes Fowler's third component: The altar "To the Unknown God" testifies of the universal attraction to "shared center(s) of value and power."

9. Kraft (1979, p. 93) lists six of his own values, including enablement to: "(1) discover some of our unconsciously employed evaluational criteria, (2) learn to employ more appropriate criteria (such as 'fit' and 'adequacy'), (3) learn to evaluate components of culture rather than whole cultures, (4) recognize the complexity of the task, (5) recognize the likelihood that we will be culturally biased in our evaluations, and (6) develop a cautious and humble attitude in our evaluating."

10. Kraft (1979, p. 30) identifies this principle as follows: "Jesus continually worked toward model and paradigm shifts on the part of his hearers. His parables were regularly introduced with some phrase such as 'The kingdom of heaven is like . . .' The whole concept of a kingdom that is to function *within* earthly kingdoms, rather than to compete with them, was a radically different model of reality. Its differentness from the models already in his hearers' minds is attested to by the extreme difficulty they had in understanding and converting to it. Then, in presenting the kingdom, Jesus continually employed model-type analogies such as mustard seed, the sower, leaven, a treasure, a pearl, etc. He presented God as 'Father' and himself as 'Son.' This is a powerful and pervasive model based on the importance in the minds of his Hebrew hearers of the first son in the Hebrew family."

11. Kraft (pp. 57–58) adds these illustrations:

> Note, for example, the conflict between underlying assumptions in the events recorded in Acts 14:8–18. Paul and Barnabas had healed a lame man in the town of Lystra. A considerable commotion arose over the event because the Lystrans assumed that only the gods could effect such a healing. When they saw what happened, they concluded that Paul and Barnabas were gods and began to worship and offer sacrifices to them. The assumption in the apostles' minds, of course, was that by healing the lame man, they would enhance their witness in that place. Typical (non-Christian) Americans observing such an event would be likely to conclude that Paul was simply a good psychologist, since they would assume a naturalistic (not a supernaturalistic) explanation for such events.
>
> In Acts 28:1–6, we see the people of Melita arriving at a conclusion similar to that of the Lystrans. They, too, assumed that only gods could survive the bite of a poisonous snake. Americans observing such an event would again come to a different conclusion because their assumptions would be different.

Appendix C: Perspectives on Persons

1. Whether the bodies of Adam and Eve were originally immortal is subject to debate (see Gen. 3:22).

2. In the early years before the flood, humankind lived longer. Adam and Methusaleh lived over 900 years (Gen. 5:5, 27). Current limits appear to be under 120 years, as indicated by the Guiness records (cf. Ps. 90:10).

3. Gundry (1987) argues that "*soma* denotes the physical body" (p. 50) and only the physical body. He claims that the term never refers to the whole person.

4. The dichotomous (two substances: body and soul/spirit) and trichotomous (three substances: body, soul, and spirit) views will be grouped together since their agreements (both hold to anthropological dualism) are greater than their differences. The trichomotous view makes a further distinction in the immaterial aspects of humanity—between soul and spirit.

5. The "extinction-recreation" view of the afterlife is the only logically defensible conclusion of ontological monism and is represented in MacKay (1980) and Reichenbach (1983—although he does not hold to an intermediate state). The other posited view, "immediate resurrection," involves an instantaneous "body switch" at death. This particular view is held by Anderson (1982) and Harris (1985), and may be inferred in Carey (1977). Yet, if continuity of existence is posited, then some form of dualism must be affirmed (Cooper 1989, pp. 180–85).

6. The monism-dualism debate has surfaced again largely due to the results of brain research. It has been found that states of consciousness are significantly dependent on brain functioning. Electrical stimulation of the brain and the use of certain chemicals can influence a person's thoughts and emotions. In response to these and other findings, MacKay (1980) and Myers (1978) have opted for a monistic view of personhood.

   For further treatment of the issue within a Christian understanding, from a social science perspective, see Van Leeuwen (1985, chap. 6); from a philosophical perspective, see Evans (1981) and Moreland (1987, chap. 3).

7. The following summaries are quoted from a forty-five-page report prepared for the Conservative Baptist Association by a committee of seminary faculty. It reviews the major terms, issues, and passages involved in the debate. The study packet can be purchased from Western Seminary, 5511 S.E. Hawthorne Boulevard, Portland, OR 97215.

8. For further study, see Hurley (1981), who represents a moderate position (yet hierarchical applications tend to be offered). For a representative of the egalitarian position, see Bilezikian (1985). For a more hierarchical presentation, see Clark (1980). Ordination of women is a related but separate issue.

Appendix J: Practical Categories of Instructional Questions from Jesus' Ministry

1. The centralized *Communion* theme was his focus.

2. The following section represents a condensation and modification of Delnay's (1987, pp. 74–83) seven categories. In addition to the passages noted here, see also John 8:10 and Luke 24:17, among others.

3. Delnay (1987, p. 75) comments: "In this case the Lord used a question to state a doctrine. While the question seems to have invited a yes or no answer, it also carried a load of meaning. The man once blind had come to some insight; he knew that Jesus was a man of God. The Lord's question dropped on him like a rock: godliness is one thing; deity is a vastly higher matter. The simple question introduced it. Earnest Jew that the man was, he understood the awesome claim and accepted it."

4. Delnay (p. 79) lists other confrontive passages like Matthew 16:8; Luke 12:26; 24:38; John 3:10–12; 4:35; 10:32; 11:26; 13:38; 16:31; 21:15–17; and especially 21:22.

5. Delnay (1987, p. 81) notes: "Some of our students may be virtual hecklers. On the other hand, some of our earnest disciples will pick up ideas that, however unscriptural, are still hard to dislodge. In such cases we might lecture, but our stubborn hearer will just tighten the strap on his protective helmet. Is there any way to pry open his mind? Lacking that, is there any way to curb his opposition?"

6. Paul's imperative is directly tied to Jesus' famous axiom (from the same Acts 20:35 verse): "It is more blessed to give than to receive."

References

Adams, Jay E. 1989. *From forgiven to forgiving*. Wheaton, Ill.: Victor.

Aleshire, Daniel. 1988. *Faithcare: Ministering to all God's people through the ages of life*. Philadelphia: Westminster.

Allen, Ronald. 1985. *Lord of song: The messiah revealed in the Psalms*. Portland, Oreg.: Multnomah.

Anderson, Leith. 1990. *Dying for change*. Minneapolis, Minn.: Bethany House.

Anderson, Norman. 1950, 1975. A Christian approach to comparative religion. In *The world's religions*, ed. Norman Anderson. 4th ed. London: InterVarsity.

Anderson, Ray. 1982. *On being human: Essays in theological anthropology*. Grand Rapids: Eerdmans.

Anderson, Ray, and Dennis Guernsey. 1985. *On being family: A social theology of the family*. Grand Rapids: Eerdmans.

Ausubel, David. 1963. *The psychology of meaningful verbal learning: An introduction to school learning*. New York: Grune and Stratton.

_____. 1968. *Educational psychology: A cognitive approach*. New York: Holt, Rinehart and Winston.

Bandura, Albert. 1977. *Social learning theory*. Englewood Cliffs, N.J.: Prentice-Hall.

_____. 1986. *Social foundations of thought and action: A social cognitive theory*. Englewood Cliffs, N.J.: Prentice-Hall.

Barber, Lucie W. 1981. *The religious education of preschool children*. Birmingham, Ala.: Religious Education.

Barbour, Ian G. 1974. *Myths, models and paradigms*. New York: Harper and Row.

Barclay, William. 1964. *New Testament words*. Philadelphia: Westminster.

_____. 1970. A comparison of Paul's preaching. In *Apostolic history and the gospel*, ed. W. Ward Gasque and Ralph P. Martin. Grand Rapids: Eerdmans.

Barna, George. 1990. *The frog in the kettle: What Christians need to know about life in the year 2000*. Ventura, Calif.: Regal.

Barth, Karl. 1961. *Church dogmatics*. Vol. 3. Edinburgh, Scotland: T. & T. Clark.

Bartlett, Josiah. 1848. *An inquiry into the degree of certainty in medicine, and into the nature and extent of its power over disease*. Philadelphia: Lea and Blanchard.

Bateman, Walter L. 1990. *Open to question: The art of teaching and learning by inquiry*. San Francisco: Jossey-Bass.

Bausch, William J. 1984. *Storytelling: Imagination and faith*. Mystic, Conn.: Twenty-Third.

Bellezza, Francis. 1981. Mnemonic devices: Classification, characteristics and criteria. *Review of Educational Research* 51 (2): 247–75.

Bennett, Christine L. 1990. Learning styles: Interactions between culture and the individual. In *Comprehensive multicultural education: Theory and practice*. 2d ed. Boston: Allyn and Bacon.

Benson, Dennis C. 1985. *Creative worship in youth ministry*. Loveland, Calif.: Group Books.

Bertolini, Dewey. 1989. *Back to the heart of youth work*. Wheaton, Ill.: Victor.

Bilezikian, Gilbert. 1985. *Beyond sex roles*. Grand Rapids: Baker.

Bloom, Benjamin, et al. 1956. *Taxonomy of educational objectives. Handbook 1: Cognitive domain*. New York: David McKay.

Bolton, Barbara, Charles T. Smith, and Wes Haystead. 1987. *Everything you wanted to know about teaching children: Grades 1–6*. Ventura, Calif.: Regal.

References

Bolton, Robert, and Dorothy Grover Bolton. 1984. *Social styles/management styles: Developing productive work relationships.* New York: American Management Association.

Bonham, L. Adrienne. 1988. Learning style use: In need of perspective. *Lifelong Learning: An Omnibus of Practice and Research* 11 (5): 14–17, 19.

Bonhoeffer, Dietrich. 1963. *The cost of discipleship.* Rev. ed. New York: Macmillan.

Borgman, Dean. 1987. A history of American youth ministry. In *The complete book of youth ministry,* ed. Warren S. Benson and Mark H. Senter, III. Chicago: Moody.

Borthwick, Paul. 1988. *Youth and missions.* Wheaton, Ill.: Victor.

Bowman, Locke E., Jr. 1990. *Teaching for Christian hearts, souls, and minds: A constructive, holistic approach to Christian education.* San Francisco: Harper and Row.

Bridgeman, Diane L. 1983. *The nature of prosocial development.* New York: Academic.

Brilhart, John, and Gloria Galanes. 1989. *Effective group discussion.* 6th ed. Dubuque, Iowa: William C. Brown.

Bronfenbrenner, Urie. 1979. *The ecology of human development.* Cambridge, Mass.: Harvard University Press.

Brookfield, Stephen D. 1987. *Developing critical thinkers: Challenging adults to explore alternative ways of thinking and acting.* San Francisco: Jossey-Bass.

———. 1990. Discussion. In *Adult learning methods: A guide for effective instruction,* ed. Michael W. Galbraith. Malabar, Fla.: Krieger.

———. 1991. Grounded teaching in learning. In *Facilitating adult learning,* ed. W. Galbraith. Malabar, Fla.: Krieger.

Brown, Harold O. J. 1977. *The reconstruction of the republic.* New Rochelle, N.Y.: Arlington.

Brown, Lowell. 1986. *Sunday school standards.* Rev. ed. Ventura, Calif.: Gospel Light.

Bruce, F. F. 1959. *The defence of the gospel in the New Testament.* Grand Rapids: Eerdmans.

Brueggemann, Walter. Covenanting as human vocation. *Interpretation* 33 (2): 115–29.

Bruner, Jerome. 1977. *The process of education.* Cambridge, Mass.: Harvard University Press.

Buechner, Frederick. 1969. *The hungering dark.* San Francisco: Harper and Row.

———. 1984. *A room called remember.* San Francisco: Harper and Row.

Bufford, Rodger. 1981. *The human reflex: Behavioral psychology in biblical perspective.* San Francisco: Harper and Row.

Burns, Jim. 1988. *The youth builder.* Eugene, Oreg.: Harvest House.

Bushnell, Horace. 1916. *Christian nurture.* New Haven, Conn.: Yale University Press.

Buss, A. H., and R. Plomin. 1984. *Temperament: Early developing personality traits.* Hillsdale, N.J.: Erlbaum.

Buzzard, Lynn R., and Laurence Eck. 1982. *Tell it to the church: Reconciling out of court.* Elgin, Ill.: David C. Cook.

Campolo, Anthony. 1983. *Ideas for social action.* Grand Rapids: Zondervan.

Carey, George. 1977. *I believe in man.* Grand Rapids: Eerdmans.

Choun, Robert J. 1988. Teaching children. In *The Christian educator's handbook on teaching: A comprehensive resource on the distinctiveness of true Christian teaching,* ed. Kenneth O. Gangel and Howard G. Hendricks. Wheaton, Ill.: Victor.

Christie, Les. 1987. *Unsung heroes: How to recruit and train volunteer youth workers.* Grand Rapids: Zondervan.

Ciccheti, Dante, and Petra Hesse, eds. 1982. *Emotional development.* New directions for child development, 16. San Francisco: Jossey-Bass.

Clark, Robert E., Joanne Brubaker, and Roy B. Zuck, eds. 1986. *Childhood education in the church.* Rev. ed. Chicago: Moody.

Clark, Stephen B. 1980. *Man and woman in Christ.* Ann Arbor: Servant.

Cole, Elbert C. 1981. Lay ministries with older adults. In *Ministry with the aging,* ed. William M. Clements. San Francisco: Harper and Row.

Coleman, Lucien E. 1984. *Why the church must teach.* Nashville: Broadman.

Colson, Howard, and Raymond Rigdon. 1981. *Understanding your church's curriculum.* Nashville: Broadman.

Conservative Baptist Seminaries. 1989. *Women's ministry roles and ordination study packet.* Portland, Oreg.: Western Seminary.

Cook, Stuart. 1988. Measurement and evaluation. In *The Christian educator's handbook on teaching: A comprehensive resource on the distinctiveness of true Christian teaching,* eds. Kenneth O. Gangel and Howard G. Hendricks. Wheaton, Ill.: Victor.

Cooper, John W. 1989. *Body, soul, and life everlasting: Biblical anthropology and the monism-dualism debate.* Grand Rapids: Eerdmans.

Copeman, W. S. C. 1960. *Doctors and diseases in Tudor times.* London: Dawsons of Pall Mall.

Cornett, Claudia. 1983. *What you should know about teaching and learning styles.* Bloomington, Ind.: Phi Delta Kappa Foundation.

Cosgrove, Mark. 1987. *The amazing body human: God's design for personhood.* Grand Rapids: Baker.

Cragoe, Thomas. 1987. An examination of the issue of infant salvation. Th.D. diss., Dallas Theological Seminary, 1987.

Curran, Dolores, 1983. *Traits of a healthy family: Fifteen traits commonly found in healthy families by those who work with them.* San Francisco: Harper and Row.

———. 1987. *Traits of a healthy family.* San Francisco: Harper and Row. [video, 55 min.]

———. 1988. *Traits of a healthy family study guide.* San Francisco: Harper and Row.

Daily Watch. 1990. Wheaton, Ill.: Pioneer Clubs.

Davis, Robert H., Lawrence T. Alexander, and Stephen L. Yelon. 1974. *Learning system design: An approach to the improvement of instruction.* New York: McGraw-Hill.

Delling, G. 1972. *Huperauxano.* In *Theological dictionary of the New Testament,* vol. 5, ed. G. Friederich. Grand Rapids: Eerdmans.

Delnay, Robert G. 1987. *Teach as He taught.* Chicago: Moody.

Dickens, Charles. n.d. *A tale of two cities.* New York: Random House.

Diehl, William E. 1991. *The Monday connection.* San Francisco: Harper.

Dieter, Melvin, et al. 1987. *Five views on sanctification.* Grand Rapids: Eerdmans.

Dillon, J. T. 1987. *Questioning and teaching: A manual of practice.* New York: Teacher's College.

Dobson, James. 1974. *Hide or seek.* Old Tappan, N.J.: Revell.

———. 1982. *Dr. Dobson answers your questions.* Wheaton, Ill.: Tyndale.

Dockery, Karen. 1989. *Combined efforts: A youth worker's guide to ministry to and through parents.* Wheaton, Ill.: Victor.

Doud, Guy Rice. 1990. *Molder of dreams.* Pamona, Calif.: Focus on the Family.

Downs, Perry. 1983. Child evangelization. *Christian Education Journal* 3 (2): 5–13.

Doyle, Walter, ed. 1990. *The handbook of research on teacher education.* New York: Macmillan.

Dunn, Rita, Jeffrey Beaudry, and Angela Klavas. 1989. Survey of research on learning styles. *Educational Leadership* 46 (6): 50–58.

Dunn, Rita, and Kenneth Dunn. 1978. *Teaching students through their individual learning styles: A practical approach.* Reston, Va.: Reston.

Dunn, Rita, and S. A. Griggs. 1988. *Learning style: Quiet revolution in American secondary schools.* Reston, Va.: National Association of Secondary School Principals.

Duska, Ronald, and Mariellen Whelan. 1975. *Moral development: A guide to Piaget and Kohlberg.* New York: Paulist.

Dworetzky, John. 1981. *Introduction to child development.* St. Paul, Minn.: West.

Dykstra, Craig. 1990. Learning theory. In *Harper's encyclopedia of religious education,* eds. Iris V. Cully and Kendig B. Cully. San Francisco: Harper and Row.

Dykstra, Craig, and Sharon Parks, eds. 1986. *Faith development and Fowler.* Birmingham, Ala.: Religious Education.

Eisner, Elliot. 1985. *The educational imagination.* 2d ed. New York: Macmillan.

Elias, John. 1983. *Psychology and religious education.* 3d ed. Malabar, Fla.: Robert E. Krieger.

_____. 1986. *Foundations and practice of adult religious education.* Melbourne, Fla.: Robert Krieger.

Elkind, David. 1978. Understanding the young adolescent. *Adolescence* 13: 127–34.

_____. 1984. *All grown up and no place to go.* Reading, Mass.: Addison-Wesley.

Elkind, David, and Irving B. Weiner. 1978. *Development of the child.* New York: Wiley.

Ellis, C. Nelson. 1971. *Where faith begins.* Philadelphia: John Knox.

Enderlein, Cheryl. 1989. *Searching together.* Wheaton, Ill.: Pioneer Clubs.

Ericksen, Stanford C. 1984. *The essence of good teaching.* San Francisco: Jossey-Bass.

Erickson, Millard. 1985. *Christian theology.* Grand Rapids: Baker.

Erikson, Erik. 1963. *Childhood and society.* 2d ed. New York: Norton.

_____. 1968. *Identity: Youth and crisis.* New York: Norton.

_____. 1982. *The life cycle completed: A review.* New York: Norton.

Evans, Stephen. 1981. Separable souls: A defense of minimal dualism. *Southern Journal of Philosophy* 19: 313–31.

Faith development in the adult life cycle. 1987. Prepared for the Religious Education Association of the United States and Canada, Minneapolis, Minn.

Farnsworth, Kirk. 1985. *Whole-hearted integration: Harmonizing psychology and Christianity through word and deed.* Grand Rapids: Baker.

Ferris, Robert W. 1990. *Renewal in theological education: Strategies for change.* Wheaton, Ill.: Billy Graham Center, Wheaton College.

Festinger, Leon. 1957. *A theory of cognitive dissonance.* Stanford: Stanford University Press.

Fine, Marvin J. 1988. *The second handbook on parent education: Contemporary perspectives.* New York: Academic.

Fisher, Kurt, and Louise Silvern. 1985. Stages and individual differences in cognitive development. *Annual Review of Psychology* 36: 613–48.

Fiske, Marjorie, and David A. Chiriboga. 1990. *Change and contriving in adult life.* San Francisco: Jossey-Bass.

Flavell, John H., and E. Markham, eds. 1983. Cognitive development. In *Handbook of child psychology,* ed. Paul Mussen. New York: Wiley.

Foltz, Nancy T., ed. 1986. *Handbook of adult religious education.* Birmingham, Ala.: Religious Education.

_____. 1988. The context of wanting. In *Does the church really want religious education?* ed. Marlene Mayr. Birmingham, Ala.: Religious Education.

_____, ed. 1990. *Religious education in the small membership church.* Birmingham, Ala.: Religious Education.

Ford, LeRoy. 1978. *Design for teaching and training.* Nashville: Broadman.

Fowler, James W. 1981. *Stages of faith: The psychology of human development and the quest for meaning.* San Francisco: Harper and Row.

_____. 1984. *Becoming adult, becoming Christian: Adult development and Christian faith.* San Francisco: Harper and Row.

_____. 1986. Faith and the structure of meaning. In *Faith development and Fowler,* ed. Craig Dykstra and Sharon Parks. Birmingham, Ala.: Religious Education.

_____. 1987. *Faith development and pastoral care.* Philadelphia: Fortress.

Frankena, William K. 1965. *Philosophy of education.* New York: Macmillan.

Fromm, Erich. 1955. *The sane society.* New York: Rinehart.

Gaebelein, Frank. 1954. *Patterns of God's truth.* Chicago: Moody.

Gage, Nathan L., and David C. Berliner. 1988. *Educational psychology.* 4th ed. Boston: Houghton Mifflin.

Gagne, Robert. 1977. *The conditions of learning.* 3d ed. New York: Holt, Rinehart and Winston.

Galbraith, Michael W. 1991. The adult learning transactional process. In *Facilitating adult learning: A transactional process,* ed. Michael W. Galbraith. Malabar, Fla.: Krieger.

Gangel, Kenneth O. 1974. *24 ways to improve your teaching.* Wheaton, Ill.: Victor.

_____. 1988. Biblical integration: The process of thinking like a Christian. In *The Christian educator's handbook on teaching,* ed. Kenneth O. Gangel and Howard G. Hendricks. Wheaton, Ill.: Victor.

_____. 1989. *Feeding and leading: A practical handbook on administration in churches and Christian organizations.* Wheaton, Ill.: Victor.

Gangel, Kenneth O., and Warren Benson. 1983. *Christian education: Its history and philosophy.* Chicago: Moody.

Geertz, Clifford. 1972. Religion as a cultural system. In *Reader in comparative religion,* ed. W. A. Lessa and E. A. Vogt. 3d ed. New York: Harper and Row.

George, Carl. 1982. Recruitment's missing link. *Leadership.*

Getz, Gene. 1974. *Sharpening the focus of the church.* Chicago: Moody.

Glatthorn, Allan. 1987. *Curriculum leadership.* Glenview, Ill.: Scott, Foresman.

Glickman, Carl. 1985. *Supervision of instruction: A developmental approach.* Boston: Allyn and Bacon.

Godin, A. J., ed. 1965. *From religious experience to a religious attitude.* Chicago: Loyola University Press.

Goldschmidt, Walter. 1966. *Comparative functionalism.* Berkeley: University of California Press.

Goldsmith, H. H. 1983. Genetic influences on personality from infancy to adulthood. *Child Development* 54: 331–55.

Goldsmith, H. H., et al. 1987. Roundtable: What is temperament? Four approaches. *Child Development* 58: 505–29.

Goleman, D. 1986, December 2. Major personality study finds that traits are mostly inherited. *New York Times,* 17–18.

Gonzales, Arturo F., Jr. 1987, February. Giving a sucker an even break. *MD:* 65–69.

Gorden, Raymond. 1980. *Interviewing: Strategies, techniques and tactics.* Homewood, Ill.: Dorsey.

Gribbon, Robert T. 1990. *Developing faith in young adults.* New York: Alban Institute.

Griffin, Em. 1982. *Getting together: A guide for good groups.* Downers Grove, Ill.: InterVarsity.

Groome, Thomas H. 1980. *Christian religious education: Sharing our story and vision.* San Francisco: Harper and Row.

————. 1991. *Sharing faith: A comprehensive approach to religious education and pastoral ministry.* San Francisco: Harper and Row.

Grunlan, Stephen A., and Marvin K. Mayers. 1979. *Cultural anthropology: A Christian perspective.* Grand Rapids: Zondervan.

Guernsey, Dennis. 1982. *A new design for family ministry.* Elgin, Ill.: David C. Cook.

Gundersen, Bev, and Linda Kondracki. 1991. *Junior electives: Teaching kids how to live in today's world.* Elgin, Ill.: David C. Cook.

Gundry, Robert. 1987. *Soma in biblical theology, with an emphasis on Pauline anthropology.* Grand Rapids: Zondervan.

Habermas, Ronald T. 1985. Even what you don't say counts. *Christian Education Journal* 5 (2): 24–27.

————. 1987, August 7. Gray matters. *Christianity Today:* 23–25.

————. 1989, Spring. Speaking in a language your family will hear. *Christian Education Today* 41 (2): 24–26.

————. 1990, Summer. Three distinctives of adolescent learning. *Youthworker* 7 (1): 70–73.

————. 1990. An examination of teaching paradigms: Three dialogical approaches which strengthen traditional androgogical practice. *Christian Education Journal* 10 (2): 47–54.

Hadidian, Alan, et al. 1989. *Creative family times: Practical activities for building character in your preschooler.* Chicago: Moody.

Hall, Edward T. 1959. *Silent language.* Greenwich, Conn.: Fawcett.

Hamilton, Ben. 1991. Kung-Fu conflict. *Sky* 20 (9): 92, 100.

Harris, Maria. 1987. *Teaching and religious imagination.* New York: Harper and Row.

Harris, Murray J. 1985. *Raised immortal: Resurrection and immortality in the New Testament.* Grand Rapids: Eerdmans.

Harrow, A. 1969. *A taxonomy of the psychomotor domain: A guide for developing behavioral objectives.* New York: David McKay.

Harner, Nevin C. 1939. *The educational work of the church.* New York: Abingdon-Cokesbury.

Harper, Norman E. 1981. *Making disciples: The challenge of Christian education at the end of the 20th century.* Memphis: Christian Studies Center.

Hauerwas, Stanley. 1985, Spring. The family as a school for character. *Religious Education* 80: 272–85.

Hawley, Gwen. 1988. *Measures of psychosocial development.* Odessa, Fla.: Psychological Assessment Resources.

Hayes, Edward. 1986. Evangelism of children. In *Childhood education in the church,* ed. Robert E. Clark, Joanne Brubaker, and Roy B. Zuck. Chicago: Moody.

Haystead, Wes. 1974. *Teaching your child about God: You can't begin too soon.* Ventura, Calif.: Regal.

————. 1989. *Everything you wanted to know about teaching young children: Birth–6 years.* Ventura: Calif.: Gospel Light.

Heinecken, Martin J. 1981. Christian theology and aging: Basic affirmations. In *Ministry with the aging,* ed. William M. Clements. San Francisco: Harper and Row.

Hendricks, Howard G. 1987. *Teaching to change lives.* Portland, Oreg.: Multnomah.

Hersey, Paul, and Ken Blanchard. 1982. *Management of organizational behavior: Utilizing human resources.* 4th ed. Englewood Cliffs, N.J.: Prentice-Hall.

Hershey, Terry. 1986. *Young adult ministry.* Loveland, Colo.: Group.

Herx, Henry, and Tony Zaza, eds. 1988. *The moral and entertainment values of 7500 movies on TV and video cassettes.* New York: Crossroads/Continuum.

Hesse, Petra, and Dante Ciccheti. 1982. Perspectives on an integrated theory of emotional development. In *Emotional development,* ed. Dante Ciccheti and Petra Hesse. New Directions for Child Development, 16. San Francisco: Jossey-Bass.

Hesselgrave, David J. 1979. *Communicating Christ cross-culturally.* Grand Rapids: Zondervan.

Hiebert, Paul G. 1976, 1983. *Cultural anthropology.* 2d ed. Grand Rapids: Baker.

————. 1985. *Anthropological insights for missionaries.* Grand Rapids: Baker.

Hoekema, Anthony. 1986. *Created in God's image.* Grand Rapids: Eerdmans.

Hoffman, Martin. 1977. Personality and social development. *Annual Review of Psychology* 28: 259–331.

Holmes, Arthur. 1977. *All truth is God's truth.* Grand Rapids: Eerdmans.

————. 1991. *Shaping character: Moral education in the Christian college.* Grand Rapids: Eerdmans.

Horne, Herman Harrell. 1982. *Teaching techniques of Jesus: How Jesus taught.* Repr., Grand Rapids: Kregel.

House, H. Wayne, ed. 1988. *Schooling choices: An examination of private, public, & home education.* Portland, Oreg.: Multnomah.

Houston, James. 1989. *The transforming friendship: A guide to prayer.* Oxford: Lion.

Hunt, Gladys. 1978. *Honey for a child's heart: The imaginative use of books in family life.* Grand Rapids: Zondervan.

Hunter, Madeline. 1982. *Mastery teaching.* El Segundo, Calif.: TIP.

Hurley, James. 1981. *Man and woman in biblical perspective.* Grand Rapids: Zondervan.

Hybels, Bill. 1987. *Who are you when no one's looking?* Downers Grove, Ill.: InterVarsity.

Hyman, Ronald. 1974. *Ways of teaching*. 2d ed. Philadelphia: Lippincott.

Ingle, Clifford, ed. 1970. *Children and conversion*. Nashville: Broadman.

Issler, Klaus. 1987. A conception of excellence in teaching. In *The best in theology*, ed. J. I. Packer. Carol Stream, Ill.: Christianity Today.

_____. 1989, Fall. Recruiting and retaining volunteer staff. *Christian Education Today* 41 (4): 6–9.

_____. 1990. Nurturing marriage and family life. *Christian Educational Journal* 10 (2): 75–85.

_____. Forthcoming. Conscience: Moral sensitivity and moral reasoning. In *Christian perspectives on being human: A multidisciplinary approach*, ed. J. P. Moreland and David Ciocchi. Grand Rapids: Baker.

Issler, Klaus, and Ted W. Ward. 1989. Moral development as a curriculum emphasis in American Protestant theological education. *Journal of Moral Education* 18 (2): 131–43.

Jaarsma, Cornelius. 1964. The learning process. In *An introduction to evangelical Christian education*, ed. J. Edward Hakes. Chicago: Moody.

Jackson, Philip. 1986. *The practice of teaching*. New York: Teacher's College Columbia.

Jeschke, Marlin. 1983. *Believers baptism for children of the church*. Scottdale, Pa.: Herald.

Jewett, A., and M. Mullan. 1977. Movement process categories in physical education in teaching-learning. In *Curriculum design: Purposes and procedures in physical education teaching-learning*. Washington, D.C.: American Alliance for Health, Physical Education and Recreation.

Jewett, Paul K. 1978. *Infant baptism and the covenant of grace*. Grand Rapids: Eerdmans.

Jones, Stephen D. 1987. *Faith shaping*. Rev. ed. Valley Forge, Pa.: Judson.

Joy, Donald. 1985. *Bonding: Relationships in the image of God*. Waco, Tex.: Word.

_____. 1986. Why reach and teach children? In *Childhood education in the church*, ed. Robert E. Clark, Joanne Brubaker, and Roy B. Zuck. Chicago: Moody.

Joyce, Bruce, and Marsha Weil. 1986. *Models of teaching*. 3d ed. Englewood Cliffs, N.J.: Prentice-Hall.

Joyce, Gruce, Marsha Weil, with Beverly Shower. 1992. *Models of teaching*. 4th ed. Englewood Cliffs, N.J.: Prentice-Hall.

Justice, William G., Jr. 1980. *Guilt and forgiveness*. Grand Rapids: Baker.

Kagan, Jerome. 1972. A conception of early adolescence. In *Twelve to Sixteen: Early Adolescence*, ed. Robert Coles et al. New York: Norton.

Kane, J. Herbert. 1981. *The Christian world mission: Today and tomorrow*. Grand Rapids: Baker.

Keesing, R. M., and F. M. Keesing. 1971. *New perspectives in cultural anthropology*. New York: Holt, Rinehart and Winston.

Kegan, Robert. 1982. *The evolving self: Problem and process in human development*. Cambridge, Mass.: Harvard University Press.

Keillor, Garrison. 1987. *Leaving home*. New York: Viking.

Keller, John. 1987. Development and use for the ARCS model of instructional design. *Journal of Instructional Development* 10 (3): 2–10.

Keyes, Ralph. 1976. *Is there life after high school?* New York: Warner.

Kibler, R., L. Barker, and D. Miles. 1970. *Behavior objectives and instruction*. Boston: Allyn and Bacon.

Kimball, Don. 1987. *Power and presence*. San Francisco: Harper and Row.

King, Lester. 1991. *Transformations in American medicine: From Benjamin Rush to William Osler*. Baltimore: Johns Hopkins University Press.

Kirkpatrick, Donald. 1986. *How to manage change effectively: Approaches, methods and case studies*. San Francisco: Jossey-Bass.

Kneller, George F. 1971. *Introduction to the philosophy of education*. 2d ed. New York: Wiley.

Knight, George R. 1980. *Philosophy and education: An introduction in Christian perspective*. Berrien Springs, Mich.: Andrews University Press.

Knowles, Malcolm S. 1980. *The modern practice of adult education: From pedagogy to andragogy*. Rev. ed. Englewood Cliffs, N.J.: Prentice-Hall.

Kohlberg, Lawrence. 1981. *The philosophy of moral development*. San Francisco: Harper and Row.

_____. 1984. *Essays on moral development*, vol. 2, *The psychology of moral development*. San Francisco: Harper and Row.

Kohlberg, Lawrence, Charles Levine, and Alexandra Hewer. 1983. *Moral stages: A current formulation and a response to critics*. Basel, Switzerland: Karger.

Kohlenberger, John. 1987. *Words about the Word*. Grand Rapids: Zondervan.

Kolb, David. 1984. *Experiential learning: Experience as the source of learning and development*. Englewood Cliffs, N.J.: Prentice-Hall.

Koons, Carolyn, and Michael J. Anthony. 1990. *Single adult passages: Uncharted territories*. Grand Rapids: Baker.

Koteskey, Ronald L. 1987. *Understanding adolescence*. Wheaton, Ill.: Victor.

Kraft, Charles H. 1979. *Christianity in culture*. Maryknoll, N.Y.: Orbis.

Krathwohl, David, Benjamin Bloom, and Bertram Masia. 1964. *Taxonomy of educational objectives—The classification of educational goals. Handbook II: Affective domain*. New York: David McKay.

Kuhmerker, Lisa. 1991. *The Kohlberg legacy for the helping professions*. Birmingham, Ala.: R.E.P.

Kurtines, William M., and Jacob L. Gewirtz, eds. 1987. *Moral development through social interaction*. New York: Wiley.

Kwast, Lloyd E. 1981. Understanding culture. In *Perspectives on the world Christian movement*, ed. R. D. Winter and S. C. Hawthorne. Pasadena, Calif.: William Carey Library.

Ladd, George. 1974. *A theology of the New Testament*. Grand Rapids: Eerdmans.

Larrick, Nancy. 1975. *A parent's guide to children's reading*. 4th ed. New York: Bantam.

Laurent, Robert. 1988. *Keeping your teen in touch with God*. Elgin, Ill.: David C. Cook.

LeBar, Lois E. 1968. *Focus on people in Christian education*. Old Tappan, N.J.: Revell.

_____. 1958, 1981. *Education that is Christian*. Old Tappan, N.J.: Revell.

Ledbetter, Mark. 1991. An evaluation of the construct validity of the Measures of Psychosocial Development using the normative sample: A confirmatory factor approach. Psy.D. diss., George Fox College.

References

Lee, James Michael. 1985. *The content of religious instruction.* Birmingham, Ala.: Religious Education.

———, ed. 1990. *Handbook of faith.* Birmingham, Ala.: Religious Education.

LeFever, Marlene. 1985. *Creative teaching methods.* Elgin, Ill.: David C. Cook.

———. 1991, Fall. Only children. *Teacher Touch.* Elgin, Ill.: David C. Cook.

Leman, Kevin. 1987. *Smart kids, stupid choices.* Ventura, Calif.: Regal/Gospel Light.

Levin, Michael. 1990, March. Can ethics be taught. *Reader's Digest:* 113–14.

Levinson, Daniel J. 1978. *The seasons of a man's life.* New York: Ballantine.

Lewis, C. S. 1950. *The lion, the witch and the wardrobe.* New York: Macmillan.

———. 1956. *The last battle.* New York: Macmillan.

———. 1959. *Surprised by joy.* London: Fontana.

———. 1970. Christian apologetics. In *God in the dock,* ed. Walter Hooper. Grand Rapids: Eerdmans.

———. 1975. *The weight of glory and other addresses.* New York: Macmillan.

Lewis, Gordon R., and Bruce A. Demarest. 1987. *Integrative theology,* vol. 1, *Knowing ultimate reality, The living God.* Grand Rapids: Zondervan.

———. 1990. *Integrative theology,* vol. 2, *Our primary need, Christ's atoning provisions.* Grand Rapids: Zondervan.

Lewis, Harold E. 1987, February. L'Amour on education. *Clearing House* 60 (6): 261–62.

Leypoldt, Martha. 1967. *40 ways to teach in groups.* Valley Forge, Pa.: Judson.

———. 1971. *Learning is change: Adult education in the church.* Valley Forge, Pa.: Judson.

Lickona, Thomas. 1983. *Raising good children: Helping your child through the stages of moral development.* New York: Bantam.

Lifton, Robert Jay. 1971. *History and human survival.* New York: Vintage.

Lingenfelter, Sherwood. 1992. *Transforming culture: A challenge for Christian mission.* Grand Rapids: Baker.

Lingenfelter, Sherwood, and Marvin Mayers. 1986. *Ministering cross-culturally: An incarnational model for personal relationships.* Grand Rapids: Baker.

Little, Sara. 1983. *To set one's heart: Belief and teaching in the church.* Atlanta: John Knox.

Loevinger, Jane. 1976. *Ego development: Conceptions and theories.* San Francisco: Jossey-Bass.

Lorayne, Harry, and Jerry Lucas. 1974. *The memory book.* New York: Ballantine.

Lowman, Joseph. 1984. *Mastering the techniques of teaching.* San Francisco: Jossey-Bass.

Lynn, David. 1988. *One-on-one.* El Cajon, Calif.: Youth Specialties.

Lynn, David, and Mike Yaconelli. 1985. *Grow for it! journal.* El Cajon, Calif.: Youth Specialties.

McBride, Neal. 1990. *How to lead small groups.* Colorado Springs, Colo.: NavPress.

McCarthy, Bernice. 1987. *The 4MAT system: Teaching to learning styles with right/left mode techniques.* Rev. ed. Barrington, Ill.: Excel.

McDonald, H. D. 1984. Man, doctrine of. In *Evangelical dictionary of theology,* ed. W. A. Elwell. Grand Rapids: Baker.

McGinnis, James. 1986. *Helping families care: Practical ideas for intergenerational programs.* New York: Crossroads/Continuum.

MacKay, Donald. 1980. *Brains, machines, and persons.* Grand Rapids: Eerdmans.

McKenzie, Leon. 1982. *The religious education of adults.* Birmingham, Ala.: Religious Education.

———. 1986. The purposes and scope of adult religious education. In *Handbook of adult religious education,* ed. Nancy T. Foltz. Birmingham, Ala.: Religious Education.

McLeish, J. 1976. The lecture method. In *The psychology of teaching methods: Seventy-fifth yearbook of the National Society for the Study of Education,* ed. N. L. Gage. Chicago: University of Chicago Press.

Mager, Robert. 1984a. *Developing attitudes toward learning.* Belmont, Calif.: David S. Lake.

———. 1984b. *Preparing instructional objectives.* Rev. ed. Belmont, Calif.: David S. Lake.

Maloney, H. Newton. 1990. The concept of faith in psychology. In *Handbook of faith,* ed. James Michael Lee. Birmingham, Ala.: Religious Education.

Mannin, E. E. 1966. *Loneliness.* London: Hutchins.

Marcia, James E. 1966. Development and validation of ego identity status. *Journal of Personality and Social Psychology* 3: 551–58.

———. 1980. Identity in adolescence. In *Handbook of adolescent psychology,* ed. Joseph Adelson. New York: Wiley.

Martin, Ralph P. 1978. *New Testament foundations: A guide for Christian students.* Vol. 2. Grand Rapids: Eerdmans.

Maslow, Abraham H. 1954, 1970. *Motivation and personality.* 2d ed. New York: Harper and Row.

Maxwell, John C. 1989. *Be a people person.* Wheaton, Ill.: Victor.

May, Rollo. 1953. The loneliness and anxiety of modern man. In *Man's search for himself.* New York: Norton.

Meier, Paul D., Frank B. Minirth, Frank B. Wichern, and Donald E. Ratcliff. 1991. *Introduction to psychology and counseling: Christian perspectives and applications.* 2d ed. Grand Rapids: Baker.

Melville, Herman. 1983. *White-jacket.* New York: Literary Classics of the United States.

Merrill, David W., and Roger H. Reid. 1981. *Personal styles and effective performance.* Radnor, Pa.: Chilton.

Meyers, Chet. 1986. *Teaching students to think critically.* San Francisco: Jossey-Bass.

Miles, M. Scott. 1990. *Families growing together: Church programs for family living.* Wheaton, Ill.: Victor.

Miller, Donald E. 1987. *Story and context.* Nashville: Abingdon.

Miller, Randolph Crump. 1956. *Education for Christian living.* Englewood Cliffs, N.J.: Prentice-Hall.

Minsky, Marvin. 1986. *The society of mind.* New York: Simon and Schuster.

Moreland, J. P. 1987. *Scaling the secular city: A defense of Christianity.* Grand Rapids: Baker.

Moreland, J. P., and Norman Geisler. 1990. *The life and death debate: Moral issues of our time.* New York: Praeger.

Morgan, Elisa. 1991. *Chronicles of childhood: Recording your child's spiritual journey.* Colorado Springs, Colo.: NavPress.

Murdock, George Peter. 1945. The common denominator of cultures. In *The science of man in the world crisis,* ed. Ralph Linton. New York: Columbia University Press.

Muus, Rolf E. 1988. *Theories of adolescence.* 5th ed. New York: Random House.

Myers, David. 1978. *The human puzzle: Psychological research and Christian belief.* San Francisco: Harper and Row.

Newbigin, Lesslie. 1969. *The finality of Christ.* London: SCM.

Newman, Barbara, and Philip Newman. 1991. *Development through life: A psychosocial approach.* 5th ed. Pacific Grove, Calif.: Brooks/Cole.

Ng, David, and Virginia Thomas. 1981. *Children in the worshiping community.* Atlanta: John Knox.

Nicholas, Ron. 1985. *Good things come in small groups.* Downers Grove, Ill.: InterVarsity.

Nida, Eugene A. 1960. *Message and mission.* New York: Harper and Row.

_____. 1964. *Toward a science of translating.* Leiden: Brill.

Niebuhr, Richard. 1951. *Christ and culture.* New York: Harper and Row.

Noll, Mark, Nathan O. Hatch, and George M. Marsden. 1983. *In search of a Christian America.* Westchester, Ill.: Crossway.

Nouwen, Henri J. M. 1989. *In the name of Jesus.* New York: Crossroad.

Owen, H. P. 1956–57. The "stages of ascent" in Hebrews V.11–VI.3. *New Testament Studies* 3: 243–53.

Packer, J. I. 1973. *Knowing God.* Downers Grove, Ill.: InterVarsity.

_____. 1983, April. Soldier, son, pilgrim: Christian know thyself. *Eternity.*

Parks, Sharon. 1986. *The critical years: The young adult search for a faith to live by.* San Francisco: Harper and Row.

Patton, Michael Quinn. 1978. *Utilization-focused evaluation.* Beverly Hills, Calif.: Sage.

Pazmiño, Robert W. 1988. *Foundational issues in Christian education: An introduction in evangelical perspective.* Grand Rapids: Baker.

_____. 1992. *Principles and practices of Christian education: An evangelical perspective.* Grand Rapids: Baker.

Pelfrey, Wanda. 1988. *Making the most of your child's teachable moments.* Chicago: Moody.

Perkins, Bill, and Rod Cooper. 1989. *Kids in sports: Shaping a child's character from the sidelines.* Portland, Oreg.: Multnomah.

Perry, William G. 1968. *Forms of intellectual and ethical development in the college years: A scheme.* New York: Holt, Rinehart and Winston.

Peterson, Eugene H. 1987. *Working the angles: The shape of pastoral integrity.* Grand Rapids: Eerdmans.

Phillips, Bob. 1989. *The delicate art of dancing with porcupines: Learning to appreciate the finer points of others.* Ventura, Calif.: Regal.

Phillips, J. B. 1956. *Your God is too small.* New York: Macmillan.

Piaget, Jean. 1977. *The development of thought: Equilibration of cognitive structures.* New York: Viking.

Piaget, Jean, and Bärbel Inhelder. 1969. *The psychology of the child.* New York: Basic.

Piper, John. 1986. *Desiring God: Meditations of a Christian hedonist.* Portland, Oreg.: Multnomah.

Plueddemann, James, and Carol Plueddemann. 1990. *Pilgrims in progress: Growing through groups.* Wheaton, Ill.: Harold Shaw.

Posner, George, and Alan Rudnitsky. 1989. *Course design: A guide to curriculum development for teachers.* 4th ed. New York: Longman.

Posterski, Donald C. 1985. *Friendship: A window on ministry to youth.* Scarborough, Ont.: Project Teen Canada.

Postman, Neil. 1985. *Amusing ourselves to death.* New York: Viking.

Postman, Neil, and Charles Weingartner. 1969. *Teaching as a subversive activity.* New York: Delacorte.

Potter, David, and Martin P. Andersen. 1976. *Discussion in small groups: A guide to effective practice.* 3d ed. Belmont, Calif.: Wadsworth.

Power, F. Clark, Ann Higgins, and Lawrence Kohlberg. 1989. *Lawrence Kohlberg's approach to moral education.* New York: Columbia University Press.

Powers, Bruce P. 1982. *Growing faith.* Nashville: Broadman.

_____. 1986a. Adults continuing to learn. In *A church ministry to adults,* ed. Jerry M. Stubblefield. Nashville: Broadman.

_____. 1986b. Mission education and involvement. In *A church ministry to adults,* ed. Jerry M. Stubblefield. Nashville: Broadman.

Presseau, Jack R. 1982. *Teach-niques.* Atlanta: John Knox.

Pulaski, Mary Ann. 1980. *Understanding Piaget: An introduction to children's cognitive development.* Rev. ed. New York: Harper and Row.

Rahn, David. 1991. Faith domain distinctions in the conceptualization of morality and social convention for evangelical Christians. Ph.D. diss., Purdue University.

Ratcliff, Donald. 1985. The development of children's religious concepts: Research review. *Journal of Psychology and Christianity* 4 (1): 35–43.

_____, ed. 1988. *Handbook of preschool religious education.* Birmingham, Ala.: Religious Education.

Redfield, Robert. 1953. *The primitive world and its transformations.* Ithaca, N.Y.: Great Seal.

Reichenbach, Bruce. 1983. *Is man the phoenix? A study of immortality.* Grand Rapids: Eerdmans.

Rest, James. 1983. Morality. In *Handbook of child psychology,* ed. Paul Mussen, 3:557–629. New York: Wiley.

_____. 1986. *Moral development: Advances in research and theory.* New York: Praeger.

Rice, Wayne. 1989. *Up close and personal.* Grand Rapids: Zondervan.

Richards, Lawrence O. 1970. *Creative Bible teaching.* Grand Rapids: Zondervan.

_____. 1982. *Teaching youth.* Kansas City, Mo.: Beacon Hill.

_____. 1983a. *A theology of children's ministry.* Grand Rapids: Zondervan.

_____. 1983b. *The Word parents' handbook.* Waco: Tex.: Word.

_____. 1987. *A practical theology of spirituality.* Grand Rapids: Zondervan.

Richards, Lawrence O., and Gib Martin. 1981. *A theology of personal ministry.* Grand Rapids: Zondervan.

Richardson, Don. 1974. *Peace child.* Ventura, Calif.: Gospel Light.

Richter, Don. 1982. A bibliographic survey of youth and youth Ministry. In *Religious education ministry with youth,* ed. D. Campbell Wyckoff and Don Richter. Birmingham, Ala.: Religious Education.

Rinehart, Paula. 1988–89. *The starting strong series.* Colorado Springs, Colo.: NavPress.

Ringer, Robert J. 1974. *Winning through intimidation.* New York: Funk and Wagnalls.

_____. 1977. *Looking out for #1.* New York: Fawcett Crest.

Rogers, Everett M. 1983. *Diffusion of innovations.* 3d ed. New York: Free.

References

Rush, Myron. 1983. *Management: A biblical approach.* Wheaton, Ill.: Victor.

_____. 1983. *Richer relationships: How to be a conflict-solver and friend-winner.* Wheaton, Ill.: Victor.

Ryrie, Charles. 1969. *Balancing the Christian life.* Chicago: Moody.

Sandberg, Mark. 1988. Paul's method in Acts 17–19: Reasoning and persuading. Unpublished paper.

Sanders, Ray E. 1990. The art of questioning. In *Adult learning methods: A guide for effective instruction,* ed. Michael W. Galbraith. Malabar, Fla.: Krieger.

Sapp, Gary L., ed. 1986. *Handbook of moral development.* Birmingham, Ala.: Religious Education.

Saxe, John Godfrey. 1953. The blind men and the elephant. In *The home book of verse,* selected and arranged by Burton Egbert Stevenson. 9th ed. New York: Holt, Rinehart and Winston.

Schaeffer, Francis A. 1968. *The God who is there.* Downers Grove, Ill.: InterVarsity.

_____. 1970. *Pollution and the death of man.* Wheaton, Ill.: Tyndale.

Schaller, Lyle. 1977. *Survival tactics in the parish.* Nashville: Abingdon.

_____. 1980. *The multiple staff and the larger church.* Nashville: Abingdon.

Schimmels, Cliff. 1984. *When junior highs invade your home.* Old Tappan, N.J.: Revell.

_____. 1989. *Parents' most-asked questions about kids and schools.* Wheaton, Ill.: Victor.

Schneidau, Herbert N. 1976. *Sacred discontent: The Bible and western tradition.* Baton Rouge, La.: Louisiana State University Press.

Seamonds, David A. 1991. Healing our innermost needs. *In Touch.* Atlanta, Ga.: In Touch Ministries.

Sell, Charles M. 1981. *Family ministry.* Grand Rapids: Zondervan.

_____. 1985. *Transition.* Chicago: Moody.

Senter, Mark. 1990. *Recruiting volunteers in the church.* Wheaton, Ill.: Victor.

Shaver, D. G. 1985. A longitudinal study of moral development at a conservative religious liberal arts college. *Journal of College Student Personnel* 26: 400–404.

_____. 1987. Moral development of students attending a Christian liberal arts college and a Bible college. *Journal of College Student Personnel* 28 (3): 211–18.

Shaw, John C. 1987. *The workcamp experience.* Loveland, Calif.: Group Books.

Sheehey, Gail. 1976. *Passages: Predictable crises of adult life.* New York: Dutton.

Simpson, Elizabeth. 1966. Taxonomy of objectives: Psychomotor domain. (ERIC ED 010368)

Singh, J., and R. Zingg. 1939. *Wolf-children and feral man.* New York: Harper and Row.

Skinner, B. F. 1953. *Science and human behavior.* New York: Macmillan.

Smalley, Gary. 1984. *The key to your child's heart.* Waco, Tex.: Word.

Smalley, Gary, and John Trent. 1990. *The two sides of love.* Pomona, Calif.: Focus on the Family.

Smart, Ninian. 1969. *The religious experience of mankind.* New York: Charles Scribner's Sons.

Smedes, Lewis B. 1970. *All things new.* Grand Rapids: Eerdmans.

_____. 1986. *Choices: Making right decisions in a complex world.* San Francisco: Harper and Row.

Smith, T. C. 1970. Acts. In *The Broadman Bible commentary,* vol. 10. Nashville: Broadman.

Snyder, Howard A. 1985. *A kingdom manifesto.* Downers Grove, Ill.: InterVarsity.

Sparkman, G. Temp. 1983. *The salvation and nurture of the child of God: The story of Emma.* Valley Forge, Pa.: Judson.

Sprinthall, Norman, and Richard Sprinthall. 1990. *Educational psychology: A developmental approach.* 5th ed. New York: Random House.

Stake, Robert. 1967. The countenance of education evaluation. *Teachers College Record* 68 (7): 523–40.

Staub, Ervin, et al., eds. 1984. *Development and maintenance of prosocial behavior.* New York: Plenum.

Steele, Les. 1989, Winter. Research on faith development. *Christian Education Journal* 9 (2): 21–30.

_____. 1990. *On the way: A practical theology of Christian formation.* Grand Rapids: Baker.

Steinaker, Norman, and M. Robert Bell. 1979. *The experiential taxonomy: A new approach to teaching and learning.* New York: Academic.

Stevens, Doug. 1985. *Called to care: Youth ministry and the church.* Grand Rapids: Zondervan.

Stewart, Stan. 1987. *Going to church with children.* Melbourne, Australia: Joint Board of Christian Education.

Stigler, James W., Richard A. Schweder, and Gilbert Herdt, eds. 1990. *Cultural psychology: Essays on comparative human development.* Cambridge: Cambridge University Press.

Stinnett, Nick, and John DeFrain. 1985. *Secrets of strong families.* New York: Berkley.

Stott, John R. W. 1964. *The epistles of John.* Grand Rapids: Eerdmans.

_____. 1988, April–June. The world's challenge to the church. *Bibliotheca Sacra* 145 (578).

Strommen, Merton P. 1974. *Five cries of youth.* New York: Harper and Row.

Strong, Augustus H. 1907. *Systematic theology.* Valley Forge, Pa.: Judson.

Stubblefield, Jerry M. 1986a. Discipleship training. In *A church ministering to adults,* ed. Jerry M. Stubblefield. Nashville: Broadman.

_____. 1986b. Learning differences in adulthood. In *A church ministering to adults,* ed. Jerry M. Stubblefield. Nashville: Broadman.

Sudman, S. and N. Bradburn. 1982. *Asking questions.* San Francisco: Jossey-Bass.

Swindoll, Charles R. 1983. *Growing strong in the seasons of life.* Portland, Oreg.: Multnomah.

Tanner, Daniel, and Laurel N. Tanner. 1980. *Curriculum development: Theory into practice.* New York: Macmillan.

The American heritage dictionary of the English language. 1971. New York: American Heritage.

Thomas, Robert L. 1991, March. Improving evangelical ethics: An analysis of the problem and a proposed solution. *Journal of the Evangelical Theological Society* 34 (1): 3–19.

Thomas, Robert L., and Stanley N. Gundry. 1988. *The NIV harmony of the Gospels.* San Francisco: Harper and Row.

Tillapaugh, Frank. 1982. *Unleashing the church: Getting people out of the fortress and into ministry.* Ventura, Calif.: Regal.

Tippett, Alan R. 1987. *Introduction to missiology.* Pasadena, Calif.: William Carey Library.

Toon, Peter. 1984. *Your conscience as your guide.* Wilton, Conn.: Morehouse-Barlow.

Tournier, Paul. 1968. *A place for you.* New York: Harper and Row.

Tracy, Myrlin. 1991, Fall. Teaching Tammy. *Teacher Touch.* Elgin, Ill.: David C. Cook.

Twain, Mark. 1912. *The adventures of Huckleberry Finn.* New York: Collier.

Van Leeuwen, Mary Stewart. 1985. *The person in psychology: A contemporary Christian appraisal.* Grand Rapids: Eerdmans.

_____. 1990. *Gender and grace: Love, work and parenting in a changing world.* Downers Grove, Ill.: InterVarsity.

VanderGoot, Mary. 1987. *Helping children grow healthy emotions.* Grand Rapids: Baker.

Veith, Gene. 1987. *Loving your God with all your mind.* Westchester, Ill.: Crossway.

Vogel, Linda Jane. 1984. *The religious education of older adults.* Birmingham, Ala.: Religious Education.

Voges, Ken, and Ron Braund. 1989. *Understanding how others misunderstand you: A unique and proven plan for strengthening personal relationships.* Chicago: Moody.

von Oech, Roger. 1983. *A whack on the side of the head.* New York: Warner.

_____. 1986. *A kick in the seat of the pants.* New York: Harper and Row.

Wallace, A. F. C. 1956. Revitalization movements. *American Anthropologist* 58: 264–81.

Ward, Ted. n.d. Development levels of the teacher. Unpublished manuscript.

_____. n.d. Non-formal education. Unpublished manuscript.

_____. 1989. *Values begin at home.* 2d ed. Wheaton, Ill.: Victor.

Watson, David, and R. Tharp. 1989. *Self-directed behavior.* 5th ed. Monterery, Calif.: Brooks/Cole.

Watson, John B. 1930. *Behaviorism.* Rev. ed. New York: Norton.

Wernick, Robert. 1987, September. Where there's fire, there is smoke—and usually a "chimney." *Smithsonian* 18 (6): 140–52.

Westerhoff, John H. 1976. *Will our children have faith?* New York: Seabury.

_____. 1982. Aspects of adult confirmation. In *Confirmation re-examined,* ed. Kendig Brubaker Cully. Wilton, Conn.: Morehouse-Barlow.

Westing, Harold. 1985. *Multiple church staff handbook.* Grand Rapids: Kregel.

Whitcomb, John C. 1977, October–December. Proof texts for semi-rational apologetics. *Bibliotheca Sacra* 134: 291–98.

White, James W. 1988. *Intergenerational religious education.* Birmingham, Ala.: Religious Education.

White, John. 1984. Parrot fish. In *The race.* Downers Grove, Ill.: InterVarsity.

Wickett, R. E. Y. 1991. *Models of adult religious education practice.* Birmingham, Ala.: R.E.P.

Wilhoit, Jim. 1991. *Christian education and the search for meaning.* Rev. ed. Grand Rapids: Baker.

Wilhoit, Jim, and Leland Ryken. 1988. *Effective Bible teaching.* Grand Rapids: Baker.

Wilkins, Michael. 1992. *Following the master: Discipleship in the steps of Jesus.* Grand Rapids: Zondervan.

Willard, Dallas. 1988. *The Spirit of the disciplines.* San Francisco: Harper and Row.

Williams, Reed G., and Thomas M. Haladyne. 1982. Logical operation for generating intended questions (LOGIQ): A typology for higher level test items. In *A technology for test-item writing,* ed. Gale H. Roid and Thomas M. Haladyne. New York: Academic.

Williamson, William. 1970. *Language and concepts in Christian education.* Philadelphia: Temple University Press.

Wittrock, Merlin, ed. 1986. *Handbook of research on teaching.* 3d ed. Washington, D.C.: American Educational Research Association.

Wlodkowski, Raymond J. 1985. *Enhancing adult motivation to learn.* San Francisco: Jossey-Bass.

Wolterstorff, Nicholas. 1980. *Educating for responsible action.* Grand Rapids: Eerdmans.

Worthen, Blaine, and James Sanders. 1987. *Educational evaluation: Alternative approaches and practical guidelines.* New York: Longman.

Wyckoff, D. Campbell. 1955. *The task of Christian education.* Philadelphia: Westminster.

_____. 1961. *Theory and design of Christian education curriculum.* Philadelphia: Westminster.

Yaconelli, Mike, and Jim Burns. 1986. *High school ministry.* Grand Rapids: Zondervan.

Yancey, Philip. 1988. *Disappointment with God.* Grand Rapids: Zondervan.

Yoder, Gideon. 1959. *The nurture and evangelism of children.* Scottdale, Pa.: Herald.

Yoder, John Howard. 1955, January–March. Discipleship as missionary strategy. *Christian Ministry* 8.

Zuck, Roy. 1984. *The Holy Spirit in your teaching.* Rev. ed. Wheaton, Ill.: Victor.

Index of Subjects

Index of Authors

Index of Scripture